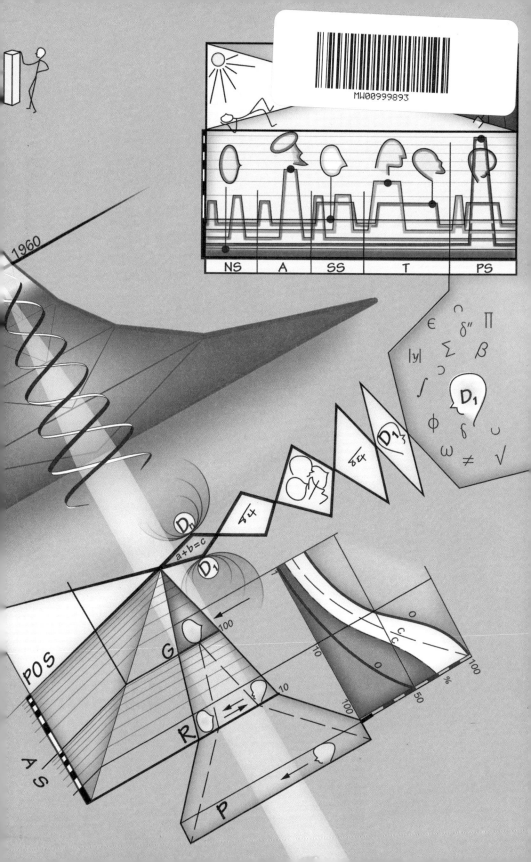

A CIVIC ENTREPRENEUR

A CIVIC ENTREPRENEUR

The Life of Technology Visionary George Kozmetsky

MONTY JONES

BRISCOE CENTER
FOR AMERICAN HISTORY
THE UNIVERSITY OF TEXAS AT AUSTIN

Distributed by Tower Books, an imprint of the University of Texas Press

Printed in the United States of America.

First edition, 2018

Requests for permission to reproduce material from this work should be sent to Office of the Director, Dolph Briscoe Center for American History, The University of Texas at Austin, 2300 Red River Stop D1100, Austin, TX 78712-1426.

∞ The paper used in this book meets the minimum requirements of ANSI/NISO z39.48-1992 (r1997)(Permanence of Paper).

Library of Congress Control Number:
2018934286

Frontispiece: As a "civic entrepreneur," George Kozmetsky (1917–2003) focused on an ever-widening community, beginning with his adopted hometown of Austin and extending around the globe. *IC² Institute photograph.*

CONTENTS

FOREWORD

As longtime colleagues of George Kozmetsky, and as three of the many people who were fortunate to have him as a mentor, we are excited about the opportunity that *A Civic Entrepreneur: The Life of Technology Visionary George Kozmetsky* provides for a wide audience to learn more about the long and distinguished career of this eminent scholar, business leader, and visionary pioneer of the global high-technology economy. We believe Monty Jones has captured in these pages the essence of George Kozmetsky, revealing his passion for learning, his boundless energy and resourcefulness, his creative and innovative approach to solving problems, and his commitment to a just and equitable social order.

We count our association with George as among the most important factors in our careers. It has been our honor to serve as fellows of the IC^2 Institute, the economic development think tank that George established in 1977 at the University of Texas at Austin. We were also faculty colleagues of George at the university's McCombs School of Business, where we were inspired by his vision. John Butler worked closely with George for many years at the IC^2 Institute, collaborated with him on research and publishing projects (including a book on immigrant entrepreneurs), and was recruited by him to serve as director of the institute in 2002. Bill Cunningham was mentored by George in his early academic career and served for many years as one of George's associate deans at the business school, before succeeding him as dean in 1982. Bob Peterson worked with George on many research projects at the business school, was one of the first fellows of the IC^2 Institute, and served as the institute's director of research and deputy director, before being appointed director in 2013.

George may be most often identified today as one of the people who helped transform Austin from a small college town into a major center of high-tech research and manufacturing, and this book offers a detailed account of his contributions to that development, but the book makes clear that he was also a figure of worldwide importance. His inspiring vision for "constructive capitalism" continues to be a guide for how the capitalist system, applied in diverse settings around the world, can be a positive force that contributes to the solution of economic and social problems. And his commitment to "shared prosperity"—among all nations and all members of society—remains a model that the world would do well to follow.

We believe we knew George as well as anyone outside his immediate family, yet each of us has learned much from this book that we did not know or did not fully understand. Through extensive archival research and interviews, the author has been able to present full accounts of episodes in George's life that had previously been understood in only a sketchy way. The reader will find here, for example, amplified accounts of George's heroic service as a medic in Europe during World War II, his extraordinary success as an industrialist in Southern California in the 1950s and 1960s, his leadership as dean of the business school at the University of Texas at Austin, and his contributions to a host of new academic disciplines and scholarly organizations.

Not least, the book provides overviews of George and Ronya Kozmetsky's lifelong partnership and their philanthropic endeavors through the RGK Foundation. Also included are absorbing accounts of the social and economic background to different aspects of George's story, including depictions of the Russian immigrant community in Seattle that shaped George's early life and a view of what Austin was like on the eve of the great changes that George did so much to bring about.

We feel fortunate that we have been able to play a part in bringing this biography project to fruition, and we are grateful to all those who have contributed in their own way. This includes the many people who shared their memories and reflections in interviews with the author, as well as the many who made financial contributions that helped to underwrite the costs of publication. Our role has mainly been as advisers and supporters, but throughout the project, Monty Jones has had editorial control, making decisions about how to organize the book, what to include, and how to present this fascinating story as it revealed itself through his research. He has succeeded in producing a thorough, insightful, and balanced book that is highly readable and accessible to a wide audience, and we hope others will find it as interesting and entertaining as we have.

John Sibley Butler
J. Marion West Chair in Constructive Capitalism, McCombs School of
    Business
Director of the IC² Institute, 2002–2013

William H. Cunningham
James L. Bayless Chair for Free Enterprise, McCombs School of Business
Dean of the University of Texas at Austin Business School, 1982–1985
President of the University of Texas at Austin, 1985–1992
Chancellor of the University of Texas System, 1992–2000

Robert A. Peterson
John T. Stuart III Centennial Chair in Business Administration,
    McCombs School of Business
Director of the IC² Institute, 2013–2016

Austin, May 5, 2017

A CIVIC ENTREPRENEUR

CHAPTER 1

GEORGE KOZMETSKY'S PIVOTAL ROLE AS A CIVIC ENTREPRENEUR

It was just barely daylight in Los Angeles on August 12, 1965, and George Kozmetsky was listening to the radio as he got ready to go to work at Teledyne Inc., the defense electronics company that he and a friend had founded five years earlier. As he looked out his bedroom window, through the twisting branches of a coral tree to a glimpse of the Pacific Ocean five miles downhill, he might have been preoccupied with the intricacies of an innovative helicopter navigation system that Teledyne was designing and building for the navy—a contract that the company had won just a few months earlier and that had suddenly made him very rich—when his attention was diverted by some disturbing news on the radio. The Watts neighborhood, south of downtown LA and about twenty miles southeast of the Kozmetskys' comfortable home in the hills of Brentwood, was on fire after a night of rioting.

It had been the beginning of what would prove to be six days and nights of clashes between police and the African American residents of the neighborhood. The violence had started after a seemingly routine traffic stop on a hot and smoggy evening; a crowd had gathered, police had argued with the onlookers, and one thing quickly led to another—resulting in one of the worst incidents of urban unrest in American history. By August 16, thirty-four people had died, one thousand had been injured, four thousand had been arrested, and looting and arson had damaged or destroyed six hundred buildings.

For Kozmetsky, the radio report after the first night of rioting produced an epiphany. For quite a while he had been mulling over a dramatic change in his way of life, thinking of returning to the university career that he had left thirteen years earlier to take up a succession of jobs in the private sector as a manager and entrepreneur. He and his wife, Ronya, had

George and Ronya Kozmetsky. *Kozmetsky family photograph.*

never expected to be away from a university campus that long, and the call of a teaching and administrative career had been growing stronger. For years he had harbored definite ideas about how a business school ought to be organized to better prepare its graduates for making contributions to a rapidly changing society. As a student at the Harvard Business School in the late 1940s he had been introduced to the fairly new idea of "corporate social responsibility," and he was now more convinced than ever that business—and the capitalist system—ought to be a force for positive change and should, instead of merely seeking profits for their own sake, join with education and government in solving society's problems.

Now the rioting in Watts lent a new urgency to those thoughts.

"I had been gone too long," he told his students many years later. "I was 48, and if I didn't get back, I wouldn't have the energy to bring about the changes that I thought should happen. That was my personal awakening."[1]

For Kozmetsky, the solution to the social turmoil that underlay the Watts riots was to be found in education and economic opportunity, with both embracing the rapid advances in technology that had defined the

A CIVIC ENTREPRENEUR

postwar years. With an optimism and a faith in technological progress that characterized many in his generation of Americans, Kozmetsky saw prosperity and self-fulfillment as within everyone's reach, and he spent the rest of his life trying to make that dream a reality.

Throughout his long career as an industrialist, an educator, a visionary supporter of new technologies, an advocate for worldwide economic development, and a philanthropist, Kozmetsky pursued and promoted constructive interactions among the often-contending worlds of academia, government, and private-sector business. He personified these interactions as a founder of Teledyne, a dean of the business school at the University of Texas at Austin, an academic researcher at the university's IC^2 Institute, a promoter of new technologies, and a far-flung consultant to entrepreneurs and government agencies.

Kozmetsky is most widely known today for two accomplishments—taking the early steps that propelled the business school at the University of Texas at Austin toward its current position as an internationally prominent institution, and playing a central role in the economic transformation of Austin from a sleepy college town in the mid-twentieth century to its present-day status as a center of high-technology research, development, and manufacturing. In the latter role, Kozmetsky has been called "Austin's equivalent of Silicon Valley's Fred Terman," the Stanford University engineering dean who fostered the growth of high-tech industry in Northern California after World War II.[2]

Kozmetsky's numerous other achievements range from pioneering the use of computers in business management; to helping establish the academic field known as management science; to forging a lucrative career as an adroit and innovative industrialist who contributed to the early application of digital technology to defense systems; to fashioning an influential theory of high-tech economic development; to serving on numerous commissions that helped shape national policies on defense, research, computers, space exploration, energy, and other fields.

Overarching one pursuit after another was his embrace of the duties of what has been called "civic entrepreneurship," which involves a merging of business acumen, a deep commitment to social responsibility, and visionary leadership for the economic development of a community. Civic entrepreneurs are known as catalysts for collaborative networks that draw on the resources of business, government, and education to work toward setting and then realizing a community's broadly shared goals.[3] Kozmetsky embodied this idea of civic entrepreneurship, to the extent that he could have been the model for the development of the concept. Inherent in Kozmetsky's role as a civic entrepreneur was the broadest possible definition of "community," beginning with one's city and region but growing outward in an ever-widening circle that enveloped the globe. This embrace of worldwide economic development sets Kozmetsky apart from a host of economic development advocates with a more parochial focus.

Principal among the themes that pervaded all of Kozmetsky's pursuits was his idea of "shared prosperity"—a belief that each of the world's nations and regions, and all socioeconomic groups within those areas, could fruitfully achieve economic advancement without necessarily harming the others. Kozmetsky embraced economic competition with a faith that transcended local rivalries. He was as eager to see China and post-Soviet Russia prosper as he was interested in the advancement of his adopted hometown of Austin. If global competition sometimes produced negative effects on employment, income, or other measures of prosperity, he saw the solution in enhanced competitiveness through reeducation, innovation, and creativity—not in protectionism and trade wars.

Other themes reflected in Kozmetsky's many projects and initiatives include an emphasis on the need to make capitalism a "constructive" force in society (something that he doubted would happen without intervention in the market); a requirement that corporations accept and act on the principle of "social responsibility"; an insistence on a new approach to business management based on the closely related ideas of creativity and innovation; and a belief that new technologies, from the computer to robotics and biotechnology, offered society far more benefits than problems.

In practice, he tended to accept the "technological fix"—the idea that technology could solve the very problems that other technology had caused. In this, as in so many other ways, Kozmetsky definitely embodied a certain optimistic and can-do way of thinking that flourished for much of twentieth-century America, although his life also testified to a much broader orientation—that of a citizen of the world, and of a person who habitually looked beyond his own time, anticipating the future and embracing its promise. He was a futurist, not only in his ability to imagine the world to come, but also in his determination to reform current education and business management to prepare people to succeed in the world of the future.

Although Kozmetsky was associated with many large corporations—as a manager, an investor, or a board member—he was often critical of big business for its bureaucratic rigidity and its slowness to adapt to new technologies or new approaches to management. He seemed much more comfortable among young entrepreneurs—people with imagination, new ideas, and flexibility—traits that he himself possessed into his later years.

A CIVIC ENTREPRENEUR

Growth and change were great attractions for him throughout his life, and these attractions were nowhere more evident than in his continuing eagerness to broaden his knowledge and to stay current with the latest developments in a multitude of fields.

From the day he joined the army in 1942, Kozmetsky was a member of large organizations, but he never worked for an organization that was standing still. It is difficult to imagine Kozmetsky in a company or a school that had stopped changing, that had settled into a comfortable way of acting and had adopted a fixed structure, and then was largely content just to keep the enterprise moving along on its established path. Kozmetsky knew that the pace of change—technological, economic, and social—outside such an organization would doom it to failure, if for no other reason than that it would become unable to respond to new challenges. The secret to success, and to survival, was to keep moving. The world outside the boardroom, the laboratory, and the factory floor was not going to stop; in fact, the pace of change was continually accelerating.

Kozmetsky's life can be seen as a laboratory for the testing of theories about economic development based on the efficacy of close collaboration among government, academia, and the private sector. This orientation may be traced to his experiences growing up in pro–New Deal Seattle as well as his experience as a combat medic during World War II. Whether as a college student fascinated by massive Depression-era dam construction projects or as a medic benefitting from the vast federal research initiative that made possible the mass production of penicillin, Kozmetsky's formative years taught him about the blessings that could flow from the constructive interaction of the public and private sectors, guided by the broad humanizing vision provided by higher education.

For much of his life, Kozmetsky pursued this collaboration between the public and private sectors as a participant in, and, indeed, an advocate for, the "military-industrial complex." As with many in his generation, the Cold War was a call to duty as much as World War II had been. He was not the only industrialist, technology pioneer, and academic researcher who saw himself as engaged in a far larger project than merely making profits for corporate America; putting capitalism and technology to work in defense of democratic principles is a motivation that later generations of Americans might find hard to understand, but it helped account for much of the drive and ambition of Kozmetsky's generation.

Kozmetsky's influence as a prophet of technological innovation for the overall good of society, despite the problems that could accompany such innovation, was felt across the country and around the globe. In recognition of these and other contributions to the advancement of technology,

President Bill Clinton presented Kozmetsky with the National Medal of Technology in 1993.

Born in Seattle in 1917 to parents of modest means who had recently immigrated from what is now Belarus, Kozmetsky graduated from the University of Washington and had been hoping to save enough money (from a CPA firm that he started) to go to graduate school when World War II intervened. After service in France and Germany as a combat medic from D-Day to the end of the war, Kozmetsky attended Harvard Business School and later taught there and at the Carnegie Institute of Technology (now Carnegie Mellon University). From 1952 to 1966, he worked in private business in Los Angeles, first at Hughes Aircraft and Litton Industries and then as a cofounder of Teledyne Inc., a company that got its start in defense electronics and became an important military contractor as well as a major conglomerate making diverse industrial and consumer products. He returned to the academic world in 1966 as dean of the University of Texas at Austin business school, where he served for sixteen years before stepping down to concentrate on the IC^2 Institute, the economic development think tank that he had established at the university in 1977.

From then until his declining health as a result of Lou Gehrig's disease, Kozmetsky continued to travel the world, consulting with governments and private-sector businesses on techniques for expanding and diversifying economic activity. Much of his message involved applying the results of years of research conducted at the IC^2 Institute on topics such as the diffusion of new technologies through an economy, new institutional arrangements for encouraging entrepreneurship, new approaches to management that met the needs of companies in rapidly changing and "hypercompetitive" high-tech environments, and the role of university research in fostering marketplace innovations.

A common thread for Kozmetsky in all these topics was that they dealt with "unstructured problems," those complex, open-ended questions that defy formulaic solutions. Another common element in the practical initiatives that arose from the work of the IC^2 Institute was that Kozmetsky viewed them as experiments that tested the viability of the institute's theories. Some of those experiments failed and some, such as the Austin Technology Incubator and a national venture capital network, were dramatically successful, but Kozmetsky knew there were lessons to be learned from the failures as well as the successes.

After the economic transformation of Austin became widely known, Kozmetsky found eager audiences for his ideas about high-technology economic development. He was active in advising state and local officials not only in Texas but also in US regions as diverse as Florida, Tennes-

Kozmetsky at
his blackboard.
*IC² Institute
photograph.*

see, Southern California, and Alaska, and he carried his message of shared prosperity and its related themes around the globe—to China, Japan, Australia, Russia, Brazil, and many other countries.

Kozmetsky had minimal personal interest in the bureaucratic procedures designed to make public academic organizations function rationally and transparently, much preferring his own entrepreneurial system of organization based on the force of his personality. He took care to hire people who could attend to the requirements of the bureaucracy, but he was willing to work around those requirements when it suited his purposes. He eschewed, for the most part, independent and peer-reviewed publishing, preferring instead to publish his research in-house through the think tank that he founded and supported financially or through subsidized arrangements with public-policy publishers. Whether this preference harmed his reputation in the academic world can be debated, but that was not something he cared much about. His speaking engagements, consulting work, and service on government and industry commissions were so numerous that he was often away from the dean's office. While these activities helped to enhance the reputation of the university and its business school, they also fueled his reputation within the institution as something of an absentee dean. And he could be as overbearing and manipulative as any university administrator or business executive determined that he knew the best course of action and intent on getting his way. More than one colleague, even some who maintained lifelong admiration and respect for him, acknowledged his manipulative prowess.

Another personality trait was his commitment to ethical business practices and a degree of courage in upholding ethical principles that may be rare in business and academia. He once faced down no less a formidable personality than Howard Hughes in defense of ethical and legal accounting practices, and he resigned from a corporate board rather than go along with a powerful CEO (and important University of Texas donor) who, Kozmetsky was convinced, wanted to act in disregard of the stockholders' best interests. Within the University of Texas System, he held for many years as much power as any staff member by virtue of his close relationship with members of the Board of Regents, and this sometimes led to conflict with the president and other officials of his campus. Yet, from all the available evidence, he wielded this power benignly. Far from seeking personal gain from his powerful positions, Kozmetsky was a major donor to the business school and other university projects. As a dean he kept to the workaholic habits that he had been accustomed to as an entrepreneur, routinely arriving at the office before 5:00 a.m. when he was in Austin, but also maintaining a travel schedule—for consulting work, academic conferences, board meetings, and congressional testimony—that exhausted many younger colleagues. Some faculty members complained that all these activities meant he spent less time on his duties as a dean than he should have; others recognized that his highly public role beyond Austin helped to enhance the stature of the business school.

Another pattern that was evident throughout Kozmetsky's life was his ability to absorb and assimilate information rapidly and with little reliance on teachers. This ability showed itself mostly with regard to scientific and technical subjects. Although apparently a less than stellar student in public school, he flourished in higher education, and early in his studies at both the University of Washington and the Harvard Business School his

Kozmetsky with a class in the master's program in technology commercialization at the IC² Institute. *IC² Institute photograph.*

teachers came to rely on him to help teach other students. While training as a medic in the army he was assigned to organize a medical library—and ended up reading most of it. He mostly taught himself about how to build and use computers while working at Hughes Aircraft and Litton Industries, and he was conversant in any number of complex subjects, including biotechnology, the management of large-scale engineering projects, and technological and policy issues related to energy and marine science.

Along with his wide learning, Kozmetsky maintained a remarkable openness to new ideas and information, just as he was open to meeting new people and encouraging them in their aspirations. "There were no barriers in his thinking or his receptiveness," said Laura Kilcrease, one of his colleagues at the IC² Institute. "Many people of his age would be negative about new ideas and would tend to say something new wouldn't work. George was always excited about something new. He wanted to try things and give them a chance."[4]

Kilcrease traced this openness partly to Kozmetsky's wide travels. "He grew up in a time when personalities and personal connections mattered. He traveled a lot, and traveling was an education for him. He learned from meeting people and seeing new things, and he was exposed to different ways of operating—on a global basis—in a much larger way than for a typical person."[5]

Kozmetsky's natural abilities to learn complex material on his own and grasp the dimensions of a new subject, with little or no tutoring and outside the confines of formal educational programs, also surely influenced his interest, as a university dean, in encouraging interdisciplinary studies, independent and self-paced learning environments, and radically new perspectives that drew connections between seemingly disparate subjects. Late in his life Kozmetsky adopted the term "transdisciplinary" as the best description of the multifaceted approach to learning that had always appealed to him.

Kozmetsky became very wealthy as a result of Teledyne's success as a defense contractor, and he made a second fortune as a major stockholder (and longtime adviser and board member) of Dell Computer Inc. These large successes in business were accompanied by a number of failed ventures in the 1980s and 1990s—businesses that he helped establish and lead but that never fulfilled their early promise.

If one includes the University of Texas business school, the IC^2 Institute, and the Austin technopolis, along with Teledyne and Dell, Kozmetsky can be credited with playing a central role in five extraordinary successes during his career—a track record that has rarely been equaled. He was, of course, not solely responsible for these successes, each of which involved the participation of a host of collaborators, but part of Kozmetsky's genius was an ability to attract and inspire capable partners and to recognize and nurture talented colleagues, particularly among younger people.

The wealth that they amassed with the success of Teledyne enabled George and Ronya to dedicate a significant portion of their lives after the mid-1960s to philanthropy. They established their RGK Foundation when George left the management of Teledyne to become dean of the University of Texas business school, with Ronya leaving her career as a teacher to take over much of the task of managing the foundation and overseeing its investments. The foundation focused mainly on medicine, education, and community development and for many years was an important source of financial support for the IC^2 Institute and the business school.

The Kozmetskys shared a dedication to helping others in many ways besides their formal philanthropic pursuits. One of the main interests that they shared was advancing the cause of rights and opportunities for women in education and business. They supported organizations that promoted women's rights, donated to political campaigns of progressive women, and served as mentors to dozens of women entrepreneurs and academics.

Most of their political contributions went to progressive candidates, such as Texas governor Ann Richards and the Democratic National Committee, with Ronya being the one who wrote most of the family's checks. As an official at a public university, George kept a low political profile, and

A CIVIC ENTREPRENEUR

he worked equally well with leaders across the political spectrum, but both George and Ronya remained liberal in their personal outlook—a perspective that may go back to their experiences as children growing up in immigrant families in the progressive environment of Seattle after World War I.

Perhaps reflective of an earlier time in American politics, the Kozmetskys had many conservative friends. They also kept in touch with people whose interests varied widely from their own immediate concerns. Robert D. King, George's friend and fellow dean, recalled a conversation he had with Elspeth Rostow, another University of Texas dean. "We were talking about George and politics, and I said George was a capitalist but was liberal in everything else. I would tell him that he could afford to be liberal because he had so much money, but that I had to be a conservative. Elspeth responded by saying that George was really a poet manqué, someone with the soul of a poet. He had an interest in matters of the intellect that business school deans don't usually have. There was a side to him that cared deeply about the humanities. You could talk to him about anything."[6]

These major sequences of events in George Kozmetsky's long and complicated life indicate the breadth and depth of his many contributions to society—contributions that rank him as one of the most important figures in twentieth-century business, academia, technology, and economic development—a true civic entrepreneur whose influence continues to be felt in Austin and around the world.

CHAPTER 2

THE IMMIGRANT EXPERIENCE

The Russian heritage of George and Ronya Kozmetsky as they were growing up in Seattle was of lasting importance in giving them insight into the immigrant experience and contributing to their outlook as world citizens. The language and culture of Russia were powerful influences from the beginning. Although George was born after his parents moved to Seattle, and Ronya moved to the Seattle area at the age of one with her parents, both of them remained fluent in Russian all their lives and on many occasions demonstrated a special attachment to the country of their ancestors and its people. When he was in his twenties, friends later recalled, George was known as a fluent Russian speaker who had a special fondness for black bread and borscht.[1]

In her youth Ronya attended a Russian school in the afternoons to improve her knowledge of the language, and she was known among her friends as "the mad Russian" for her wild driving habits.[2] George's first appearance in the news media was as an interpreter for a group of Russian aviators who landed unexpectedly in Washington State in 1937. When they were rearing their own family in the 1940s and 1950s, George and Ronya sometimes switched to Russian when they wanted to confer with one another without their children knowing what was being said. After the fall of the Soviet Union and the rise of entrepreneurial opportunities in Russia, George and the IC² Institute, his economic development think tank, jumped at the chance to nurture that emerging spirit of capitalism. Ronya also embraced those efforts through one of her roles as a sort of social and cultural ambassador associated with George's activities.

George's and Ronya's families were part of a diverse stream of emigration from Russia and adjacent lands that began with political opposition to the czar in 1905 and continued during and after World War I. In the early twentieth century there were many reasons for leaving Russia and Eastern Europe—economic hardship, war, anarchy, political and religious oppression, autocratic government, the disorder and repression that followed the Bolshevik revolution, and the lure of reports of freedom and opportunity in America.

The victory of the Bolsheviks in 1921 ended a civil war and prompted many on the losing side, eventually as many as three million by some estimates, to leave the country. At first some of these emigrants thought of themselves as seeking only temporary refuge, with continuing close ties to Russia, but as the 1920s wore on, more and more of them saw themselves as members of a permanent community abroad, never completely losing their attachment to Russia but becoming more integrated into the life of their new countries.[3] The waves of émigrés included thousands of Russia's intellectual and artistic elites, as well as more humble citizens. George's father and stepfather were tradesmen (a butcher and a welder, respectively), and Ronya's father, who had been a librarian in Russia, operated a restaurant with his wife after they came to America.

Seattle, perhaps because of its long-standing connections with Russian settlements in Alaska and the Pacific Northwest, as well as because of its ease of access as a relatively close port city, was a popular destination for the prerevolutionary emigrants, although they were also attracted, and in far greater numbers, to larger US cities.[4] Many Russians and others who arrived in America from across the Pacific were processed by immigration officials at Angel Island in San Francisco Bay—a West Coast version of New York's Ellis Island—but many others arrived at other West Coast ports, including (like George's and Ronya's parents) the thriving city of Seattle.

Several aspects of Seattle during George's and Ronya's formative years had a lasting influence throughout their lives. These included the international orientation of the city, looking outward to the world of the Pacific; its large population of immigrants from Russia and Eastern Europe; this immigrant community's commitment to education and entrepreneurship; and the city's tradition of liberal and progressive politics and social commitment. These and other features of life in Seattle in the first half of the twentieth century echoed again and again as themes in George and Ronya's personalities, their careers, and their philanthropic endeavors.

Because of its location in the Pacific Northwest and its status as a major port city, Seattle has always had a strong international flavor. Quite early, the city saw itself as intimately linked, economically and socially, to other places on the Pacific Rim, from Alaska to Russia and East Asia. George and Ronya could have become "citizens of the world" wherever they might have grown up, but it is easy to see the fact of Seattle's international and global orientation as part of the background of many of their interests and activities throughout their lives.

By the time that George was born in Seattle in 1917 and Ronya's family arrived in 1923, the city was already home to a well-established community of Russian immigrants. As early as 1905 there were some one thousand Russian Jews in Seattle, refugees from religious persecution under the czar. Additional waves of immigrants—Russian Orthodox as well as Jewish—arrived during World War I and as a result of the Bolshevik revolution of 1917 and the subsequent establishment of the Soviet Union. By 1925 there were an estimated five thousand people of Russian heritage in the city. The Russian community continued to grow throughout the years that George and Ronya lived there, with much of the later immigration spurred by events such as the Japanese occupation of Manchuria in the 1930s and the repressive policies of Joseph Stalin. A newspaper report in 1925 described the Russian Orthodox community as tight-knit and concentrated around Saint Spiridon Orthodox Church, then on Lakeview Boulevard, while an earlier report said the Russian Jews were concentrated in a business and residential district around Railroad Avenue, much farther south. Many of the immigrants were well-educated professionals, but it appears that night classes for the study of English and to prepare for citizenship tests were popular among all economic levels. On February 25, 1925, when George was seven and Ronya was three, the community held a "Russian Evening" with music and dancing in ethnic costumes to raise money for employment programs for new immigrants and to help build a church. Publication of the *Russian Gazette*, a newspaper mostly in Russian, began that year. A common preoccupation of members of the community was the process for becoming a citizen.[5] Free weekly classes preparing immigrants to pass the tests for citizenship were provided by the Seattle YMCA and the Municipal League of Seattle, a civic group, beginning in 1912.[6] Russian-language schools were also popular, with children taking classes in the late afternoon after their regular school classes.

Much of the Russian community's life revolved around the Russian Orthodox Church. The first Orthodox church in the city was Saint Spiridon, which opened in 1895 on Lakeview Boulevard with services catering to immigrants of Russian, Greek, and Serbian descent. Czar Nicholas II provided money to expand the church in 1901, as well as a stipend for the parish priest. After the Russian Revolution, Soviet-era politics invaded Saint Spiridon and other Orthodox churches outside Russia, as Soviet-backed factions fought for control against more traditional church members. The pro-Soviet faction failed to make much headway in Seattle. The

Saint Spiridon Orthodox Cathedral, Seattle. *Photograph by Monty Jones.*

church, designated as Saint Spiridon Orthodox Cathedral, moved in 1938 to its present location at 400 Yale Avenue North, well north of the neighborhood where the Kozmetskys lived. George's sister, Luba, was married there in 1941. In the early 1930s a second Orthodox church was established in Seattle, now known as Saint Nicholas Russian Orthodox Cathedral. Its founders included a group of former Russian naval officers who were loyal to the last czar. The church opened in 1937 at 1714 Thirteenth Avenue, a few blocks east of Saint Spiridon. Funeral services for George's mother, Nettie Kozmetsky Liszewski, were held there in 1978. Both churches feature the distinctive traditional domed architecture of Russia. Although they are designated as cathedrals, they are relatively modest in size.

Russian immigrants in Seattle encountered several incidents of suspicion, if not outright discrimination, during the years that George and Ronya were growing up. An incident that reverberated throughout the Russian community while they were in high school was the firing in 1932 of a librarian at the Seattle Public Library (one of George's favorite haunts) on charges that she was a member of the Communist Party and had filled the library's large foreign-language section with subversive publications from Russia. The librarian, Natalie Notkin—herself an immigrant from Russia whose family, like Ronya's, had lived in China briefly before coming to the United States—steadfastly denied the accusations that she was a communist, but library and city officials gave in to public pressure and fired her (after she refused to resign). Notkin's case was in the Seattle headlines throughout 1932. A number of prominent Seattle citizens came to her defense, and more than one hundred Russian-language readers signed a letter protesting her firing. After an unsuccessful lawsuit against the city seeking reinstatement, Notkin worked for many years as a librarian at the University of Washington, where she was in charge of the Russian collection.[7] The incident was one of several in the 1930s in which members of Seattle's Russian community were accused of communist sympathies.

Seattle had a heritage of left-leaning politics, from the more ordinary liberals and progressives to socialists and a few communists. Union activity was strong, from the docks to the shipyards to the nearby lumber camps. Particularly in the years before and immediately after World War I, the radical Industrial Workers of the World had a strong presence in Seattle, often holding street rallies attended by thousands of people. Seattle was the site of a five-day "general strike" in 1919, one of the few such citywide labor protests in the history of the United States. In 1935 and 1936, when Kozmetsky was a student at the University of Washington, Seattle was the site of extensive labor strife, with prolonged strikes by union workers in sawmills, flour mills, wooden-box factories, oil storage facilities, docks, clothing factories, and other industrial facilities. A Committee of 500, composed of the city's business leaders, fought the strikers with "private guards, gunmen, strike-breakers, and newspaper propaganda."[8]

George and Ronya were definitely capitalists and were anything but radical in their politics, but throughout their lives their political views continued to reflect the progressive attitudes prevalent in Seattle during their formative years. They were consistent supporters of Democratic Party candidates, upheld the ideals of an egalitarian society, endorsed minority economic and social advancement, and espoused feminist political causes—all positions that were consistent with the predominantly progressive political climate of Seattle in the first half of the twentieth century. George's early academic research concerned the management of labor unions, and he was known as someone who could easily ingratiate himself with union officials and get them to cooperate with his research. His brand of capitalism always emphasized corporate social responsibility and

A CIVIC ENTREPRENEUR

close alliances among private enterprise, government, and universities. George and Ronya's RGK Foundation, established in 1966, when George left Teledyne and returned to the academic world, embodied their values of social responsibility.

SEATTLE IN THE DEPRESSION

Kozmetsky had just turned twelve at the time of the stock market crash in October 1929, so his last years of elementary school and all of his years in high school and at the University of Washington were times of continued economic crisis. Seattle was shaken like the rest of the country with high unemployment, depressed wages, and stalled business conditions, but despite the persistent hard times there was never any serious question about George finishing his schooling. The family never lost sight of his father's admonition, made as he was dying when his son was five, about the importance of getting an education. In any case, there were hardly any jobs to be found, so staying in school during the Depression was a realistic option. In fact, the Depression may have had a positive effect on George. As he recalled near the end of his life, he found ready employment during the mid- and late-1930s teaching at the University of Washington, which needed cheap labor to deal with its burgeoning enrollment. "Thank God for the Depression," he told a friend.[9]

High unemployment had been familiar in Seattle for years before the Depression because of the seasonal basis of much of the local economy. In 1930 the city was heavily dependent on agriculture and the lumber industry, and even some of the major manufacturing operations—bread making and grain milling—were related to agriculture. Every winter, in good times and bad, temporarily unemployed loggers and farmworkers flocked to Seattle and Portland, so high levels of unemployment were familiar to residents of both cities well before the Depression.[10]

Leaders of Seattle and other West Coast cities expressed confidence immediately after the crash that their region was healthy enough to avoid the worst effects of a national downturn. One reason was that numerous large private and public construction projects were under way or being planned. In Seattle, for example, projects being planned in late 1929 included a new federal building and expansions of an automobile factory, a steel mill, a cement company, and a railroad equipment manufacturer. In addition, a new municipal hydroelectric dam was under construction. Almost complete was a massive project known as the Denny Regrade, which involved leveling a large hill in the middle of downtown to make the site suitable for construction (this was one of the largest of some sixty projects undertaken by the city through its first century to level much of the naturally hilly terrain). In January 1930, Seattle was behind only New York City, Chicago, and Los Angeles in the number of building permits.[11]

The city's optimism was challenged in the early 1930s, as unemployment continued to rise and wages sank precipitously in a deflationary spiral. As in many cities during the Depression, people in Seattle who had lost their jobs and homes sometimes formed squatters' communities known popularly as Hoovervilles. There were at least eight of these shantytowns in Seattle, with the largest (numbering sometimes 1,200 residents) built on the lowlands near a shipyard fronting Elliott Bay west of downtown. It arose in 1931 as a haphazard congregation of unemployed workers from the logging, fishing, mining, and agriculture industries. Although the city tried at first to tear down the shacks cropping up throughout the city, officials soon reached an accommodation with the squatters, and the city's Hoovervilles remained in place until the start of World War II.[12] Several shantytowns were near the neighborhood where Kozmetsky grew up. The closest one, known as the Airport Way Hooverville, was a group of shacks that lined a street south of downtown, just west of the present-day intersection of Interstate 5 and Interstate 90. George would have walked past the shacks on his way to the downtown library. In 1935, the Seattle Health Department estimated that the various shantytowns had a total population of four thousand to five thousand people.[13]

FAMILY HISTORIES

Tracing the participation of George's and Ronya's parents in the history of social and political upheaval in Russia and Eastern Europe in the early twentieth century and the resulting successive waves of immigration to America is complicated by the varying spelling of last names in historical documents and the incompleteness of the historical record.

George's father and mother, George Kozmetsky and Nadya Omelanetz, immigrated separately, in 1909 and 1916, respectively,[14] and met and married in Seattle. Little is known about the background of George Sr. until he was listed in the US Census for 1920. He came from Grodno,[15] a city in present-day Belarus close to the borders with Poland and Lithuania that had been an important center of international trade since the twelfth century. The city became part of the Russian Empire in the late eighteenth century but always maintained its mix of cultures—Polish, Lithuanian, and Russian, with a large population of Jews—at least until the rise of the Soviet Union and then occupation by Germany. In the Soviet era, Grodno was part of the Belarusian Soviet Socialist Republic, now the nation of Belarus.

In later years, Kozmetsky sometimes identified himself as Jewish when he was speaking with Jewish friends, apparently a reference to his father's background, although his mother and sister had connections with the Russian Orthodox Church. Both he and Ronya were secular in outlook.[16]

George's mother's family, the Omelanetzes, came from Sharashova,[17] a smaller town in present-day southwestern Belarus close to the regional capital of Brest. The town was part of Poland when members of the Omelanetz family emigrated in 1916 but became part of Belarus after that country declared its independence during the turmoil surrounding World War I. Nadya, known as Nettie, was born there on May 9, 1896, one of nine children (six girls and three boys) born to Alexander and Alexandria Omelanetz (also spelled Omelyanetz or Ormelanitz in some family records). The father, who disliked farmwork, was employed as a secretary to the town council, while the mother tended crops that the family depended on for food. Alexander was thirty-two and Alexandria was sixteen when they married.[18]

Nettie's niece, Nena Running, was a daughter of Nettie's older sister, Pauline, and a lifelong friend of Nettie's children, George and Luba. She recalled in the 1990s that her mother and her Aunt Nettie had grown up under harsh conditions before moving to America. Pauline was the second oldest of the six girls and was said to be a disappointment to her father, who worried about having enough land for dowries when his daughters married. The family lived in a primitive log cabin that had no more than two or three rooms and was heated by a large brick oven. On cold nights, family members could sleep on top of the oven. A loft, reached by a ladder, was spread with sand as insulation and was used for drying clothes. There was no running water in the cabin, and water was supplied by the family's well and by a communal well in the town square. Each family had a long plot of ground for growing vegetables and fruit trees. Most of the residents were Orthodox Christians, but there was a small Jewish population in the town. As in much of Europe, Jews generally served as merchants because they were not allowed to own land.

Often the Omelanetz family did not have enough pairs of shoes for all the girls to go to school at the same time—a deprivation that instilled in Pauline a commitment to education for herself and her children.[19] This early lack of educational opportunity also seems to have had a profound lifelong effect on Nettie. Late in his life, George Kozmetsky recalled that his mother was "an intelligent woman who had wanted to be a school teacher all her life but had never felt comfortable that she could pass the written or oral examination in English to become an American citizen."[20]

The Kozmetsky family—George Sr., Nettie, and two-year-old George— first appear in the US Census in 1920, although their surname is erroneously listed as Kosman. Kosman and Kozman are much more common names than Kozmetsky (which appears to belong to only one family in the United States), and the census enumerator for the Kozmetskys' neighborhood in 1920 (one Albert C. Moses) could have easily written down a name with which he was more familiar instead of the correct one.[21] That this census record is for the Kozmetsky family is certain from several pieces of evidence—the address, at 816 Norman, is the same as the one listed for the family in early city directories and school records; the first names of the three family members fit the Kozmetsky family; and the age of the youngest member of the household is given as two years and three months. The census taker filled in the form on January 8, 1920, so young George would have been three days shy of that age. He was born on October 5, 1917, very likely at home attended by a midwife rather than in a hospital. Young George's sister, Luba, was born in 1923. (Their cousin, Nena Nehoda, later Nena Running, was born in Seattle in 1922 with a midwife, a Mrs. Konovoloff, in attendance.)[22]

The census record also provides this information: George the elder owned the house at 816 Norman, free of any mortgage. He was twenty-eight years old, making him born in 1891 or 1892, and he emigrated in 1909 from Poland[23] and was still an "alien." His occupation is listed as a "bolter up" in a shipyard. He could not read or write and, according to the census taker, did not speak English, despite having been in the United States for eleven years. Young George's mother is listed as Nettie, twenty-five at the time of the census. The form states that she could not read or write, but it is blank regarding whether she spoke English. On a delayed birth certificate for her niece, Nena, issued in 1942, Nettie did sign her name to a supporting affidavit.[24]

Two other people were living in the Kozmetsky house in 1920, probably as boarders. They were K. Zubal, twenty-three, and Sten Green, twenty-eight, both immigrants from Poland, in 1910 and 1912, respectively. Like George Sr., Zubal was a bolter up in a shipyard, and Green had a job as a brush maker in a brush factory. Neither could read or write, but Zubal, unlike Green, was said to be able to speak English, so he might have assisted in providing information for the census form. Russian was listed as the "mother tongue" for everyone in the household.

Only four houses were occupied in the 800 block of Norman Street when the census taker came by—all of them occupied by Russian speakers from Poland, Russia, or Siberia. City maps from the 1920s show only a few structures on Norman and adjacent streets, with much vacant land on every block.[25]

Although George's father was listed as working in a shipyard in the 1920 census, he was described as a sausage maker in the 1919 Seattle city direc-

A Civic Entrepreneur

tory and again in 1920 and 1923. In 1921 he was described as a butcher. In the earlier editions of the directory he was listed as working for Jas Henry. A person with that name owned a restaurant at 2101 First Avenue, a few blocks west of the Kozmetsky residence.[26] The city directories for 1921 and several more years in the 1920s show the Kozmetsky family still living at 816 Norman, but in later years they moved a little south, first to nearby houses on Atlantic and Judkins Streets and then on Ninth Avenue South.

The elder George Kozmetsky died in 1923 of influenza or pneumonia when young George was five years old and his sister Luba was one. The loss plummeted the family into a period of economic hardship that required Nettie, and, before long, her young son, to seek work outside the home. For several years after her husband's death, Nettie worked cleaning Pullman cars. She would have worked either at the King Street Station, then the home of the Northern Pacific Railway and now an Amtrak station, or at the adjacent Union Station, then serving the Union Pacific Railroad and now the headquarters for the regional bus and rail systems. The stations are just south of downtown between Second and Fourth Avenues and a few blocks west and north of the neighborhood where the Kozmetskys lived. George remembered going to the docks west of his home to get fish for the family's meals, and he was about nine when he started working at a warehouse for the S. H. Kress dime-store company.[27] The warehouse was in a row of modest one-story warehouses on Sixth Avenue just two or three blocks west of the Kozmetskys' house and is still standing. George also assumed at a very early age many household duties, such as gathering firewood and helping with cooking and cleaning.[28]

George always felt that these early experiences, despite the economic hardships, had a positive effect on developing his character. His optimistic interpretation of that time was paraphrased by Nancy Ritchey: "The fortunate result of the family's straits was that Nadya taught George responsibility and accountability, which became a pervasive theme in his life. As the older child, he was responsible for many of the tasks necessary to care for the family of a single working mother. . . . Perhaps even more important to his development as an accountable, responsible person, his mother talked to him about family issues, using him as her adviser."[29]

The illness and death of his father also gave the entire family an occasion to focus on the importance of education for the children. One of George's father's last admonitions to his son was that he get an education, and his mother was so much in agreement with this goal that she had the family set aside $10 in 1923 ($142 in 2017) as the beginning of a savings fund to pay for college.[30] The money was probably secreted away under a mattress because the Kozmetsky family, like many immigrants of their time and social class, had little use for banks. When Nettie died in 1978, her mattress was still found to contain household money.[31]

A working-class background and the economic hardships typical of many immigrant families did not prevent the Kozmetsky family from looking their best for family photographs taken at a photography studio. One such photograph shows George Sr. as a tall, handsome man in a stylish three-piece suit standing behind his wife and his son, who appears to be about two years old. Another early studio photograph shows young George at about age eleven, with his mother, sister, and stepfather, Stanley Liszewski, all of them decked out in the latest fashions. The family might have rented clothes for these portraits, a common practice at the time.

When George was eleven and Luba was six, their mother married Stanley Liszewski, a welder by trade who was remembered as a kind, hardworking parent who provided well for his new family despite the precariousness of immigrant life and the hardships of the Depression. "Stanley raised George and Luba as a father figure; he was a very good person, solid and easygoing," said George's elder son, Greg.[32] Another family member described him as "a gentle soul."[33] George grew close to his stepfather and relied on him for guidance through the traditional rites of passage, such as learning to drive.[34]

Born on April 12, 1896, in Maje, Poland (later Russia), Stanislaw Lischewski (as he was called on his certificate of arrival) sailed to America from Hamburg, Germany, on the SS *Kaiserin Auguste Victoria*, arriving in New York on May 24, 1913.[35] The ship, named for the last German empress and queen of Prussia, was launched in 1905 by the Hamburg-America line and was the world's largest ocean liner until the launching of the *Lusitania* the next year.[36] Family reminiscences held that Stanley's parents encouraged him to emigrate, just after his seventeenth birthday, to escape conscription in the army of Russia, which dominated Poland at the time.[37]

In 1934, in his declaration of intention to become a US citizen, Liszewski was described as a laborer, but in other sources he is called a blacksmith or a welder. He first filed a petition for naturalization in November 1933, but it was denied because of a conviction under the National Prohibition Act. He filed again in November 1936, three years after Prohibition ended. This time the application was approved, and he became a citizen on July 12, 1937.[38]

Liszewski found employment as a metalworker, sometimes in the shipbuilding industry in Seattle. In 1942, when he registered for military service (in a special category for men who had been born between 1877 and 1897, ages forty-five to sixty-five in 1942), he was working at the Washington Iron Works at Sixth Avenue and Atlantic Street.[39] While George served in the army in Europe, his stepfather did his part for the war effort by helping to build freighters. Washington Iron Works was among eighteen Washington State companies with contracts from the US Maritime Commission for construction of "fighting freighters."[40]

Stanley and Nettie were married on March 4, 1930. The Kozmetsky-Liszewski family moved several times during the 1930s, first leaving the house at 816 Norman to move to 815 Atlantic and then to 814 Judkins before moving in 1936 to 1402 Ninth Avenue South, where Stanley and Nettie continued to live at least through the mid-1950s. All these addresses were within a few blocks of each other. From an early date the neighborhood was well served by streetcar lines, at least four of them within a few blocks of the Kozmetskys' house on Norman, running north–south as well as diagonally.[41] The house on Ninth Avenue was a two-story structure with bedrooms for the children upstairs and a large yard and garden that Nettie enjoyed tending.[42] To George's regret, the entire neighborhood was leveled in the 1950s and 1960s to make way for Interstate 5 and Interstate 90. The site of the Kozmetsky house on Norman Street lies almost under the middle of the interchange where those two massive freeways meet.[43]

Stanley Liszewski died in 1975 at age seventy-nine, and Nettie died in 1978 at eighty-three. They had continued to live in Seattle, where George and Ronya and their children were regular visitors. George told friends that when his mother was near the end of her life he visited as often as he could, and one day she opened the door for him and fell into his arms and died. "She waited for me," George said.[44]

Nettie Liszewski was survived by four grandchildren and seven great-grandchildren. The services at Saint Nicholas included a traditional vigil and memorial service known as a *panikhida* and, the next day, the church's divine liturgy and last rites.[45] The two days of elaborate services impressed some of her grandchildren for the rigor of the traditions of the Russian Orthodox Church, where there are no pews and the congregation generally stands throughout services.[46]

Similar discrepancies such as those in the historical records of the Kozmetsky family also occur in the records related to Ronya's family, the Keosiffs. For example, immigration and naturalization records give the family name as both Keoseff and Kiseleff (or Keseleff), even when Fedor, Ronya's father, signed his name as Keoseff. The family spelled the name as Keosiff in later years.[47]

A certificate of arrival filled out in 1930 by the assistant commissioner of immigration in Seattle states that the Keosiff family (Fedor, wife Fania, and one-year-old Ronya) arrived in Seattle from Shanghai on November 1, 1923, aboard the SS *President Jackson*. The ship, sailing under the US flag, carried freight (mostly Japanese raw silk) and passengers between Seattle and Asian ports in the 1920s and 1930s and was known to dock at the Smith Cove Terminal near the present-day Space Needle. The ship served as a naval transport in World War II and was scrapped in 1948.[48]

Fedor's birthplace is uncertain. Immigration documents state that he was born in Tevres, Russia, on August 15, 1885, but his World War II draft records give his birthplace as Berdinsk, Russia,[49] and the birthplace of Fania (also spelled Fedoaia) as Hesinpot, Russia, on October 20, 1898. Neither Tevres nor Hesinpot appears in the most common present-day reference works. The family was of Jewish heritage, but religious background is not indicated on immigration documents, and the extent to which the family practiced any religion is uncertain. Fedor became a US citizen in 1931, having sworn, in accordance with the requirements of the time, that he was not an anarchist or a polygamist and that he renounced any allegiance to Russia.[50] It is unclear whether Fania Keosiff became a citizen.

Fedor (also sometimes spelled Feodore and later sometimes Americanized as Theodore) was described as an engineer in his declaration of intention to become a citizen, but he was listed as a box maker in his petition for citizenship in 1930. Immigration documents state that the Keosiffs lived at various times at 3000 Yesler Way and around the corner at 115 Nineteenth Avenue, about twenty blocks north of the Kozmetskys' home on Norman Street. The family later moved to the Olympia area, where they operated a café. Although they lived close to each other for several years in the 1920s, George and Ronya did not meet until they were students at the University of Washington in the 1930s.

The Keosiffs were among the tens of thousands who left Russia or Russian-controlled territory at the time of the Bolshevik revolution. Before coming to America, they had been among the many Russians who, fleeing oppression and violence, were drawn by economic opportunities to the northeastern Chinese city of Harbin, Ronya's birthplace. The Harbin area had been seized from China by the Russian government in 1896 as a center for construction of the Chinese Eastern Railroad. With the influx of Russians, Harbin grew from a minuscule village at the end of the nineteenth century to a city of more than one hundred thousand by the beginning of the Russian Revolution. Harbin had the largest concentration of Russians outside the official borders of the czar's empire, and it was complete with Russian schools, churches, newspapers, and other features of Russian culture. Chinese, Japanese, and Russian armies fought in Manchuria off and on from 1896 through 1945, with continuous conflict from 1917 to 1922, the year before the Keosiff family left for the United States.[51] Fedor and Fania were married in Harbin on September 11, 1918. Ronya, their only child, was born on June 8, 1921.[52]

The Keosiffs continued to live and work in Olympia until they moved to Massachusetts after World War II to be near George and Ronya (and the Keosiffs' grandchildren). They then moved to the Los Angeles area when George began working there in the 1950s. In the summer of 1966, George and Ronya helped the Keosiffs make a trip to the Soviet Union to relive some of their early memories. After George and Ronya moved to Austin in 1966, the Keosiffs stayed in Los Angeles and helped to look after the Kozmetskys' house in Santa Monica. For part of her years in California, Fania, known as Fanny, worked in the cafeteria at University High School, more to have some activity outside the home than for the money.[53] Fedor died in 1973 just shy of his eighty-eighth birthday, and Fanny died in 1978 at age eighty-nine.

CHAPTER 3

SCHOOL AND COLLEGE

In 1923, when George was six, his mother took him to Beacon Hill Elementary School and enrolled him in the first grade. The school, at 2524 Sixteenth Avenue South, was more than a mile from the Kozmetskys' house and was up at least one steep hill, but it was on a convenient streetcar line. The school's two-story building had opened in 1904 and provided classes for grades one through eight when George went there. The building still stands, but since the 1970s it has been used as a social and cultural center for the surrounding Latino community.

At some point George transferred to Central Elementary, a three-story building at Seventh Avenue and Madison Street, about as far north from the Kozmetskys' home as Beacon Hill had been to the south. The ornate building had been constructed in 1889, with the third floor used for high school classes and the two lower floors for elementary pupils. The building was damaged in an earthquake in 1949 and was later demolished. The site is now under Interstate 5.

George completed the eight grades of "grammar school" in about seven years, transferring to the ninth grade at Franklin High School in February 1931, when he was thirteen.[1] Although this rate of progress seems to indicate that he was an outstanding student, his permanent record shows that he had only an overall B average in scholarship in elementary school, while attaining an A in citizenship. Perhaps more revealing than these letter grades are his scores on standardized tests. The permanent record indicates that he scored 113 on an IQ test and 131 on an academic aptitude test.[2] The aptitude test was designed by Arthur Sinton Otis, a pioneer of standardized testing, and was a forerunner of the tests used today to assess academic ability. A score of 131 on today's Otis-Lennon School Ability Test could be at the cut-off point for placing a student in an academically

Beacon Hill Elementary School, Seattle. *Photograph by Monty Jones.*

"gifted" program. An IQ of 113 as measured by modern tests could place a student in a "high average" category.

Years later, Kozmetsky spoke of his early schooling as if he himself were an immigrant, even though he had been born in Seattle. It seems clear that he identified with the immigrant experience when he went to school, perhaps because he grew up in a relatively poor neighborhood that was heavily populated by immigrants and Russian was his first language. He recalled that "no one told immigrant children they were gifted [and] they always thought they were average at best and probably below average in reality. Because everyone else in school lived in better conditions and seemed more intelligent, immigrant children . . . thought living conditions and intelligence went hand in hand."[3]

George learned to read with ease, and the city's public library became a favorite haunt from an early age. He frequented the main library, which was housed in an imposing neoclassical building that had opened in 1906, having been financed with donations from Andrew Carnegie. The build-

Throughout his youth Kozmetsky was a frequent patron of Seattle's downtown public library, which was housed in this building from 1906 to 1957. *Courtesy of the Seattle Public Library, spl_shp_27887.*

ing occupied the same downtown block that houses the city's present-day main library. The building that Kozmetsky used was replaced in 1960, and then that newer building was replaced in 2004 by the present structure. To get to the library from his home, George could have taken a streetcar for part of the twenty-block journey. When George was twelve and his cousin Nena Nehoda (later Nena Running) was seven, he showed her the way to the library, starting her on her own journey to becoming an avid reader the same as he.[4]

The public schools in Seattle (and in most of the country) in the 1920s were organized mainly on two levels—grammar schools for the first eight grades and high schools for the last four. The first junior high schools in Seattle (for grades seven through nine) opened in 1927 in the north end

A CIVIC ENTREPRENEUR

of the city, but that innovation did not affect Kozmetsky's school career. Franklin High School, a four-story neoclassical building on Rainier Avenue south of Mount Baker, opened in 1912 and was expanded several times over the years. The building was restored in the late 1980s, and additions that had obscured the original facade were removed, so that the front of the building today looks much the way it did when Kozmetsky was a student there. The school is named for Benjamin Franklin, and the school teams, wearing green and black, are the Quakers.

Franklin High sits on a hill and until after World War II it had been surrounded by considerable open space. Most of the hillside has since been developed, and houses now surround the school, which is still in use. The school's traditions included an assembly to commemorate the birthday of Benjamin Franklin (January 17), an annual kite-flying contest, and an annual White Clothes Day, when all the students dressed in white.[5] The school attained a record enrollment of 2,304 students during Kozmetsky's junior year, a total that included 100 "post graduate" students.[6] Broad programs were offered in both academic and vocational subjects.[7]

An emphasis on "character education" was as important in the Seattle public schools in the 1920s and 1930s as their academic and vocational programs, at least judging by a two-hundred-page guide prepared by a committee of teachers. The guide, *Successful Living*, promoted the "four Cs" of Cleanliness, Country, Citizenship, and Character and was designed to help teachers in the school district incorporate these values in all classes, regardless of the other content. This emphasis was heavily motivated by a desire to transform recent immigrants into model citizens. The earnestness with which Seattle schools pursued this program was highlighted by the practice of beginning each school day with two minutes of silence— not for prayer but to give students and teachers an opportunity to focus their attention on the coming day's academic work.[8]

Many people who knew Kozmetsky as an adult, when he was often described as "the smartest person in the room," would be surprised to learn that he was not a particularly distinguished student in high school. Although he excelled in some subjects, he also had trouble with some. He made As in world history, US history, and economics, but Bs and Cs in Latin and Ds in French. His grades in composition were uneven—C, B, and A—while he made Bs and Cs in literature. He earned two Cs in algebra but did better in geometry, with grades of B and A. He took seven semesters of science courses, earning two Cs in botany, a B and a C in chemistry, a B and an A in general science, and a B in physiology. He tried one course in journalism and made a D, as well as one vocational course, in electricity, for which he received an enigmatic E on his permanent record. In his academic favor, he earned his high school diploma in only seven semesters instead of the usual eight. This was despite the fact that in his first semester as a freshman he took only three classes, a light academic load that suggests he was also working to help with the family's finances.[9]

The grades as entered on Kozmetsky's permanent school record conflict with some of his reminiscences, as recorded by Nancy Ritchey in the "Brief Biography" compiled in the 1990s. For example, the biography states that his high school algebra teacher, "one of the first to note how far he was from average, told him he didn't have to come to class except to take the exams . . . he could simply study at his own pace." This is inconsistent with his grades of C in algebra in his freshman and sophomore years. The biography also states that his physics and chemistry teachers asked him to help conduct experiments and grade papers. The school record indicates that he earned grades of only B and C in two semesters of chemistry that he took as a junior and senior, and that he did not take a physics course. Perhaps he was referring to the two semesters of general science that he took as a sophomore, earning grades of B and A.[10]

Sixty-four years after leaving Franklin High, Kozmetsky was inducted in 1998 into the school's Hall of Fame. He was honored in recognition of his "distinguished career in both business and academia." Others who were inducted that year include George Hitchings, a Nobel laureate in medicine; Fred Hutchison, a professional baseball player for whom the Fred Hutchison Cancer Research Center is named; Gary Locke, a former governor of Washington and US secretary of commerce; Mark Morris, a modern dance choreographer and company director; and Al Moen, the inventor of the single-handle mixing faucet (and a member of George's class of 1934).[11]

LEARNING AND TEACHING AT THE UNIVERSITY OF WASHINGTON

After graduating from high school in the spring of 1934, a few months shy of his seventeenth birthday, Kozmetsky began studies at the University of Washington in Seattle, where he thrived in an unusual new undergraduate program combining business, economics, political science, and law. The program was Kozmetsky's first experience with interdisciplinary learning, which would become a lifelong passion.[12] His bachelor's degree was awarded in political science, but he took a large number of courses in business, particularly in accounting and statistics.

Kozmetsky blossomed as a student at the university, far surpassing his achievements in public school. Often there is a particular mentor who plays a pivotal role for such a student, and in Kozmetsky's case that person

A CIVIC ENTREPRENEUR

was his statistics teacher, Grant I. Butterbaugh. Kozmetsky often praised Butterbaugh for his deep interest and guidance, which went far beyond work in the classroom. Butterbaugh "was a gifted giant of a teacher whose life was student-oriented," Kozmetsky recalled. "It transcended his academic classes and flowed out to student chapters and professional sections in Seattle and around the world."[13] Kozmetsky said that "to challenge the mind of the young, to drive them to excellence, to be creative—these were Grant's legacy to his students."[14]

Kozmetsky shared with friends some of the extraordinary assistance that he received from Butterbaugh, who introduced the young student to the worlds of art and culture and on one occasion gave him a print of a painting, which Kozmetsky seemed to prize above most of his possessions. The print was destroyed in a fire at the Kozmetskys' Los Angeles home in 1961, but Kozmetsky acquired another copy that he kept on his wall ever afterward. Butterbaugh helped in other ways to broaden the experiences of Kozmetsky, whose early life in a working-class immigrant household must have left him rough around the edges, compared with many middle-class university students. There were times, for example, when Butterbaugh took Kozmetsky to restaurants for lunch and showed him how to order from the menu—a seemingly simple skill that could have been as remote to Kozmetsky's experience as the glitter of a 1930s Hollywood movie. "George had such a high IQ that he could learn all about any subject on his own, but he said that in those days he was socially awkward and had no self-confidence. Butterbaugh helped give him social refinement," said Kozmetsky's friend Kenneth D. Walters.[15]

Butterbaugh, who held a doctorate from the University of Chicago, had done his dissertation on a pioneering project for establishing economic indices for the Pacific Northwest, and it laid the foundation for the university's Bureau of Business Research. He taught at the University of Washington for thirty-two years, beginning in 1928. He was the editor of the *International Journal of Abstracts on Statistical Methods in Industry* and was an expert on statistical methods for ensuring quality control. He was also an early member of the Institute of Management Sciences, which Kozmetsky helped found in the early 1950s. When Kozmetsky was in his junior year, Butterbaugh recruited him to teach the beginning statistics lab, one of a series of teaching jobs that helped Kozmetsky work his way through the university (Kozmetsky also earned money by tutoring football players, work that he continued after he graduated in 1938).

Thirty years after he graduated, Kozmetsky honored the memory of his old professor by endowing a professorship in Butterbaugh's name, the first named professorship established at the University of Washington.

The endowment, to support a faculty member specializing in quantitative methods, was created with a gift of $100,000 from the RGK Foundation.[16]

In remarks at a dinner to present the gift, Kozmetsky reminisced about the influence that Butterbaugh had on his life: "To me, Grant I. Butterbaugh was the teacher who touched my life. He was a gentle man, a noble person with an artist's depth of understanding of individuals. He had the ability of the performing artist to make you feel better because of the time and counsel he would give you if you became one of his students. Nor would he forget you when you left his classes. His warm letters of understanding and encouragement would find you in your time of need. Your family was easily encompassed in the warmth radiated by him and Laurie. Grant was an artist. His personally drawn Christmas cards were artistically complete for mounting in a corner of your study or family room. . . . In short, he was a Renaissance man."[17]

Classes at the University of Washington were organized by quarters, with a typical student enrolled for the autumn, winter, and spring quarters each year. Admission was generally open to any Washington high school graduate who had taken a minimum of twelve units of courses.

For undergraduates who were residents of Washington or the Territory of Alaska, tuition was $10 per quarter in Kozmetsky's freshman year, with an additional "incidental fee" of $11 per quarter. A $5 fee for the university's student association brought the total to $26 for the autumn quarter. The student association fee was less for the winter and spring quarters, so tuition and fees for Kozmetsky's freshman year totaled $73 (or $1,323 in 2017). Tuition went up to $15 per quarter in 1935–1936, and the incidental fee rose to $12.50 in 1936–1937, but the expenses stayed at those levels until after Kozmetsky graduated. Students who demonstrated a "marked capacity" for their academic work could defer these costs until after graduation (when, presumably, they could find employment) through a loan from the university at 4 percent interest per year.[18]

Kozmetsky's expenses would have been less than those of many students because he was able to live at home throughout his years as an undergraduate. The campus on Union Bay was more than five miles north of Kozmetsky's neighborhood but was accessible by bus or streetcar.

The business school was formally the College of Economics and Business, and classes were taught in Commerce Hall (now Savery Hall), one of the Gothic-style buildings on the university's quadrangle. Like most business schools of its time, it also offered courses in office skills, such as typing and shorthand. In addition to standard courses in the "functional" areas of business, such as marketing and accounting, the school in the 1930s offered courses on topics that reflected the university's region—

maritime commerce, the cooperative movement, labor union issues, and trade issues related to the US foreign service.

One of Kozmetsky's favorite pastimes during his college years was to go with his friend Herman Feinberg and others to observe the construction of hydroelectric dams east and south of Seattle.[19] Spurred by New Deal programs to expand the availability of electricity and stimulate the economy, the 1930s was a decade of extensive dam construction across the country—a period of epic projects that often stirred patriotic pride and even inspired folk singers and poets.[20] Some of the most massive of these public works projects arose on the Columbia and Snake Rivers and their tributaries in Washington and Oregon. Two projects that attracted Kozmetsky and his friends were the Bonneville Dam on the Washington-Oregon border, completed in 1937, and the Grand Coulee Dam, 230 miles east of Seattle, completed in 1941. Weekend excursions to such sites, with the inherent appeal of observing these epic engineering and organizational feats as they slowly took form and transformed the landscape, made for a popular form of inexpensive entertainment. It is not difficult to see in such trips the beginnings of Kozmetsky's later absorption in the challenges of managing the construction of large-scale projects.

Kozmetsky and Feinberg were close friends throughout their early years, until World War II sent them in separate directions. Feinberg was two months older than Kozmetsky and, like his friend, was also the oldest child of Russian immigrants. His father, Jacob, was a fruit merchant, and the family lived not far from the neighborhood where Kozmetsky grew up. The two friends were students together at the University of Washington, and they were so inseparable during their college years that friends called them the "Gold Dust Twins."[21] After they graduated, they studied together for the CPA exam and both opened accounting firms.

For at least some of the time that he attended the university, Kozmetsky had a car, as his cousin Nena Running recalled: "Many was the time that George would pick me up when I was a senior in high school, then pick up Herman, and we would all drive to the U. I would spend several hours typing for them while they play[ed] handball. Later George would be my teacher in an advanced accounting class."[22] Running also opened a CPA firm in Seattle and practiced well into her eighties.

An Encounter with Russian Aviators

Kozmetsky first appeared in the national news media as a nineteen-year-old university student, when his unit of the Reserve Officers' Training Corps was undergoing summer field training at Pearson Field, an army airport in Vancouver, Washington.[23] He was recruited to translate for a trio of Russian aviators who landed by surprise at the airport after making the first transpolar flight from Europe to North America. The Russians had been hoping to fly all the way to Oakland, California, but bad weather forced them to end the flight of their Soviet-built ANT-25 monoplane six hundred miles short of the goal, on June 20, 1937. It appears that Kozmetsky was the only person at the airport who spoke Russian, although other Russian speakers arrived when they heard news of the plane's arrival. Kozmetsky and two other cadets and a few army soldiers were the first to see the long-winged, red-and-gray plane emerge from overcast skies and set down.

The flight, which set a world record for long-distance flight and opened a new air route between the Soviet Union and North America, made celebrities of the three aviators. The story made the front page of the *New York Times*, but Kozmetsky was not mentioned until the continuation of the story on page 3. The article described the emergence of the pilot, Valery Pavlovich Chkalov, who peered "at the rain-soaked country through eyes reddened by lack of sleep" and then received his first greetings on US soil from Kozmetsky.

"I saluted him and said 'Zdrastvooitie' (Hello) and he shook my hand," Kozmetsky told the reporter.[24] A crowd, including members of the press, quickly gathered around the fliers and tried to ask them questions, but they and their impromptu interpreter were whisked away to the field office of the commandant of the Vancouver barracks, who was none other than Brig. Gen. George C. Marshall (chief of staff of the US Army during World War II and later secretary of state and secretary of defense, as well as the architect of the Marshall Plan). Also on the staff was Maj. Walter Bedell "Beetle" Smith, who later became chief of staff to Gen. Dwight D. Eisenhower and directed the Central Intelligence Agency.

Cadet Kozmetsky stood between Marshall and the Soviet aviators and relayed Chkalov's emphatic denial of a report that a faulty fuel pump had caused the early end to their flight. "He declared the ship still had enough gasoline to fly 750 miles further, or more than enough to reach Oakland. As he talked the pilot licked his parched lips and asked for a glass of water. He gulped it eagerly."[25]

Newspapers across the country, including the two in Seattle, carried the story. The *Seattle Post-Intelligencer* even ran a 350-word first-person account by Kozmetsky, "as told to" a reporter. Kozmetsky said, "I don't know whether I was more surprised at the part I had at the finish of this flight or whether the flyers were more surprised at being greeted in Russian. Anyway, I was glad I could understand and glad I was there to talk to them."[26]

A CIVIC ENTREPRENEUR

The arrival of Russian aviators after a transpolar flight in 1937 was major news in newspapers in Seattle and across the country. Pilot Valery Chkalov is shown with his plane. *Museum of History and Industry,* Seattle Post-Intelligencer *Collection (2000.107.036.16.01).*

Kozmetsky then recounted his first greetings to the fliers and his relaying of questions from Marshall. After this initial interview with the aviators, he went with them to Marshall's house, where they recovered from their exhausting flight and answered more questions. "My Russian must have sounded a little bit funny to them because I learned it at home from my folks and either it was too slangy or a different dialect," Kozmetsky said. "We got along pretty good though and I'm certainly glad that I had the chance."[27] The newspaper coverage also included extensive quotes from the aviators, as translated for reporters by Kozmetsky.

Kozmetsky stayed around after the Russians had eaten breakfast and continued to translate as Chkalov recounted details of the flight, and he ended up spending three days with Marshall and Smith, translating for the Russians at a variety of events. Eventually the Soviet ambassador to the United States, Alexander A. Troyanovsky, who had traveled to the West Coast in anticipation of the aviators' arrival, came to Vancouver and took over the translation duties. Kozmetsky's role as a volunteer translator is mentioned briefly in a biography of Chkalov written by his copilot, Georgy Baidukov. The book adds one detail that was not covered in contemporary press accounts—Kozmetsky's assistance in translating the markings on the plane's engine (he apparently climbed a stepladder to look inside the engine cowling), to verify for reporters that it had been made in Moscow and was not of foreign manufacture. Baidukov also confirms the newspaper accounts that Kozmetsky was the first person to greet Chkalov.[28]

Many years later Kozmetsky recalled the experience with the aviators for biographer Nancy Ritchey, who wrote: "It was eye-opening for him to watch the way these important people conducted themselves. It was also his first experience dealing with the press. One indelible memory Kozmetsky has of this experience is of the occasion when General Marshall chewed him out for speaking to reporters without first clearing [it] with him." Kozmetsky also recalled that it was the first time he had met any important Russians, but, Ritchey noted, "it would not be his last"—a reference to his numerous later consultations with Soviet and Russian government and business leaders.[29]

The Russians' nonstop flight from Moscow took sixty-three hours and seventeen minutes and covered 5,288 miles. It was one of the notable flights in a heroic era of aviation that captured the international public's imagination. The flight has been seen as evidence of the Soviet domination of exploration of the North Pole region in the 1930s. Chkalov, Baidukov, and Alexander Beliakov (the navigator on the flight) made a triumphant tour of the United States by train and met President Franklin D. Roosevelt in Washington, DC, on their way home to the Soviet Union (their plane was disassembled and shipped back). At home they were celebrated as national heroes. Troyanovsky, the Soviet ambassador, declared that the flight demonstrated "great possibilities for communication between two great nations."[30] Today the flight is commemorated with a historical marker and an exhibit at Pearson Air Museum in Vancouver, Washington, where a city street is also named for Chkalov.

Kozmetsky had served as a translator for one of the most honored figures in the history of Soviet aviation. Chkalov, who was named a Hero of the Soviet Union, the USSR's highest distinction, was popularly seen by the Soviets as their equivalent of Charles A. Lindbergh, and his achievements became a rallying point for patriotic sentiment. His career ended

George Kozmetsky (far left), who was an ROTC cadet, served as a translator for the Russian aviators. Others pictured are Major Paul Burrows, Harry Coffey, and pilot Valery Chkalov. *Museum of History and Industry,* Seattle Post-Intelligencer *Collection (2000.107.036.16.02).*

only eighteen months after the transpolar flight, when he died, at age thirty-four, in the crash of a plane that he was test piloting.[31]

Joining the Faculty

The episode at Pearson Field came at the end of Kozmetsky's junior year, and a year later, at age twenty, he graduated and immediately accepted an offer to join the faculty as an instructor of accounting, later adding economics and statistics classes to his teaching duties. For the next three and a half years, from the fall of 1938 until early 1942, Kozmetsky pursued a career as a teacher. He also spent those years running his one-person CPA firm.

The university also assigned Kozmetsky to teach business courses at Saint Martin's College (now Saint Martin's University), a Jesuit school in Lacey, a suburb of Olympia, the state capital. Football players from the University of Washington often went to Saint Martin's to fulfill various academic requirements, and Kozmetsky taught them business courses, including commercial law and economics.[32] With his teaching assignments at the University of Washington and Saint Martin's, and with his CPA business up and running, Kozmetsky found himself with three jobs, making him more fortunate than many who graduated from college during the "Roosevelt recession," the late-1930s setback to the economic recovery that followed cuts in federal spending.

The years that he spent teaching at the University of Washington had a profoundly broadening effect on Kozmetsky, as he "was exposed to people of unusual intellectual quality." These included Clark Kerr (later to become president of the University of California, Berkeley), who was a teaching assistant at the university, and several faculty colleagues who had been students of the economist John Maynard Keynes. Nancy Ritchey noted that "reflecting in recent years on this exposure to 'fabulous role models,' Kozmetsky came to understand that when you work with world-class people and you perform well, you have a chance of becoming world class yourself." These experiences led Kozmetsky to start thinking for the first time about pursuing a doctoral degree, and he set his sights on the Harvard Business School. In an era of relatively few financial aid programs, Kozmetsky's various jobs as a teacher and an accountant contributed to his ability to finance a graduate school education.[33]

In addition to those jobs, Kozmetsky also served during part of 1940 and 1941 as an assistant personnel director for the Seattle-Tacoma Shipbuilding Corporation, which had been gearing up for war production with financing from the navy. The shipyards had been active during World War I but were closed until the navy began in the late 1930s to make preparations for the new war that many in the military were expecting. Sea-Tac, as the company was known, became the third largest producer of navy destroyers during World War II.[34]

One of Kozmetsky's students at the University of Washington was Marion Oliver, one of the earliest female accounting graduates at the university and later, as Marion McCaw Garrison, one of the leading businesswomen and philanthropists in the state. Kozmetsky was proud of having helped to advance her education, one of the first instances of his continuing interest in furthering opportunities for women in education and business.[35] In 2001, the University of Washington business school honored Kozmetsky and Garrison with its Alumni Leadership Award.[36]

Kozmetsky's CPA firm was the first such business in Olympia, sixty miles south of Seattle. "Demonstrating a bent that would continue throughout his life for achieving goals as economically as possible," Kozmetsky worked out a deal with an Olympia secretarial school, where he set up his firm rent-free, an arrangement that benefitted the school because he provided training to its secretarial students at no cost. He also received free room and board at Saint Martin's, where he continued to teach. These arrangements allowed him to save almost all his CPA fees and begin building up a nest egg for Harvard.[37] The arrangements in Olympia and Lacey also placed Kozmetsky close to the home of the parents of his new girlfriend.

Finding a Partner

In 1940, as his efforts to save money for graduate school were well under way, George met Ronya Keosiff for a date at a wedding. Herman Feinberg recalled that one weekend when George was visiting home in Seattle, Feinberg's sister, Margaret, recommended that he call "a Russian girl" who was one of her sorority sisters at Phi Sigma Sigma and ask her to attend an upcoming wedding. "After George expressed some interest," Feinberg wrote, "Margaret called the sorority house and asked to speak to Ronya. After Ronya answered the phone, she was told by my sister that someone wanted to speak with her. George picked up the phone and commenced speaking immediately in a burst of Russian."[38]

The date did not go very well. In fact, "they took an instant dislike to each other," despite the many things they had in common—they were both children of Russian immigrants, they were both intellectually brilliant, and they shared the same political views, culture, and values. Friends later observed that they had very different personalities, though as it would turn out, perhaps complementary ones. Ronya's best friend since before she had started the first grade contrasted George's "perfect balanced influence" with Ronya's "big commotion."[39] Despite a perhaps challenging start to their relationship, George later decided he wanted to see Ronya again, and he visited her while she was staying with her parents in Olympia. Before long George had a girlfriend and a new client, as the Keosiff family began using his CPA services.[40]

Ronya was studying sociology at the university in preparation for a career as a social worker before marriage and family interrupted those career plans. Her independent spirit, energy, and social consciousness—traits familiar to all who knew her in later life—were evident during her college years, not least in her choice of sorority. Phi Sigma Sigma was a pioneering sorority, having been established in 1913 at Hunter College in New York with the purpose of admitting students of all religious and ethnic groups—a progressive social response to the widespread discrimination against immigrants, particularly against Jews and people from Eastern and Southern Europe, who in the late nineteenth and early twentieth centuries had increased the populations of many US cities.[41] A half dozen nonsectarian fraternities were established during this period, but Phi

Sigma Sigma was the only nonsectarian sorority founded in that era. The founders "believed that women of different faiths could come together and work toward common goals," and the sorority's rituals made no mention of religion.[42] Before groups such as Phi Sigma Sigma began to broaden the definition of Greek letter societies, college fraternities and sororities were segregated by religion and ethnicity, and national organizations were either reserved for "WASPs" (white Anglo-Saxon protestants) or were established to serve the interests of particular religious or ethnic minority groups.

Ronya's independent spirit extended beyond this pioneering sorority to her other activities. She had an early interest in aviation and learned to fly, sometimes buzzing George as he played tennis.[43] One can imagine that because of her adventurousness and her feelings about the war against fascism, Ronya might have joined the Army Air Forces as a pilot if the opportunity had been open to women.

After graduating in 1943 Ronya worked for several years as a social worker with Thurston County (home of Olympia and Lacey) before she and George finally decided to marry. From the beginning, Ronya appears to have had a profound influence on George's view of society. He said he was fascinated by the importance that she placed on contributing to her community, and they easily began to share the same social consciousness. She brought him clients who needed the help of an accountant but couldn't afford to pay, and George also began doing the books, without charge, for a charity (run by the Weyerhaeuser timber company) that assisted unemployed people. It was the beginning of a lifelong partnership to which both contributed intellectual curiosity, broad ambition, a flair for making money, and a dedication to sharing their good fortune with others.[44]

George recalled that soon after he met Ronya, "he knew she was the one for him, though, in his account, *she* was never sure." Three years later, on the day they were married—November 5, 1943—Ronya told George "she gave the marriage five years."[45] More than fifty years later, George's reflections on this beginning were recorded by a biographer: "Kozmetsky believes what his mother said . . . that if the man is more in love than the woman, the marriage will last. It wasn't that Ronya didn't love him, he believes, just that at the beginning it was more one-sided. Deciding to marry was a difficult choice for Ronya because there were so many things she wanted to do at the same time: She wanted to go save starving Chinese children, fly airplanes during World War II. . . . Through all the years that followed, Kozmetsky has been grateful for the good fortune that Ronya decided to marry him. He credits marriage to her with making a major

A CIVIC ENTREPRENEUR

difference not only in his personal life, but more important, in his attitudes, value system, and morals."[46]

Despite their attraction, George and Ronya faced some opposition from George's sister, Luba, that Ronya was not "good enough" for him.[47] Nevertheless, they proceeded with their decision, and the marriage was performed by a justice of the peace at Seattle's King County Courthouse. George had been drafted into the army and was training in Texas as a medic, so he took advantage of a brief leave of absence to get married. Their marriage certificate indicates the issuance of a marriage license on November 4, the day before the ceremony. The certificate shows George's residence as Coryell County, Texas, which would have been Camp Hood (renamed as Fort Hood in 1950). The witnesses listed on the certificate are Mildred Goldberg, one of Ronya's sorority sisters (as shown in the University of Washington yearbook for 1941), and Milan Neslin, who was studying engineering at the university.[48]

The choice of a justice of the peace (JP) to perform the ceremony could not have been more fitting, given George and Ronya's views on opportunities for women. The JP was Evangeline Starr, who became King County's second female JP in 1941, when she was appointed to complete the term of the county's first woman in that job, Reah Mary Whitehead, who had died while in office. Starr served as a JP until 1963 and then as a district court judge until her retirement in 1970. She became in 1967 the first member of Washington State's branch of the newly established National Organization for Women, and she organized a Seattle chapter of the group in 1970. Starr had earned a law degree from the University of Washington in 1920 and was the only woman to take the state bar exam that year.[49] Whether by coincidence or planning, George and Ronya began their marriage with the formal imprimatur of a kindred spirit.

After a brief honeymoon at Snoqualmie Falls, a popular resort thirty miles east of Seattle centered on a 270-foot waterfall on the Snoqualmie River, George and Ronya returned to Texas, where George's unit was continuing to train for the anticipated invasion of Europe. Another remarkable coincidence soon occurred, concerning George's purchase of a wedding ring for Ronya. This occurred in Waco, which with a 1940 population of almost fifty-six thousand was by far the largest city in the vicinity of Camp Hood. The young couple happened to walk into Art's Jewelers—a store owned by Bernard Rapoport and his mother-in-law's second husband, Ben Art, on downtown Waco's Austin Avenue. The Kozmetskys bought a wedding ring from Rapoport himself.[50] Rapoport owned and operated the store from 1944 to 1949,[51] before moving on to other ventures and eventually making a fortune in the insurance business. George and Ronya's purchase of the ring would have had to have been in the spring of 1944 because they were not in Waco again until many years after the war, long after Rapoport had gotten out of the jewelry business. Rapoport became a major donor to Democratic Party candidates and various progressive and human rights causes that coincided with the Kozmetskys' interests. A University of Texas at Austin alumnus, Rapoport was appointed in 1991 to the University of Texas System Board of Regents by Governor Ann Richards, the Kozmetskys' friend, and he served as chairman of the board from 1993 to 1997. His service on the board overlapped with George's final years as an adviser to the regents. To be married in Seattle by a champion of feminist causes and then to buy a wedding ring from a soon-to-be liberal Texas powerbroker and philanthropist aligned with so many of George and Ronya's own viewpoints and could be seen as blessings that helped guarantee a successful marriage.

George's sister had married two years earlier then he, on October 27, 1941. Luba's husband was Lubi Paul Cheskov, who was active in the Croatian Fraternal Union of America and played for many years in bands that performed traditional Serbo-Croatian music, known as *tamburitza*, throughout the western United States. Two of his fellow musicians were witnesses at his wedding to Luba, which took place at Saint Spiridon Orthodox Cathedral. George and Ronya were also in attendance, with Ronya serving as one of the four bridesmaids—clearly a sign of the seriousness of George and Ronya's courtship at that stage. In 1945, Cheskov joined a popular Yugoslavian-American folk music group called the Serenaders, which in 1947 represented Yugoslavia in a United Nations Festival at the University of Washington.[52]

Whatever tension might have existed at first between Luba and Ronya, it didn't prevent George and Ronya from maintaining close relationships with the Liszewski and Cheskov families in Seattle, and from regularly visiting the city for family reunions and hosting their Seattle relatives in their homes in California and Texas. George helped family members with financial needs and generally continued to play the role of older brother, long after he had found wealth and fame in Southern California and Texas. George and Ronya also found solace in visits to the Cheskovs' recreational cabin in the village of Lilliwaup on the west side of Hood Canal, a natural waterway that forms one of the basins of Puget Sound west of Seattle.[53]

"George was the best," recalled his niece, Elaine Wiley. "He looked out for everybody in his family. The older he got, family became even more important to him, and he helped everyone financially as well as every other way. As the oldest in the family, he looked out for my mom and dad and for my sister and me. When he would come for a visit, there would be

George and Ronya (far right) at the wedding of his sister Luba and Lubi Paul Cheskov, 1941. *Kozmetsky family photograph.*

a time when he and my mom would go off and start talking, and I know he would be giving her financial advice. The way they had grown up, they went through hard times, and he always had that sense of responsibility for his sister and other family members. When my mom and dad died, George and Ronya talked to me and said, 'You're the oldest, we want you to look out for your sister.' If something was needed or we had any kind of problem, they were always there for us."[54]

The family get-togethers, particularly in Southern California, could be unpredictable. One Christmas, when George and Ronya and their daughter Nadya were joined by Luba and her family, George suddenly decided everyone should tour the hilly neighborhood around their Saltair Avenue home to sing carols. Some in the party were reluctant, but George insisted, and he led everyone up and down the hills bravely belting out one carol after another. George was full of enthusiasm, but that was the best that could be said for his singing.[55]

Ronya also had her enthusiasms during family gatherings—as when she would round up visiting family members and take them to the beach to be astounded by the spectacular running of the grunion, a small silvery fish that comes up onto the beaches of Southern California by the millions to spawn in the moonlight on spring and summer evenings.[56]

The course of World War II would bring George and Ronya's Seattle years together to an abrupt close, delaying George's plans for further education and the couple's plans for starting a family. Ronya stayed in Seattle throughout the war, but George would not return until after the surrender of Germany in 1945, when George and Ronya picked up their lives where they had left off.

CHAPTER 4

THE WAR INTERVENES

Like many veterans of combat, Kozmetsky rarely talked, in later life, about his experiences as a medic in Europe in World War II.[1] When the subject did come up, he often gave the shortest of summaries about his experiences, and sometimes offered only a cursory account of the many months he had spent in battle as a medic in charge of a forward aid station within yards of the front lines. On one occasion he summarized his entire wartime experience this way: "During the war I was very lucky and very fortunate. I never had to shoot at anyone. I was in the infantry, but I was a battalion surgeon assistant. I was given some special training. One hundred twenty-five of us were picked, sent for rapid training to get ahead of MASH. Before MASH got them we were supposed to look at them and get them out of there to MASH."[2] He also recalled that during his training at an army hospital in San Antonio he was assigned to organize the hospital's medical library. "Nobody told me in establishing it that I wasn't supposed to read it, so I read it. That got me very interested in medicine."[3]

Surviving army records provide only a sketchy outline of Kozmetsky's service. His detailed military records were destroyed, along with sixteen to eighteen million other military records, in a fire in 1973 at the National Personnel Records Center in St. Louis.[4] Whatever letters he wrote to Ronya and other family members appear to have been lost in the wildfire that consumed the Kozmetsky residence and many other homes in the Brentwood and Bel Air areas of Los Angeles in 1961. Kozmetsky did provide through the years some sketchy information about his military service, and he included some details in an interview in the mid-1990s for a brief biography compiled by a colleague at the IC² Institute (he provided, however, more information about his training in Texas than about his deployment to Europe). In addition, a list of his wartime medals—a Silver Star, a Bronze Star, and a Purple Heart—has been included in many summaries of his life, although only documents about details of the Silver Star appear to have survived.

In most published accounts, Kozmetsky's wartime experience has been summarized in two or three sentences. Research reveals, however, that much more information is available. Many details about Kozmetsky's battlefield experiences are contained in two interviews that he participated in *during the war*—an astounding coincidence given that there were 16 million Americans in uniform during the three years and eight months that the United States was at war, and most of them were never interviewed even once. The first interview was conducted by an army historian traveling with the troops and took place in December 1944 just after Kozmetsky's unit had been engaged in the horrific Battle of Hürtgen Forest. The second interview was conducted by an Associated Press reporter in February 1945 on the battlefield as Kozmetsky's unit was attempting to penetrate the German defenses known as the Siegfried Line. A portion of that interview was published in the *Seattle Times* a day or two later.

Identifying Kozmetsky's unit is all-important because it allows his whereabouts to be tracked during the fighting in Europe. The army history is particularly valuable because it lists Kozmetsky's unit as the Twenty-Second Infantry Regiment of the Fourth Infantry Division. Until September 1944 he was a medical administrator, probably assigned to the division's headquarters, but from September through the end of the war in Europe he was a combat medic assigned to the regiment's First Battalion. Documents from the IC² Institute have given the unit as the Twenty-Third Infantry Division, and many other biographical summaries have repeated that misinformation. The army did have a Twenty-Third Infantry Division (also known as the Americal Division), but it fought in the Pacific. There was also a Twenty-Third Infantry Regiment, which fought in Europe (landing in Normandy two days after D-Day) and continued to fight in many engagements in a pattern similar to that of the Twenty-Second Regiment, but the army historian's report and another army document clearly place Kozmetsky in the Twenty-Second Infantry Regiment.[5]

Other circumstances confirm that Kozmetsky's unit was the Twenty-Second Infantry Regiment. The army history includes interviews with several of Kozmetsky's fellow medics and a physician in the Twenty-Second Regiment. Kozmetsky recalled in later life that his unit had participated in the D-Day landings, but that he joined the unit soon afterward. This would fit the Twenty-Second Regiment, which did land on Utah Beach on June 6, but would not fit the Twenty-Third Regiment. The Associated

Press report, written in February 1945, says Kozmetsky had an administrative job when he first got to Europe and was transferred three months later to aid stations near the front lines. This would explain why he did not set foot on French soil until two days after D-Day. Working in medical administration, he would have been part of the support staff or headquarters, not part of the first advances of the regiment fighting its way onto the beach.

Training as a Medic

When Kozmetsky received his bachelor's degree from the University of Washington in the spring of 1938, at age twenty, he had finished all his Reserve Officers' Training Corps (ROTC) courses and fieldwork but was too young to be commissioned as an officer, so he pursued his career in teaching and running his CPA business. Three years later, after the attack on Pearl Harbor, he wanted to become a pilot in the Army Air Forces (the forerunner of the US Air Force as a separate military service), but he was disqualified from pilot training because of his vision, corrected from an early age with glasses. Instead, he sought an officer's commission in the army based on his ROTC training, but according to later interviews a physical exam revealed a heart murmur that disqualified him for a commission but still left him eligible for the rank of private.[6]

Kozmetsky was drafted in Seattle on April 25, 1942. His enlistment records give the standard terms of enlistment: "for the duration of the War or other emergency, plus six months, subject to the discretion of the President or otherwise according to law." The record notes that he had achieved four years of college, and his civilian occupation was given, inexactly, as in the category of "Teachers (secondary school) and principals." The form gives his height as 67 inches and his weight as 160 pounds.[7]

He was first assigned to the Army Air Forces and was sent to Lemoore Army Airfield, a newly established base in the San Joaquin Valley of central California (part of the old airfield is now the site of Lemoore Naval Air Station). The airfield had a dirt landing strip that was usable only in dry weather, but it was employed by the Fourth Air Force as a processing and training base.[8]

Kozmetsky's first assignment at Lemoore was to apply his CPA background to the job of reviewing and organizing the accounting records of the airfield's hospital. This was in response to questions raised by the inspector general. After a week of Kozmetsky's putting the books in order, the unit received a favorable report. Kozmetsky, who had been quickly promoted to the rank of sergeant, said years later that he had hoped to be assigned to teach mathematics to military personnel at the University of Southern California, a job that would have carried an officer's commission, but because of a shortage of doctors and medics, the army had other plans for him. Instead of sending him to the University of Southern California for a job that would have fit his academic experience and skills as well as his long-term career goals, the army assigned him to the officer candidate school run by the Medical Administrative Corps at Camp Barkeley, about eleven miles southwest of Abilene, Texas. It appears that the heart murmur that had been detected earlier was not serious enough to disqualify him from this training, although the physical demands of a medic's job could be as strenuous as those of an infantry rifleman.

Camp Barkeley in West Texas and Carlisle Barracks in Pennsylvania were the main officer training facilities for the Medical Administrative Corps, although many other facilities around the country trained other medical department personnel. Camp Barkeley and Carlisle Barracks together commissioned almost 17,100 officers during the war. The two training facilities shared a common curriculum of six basic subjects: tactics (including map reading, army organization, military operations, deployment of medical units, and a field training exercise), administration, logistics, first aid and related training, sanitation, and chemical warfare.[9]

The daily routine that Kozmetsky faced during this training began at 5:45 a.m. and usually ended at 8:00 p.m. Academic progress was measured with tests and quizzes, and a grade of 75 was required in all subjects. Classroom instruction was supplemented with outdoor demonstrations, and physical training included calisthenics, an obstacle course, and marches. Saturday afternoons were usually free time.[10]

The training for medics was fairly demanding, with the pass rate at Barkeley only 65 percent. A majority of class groups in 1943 and 1944 had more candidates who failed than passed, so the army set up an intensive remedial program that had some success in salvaging some of those who had failed. Officers in charge of the Barkeley program said the high attrition rate resulted from poor selection methods; also cited were the poor living conditions at the isolated camp out on the windy, treeless prairie of West Texas. One official attributed the high failure rate more to inappropriate instruction than to the inadequacies of the candidates.[11]

Officer Candidate School (OCS) training for the medical corps began at the seventy-thousand-acre Camp Barkeley in May 1942, and in a few months the camp was enrolling a new class of five hundred students every two weeks. The school occupied ninety-three buildings, most of which were constructed of wood and tar paper, including "hutments" that housed from five to fifteen men each.

A Civic Entrepreneur

The school included a miniature battlefield for instruction in how medical support would be organized in an actual battle. The model was 60 feet by 349 feet and displayed the locations of various types of medical support, including the point where litter carriers would collect the wounded at the front, forward aid stations (like the one Kozmetsky would operate in Europe), regimental aid stations, field hospitals, and the permanent hospitals in the "zone of the interior," which included the United Kingdom and the United States. There was even an artificial pond symbolizing the ocean that separated the battlefield from the United States. In addition to extensive field exercises on this model, the students carried out a six-day bivouac, which included the same kind of practice but on the actual scale that would be encountered in a battle.[12]

A few of the soldiers who received training as medics at Camp Barkeley recalled the experience in later life, and their memories reveal the challenges that an intellectual such as Kozmetsky would have faced. Elliott Richardson, who held four cabinet positions in the Nixon and Ford administrations, completed the Barkeley OCS in 1942 just ahead of Kozmetsky. He later wrote that he thought Barkeley was "a very tough school." Vernon McKenzie, who served in the army from World War II until 1967 and then was an assistant secretary of defense, was at Camp Barkeley early in the war. He said of his experience: "I went to a miserable place called Camp Barkeley, Texas, and decided shortly thereafter that I could withstand any form of psychological warfare that the Army could wish to apply to me for three months."[13]

A small number of African American soldiers attended the OCS training at Camp Barkeley, recording a success rate equal to that of the white soldiers. They did, however, experience morale problems because of strictly enforced segregation in Abilene, where the OCS candidates went for recreation. At one point the commanders at Camp Barkeley requested that African American soldiers be sent only to Pennsylvania for their training as medics, since it was thought that they would face less discrimination there.[14]

At the end of his training, Kozmetsky was commissioned as a second lieutenant in the medical corps and was assigned to the hospital at the Army Air Force's Brooks Field in San Antonio, a major flight-training facility during World War II.[15] War was already raging in the Pacific, but Kozmetsky was at first assigned to the Ninetieth Replacement Battalion rather than sent into battle. Later, he was assigned to units that were clearly among those being prepared for action in Europe, when the Allies were in a position to stage an invasion. There was no immediate need for as many medics as were stationed at Brooks Field, so Kozmetsky was given a job that turned out to be ideally suited to his interests and talents—organizing a medical library for the base. As he later explained, the job fit perfectly with his lifelong interest in learning new subjects and his ability to master them quickly, and he not only organized the library but also found time to read many of the medical books. He also found Brooks to have a wealth of medical experts who could answer all his questions about what he was reading—"just one of the many instances in his life where he was able to develop understanding in a new field without formal instruction in a degree program."[16]

The army next sent Kozmetsky with a group of other officers in the Medical Administrative Corps back to Abilene for concentrated training as assistant battalion surgeons. In that role, Kozmetsky would usually be the first medical officer to attend to wounded soldiers, who were walking on their own or being carried by stretcher-bearers to a forward medical station as close to the front as was practical. The assistant battalion surgeon would administer first aid and organize evacuation of the wounded to a field hospital. Part of the job was also to keep the fighting units apprised of the location of the medical station, which moved with the course of the fighting.

The medical care provided by the assistant battalion surgeons was generally limited to first aid. Wounds were cleaned and given field dressings, tourniquets and slings were put in place, and sulfa drugs, penicillin, blood plasma, and morphine could be administered. The wounded were then evacuated to a field hospital, where teams of doctors and nurses carried out operations. Every stage involved a process of triage.[17]

"Wonder drugs" and other life-saving techniques that had been unknown in previous wars were available to medical personnel in World War II. The first of the sulfa drugs, which kill bacteria and fungi, was discovered by a German chemist in 1935, and such drugs were in wide use during the war. Penicillin had been known to medicine since 1928, but formidable problems in mass-producing the drug delayed its availability during the war. It was reported that in June 1942 enough penicillin had been manufactured to treat just ten patients, but a breakneck R&D program, sponsored by the US War Production Board, resulted in the production of 231 billion units by 1943, 1.63 trillion units in 1944 (including 300 billion units available on D-Day), and 7.95 trillion units in 1945. A large supply was needed because a single case of pneumonia could require treatment with millions of units of penicillin daily.[18]

During Kozmetsky's early training as a medic, the use of penicillin would have been, at best, a tantalizing prospect for the dreamed-of future; but by the time he was running battalion aid stations in France and

Germany, penicillin had become an essential tool in the fight to save the wounded from infections, which throughout history had killed far more soldiers than the weapons of war. The clinical use of blood plasma to treat shock and hemorrhage was also developed because of battlefield needs during World War II, as was the concept of hemorrhagic shock itself. The technology of dried plasma was another outcome of the massive R&D collaboration of government and industry during the war.[19]

The Twenty-Second Infantry Regiment

During his second year of training as a medic, in September 1943, Kozmetsky took the occasion of a leave of absence to be married. He and Ronya could have managed only a very short honeymoon because his unit was nearing the most intensive period of training in preparation for sailing to Europe and the anticipated Allied invasion. Kozmetsky's First Battalion was one of three in the Twenty-Second Infantry Regiment (Fourth Infantry Division, First Army). The division, which also included the Eighth and Twelfth Infantry Regiments, took part in the D-Day landings on Utah Beach and was in battle almost continuously until the late spring of 1945, by which time the unit had taken up duties as part of the occupying forces in Germany. The division fought in the campaigns of Normandy, northern France, the Ardennes, the Rhineland, and central Europe. By the German surrender in May 1945, the division had experienced 35,545 casualties, including 4,488 killed, 16,985 wounded, 860 missing, and 121 captured. The division took 75,377 prisoners of war.[20]

Kozmetsky served alongside several famous people. The Pulitzer Prize–winning fiction writer John Cheever was a member of the Twenty-Second Infantry Regiment, and the war correspondent Ernie Pyle traveled with the regiment for part of the time that it fought its way across northern France and into Germany. Ernest Hemingway dropped in on the regiment from liberated Paris to report on the progress of the war for *Collier's* magazine and to visit with his good friend Col. Charles T. "Buck" Lanham, the commander of the regiment from July 1944 to March 1945. Hemingway was with the regiment on three occasions—in late July and early August as the regiment took part in the "breakout" from Normandy, for two weeks in September as the unit pushed into Belgium and across the German border, and from November 9 to December 3 as the unit was engaged in the Battle of Hürtgen Forest. Hemingway described Lanham as "the best military commander I have known." Lanham also was the model for the main character in Hemingway's 1950 novel *Across the River and into the Trees.*[21] Late in his life, Kozmetsky often spoke to his grandchildren about meeting Hemingway during one of the author's visits with Lanham.[22]

Lanham, one of four commanders of the regiment from D-Day to the end of the war, was a hard-charging leader described by one fellow officer as someone who appeared to want to win the war entirely by himself. "Lanham led from the front," as one historian described him, "even to the point of foolhardiness, and expected his leaders to do the same. His first words to his officers on assuming command were if they retreated one step without permission, they would be court-martialed. Rumor at the time was that he had relieved, reclassified, and reassigned more officers than the two other infantry regiments in the 4th Division combined. Emphasis on heroic leadership had a cost. From 10 July to 16 November, four battalion commanders and eighteen rifle company commanders were killed, wounded, or relieved of command."[23]

A summary of the experiences of the regiment after D-Day provides a broad understanding of where Kozmetsky was and suggests the enormous physical and mental demands that were placed on him and his comrades. Throughout the summer of 1944, Kozmetsky would have been some distance from the front lines as he carried out his medical administrative duties, but beginning in September, as the fighting continued to take its toll on the manpower of the regiment, Kozmetsky was assigned to run a forward aid station. From then on, he was often within a few hundred yards of the front and would have kept moving his station as the regiment advanced. He and the regiment would face two hundred more days of almost continuous combat before the war ended.

After training at several East Coast forts, the regiment sailed from New Jersey on January 17, 1944, aboard the British troopship *Capetown Castle*. The weather was cold and rainy and many of the men were seasick during the thirteen-day crossing to Liverpool, England. From January to May, Kozmetsky's unit, the First Battalion, was billeted at the Devonshire town of Newton Abbot, in southwestern England, and underwent training at the US base established at nearby Denbury.

Parts of the regiment participated in the D-Day landings on Utah Beach and then fought across the fortifications and hedgerows of the Cherbourg Peninsula. The regiment then participated in the Battle of the Hedgerows, the St. Lô breakout from Normandy, the march toward Paris, and by late August the crossing of the Seine to take part in the final drive to Paris. Other units liberated Paris on August 25, 1944, and the Twenty-Second Regiment entered the city on August 27. According to a regimental history, "upon the troops were heaped the plaudits and gratitude of the now laughing, now crying, flag waving, kissing, hugging, wine dispensing, champagne drinking, hysterical populace."[24]

The fighting resumed the next day as the regiment joined the effort

A Civic Entrepreneur

to push on toward Belgium and drive the German army out of France. By September 11, leading elements of the regiment were among the first Allied ground forces to enter Germany, and the next day patrols reached the extensive defensive fortifications and obstacles that the Germans called Westwall and the Allies referred to as the Siegfried Line. Some of the heaviest fighting of the war ensued as the regiment moved back and forth between France, Belgium, and Germany. On October 5, Kozmetsky's twenty-seventh birthday, the regiment was occupying a portion of the front line near Krinkelt, Belgium.

On November 8 the regiment moved to Zweifall, Germany, just west of the Hürtgen Forest, to prepare for an attempt to drive the Germans through the forest. The attack began on November 16 and heavy fighting continued until December 3, after which the regiment was relieved and moved to a defensive position near Luxembourg City. The regiment had advanced only 7,500 yards while taking more than 2,800 casualties in eighteen days of fighting in the Hürtgen Forest. Despite everything, the regiment had a turkey dinner for Thanksgiving.[25]

The regiment enjoyed a period of relative quiet until December 16, when a massive German counterattack began, the start of what became known as the Battle of the Bulge, or the Ardennes Offensive. The Twenty-Second Infantry fought on the southern shoulder of the bulge in the Allied lines created by the German attack. The First Battalion celebrated Christmas and New Year's in defensive positions near the towns of Dickweiler and Osweiler in Luxembourg. In early February 1945 the regiment was ordered once again to try to penetrate the Siegfried Line—at the identical point where it had attacked four months earlier. After nine days of fighting, the regiment had advanced about ten thousand yards and captured the towns of Brandscheid and Prüm, Germany. From there the regiment advanced slowly into Germany, not seeing a few days' respite from battle until mid-March. On March 20 the regiment crossed the Rhine at the ancient city of Worms and continued moving east with relatively little resistance. April continued as a period of rapid advance against generally little resistance. The soldiers often covered fifteen miles a day, but at times their advance was punctuated by intense local fighting. The regiment crossed the Danube near Lauingen on April 26 and moved to the foothills of the Bavarian Alps. On May 3, the regiment moved to the vicinity of Nuremberg and took over the occupation of the Nuremberg-Ansbach area. After the German surrender on May 5, the regiment continued to occupy the region around Ansbach, guarding military installations, operating camps for displaced persons, processing prisoners, and maintaining military control of the area.

The soldiers had been expecting an extended tour of occupation duty in Europe, but in early June they received word that the regiment was to prepare to return to the United States for thirty days of R&R, and then to proceed to the Pacific to fight against the Japanese, including in the anticipated invasion of Japan. After landing in New York on July 11, the men of the regiment dispersed and were told to reassemble at Camp Butner, North Carolina, on August 28. By that time, of course, the war in the Pacific was over.[26]

The Battle of Hürtgen Forest

One of the most intense and extended periods of fighting in which the Twenty-Second Infantry participated was the Battle of Hürtgen Forest in the fall of 1944. It was also one of the most futile and disappointing engagements of US troops, and one that is now judged to have had little importance in the overall war effort.[27] The army's hope had been to make a rapid advance through the forest, south and east of the city of Aachen, driving the Germans back across the Rur River and taking control of the system of seven flood-control and hydroelectric dams on the river and its tributaries. Historians have cited many reasons for the failure of the plan in the fall of 1944, among them a poorly conceived strategy by US commanders and their focus more on the Hürtgen Forest instead of the ultimate objective, the steep terrain in the dense forest, bad weather, poor roads or a lack of roads altogether, mechanical problems with US tanks and other equipment, supply problems, poorly trained replacement troops, and, not least, stiff resistance by the Germans, who may have been more determined than in some previous battles because they were now defending their own heartland.[28]

The Twenty-Second Infantry was engaged in the battle for eighteen days from mid-November to early December, by which time the strength of the regiment was so depleted that it was removed from the fighting and sent to defensive positions in Luxembourg to recuperate and rebuild. The casualty rate for the regiment was extraordinary: 2,805 men killed, wounded, captured, or otherwise incapacitated. That was 86 percent of the regiment's usual strength. Among the rifle companies, 91 percent of the enlisted men and 93 percent of the officers were casualties by early December. All the original battalion commanders were lost within the first three days of fighting, and by early December the regiment was no longer able to stage an attack because it had lost the last of its veteran junior leaders. The attrition rate among commanders of the regiment's nine rifle companies was so high that at least thirty-one different commanders were in charge of them during the battle. In addition to wounds from bullets, shelling, and mines, the soldiers suffered from trench foot, frostbite, battle fatigue, and other physical and mental ailments. The overall casualty rates of the regiment have been compared to the most horrific battles of the US Civil War.[29] Members of the regiment killed in the battle included eleven members of Kozmetsky's medical detachment—two sergeants and nine privates, who would probably have been assigned the job of carrying the wounded back to aid stations.[30]

A summary based on the regimental journal focuses on some of the effects of the battle on aid workers such as Kozmetsky: "The trek of wounded to the rear became a continuous stream, and the medical detachments were hard-pressed because of the extremely long handcarriers [stretchers] made necessary by the dreadfully inadequate road net. Snow and rain were incessant; trench foot added to the casualty rate; blankets at night for the forward battalions were luxuries seldom enjoyed; shaving was impossible. German counterattacks increased in viciousness and constant infiltrations made communication extremely dubious and unreliable; radios and telephones were destroyed by mortar and shell fire in wholesale lots. The long, thin line of replacements filing to the front passed the long, thin line of the wounded limping to the rear."[31]

The official army history of the campaign describes the conditions this way: "Seeping rain turned radios into useless impediments. So choked with debris was the floor of the forest that men broke under the sheer physical strain of moving supplies forward and evacuating the wounded. The fighting was at such close quarters that hand grenades were the decisive weapon. The mine fields seemed endless. A platoon could spend hours probing, searching, determining the pattern, only to discover after breaching one mine field that another just as extensive lay twenty-five yards ahead. Unwary men who sought cover from shellfire in ditches or abandoned foxholes might trip lethal booby traps and turn the promised sanctuary into an open grave."[32]

Thanks to the army's practice of sending historians to document the course of the fighting almost as soon as a particular engagement had ended, some of Kozmetsky's own reactions to the battle in the Hürtgen Forest have been recorded. Capt. K. W. Hechler of the Second Information and History Service (VIII Corps) interviewed Kozmetsky and other medics on December 20, 1944, in the vicinity of Gostingen, a hamlet in Luxembourg just a few miles from the German border. Given Kozmetsky's reluctance in later life to dwell on his wartime experiences, these interviews provide a rare revelation full of detail (down to the numerical locations indicated on military maps) for which there are no other sources. Hechler's account quotes Kozmetsky and includes extensive paraphrases based on information he and the other aidmen provided:

> The work of the aid men during the battle of Hürtgen Forest, and the operation of the battalion aid station, presented many difficulties, according to Lt. George Kozmetsky, Assistant Battalion Surgeon. The tangled and felled trees made vehicular traffic often impossible and hand carrying parties with litters advanced with difficulty. . . . Litter teams, including three from the collecting company to augment the regular number, worked during the evening, night and early morning evacuating casualties, the greater portion of which were sustained from shell fire. On 17 November . . . the task of the aid men increased in difficulty; the litter haul was 1,000 yards in length, under constant fire, and evacuation was made from an area where there were many booby traps and mines. The shelling increased in intensity; Major Drake, the battalion commander, was killed and Capt. Neil Elzey, the battalion surgeon was wounded. It was not easy for the aid men to work—not only because of the heavy casualties but because of the nervous strain of the constant pounding.[33]

Kozmetsky told the historian that a private who had worked as a litter bearer and had been "an absolutely fearless man" had cracked under the strain on November 17. "He had gone out and been the leading man on infantry patrols, had become so attached to his company that he slept and ate with the A Company riflemen. On the 17th, he had carried out two men on his back and made his way back to the aid station when the shelling started getting more heavy. 'They're killing my boys, they're killing my boys,' he kept repeating. Finally he tried to get a hold of a gun to overcome the feeling of helplessness at inability to fight back . . . and had to be evacuated for combat exhaustion."[34]

On the next day Kozmetsky's forward aid station was moved about one hundred yards to a somewhat safer location. During this part of the battle, the aid station began sending the more serious casualties directly to the rear without even tagging them, an expedited process that probably helped save lives but also reduced the number of casualties listed on the battalion's records. During November 20 to 22 the litter bearers "had a 2½-hour haul to evacuate each litter casualty, across steep, rocky slopes and the north-south stream." By the twenty-fourth, the aid station was near a road that allowed evacuation by jeep, but the shape of the battle had changed again by the twenty-sixth, so that causalities again had to be carried more than two hours across steep terrain to an evacuation point.

Hechler also interviewed Kozmetsky and others regarding battlefield replacements and noncombat casualties: "There were 28 cases of trench-foot in the 1st Battalion, and 63 cases of combat exhaustion. The rain and sleet encountered throughout the forest campaign, the constant damp-ness and cold with which the men had to contend, their inability to dig deep and comfortable entrenchments because of the rocky rooted soil and almost constant (though slow) forward movement, the tendency to throw away overshoes which became heavy with mud, and lack of oppor-tunity ever to get thoroughly dry all contributed to the trenchfoot cases. The combat exhaustion cases were not unusually high, according to Capt. Frye. A possible reason advanced by both Capt. Frye and Lt. Kozmetsky was that, with the high number of casualties suffered among the veterans in the battalion, the percentage of replacements was unusually high."

One of the soldiers whose main job was to collect the dead described the conditions under which he worked: "The forest up there was a helluva eerie place to fight. . . . Show me a man who went through the battle of Hürtgen Forest and who says he never had a feeling of fear and I'll show you a liar. You can't get all of the dead because you can't find them, and they stay there to remind guys advancing to what might hit them. You can't get protection. You can't see. You can't get fields of fire. The trees are slashed like a scythe by artillery. Everything is tangled. You can scarcely walk. Everybody is cold and wet, and the mixture of cold rain and sleet keeps falling. Then they jump off again and soon there is only a hand-ful of the old men left."[35] Kozmetsky told the historian that considering such conditions, it was "a wonder that the combat exhaustion figures were not higher."[36]

Until the German counteroffensive began on December 17, the Fourth Infantry had a period of unusual rest after more than five months of fight-ing. The division "began to send groups of its veterans on leave—to Paris, to Arlon in Belgium, even a fortunate few to the United States. Rotation in the line allowed others a few hours in Luxembourg City, ice cream in sev-eral flavors, and the dubious pleasure of hearing accordions squeeze out German waltzes and Yankee marching songs of World War I vintage."[37]

Just days later, on December 18, Kozmetsky's battalion put aside all thoughts of ice cream and accordion music as they suffered casualties in a confused incident that involved friendly fire. The battalion had met a Ger-man column in the woods west of Osweiler (a village in Luxembourg held by the Americans) on December 17, and the next day they headed for the village. "The last word to reach Osweiler had been that the 2nd Battalion was under serious attack in the woods; when the battalion neared the village the American tanks there opened fire, under suspicion that this was a German force. After two hours, and some casualties, a patrol bearing a white flag worked its way in close enough for recognition." The battalion then came out of the woods and joined the garrison inside the village.[38]

Several members of Kozmetsky's regiment have written about their war experiences, including the fighting in the Hürtgen Forest. One of these accounts is a memoir by James Marion Kirtley, MD, a surgeon at the Twenty-Second Regiment's regimental aid station, where the wounded were taken after being assessed and treated at Kozmetsky's battalion aid station. Kirtley wrote of the battle in the Hürtgen Forest: "Contact with the enemy was immediate and severe with mortar fire and machine gun fire cutting the first soldiers to pieces as they advanced. German artillery fire was extremely bad and our boys were subjected to another terrible hazard, the tree bursts of the artillery shells that rained a deadly shower on them. . . . Severe casualties were encountered during the entire battle and our aid men were real heroes in responding to the calls for medics and going to the fallen comrades without regard for their own safety."[39]

Kirtley also wrote about the stress of battle causing "the complete collapse of one of my battalion surgeons who [was suffering] from extreme battle neurosis and had to be strapped to a litter so that he could be evacuated to the rear. He was certain that his entire group was going to be killed and that the Germans were moving toward us in an unstoppable fashion. He was the only officer I lost in such a way but there might have been many more . . . because of the long times that they had to serve." While Kozmetsky, in his interview with Hechler, had discussed the presence of replacements, Kirtley commented on a lack of replacements for the medical officers themselves. "We had no system of rotation of medical officers that would have allowed fresh men to assume the duties of their peers and let them get away from such stressful responsibilities."[40]

Many of the wounded were patched up at the field hospital to which Kozmetsky and other medics sent the soldiers after they had performed triage and administered emergency aid, but many others were evacuated to hospitals in the United Kingdom for additional surgery. An American surgeon at a hospital outside London gave this account of the aftermath of the action in the Hürtgen Forest: "I remember *Stars and Stripes* [US military newspaper] in either October or November 1944 stating that there was light action in the Hürtgen Forest, and my God, we were getting back wounded like I could not believe. We operated for three or four days, day and night, and at the end of that period there would be a lull. There wouldn't be any more convoys coming for a couple of days or a week, then a new convoy would come in."[41]

Another account of the fighting in the forest and the treatment of the wounded was provided by William S. Boice, the chaplain of the Twenty-Second Infantry Regiment, who worked alongside the medics: "Perhaps [the wounded] had been patched up after a fashion by the forward aid men, but the casualties were too great and the wounds too many for him to be able to see all of them, and so back they came in an ever-increasing stream, some of the litters having to be carried through the mud, setting their teeth at every jar, or crying out in pain as the litter bearer slipped and perhaps dropped his end of the litter. Streams had to be forded, and, indeed, it seemed as if nature and God himself had turned his face away from this embittered and tragic regiment."[42]

A frontline soldier in the Twenty-Second Regiment (one who sometimes served as a stretcher-bearer carrying the wounded back to aid stations run by Kozmetsky and others) was interviewed about his experience in the Hürtgen Forest by historian Robin Neillands: "By the end of the first afternoon we were stretcher-bearers, taking out the wounded. There were only five members of the 3rd Platoon left and it went in at full strength. . . . There were a lot of people my age there but I aged very rapidly then. What I remember about that afternoon was not that I expected to be hit but when I would be hit and how badly I would be hurt. It didn't seem that anyone could live through that day. . . . When we got back to Luxembourg City we slept in beds, in houses, for the first time since Normandy and all those that had been in the Hürtgen developed trench foot, which was very painful . . . but after a week or so, feet or not, we had to get going again, because of the Bulge."[43]

The effort to capture the Rur River dams was interrupted by the German counteroffensive that led to the Battle of the Bulge. After that attack was repulsed, the dams were finally captured in early February 1945 by other units, while Kozmetsky's regiment was engaged elsewhere.

Report from a Captured Pillbox

Another remarkable account of Kozmetsky at work on the battlefield is provided by an Associated Press report in early 1945. Kozmetsky was interviewed while tending to the wounded during an ultimately successful effort to penetrate the Siegfried Line in the Buchet-Brandscheid sector. Kozmetsky's hometown newspaper printed the report, rewriting the lead paragraph to emphasize local facts and accompanying the story with the Reserve Officers' Training Corps photograph that had been used in the story about the Russian aviators in 1937 (see chapter 3).

"A former instructor in the University of Washington School of Economics and Business Administration, George Kozmetsky, is doing practically a physician's work on the Western Front, the Associated Press reported today," said the report. The Associated Press reporter described Kozmetsky as "a slight, bespectacled lieutenant in a blood-stained G.I. mackinaw . . . working quickly and calmly in the dark interior of a captured German pillbox."

After he bandaged a man's hip, put a dressing on another soldier's leg, and gave instructions for taking extra water with sulfa pills, Kozmetsky telephoned to the rear for more litter bearers. "In general, he was doing the work of a front-line surgeon, but when he was asked his name he said quickly, 'I'm not a doctor, and all I do is patch them up a little bit until our surgeon can take care of them properly at a collection point farther back.'" The reporter asked Kozmetsky if his job appealed to him, and he "answered thoughtfully, 'I don't think anyone likes such work. But at least it does make me feel that I am helping a little.'"[44]

In keeping with security protocol, the Associated Press report does not mention the name of Kozmetsky's unit or the exact location where the reporter encountered him, but other sources make it clear that Kozmetsky was tending to the wounded during an American attack on an area known as the Schnee Eifel, a ten-mile-long ridge that runs parallel to the Belgian border near the town of St. Vith. The ridge, which rises abruptly two thousand feet above the surrounding countryside, was studded with German pillboxes that were part of the defenses of the Siegfried Line, and it was the same area that the Fourth Infantry Division had fought for during the previous September.

At 7:00 a.m. on February 4, 1945, during a snowstorm, Kozmetsky's First Battalion was ordered to join a battalion of the Eighth Infantry Regiment in an attack up the ridge. The official army history of the war tells what happened:

> The first objective of both battalions was a road along the crest of the
> Schnee Eifel, a string beaded with pillboxes. Follow-up battalions . . .
> were to turn left and right and strip off the beads. As in September,
> success the first day was complete. . . . On the second day, 5 February,
> German artillery and mortar fire increased considerably. A battalion of
> the 22nd Infantry toiled all morning to clear 11 pillboxes in and around
> the crossroads above Brandscheid. Thereupon 2 companies poised for
> a final assault out of the woods across five hundred yard[s] of open
> ground to the village. With them were 10 medium tanks and 7 tank
> destroyers equipped with 90-mm. guns.

Shortly after midday, tanks and tank destroyers opened fire against all visible pillboxes along the road into Brandscheid. Heavy machine guns from the woods line chattered support. Infantry men burst from the forest cover, shooting their rifles and bazookas and tossing white phosphorous grenades as they ran. Although the Germans returned the fire at first, it diminished as the Americans closed in. Within three hours, the 22nd Infantry held Brandscheid and a formidable ring of pillboxes. The cost was surprisingly light, a total of 43 casualties, of which 3 were fatalities.[45]

Two days later, on February 7, the Seattle newspaper published the news story about Kozmetsky tending to some of the forty-one wounded in one of those captured pillboxes (this would have been before the final outcome of that day's fighting had become clear). Even as Ronya and others in Seattle were reading the account, without knowing exactly where the action was taking place, the Germans had already staged a counterattack against the American forces holding the village and had overrun the Twenty-Second Infantry's defenses. Although they took heavy casualties in that fighting, the Americans eventually recovered control of the village and captured 150 Germans. The Twenty-Second Infantry then moved on to the east to continue the attack farther into Germany.[46]

"Gallantry in Action"

By February 9, 1945, Kozmetsky's regiment was near the village of Sellerich, Germany, still engaged in heavy fighting. Kozmetsky's battlefield heroism that day resulted in his being awarded the Silver Star, an honor that dates to World War I and is the third-highest US award given exclusively for combat bravery (or "conspicuous gallantry and intrepidity in action"), following the Medal of Honor and the Distinguished Service Cross.

The official citation for Kozmetsky's Silver Star, signed by Maj. Gen. George P. Hays, reads as follows:

George Kozmetsky, 01545825, First Lieutenant, Medical Administrative Corps, 22nd Infantry, for gallantry in action near Sellerich, Germany, 9 February, 1945. In order to hasten the evacuation and treatment of increasingly heavy casualties during an attack, Lieutenant Kozmetsky established his forward aid station directly behind the attacking companies. Moving at great risk through withering artillery and mortar fire, he determined the number of casualties and the best routes of evacuation. He then led his litter bearers to the locations of the wounded and directed their removal. Whenever a litter bearer, due to sheer physical exhaustion, was unable to carry on, Lieutenant Kozmetsky took the man's place. He gave emergency aid to a number of litter bearers who had been wounded by direct tank fire. He was severely shaken by enemy mortar fire, but refused to leave his post and led searching parties over the fire-swept area to locate and evacuate serious casualties. Due to his heroic actions, over 120 battle casualties were evacuated. Lieutenant Kozmetsky's gallantry is in keeping with the finest traditions of the military services.[47]

Kozmetsky also received a Bronze Star with Oak Leaf Cluster (meaning the medal was awarded twice) and a Purple Heart, but the citations for those medals have apparently been lost. The official file of his military records apparently was lost in the fire that destroyed the military records storage facility in St. Louis in 1973.[48] The Bronze Star, created in 1944, is the fourth-highest military award and is given for acts of "heroism, outstanding achievement, or meritorious service" in combat. The Purple Heart is awarded to those wounded or killed in action. Kozmetsky was wounded near an eye, but it seems that the injury did not cause any lasting problems.[49]

When he was almost eighty, Kozmetsky reflected that he had learned important lessons from his war experience: "The conditions of war train people from all levels of society (whatever their intellect or education) for a quality of leadership that is missing today. Being frightened is a normal response to crisis, particularly to battlefield conditions. It's a hard way to learn it, but it shows you what you're made of and where your breaking point is." Kozmetsky also said he had learned that "if you care about people and want to help them, caring does more for you than them."[50]

Kozmetsky contributed to the historical record of the regiment's experiences, including, in an interview at the IC² Institute, what he said was his most vivid memory of the war. His job had been to "go out with the leading company under attack to be sure they knew where the aid station was. During lulls in the fighting he would tell the men how they could help themselves by coming to him. He made an intense effort to see that the men got to the aid stations within the 'four golden hours'—the crucial four hours after a man was wounded when medical attention had the greatest chance of saving his life. His most vivid memory from the 200 days of battle is of a soldier who walked in and said, 'I remember what you told me, and here I am. I got hit by shrapnel.' Cutting the wounded man's pants off revealed that the shrapnel had taken the man's whole hipbone out. Kozmetsky doesn't know how the soldier walked to the aid station— only that he did."[51]

A CIVIC ENTREPRENEUR

Coming Home

The Twenty-Second Infantry Regiment departed from France as a group, sailing from Le Havre in July aboard the ten-thousand-ton troopship SS *James B. Parker*. They arrived in New York on July 11.[52]

Kozmetsky had thirty days before he was due to report with the rest of the regiment at its headquarters at Camp Butner in North Carolina, so he took the train home to Seattle—fully expecting that by the end of the summer or early fall he would be departing with the regiment for the Far East to take part in a planned invasion of Japan.

Getting to Seattle from New York in 1945 required a certain amount of stamina and determination, whether one traveled by train, bus, or plane. Even the expensive trip by plane took almost twenty-two hours and required stops along the way. A United Airlines flight from New York's La Guardia stopped at Chicago Midway before traveling on to Seattle.

Train service between New York and Seattle was frequent, with one of the fastest routes taking at least eighty-five hours. Kozmetsky would have traveled by coach first to Chicago, boarding the New York Central Railroad's Twentieth Century Limited at Grand Central Station in New York. Travelers headed to the West Coast changed trains at Chicago, and there could be a four-hour wait for the connection, so it was common to spend the time shopping or sightseeing in the Loop area, where the train stations were concentrated. From Chicago, a popular choice was the Northern Pacific's North Coast Limited, which left Chicago at 10:45 p.m. Sunday and arrived at Seattle at 8:05 a.m. Wednesday. Another train across the continent was the Great Northern Railway's Empire Builder, which crossed the northern tier of states before winding through the Rockies and the Cascades and descending to Spokane. At Spokane the route split in two, one line heading southwest to Portland and the other going northwest to Seattle, where it terminated at the King Street Station. (Passenger service continues today on the Empire Builder, which is one of Amtrak's most popular routes.)[53]

Soldiers coming home from combat in World War II had little, if anything, in the way of formal government-sponsored social services to help them cope with the psychological effects of battle and readjust to civilian life. They could fall back on the support of their families or their inner resources, but the sudden contrast between the battlefields of France and Germany and the tranquility of Seattle must have been staggering for Kozmetsky.

George and Ronya apparently did not leave a record of their reunion after two years of separation. At first a shadow would have been cast over

Newlyweds George and Ronya Kozmetsky. The Kozmetskys were married in Seattle in 1943 when George, a newly commissioned lieutenant, took a leave from his training as an army medic in Texas. *Kozmetsky family photograph.*

the reunion by the prospect of Kozmetsky's regiment being sent to the Pacific in only a month or so, but the dropping of atomic bombs on Hiroshima and Nagasaki in the first week of August and the subsequent surrender of Japan relieved Kozmetsky and millions of other servicemen and women from further military obligations.

Overnight, George and Ronya were free to start planning their civilian life together in earnest. Kozmetsky reported to Camp Butner as scheduled and soon began the process of being discharged from the army, a process that was not officially complete until December 16, 1945. By then he had been in the army for three years and eight months. He was twenty-eight years old, about to start over as a university student once again, and soon to set out with Ronya to raise a family.

CHAPTER 5

BACK TO SCHOOL

When George and Ronya moved to Boston in late 1945 so George could at last pursue graduate studies at the Harvard Business School, they resumed an academic pursuit that the war had interrupted. George's plan before the war had been to use income from his CPA business to save money for graduate school. There was no large-scale government program of financial assistance, such as was introduced after the war, so students could expect to bear most of the costs of education themselves unless they obtained a scholarship. In many cases this meant that attending one of the elite private institutions such as Harvard, which was George's goal, was possible only for people from wealthy families.[1] The Kozmetskys and the Keosiffs were not wealthy, but through industry and thrift (including money saved by Ronya during the war), George had hopes of continuing his education among the elite at Harvard.

Kozmetsky was among sixteen million Americans in the military during the war, so many others experienced the same kind of interruption in their career plans. For some of Kozmetsky's contemporaries and later academic and business associates, however, the war had not meant such a complete interruption in progress toward their lifetime goals. For those select few, the war turned out to be largely a continuation of their civilian work experience or a path toward new and highly rewarding fields of endeavor that eventually gave their postwar careers a boost and a head start. Among those in Kozmetsky's generation who found such opportunities during the war, and with whom Kozmetsky was later closely associated, were the following:

Roy Ash (1918–2011), a fellow MBA student at Harvard and later an executive at Hughes Aircraft and Litton Industries, spent the war as a captain at the Office of Statistical Control.

Abraham Charnes (1917–1992), a colleague of Kozmetsky's at the Carnegie Institute of Technology and the University of Texas at Austin, worked during the war as a researcher and operations analyst in the naval reserve.

William W. Cooper (1914–2012), also a colleague at the Carnegie Institute of Technology and the University of Texas at Austin, spent the war teaching at the University of Chicago and serving with the US Bureau of the Budget (now the Office of Management and Budget).

Robert S. McNamara (1916–2009), who ran the Department of Defense in the 1960s, when Kozmetsky's company Teledyne was getting its first big military contracts, had been a captain in the Office of Statistical Control and an assistant professor at Harvard.

Simon Ramo (1913–2016), a colleague at Hughes Aircraft and later a founder of TRW Inc., spent the war as head of electronics research at General Electric.

Melvin E. Salveson (1919–2014), a management professor at the University of California, Los Angeles, as well as an engineer, an inventor, and a founder (with Kozmetsky and others) of the Institute of Management Sciences, spent the war in charge of submarine construction in San Francisco.

Herbert A. Simon (1916–2001), a colleague at the Carnegie Institute of Technology and a Nobel laureate in economics, spent the war as a faculty member at the University of Chicago and other institutions.

Henry Singleton (1916–1999), a colleague at Hughes Aircraft and Litton Industries and the cofounder, with Kozmetsky, of Teledyne, spent the war with the Office of Strategic Services.

Charles B. "Tex" Thornton (1913–1981), a colleague and mentor of Kozmetsky at Hughes Aircraft and Litton Industries and later a founder of TRW Inc., was a colonel during the war, in charge of the secret programs run by the Office of Statistical Control.

Andrew Vázsonyi (1916–2003), a mathematician and an engineer who was a colleague at Hughes Aircraft, spent the war as a graduate student at Harvard and as a worker in a Harvard lab for the design of supersonic aircraft.

Dean Wooldridge (1913–2006), a colleague at Hughes Aircraft and a founder of TRW Inc., spent the war as a researcher at Bell Laboratories in New Jersey.

The wartime service of these men might have been intellectual instead of physical—largely a matter of chalk dust, fountain pen ink, slide rules, and, in some cases, fledgling computers—but their work was no less necessary to the war effort than that of the individuals who, like Kozmetsky, labored in the mud and snow of the battlefields. Kozmetsky's mind, no less brilliant than the minds of these later colleagues, had been preoccupied during the war with the wounds of fellow soldiers rather than equations, state secrets, and ingenious new technologies. Kozmetsky lost no time catching up after the war, and it was not long before he was recognized by these other men as one of their group—and one of the brightest of them all.

The wartime experiences of these future colleagues involved activities that were to have a profound effect on postwar America and would shape Kozmetsky's career in numerous ways. All of these men were engaged during the war in efforts to maximize the production and optimize the efficiency of weaponry and other war materials. This effort, on such a massive scale and with such pressing timetables, called for new approaches to the management of the entire process of production—extraction of raw materials, laboratory design and experimentation, factory production, labor relations, transportation, training, and all other phases of equipping the military forces to carry out their mission. The war's impact on the theory and practice of management, whether of government agencies or private enterprise, was enormous. The demands of the war required a departure from the old anecdotal and largely intuitive approaches to management and spurred new and more rigorously scientific techniques, including development of computers as a manager's essential tool. These new approaches were reflected after the war in changes in management education at universities across the country, and it was at this stage that Kozmetsky's path, as a business school student and a young faculty member, crossed the paths of these other men who had spent the war in more technical and scientific pursuits. Together, they contributed to revolutionary changes in management and management education in the postwar period, as well as in the technologies that were brought to bear on these endeavors. In later years Kozmetsky was often preoccupied with the special requirements of "large-scale projects," and the entire Allied effort in World War II was a scientific, technological, and managerial challenge on about as large a scale as anyone had ever imagined.

Harvard

With enough money saved for George and Ronya to start a family and for George to go to school, and realizing that the newly instituted GI Bill would pay a major part of their expenses, the couple considered several possibilities after George was released from military service in the fall of 1945. He had at least three tempting offers, based on his academic record and the recommendations of influential faculty at the University of Washington, such as his mentor, Grant Butterbaugh. Columbia University offered him an instructorship with a decent salary while he would pursue a PhD in economics. The University of Michigan offered him a job as an instructor while he studied for a doctorate in accounting and worked with William A. Paton, a pioneer accounting theorist, a founder of the American Accounting Association in 1916, and the author of the leading accounting textbooks of the time. And Harvard, which had the nation's most prestigious business school, granted him admission, but that was all—there was not even an offer of financial aid. George and Ronya mulled over the opportunities and chose Harvard.[2]

More than forty years later, Kozmetsky said his decision to go to Harvard was based on the university's new approach to business education. "I went to Harvard because they were teaching a new course called Control," he said. "Before World War II, we taught accounting and statistics in the business schools. . . . Harvard combined those two courses with economics and called it 'Control.' I have spent my lifetime on problems of planning and control."[3]

Harvard estimated the cost per term for the MBA program at $655. That total included $300 per term for tuition (increased to $400 in 1947–1948), $130 for housing, $150 for board, $25 for books, and $50 for personal expenses (excluding the cost of clothing).[4] The living expenses were for one person. These costs would be doubled when Harvard returned to a normal two-term schedule for each school year. The cost of $655 per term was the equivalent of $8,157 in 2017. The cost of tuition alone for one term in 1946 had a value of $3,736 in 2017. The Kozmetskys were a three-person family by 1946, when Gregory was born, and their daughter Nadya joined them in 1948, so their actual living expenses were considerably higher than the official Harvard estimate for one person.

Benefits provided by the GI Bill went a long way toward helping the Kozmetskys meet these costs. The legislation, officially called the Servicemen's Readjustment Act of 1944, provided a veteran with $500 a year in higher education benefits for tuition, books, and other expenses, plus $50 a month in additional aid for a single veteran, or $75 a month for a veteran with at least one dependent. After he received his MBA and entered the business school's doctoral program, Kozmetsky also began receiving a paycheck from Harvard for his work as an instructor on the school's faculty.

Classes in the MBA program would not begin until early in 1946, but George and Ronya moved to Boston as soon as possible, partly because they were planning to start a family. To make the trip as economically as possible, George bought a trailer and a trailer hitch at Sears.[5] The couple set out on the cross-country journey in September 1945 but were only about three miles outside Seattle, on a winding road in the Cascade Mountains, when disaster struck: "Ronya said, 'Some fool has lost a trailer and it's passing us.' As the runaway trailer went over a cliff, George said, 'That's *our* trailer.' He stopped the car and they both got out and looked down: The trailer, containing all their worldly belongings, had landed upside-down in the ravine below, the wheels spinning in the air. George said, 'I never wanted the damn thing in the first place.' Ronya said, 'Neither did I.'"

When they recovered the trailer, enlisting the aid of a wrecker, they found that the damage was minimal: "In part because George had worked at a warehouse during college and learned to pack things extremely well, the only thing damaged was a whistling tea-kettle that got bent. The trailer suffered no damage that needed repairing. The incident taught them that luck meant a great deal—and provided one of the best methods in communication for the rest of their lives; all they have to do is look at each other and say, 'Is this another trailer?'"[6] Although they were fortunate that the trailer was undamaged, in some tellings of the story George and Ronya said some of their valuable family possessions had been lost in the wreck.[7]

The rest of their trip east was apparently uneventful, and they were soon settled into an apartment in Boston's Allston neighborhood, a popular residential area for students. It was a short walk to the Harvard Business School at Soldier Field, across the Charles River from Harvard Square. In the 1948 city directory for the Boston area, George and Ronya are shown as living in a three-bedroom bungalow in the town of Waltham, about seven miles west of Harvard. If they had bought that house, they could have used the mortgage benefits of the GI Bill, which provided federal guarantees for home loans as well as subsidies to help with the mortgage payments.

Kozmetsky did not begin classes until February 1946, because in the fall of 1945 the business school was still winding down its participation in the war effort. No strictly civilian classes had been offered since 1942, when the faculty had begun focusing its attention on training military officers. During the fall of 1945 the school was preparing for resumption of civilian programs with a drastic overhaul of its MBA program, but it also focused on training business leaders to deal with the "reconversion" of the economy to peacetime activities.[8]

The world learned in October 1945 of another contribution that the business school had made to fighting the war when a heretofore secret program of statistical planning was made public. The program—now famous in the annals of statistics, military planning, and the application of quantitative methods to large management problems—concentrated on creating a scientific approach, through sophisticated mathematics, to the problems of carrying out bombing campaigns, such as how to make the most efficient use of planes, personnel, and supplies, and how to ensure that equipment and personnel were available when and where needed. The program also was responsible for assessing the results of bombing runs. The program, credited with introducing revolutionary approaches to statistical analysis, was run from Washington, DC, under the direction of Tex Thornton, who led a secret War Department entity known as the Office of Statistical Control. The training of his large staff was undertaken by professors at the Harvard Business School under the wartime Army Air Forces Statistical School, known as the Stat School. During the war the business school faculty instructed 3,113 officers and officer candidates in the advanced statistical methods they would need to carry out the mission of the Office of Statistical Control. The whole operation was first made public in the *Harvard Alumni Bulletin* in fall 1945, almost as soon as the Stat School was disbanded, and then was widely reported in newspapers.[9]

Given his interest in accounting and business control, Kozmetsky followed the revelations closely. He had, of course, no way of knowing that Thornton would gather a group of veterans of the operation and put them to work on behalf of postwar American business (as his "Whiz Kids"), or the extent to which Thornton would play a continuing role in his career, first at Hughes Aircraft and then at Litton Industries (see chapter 6).

As it became clear in early 1945 that the war in Europe was drawing to a victorious conclusion, Dean Donald K. David and his business school faculty began to plan for a revision of the school's curriculum to meet the anticipated needs of the postwar era. They kept the "case method" of instruction, for which the school had been known since its founding in 1908, but reorganized and amplified the content of the curriculum. The changes that they devised, implemented with Kozmetsky's entering class of February 1946, made radical revisions in the program as it had been offered before the war. The changes reflected the growing demand for business managers in the civilian economy; changes in management requirements and techniques stemming from the country's experience during the war; a sense that the US economy would be vastly more complex after the war, as the country emerged as a superpower with new international commitments; and new relationships between labor and management stemming from the war effort. Another important factor was the personal approach to business education of Dean David, who advocated what he

A CIVIC ENTREPRENEUR

called a more "constructive" form of capitalism, including a greater role for business leaders in solving social, economic, and political problems.[10]

The Influence of a Dean

Donald David would prove to be of pivotal importance in the development of Kozmetsky's thinking and a continuing influence when he became a business dean himself. David had served as assistant dean at Harvard for twenty-two years when he was named dean in 1942, just as the business school was shutting down its civilian programs and beginning its role of providing management education to military officers. The revision of the curriculum in anticipation of a return to civilian programs in 1946 gave him a chance to incorporate ideas about the purposes of business education that had been percolating for some time. One of his central ideas, which he spoke and wrote about frequently during the rest of his deanship (he stepped down in 1955), was that business leaders had obligations to society beyond the efficient organization of their companies and the generation of profits. They had an obligation, he often said, to serve as "trustees of the public interest." They needed to be "sensitive and responsive to their economic, social, political, and moral responsibilities"[11] A "businessman" must be "a constructive and courageous participant in the affairs of society in general, similar to that which he offers to those in the business society which he guides. He must find ways of integrating his own and his organization's activities into a positive force for general social welfare."[12]

These thoughts were summarized in a phrase that became a slogan of David's deanship—"education for business responsibility." The phrase "corporate social responsibility" was not yet in vogue, but David and his colleagues were helping to move corporations toward the idea that they should do more than serve their shareholders through profits and dividends and should acknowledge "the public responsibilities of enterprise." These responsibilities included fair treatment of employees, opposition to racial discrimination, and helping with the economic development of poorer countries.[13] Students at the Harvard Business School beginning in 1946 found these ideas incorporated throughout the curriculum, and the influence of these ideas would be evident throughout the rest of Kozmetsky's life.

David was explicit about his motives for this expansive view of business, saying it was one of the necessary underpinnings of a democratic society but was also essential in strengthening the capitalist system and bolstering the United States as capitalism's chief exemplar in the competition with communism. The specter of the Soviet Union, the "uncertain

Dean Donald K. David of the Harvard Business School in 1947. *Photograph by Tommy Weber, HBS Archives Photograph Collection: Faculty and Staff, Baker Library, Harvard Business School.*

world" following World War II, and the emerging Cold War were never far from David's mind.[14] These, too, continued to be influential ideas for Kozmetsky as his career developed.

Kozmetsky's later approach to capitalism and business education differed from David's somewhat, reflecting shifting conditions in the economy and society. For example, David's approach makes no mention of themes that were of pervasive importance to Kozmetsky during the last thirty-five years of his life, such as computer literacy, regional economic development based on technology, transferring university-developed technology to the marketplace, entrepreneurship, venture capital, and

　　　　　　　　　　　A CIVIC ENTREPRENEUR

collaboration among business, government, and higher education. But the similarities are also striking—the sense that dramatic new realities in society required a new kind of business education; that educational programs for the managers of the future needed to be interdisciplinary; that business should accept responsibility for leading constructive change in both the capitalist system and society as a whole; and that a business school ought to be a center of intellectual ferment and not just a routine training ground for managers.

There is other striking evidence for the continuing influence of David's views on Kozmetsky, even when the economic and societal context had shifted. In his Management 385 class at the University of Texas in the 1980s, on "creative and innovative management," Kozmetsky discussed his view that the times called for a new type of business manager, one who excelled at, among other things, manipulating information through technology. But he described this manager of the future in language that sounds like David's, emphasizing a nontraditional view of "profitability" that took into account not just the benefits accruing to shareholders but also the benefits that a company could bestow on society at large.[15]

LIFE AT HARVARD

One of the biggest innovations in the curriculum that the Harvard Business School inaugurated with Kozmetsky's entering class was to combine a series of first-year classes into one multidimensional course, called Elements of Administration, that filled the entire first year of coursework. The course integrated the study of production, marketing, finance, control (accounting and statistics), administrative practices, and "public relationships and responsibilities." Often during the course, a single problem drawn from real-life cases in business would be studied from each of these six points of view.

In second-year classes, the emphasis on integrated study of business problems was continued, but students also specialized in a particular area. They were also required to take a two-term course called Administrative Policy, in which problems were considered from the viewpoint of the top levels of management. This required students to think about company-wide objectives and the coordination of all of a company's policies and activities.[16]

One broad subject that is strikingly absent from the curriculum designed for Harvard's first postwar MBA class is the use of the computer in business management. There is good reason for this omission. The world did not learn about the secret wartime development of the first electronic computer, known as ENIAC (Electronic Numerical Integrator and Computer), until a news conference in Philadelphia on February 14, 1946—the very same day that Kozmetsky and his classmates were going to their first classes of the spring term—when the government and the University of Pennsylvania announced what they had been working on since 1943. Newspapers reported on the machine and its wonders the next day, and at least one report, on the front page of the *New York Times*, accurately pronounced the beginning of an economic, social, and techno-logical revolution. Given the broad influence of the computer revolution on the rest of Kozmetsky's life and career, it is a fitting coincidence that this first news about ENIAC arrived just as he was beginning his graduate studies. As the *New York Times* reported:

> One of the war's top secrets, an amazing machine which applies electronic speeds for the first time to mathematical tasks hitherto too difficult and cumbersome for solution, was announced here tonight by the War Department. Leaders who saw the device in action for the first time heralded it as a tool with which to begin to rebuild scientific affairs on new foundations. Such instruments, it was said, could revolutionize modern engineering, bring on a new epoch of industrial design, and eventually eliminate much slow and costly trial-and-error development work now deemed necessary in the fashioning of intricate machines. Heretofore, sheer mathematical difficulties have often forced design-ers to accept inferior solutions to their problems, with higher costs and slower progress. The "Eniac," as the new electronic speed marvel is known, virtually eliminates time in doing such jobs. The inventors say it computes a mathematical problem 1,000 times faster than it has ever been done before.[17]

The *Boston Globe* carried a much shorter version of an Associated Press story about the thirty-ton machine—without a photograph, as appeared in the *Times*, and on page 7—but the idea that something revolutionary had been announced still came through: "Improved industrial products, better communication and transportation, superior weather forecasting and general advances in science and engineering may be made possible, the Army said, from the development of 'the first all-electronic general purpose computer.'"[18]

The 320 members of the class that Kozmetsky began with had been selected from what David called "an exceedingly large number of appli-cants." By January 1946, the business school had received more than 1,300 applications for the spring term, and applications were still arriving every day in the mail, even though there were no more places available in the starting class.[19] The demand at Harvard was one reflection of a social revolution spurred by the GI Bill, which caused a nationwide surge in college enrollment. In 1947 veterans made up 49 percent of college admissions across the country, and by the time the original GI Bill ended in 1956, 7.8 million of the 16 million World War II veterans had enrolled in an education or training program.[20]

Recognizing the urgency with which many returning veterans wanted to get started on their business careers, as well as trying to accommodate the greatly increased demand for education, Harvard offered an accelerated program under which students could complete an MBA in only sixteen months instead of the usual twenty-four. Kozmetsky, a fast learner anyway, took this option (concentrating in the subject of accounting and control) and received his MBA at the end of the spring term in 1947, after which he immediately began work on a doctorate. He was among only twenty-six doctoral candidates when he began the program in 1947–1948.

Kozmetsky undertook his MBA studies with great interest, and he quickly impressed his professors with his advanced mastery of certain subjects, including those related to accounting and statistics. Repeating a pattern that had occurred when he was in high school and a student at the University of Washington, his professors at Harvard recruited him to assist in teaching the other students. In his second year, he was given the task of writing cases for the first-year sessions dealing with control.[21] He completed his MBA degree "with high distinction," earning him the school's honorary designation as a Baker Scholar.[22]

Some of the relationships that Kozmetsky formed as an MBA and doctoral student continued for the rest of his life. Judson Neff, an assistant professor when Kozmetsky arrived at Harvard, eventually moved to the University of Texas at Austin and was Kozmetsky's greatest advocate when he was being considered in 1966 for the deanship of the university's business school. Other faculty members whom Kozmetsky considered mentors[23] and with whom he maintained long friendships were Edmund P. Learned, a professor of marketing and business administration who in the 1950s shared Kozmetsky's interest in using computers to analyze business problems, and Benjamin M. Selekman, a professor of labor relations and an author of books on business ethics.

Many years after he left Harvard, Kozmetsky recalled that he had been "blessed as a graduate student to have worked for [Elton] Mayo, [Fritz J.] Roethlisberger, and George Homans, the so-called early giants" of the field of human relations. In discussing them during a class he was teaching at the University of Texas at Austin, Kozmetsky revealed something of the high stress that often prevailed at Harvard. He said those three faculty

Professor Judson Neff in 1942. Neff was one of Kozmetsky's teachers at Harvard and later a faculty member at the University of Texas. *HBS Archives Photograph Collection: Faculty and Staff, Baker Library, Harvard Business School.*

members had a hard-driving, high-pressure managerial style based on manipulating people, sometimes harshly. "Every outstanding professor I had in this area [human relations], with the exception of [Herbert] Simon [at Carnegie Tech], always had his secretaries cry or quit," Kozmetsky recalled. "The first thing I noticed as a graduate student is that their secretaries cry. I also found that as a graduate student I was sick and tired of them trying to [manipulate] me."[24] By the time he made that comment, Kozmetsky had developed a theory that the best managers broke from the old-style approach of manipulating people and had learned to focus their energies on manipulating information. Despite this theory, many of his colleagues at the business school and the IC^2 Institute considered Kozmetsky himself to be an expert at manipulating others in order to get his way.[25]

Fritz Roethlisberger was a leading management theorist who was associated with the "Hawthorne experiments," a series of landmark studies of factory conditions and worker efficiency at a Western Electric plant near Chicago. He was a professor of industrial research and human relations at Harvard. Elton Mayo, an Australian, was an industrial psychologist, sociologist, and organizational theorist. Considered the founder of the "human relations movement," he was a professor of industrial research at Harvard. George Homans was a sociologist and the founder of the field of behavioral sociology. He drew on economics, psychology, and other fields for his studies of human group behavior.

These and other Harvard faculty members carried on an informal discussion group in the late 1940s about the "behavioral sciences," an academic field that was then in its formative years. Kozmetsky was only a doctoral student with the lowest faculty rank of "instructor," but he was invited to participate in these weekly meetings. The group met on Sunday mornings in the homes of various senior professors from Harvard and other higher education institutions in the Boston area. The group would meet for brunch, followed by wide-ranging discussion. In his late seventies, Kozmetsky looked back on this discussion group and other aspects of his years at Harvard, such as his work with labor unions and his exposure to other fields like business history, as experiences that had given him "a grounding in the sources of societal change" that had been useful throughout his career in business and the academic world.[26]

The Harvard classes could be very stressful, as Kozmetsky related to one of his own graduate management classes at the University of Texas at Austin. A course taught by the legendary Georges F. Doriot, founder in 1946 of American Research and Development Corp., the first publicly owned venture capital firm, presented some particularly high-stress moments: "He had 300 students in his class. He lectured only, and then he gave us a pop quiz and came back the next class period and asked the front row to move out and go to the back and called five names and said, 'From here on in, I am teaching at the speed that these five can learn. If you want to stay in the class, you are welcome. If not, leave.' Then he worked the be-Jesus out of us five. He said you had to start thinking about new ideas. We had to submit five new ideas every day in writing. Then you got the shock of your life. You found that somebody else had these same ideas years ago. Then you wondered if he was going to flunk you. Other times I wondered if he ever read all five ideas . . . but you got in the practice of doing it."[27] Kozmetsky kept in touch with Doriot through the years, and in 1970 Doriot visited the University of Texas business school at Kozmetsky's invitation to speak about venture capital.[28]

Despite its many innovations during and after the war, Harvard was in many ways an institution still clinging to an earlier era. Only men were admitted, and, in fact, it was not until 1963 that all programs in the business school began admitting women directly. That same year saw the closing of the nondegree Harvard-Radcliffe Program in Business Administration, through which Harvard faculty, including Kozmetsky in the late 1940s, had taught at Radcliffe College.[29] The Harvard Law School had moved faster, admitting women for the first time in 1950. That left only the business school off-limits to women, as the undergraduate program and other graduate programs had begun admitting women in the 1940s. The first female faculty member to attain the rank of full professor (in history) was announced in 1948, and the first African American full professor (at the medical school) was announced the next year.

Although the campus was increasingly open to women while Kozmetsky was a student, there were still many pockets of discrimination. The university's undergraduate library, for example, was off-limits to women, including the wives of professors, except for Saturday afternoons, as a security measure. "There are far too many corridors and alcoves," the head librarian told a reporter. "Why, if we let girls in we should have to hire a force of patrolmen to watch the dark corners, at tremendous expense."[30]

In later years, Ronya told some friends that she had been unhappy at Harvard because of the discrimination against women, and she also indicated that she had felt the sting of anti-Semitism. Those experiences accounted for the lack of donations to Harvard by the Kozmetskys, friends said.[31]

The Doctoral Program

After earning his MBA in 1947, Kozmetsky became an instructor in accounting and finance courses while also pursuing his doctor of commercial science degree. The school began a new system in 1947, providing a doctoral student with $10,000 over three years—two years of salary for teaching in the MBA program (while also taking a full load of courses), followed by a year's stipend while the student completed a thesis. Kozmetsky negotiated with the school to reverse this pattern, writing his thesis the first year and teaching in years two and three.[32]

Whether or not he anticipated in 1947 that he might leave Harvard before completing all the requirements for a doctorate, the reversal of the standard order in teaching and thesis writing turned out to serve his needs in 1950, when he left Harvard for the Carnegie Institute of Technology. He had his completed thesis in hand (and even published by the university), but he was not awarded his doctor of commercial science degree until 1957 because he kept putting off his oral defense of his thesis. As he explained years later to one of his University of Texas classes: "I wanted my doctorate to be perfect. Ten years after I wrote it and after it was published, I did my oral defense. That is why my doctorate is 1957 instead of 1947. That was silly. I wanted to be a perfectionist, but you never reach that.

A Civic Entrepreneur

Kozmetsky (back row, far right) and other members of the staff of the *Harbus News*, the student newspaper at Harvard Business School, August 1946. *HBS Archives Photograph Collection: Student Life, Baker Library, Harvard Business School.*

It makes more sense to stop worrying and get far enough down to get it out." Kozmetsky also applied that lesson to his experience as a manager of research and development projects in private industry: "As a manager of R&D, you have to learn to take a project away and get the researchers excited about the new project."[33]

Among Kozmetsky's students in his final year at Harvard were Arthur Rock and Fayez Sarofim, both of whom received their MBAs in 1951. Rock went on to become a pioneer of the venture capital industry and an early source of financial support for Silicon Valley companies, as well as one of the early investors in Teledyne. Sarofim built a leading investment firm based in Houston and also invested in Teledyne. His numerous philanthropic activities have included endowed faculty positions at the University of Texas business school.

In addition to teaching in the MBA program at Harvard, Kozmetsky was sent by the business school to teach at Radcliffe, a women's liberal arts college that merged with Harvard in 1977. He taught Radcliffe courses in accounting as well as in social, economic, and political problems. His participation in the Radcliffe program is an indication that Kozmetsky was ahead of many of his male colleagues in supporting business education for women. "Harvard only sent to Radcliffe professors who were willing to teach women and would be supportive of women, so George obviously already had a temperament that was receptive to women getting an education in business," said Janey Lack, a friend of Kozmetsky who started her business studies in the Harvard-Radcliffe program but was among the first women (in 1964) to earn an MBA from Harvard itself.[34]

On the Harvard campus, Kozmetsky taught classes in control, finance, and labor economics. He had no teaching duties in the summers (and no paychecks from Harvard), so he picked up extra money by teaching special classes for the local union of the United Steelworkers of America. His contacts with the union when he was doing research introduced him and his teaching skills to union officials, so it is understandable that he was able to parlay those contacts into a summer job. He taught the union members how to read contracts and financial reports, with the goal of putting them in a better position to negotiate with management.[35]

While working on his thesis, Kozmetsky first encountered the research on the behavior of administrators by Herbert A. Simon, who would become a colleague of Kozmetsky's at Carnegie Tech and would eventually win the Nobel Prize in economics.[36] Simon had published several articles in journals in the 1940s, but his first book, *Administrative Behavior* (based on his doctoral dissertation at the University of Chicago), was published in 1947, just as Kozmetsky was beginning his own doctoral studies. Simon was a pioneer in several fields that would be central to Kozmetsky in his business and academic pursuits, including the science of decision-making and the use of computers for problem-solving in management. One of Simon's central ideas was what he called "bounded rationality," the idea that decisions can never be entirely rational because of constraints such as lack of knowledge and the complexity of the environment. Like Henry Singleton, Kozmetsky's business partner at Teledyne, Simon was an enthusiast of the game of chess. While Singleton's specialty was playing the game without looking at the board, Simon was an early experimenter with chess-playing computers. For such qualities, Simon was the kind of personality that Kozmetsky delighted in conversing with all his life.[37]

For his thesis, Kozmetsky undertook an extensive research project that gathered and analyzed information about how unions reported their finances. This study, which resulted in the publication of Kozmetsky's first book (*Financial Reports of Labor Unions*, Harvard University, 1950), may appear at first to be a highly specialized and technical project that would be of little interest to those outside the accounting profession, but it dealt with several issues that were of significance to business in general and

The first six students of the Graduate School of Industrial Administration (GSIA) at the Carnegie Institute of Technology gather with the school's initial faculty in 1949. Professor William W. Cooper is seated at the center of the table. Standing is Herbert A. Simon. To Simon's left are Elliott D. Smith, provost of Carnegie Tech, and George Leland Bach, the first dean of the GSIA. Kozmetsky would join the faculty in 1950 and become a longtime collaborator with Cooper and Simon. *Courtesy of the Carnegie Mellon University Archives.*

the wider society in the late 1940s. In a preview of his study published in 1949 in the *Harvard Business Review*, Kozmetsky expressed a hope that the research would help management and labor better understand each other and develop more productive relationships. He also hoped it would lead to more enlightened public debate by promoting accurate and reliable financial data from both labor and management, replacing the "propaganda" that each side often distributed about the other.[38] Also in 1949, Kozmetsky published another article that grew out of his dissertation research, on the types and quality of data that management and labor would need for successful collective bargaining.[39]

The choice of subject may be further explained by several factors: Kozmetsky's background in working-class Seattle, which had been the home of a vigorous labor movement throughout his years there; the large role that unions played in the economy in the immediate postwar years; the incorporation of labor economics and labor-management relations as important elements in the graduate school curriculum; and perhaps even the school's broad emphasis on the social responsibility of business in a democratic society.

The book contains a wealth of details about labor union history in the first half of the twentieth century—information that does not appear to be readily available elsewhere today. The study is also important in Kozmetsky's career because it was his first major project in field research, and it helped lay the groundwork for the early phase of his own work within private-sector corporations, which focused on accounting and financial control.

Compared to their relative influence today, labor unions were a much more important element in the economy and in politics in the immediate postwar years, when more than one-third of private-sector workers in the United States belonged to a union. Union membership was peaking during the years that Kozmetsky undertook his study, largely because of pro-union federal legislation and the effects of World War II on economic growth and industrial policy. The nation's basic manufacturing industries were almost completely unionized, and labor-management conflicts, including strikes, were a much more common feature of the economy than they are today. Union membership, as a percentage of nonagricultural employment, had shot up from only 13 percent in 1935 (when the National Labor Relations Act was signed into law) to about 35 percent by the end of the war, and it stayed well above 30 percent for many years thereafter.[40]

Although unions were in their heyday after the war, they were also under increasing scrutiny for the way they managed their financial resources (estimated at more than $2.5 billion in 1950), and charges of mismanagement and corruption were common from anti-union segments of society as well as from some reformers within the labor movement. The accuracy and usefulness of unions' financial reports not only were of interest to the unions' members, but also could affect issues in the management of the businesses that employed the members. Kozmetsky's project sought to analyze, for the first time in an academic and professional study, what unions were actually doing with their money and how well union officers were reporting their organizations' finances to the members and the public at large. He sought answers to these questions by interviewing officials of twenty-seven international unions in fifteen basic industries, examining more than one hundred union financial reports, and studying more than 150 other official union publications. The study focused extensively on the International Ladies' Garment Workers' Union and the United Steelworkers of America, with officials of both of those large and influential unions opening their records to Kozmetsky for his inspection.[41]

From the fact that these unions were willing to provide Kozmetsky with extensive data about their internal operations, it seems clear that Kozmetsky had won the confidence of the unions' auditors, treasurers, and other officials, persuading them that he was intent on conducting a sound and fair research study. Given the wariness between labor and management, they certainly could have been suspicious of a young Harvard Business School instructor asking to see their files. In putting them at ease, he could have related to them on a personal level by drawing on his and Ronya's working-class backgrounds, as well as their liberal politics. Kozmetsky's rapport with the union officials led to at least one lifelong friendship—with Thomas Murray, an official of the United Steelworkers.

With some exceptions, union officials would have found little to complain about when they read the major conclusions that Kozmetsky reached. He found that the unions' financial reports generally contained highly detailed accounts of receipts and disbursements, including donations to local unions, other unions, and charitable and political institutions. Kozmetsky was struck, however, by the reports' lack of information about direct contributions for political purposes. He also concluded that the unions had worked hard to maintain a high standard of honesty in handling their funds and that most financial reports were audited by independent accounting firms, although no government regulations required such audits.[42]

Reviewers found some points to criticize even as they praised the book as a pioneering effort that placed important issues before the public for the first time. A union official said in a review that Kozmetsky had glossed over the differences between the accounting needs of for-profit corporations and unions,[43] while a professor of industrial relations thought Kozmetsky had paid too little attention to accounting issues of local unions and had misrepresented aspects of union history.[44] There was one other review, a short notice that said the book was the first one on its subject and ought to be an aid to union administration.[45]

Carnegie Institute of Technology

One day in early 1950, Kozmetsky was walking across the Anderson Memorial Bridge, which spans the Charles River and connects Harvard Square in Cambridge with the Allston neighborhood, where the business school is located, when he was struck by the realization that it could be at least ten years before he achieved the rank of professor at Harvard and had the control over his academic work that he longed for. He didn't want to wait that long.[46] Because the war had delayed his pursuit of graduate degrees, he was, at thirty-two, older than many of his fellow assistant professors. He would be forty-three in 1960, with not much more than twenty years left in the typical academic career of that era (when retirement was often mandatory at age sixty-five).[47]

Not long after that epiphany on the bridge, Kozmetsky was contacted by officials of the recently established Graduate School of Industrial Administration (GSIA) at the Carnegie Institute of Technology in Pittsburgh.[48] The inquiry was whether he would be interested in the possibility of moving to Pittsburgh to join the faculty and help the new school implement its radically new approach to business education. He lost no time in pursuing this opportunity.

Despite the prestige of the Harvard Business School, there was significant opposition to its approach to business education in the 1940s and 1950s. New ways of thinking had begun to emerge about the academic study of business issues and the education of business managers who could cope with the new world that was coming into being after the war, and these trends were nowhere more evident than at Carnegie Tech. The GSIA was established in 1949 with a $6 million gift from William Larimer Mellon Sr., a trustee of Carnegie Tech and a founder and former chairman of the board of Gulf Oil Corp., which had its headquarters in Pittsburgh. Robert Doherty, Carnegie Tech's president, planned to use at least $1 million of the Mellon gift to erect a building for the GSIA and the rest for an endowment for the school.[49] Under Doherty and the economist George Leland Bach, the first dean of the business school, the GSIA became one of the central vehicles through which Carnegie Tech was to transform itself in the postwar period from "a second-tier engineering institute"[50] into a major research university.

The GSIA was brand new, unranked, and unaccredited, and it was clearly a "renegade" school in the world of business education, but it had $6 million from Mellon and had begun a long and fruitful financial relationship with the Ford Foundation. It had also attracted several dynamic and innovative scholars—among them William W. Cooper and Herbert A. Simon from the University of Chicago—who were joining with Bach to revolutionize business education.

Their vision for the new school was heavily influenced by the theories of education propounded by Robert Maynard Hutchins, president of the University of Chicago, as well as the interest of the Ford Foundation in reshaping university education after the war. Hutchins argued, first, that universities should concentrate on the production and dissemination of fundamental knowledge based on research and with strong theoretical foundations; and, second, that the faculty and students should pursue knowledge wherever their studies took them, regardless of the lines separating the traditional academic disciplines. For Hutchins, the ideal undergraduate curriculum surveyed the entire spectrum of knowledge and was heavily engaged in reading and discussion of the "great books" that were everyone's cultural heritage. He had no interest in the prevailing approach to professional education, which he saw as overly focused on the accumulation of facts from current practice (such as the Harvard Business School's use of case studies), common sense, and vocational training. Hutchins's ideal was for professional schools to shift their emphasis toward basic research, interdisciplinary studies, and the underlying principles of knowledge (based, whenever possible, on mathematics). He saw institutions such as the Harvard Business School as offering only fragmentary courses, being too little concerned with theoretical studies, and being overly influenced by "the pressure of the practical."[51]

These and related ideas from Hutchins, along with studies conducted by the Ford Foundation and lessons from the military's experience in scientific planning during the war, influenced the leaders of the GSIA as they designed a school to offer a new kind of management education to Carnegie Tech's engineering graduates. Bach, Cooper, Simon, and others had studied at the University of Chicago and "were steeped in the Hutchins ethos and catechism."[52]

On his first visit to the Pittsburgh school, Kozmetsky met with Bach, Simon, and Cooper, and he was an immediate convert to their cause. Simon seems to have done the initial recruiting, but Kozmetsky's meeting with Cooper was decisive. They became instant friends, as Kozmetsky recalled almost forty years later: "What I thought was an interview actually turned into an exciting discussion of what could be done to bring accounting, quantitative methods, finance, and organizational and behavioral theory into a more modern managerial context." Kozmetsky said this was a discussion "that was impossible to have participated in at that time at the Harvard Business School, even among the junior faculty."

Kozmetsky recalled, "I was so excited that I couldn't wait to meet with Ronya to discuss moving from Harvard to Carnegie Tech, if they offered me an assistant professorship." The offer was soon made by Bach, and Kozmetsky later wrote that the friendly welcome accorded to Ronya and their children (four-year-old Greg and two-year-old Nadya) by

Ruth Cooper and Dorothea Simon made it easier to accept the new opportunity.[53]

Bach asked Ruth Cooper, William Cooper's wife, to entertain Ronya and the children while George was busy with his interviews. Ruth was one of the few women enrolled in law school at the University of Pittsburgh, and Bach sensed that Ruth and Ronya would be kindred spirits. Ruth Cooper later recalled that day, which included lunch at the very formal University Club:

> Just as we sat down at our table, Dean [Judson A.] Crane of Pitt Law School came in. I was in his school then, without his welcome because he did not want women in his school, or in the legal profession. Crane was something of a man-about-town, a ladies' man, but not a lady lawyer man. He acknowledged my greeting with a nod of the head. Ronya and I began a lively discussion . . . ignoring Greg's "all little boy" restlessness. I did vaguely notice Greg was beginning to take notice of Dean Crane but ignored it because of being deep into making a new friend. But Greg got all of my attention when he slid out of his chair, went over to the dean, and wiped mashed potatoes on the dean's suit coat. The dean became red-faced and gave me a look meant to kill. I just pretended I didn't know what happened. Ronya and I went on enjoying ourselves—and haven't stopped.[54]

The trip to Pittsburgh seems to have been a success for everyone except the former law dean, and soon Kozmetsky accepted the GSIA offer to become an assistant professor teaching corporate finance. The job would also involve a substantial commitment to research, and Kozmetsky's successful experience conducting field research for his book on labor unions was obviously one of the factors that attracted GSIA leaders to him.

From all reports, Kozmetsky was popular with his Carnegie Tech students, all of whom in the early days had graduated from an engineering program. On one occasion he passed around a transistor, which few people in the early 1950s had ever seen, and assigned the students the task of thinking of possible practical uses for the device—uses that an entrepreneur might make the basis of a start-up company.[55] The transistor had been invented at Bell Labs in 1947, but the first commercial silicon transistor would not be developed until 1954 (at Texas Instruments), thus beginning the process of using transistors instead of vacuum tubes in electronic devices.

When Kozmetsky became dean of the University of Texas at Austin business school in 1966, his vision for what he wanted to achieve was heavily influenced by the philosophy and practice of the business school at

A CIVIC ENTREPRENEUR

Carnegie Tech. He attracted to the University of Texas faculty several of the people who had been instrumental in shaping the GSIA and making it an important national and international force in business education, and the continuing interactions between the faculty of the business schools at the University of Texas and Carnegie Mellon University are an important theme in the history of both schools (see chapter 10).

A distinguishing trait of the GSIA was the "academic entrepreneurship" of the faculty, who were leaders in the new approach of securing large research grants and contracts from government agencies, foundations, and business groups. Cooper won a large research grant from the air force in 1950 for a study of new analytical methods of planning, and Simon and another colleague received grants from the Office of National Research for a study of inventory and production rates. Simon and Kozmetsky soon followed by persuading the Financial Executives Institute to make a large research grant, and Kozmetsky was credited with securing another grant from the Controllership Foundation. That grant paid for a field study of how large corporations organized the controller's function—a study that led to the publication of Kozmetsky's second book, coauthored with Simon and others.[56] Much later, Kozmetsky reflected on the historical significance of the way the Carnegie Tech faculty sought outside financial support for their academic work: "Note how education and research were thus brought together in a new and significant way. This helped to set the sights for combining significant research with business education at GSIA and elsewhere. As academic entrepreneurs, we helped change graduate business and managerial education at Carnegie Mellon, Harvard Business School, the University of Texas, and elsewhere."[57]

The Controllership Foundation was motivated to sponsor a research project partly because of national defense issues arising from the Cold War, a common justification at the time for a wide assortment of government, academic, and corporate activities. T. F. Bradshaw, research director of the foundation and an assistant professor of business administration at Harvard, observed that the study, as the *New York Times* paraphrased, "comes at a time . . . when decentralization of production, warehousing, and distribution in the defense program is uppermost in the minds of industrialists because of global political developments."[58]

The research engaged Kozmetsky in a large and complex interdisciplinary study with Simon, and it turned out to be one of numerous pieces of Simon's larger academic interests in the structure and management of large organizations, focusing mainly on "the descriptive study of organizational decision-making."[59] The controllership study was one of three early research projects that Simon directed as part of his interest in decision-making and behavioral economics. Kozmetsky's association with Bradshaw at Harvard would have been an asset in bringing the project to Carnegie Tech.[60] These projects came at the beginning of Simon's lifelong achievements in such research, for which he was awarded the Nobel Prize in economics in 1978.

The controllership study sought to answer the question of how a large company should organize the controller's function for greatest effectiveness, that is, in order to provide high-quality services to the organization at minimum cost while also facilitating the development of competent accounting and operating executives. Seven large companies, including Eastman Kodak and H. J. Heinz Co., agreed to cooperate with the researchers. The study included interviews with controllers and their staffs, analysis of the controllers' reports, and observation of the staffs as they carried out their work. Kozmetsky was responsible for organizing the field research and analyzing the data. He also collaborated with others on the research staff and with graduate students in conducting the interviews.

The project was the first large empirical study that Simon organized at Carnegie Tech. In his 1991 autobiography, Simon recalled the study and the contributions that Kozmetsky made through the combination of his "people skills" and his analytical talents. The study, Simon said, "took us into factories and sales offices to see what use was made by operators of blast furnaces and sales managers, as aids to their decision-making, of the company accounting and cost accounting records and of the services of the accountants. [It] was an adventure to me, both watching George Kozmetsky (whom we hired from the Harvard Business School as a young Ph.D. [*sic*], and who already had extraordinary facility in analyzing accounting records) extract information from our respondents, and trudging through the reddish brown dust of the National Works of U.S. Steel in McKeesport [Pennsylvania] to learn how a steel mill was actually managed and how its decisions were made."[61] Simon's colleague William Cooper recalled that the resulting report on the research "left the [Controllership] Foundation unhappy because of its science-based rather than practical orientation. Nevertheless it led to *Centralization vs. Decentralization in Organizing the Controller's Department*, a book published by the Controllership Foundation which has had considerable impact on the literature of cost and managerial accounting."[62]

In the eyes of the Carnegie Tech faculty members, this type of research was important pioneering work for the nation's business schools, which they said typically were composed of faculty who had little or no experience of what operating a company actually involved. In this and other projects, Kozmetsky collaborated with a team of researchers that included future stars in a variety of academic disciplines—scholars who in many cases maintained lifelong professional and personal associations with him. One of the coauthors on the project, Harold Guetzkow, was director of the Social Science Laboratory at Carnegie Tech, and his later scholarship encompassed the fields of political science, psychology, and sociology. Others who were recruited to GSIA in its early days included Richard Cyert, an economist and statistician who served as Carnegie Mellon University's president during its transformative period in the 1970s; James G. March, who later held appointments in management, education, political science, and sociology at Stanford and participated in a "knowledge economy" research institute that Kozmetsky helped support financially; and Charles C. Holt, an expert on computer simulation and operations research who years later was recruited to the University of Texas business school by Kozmetsky and became director of the university's Bureau of Business Research.

The atmosphere at Carnegie Tech was intellectually intense and highly competitive, and Simon was the acknowledged leader. He was said to tolerate and even encourage "mavericks" on the faculty, and Kozmetsky has been cited as one of those, since he was a product of the Harvard Business School and its case method of instruction, which GSIA was seeking to overturn. It has also been suggested that Kozmetsky was sought out by Simon and the others at Carnegie Tech partly because of his immersion in Harvard's case method, since they did not want to leave their students without any familiarity with that approach to management education.[63]

The association with Simon at Carnegie Tech had a lifelong effect on Kozmetsky. When Simon died in 2001, Kozmetsky reflected on their long friendship:

> [Herbert Simon] was an example of a man I prized most highly as a remarkable human being—a very special transdisciplinary researcher, a beloved teacher and academic colleague. I prized Herb for his humility, integrity, humanity and scrupulous regard for sensibility, individual freedom and personal affection. Herb was quite a man for all seasons. Herb had that rare quality of transforming his academic and professional colleagues, students, alumni and those professionals who labored in the world of ideas in which he labored and made a lasting contribution. Herb touched people for their lifetimes. I can attest to his impact on the lives of the Kozmetsky family. It was Herb Simon who started me on my life's journey in application research in academia, business and technology in 1950 in the field research for the book *Centralization vs. Decentralization in Organizing the Controller's Department*. Herb's work is timeless.

. . . Ronya and I and our entire family will miss Herb. We are honored that he and Dorothea embraced us as part of their extended family.[64]

Despite the intellectual stimulation that Kozmetsky found at the GSIA, he stayed there less than two full years, moving in January 1952 to a job at Hughes Aircraft in Los Angeles. The move might seem surprising, given Kozmetsky's obvious comfort within the academic world and his lifelong self-image as, more than anything else, a teacher. Roy Ash, his friend since their student days together at Harvard, had helped recruit him to Hughes, having called him in 1951 to talk about the unusual opportunity to work with Tex Thornton, who had moved to Hughes Aircraft from a brief stint at the Ford Motor Co. and was carrying out innovations in the for-profit corporate world that were as far-reaching as any being implemented at academic institutions like Carnegie Tech. In addition to enabling Kozmetsky to be part of those changes in the way business was conducted, moving to Hughes would have the advantage of giving him experience in the day-to-day practical work of running a business.

Another important factor was the potential for making money, which within the academic world must have seemed very slight in those days, particularly for someone with Kozmetsky's large ambitions. Even at that early date, however, he seems to have been interested in making money only as a means toward other accomplishments, and he had in mind an eventual return to academia. He told Ronya, who needed to be persuaded that the move to private business was wise, that he was attracted to the opportunity to see what life was like within the corporate world, and that he thought he might want to do that for a few years before returning to an academic job, where he could incorporate his newly acquired knowledge into the challenge to educate new generations of managers. "He always thought of himself, first and foremost, as a teacher," said Greg Kozmetsky. "When he left Carnegie Tech for Hughes Aircraft, he told our mother, 'Let me go for a year. It will make me a better teacher to have the real-world experience.'"[65]

George was also trying to look well into the future. As William Cooper recalled: "George told us [at Carnegie Tech] that his plan was to go out and work in the private sector for a period of time and make a lot of money and then get his own business school and run it according to his own principles. I don't think anyone at Carnegie Tech quite believed he was serious, or that he would pull that off. But that is pretty much what happened, although it may have taken him a little longer than he thought at first. He had a knack for making lies come true."[66]

A CIVIC ENTREPRENEUR

CHAPTER 6

A CAREER IN BUSINESS I

Hughes Aircraft and Litton Industries

When Kozmetsky accepted the job offer from Charles B. "Tex" Thornton and Roy Ash and moved his family to the Los Angeles area in 1952, he was entering a region with a burgeoning postwar economy that thrived on what was to become known as the nation's "military-industrial complex." The region's long tradition in the aircraft industry was transformed after the war through participation in the new field of aerospace, as well as through the wide development of the electronics industry, beginning with military needs and extending quickly into products for private industry, business management, and the household consumer market. These forces, together with the area's successes in higher education, led during the 1950s and 1960s to the development of one of the nation's first technology-based regional economies—an emerging "technopolis" well before that word would be widely applied to such developments.[1] Kozmetsky's activities in the business world benefited from and contributed to these trends.

The origins of the Southern California technopolis have been traced to a variety of factors, including the technological breakthroughs in the 1930s of the Lockheed L-10 Electra airplane (1933) and Douglas's DC-3 (1935). The overwhelming superiority of these airplanes in speed, efficiency, and safety spurred an expansion of aircraft manufacturing in the region and led to the region's national dominance in the industry, and that helped position the area to take full advantage of the military production requirements during World War II and then (after a brief postwar slump) during the Korean War and the Cold War. The expansion of the region into advanced electronics after World War II—including the work of the three companies with which Kozmetsky was associated—was in response to the rapidly expanding demand by the military for airplanes, missiles, satellites, and other armaments that relied on high-tech components.[2]

The dominant role of California in the military-industrial complex is clear from its leading position in the winning of prime contracts from the Department of Defense. New York and Michigan had been ahead of California in military contracts during World War II, but California surged into first place in the 1950s, and the state stayed there. California had 26 percent of all defense prime contracts in 1954 (the year Kozmetsky moved from Hughes Aircraft to Litton Industries) and still had 21 percent of the contracts in 1960 (the year that Kozmetsky and Henry Singleton founded Teledyne). About 70 percent of the state's military contracts were consistently in the seven counties of Southern California, with about half of them in Los Angeles County. By the early 1960s, over 170,000 people were employed in the aerospace-electronics industries in Southern California.[3]

Kozmetsky's sojourn in the Southern California technopolis included associations with three of the corporations that contributed most significantly to the high-tech economic development of the region. At each company he played a major role, whether as a strategic planner, an accountant, a manager applying the techniques and strategies of management science, a hands-on computer designer, or an entrepreneur. Along the way he amassed a fortune of many millions of dollars; developed a wide network of contacts in business, engineering, and government; and gained a national reputation as a pioneering industrialist with a broad vision for policy decisions at the intersection of business, higher education, and government.

More than thirty years after Kozmetsky left Los Angeles to become the dean of business at the University of Texas at Austin, business leaders in Orange County were interested in talking with him about the successes he had been part of in the economic development of Austin. He compared what had happened in Austin to his early days in Southern California: "I was one of the 20 or 30 people that had a dream of what was going to be done with California. Just about the time Sputnik went off, we laid out a 50-year plan. When I came down to Orange County this was nothing but country roads and farms. We visualized what you are now seeing. We saw technology coming. We took the defense part and put it into Los Angeles. What we saw here [in Orange County] was the commercial stuff coming out. Most people don't think of Disneyland as based on technology, [but] they hired people out of Hughes Aircraft to help design and develop it. It is loaded with technology. . . . The most important thing was that we had the talent—the scientists and the engineers—and we started to concentrate on commercialization."[4]

Kozmetsky often looked back on the early years of his business career and the beginning of the computer age with an awareness of how fortunate he had been. "I couldn't have been born at a better time," he told his University of Texas at Austin students. "There were so few of us that all you had to do was be halfway smart and be willing to work, and you got all kinds of opportunities. There was nobody to compete with you. You could do anything you liked because the other part of the world's market had great demands and needs."[5]

Hughes Aircraft

Roy Ash, a good friend of Kozmetsky's since their days as students at the Harvard Business School, helped persuade Kozmetsky to leave Carnegie Tech and join the team of young and ambitious managers, scientists, and engineers who were transforming Hughes Aircraft Company, which was based in Culver City. When Kozmetsky began working with them in 1952, some of them had already been with the company for more than four years, after Howard Hughes had begun expanding the staff and providing the capital that allowed the company to develop rapidly from a "putterer on the fringes of the aircraft industry" into a specialist in advanced electronics for the military.[6]

One of Hughes's first steps, in 1946, had been to hire Simon Ramo, an electrical engineer, away from General Electric to run the company's electronics R&D lab, and by the early 1950s Ramo was understandably pleased with the operation he had created and the quality of talent he had been able to attract. He called the lab "the largest concentration of technical college graduates, including the greatest number of Ph.D.s, in any single industrial facility of that period, except for the Bell Telephone Laboratories in New Jersey."[7] Dean Wooldridge, a friend of Ramo's from the California Institute of Technology, where they had been graduate students, moved in 1946 from his job at Bell Labs to help Ramo run the R&D program.

Encouraged by the early successes of the R&D lab, Hughes began investing more resources in the aircraft company in the late 1940s, and he recruited a management team that was led by two retired air force generals. The team included Gen. Ira C. Eaker, who had ended the war as deputy commander of the Army Air Forces and was named general manager of Hughes Aircraft in late 1947; Gen. Harold L. George, who had led the Air Transport Command during the war and became assistant general manager at Hughes in 1948; and Thornton, who had led the wartime Office of Statistical Control and was named Gen. George's assistant. Immediately after the war, Thornton and a group of his "Whiz Kids" from Statistical Control had joined Ford Motor Co. Most of them stayed on to help reorganize Ford over the long term, but Thornton left in 1948 for the job at Hughes.

Hughes Aircraft was a division of Hughes Tool Co., which had its headquarters in Houston and was wholly owned by Howard Hughes, who had inherited the company—and its patented drilling-bit technology—from his father. Hughes had started the aircraft division in the 1930s, and it had won a few military contracts during the war, but it had been largely a plaything through which Hughes could indulge his personal interest in aviation. When he began to try to make something more out of the division after the war, there were many skeptics. Thornton and the other new managers had hesitated to join the company because of Hughes's reputation as an erratic and eccentric businessman, but Hughes won them over with promises to provide ample working capital and not to interfere in operation of the company. Thanks in part to an increase in air force contracts during the Korean War, the new team quickly turned the division around. It went from being a money loser in 1948 to turning a $1.7 million profit in 1951, and by 1953 the division had a backlog of $600 million in air force orders. It had also acquired, thanks to the expertise of Ramo and Wooldridge's electronics laboratory and the success of the management team in putting together highly competitive bids, a virtual monopoly on the air force and navy contracts for the fire- and flight-control systems of all of their interceptor airplanes (the main line of defense against a feared Soviet attack on North America).[8]

Beginning in 1950, however, there were signs that Hughes and his longtime chief executive, Noah Dietrich, were going to try to exert more direct influence on how the division was run. The standard account in the news media at the time and in many subsequent retellings is that Dietrich had been content to leave the division alone, and had even hoped for its demise, when it was losing money, but that he sought to exercise control after the new team demonstrated just how profitable it could be. Three years of conflict ensued, with dramatic consequences for the careers of Ramo, Wooldridge, George, Thornton, and scores of other managers and engineers whom they had recruited—including Kozmetsky.

The turmoil was well under way when Kozmetsky joined the company in 1952, but no one predicted the ultimate crisis that would come over a year later. The company was definitely on the move, and it must have seemed to Kozmetsky, as it still did to those who had preceded him in going to work there, that the opportunities were limitless. In addition to the possibility of making a lot of money and moving quickly into positions of increasing responsibility, the employees shared a heady idealism about the importance of what they were doing on behalf of the country. Although Hughes Aircraft was privately held and its main purpose was to turn a profit, its managers and engineers also felt patriotic pride in their achievements in developing technologies that were important to the nation's military effort, and they saw the company as performing a public service that was vital to national security.[9]

Kozmetsky was at first reluctant to leave the Carnegie Institute of Technology, but Ash persisted, and his arguments were finally persuasive. In later life, Kozmetsky called Hughes Aircraft "a marvelous post-graduate school" at which he expanded his knowledge of emerging technologies. "I found when people want you, you could ask for everything—it is not all salary," he told one of his classes at the University of Texas. "I insisted that I be allowed to be on the computer policy committee, and I insisted that I get into semiconductors. The first thing I knew, I got all my technology training at Hughes Aircraft. I made the first market projections for digital computers. . . . I got an opportunity to work on digital computers, mathematical modeling, semiconductors, and so on."[10]

Many of the challenges that science and technology companies such as Hughes faced in the early 1950s were so new that Kozmetsky and his colleagues found their career opportunities to be wide open. "When I was at Hughes," Kozmetsky recalled, "I was excited about participating on all of the policy groups in setting the direction in which the company was to go. In the electronics lab, there was no design theory. How do you design a black box? There is no theory for it. I knew absolutely nothing about configuration control. It didn't exist, so we had to invent a way to control design and a way to make changes. Nobody knew how much to block into production lines. Nobody knew what the impact on costs would be. Nobody knew the impact on financing or sales. I learned all of that at Hughes. In effect, my Hughes experience trained me to be a generalist. I had to work with the R&D people. During that time, the digital computer didn't have an academic discipline. There was no university to go to, to learn about computers."[11]

As a brand-new business manager with little management experience but a lot of ideas learned in business school, Kozmetsky had a rocky start at Hughes Aircraft. As he recalled:

> When I . . . went to Hughes Aircraft and I started making decisions like they taught me at the Harvard Business School by the case method . . . how nice it was [for] the first day or two. I solved one case problem after another and toward the end of the week, there were so many case

problems walking in [to] my office that I even . . . barked at my kids, and fussed at my wife, as well as my secretary. One day my secretary sat me down and said, "Look, you may think you are the boss and you may be a professor and you may be smart, but let me tell you that I am going to outlast you here. You are the third boss that I have had that I am training for this job, and you start treating me like I am a person and not somebody that doesn't have a brain in their head and I don't care that I only went to [business] college." Then I realized I had been taking advantage of things and she was absolutely right. I was worse than a chauvinist. Things changed after that.

We had to put in a management control system, and she wrote it. She not only typed up the stuff, helped me draw the charts, but we only had a four-hour open window before we had to go to a meeting. She would do the analysis too. I had my master's students from Harvard on my staff and I couldn't even get them to do analysis.[12]

As assistant controller when he joined the company in 1952, Kozmetsky's first assignment was to create an integrated accounting, control, and project management system through which the company could better manage its defense contracts. He brought in his friends William Cooper and Abraham Charnes from the Carnegie Institute of Technology as consultants to help design and install the system.[13] Their work corrected the kind of problems that had shown up in the company's audit for 1951, such as disparities in inventory accounting (and an apparent shortage of $500,000 worth of aircraft parts) that were traced to sloppy paperwork and poor communications between the assembly line and the accounting department. The company had expanded so fast and had taken on such complex projects that its antiquated control system could not keep up, and resulting problems, such as the inventory issues, had been used by Dietrich as ammunition in his running argument with the management team.[14] Gen. George acknowledged that the company's accounting system during its first period of expansion was "rather rotten,"[15] and overhauling the system was a challenge tailor-made for the accounting skills of Kozmetsky and the interests of Cooper and Charnes in applying academic skills to complex real-world problems.[16]

Despite the efforts to fix the company's accounting system, some production demands required a high level of "creative" management. Hughes had a contract from North American Aviation to produce a certain number of fire-control systems for the F-86 Sabre fighter aircraft (a mainstay of the air force during the Korean War). The contract would be canceled after a year if Hughes did not meet the production schedule, and

Kozmetsky recalled that those circumstances caused him and other managers to make exceptions to the usual accounting procedures.

"That is when I learned such things as midnight requisitioning [a World War II term for acquisitions by irregular means]," he said. "You climb over the fence for a part because there is no clerk there and you take the part out and you let them catch up later. We had to move the stuff through. Then we had big inventory adjustments." Kozmetsky joked that that was "when I learned to be creative and innovative," using his favorite adjectives for successful managers.

"The other thing I found out at Hughes was that we had so many small parts that it cost more to write a requisition to issue them fom the storeroom than to buy the parts," he said. To keep the production line moving in a cost-effective manner, Kozmetsky bypassed the usual accounting procedures, and then once a week he would correct the books. "It used to take me [and] four girls calculations on a comptometer [a mechanical calculator] for four hours every Tuesday morning," he said. "I weekly presented to management what was happening."[17]

Another early assignment for Kozmetsky was to conduct a marketing study of the business opportunities available to the company, particularly within the arena of military contracting. His study concluded that the most profitable future for the company would lie in the development and manufacture of electronic components rather than in the design and production of entire aircraft. His report reinforced the focus that Ramo and Wooldridge had brought to the company, and it laid the groundwork for the company's growth during the rest of the century, long after the wholesale changes in the management team that occurred in 1953 and 1954.[18]

After these quick successes, Kozmetsky moved to the company's Advanced Electronics Laboratory, where he became part of the team that was designing and producing the electronic fire- and flight-control systems for interceptor airplanes and key guidance components of the air force's missile systems. No other company in the country had the electronics capabilities of this team, yet Kozmetsky, who had no formal training in electronics or other fields of engineering, appears to have been at home. His ability to learn new subjects quickly and to teach himself was a valuable asset at Hughes. His assignments included designing and building digital computers for use by the engineers—a field that at the time was wide open to anyone with the aptitude for it, regardless of their formal education. As he would on many occasions throughout his career, Kozmetsky had found a single outlet through which he could pursue his twin interests in business management and advanced technology.

Kozmetsky also had an opportunity at Hughes to be involved in higher education. The company adopted an innovative hiring policy, scouring the country for the best undergraduates in science and engineering, and then the company paid for these new employees' graduate education at the California Institute of Technology and the University of California, Los Angeles. Part of Kozmetsky's job was to help coordinate the education of the employees, who divided their time between their jobs at Hughes and their studies. The institutions did not always provide the kind of academic programs that the company thought was best, as Kozmetsky recalled many years later. "I remember going to Cal Tech in 1952 trying to get them to teach quantitative methods. No way were they interested in it, so we went into extension departments and taught at nights and wrote the textbooks. Then we [Hughes Aircraft] became the big tax base so we lobbied the state legislature to build up education."[19]

Kozmetsky developed a lasting friendship with Ramo. When Kozmetsky was in the controller's office and Ramo was in charge of R&D, they worked together on several projects, including a long-range business plan for the company. They also developed some unusual methods of relieving stress and taking a break from long hours on the job. Kozmetsky later recalled, "It was the first time in my life I ever did any long-range planning. We did a 20-year plan for Hughes Aircraft. Ramo and I were there, and you get tired of being creative, and do you know what we did to break ourselves up and come up with issue generation? His wife insisted that he learn ballroom dancing, so he would lock the door, turn on the record, and he and I would dance. We found it very productive."[20] Those late-night dance sessions proved valuable to Kozmetsky almost fifty years later, when he danced with one of his granddaughters at her wedding. Her husband once asked Kozmetsky if he had known the legendary Ramo, and he replied, "Oh, Si taught me how to dance."[21]

Howard Hughes rarely showed up at the company, preferring to stay in his home in Las Vegas and let Dietrich handle face-to-face meetings. But occasionally his battered Chevrolet would be seen in the company parking lot, and that made many employees nervous. Kozmetsky had at least one confrontation with the eccentric and unpredictable owner, when Kozmetsky advised Hughes and Ash that one of the company's practices was illegal. Kozmetsky had discovered that six of Hughes's personal airplanes were being guarded around the clock by people paid from an air force contract. Hughes told Kozmetsky to continue authorizing the payments, but he refused. When he went home that night he told Ronya he might lose his job the next day, but he'd had to do what was right. In the end, Hughes acquiesced.[22]

The Crisis at Hughes

For many members of the Hughes Aircraft management team, the excitement and fulfillment of working for a first-class organization with creative and forward-thinking teams of engineers and managers started to fade as early as 1951 and 1952 when Hughes and Dietrich began to exert more control over the division. The turmoil surrounding Hughes's conflict with the management team was a regular feature of the work environment during Kozmetsky's years at the company. For more than two years Hughes had kept his promise not to interfere with the stellar management and technical team that he had recruited and that Ramo and others had augmented, but beginning in 1951 he and Dietrich increasingly threw roadblocks in the team's path regarding budget decisions, contracting authority, employee assignments, and other details. Hughes's motives were, typically, hard to discern. He acted in a capricious and unpredictable manner that was all too familiar in many of his other business operations, such as Trans World Airlines (TWA) and the RKO Pictures movie studio, and for much of this period he lived a reclusive life in Las Vegas hotel suites, a foretaste of the better-publicized eccentricities of the last years of his life. Dietrich's motives appear to have been simply to take personal control over the now-successful division, as he had done with other divisions of the Hughes empire when they became large enough and profitable enough to interest (or perhaps threaten) him.[23]

Meanwhile, the leaders of the management team had developed a great sense of pride in what they were accomplishing, a sense of pride that evolved into a feeling of ownership of the company. They had given the company its direction, had overseen its engineering successes, and had won back the respect and trust of the Department of Defense, and they saw Hughes and Dietrich as direct threats to everything they had built.

Before the management team left, they made efforts to buy the company so they could continue what they had started, but talks with Howard Hughes were unfruitful, as were further efforts to win concessions from him. By September 1953, George, Thornton, Wooldridge, and Ramo had resigned, and many other managers and engineers (including sixteen senior members of the technical staff) were also preparing to leave. Air Force Secretary Harold Talbott flew to Culver City and persuaded many employees to stay for a while, arguing that a sudden demise of the company would create a national security crisis.[24] Nevertheless, throughout the fall of 1953 and early 1954, many more employees, including Kozmetsky, found other places to work.

By the time Kozmetsky left in the summer of 1954 for a job at Litton Industries, Hughes Aircraft was struggling to maintain its leadership in defense electronics. The air force had decided to cultivate competitors for its advanced electronics contracts and to break the virtual monopoly that it had allowed Hughes to develop. By late 1953 the division was being left out of much of the new business from the air force, and the retrenchment and uncertainty made the division suddenly a gloomy place to work. The company managed to continue to meet all its schedules for the military, and Howard Hughes succeeded in attracting new management expertise, but more and more air force business for which Hughes Aircraft had been the sole source was now going to other companies, such as RCA and Philco.[25]

In this troubled environment, it must have been a relatively easy decision for Kozmetsky to make when Ash, who had already moved to Litton Industries, called him in 1954 and offered him a job building computers for that company, which was now controlled by another of Kozmetsky's friends, Tex Thornton. Throughout the first half of 1954, the exodus from Hughes had been renewed, and the entire West Coast avionics industry had been "buzzing" about the large number of Hughes technicians who had either left the company or were "feeling around for new jobs."[26] Kozmetsky was part of this second wave of departures. Many of the departing employees went to work for Ramo and Wooldridge at the company they had established after leaving Hughes (eventually to become known as TRW, for Thompson Ramo Wooldridge), while many others, including Kozmetsky, went with Thornton's new company.[27]

Litton Industries

At Litton Industries, Kozmetsky was joining a newly organized company with an old name. Thornton had left Hughes in the fall of 1953 with the goal of running his own electronics company and rapidly becoming one of the dominant companies in the field. His strategy was to buy a successful existing company and use it as a base for expansion through a combination of internal growth through research and acquisition of additional companies—aiming primarily at providing products to meet the growing needs of the Department of Defense. By growing the company quickly and establishing its dominance in the market, Thornton hoped to keep control of the enterprise and fend off the common fate of fledgling electronics companies of that era, which was to be acquired by larger and stronger companies. He wanted to be one of the hunters, not one of the hunted. In his overall business strategy, the way he financed his initial operations, and his method of decentralized management of the companies he acquired,

Thornton set precedents that Kozmetsky and Henry Singleton emulated when they set off on their own entrepreneurial adventure with the founding of Teledyne in 1960. The Litton Industries example, and the lessons that Kozmetsky and Singleton learned from Thornton during their six years at Litton, were a foundation for much of their success with Teledyne.

With the Cold War in full force, Thornton aimed at the Department of Defense as his main market. It was Thornton's "early and unshakable conviction that the government would be buying weapons of constantly increasing complexity for many years to come. The way to sell to that market, Thornton thought, was to build a company loaded with knowledgeable men who could come up with the weapons,"[28] beginning with individual components and then expanding to entire weapons systems. The concept, Thornton told a reporter, "would have been evident to any nine-year-old child willing to think about it."[29] For the longer term, the goal was to become "a multi-product, multi-industry, multi-national company."[30]

At first Thornton, Ash, and Hugh W. Jamieson, another Hughes Aircraft alumnus, founded a company that they called Electro Dynamics Corporation, but its only reason for existence was as a vehicle for making the first in the long series of acquisitions that the founders were planning. They decided to go after a small and specialized company near Stanford University called Litton Industries. By the time the owner, Charles V. Litton Sr., agreed to sell his vacuum tube manufacturing operation to Thornton and concentrate on his remaining business, he had established a solid reputation among the military for the high quality of his main product—a mass-produced magnetron, a device that was then a key component of radar systems but is today more commonly used in microwave ovens. A magnetron is a vacuum tube that produces microwave radiation by using a magnetic field to guide electrons through a copper cylinder. Litton's magnetrons were far more reliable than those made by his competitors, partly because of his more exacting quality-control measures. Thornton saw the wisdom of taking advantage of the prestige that the Litton name carried with the navy and other buyers, so in 1954 he acquired the rights to the name, and Electro Dynamics disappeared inside the new Litton Industries.[31]

During the first twelve years of Thornton's company, it recorded the fastest growth rate of any company in the history of US business up to that time, with average yearly increases of 59 percent in sales and 44 percent in earnings per share.[32] The growth was fueled by mergers and acquisitions, together with an emphasis on internal research and development of advanced technologies, as well as a highly decentralized approach to management of the company's many divisions and subsidiaries. As one of the most prominent of a new breed of corporation known as conglomerates, Litton operated as a vast holding company, eventually commanding more than two hundred operating units, but with a coordinated research program. This "free-form management," as it was called, combined centralized planning and research with decentralized administration of the separate business units, and it was often given much of the credit for Litton's rapid growth. All these characteristics made Litton Industries a model not only for Teledyne but also for many other new companies that departed from the traditions of the more narrowly focused and more tightly structured industrial corporation.[33]

As with his management of Hughes Aircraft and the Office of Statistical Control, one of Thornton's greatest strengths at Litton was his ability to attract highly talented staff members. A significant part of the staff's compensation at Litton was in generous stock options, which Thornton paid out of his own supply of stock and which gave the employees a direct stake in the risks and rewards associated with the business. The stock options also helped Kozmetsky and Singleton accumulate the money that they eventually invested in Teledyne.

Among the core of Thornton's management and research staff, Kozmetsky and Singleton have been cited as examples of the high quality of employee he recruited. At first Singleton headed the company's Inertial Guidance Division and then took over the Electronic Equipment Division. Kozmetsky, who was recruited to lead Litton's digital development as director of the company's computer and controls development work, soon became assistant general manager of the Electronic Equipment Division under Singleton. In mid-1959, Kozmetsky was promoted to the position of vice president of the corporation.[34] Singleton and Kozmetsky began sharing the leadership role at the Electronic Equipment Division, where they soon "had shown themselves capable of turning out a steady stream of technologically advanced products."[35]

Kozmetsky later said he had been worried at first about how well he could make the transition from accounting to direct management of engineering projects:

> When Hughes Aircraft broke up, I had a reputation for being an exceptional accountant and so was on the forefront of management planning and control. I was scared to death [leaving that job]. As an academician, I never took a course in engineering. . . . When Hughes blew up, there was a big management fight and I learned what loyalty is all about and how ephemeral it is. I was offered a job in the controller's office at Ford,

which was at that time run by [Robert] McNamara. I went to the other side of town and was offered the same type of job at Chrysler. I really didn't want to be a controller. I had served as that once in my life and I never wanted to be a staff person again. That is a terrible position to be in. You get beat up all the time. You always have to persuade people to do things. You can't see the results of anything you do.

It was then that "Tex" Thornton agreed to let me head up digital computers at Litton Industries. I didn't think engineers would work for me. I didn't think I would know how to manage or contribute to engineers. . . . I think the best advice I ever received as a graduate student was [from] the president of Harvard, Dr. [James B.] Conant, who told us that if a scientist or engineer couldn't explain in simple language what he was doing, then he didn't know what he was doing. So I went in and worked in the lab [at Litton]. The first shock I got was that I could make some contribution. . . . I found out that when you get into the technology of a science in its early phases, nobody knows anything about it and you have just as much knowledge to bring to bear as everyone else.[36]

The Litton years gave Kozmetsky valuable experience in ensuring the quality of work on a production line and keeping his customers satisfied—experience that he would put to good use at Teledyne. He said that at Litton he learned to rely on reports of the quality assurance (QA) staff rather than accounting reports because QA made information available faster. In one case, he read a field engineer's report that said some circuit boards (which were installed in a guidance system on an aircraft carrier off the coast of Southern California) had "coffee" stains on them, and he knew something must be wrong because the boards could not be near any coffee cups. The problem was traced to a leak in a capacitor, and then Kozmetsky came up with a solution: "We sat down and worked for a couple of days and nights on the crisis and figured out how to encapsulate the leaky part of the capacitor so it would stop leaking. Then we made up some kits and took off for the aircraft carrier and started encapsulating. Later we removed those we encapsulated and put solid ones on. It is when you don't do anything that you get into trouble. When you have tried to do something and have some answers for it, then people usually respond to that. It is important that you are not going to turn out bad quality."[37] He also began making plans to buy the plant where the capacitors had been manufactured so Litton could better control the quality of its products.[38]

Kozmetsky also recalled how his work at Litton made him wish he had taken a course on the subject of selling. Thornton had promised him a $5 million budget to start the company's digital computer operation, but on his first day on the job, about two months later, he learned that the money had evaporated on another project and he was going to have to concentrate on drumming up customers to bring in revenues. This prospect gave him a moment of panic:

> I remember walking to the water fountain, taking a drink, saying, "Oh, gosh, what do I tell Ronya when I get home? What a fool I was taking that kind of job. What do I do now?" My office, along with the engineers at that time, was in a great big auditorium of an ex-sewing machine company in Beverly Hills. I had to get permission from Gertrude, who was the one secretary there, to spend money to telephone IBM to make an appointment to see if I could get something to subcontract from them. I started to learn to sell the hard way.
>
> I discovered that you sell all the time. All leaders are involved with selling no matter what other words we use for it. You must be persistent. You can't get discouraged, can't give up. I kept pushing away. If it doesn't go this way, go that way. Usually I tell students, "Listen, there is a time when you have to learn something. You can be persistent, but think of it as hitting your head on a brick wall. One day you ought to go look. If there is blood, stop it. Then figure out a way where the end of that wall is and come around it, go another direction, another way, or go back and come up with other alternatives and try them."[39]

One of the earliest successes of Litton's R&D program was the miniaturization of inertial navigation technology so it could be incorporated into aircraft design.[40] An inertial navigation system (consisting of motion sensors, gyroscopes, and a computer) allows an airplane, missile, or other vehicle to stay on course by measuring its speed and direction relative to a beginning point and providing that information to the engines, steering mechanisms, and other onboard equipment. Singleton, always more adept at engineering than his partner Kozmetsky, was responsible for several improvements in the design of inertial navigation systems while he worked at Litton, and the company eventually won the contracts to provide systems for the F-104 Starfighter aircraft and other vehicles. Singleton held at least six patents based on research he conducted at Litton related to improved inertial navigation systems, including an "ultra-precision" gyroscope,[41] a programmed computer,[42] and an acceleration measuring system.[43] This technology would be crucial to Teledyne's early success.

A large group of engineers worked under Singleton and Kozmetsky, whose duties included managing Litton's computer avionics organization.

Kozmetsky's supervision of the office was not always appreciated by the professional engineers on the staff. One of them, Harold "Hal" Erdley, an expert on gyroscopes who had also worked with Singleton at North American Aviation, later wrote that Kozmetsky "was especially difficult for me to deal with, as he had no real understanding of our problems and continued to attempt to micromanage my organization and hold a number of time-wasting meetings."[44] Erdley's difficulties in working with Kozmetsky were so great that when Singleton later tried to recruit Erdley to work at Teledyne, he "politely declined, letting Singleton know the principal reason for this was my inability to get along with Kozmetsky."[45] After Kozmetsky left Teledyne management in 1966, Erdley did move from Litton to Teledyne and stayed there until his retirement in 1990.

At about the time that Kozmetsky and Singleton left Litton, the Electronic Equipment Division entered the commercial computer market with its Litton C 7000 and Litton Data Assessor, two general-purpose computers developed under Kozmetsky's and Singleton's guidance. The Data Assessor, the larger and faster of the two, performed about seventy-five thousand operations per second. The machine weighed five hundred pounds and occupied nine square feet of floor space.[46] These machines were short-lived in the rapidly advancing field of designing computers as tools for business management, a field that Kozmetsky had paid close attention to throughout his years at Hughes Aircraft and Litton Industries. In addition to computers that bore the Litton brand, the company marketed computers under other logos. One of the most significant of these was Monroe, a maker of office machines that Litton acquired in 1957.

As he had at Hughes Aircraft, Kozmetsky called on Abraham Charnes and William Cooper to serve as consultants on a variety of management issues that Litton was facing. These included planning and control issues, artificial intelligence, and systems analysis.[47]

During Litton Industries' first six years, when Kozmetsky and Singleton worked there, the company's annual revenues grew from $8.9 million to $187.8 million. Annual earnings rose from $436,000 to $7.5 million, and earnings per share increased from five cents to thirty-eight cents. The number of employees rose from 1,100 to 17,400.[48] Revenues generated by the Electronic Equipment Division under Singleton and Kozmetsky grew to $80 million a year at the end of those six years—accounting for over 42 percent of the company's total revenues by 1960. The division employed five thousand people by the time Singleton and Kozmetsky left that year.[49]

When almost forty years later Kozmetsky looked back on his years at Hughes Aircraft and Litton Industries, he emphasized the intellectual ferment among the managers, engineers, and scientists at those and other companies in the electronics and aerospace industries in the Los Angeles area. He recalled a regular series of "industry seminars" involving the relatively young employees from Litton, Hughes, the Rand Corporation, and other organizations, such as the California Institute of Technology and the University of California, Los Angeles—meetings reminiscent of the Sunday morning sessions that he had participated in while at Harvard and the interdisciplinary conversations he'd had at Carnegie Tech. He remembered that he and his colleagues "would get together on Thursday nights to trade ideas about high energy physics and the companies we were working for. One meeting a week wasn't enough, so we'd have picnics on the beach at weekends." A reporter summed up the result of that confluence of ideas in the sweeping dimensions typical of Kozmetsky: "What resulted was a cross-fertilization of ideas that helped launch the U.S. space program and the modern electronics industry too."[50]

Those reminiscences by Kozmetsky of his early days in Southern California came on the occasion of an initiative in 1997 by the IC[2] Institute to join with Pepperdine University and the Orange County Business Council to facilitate venture capital and entrepreneurship activities in the region. Kozmetsky expressed high hopes for a renewal of the entrepreneurial spirit of those earlier days, and he observed that the new entrepreneurs in the Los Angeles area in the 1990s had an advantage in being able to tap into local venture capital funds, whereas the earlier generation was largely dependent on Defense Department contracts to get their businesses up and running.[51]

KOZMETSKY AND THE COMPUTER

In 1953, when Kozmetsky was still working at Hughes Aircraft, he and a friend in the accounting department at the University of California, Los Angeles, Paul Kircher,[52] began work on a book to explain to business managers, using largely nontechnical language, the new world of digital computing. When they started there were no books of that kind, but when their *Electronic Computers and Management Control* (McGraw-Hill, 1956) was published, it was one of three books published that year aimed at giving business managers the information they would need to understand how computers could be used in their businesses. In the mid-1950s many business executives, particularly those from the generation before Kozmetsky's, needed a concise and reliable guide to the new technology.

Kozmetsky and Kircher provided enough detail to give higher-level executives the information they would need to begin making decisions about acquiring a computer and putting it to use to keep their companies competitive. Richard G. Canning, an engineer at the University of California, Los Angeles, and a business consultant, produced a book aimed more at middle managers involved in the day-to-day work of organizing companies' data-processing activities.[53] The third book was by Howard S. Levin, who taught mathematics at the University of Illinois and founded a computer leasing company.[54] Before these three books, the available literature on the subject had been limited mostly to a scattering of technical articles in academic journals, reports from professional societies and government agencies, and several computer magazines.[55]

Kozmetsky and Kircher produced a remarkable book that was influential at the time and remains valuable for its historical information on the early use of computers in business, its comprehensive presentation of the factors to consider before installing a computer for business operations, and its discussion of the economic and sociological aspects of the emerging computer revolution.[56] In 1971, a *New York Times* reporter called it "a prophetic book."[57]

The authors did not discuss their process of researching and writing the book, but given the relative paucity of academic or popular literature on the subject at that time, they must have generated much of their information through direct contact with a host of companies across the country, as well as by drawing on their own experience. The book includes numerous brief descriptions of how various companies had begun to use computers—descriptions that bear comparison with the material that Kozmetsky had generated through interviews with labor union officials and corporate controllers for his earlier books (see chapter 5).

The book holds up well as an introduction to computers in general and their use in business operations, although large parts of it now have purely historical interest. The newness of the subject is evident in the fact that Kozmetsky and Kircher found it necessary to define, and often put in quotation marks, many terms that were not yet fully incorporated into the ordinary person's daily vocabulary—terms such as automation, command, computer memory, computer program, diode, management sciences, modular, random access, transistor, and input and output.

The authors described their reason for writing the book as "to explain certain new developments which may have a greater influence on the management of enterprise than any single group of events since the first industrial revolution."[58] They advised that the computer was likely to "revolutionize management planning and control" by organizing information to allow for better decision-making, by leading to efficiencies that would increase profits, by ensuring that a company could make the best allocation of its resources, and by overhauling the traditional management functions, eliminating some and strengthening others.[59]

At the time there was debate about how much technical and mathematical knowledge a business manager would need in order to have his enterprise take advantage of the new technologies, and Kozmetsky and Kircher spent some time on issues of business education. They argued that employees with entirely new types of training would be needed to operate a company's computers, but that executives would still need a broader education, with only a general understanding of computer technology.[60]

Many executives were hesitant to invest in a computer because of concerns that whatever kind of equipment they bought would soon be made obsolete as the technology continued its rapid development. Kozmetsky and Kircher advocated going ahead and purchasing (or leasing) available equipment as soon as possible. The arguments they used are similar to those Kozmetsky presented to the University of Texas System Board of Regents thirty years later when the board was considering acquiring a supercomputer and some regents were hesitant because of the obsolescence issue (see chapter 13). Kozmetsky and Kircher wrote that the reasons against waiting for newer equipment to come on the market included that much of the fundamental experimentation in the field had already been accomplished; the productiveness and efficiencies of a computer meant the equipment would pay for itself long before it became obsolete; and the experience gained with a computer would reduce the expense of installing and learning to use any subsequent equipment.[61]

Kozmetsky and Kircher devoted considerable space to surveys of how companies had begun, however tentatively, to use large-scale computers in one or more areas, such as accounting (payroll, receivables and payables, and general and cost accounting); inventory and sales (retail record keeping, mail-order sales, airline reservations, and stock quotations); production, control, and scheduling; and document handling. Many companies decided to limit their early experiments with computers to managing payroll, since that was a relatively straightforward activity that had also involved substantial clerical costs before computers were available, and then to branch out gradually to other business functions.[62]

Most of Kozmetsky and Kircher's examples in the book are of companies that had ordered a UNIVAC (Universal Automated Computer)[63] or one of the IBM 700 series computers. The UNIVAC I (so designated after 1955, when the UNIVAC II was introduced) was marketed from 1951 to 1958. When Kozmetsky and Kircher published their book the manufacturer of UNIVAC was known as Sperry Rand, a company that evolved to become the present-day Unisys. The first UNIVAC was acquired by the US Bureau of the Census in 1951, and forty-three of the machines were eventually delivered to companies and institutions. In 1953 IBM delivered its first 700 series computer, a 701 Electronic Data Processing Machine. The IBM 702 was introduced in 1955. By the end of the 1950s a dozen US manufacturers had delivered about 450 large-scale computers to businesses and institutions; 350 of those were from IBM.[64]

The book traced in considerable detail the early experiences with computers at major insurance companies, manufacturers such as General Electric and Sylvania, and a range of other companies, from DuPont to Commonwealth Edison to Bank of America. Also included was an extensive account of a computerized reservation system installed at American Airlines in 1952—the first such system in the world.

Kozmetsky and Kircher also discussed the extensive administrative problems that companies faced when introducing computer systems, drawing in detail on the experiences of General Electric employees in GE's large consumer-appliance manufacturing complex in Louisville, Kentucky, where their friend Melvin E. Salveson had begun working in late 1953 as the manager of the company's advanced data systems. Construction had started in 1951 on the Louisville complex, known as Appliance Park, and in 1953 it was the site of the first installation of a UNIVAC at a business site. GE had not solved all the problems with the computer installation by the time of Kozmetsky and Kircher's book, and, indeed, many companies were still facing such problems ten years later, when Kozmetsky took on the challenge of helping to educate the next generation of business managers. The problems, as outlined in the 1956 book, included replacing old equipment in an orderly manner, retraining and regrouping employees, hiring new kinds of experts and fitting them into the organization, and revising a company's methods of gathering, processing, and reporting information. Resistence to the new machines by managers was also a common problem.[65]

Kircher and Kozmetsky made money on the book, and the new income helped raise the Kozmetsky family's standard of living. Ronya used the royalties for two major upgrades to their lifestyle—first to buy a washing machine and then to hire a gardener who would regularly maintain the yards and flower beds of their home. George had many talents, but he had not inherited his mother's interest in working in the yard or growing vegetables and flowers.[66]

When the book was finished, Ronya made a comment that kept Kozmetsky occupied for the rest of his life. As he told one of his classes: "When I finished writing [the computer book] Ronya said, 'Now that you have taken care of all the smart people, what are you going to do with us average?' The only thing I could come up with was conceptual thinking—teaching people at all levels to organize thoughts into a framework or paradigm so they can adapt to change."[67]

By 1960, after eight years in Los Angeles, Kozmetsky and Singleton had had enough of working for other people, regardless of how rewarding that experience had been. The entrepreneurial spirit that had motivated Tex Thornton and their other bosses proved to be infectious, and Kozmetsky and Singleton both had strong ideas about technology and business management that they wanted to put into practice on their own behalf. Making money was another major motivation, but as members of the postwar generation that was dedicated to winning the Cold War, they also shared with Thornton and others the conviction that producing products for the Department of Defense was a patriotic calling. Out of that mixture of motives and drives, Kozmetsky and Singleton decided to create a new company, which they named Teledyne.

CHAPTER 7

A CAREER IN BUSINESS II
Teledyne

D espite its rapid growth and impressive profits, all was not well at Litton Industries, and within a few years of its founding many of the early managers that Tex Thornton and Roy Ash had recruited began to leave the company, often to start their own entrepreneurial ventures. Some of these ventures remained small proprietorships, while others grew into conglomerates that rivaled Litton's own success. When they left to form Teledyne in 1960, Singleton and Kozmetsky were not the first to cut their ties to Litton, but they were among the most prominent departures, joining an exodus of executives who became known in the business world and the media as "Lidos," or Litton Industries dropouts.[1] Hugh Jamieson, one of the Litton founders, started this exodus in 1958 when he left to form his own electronics company after he grew concerned that Thornton was paying too little attention to the management of existing business units and too much attention to acquiring new ones. Singleton and Kozmetsky also had disputes with Thornton and with Ash, Thornton's right-hand man. One of their concerns was that they thought Thornton and Ash were mistaken in their refusal to enter the semiconductor business. As George A. Roberts, Henry Singleton's friend and successor as Teledyne president, has written: "Henry had become convinced that digital technology would be the dominant force in future developments in control systems and virtually every other electronic field, and that semiconductor technology would be critical to future developments in those fields. He felt it was important that Litton should enter the semiconductor field in order to control the design of the components used in control systems, and create a synergism between semiconductor component designs and control system design, each contributing to new developments in the other field. . . . [Ash] felt the semiconductor component business was too crowded and competitive, and not profitable enough. At that time this was certainly so. But Henry had faith in his convictions."[2] There are also reports that Singleton had come to realize by 1960 that he was unlikely ever to rise much higher at Litton, since Ash's position as the No. 2 executive behind Thornton seemed completely secure.[3]

Litton's Electronic Equipment Division, run by Singleton and Kozmetsky, was one of the brightest stars in the Litton constellation and was doing $80 million in business by 1960, and Singleton and Kozmetsky saw no reason that they could not repeat their success on their own. Thornton and Ash tried to cast such departures in a positive light, not always with success. They wanted the world to view the exodus of people like Singleton and Kozmetsky as a sign of Litton's strength rather than weakness, since the company was, in a sense, graduating the managers that it had cultivated and sending them out into the world on their own.

Thornton and Ash, it was reported, "took an almost missionary attitude toward the departures, as though the Lidos were going to spread the word to others. Ash suggested there was room for about half a dozen firms like Litton, expanding rapidly into related areas and producing crops of executives who later would take up the banner at some other company. Moreover, Ash suggested that while the Lidos were talented, their replacements were equally so. But that wasn't true. Singleton and Kozmetsky . . . were sorely missed, and the magnitude of their loss would be recognized in the 1970s, when Teledyne grew rapidly and Litton ran into serious difficulties."[4]

The departures from Litton were a natural outgrowth of a company that fostered an entrepreneurial environment among employees, tended to hire people who were highly motivated to take risks on new ideas, and rewarded those who took their responsibilities as seriously as if they were working for themselves. At one point Ash estimated that close to one thousand of its employees approached their jobs with this entrepreneurial spirit,[5] so it would not have been surprising when many of them struck off on their own. Singleton was always positive about his years at Litton, where he gained experience and was allowed to test his theories, and where he and Kozmetsky made enough money to finance the initial investment in their own company.[6]

Singleton and Kozmetsky had a natural affinity for the style of doing business that was reflected in the growth of conglomerates. In an editorial at the height of the conglomerate boom for both companies, the editors of *Fortune* traced the growth of conglomerates like Litton and Teledyne to the technology-driven management approach that Kozmetsky had been introduced to at Harvard and the Carnegie Institute of Technology.

The concern for profitability by business executives "has been far more sharply focused and systematic than it used to be," the editorial said of postwar managers. "Heavily influenced by the advent of computers, and the related requirement to engage in organized long-term planning, businessmen have increasingly found themselves in an environment dominated by the 'systems' approach to decision making. The approach forces decision makers to keep on asking themselves about their ultimate objectives and to keep on challenging any conventional notions about the way to achieve."[7]

This way of explaining business trends of the 1950s and 1960s suggests a natural linkage among three of the dominant features of Kozmetsky's early business career—the theories of management science, the computerization of management decisions, and the emergence of the conglomerate as a new way of organizing corporations.

Ash, Singleton, and other managers of conglomerate corporations professed not to like the term "conglomerate," but it gained widespread currency in the 1950s to describe large, multidimensional companies like Litton and Teledyne. The term had negative connotations for many government regulators, politicians, journalists, and more traditional business leaders. Litton Industries was the prototype for the kind of company that Teledyne would become, but there were many other examples of this type of corporate organization, including TRW, Ling-Temco-Vought (LTV), Gulf and Western Industries, and Textron. Several older and more traditional companies, such as General Electric, also adopted much of the conglomerate model.

A study by the Federal Trade Commission identified a major movement of mergers and acquisitions in US business beginning in 1948 and extending at least through 1968, when a recession and an accompanying decline in stock prices interrupted the trend.[8] Conglomerates grew, typically, by acquiring businesses in unrelated sectors, so their acquisitive ways tended not to raise red flags among antitrust regulators, who concentrated on the anticompetitive potential of horizontal and vertical mergers.[9] Teledyne was prominent among conglomerates of the period, making a list of the twenty-five most active acquiring companies among the two hundred largest manufacturing corporations from 1961 to 1968. In that period Teledyne concluded 125 mergers and acquired assets of $1.03 billion. Relatively few of those acquisitions were of large companies. In the same period, LTV made only 23 acquisitions, but they involved companies with assets totaling $2.9 billion.[10]

Singleton explained the reasoning behind the company's diversification as if it was, at least in part, a way of hedging one's bets: "The principle reason is the natural desire of companies to survive. If you remain in one single line, you will not survive. Everything has its day. You can't wait to see what is going to replace what you are doing. Concurrent with the instinct for survival is the desire to grow. If you want to grow—the purpose being clearly to increase the company's strength and give it greater potential for survival—this can be accomplished by having a number of lines and phasing out the old ones as time goes by. I'm talking about the long term."[11]

Starting Teledyne

Kozmetsky traced the origin of Teledyne to a conversation he had with Singleton while they were managing the electronics business of Litton: "Henry Singleton said to me, 'George, do you think we could start a company that is better than Litton?' I said, 'Yes.' He said, 'Would you be interested?' I said, 'There is one thing I haven't done in business. I have never had to finance myself, so let's go out and start it.' That is how we started Teledyne."[12]

They organized their new company with a similar simplicity, as Kozmetsky recalled, with Singleton being the natural choice to become president. "He was definitely a president. Henry is from Fort Worth, beautifully tall 6 foot-2 Texan, blue flashing eyes, and when he gets angry, the sparks fly out. It raises people in their seats. He wears a cowboy hat to this day and has all the manners of a Texan. Then you have me, inconspicuous little guy—that is not an image of a president of a dynamic company that is going to start and become one of the Fortune 500. There was never a question who was going to become president."[13]

Teledyne began in the semiconductor business and as a producer of precision instruments, including electronic and aviation control systems for the military, and although the company made many important acquisitions in its early years it did not become a full-fledged conglomerate with numerous unrelated business units and products in diverse fields until after Kozmetsky stepped down from his management role in 1966. He was, however, still on the board during the time that Teledyne broadened its acquisition strategy.

To help get the company started, Singleton and Kozmetsky each contributed $225,000 ($1.85 million in 2017), derived partly from their stock options. They also had resources accumulated from their salaries as Litton executives (Singleton's salary in his last year at Litton has been reported as $35,000, or more than $287,000 in 2017), and within a year or so of establishing the company they each increased their personal contributions of capital to a total of $500,000. Some of this money may have come from the invention of an autopilot for jet fighters, which Singleton was reported

The Teledyne board of directors in 1987. Left to right, Arthur Rock, Henry Singleton, George Roberts, George Kozmetsky, and Fayez Sarofim. *Photograph from Teledyne, Inc.*

to have worked on in his garage, with Kozmetsky's help, and which they apparently sold to the military.[14]

An additional $1.8 million was raised in 1961 in a private stock issue that was organized by the pioneering venture capitalist (and Kozmetsky's former student at Harvard) Arthur Rock and the firm he worked for at the time, Hayden Stone.[15] In the fall of 1961, Rock and his partner in a private investment organization, Thomas J. Davis Jr., invested $200,000 of their fund's money in Teledyne, and they later purchased additional stock to bring their total investment in Teledyne to just over $1 million. (By August 1967, that investment was worth $7.25 million.)[16] Rock's longtime friend Fayez S. Sarofim, a Houston investor and another former student of Kozmetsky's, also put money into the company at the beginning and remained an investor for decades. By the mid-1980s, he owned 1.7 million shares of Teledyne, 8.3 percent of the common stock.[17]

The company also had early financing from J. P. Morgan & Co. Years later, one of the J. P. Morgan bankers who approved a loan to Teledyne related a story to one of Kozmetsky's friends about how that came about. He said he and a colleague were sitting across a table from Kozmetsky and Singleton as Kozmetsky explained the company's finances and its need for capital to fulfill its government contracts. After a long presentation that included Kozmetsky going into details that involved calculus, the bankers took a break, and one of them asked the other, "Do you know what he was saying?" "No," the other banker said, "but I saw he was doing the math for us upside down. Let's give him the money."[18]

The early days of the company were a financial struggle. Many years later Kozmetsky took his friend Laura Kilcrease on a tour of the neighborhood where the company got its start, and he showed her a now fully developed area behind the Teledyne building that had been an orchard in the early 1960s. "George said that in the first year they made more money off the orchard than the company's products," she said.[19]

Throughout its early years, and for quite a while thereafter, Teledyne was governed by a six-member board made up of technology-savvy men. In addition to Singleton, Kozmetsky, and Rock, the early board also included Claude E. Shannon, who was an MIT electrical engineer and mathematician, the founder of information theory, and a friend and chess partner of Singleton since they were MIT students. Robert Sprague, founder of Sprague Engineering, joined the board after Teledyne acquired his company in 1963. George A. Roberts, Singleton's friend since they were students at the US Naval Academy, joined the board when his company, Vasco Metals Corp., was acquired by Teledyne in 1966.

First called Instrument Systems but quickly renamed Teledyne Systems Corp.,[20] the company opened in nondescript offices on North Beverly Drive in Beverly Hills but later moved to offices on Panama Street not far from the Los Angeles airport and on South Daphne Avenue in nearby Hawthorne. (The facility in Hawthorne, where Kozmetsky worked, is now the home of Teledyne Relays, a maker of electronic switches and a subsidiary of Teledyne Technologies Inc.) In 1967 Teledyne moved its corporate offices to a high-rise building at 1901 Avenue of the Stars in Century City, where the firm Hayden Stone also had offices.

Although Singleton's background was mainly in engineering and Kozmetsky's was in management and accounting, both understood the basics of the other's specialty, and on any given day or any particular project they could change places and operate in the other's primary realm.[21] From the start, they shared the top management jobs. An early press account described their relationship and demanding work habits:

> Teledyne executives say Singleton is "more than an engineer," and
> understands the financial aspects of building a company, too; his titles
> of chairman, president, and treasurer reflect this. But on this side he
> obviously gets much help from Kozmetsky, who has been operating
> on the frontiers of management science and is author of an important
> book on the functions of the comptroller. As executive vice-president
> and secretary, Kozmetsky shares master planning with Singleton.

A CIVIC ENTREPRENEUR

Obviously, the Singleton-Kozmetsky plan for growth is tailored to an industry subject to quick changes of fortune and sudden obsolescence of products. . . . With Singleton and Kozmetsky, growth is a religion and their desire to boss a very large company is almost fanatical. Singleton quite obviously is in favor of any policy that will speed Teledyne along the road to bigness. To achieve this, they operate on a grinding schedule—Kozmetsky has ruled out vacations for himself for at least three years, and one employee says Teledyne's policy is to pay employees for vacations they don't take rather than slow production.[22]

The breakneck pace and workaholic zeal led some executives to turn down offers to join the organization. "Singleton and Kozmetsky scared me to death," one of them was reported to have said, but many others, including some who had been working at such a frenetic pace since their days at Litton Industries, were attracted to the new opportunities at Teledyne.[23]

Singleton and Kozmetsky concentrated much of their energies on maintaining high-quality products and a highly productive workforce. They could be extremely demanding of their employees. Kozmetsky recalled one of his policies: "I used to tell my creative people that they were allowed to make one mistake in a certain area. The second time, they received a reprimand. The third time, they might as well leave. However, they could make a mistake in a different area and go through the same process."[24]

Singleton was usually averse to discussing his operation of the company with the news media, and when he did grant interviews, reporters and editors often found his answers evasive. He once claimed that he had no real plan in operating Teledyne, but simply went with his instincts on any particular day. He was quoted from time to time as saying he had always wanted to build a company as big and powerful as General Electric. On another occasion he outlined a comprehensive business plan for Teledyne that contained three specific goals: to make a large number of products in the fields of automatic controls and communications systems; to produce all or almost all of the components that went into those systems; and to establish a strong capability in the fields of semiconductors and integrated circuits.[25]

One of Singleton and Kozmetsky's most important early decisions was to begin designing and manufacturing semiconductors—setting the company on a course that helped make it successful in competing for military contracts. Teledyne's first acquisition, in October 1960, was a small electronics company called Amelco, which had offices and a job-shop manufacturing facility in Los Angeles, but Amelco's main usefulness was simply that it provided a place to work as well as a corporate structure for organizing various business units. Teledyne began its semiconductor business in February 1961 as a subsidiary of Amelco (under an organizational plan designed by Kozmetsky to take advantage of tax laws)[26] but set up the operation in Mountain View, in the region of California that was to become Silicon Valley.

That location for the Amelco Semiconductor Division was chosen because Singleton and Arthur Rock had persuaded Jay T. Last and his friend Jean Hoerni, two of the pioneers of integrated circuits at Fairchild Semiconductor, to leave that company and help start Teledyne's semiconductor operation. Last and Hoerni rejected a plan by Singleton that they move to Los Angeles, since they were already established in the San Francisco Bay area and could draw on an already significant semiconductor labor force in that region. Rock, who had helped finance both Fairchild and Teledyne, brought Singleton and Last together and they hit it off at once. Last and others had founded Fairchild in 1957 after a famous exodus of engineers from the company run by William Shockley, one of the inventors of the transistor, but by 1960 Last was dissatisfied because new managers were more interested in building discrete components like transistors and diodes rather than complete integrated circuits. Just before Teledyne was established, Last and Hoerni had developed the first practical integrated circuits (Hoerni having invented the planar process for reliable production of semiconductors), and they found that Singleton and Kozmetsky shared their view that those devices would be a key part of the future of electronics.[27]

Last explained the attraction that Teledyne held for him: "What really impressed me about [Singleton] was that he really wanted to use integrated circuits in his systems, and he really wanted to have the capability to make them himself. He knew my background and wanted me to start up an operation for doing that." Using integrated circuits "fit in perfectly with [Singleton's] plan to build electronic systems for military and space applications where low power dissipation, low weight and small size were of prime interest, cost was not so important."[28]

Last invested his own money in Teledyne and would eventually become its corporate vice president for technology. His operation in Mountain View was a stunning success and proved to be one of the decisive factors in Teledyne's early victory in the competition for a contract to produce an advanced helicopter control system for the navy and marines, as well as Teledyne's subcontracts to produce electronic devices for NASA's Apollo program.

In one of his rare interviews with the news media, Singleton explained the rationale for deciding to start the semiconductor operation: "It was our conviction that the classical electrical manufacturing process was about to undergo an interesting and decisive change in basic direction. Instead of buying electronics components from specialty houses, manufacturers [would] more and more be forced to make up their own circuit elements, particularly semiconductors."[29]

Kozmetsky told his students at the University of Texas at Austin that starting the semiconductor operations was "the most creative period I ever had in my life. . . . [W]e were starting what today are called chips. We were making hybrids ourselves. We designed all of the equipment, we went to the junkyards and picked up things. We worked seven days away around the clock and did the machining if we had the talent ourselves. We were making hybrid circuits at the rate of 500 a month on just $60,000 that we wheedled out of management."[30]

Other veterans of Fairchild Semiconductor soon joined Last and Hoerni at Teledyne's Amelco operation, and Amelco emerged as a major semiconductor manufacturer that also designed a variety of microelectronic components for other Teledyne divisions. That work gave Teledyne the technological capabilities that enabled it to compete for a host of military and NASA contracts. Amelco's high-performance transistors and miniature circuits were key components of Teledyne products such as tracking receivers, airborne digital computers, inertial guidance systems, and miniature gyroscopes.[31]

Despite its advanced technical capabilities, Amelco lost money in 1963, partly because of problems in coordinating sales and manufacturing, and one version of what happened next is that Kozmetsky decided to remove Hoerni from his role as general manager of the division and replace him with someone with more management skill. According to background materials provided to a writer by Last, Kozmetsky hoped to let Hoerni save face by naming him director of research and development at Teledyne's corporate headquarters, but Hoerni declined that offer and insisted that Kozmetsky fire him. Kozmetsky then hired Jim Battey, a manager at Clevite Corp., to manage Amelco, and Hoerni took a job at Union Carbide Electronics, where he started another semiconductor operation. Under Battey, Amelco became profitable by 1964 and soon played a key role in Teledyne's successful bid for the contract for a helicopter avionics system.[32]

Hoerni had a different view of the problems at the Amelco division. He said the division was underfunded by Teledyne and had trouble fulfilling military contracts that were for low quantities of highly specialized semiconductors. In Hoerni's view, Kozmetsky knew little about manufacturing integrated circuits and had decided unfairly that Hoerni was the problem rather than the difficulties presented by the way the contracts were written. Hoerni's version was that he abruptly quit before Kozmetsky could fire him.[33]

Another perspective on those early days at Teledyne and Amelco is provided by Isy Haas, an engineer who left Fairchild Semiconductor to work with Last and Hoerni at Amelco and eventually was placed in charge of R&D at Amelco after Last left in 1966 to take a corporate job (vice president of technology) working with Singleton in Los Angeles. Haas said he and Hoerni had their differences, perhaps related to the different kinds of electronic devices in which they specialized. Hoerni and Kozmetsky also had a number of differences, Haas said: "I know that Jean and George used to go at each other in meetings. George told me so himself after I left Teledyne. . . . I asked him to help me organize my efforts to start a semiconductor company. And he helped me for a couple of months at that; we talked. He used to tell me stories about he and Jean. Jean was a very emotional, dramatic person. George was a very cool person."[34]

Last agreed with others that Teledyne and Amelco were underfunded: "I remember one day I was having trouble meeting payrolls and I just got on the plane and flew down to Henry and said, 'Look I need $100,000 right away. I've just had it.' And he turned to Betty, his secretary, and mumbled something and he came back and said, 'Here's a check for $60,000, not $100,000. I'm giving you $60,000 because that's all the money there is in this whole goddamn company.' So that was the shoestring we were doing it on and that came later on to haunt us because we didn't have the resources to build the mass of low-cost production lines."[35]

Kozmetsky recalled that one of the lessons he learned from his years at Teledyne was that money spent on research and development ("if it is done well") should be considered an investment rather than an expense. R&D "has a funny attribute," he said. "The more you use technology, the more you have. It doesn't disappear. As a matter of fact, the worst thing you can do is not use it."[36]

On another occasion Kozmetsky described for his University of Texas students his and Singleton's hopes for enlarging Teledyne, and, in a rare depiction of the inner operations of the company, he recalled a series of management techniques designed to speed up that growth. "At Teledyne we had a fairly simple idea that in 10 years we would be at $1 billion of sales," Kozmetsky said, "and our profits would double each year and our sales would double each year. If we came down to the base, this was $4 million of sales, and at the end of 10 years you would have $1 billion if it doubled every year." Kozmetsky continued:

A CIVIC ENTREPRENEUR

One of the things we could get some work on was to assemble components on an old-fashioned circuit board. If you look at any circuit board, you put resistors on, capacitors, and then transistors. In those days, a resistor cost you a penny, a capacitor 40 cents, and a transistor $5. If you wanted to grow your sales . . . you had to be among the best subcontractors. How do you get to be number one? The board, when tested, always had to be good quality work. That gets you the sale, but if you put too much labor in it that is all you had. Then you wouldn't make the profits. So how do you increase profits? We did a simple thing. At that time beginning wages were $1.25 so we had all our beginning people put in to making resistors. If they did a bad job and we had to replace it, it would only cost their labor hours plus a penny. Those who had [less] skill we put them here, and the most skilled went on the transistors because if you damaged a transistor, you really looked bad. So we got our labor rates down because in the past you would take a $4 or $5 an hour person and they did all of it. We also . . . organized it so that everybody could see a promotion. Those were our circumstances.[37]

Kozmetsky said Teledyne's bids for contracts from the government and subcontracts from other defense companies included a high calculation for overhead costs, and then "we used every management science technique in the world so we could operate at 80 percent" of what was originally budgeted for overhead. That gave the company extra resources for financing special projects by the engineers that improved quality and led to new products.[38]

NASA was a significant source of work for Teledyne, and the connections that Kozmetsky developed with the space agency proved to be important throughout his career. One of the most important NASA contracts won by Teledyne involved a study of "man-machine methodology"—applying computer-based analysis to the interaction between people and the complex technological systems involved in space exploration. Kozmetsky was the author of the study's report, which was one of the foundations for the space agency's development of management techniques for large, complex projects. An appendix to the report applied the management techniques to a proposed helicopter avionics system that the navy was considering—a system for which Teledyne eventually won the production contract.[39]

Other work for NASA included development of a miniature television camera that was the size of a small paperback book and weighed one and a half pounds. The camera used a vidicon tube (which scanned a surface with an electron beam) and integrated circuits, and it had a resolution equal to that of commercial broadcast cameras of that era. NASA used the camera inside spacecraft to observe astronauts during flight.[40] Several other Teledyne products were aboard the Apollo spacecraft that went to the moon, including a Doppler radar device.[41]

Of all his NASA connections, Kozmetsky may have been most proud of his work in advising President John F. Kennedy on his 1962 speech in which he dedicated the United States to going to the moon by the end of the decade. Kozmetsky, who often mentioned his work on the speech to friends and students, apparently had been asked to help through his and Kennedy's mutual connections at Harvard.[42]

INTEGRATED HELICOPTER AVIONICS SYSTEM

Teledyne's success in early 1965 in winning the prime contract for the navy's Integrated Helicopter Avionics System (IHAS) was the culmination of decisions made by Singleton and Kozmetsky since they founded Teledyne, and it was a major turning point for the long-range economic viability of the company even though the system eventually proved to be so far ahead of its time that it was unworkable. Teledyne, Northrop Corp., and Texas Instruments had been named as finalists for the avionics program in 1963, beating out an impressive list of more than a dozen experienced defense contractors that included IBM, GM, North American Aviation, Bendix, Burroughs, and Honeywell. In early 1965, in a decision that surprised many in the defense industry, the Pentagon named Teledyne as the prime contractor.

The success resulted from an intricate combination of three strengths: The company's pursuit of its own R&D capabilities in inertial guidance systems and computer technology, including the design and manufacture of integrated circuits; the application of techniques from the field of management science to complex manufacturing challenges; and an approach toward acquisitions that emphasized companies that could contribute to Teledyne's overall self-sufficiency in manufacturing electronic components and systems.

The techniques of management science were at the heart of the successful bid. As Kozmetsky condensed the story for his management class at the University of Texas: "If I did not develop chance constraint programming, Teledyne would never have gotten its first defense contract, which pushed it into the big leagues. TI [Texas Instruments] was our competition and we had to knock them out."[43]

The helicopter avionics program, which involved multiple contracts, made a lot of money for Teledyne, and it positioned the company for continued highly profitable projects for years to come. One aspect or another of the pursuit of the contracts occupied various units of Teledyne for almost the entire six years that Kozmetsky was involved in management of the company, and revenue from the contracts was one of the main sources of the wealth that helped give Kozmetsky the ability and motivation to return to the academic world in 1966. That wealth would not have materialized as quickly if Teledyne had failed to win the helicopter program. In addition, the story of how Teledyne applied techniques from the field of management science to win the program became one of Kozmetsky's chief exhibits, when he became dean of the University of Texas at Austin business school, in his argument for how business education needed to be reformed.[44]

For all these reasons, winning the IHAS contracts has to be seen as the seminal event of Teledyne's early years and one of the central events in Kozmetsky's career. Kozmetsky was codirector of the program from its inception, along with Teck Wilson, a Teledyne vice president. Wilson, an electrical engineer, came to Teledyne in its first year with other associates of Singleton and Kozmetsky at Litton, and he remained with the company until his retirement in 1980. He had a talent for writing and presenting contract proposals and was one of Teledyne's leaders in pursuing government contracts and searching for new companies to acquire.[45]

The avionics system was intended to enable helicopters to fly in automatically controlled formation in zero visibility in all kinds of weather, and to fly very close to the ground over hostile terrain.[46] If it had worked properly, it would have been the first system to allow a helicopter to "hug the ground" automatically, avoiding obstacles without losing speed, while controlling and coordinating all of the aircraft's major electronics components. Designed for installation in the navy's CH-53 heavy assault helicopter (built by Sikorsky) and its companion CH-46 helicopter (built by Boeing through its subsidiary Vertol), the system was meant to enhance the ability of those aircraft to carry large numbers of marines and their equipment into battle from navy assault transports, giving the aircraft "a flight control capability far in excess of that provided by any prior developments."[47]

Teledyne engineer James P. Murphy and two others who worked on the IHAS described the hoped-for functions of the system when installed in the CH-53 in this way (well before the technology was to prove unworkable): "The mission of that aircraft is the rapid movement of troops and heavy cargo in the 'vertical envelopment' tactic in a Marine Corps amphibious assault. To perform that mission in day or night and all weather, the IHAS first provides the total Weapons System with the precision navigation system required to locate the landing zone without terminal aids and to precisely schedule succeeding waves. Second, the IHAS provides a low altitude terrain following and avoidance capability; at low altitudes the probability is relatively high that local topology will conceal the aircraft. Further, when it is detected, the aircraft will be passing hostile ground forces at a high angular rate and will remain in view a much shorter time. With this limited time for enemy action, the greater number of aircraft suddenly appearing as targets, the greater the probability of survival for each. Therefore, the third major IHAS function is close-formation flight or stationkeeping."[48]

The heart of the system was a "Computer Central Complex," which consisted of three digital computers designed by Teledyne to analyze data from sensors and radar, to give the pilot precise information about the aircraft, and, as needed, to automatically control the flight. Each computer weighed no more than seventeen pounds, and the largest measured only 3 inches by 7.5 inches by 23.25 inches.[49] The system was built on the principle of "functional modularity," allowing various components to be inserted or removed easily, limiting the adverse effects if a particular module failed, and simplifying maintenance and repair.[50]

The Teledyne contract represented the first time in the postwar era that the navy had given a single contractor complete responsibility for the entire avionics aboard an aircraft, and it was the first avionics system pursued through a new Defense Department procurement program based on rigid performance and cost-effectiveness requirements. The system was designed to overcome the high failure rates and maintenance costs that the military had experienced with much of its advanced technology. The army, which was interested in using the system in its own helicopters, contributed 40 percent of the initial $26.6 million contracts awarded to Teledyne Systems Corp. (a subsidiary of the parent company) for a twenty-three-month development program beginning in April 1965. A production contract would follow worth more than $100 million ($771 million in 2017).

Singleton attributed Teledyne's success in competing for the development contract to, in large measure, the company's strength in semiconductor design and manufacturing because that helped its engineers design a simpler and more reliable computer that was intended to be the key to the avionics system.[51] From Kozmetsky's perspective, an essential element was his work with his old friends Abe Charnes and Bill Cooper in applying the techniques of management science to the complex manufacturing procedures, production schedules, and quality control measures that would be required of whatever company won the contract. Charnes and Cooper brought their analytical skills to the challenge of demonstrat-

A Civic Entrepreneur

ing how Teledyne could do a better job with the avionics project than far more experienced defense contractors. This kind of analysis appealed to Defense Secretary Robert S. McNamara, whose management style continued to be influenced by his work in the field of operations research during World War II, and it helped persuade the Defense Department that a newcomer like Teledyne was up to the challenge of manufacturing the system and delivering it on time and within the budget (none of which, as it turned out, proved to be the case).

William Cooper recalled the story of winning the contract:

> George called me and explained the problem they were facing in putting together their proposal for the contract. I didn't think Teledyne had a chance. They only had a couple hundred employees and no track record in defense procurement, and they were competing against companies like Boeing and Lockheed. But I agreed to see what we could do to help, and we arranged a meeting with Abe Charnes and Teledyne engineers in Evanston, Illinois, where Charnes was on the faculty [at Northwestern University]. We worked for three days, without sleep, trying one idea after another. Charnes and I finally worked out the complete mathematical model for estimating the process and cost of production, and George looked at it and was satisfied.
>
> I can still remember saying, "OK, let's go home and get some sleep," but George said, "What are you talking about?" He went to the bathroom, washed up, put on a clean shirt, and then packed up his suitcase and was off to Washington to make a presentation to McNamara. Then he made a trip to New York to arrange for more financing.[52]

Cooper said the mathematical models backing up Teledyne's claims for the system were crucial to McNamara's decision to award the contract to Teledyne. As secretary of defense, McNamara had introduced new concepts of "cost-effectiveness" in defense planning, an approach that required competitors for weapons contracts to demonstrate that their proposals were the most favorable in comparison with competing approaches or designs.[53]

Not long after he became dean of business at the University of Texas, and four years before the avionics system proved unworkable, Kozmetsky recounted the challenges of the helicopter contract in a lecture at Harvard on the use of computers in business management: "The [Department of Defense] requirements stated explicitly that one must demonstrate that the proposed item has been determined to be the most favorable in the relationship to the cost-effectiveness of competing items on a DOD-wide basis. The end item was an avionics package for a helicopter, and the competing items ranged from other avionics, to other helicopters, STOL [short takeoff and landing] aircraft, COIN [counter-insurgency] aircraft, etc. The context of the request was such that analysis was required to prove that the proposed plan was best suited for designated missions to be used with unspecified forces, using yet-to-be-developed tactics, to best accomplish more explicit strategies for four major classes of war and at the same time be capable of demonstrating that the best national defense posture was maintained. In short, looking at the problem as an organic whole."

Kozmetsky said that the company had been able to attain the contract not as "the sole result of utilization of a computerized management model or the brilliant engineering breakthrough or an advanced management system. Nor was it the collection of a group of the most capable engineers, scientists, and managers. It was actually the ability of top management to coordinate from just a conceptual point of view the various required technical and engineering techniques [and] the formulation of the end goals as well as the sub-goals at each level . . . so that existing technical and engineering techniques . . . could be utilized in meeting DOD's cost-effectiveness requirements. This could not have been done prior to the days of a computer."[54]

Kozmetsky also made presentations about aspects of the IHAS project to at least two scientific meetings. He discussed the system's use of semi-conductors at an Office of Naval Research conference on microelectronics in 1965, and he talked about economic considerations of the application of microcircuits to systems at the 1966 Aerospace and Electronic Systems Convention in Washington, DC, sponsored by the Institute of Electrical and Electronics Engineers. At the Office of Naval Research conference, Kozmetsky commented on the irony that although microelectronic circuits had provided three major benefits in systems technology—reduced size, weight, and power requirements for the performance of a given function; a marked increase in reliability of a system's components; and greatly reduced costs—such circuits were not a panacea for engineering problems because of "the ever-increasing rate with which demands for precision in system performance and breadth of system capability are rising." He traced these increasing demands to the upward spiral of competition with "the potential enemy" (the Soviet Union) and vigorous competition in the civilian market.

Kozmetsky said the techniques of cost-effectiveness analysis had provided a rigorous and objective way of determining whether the technological advances of the system were truly worth their cost—particularly whether they could be justified in terms of increased reliability. He lauded the "comprehensive integral self-testing capabilities" of the IHAS computers, which permitted "the automatic detection and isolation of faults in the system during operation." The modular design of the system and its "triple redundancy" would make it much more reliable, he said, than the usual scientific or business computers, where the techniques for detecting errors were less rigorous. Those techniques "are meaningless in the central computer of an avionics system," Kozmetsky said, "where the problem is not merely to inhibit the outputting of wrong answers but, rather, to ensure the outputting of right answers. If these right answers do not continue to be forthcoming, we do not merely have a balance sheet printout which is gibberish but instead run the risk of losing an aircraft."[55]

The selection of Teledyne had effects that reverberated through the company for many years. As if overnight, Teledyne had become a force to be reckoned with in the aerospace and military industries. Investors were impressed with the company's capabilities and track record, and within a year of the contract award Teledyne's stock had risen from $15 a share to $65. One benefit of that increase in stock price was that it gave the company the financial resources to make much larger acquisitions than it had been capable of in the earliest years.[56]

The shell of a navy helicopter was soon installed in one of the Teledyne buildings on Panama Street so engineers could outfit it with pieces of the prototype avionics system as they became available. Teledyne was originally expected to produce four prototypes before production would begin. The helicopter and the engineers eventually moved to a 250,000-square-foot plant that was built for Teledyne Systems in Northridge, in the San Fernando Valley.[57] That plant was eventually doubled in size, providing space for four thousand employees for the IHAS contracts and other Teledyne Systems projects before the helicopter program was canceled.[58]

Failure of the technology was a major setback for the military's plans for advancing the design of helicopters, which still largely relied on avionics systems borrowed from fixed-wing aircraft. It had been the military's hope "that at long last helicopters would have a full instrument capability in rough terrain. Then, in one of the more frustrating chains of events experienced by the Navy and Marine Corps, the entire concept began to run into difficulty. Testing fell 26 months behind schedule. Cost overruns were encountered which required delicate and lengthy negotiations between the Navy and Teledyne."[59]

One problem was that the self-contained navigation system caused the helicopter's radio transmissions to be blanked out. According to a history of marine helicopters, "in July 1969, after five months of reengineering in a shielded hangar at Vertol [the Boeing subsidiary that built the CH-46 and

CH-47 helicopters], the problem remained unsolved. The last months of 1969 and the spring of 1970 saw one contract after another cancelled due to cost and delays. By the middle of the year, IHAS and all its components were, for all practical purposes, no longer an active program."[60] A similar terrain-following radar system installed by Teledyne in a smaller army helicopter also failed an early series of tests.[61]

Given the great importance of the helicopter contract in the fortunes of Teledyne and Kozmetsky regardless of the final outcome, the ultimate failure of the system is almost beside the point—except, of course, for the marines.

Growth through Acquisitions

Throughout the period that Kozmetsky was directing the IHAS project and providing other management oversight, Singleton was continuing to work on expanding Teledyne's technical capabilities and market strength through a series of acquisitions—mostly of small electronics companies that specialized in designing and manufacturing one or a few types of products. After the first acquisition—Amelco in October 1960—many others soon followed. Teledyne was seeking companies that, among other things, would help the parent company develop the self-sufficiency in electronic systems that Singleton and Kozmetsky were aiming for. There were seventeen such acquisitions in Teledyne's first three years and a total of 127 during the company's first eight years, most of them through transactions that involved an exchange of stock or other securities. The Teledyne stock was often restricted, so it could not be sold for a particular length of time, a provision that sometimes left holders of the stock quite disgruntled.[62]

Singleton sometimes oversimplified the acquisition strategy when talking with outsiders. He told *Businessweek*, for example, that Teledyne simply looked for companies in a field or with a product that "interested" him and the other directors, and that had the potential for high growth through technological innovation. All the board members were either engineers or, like Kozmetsky, were easily conversant with high-tech topics. It was not surprising, wrote *Businessweek*, "that the things that interest this board in the way of acquisitions sound a bit far out to the layman. Technical talk of inertial guidance systems, telemetering applications, servomechanisms, superalloys, nuclear cross sections, photo-instrumentation, and seismic profilers is their métier."[63]

Teledyne acquired two other companies in 1960—Handley Inc., a small company that made potentiometers (devices to measure voltage and control other electrical components, used in everything from nuclear weapons to electric guitars), and Mercury Transformer Corp., which specialized in making the electromagnetic devices that transfer energy between circuits. Those first three acquisitions gave Teledyne eighty thousand square feet of facilities devoted to the manufacture of electronics systems, data entry and readout equipment, magnetic devices and transformers, high-quality etched circuits, and miniature potentiometers. By the end of its first calendar year Teledyne had more than four hundred employees in these operations.

In 1961, Teledyne acquired Palmer Instruments, a small maker of electronic measuring devices, and Linair Engineering Inc., which had $2 million in sales and made instruments such as pneumatic fittings, potentiometers, and relays. With the Linair acquisition, Teledyne went public, and its stock began trading over the counter. Pieces of Handley, Palmer, and Linair were joined to form Teledyne Precision Inc., which soon added other products, such as quartz crystals and slip rings (electrical connectors that carry signals from a stationary wire to a rotating device).[64]

In 1962 there were two acquisitions—Crittendon Transformer Works Inc., which had sales of $1 million, and American Systems Inc., a small company that conducted research and development of computer technology, antennas, and other electronic equipment. It was renamed Teledyne Systems Corp. and was greatly expanded, eventually acquiring the size and expertise to manage large, complex projects such as the IHAS.

Ten more acquisitions came in quick succession from 1963 to 1965, including companies engaged in making geodetic engineering and mapping systems, microwave components, explosive devices, electronic switches, optical technologies, circuits for temperature sensing and control, hydraulic components, communications equipment, ordnance systems, industrial controls, seismographs, traveling-wave tubes, transistors, diodes, aircraft controls, and telemetry equipment, as well as providing engineering and design services.[65]

By the end of 1965, Teledyne had become the nation's seventy-ninth-largest defense contractor, with contracts valued at $30.7 million, most of that a result of winning the IHAS competition. Although Teledyne impressed many observers with its rapid growth during its first six years, it was still a relatively small player in the military-industrial complex. Forty-one companies had more than $100 million in defense contracts in 1965, and Lockheed Aircraft Corp. led them all with $1.7 billion.[66] (By 1980, Teledyne had climbed to No. 28 with $399.7 million in contracts, and General Dynamics was then in first place with $3.5 billion.)[67]

The rapid pace of acquisitions continued in 1966, Kozmetsky's last year in management of Teledyne, with companies engaged in oil-field services, offshore drilling, and research, as well as more manufacturers of electronic devices.[68]

Teledyne's biggest acquisition in 1966 was Vasco Metals Corp., a $43.4 million operation in Latrobe, Pennsylvania, that brought its president, George A. Roberts, to Teledyne as Teledyne's new president and a member of the board of directors (with Singleton continuing as chairman and chief executive officer). Roberts remained as Teledyne's president for twenty-four years and effectively took Kozmetsky's place as Singleton's top management partner. Vasco was a manufacturer of ultra-high-strength and high-temperature alloys, specializing in alloys important to the defense and space industries. After its acquisition, the company served as a center of materials R&D for Teledyne.[69] In 1967 Roberts helped Teledyne acquire another major metallurgy company, the Wah Chang Corporation of Oregon and Alabama—the world's leading producer of many rare metals—and, in 1968 alone, twenty-one other metals companies that gave Teledyne a leading position in the metals, metallurgy, machine tool, and tool-and-dye industries.[70]

The acquisition of Vasco Metals Corp., announced in March 1966, facilitated the transition to a Teledyne without Kozmetsky in its management and eventually resulted in several dramatic changes in direction for the company. At least by the previous summer, Kozmetsky had been exploring the possibilities of a top management position at a major university, and by the spring of 1966, he was well along in his pursuit of the dean's office at the University of Texas business school. His acceptance of that job by early summer was made easier by his knowledge that Singleton now had another trusted friend to help him run the day-to-day operations of the company. Many years later, Roberts recalled a conversation he had with Kozmetsky, when they first met, about the transition at Teledyne: "George Kozmetsky assured me that he had asked Henry [Singleton] many times to find someone to take his position so that he could achieve his lifelong goal of returning to academia" (see chapter 8).[71] Another observer, Vasco official James D. Nisbet, said he thought Kozmetsky was unsuited to running the type of conglomerate that Singleton was putting together. "Kozmetsky was oriented toward the academic community, and I believe he was uncomfortable in the rough and tumble world of operating the business," he wrote.[72] Nisbet became a vice president of Teledyne and helped it evaluate companies for possible acquisition.

The Vasco acquisition was one of the reasons for large gains in sales and earnings for Teledyne in 1966. Net income rose to $12.04 million from $3.4 million the previous year. That was equal to $3.67 per share (on 2.7

million shares), compared with \$1.98 per share (on 1.7 million shares) a year earlier. Total sales were \$256.8 million, compared with \$86.5 million a year earlier. The year's acquisitions, as well as internal growth, greatly swelled Teledyne's employment, which stood at 14,000 at the end of the year, up from 5,400 a year earlier.[73] From its beginnings in a single Los Angeles building that it inherited from Amelco, Teledyne now had one million square feet of manufacturing space, at plants at several locations in Southern California as well as the San Francisco Bay area, Boston, Dallas, Houston, New York, Virginia, Florida, and Alabama. It had been a whirlwind six years for Kozmetsky and Singleton.

The growth of Teledyne during the years that Kozmetsky was in management (1960–1966) or on the board (through 1995) often astounded observers. From 1961 to 1971, Teledyne led the Fortune 500 ranking in earnings and the growth of its earnings per share. By the end of 1966 Teledyne had reached the 293rd spot on the Fortune 500 with sales of \$256.8 million—almost three times the sales of the previous year.[74] The growth in sales was more spectacular in subsequent years, although by other measures, such as the stock price, the company's record was more spotty. Sales exceeded \$1 billion in 1969 and never again fell below that figure. After 1984 sales were well above \$3 billion a year.

Teledyne's stock price closed 1966 at \$85.60 per share, although it had been as high as \$129.50 that year. Kozmetsky was reported to own 130,000 shares of Teledyne when he left for the University of Texas business school,[75] holdings that would have been worth \$11.1 million at year's end (\$83.2 million in 2017). In 1967 the stock rebounded to more than \$200 a share, which would have made Kozmetsky's holdings worth more than \$26 million at the time (\$195 million in 2017), but the price was highly variable for many years. The stock price, along with that of many other conglomerates, slumped in the early 1970s, but Teledyne posted significant gains in subsequent years, trading at well over \$300 a share by the mid-1980s.[76]

After 1966 Teledyne continued its work in electronics but soon branched out to other fields, including expanded work in metallurgy and geophysics as well as expansion into new fields such as consumer products, insurance, airplane manufacturing, engine manufacturing for cars and other vehicles, phonograph speakers, and televisions. Teledyne even acquired the company that made the Waterpik oral irrigator and shower massage devices.

The great surge in acquisitions that had been Teledyne's way of life since its founding came to an end by 1970, after Singleton and the board decided that prices for companies were too high and there were few companies available that Teledyne had much interest in.[77] There was speculation that accounting changes adopted in early 1970 by a board of the American Institute of Certified Public Accountants would discourage mergers and acquisitions, but Singleton downplayed the possible effects of the new rules.[78] Since there was not much left to buy outright, Teledyne began a new phase of growth by reorganizing and consolidating what it had already acquired, and by a greater emphasis by Singleton on asset management, including investing through Teledyne's insurance companies in the securities of other companies. Teledyne gained effective control of several major companies in this period. At one point in the late 1970s, Teledyne owned 25 percent of the common stock of Litton Industries. Among many other companies in which Teledyne had a significant stake were General Electric, the conglomerate TRW, H. J. Heinz, Occidental Petroleum, International Harvester, Walter Kidde (a maker of fire extinguishers), and Curtiss-Wright (a diversified aerospace company).

As such investments grew, Teledyne devoted less attention to R&D, and there were several dramatic examples of decline in some of its technology-based operations and subsequent losses of important contracts. After these and other setbacks, Singleton stepped down from his management responsibilities in 1986 and turned over the management to George Roberts. Many other changes in the direction of the company were to follow, and in 1995, the year Kozmetsky left the Teledyne board, almost all the business and assets of Teledyne Electronics Systems were sold to Litton Industries, thus ending Teledyne's participation in the defense electronics business, the field that had drawn Singleton and Kozmetsky to start the company thirty-five years earlier.[79] The next year, Teledyne was acquired by Allegheny Ludlum Corp., a steel company in Pittsburgh, and a new company, Allegheny Teledyne, was formed. In 1999 many of that company's technology-based operations were spun off into what became known as Teledyne Technologies, which continues to exist.[80]

One of the continuing legacies of the Singleton and Kozmetsky years in Teledyne management was the company's streamlined executive offices. In the mid-1970s, for example, the company had forty-five thousand employees in all its divisions but only 150 employees in its executive headquarters in Century City. Two-thirds of those were members of the controller's staff.[81] Teledyne's long-established practice of granting a high degree of autonomy to its divisions and subsidiaries (while requiring rigorous financial control and planning) helped keep down the size of the central management. Kozmetsky and Singleton also saw it as one of the keys to their company's profitability. As Kozmetsky told one of his management classes at the University of Texas: "At Teledyne we had 135 companies and 135 presidents. They all knew their operations. We had a management style that was very simple. We decentralized decision-making. A horrible example to me was always U.S. Steel. At U.S. Steel if they wanted a capital investment of $500 or more, the board decided who was going to spend it. We wouldn't waste our time on that. The critical test to see if management has decentralized decision-making is to ask who sets the price? Teledyne was the bank for the 135 companies. The presidents thought that they could get money from Teledyne but they were wrong. They had to make their money from their operations."[82]

Teledyne's policy was not to interfere in the management of the companies it owned as long as a required amount of cash was sent to the corporate headquarters each month, representing Teledyne's return on its investment. "Then if they needed money, they had to come and ask us," Kozmetsky recalled. "I can remember looking people in the eye and being hard and saying, 'If you think getting money out of me is easier than getting money out of your customers, you are mistaken. Go collect on your receivables, sell your inventories.'"[83]

The growth of Teledyne during the 1960s was one factor underlying a surge by the end of the decade in the venture capital industry, which further stimulated the development of Silicon Valley companies. The spectacular capital gains earned by Arthur Rock and his partner Thomas Davis through their investment in Teledyne and another electronics company, Scientific Data Systems, attracted the notice of other investors and is credited with a surge in new capital available for new technology companies in California. By the time the Davis and Rock partnership was dissolved in 1968, the $3 million that it had invested in Teledyne and Scientific Data Systems had grown to $90 million ($628 million in 2017).[84]

After defense contracts started coming in, and after the company's aggressive acquisition program and investments by Teledyne in the stock of other companies proved enormously profitable, Singleton and Kozmetsky became very wealthy. When *Forbes* magazine in 1982 began its annual listing of the four hundred richest Americans, Singleton made the list with an estimated net worth of $100 million. Kozmetsky may have come close to making the cut from the beginning, because when he appeared on the list for the first time in 1984, his net worth was estimated at $185 million ($432 million in 2017). Singleton's net worth had climbed to $450 million by 1984 ($1.05 billion in 2017).[85]

Being listed among *Forbes*'s richest people was an occasion for local media attention, but for George and Ronya Kozmetsky it was not a kind of publicity that they sought. Their wealth gave them increased credibility in the judgment of many people, but they were more interested in what could be done with money rather than merely having it.

Singleton remained on the *Forbes* list each year until his death in 1999, with a net worth estimated at $750 million by the end. Because of inflation and the rapid accumulation of wealth by the richest Americans beginning in the 1980s, the minimum net worth for being listed had climbed to $500 million by 1999.[86] After his initial listing in 1984, Kozmetsky appeared three more times—in 1985 ($175 million), 1986 ($200 million), and 1988 ($240 million).[87] After that the cutoff point was so high that Kozmetsky was not listed again.

Although Kozmetsky traded his management job at Teledyne for the management of the University of Texas business school in 1966, it would be a mistake to say that he "left Teledyne." He was employed as a consultant to George Roberts, the new president, until 1971, and he continued as a member of the board of directors until 1995. It was said that throughout those years he never missed a board meeting or annual shareholders meeting. For many years he continued to own more than 5 percent of Teledyne's stock, remaining the company's second-largest shareholder.

Singleton stepped down as CEO in 1986 but continued as chairman until 1991 and as a director until 1997. When he left the board he still owned 7.2 percent of Teledyne's stock.[88] After the mid-1980s he devoted much of his time to managing San Cristóbal, his 81,000-acre ranch south of Santa Fe, and other ranches totaling more than one million acres in New Mexico and California.[89]

LIFE IN SOUTHERN CALIFORNIA

For the Kozmetsky family, life in Southern California was a time of growth and adventure. It also brought an encounter with the region's infamous wildfires—an episode that severely tested the family's strength and resilience.

In November 1961, Teledyne's second year, the worst wildfire in Los Angeles up to that time swept through Bel Air and other sections of the city and destroyed 484 homes, including the Kozmetsky family residence at 421 North Saltair Avenue. Driven by fifty-mile-per-hour Santa Ana winds and racing through extremely dry and brushy terrain, parts of which had not burned in more than fifty years, the Bel Air–Brentwood fire consumed more than 6,000 acres within a 19.5-mile perimeter and prompted the evacuation of 3,500 residents. More people would have been forced to flee, but the fire began on a Monday morning after many residents had already gone to work or school.

The fire, believed to be accidental, was sparked under extremely flammable conditions of low humidity, high winds, and abundant natural and man-made fuel. On the morning of the fire the relative humidity in the area stood at 3 percent, and the area registered an almost unheard of 84 (out of a possible 100) on a fire hazard index from the US Forest Service. At the height of the fire, it was fought by 85 percent of all the available firefighting equipment in the region. Over the three days it blazed before it was brought completely under control, the fire caused $25 million worth of damage—the fifth-costliest fire in US history up to that time.[90]

The Kozmetsky house, which had been built in 1936 and had a wood-shingle roof, was on a large piece of property and, like many houses in the area, had an orchard behind it. The fire consumed the house directly across the street and its orchard and then jumped across to the Kozmetskys' side, burning their house and orchard. George was at work and the children—Greg, who was sixteen and a junior in high school; Nadya, thirteen and in the seventh grade; and Georgie, eight and in the second grade—were safe at school when the fire struck. Ronya got out of the house just ahead of the fast-moving wall of fire, able to escape with only the family's tax and bank account records and some of the family's clothes. Most family photographs and other documents and keepsakes, as well as manuscripts and other papers from George's academic and business careers, were lost. All of his library was destroyed, except for a few items that were in his office at Teledyne. Later a diamond ring was found in the rubble.[91]

Singleton and his family were more fortunate. Their home, at 15000 Mulholland Drive (6.5 miles north of the Kozmetskys' home), was spared when the fire, which had been moving up the canyon wall toward the house, suddenly stopped in the Singletons' backyard and veered in a different direction.[92]

The Kozmetsky family moved into an apartment and fell back on Ronya's salary as a schoolteacher while Teledyne was continuing to get established. The family delayed rebuilding their home when George proposed that the insurance money from the destroyed house be applied to Teledyne's needs to meet its payroll. Amelco, the company that Teledyne had acquired, owed $1 million to the Bank of America, which was not willing to loan any more, and Teledyne needed cash right away. Ronya agreed to give up the insurance money temporarily. By January, Teledyne had managed to borrow $1.2 million from a bank in New York; most of the money went to the Bank of America, but Ronya got enough to rebuild their house.[93]

"My parents are fighters and survivors," Greg Kozmetsky said. "Their attitude was, 'This disaster has happened, and now we are going to move forward and build this company,' and that is what they did."[94] The family also drew comfort from the fact that Ronya's parents, Theodore and Fania Keosiff, had followed them to the Los Angeles area and still lived not far away in Culver City.

As Teledyne gained its footing, the house in Bel Air was rebuilt, with a design by the prominent Los Angeles architect Alfred T. Gilman, who had been an associate of Frank Lloyd Wright. The house was included in a 1968 tour of "distinctive homes" that raised money for the Palisades High School PTA. The house was described as having "green slate floors and wormy chestnut and walnut woods." The Keosiffs often stayed at the home when George and Ronya were in Austin, and Theodore was said to spend a lot of time in a toy workshop that he had installed in the home.[95] Today a high wall extends across the property's frontage on Saltair Avenue, with only a portion of the house's roofline visible from the street.

When the Kozmetskys had first moved to the Los Angeles area in 1952, they had rented a house in the Pacific Palisades section of the city before moving to Bel Air. They later moved to Santa Monica, partly to take advantage of the lower property taxes. The Santa Monica house, at 516 Nineteenth Street, was also closer to the beach. In 1985, a landscape firm hired by the Kozmetskys, Pardee & Fleming Landscape, won first place for their large renovation project in the annual awards sponsored by the local chapter of the California Landscape Contractors Association.[96]

When the Kozmetsky children were growing up in the 1950s, the Bel Air house was frequently full of visitors. Herbert Simon and his family were frequent houseguests, as were scholars visiting the Rand Corporation and other Southern California institutions. The house was also often full of children from the neighborhood, and George sometimes tested his ideas on them or their parents. "He always kept a blackboard in his bedroom, as in his office or study," Greg Kozmetsky said. "Sometimes he would bring in the children or others from the neighborhood and go over concepts that he was working [up] on the blackboard. This would usually be from 30,000 feet. He always said that if he could explain his ideas to children he must have them clearly in mind. Everywhere we lived we had blackboards."[97] It may not be a coincidence that Henry Singleton also kept a blackboard in his office at Teledyne, using it, among other things, for "rapid-fire chalk talks" on the workings of the company.[98]

When Greg was in junior high he would ride with his father as far as his school bus stop, where George would turn to go to the Litton offices. On a few occasions Greg would go with his father to Litton, with a visit to the company's computer—which occupied a large room—a highlight of the trip. At home around the dinner table, George would lead discussions of current events and would ask the children questions about items in the news or about subjects such as physics. There were also outings to fast-food restaurants near the Fox Hills shopping center, including a drive-in hamburger place where George enjoyed eating in the car. There were frequent trips to the beach, and vacations often included trips to Seattle to visit relatives, as well as trips to Palm Springs for Easter. But as much as George enjoyed such family activities, these were also years in which he was often away from the family.

"He was gone a lot when we were growing up," Greg Kozmetsky said. "This was a time that was very important in the country's history, and he and his peers were building things that people today don't know much about. But it was very important work. He always tried to share with us the excitement of building a business, particularly after the fire."[99] Greg worked at Teledyne in the summer of 1964, but it was understood to be only a summer job, as Kozmetsky and Singleton had agreed that they would not bring members of their families into the business with permanent jobs. Kozmetsky also found part-time work for Nadya at Teledyne, but neither Greg nor Nadya was given an easy job in an office. Instead, they were put to work in storerooms lifting boxes or doing other chores that got their hands dirty.

Although business occupied a major portion of George's time, "if you needed him he would be there," said Greg, who entered the army after high school and served in Vietnam. "When I was injured in Vietnam, he went to UCLA to talk to specialists there about my injuries, and then he flew to Japan to talk to my doctors. He was always busy building companies, and he had many concerns, but he made time for you when you needed him."[100]

Throughout his years at Teledyne, Kozmetsky maintained the diverse intellectual pursuits that had been his passion since his early life in Seattle. A continuing feature of these interests was the gathering of brilliant minds for freewheeling discussion. The Kozmetskys' home was often full of overnight guests from the worlds of acadamia, government, and industry. Wlodzimierz Szwarc, whose research into solving complex scheduling and transportation problems was published in the journals *Management Science* and *Operations Research*, stayed with the Kozmetskys in Brentwood for a week in May 1963 for a series of meetings in the Los Angeles area. Bill Cooper had arranged for Szwarc to stay with the Kozmetskys.

"George picked me up from the airport and sang old Russian songs," Szwarc recalled. "Bill [had] asked me to check whether George spoke good Russian. He did." One day during the visit George took Szwarc across the street to swim in the backyard pool of LaVerne Andrews, the oldest member of the singing trio the Andrews Sisters, popular in the 1940s and 1950s.

Szwarc said Ronya was not amused when he and George returned with LaVerne's lipstick on their cheeks.[101] Ronya may have feigned displeasure, but she also sometimes enjoyed taking friends across the street to visit LaVerne and view her collection of gold records and stage costumes.[102]

One evening during his visit, Szwarc invited to dinner at the Kozmetskys' home his friend Richard E. Bellman, an applied mathematician who worked at that time at the Rand Corporation in Santa Monica and who had invented the technique of "dynamic programming" in the early 1950s. Bellman and Szwarc had begun corresponding before Szwarc emigrated from Poland. Also at the dinner were Andrew Vázsonyi, a mathematician who had been a friend and colleague of Kozmetsky's at Hughes Aircraft and since the early days of the Institute of Management Sciences, and George W. Hoover, a retired navy commander who as an official of the Office of Naval Research had worked closely with Wernher von Braun on the US missile and satellite programs at Huntsville, Alabama. Hoover and Kozmetsky had known each other at Litton Industries, which had worked on various navy contracts in the 1950s. The evening did not go as well as the Kozmetskys had hoped. When Bellman arrived, Kozmetsky told him he had a real treat for him—that Commander Hoover would be coming to the dinner. Bellman was noncommittal, but when Hoover arrived and had been introduced, Bellman asked him, "How does it feel to work with a Nazi war criminal?"—a reference to von Braun's wartime work on the Germans' V-2 rocket, which was produced in a factory that used forced labor. Szwarc and Vázsonyi had numerous relatives who were killed by the Nazis, but they apparently were more polite to Hoover. Bellman noted in his autobiography that he was not invited back to the Kozmetskys' house.[103]

As his income increased in the 1950s and 1960s, Kozmetsky developed an interest in collecting rare books and other objects of historical or scientific interest. He recalled: "While an executive, I began to collect old scientific books and instruments as well as Old Masters' etchings. In the process, I met many of the experts in the universities, galleries, and museums who educated me. In the process, I found myself more and more exchanging expertise between us. In other words, art expertise and knowledge for business expertise and knowledge."[104] One of his favorite bookstores in Los Angeles was Zeitlin & Ver Brugge, one of the leading antiquarian booksellers in the country, which occupied a barnlike building on La Cienega Boulevard in West Hollywood. The store was run by Jake Zeitlin and his wife, Josephine Ver Brugge, from the late 1940s through the 1980s, and Kozmetsky would often take his daughter, Nadya, with him on expeditions to browse the store's collection of works of fine art, which were kept in a loft.[105] The store also specialized in old scientific journals and related books.[106]

The move to Austin in 1966 did not pull the Kozmetskys entirely away from the life in Southern California that they liked so much. They kept their house in Santa Monica and regularly spent the summers and Christmas holidays there and often visited the Keosiffs and old friends, in addition to frequent business trips that George made to the area.

CHAPTER 8

RETURN TO ACADEMIA

The University of Texas at Austin was searching for a new dean of its business school at the same time that Kozmetsky began looking for an opportunity to return to the academic world. He had several reasons for wanting to make this transition. In later years he told friends that he decided to leave Teledyne when he finally realized that Henry Singleton was never going to let him have a greater role in making key management decisions.[1] Some believed Kozmetsky was "eased out" of his management role by Singleton's desire to bring in another old friend, George A. Roberts, to take over more of the day-to-day operations, but Kozmetsky never discussed this publically, and Roberts claimed that the management changes had been Kozmetsky's preference.[2] Any rift that might have developed between Kozmetsky and Singleton appeared not to be very deep because Kozmetsky remained on the Teledyne board of directors for many years after leaving his management role. He also had other motives for wanting to make a change.

Kozmetsky had never given up his long-term dream of returning to the academic world, including a long-held desire to be in charge of a business school. He had promised Ronya in 1952 that his move from Carnegie Tech to Hughes Aircraft would be a short-term venture into private business, but by the time he left Teledyne, fourteen years had elapsed. They had been exciting and highly lucrative years for the Kozmetskys, and George seemed to have a natural talent for making business decisions (and making money), but he had never given up a desire to return to a university. Only in such a setting could he fully pursue his intellectual interests and associate with the broad spectrum of scientists, engineers, and humanists whose company he craved. Only there could he fully pursue his love for teaching and fully indulge his flair for creative thinking, drawing ideas from across multiple disciplines. He had no intention of retreating to an ivory tower unconnected to the outside world; instead, he saw a position in academia as the best vantage point from which to explore his ideas about how the realms of business, government, and academic institutions could collaborate on solving the problems of society.

These themes came together for Kozmetsky one morning in the summer of 1965 as he listened to news on the radio about the first night of the rioting in Los Angeles's Watts neighborhood, about twenty miles from his home in Brentwood. As recounted in chapter 1, news of the rioting, which continued for six days, resulted in an awakening for Kozmetsky, who realized with a sense of finality that his true calling was as a leader in the academic world and not as an industrialist.

Many years later, he recounted this experience for his management students at the University of Texas at Austin. The class had been discussing ideologies, and Kozmetsky had expressed his view that the traditional American ideology of capitalism had broken down. A student asked if he could "pinpoint historically" when that process had started, and Kozmetsky had responded without hesitation: "Oh, I have no trouble. Can I personalize it? Yes, the morning I woke up in my bedroom in Los Angeles and I looked out through our coral tree to the Pacific Ocean and listened to the radio telling me Watts was burning. That is when it struck me. That is when I decided to give up being an executive. The time had come to go back to the university. I had been gone too long. My one year out of the university had stretched into fifteen. I was forty-eight and if I didn't get back, I wouldn't have the energy to bring about the changes that I thought should happen. That was my personal awakening."[3]

In that same class period Kozmetsky emphasized his view that profits in the business world were not an end in themselves and that "ends do not justify the means." These views were one reason that being an industrialist had left him unsatisfied.

So it was that by the mid-1960s Kozmetsky was motivated by social concerns to look for an opportunity to return to the academic world, and thanks to the success of Teledyne and its now steady income from defense contracts, particularly the helicopter avionics contract, he was in a financial position to make the long-delayed move back to a campus environment. Another factor that would have influenced the timing of his decision to go back to academia was the new direction in which Singleton wanted to take Teledyne, broadening the scope of its acquisitions and eventually calling in George Roberts to help manage the company. Kozmetsky began looking seriously for an academic job several months before Roberts arrived at Teledyne, but he later expressed relief that the presence of Roberts gave him confidence that he could leave without harming the company. Those three factors—the independence that came with Kozmetsky's new wealth, the new directions in which Singleton wanted to take Teledyne, and the epiphany that Kozmetsky experienced when hearing about the Watts rioting—combined to make that the year that Kozmetsky would enter the academic job market, looking mainly for an appointment as dean of a business school or other high administrative role that would give him an opportunity to carry out the dreams that he had been nurturing since his days at Harvard and the Carnegie Institute of Technology.

He had an offer of a professorship from Carnegie Tech, and his friend Judson Neff, a University of Texas management professor who had been a mentor since the days when he supervised Kozmetsky's dissertation at Harvard, once reported that the University of California, Berkeley, came close to hiring him as dean of its college of engineering.[4] That position also involved a joint appointment at the Berkeley business school.[5] There were also reports that the University of California, Irvine, which opened in 1965, had been interested in Kozmetsky as one of its deans.[6] And a few months after he moved to Texas, one of his friends at Harvard asked him discretely if he thought he wanted to stay there—apparently an overture about opportunities that might remain open at Harvard.

There might have been additional universities that were interested in Kozmetsky, or that he was interested in, but it was the University of Texas that eventually offered him the kind of opportunity that he had first dreamed about in the early 1950s—a chance to transform a business school in his image, even going beyond the innovations that he had witnessed and been part of at Harvard and Carnegie Tech. Kozmetsky recalled that Texas had a strong pull for him partly because investors from the state (including Fayez Sarofim and University of Texas alumnus Foster Parker of Houston) had provided as much as a fourth of Teledyne's early capital and the company's early sales in Texas had been robust.[7]

Kozmetsky later elaborated on the reasons that he was attracted to the opportunity at the University of Texas business school. He said that the southwestern region of the country had seemed to him to be the most promising place for the next surge of technology-based economic development. He cited the concentration of industrial activity in the Dallas area, the presence of two national laboratories in New Mexico, and the extensive engineering education programs at the Monterrey Institute of Technology in northern Mexico as the outer boundaries of a potentially dynamic new regional economy, with, as it happened, Austin and its growing university right in the center.[8]

In claiming such prescience, Kozmetsky might have been projecting backward, to some extent, from the regional economy as it was developing in the 1980s and 1990s back to his motivations in the mid-1960s. There is no doubt, however, that he saw the potential for such a regional economy centered on Austin and the public university there long before other people did. In the words of Fred Phillips, a longtime colleague of Kozmetsky's at the IC^2 Institute, "George came to Texas and started preaching about technology-based entrepreneurship, and he had to do that for years before anybody listened. Rich Texans respected George, but they made their money from oil, cattle, and real estate, and they weren't going to change. That is, until the 1980s when all three crashed, and rich people began to think maybe they should listen to George."[9]

Joe B. Frantz, for many years a prominent history professor at the University of Texas, has written about the flurry of rumors leading up to Kozmetsky's move to the university: "In the mid-1960s I began to hear rumors that Kozmetsky was going to succeed the congenial John Arch White . . . as dean of the College of Business Administration. I couldn't believe George would give up Teledyne for an academic career. The rumors gained in scope. Kozmetsky was going to Stanford. Kozmetsky was going to—you name it. He seemed to be the hottest nonacademic academic in the nation. The most intriguing rumor held that Kozmetsky was now worth $35 million with his Teledyne holdings alone, and that he had threatened Texas: either make up your minds and make me your dean or I will found my own business school and compete you out of business. I never asked Kozmetsky whether the rumor was true, but the university made its move with an offer. The College of Business Administration has not been the same since, to its everlasting credit."[10]

The Search for a Dean

By 1964 University of Texas officials had begun the process of looking for a successor to John Arch White, dean of the business school since 1958. White would turn sixty-five in the summer of 1966 and would be subject to the then-mandatory retirement age for university administrators.[11] About midway through the search for a successor, in October 1965, White had a minor stroke, but he recovered well enough to complete the remaining months of his deanship, and he retired from the faculty in 1968 after more bouts of poor health.

The appointment of a new dean provided an opportunity for Chancellor Harry Ransom (who was serving as chief executive officer of both the University of Texas System and the University of Texas at Austin), Vice Chancellor for Academic Affairs Norman Hackerman, and the University of Texas System Board of Regents to try to elevate the academic quality of

John Arch White, Kozmetsky's predecessor as dean. *Texas Student Publications (Cactus).*

the University of Texas at Austin beyond its traditional level of regional prominence. The vision was for dramatic improvement on all fronts, and Ransom was an enthusiastic supporter of a ten-year development plan that the regents had adopted in 1960, just as he became the University of Texas at Austin's top campus administrator. The goal of the plan (an outgrowth of the work of a committee that helped commemorate the university's seventy-fifth anniversary in 1958) was nothing less than "to place the University of Texas in company with the best institutions in the nation." The regents would attempt to achieve this through an increase of at least $61.88 million in spending for "greatly improved teaching and research" at the University of Texas at Austin as well as an ambitious construction program that would, over the course of the ten-year plan, involve $52.5

A CIVIC ENTREPRENEUR

Members of the UT System Board of Regents in 1966. From left, Rabbi Levi Arthur Olan, Walter P. Brenan, Frank C. Erwin Jr., Frank Neville Ikard, William W. Heath (chairman), Jack S. Josey, Ruth Carter Stevenson, William H. Bauer, and Herschel F. Connally Jr. *Texas Student Publications (Cactus).*

million worth of new and renovated buildings ($507.7 million and $430.7 million, respectively, in 2017).[12]

Most of this new funding would be derived from the Permanent University Fund, but the regents also envisioned aggressive efforts to obtain federal grants and to increase fundraising from the private sector. The plan had lasting effects across the campus, at the professional schools as well as in the arts and sciences, and in both undergraduate and graduate programs. It included increases in faculty salaries, growth in the number of faculty members, enhanced teaching equipment such as computers, and subsidies to support research. The regents said the plan was designed to "build a floor" under the university's aspirations for excellence. For Ransom, the most important result of the new spending was that it meant the university "can hold and add first-rate teachers and scholars" in competition with the nation's leading institutions.[13]

Kozmetsky began serving as dean of the business school halfway through this ambitious program of academic enhancement, and expectations were high. Ransom and others often expressed their ambitions for the business school as having it join the ranks of the top five business schools in the country. How such a status would be demonstrated was uncertain, but by whatever measure, achieving their ambitions would require radical change.[14] Although the business school had made progress under White, it was still widely acknowledged to be lagging in the university's push for national recognition. The conventional view is that the business school before Kozmetsky was no more than a good regional school and was far behind the times in comparison with institutions such as Harvard, the Carnegie Institute of Technology, and the University of Chicago. The Department of Accounting had a high reputation beyond the Southwest, but this has been seen as an exception to the general level of teaching and research at the business school in the era before Kozmetsky's arrival. Ransom and Hackerman pursued the search for a new dean with the goal of finding a leader who could make their and the regents' lofty ambitions a reality.

Finding the right person to lead this effort was not easy. The search process that resulted in the appointment of Kozmetsky in June 1966 had lasted more than eighteen months, had led to the first chairman of the faculty search committee resigning in frustration, and had included offering the job to four other nationally prominent academics or professional leaders, each of whom, for various reasons, had turned down the university. The difficult course of the search was not widely known at the time, but a thorough record of the process survives in the university's archives.[15]

Ransom formally began the search process in October 1964, when he appointed a seven-member faculty committee to advise him and Hackerman on a successor to White. John R. Stockton, a professor of statistics at the university since the 1930s, was the chairman, and the other members were John V. Bickley, chairman of the finance department; Calvin P. Blair, professor of marketing; William S. Livingston, professor of government; Stephen L. McDonald, professor of economics; Keith Morrison, professor of law; and C. Aubrey Smith, professor of accounting. Ransom told the committee he intended to name "two or three" additional members who had no formal affiliation with the university, but he never did so, although he did receive informal advice from various alumni and others as the search proceeded.[16] In late May 1965, Ransom and Hackerman apparently decided against naming anyone from off campus to the committee.[17]

William S. Livingston, vice chancellor for academic programs, in 1970. Earlier, he served on the search committee that led to Kozmetsky coming to the University of Texas. *Texas Student Publications (Cactus).*

In his own mind, Ransom had begun the search several months earlier, when he talked about the job that summer with Charls E. Walker, an executive vice president of the American Bankers Association from 1961 to 1969, a former vice president of the Federal Reserve Bank of Dallas, and an assistant to the secretary of the treasury in the Eisenhower administration.[18] Walker had earned a bachelor's degree and an MBA from the University of Texas at Austin (and later earned a PhD in economics from the Wharton School of Finance at the University of Pennsylvania), and he had taught in the University of Texas finance department from 1948 to 1954. Ransom also could have known him through visits that Walker had made to the Austin campus to deliver speeches or participate in executive development programs.[19] Walker was Ransom's clear first choice for the deanship, and the search committee understood its initial assignment very well, as Livingston recalled: "Harry believed the university needed a first-class leader with national stature to bring dramatic change to the business school, and he knew Walker and trusted him to do the job. Harry perceived the business school as one of the weakest areas of the university academically, and he was determined to do something about it. In the beginning, the work of the committee was rather simple—ratify Harry's first choice for the deanship. We took our assignment seriously, and we suggested a backup candidate as well, but I believe the deanship was clearly Walker's if he wanted it. I don't think there was any awareness at the beginning of Kozmetsky as a potential candidate. His name emerged only much later, after many others had been considered."[20]

On January 22, 1965, after spending only about three months conducting the "careful study" that Ransom had asked for, the committee recommended that the deanship be offered to Charls Walker. Stockton wrote to his bosses that the faculty of the business school was unanimous in support of Walker, although he cites no vote of the faculty on the matter. If Walker should decline—and many people on and off the committee doubted that the university could succeed in attracting a nationally prominent business leader like Walker—the committee recommended that Ransom and Hackerman offer the job to Davis Gregg, then president of the American College of Life Underwriters in Bryn Mawr, Pennsylvania. Gregg, a native of Austin and an alumnus of the University of Texas at Austin, was also well known to Ransom, and he had been the first choice of a faculty search committee for the business school deanship in 1958, when White had been appointed.[21] Gregg's name soon disappeared from the record of the search process, leading to the supposition that he was not interested.

The details of Ransom's offer to Walker are not in the university's records, but on February 17, 1965, Walker wrote to Ransom that, as he said he had discussed with the chancellor the previous summer, he would be interested in discussing the university job if his upcoming negotiations for a new contract with the American Bankers Association were not successful. He said the negotiations should be complete by mid-April, and he said the prospects were "strongly in favor" of a new contract with the association.[22] (Walker did remain at the association, although he later served as an adjunct professor of finance and public affairs at the University of Texas and maintained many other ties to the university, including serving in 1980 on the committee that raised money to create an endowed chair in Kozmetsky's honor.)

By the spring of 1965, the search committee had clearly given up on Walker as well as Gregg. After a meeting on April 29, presumably with Hackerman, the committee turned to an evaluation of a list of forty current or former deans of business schools around the country. On May 27, Stockton sent Hackerman a list of six deans or former deans whom the committee was willing to endorse for the job and also believed "there is a reasonable chance that they would be interested in it." Stockton listed them in the order of his personal preference: Eugene L. Swearingen, Oklahoma State University; Joseph W. McGuire, University of Kansas; Robert

O. Harvey, University of Connecticut; Paul. B. Blomgren, former dean at Montana State University; Paul L. Noble, former dean at Ohio University; and James A. Morris, University of South Carolina. There is a note of resignation, if not defeat, in Stockton's letter: "It has been difficult to avoid the temptation to list an outstanding individual who would make a fine dean but who would almost certainly not be willing to accept the position."[23] Hackerman wrote back within the week asking the committee to produce a list of three to six names and to rank them in order of the whole committee's preference, "so that we may proceed to the business of making offers, if an offer seems indicated, to the first man, then the second, etc."[24]

Those instructions produced, on June 15, a list from Stockton of three names from the earlier list—McGuire, Morris, and Swearingen—but Stockton said it was only a preliminary ranking and the committee would want to interview all of them before expressing final preferences. Hackerman wrote back that he and Ransom had discussed the three candidates at length and wanted Stockton to invite them to the campus for interviews as soon as possible.[25]

There was some dissatisfaction within the business school over the three named candidates, and faculty members began to make new recommendations. One professor sent in a twelve-page memo advocating that Glenn A. Welsch, a University of Texas professor of accounting, be considered,[26] and White suggested that Hackerman and Ransom might want to consider John T. Wheeler, an accounting professor at Berkeley who had made a favorable impression on university faculty members when he visited the Austin campus that year as part of work he was doing for the Ford Foundation.[27]

At the end of July, after several campus interviews, the search committee had a new recommendation—that the university offer the job to Morris, and then to McGuire if Morris did not accept.[28] Ransom and Hackerman balked at that idea and told Stockton that the committee's two-person list was too restrictive. After beginning the process by advocating nonacademic leaders of business associations and then urging the committee to switch gears and review current and former deans, Ransom and Hackerman shifted again and urged the committee to cast a new net for candidates and look again beyond those who had experience as deans of business schools.[29]

Little was accomplished for the next two months because of summer travel schedules, but in September Stockton decided he had served as long as he wanted to as chairman of the search committee. He asked Hackerman on September 13 for a meeting with the full committee "to discuss the whole problem before we make any moves,"[30] and Hackerman met with them on the twenty-second (Ransom was out of town). Whatever was discussed at that meeting about the "problem," it was enough for Stockton, and two days later he informed Hackerman that he wanted to resign as chairman. Hackerman thanked him for his contributions and named as his replacement Eugene W. Nelson, a longtime professor of business law and the secretary of the General Faculty.[31]

In October several other new candidates were under review by the committee, including John Bickley, who had resigned from the search committee because he wanted to be considered for the deanship.[32] He was replaced by Charles T. Zlatkovich, a professor of accounting.

New prospects emerged in November. The committee was continuing its interest in Morris, the South Carolina dean who had first been considered the previous summer, and they now added a University of Texas faculty member, Lanier Cox, who had taught business law at the university since 1937, when he was twenty-one years old.[33] The committee was also considering three others from outside the university—Paul G. Craig, the chairman of the economics department at Ohio State University; Frederick F. Balderston, a professor of economics and an expert on banking at Berkeley; and, as if from out of nowhere, George Kozmetsky. Others remained under consideration for a few more weeks, but these five were the ones that the committee ultimately recommended.[34]

Kozmetsky's name enters the record of the search on November 4, 1965, when Judson Neff, Kozmetsky's friend from Harvard, sent Hackerman information about his old student's background and his achievements in business. The one-page summary of Kozmetsky's qualifications reproduced his Who's Who–type entry in *American Men of Science* (1962), provided the library call numbers for his books on computers and labor unions, and included several brief but telling remarks by Neff. Kozmetsky was described by Neff as "an educator, and perhaps most successfully a promoter and innovator; especially the Institute for Management Sciences, its journal *Management Sciences* and its international expansion. An able speaker and negotiator—and manager." After also noting that his "wife is a teacher; Dr. Kozmetsky finds time to lecture and to teach; children grown up," Neff concludes: "Hopes to make Teledyne stock worth enough he can found and run his own GSB [graduate school of business]."[35]

The idea that Kozmetsky's personal wealth could benefit the business school cropped up again in December, when the highly regarded C. Aubrey Smith wrote to Ransom and Hackerman that "Dr. Kozmetsky might be persuaded to make a substantial endowment for the College

Norman Hackerman, UT Austin president, in 1970. *Texas Student Publications (Cactus).*

immediately, as well as in the future, should he be selected."[36] It seems inconceivable that anyone connected with the university would have suggested to Kozmetsky that one of his roles as dean of business would be to give money to the business school, so Kozmetsky himself is the most likely source for this idea. The record does not indicate whether any of those officials had premonitions about the various difficulties that might arise if a dean did indeed treat the school as "his own GSB."

Neff followed up through Nelson with a request to meet with Hackerman, and the note made by the secretary who took the call suggests that Kozmetsky was then an unknown quantity, at least to her, and perhaps also to Hackerman: "Mr. Nelson called to ask if you would meet for 15 min with Mr. Judson Neff and answer some questions about position Dean of Business College. Mr. Neff has an acquaintance here in Austin, executive in large business with Ph.D. from Harvard, who would like to get back in Academic field. Man's name is Dr. Koznetsky. Koznetsky doesn't want to apply for the job until he knows more about it, and Neff is supposed to get some answers for him."[37]

With Nelson's blessing, Neff met with Hackerman on November 12 to discuss Kozmetsky. The notes he made in preparation for that meeting ended up in Hackerman's presidential papers,[38] and they make it clear that Neff was pushing hard for Hackerman and Ransom to take the Kozmetsky candidacy seriously. Neff noted that the business school had tried to recruit Kozmetsky to the faculty in 1963 but he was "busy consolidating 8 co's" (a reference to Teledyne's acquisitions), and that the University of California, Berkeley, "nearly got him for Dean of Engineering (but did not do their homework)."[39] Neff then noted that he had phoned Kozmetsky the week before and observed that Kozmetsky had business interests in Texas through some of Teledyne's acquisitions and that he "meets with some of the board of Rice U."

After telling Hackerman that "normally, we could not hope to attract a man such as Kozmetsky," Neff laid out another of his highly revealing descriptions of his friend at that stage in his career: "Here is a man who does not set much store by this world's goods as an end in themselves. He holds high the challenge of academic life: 1. Provided the men at the top of the institution are determined to mount a substantial program for rapid and radical advances. 2. Provided the plans are for immediate and, in his words, 'exponential change'—with the major lines established within five years."

Neff compared Kozmetsky with Edwin Land, the inventor and entrepreneur behind the Polaroid Corp., "but who in addition is qualified for the deanship." He added that Kozmetsky's "contribution will be in shaking up the show—sixteen years of it, since he is only 49."[40]

Hackerman's response, as relayed to Nelson by Neff, was noncommittal, but he was willing to include Kozmetsky in the list of nominees under consideration. Neff quoted Hackerman as saying "there is no bar from me" with regard to adding Kozmetsky's name to the list of candidates acceptable to the faculty. "Once Dr. Kozmetsky is nominated to the list by your committee, Dr. Hackerman will take it from there. He will work with your list," Neff wrote.[41]

Livingston said Neff's advocacy was the major factor that turned the committee's attention (and Hackerman's and Ransom's) toward Kozmetsky. "There was no doubt Neff was pushing very hard, and I think it is reasonable to assume that he and George were consulting with one another very closely in an effort to bring his name forward. It can be counterproductive to campaign too openly for an academic appointment, but in this case the campaigning by Neff had a positive result. George's eminent qualifications made the difference."[42]

The committee spent the next month interviewing eight candidates (in addition to the ones they had interviewed in the summer), and the candidates also met with larger groups of faculty. Kozmetsky met with Ran-

Harry Ransom
as chancel-
lor, 1966.
*Texas Student
Publications
(Cactus).*

som in his office at 9:00 a.m. on November 30, followed by other campus interviews.[43] On December 8 the committee sent Ransom and Hackerman an elaborate ranking of their five leading candidates (Balderston, Cox, Craig, Kozmetsky, and Morris). Each committee member assigned points to the candidates in two categories, their personal preference and their appraisal of each person's qualifications. In each case, the lowest score was the best. In the ranking by preference, Craig led with 15 points, followed by Kozmetsky and Cox at 19 each, and then Balderston with 21 and Morris with 31. In the assessment of qualifications, Craig was again in first place with a score of 11, Balderston was second (14 points), Kozmetsky was third (16), Cox was fourth (21), and Morris was last (27).[44]

Two days later C. Aubrey Smith sent Hackerman a separate recommendation—that Kozmetsky be named dean of the graduate school of business while Cox was appointed dean of an undergraduate business school.

This idea had gone nowhere in the committee, and it went nowhere with Hackerman, but it does reveal one of the doubts that some people had about Kozmetsky after his first campus interviews. "It seems likely that Dr. Kozmetsky, who has little interest in undergraduate work, nor Mr. Cox, who lacks graduate stature, would individually and separately be acceptable to the faculty," Smith wrote. He went on to say he had taken an "informal poll" of the faculty "and have found general acceptance and support for the two men as a team."[45] Ransom and Hackerman might well have been skeptical about the accuracy of Smith's "informal poll" and about how long that "general acceptance" of two deans, or one divided deanship, would have lasted in practice.[46]

Meanwhile, Neff was continuing to lobby heavily for Kozmetsky, writing to Ransom and Hackerman: "Personally, I believe Kozmetsky will be our dean if you have time to check your sources and to work on him. . . . The general reaction here is that Kozmetsky is beyond our dream. But, this is *not* a dream. Harvard Business School got Donald K. David away from American Maize, et al., at age 50 and kept him for 10 years. *We* can get Kozmetsky. He and David are alike—they are close friends."[47]

After all five finalists had undergone more interviews Craig received at least one emphatic endorsement from a faculty member not on the committee—Ray M. Sommerfield, then a young member of the accounting department and later one of the business school's most powerful faculty members. He wrote to Hackerman to express "my personal and very strong preference for professor Paul G. Craig . . . [who] was the only one of the dean candidates who, in his appearance before the faculty, appeared to understand the dimensions of our more serious problems and who recommended reasonable solutions to them."[48]

The day after Sommerfield's letter, Kozmetsky's prospects got an important boost through a phone call to Hackerman from Jack G. Taylor, an Austin investor who was an alumnus of the business school and one of its major donors. According to Hackerman's handwritten notes, Taylor listed his preferences, in order, as Kozmetsky, Balderston, and Craig.[49]

Although there are indications that Hackerman made it clear to Craig that the job was his if he wanted it, Craig told the university on November 16 that he wanted to withdraw so he could accept new administrative duties offered by Ohio State.[50] From then on, the focus of Ransom and Hackerman was on Balderston and Kozmetsky, and their first step was to pursue Balderston immediately. Hackerman offered him the job by phone on December 17. Hackerman's report on the call says he offered Balderston a salary of $30,000, with the addition that Balderston could continue his

A CIVIC ENTREPRENEUR

outside consulting jobs. He also told Balderston that $60,000 had been allocated for hiring new faculty for the next academic year, and that he was willing to ask the regents immediately for additional money for more faculty positions.

"Also, I told him I was pretty sure that he would be treated generally well in view of the regents' interest in the college," Hackerman wrote. Balderston replied that he was "highly interested" in the deanship but was uncertain whether he wanted to reduce his teaching and research and take on such large administrative duties at this stage of his career. "He will determine whether he should pursue this further and let me know soon," Hackerman wrote. "If he does he would want to make another campus visit, and I said fine."[51]

For Balderston, letting Hackerman know "soon" meant calling more than three weeks later to turn down the job. In a brief follow-up letter, Balderston explained: "My request to have my name withdrawn was based on the conclusion that the tasks of institution-building would be very demanding in view of the opportunity and aspirations of the university, and would require essentially exclusive attention and administrative leadership over a period of years."[52]

After his call from Balderston, Hackerman wrote a brief note for the files: "I received a call from Dr. Balderston while I was in Washington on January 10, 1966. He said no. I now have to get Kozmetsky." He called Kozmetsky that same day.[53]

Over the holidays, Neff had kept Hackerman advised about Kozmetsky's travel plans and assured him that Kozmetsky was still interested in the deanship: "I have had several conversations with Dr. Kozmetsky, and he is interested. I have known him for twenty years, and he has never let anyone down on any commitment. I believe he will put the University of Texas a decade or two ahead of all the others in Business Administration." Neff advised Hackerman that Kozmetsky would be in Washington in the first week of January to take part in meetings related to three government projects—a committee led by Vice President Hubert H. Humphrey on the National Science Library, an advisory committee on a proposal for a federal computerized data bank, and a "Man-Machine Study" connected with NASA.[54]

There are few details in the university's archives about the substance of Kozmetsky's visits to the campus early in 1966. As part of his efforts to find a date when Kozmetsky could visit, Hackerman informed Kozmetsky that "the salary we have in mind is in the range of $25,000"—$5,000 less than he had offered Balderston a month earlier.[55] "The duties," Hackerman wrote, "will be best described in our conversations but they involve the administration of the college and, more important, the building of an academic program for the present and for the future."[56]

Kozmetsky had lunch with Ransom and Hackerman on February 10 and then continued talking with them in Ransom's office. (The chancellor's office in those days was in the Main Building on the campus rather than, as today, in downtown Austin.) Kozmetsky spent the rest of that day and the next in interviews with faculty and others associated with the business school.[57] At least one off-campus group with an interest in the school—an association of professional accountants—also met with Kozmetsky during those days.[58]

Kozmetsky returned to the campus in mid-April for another round of meetings with the faculty and others. On his other visits he stayed at the Forty Acres Club, a faculty dining club at Guadalupe and Twenty-Fourth Streets with two floors of hotel-like rooms for short-term guests, but that facility was full in April so the university booked a room for Kozmetsky at the Villa Capri motel, a long-popular inn that was just east of the campus and adjacent to Interstate 35 (now the site of a football practice field). Dean White met Kozmetsky's flight from Dallas (at that time the airport was on Manor Road two miles east of the campus) in time for a 9:00 a.m. meeting with Hackerman.[59]

Kozmetsky did not always make a good first impression in his meetings with faculty members. Floyd Brandt, whom Kozmetsky later appointed chairman of the Department of Management, recalled that when Neff brought Kozmetsky by his office to say hello he was struck by how disjointed Kozmetsky's conversation seemed to be, jumping from one subject to another. "I remember being kind of puzzled. I asked Neff, 'Is this guy for real?' He didn't seem to stay on one subject long enough to complete a thought. I questioned his credentials and talked to Neff about that. And then a little later [Neff] and George showed up in my office again. Neff had told George everything I had said, and George wanted another chance to answer any questions I had. This was my first encounter with George strictly one on one, and I had a better impression of him after that conversation."[60]

The conversations with faculty, staff, and regents continued off and on for two more months before the university was able to announce that Kozmetsky had been hired as dean.[61] One reason for the extended discussions had been the need to work out arrangements by which Kozmetsky also was named to a newly created position as the regents' executive associate for economic affairs. The duties of the position were designed to take full advantage of Kozmetsky's unique background in management, investing, and economic development. Another unique attribute of the new dean was that he probably possessed more personal wealth than any of the regents.

The duties of the regents' new executive associate were stated as follows: "The executive associate on a continuing basis conceives and develops long-range plans and studies with respect to the development and management of the economic resources of the university system and its component institutions, and, upon request, consults and advises with the Board of Regents and the executive director of investments, trusts and lands regarding such plans and studies."[62]

The "economic resources" in question were the assets of the Permanent University Fund, which included two million acres of land, mostly in West Texas. After oil had been discovered on the land in 1923, the value of the fund had grown to $438.6 million by 1966.[63] For the next thirty years, the regents would seek expert advice from Kozmetsky on a wide range of issues—from investment decisions to the purchase of a supercomputer, and from energy policy and research to economic development projects at various University of Texas System campuses. The job of executive associate for economic affairs was designed exclusively to fit Kozmetsky's experience and abilities, and no one other than Kozmetsky has held such a position.

Kozmetsky's appointment was covered by the student newspaper, drawing heavily on the university's press release. The story quoted Ransom: "Dr. Kozmetsky will now undertake new developments in education designed to bring the college and university into close contact with American industry and business. Texas could not have made a better appointment for this important task."[64] (In referring to "Texas," Ransom was using the then-current shorthand term for the university, a usage that is now mostly reserved for sports coverage.) On the same day, the newspaper published an editorial that viewed the appointment not as a sharp break with White's deanship (as many during the next decades would view it) but as a way of securing and broadening reforms that White had initiated. The editorial credited White with "able leadership in a time when the emphasis on business education was shifting from the classical approach to the quantitative and behavioral science approach," and it implied that Kozmetsky's success in business would be inspiring to students. "In this, Dr. Kozmetsky's presence in the university community is certainly welcome."[65]

The appointment drew national attention as part of a trend of business executives taking leadership roles at universities, whether as president, business dean, or senior faculty member. The *New York Times* noted six other business executives who had recently returned to academia, all of them sharing Kozmetsky's view of the value and purpose of higher education. As Kozmetsky expressed it: "It is my personal belief that the role of education is to provide balanced leadership to our society. The task of American education is therefore to keep ahead of our fast-moving world. To lead and not follow it."[66] The newspaper continued:

> Dr. Kozmetsky sees the field of education as "providing a bridge to enrich research." He looks forward to the opportunity of supplying, through his faculty and students, a mixed-discipline approach to the peripheral problems, "those that have not yet been solved," for industry. "Undergraduates," he said in a recent visit to New York, "need people who have done something, who can establish a motivation for them to follow." He strongly believes the stimulus for this, as well as solutions or approaches to such matters as urban transportation and water and air pollution, will come from the kind of informal working arrangements that may be found in a university setting where students and professors in diverse fields can be brought together to consider a problem.
>
> He looks ahead not just to new products [for industry] but [to] new methods of solving problems. "Sooner or later," he says, "education has to get out ahead of these problems and not simply try to keep up with them."[67]

During the sixteen years that Kozmetsky served as dean, it became clear that Ransom and Hackerman had found the kind of person they had been looking for—someone who would bring fundamental and lasting change and propel the business school into the upper ranks nationally. They may not have realized, in the spring and summer of 1966, the full dimensions of their success, since Kozmetsky, after all, was their fifth choice for the job, after they had been turned down by Walker, Craig, Balderston, and Gregg. Ransom and Hackerman both had long and distinguished careers at the University of Texas, and in Hackerman's case, also at Rice University, and they did as much as anyone in the mid-twentieth century to move the University of Texas at Austin toward the top ranks of American universities. They have been praised for many achievements, but their pivotal role in bringing Kozmetsky to Austin has not been recognized for the triumph that it turned out to be.

The Kozmetskys Find a Home

The Kozmetskys arrived in Austin soon after the announcement of George's appointment and rented an apartment in the recently opened Cambridge Tower high-rise while they looked for a house to buy. Cambridge Tower, at 1801 Lavaca, was only three blocks from the Business-Economics Building at Twenty-First Street and Speedway, so it could not have been more convenient. It also boasted the Table Royal restaurant, advertised as one of the finest in the city, and other amenities such as a barber shop and a rooftop garden. The building, now a condominium project, was a favorite stopping place for many new faculty members while they were getting settled in Austin. Abraham and Kay Charnes also lived there for a while when Kozmetsky recruited Abe to join the university faculty in 1968. The Charnes children and the Kozmetskys' youngest son, Georgie, sometimes amused themselves by dropping water balloons and ice cubes from the building's roof garden, but there are no reports of any direct hits on pedestrians fifteen stories below.[68]

By late 1966 the Kozmetskys had found the kind of house they were looking for, a home at 1001 West Seventeenth Street, in a close-in neighborhood known as Judges' Hill (because of the large number of judges and lawyers who had lived in the area since the nineteenth century). The house was just four blocks south and seven blocks west of the business school—an easy walk for a vigorous, energetic, forty-nine-year-old Kozmetsky despite several steep hills on whatever route he chose. The house was also attractive to Ronya because of the centuries-old live oak in the front yard.

The Kozmetskys' oldest son, Greg, was twenty and in the army when the family moved to Austin, and he would be sent to Vietnam that December. Their daughter, Nadya, was eighteen, had just finished high school, and was preparing for a trip to Europe before going to college (first at the University of California, Santa Barbara, and finishing her degree at Carnegie Mellon University), and Georgie was twelve and was about to enter junior high school.

The house on Seventeenth Street was designated a historic landmark by the Austin City Council in 2010, in large part because of its long association with the Kozmetsky family and the numerous connections of the house with the economic, social, and academic history of Austin when they lived there. Apart from its general association with the economic transformation of Austin in the last half century, the house may be best known in Austin folklore for the visits of Michael Dell to seek advice and counsel from Kozmetsky in the early days of planning for his computer manufacturing company. After a library was added on the lower level of the house, Kozmetsky would receive Dell and other visitors there.

Thanks to the extensive research conducted for the effort to obtain the historic designation, the history of the house on Seventeenth Street is well documented.[69] The single-level, brick-veneer house was built in 1955 and was designed, probably by the Austin architectural firm of Page Sutherland

Page, in the style known as midcentury modern. The house was oriented to the east and west, with deep southern eaves and no eaves on the north side, a design that, along with the surrounding trees, a steep roof, and a system to draw air from shaded areas through the attic, reduces heat in the summer while letting in ample light during the winter—an example of passive solar design. The Kozmetskys would have been accustomed to this style of residential architecture from their days in California, and, indeed, the Austin house shared many design elements with their house in Brentwood and the house of Henry Singleton and his family on Mulholland Drive.

The Austin house was built for retired justice James W. McClendon and his wife Anne Watt McClendon, whose father had given the property to her as a wedding gift in 1909. McClendon had been chief justice of the Texas Court of Civil Appeals and in 1948 had presided in the case of *Sweatt v. Painter*, in which the appeals court upheld segregation in the University of Texas's graduate and professional schools, a decision that was overturned in a landmark decision by the US Supreme Court in 1950. After his wife's death, McClendon moved in 1966 to the recently completed Westgate Towers next to the capitol, and his wife's estate sold the house to the Kozmetskys in December of that year. The Kozmetskys finished moving into the house in early 1967.

Over the years, the Kozmetskys made several significant changes to the house, overseen by Roland G. Roessner Sr., a University of Texas architecture professor who had become their close friend and who worked on several other projects for them. They renovated the house and added a swimming pool in 1967, and in 1985 they added a nine-hundred-square-foot, wood-paneled library and made other changes to the interior. The library, placed at the back of the west facade, was designed to meet George's desire for a private, comfortable place to study and to receive students and colleagues away from the interruptions of his campus office. The library included a dumbwaiter used to retrieve books and papers from a basement vault.

The swimming pool carried forward the Kozmetskys' informal Southern California lifestyle. Robert D. King, a linguistics professor who came to the university a few years after the Kozmetskys and moved with his young family into a house on Seventeenth Street catty-cornered from the Kozmetskys' house, recalled that his wife and children were in their front yard one summer afternoon soon after they moved in, and Ronya was in her front yard tending to plants. The women waved at one another across the street and soon began talking, and before the conversation was over Ronya had invited the King family to use their swimming pool whenever they wanted. A common sight after that was for the King children to troop through the Kozmetskys' side yard to get to the pool.[70]

In later years, George enjoyed exercising in the pool and could be found walking through the water singing to himself. When his grandchildren came over, he would get out of the pool and serve as the judge as they practiced diving.

Austin and the University in 1966

For those familiar only with twenty-first-century Austin, the appearance of the city when the Kozmetskys arrived from California in the summer of 1966 would be startling.[71] On whatever route travelers took to approach the city—Route 290 or Highway 71 from the west and east, or the new four-lane Interstate 35 from the north or south—they would not have been within significantly built-up areas until well within sight of the capitol dome or the University of Texas Tower, at that time the two vertical landmarks that dominated the city's skyline. Farm and ranch lands were still prevalent in areas on all sides of the city that are now well within the area of urban development.

The population of Austin in 1966 was 218,981, making it the sixth largest city in the state, compared with more than 930,000 within the city limits and a fourth-place ranking today (having surpassed El Paso and Fort Worth). More than two million people currently live in the Austin Statistical Metropolitan Area, which includes Round Rock and other cities that in 1966 were still widely separated from Austin by agricultural lands. The population of Texas was about 10.5 million in 1966, about 40 percent of what it is now.

High technology barely registered on the city's business and industrial map in 1966. The city's leading technology companies included Tracor, a homegrown R&D and manufacturing company, as well as a few scientific instrument manufacturers, a maker of control valves, and a petrochemical research company. In 1967, IBM would open a factory in northwest Austin for assembly of Selectric typewriters. Other major industrial concerns included Glastron Boat Co., which made fiberglass pleasure boats, and Ward Body Works, which made bodies for school and commercial buses. Other "large" employers included Adams Extract Co., Steck Co. (publishers and printers), a maker of plastic cups, a limestone quarry, and two furniture factories.

The city's Mueller Airport was a little northeast of the campus on Manor Road, a drive of less than ten minutes from downtown. The city was served only by Braniff International and Trans-Texas (later Texas

International), with a total of thirty-one daily flights. Southwest Airlines would not begin Austin service until 1977. The site of the current Austin-Bergstrom International Airport was then Bergstrom Air Force Base, which closed in 1993.

There were 28,868 students at the University of Texas the year before Kozmetsky came to Austin, 4,350 of them in the business school. That made it the largest of the university's colleges and schools except for the College of Arts and Sciences. In keeping with the populist traditions of the state, tuition at state universities was only $50 a semester ($200 for out-of-state students), although mandatory and optional fees at the University of Texas could add another $50 to the bill. The low costs kept attracting ever-greater numbers of students, and the university, including the business school, faced a perennial problem of meeting this demand with enough classroom and laboratory space, teachers, and student services. The difficult equation among these quantities—while not losing sight of the issue of quality—was one of the main challenges for every University of Texas administrator.

In the mid-1960s the university was in many respects still focused on the South and the Southwest instead of on the national and international role it would begin to occupy in the last decades of the century. The institution's academic standing was still symbolized by the legacy of the triumvirate of folklorist J. Frank Dobie, historian Walter Prescott Webb, and writer Roy Bedichek, who were identified mostly with the 1930s and 1940s and all of whom were preoccupied with regional subjects. Harry Ransom had been leading an effort to shatter the university's insularity, but as late as 1962 Carl J. Eckhardt, a longtime engineering faculty member and a University of Texas historian, could seriously propose that the entire university pause twice a day to celebrate its heritage by playing over loudspeakers "The Eyes of Texas" at noon and "Dixie" at 5:00 p.m.[72]

The federally funded urban renewal program of President Lyndon Johnson's Great Society had not yet, in 1966, destroyed the large residential and retail neighborhoods (with many structures dating to the late nineteenth and early twentieth centuries) that separated the university from the capitol and from Interstate 35, then still under initial construction.

The university was in the midst of a major construction program when Kozmetsky became dean, and the boom would continue off and on for many years as the university continued to seek to meet the needs of an ever-increasing student population and to make its teaching and research programs more competitive nationwide. Well over $21 million worth of construction projects (more than $157 million in 2017) were under way or about to begin in the fall of 1966, including new facilities for biological sciences, geology, liberal arts, physics, mathematics, and astronomy, as well as new campus dormitories and a library storage facility.[73] The business school's undergraduate and graduate programs shared the Business-Economics Building (known as the BEB) with the economics department, which was a unit of the College of Arts and Sciences, and Kozmetsky soon began planning for an additional building to house the Graduate School of Business.

The rapid academic progress of the University of Texas at Austin in many fields during the late 1950s and early 1960s had begun to gain national attention. At about the time of Kozmetsky's appointment as dean, an opinion survey conducted by the American Council on Education found that thirteen PhD programs at the university ranked among the top twenty in the nation. German and botany were ranked fourth and eighth, respectively, and programs ranked from eleventh to eighteenth included geology, linguistics, chemical engineering, civil engineering, French, Spanish, microbiology, classics, philosophy, sociology, and zoology. Seven years earlier, a comparable survey had ranked only two university doctoral programs among the top twenty. In the business school, only the graduate program in accounting would have been ranked as one of the best in the country, if the education council survey had included business programs.[74]

The university had begun laying the foundations for progress in numerous other academic fields, and Kozmetsky's explicit assignment to transform the business school and develop the business program into one of the best in the nation was only one of many such assignments from Ransom and the Board of Regents. Another example of such lofty aspirations in 1966 was the university's American studies program. Ransom had recruited nationally prominent scholars in history, classics, philosophy, art history, linguistics, English, and other fields. The hiring of senior, high-profile faculty members from other institutions was at the heart of Ransom's efforts to elevate the university's academic standing, and he generally paid these recruits more than other faculty and gave them reduced teaching loads and generous internal research grants. These favorites also had ready access to Ransom, and they became known to the ordinary faculty as "Harry's Boys."[75] Kozmetsky would use similar techniques in his efforts to elevate the business school.

In 1966 Austin was still in many ways a small town, and the University of Texas was still a regional university, but Austin was on the verge of a new identity as a flourishing technopolis that was home to one of the world's major research universities. In the mid-1960s, no one could have predicted the dimensions of the transformation that awaited the city and the university during the next four decades, or the important role that Kozmetsky would play in that transformation. Many others would play roles as well, drawn to Austin, in some cases, by word of the changes under way at the business school under its new dean. In the early years of Kozmetsky's tenure, few people outside the world of business education paid much attention to those changes, but his work as dean was to gain an outsized significance in retrospect.

A FAMILY TRAGEDY

During the Kozmetskys' early years in Austin, their youngest son, Georgie, was still in school. For a while after graduating from Austin High he took a job as a production worker at IBM's plant in north Austin and continued to live with his parents in the house on Seventeenth Street, but in November 1972, he died of a drug overdose. Friends had noticed him in distress and tried to revive him with mouth-to-mouth resuscitation, and when that failed they took him to Brackenridge Hospital. He died early on the morning of November 23 (Thanksgiving Day), just two weeks after his nineteenth birthday.[76]

George and Ronya rarely talked about the death, but occasionally Ronya would confide that the sorrow never healed, or she might make an oblique reference to the loss. Describing her approach to marriage and family life, she told a reporter, "Laugh a lot and save your energies to fall apart on something heavy. If children aren't dying, nothing is that important."[77]

In the years after Georgie's death, there was a somber mood at the family's Thanksgiving meals. Ronya might have been particularly close to Georgie because his birth had been so difficult, even causing her heart to stop beating at one point during labor. Georgie had had learning problems throughout school, and his parents had sought numerous doctors and counselors to help him, with Ronya taking the lead with her characteristic determination to overcome any challenge, based in part on her background in social work and education. However, knowledge about learning disorders was limited then, and little help was available in that era. A drug culture was widespread among young people in Austin and many other college towns in the 1960s and early 1970s, and Georgie once told his mother that taking drugs made him feel "normal."[78]

In later years, George sometimes told close friends that he felt responsible for his son's death, that he had pushed him too hard and demanded too much.[79] It was a subject he rarely opened up about, and such feelings of guilt are a common response to the loss of a child.

The Kozmetskys established several endowments commemorating Georgie, including a scholarship fund at the University of Texas at Austin and an academic position at the University of Washington. One of the campuses of the charter school operated by the University of Texas is named for George M. Kozmetsky.

CHAPTER 9

TRANSFORMING THE BUSINESS SCHOOL I

Laying the Groundwork for Change

George Kozmetsky's arrival in Austin in 1966 marked the beginning of an extended period of wide-reaching change within the University of Texas business school. By the time he stepped down as dean sixteen years later, the school had been transformed from a regional institution that was strong in accounting but little else to one of the country's major business schools. The Kozmetsky years saw radical advancement in the quality of every aspect of the school—faculty and students, curriculum, research, endowment, student services, physical facilities, and relationships with the business community. Many of Kozmetsky's initiatives centered on interdisciplinary studies, new technology, quantitative studies of management problems, entrepreneurship, regional economic development, and the role of business in solving social and economic problems. These areas of emphasis gave the school a dramatically different focus from the pre-Kozmetsky era.

Kozmetsky was only the fifth dean in the history of the business school, which traces its origins to classes in "business training" that were first taught in 1912. The School of Business Administration was established in 1922, with Spurgeon Bell, who had been in charge of the program since its inception, serving as the first dean. Bell was succeeded in 1926 by J. Anderson Fitzgerald, who served as dean until 1950. It was under Fitzgerald's deanship, in 1945, that the school was renamed as the College of Business Administration and organized into academic departments. The third dean was William R. Spriegel, who served from 1950 to 1958. The next dean, Kozmetsky's immediate predecessor, was John Arch White, who served as acting dean in 1958 and then dean from 1959 to 1966. It was under White that the Graduate School of Business was created as a separate administrative unit.[1]

Kozmetsky's Inheritance at the Business School

The changes under Kozmetsky were so great that the considerable achievements under White have been overshadowed. The conventional wisdom is that the business school before Kozmetsky was a provincial operation, sort of an old boys' club, with no great academic distinction apart from the perennially prominent accounting department. The emphasis was on undergraduate education (one goal being to provide the state with a steady stream of graduates capable of running small businesses), and faculty members who made a mark with their research were rare. While broadly accurate, this view obscures the areas where progress had been made under White. A more precise picture is that of a regional business school that had begun to develop into a more prominent and competitive center of business education, but that still had a very long way to go and was definitely still a follower rather than a leader on the national stage.

One example of the way White's achievements have been obscured has to do with computers. Some colleagues of Kozmetsky emphasize quite rightly his passion for applying computers to problems of business management as well as academic research, and for incorporating the computer into students' assignments, but their memory has sometimes also attributed to Kozmetsky the idea that he first introduced the use of computers to a largely backward and recalcitrant faculty. In its most extreme form, this mythologizing about Kozmetsky has given him credit for purchasing the business school's first computer, even against the wishes of some older faculty members.[2] Kozmetsky did greatly expand the school's computer facilities, and he was largely responsible for attracting new faculty members whose research required advanced computing capabilities, but White was actually the dean under whom the business school first acquired a computer of its own (apart from the equipment managed by the campus-wide Computation Center). This was an IBM 1620 purchased in 1962 with funds provided by the chancellor's office and used first in business statistics classes and later by students in accounting, finance, management, and marketing.[3]

As White prepared to turn the business school over to his successor at the beginning of the 1966–1967 academic year, he made an assessment of the progress since 1958 that shows the older dean to have been interested in many of the academic matters that were to preoccupy Kozmetsky. Among other achievements during his deanship, White noted that the school revised all its degree programs and core courses, with a new emphasis on applications of mathematics and the behavioral sciences; moved (in 1962) into the newly constructed Business-Economics Building; established the

Graduate School of Business; established the College of Business Administration Foundation, with an advisory council of "leading businessmen"; began a college-wide research program; and started a program of computer instruction required of all students.[4]

Numerous subjects that would interest Kozmetsky were missing from White's list (such as interdisciplinary studies, a full-fledged management science program, and advanced research centers operating outside the traditional department structure), but the business school had taken initial steps in directions to which Kozmetsky would give greater emphasis.

At the end of September 1965, after the search for a new dean had been under way for almost a year and about a month before Kozmetsky's name first appears in the records of the search committee, White produced another summary of the business school's efforts in one of the areas of special interest to Kozmetsky—the use of "quantitative methods" in dealing with management problems. While White said he was not able to report as much progress as he would have liked, this document directly addressed many of the subjects on which Kozmetsky would concentrate the most when he became dean—including computer programming, systems analysis, and management science—and it lends credence to the idea that Kozmetsky's deanship can be seen as partly a continuation and acceleration of initiatives undertaken by White, rather than a simple and dramatic break with the past. Faced with the arrival on the campus for the past year of a steady stream of candidates to replace him, White might have been defensive about the achievements in this area.[5]

The focus of Harry Ransom, Norman Hackerman (Ransom's second-in-command), and the regents in the mid-1960s was more on what remained to be done, not on what had already been accomplished, and it is by that measure that the business school was judged to be still in need of a major overhaul. White, not surprisingly, applauded the choice of Kozmetsky as his successor. "I know of no one who is better qualified from the standpoint of experience, educational background, and real ability than Dr. Kozmetsky," he wrote in his final annual report as dean. "It is my belief that Dr. Kozmetsky, with the support of the faculty, will establish the College and the Graduate School of Business as among the top three or four institutions in the country."[6]

A glimpse of Kozmetsky in his early days as dean is provided by Joe B. Frantz, a longtime history professor at the university. Frantz had met Kozmetsky in 1948 when they were both graduate students at Harvard, where he remembered Kozmetsky as "a slight, amiable, fragile-looking student." "I thought he was highly nervous. I didn't recognize that he was a genius."[7] By the time Kozmetsky arrived in Austin, Frantz was in the

George Kozmetsky in his first year as dean. *Texas Student Publications (Cactus).*

midst of a career in the history department, but he was in a position to observe the new dean because his courses in business history were often cross-listed in the business school.

Frantz reported that there was considerable opposition to Kozmetsky from his earliest, frenetic days at the university. "My friends in the Business-Economics Building began to tell me horror stories—from their viewpoint—about the new dean," Frantz wrote. "Kozmetsky never rested, like Lyndon Johnson. Like Johnson, he thought that if he was up and flying, they should be up and flying. He started calling faculty meetings before dawn, an unheard-of practice to academics, most of whom don't like faculty meetings at any hour but certainly not before late afternoon. Kozmetsky never runs when he can gallop. He's never heard of walking. Ideas and words foam from his head like detergent spilled in a fountain."[8]

Kozmetsky's View of His Achievements as Dean

Late in his life Kozmetsky asked his friend William W. Cooper to help compile a report of his achievements as dean, and the result was a memorandum that described four periods of progress at the school during the Kozmetsky years. This report, based on conversations between Kozmetsky and Cooper, is not the last word on Kozmetsky's work as dean, but despite several errors of fact it is an important document that provides the most complete and detailed account of Kozmetsky's own view of what he accomplished at the business school.[9]

The first period described by the memo, from 1966 to 1969, was characterized by three closely interconnected objectives—to modernize the school's technological infrastructure, to improve dramatically the quality of academic programs, and to set a course toward achieving the goal of becoming one of the nation's five best business schools. The first step was relatively easy, as Kozmetsky acquired upgraded computer equipment (using, in 1966–1967, for example, University of Texas System appropriations and a federal grant approved before he became dean). The second involved changes on multiple fronts—recruiting distinguished senior faculty, expanding research, raising admission standards, revising the curriculum, increasing private-sector fundraising, and beginning a series of long-range strategic plans. These areas of progress were at the core of the transformations under Kozmetsky's leadership, and they continued as priorities throughout his deanship. The third goal—working to become one of the five best business schools—was so uncertain in its measurement that just about any progress could be counted as a step in that direction, but Kozmetsky and Cooper could cite any number of achievements that demonstrated the school was on the move.

The second phase of Kozmetsky's tenure as dean, as he and Cooper characterized it, ran from 1970 to 1974 and involved two major new initiatives—planning a building for the Graduate School of Business and improving the business school's day-to-day operating efficiency. The goal of greater efficiency was made more urgent by a decline in state appropriations during these years. Kozmetsky turned to his newly installed computer managers to provide models for budget-cutting options that could be implemented without impairing efforts to advance the academic standing of the school. The budget problems also were a motive for increased outreach efforts in this period. Kozmetsky began a series of weekly speeches that took him across the state to meet with businesses, civic clubs, and newly organized business school alumni clubs.

The third phase described in Cooper's memo ran from 1975 to 1980 and focused on three broad classes of issues that were increasingly relevant to business—economic globalization, environmental issues, and social issues. The major development in this period was the creation of the IC² Institute, originally known as the Institute for Constructive Capitalism.

170   A CIVIC ENTREPRENEUR

Other events in this period were the reorganization and expansion of the business school foundation and the beginning of a major fundraising campaign that benefitted from matching funds provided by the regents as part of the university's centennial.

The fourth period ran from 1980 to 1982 and witnessed construction of the University Teaching Center and renovation of the business school's other facilities. Other actions included the beginning of joint MBA programs with law, architecture, engineering, communication, and public affairs, as well as the inauguration of the Option II executive MBA program.

The summary presented by Cooper is heavily weighted toward dramatic change in the earliest years of Kozmetsky's deanship. While many years of effort were required for the full effect of Kozmetsky's changes to be felt, the new direction and major areas of achievement were determined quite early. Underlying all these changes was Kozmetsky's unifying vision of the needs of business education as well as his vision of business itself as a force for good in society.

Kozmetsky's Vision for Business Education

Kozmetsky often set forth his view that the challenge facing business schools was to educate managers who could meet new and distinctive needs of business in the last third of the twentieth century. (As he neared the end of his tenure as dean, he often shifted this formula to the need to meet the rather different challenges that he foresaw as emerging in the twenty-first century.) When he spoke or wrote about "business" he usually meant large corporations, or start-up companies that aspired to become large organizations, and when he discussed the distinctive needs of such organizations early in his deanship he was usually referring to their use of computers and other advanced technology, not only to solve the increasingly complex problems of production, control, and research and development within industry, but also to contribute to the solution of larger problems in society. He also consistently emphasized the need to educate managers who could cope with "unstructured problems" and the new "nonroutine" industries of the computer era. Throughout his statements of purpose for business education and for business itself, broader issues of society—such as education, health, urban affairs, poverty, the environment, and national security—were never far from the surface.

This was an expansive view of the role of business that certainly did not disdain the making of profits and providing a return on investment but did include a requirement that making money must be accompanied by a commitment to socially responsible behavior by corporations—an approach that echoed the views of Kozmetsky's dean at Harvard, Donald

K. David. Kozmetsky's views on this subject did not always go down easy in the Texas business community. "I remember how I shocked the Texans when I first came here in 1966," he told one of his classes at the University of Texas, "and said that if all business does is make a buck . . . they won't be in business, and if they don't make a profit, they won't be in business. Therefore, making a buck is not the objective of business."[10]

Kozmetsky's views of how corporations should act, and how best to train their managers, were consistent with the "corporate social responsibility" movement, which had gotten its start at the Harvard Business School and other institutions after World War II and gained momentum in response to the social problems of the 1960s and 1970s.[11] Kozmetsky's ideas on new ways of evaluating corporate profits (with an emphasis on the overall value, on balance, of a corporation to society, rather than the simple bottom line on a spreadsheet) were included in a major study of information technology that he and Timothy W. Ruefli, his colleague at the business school, conducted for the Conference Board in the early 1970s.

Kozmetsky became dean amid the expansion of US military involvement in Vietnam, a period of increasing racial unrest in American cities, a growing environmental movement, a new phase of the women's rights movement, the rise of the "counterculture" among young people, and an ever-increasing pace of technological change—all of which provided the context for his contemplation about how best to educate the next generation of business managers. These events resulted in new challenges to the assumptions about business, social organization, and world affairs under which Kozmetsky's postwar generation had operated. A few years into his deanship he wrote: "After a world-wide depression, a second World War, and a Korean conflict, we are agonizing in the midst of the longest war that our nation has ever participated in even though unpopular, raising a generation under an uneasy Cold War environment, reaching an economic affluence unprecedented in the history of mankind, and nurturing an explosive growth in technology. At this moment, many of us believe . . . we live in an unparalleled period of social upheaval in a society marked by man's meaningless inhumanity to man under ideological conflict that has already led to agony and bloodshed. In the words of the late John F. Kennedy, we as educators must 'confront the unfinished business of our generation.'"[12]

When Kozmetsky talked about business education for "the last third of the 20th century," he drew sharp contrasts with earlier decades, and the main difference concerned the advance of information technology. There is often a tone of impatience in his descriptions of how much remained to be done to take advantage of computer technology in both education and

A CIVIC ENTREPRENEUR

Computer terminals in the business school, 1960s. *Texas Student Publications (Cactus).*

business management. At Teledyne and earlier he had been at the forefront of a computer revolution, but society as a whole had hardly begun
to participate in that revolution by the mid-1960s.

The "digital divide" was far deeper and broader when Kozmetsky was
beginning to serve as dean than it is in the early twenty-first century. In
1967 it was estimated that only about half of US colleges and universities
were using computers in the "functional" areas of administration, such
as class scheduling and grade reporting. A government report quoted by
Kozmetsky in 1967 concluded that less than 5 percent of the country's total
higher education enrollment had access to computing services, and the

report recommended massive federal spending on a program to make students in the 1970s as familiar with using a computer as driving a car.[13]

Kozmetsky found that in both industry and higher education, too many leaders, most of whom had been educated well before the postwar computer era, were woefully behind the times and were unprepared to make the changes that new technologies were demanding.[14]

The changes that Kozmetsky undertook as dean were intended to prepare the business school's students for jobs within the corporate structure as it had evolved after World War II, as well as to educate them to meet the challenges of a time of continuing rapid change. In his 1967 book *The New Industrial State*, the economist John Kenneth Galbraith explained how the advance of technology, particularly in the postwar period, had created new requirements for sophisticated planning within business and government, close interaction between business management and science, and new approaches to education—leading to the emergence of what he called a "scientific and educational estate."[15] Kozmetsky, who had a first edition of Galbraith's book in his personal library, referred to the book on several occasions (such as in his 1970 paper "How Much Revolution Does American Business Need?"), and he wrote about his experience in winning the helicopter avionics contract at Teledyne in terms that echo much of Galbraith's analysis of contemporary specialized decision-making in industries that are heavily involved with advanced technology. Kozmetsky also cited the avionics project as an example of the necessity of using computers in managing the development and production of advanced technologies, another of Galbraith's themes. It is clear that Kozmetsky, like Galbraith, understood that the computer was both a cause and an effect of advances in technology.

As the decade of the 1970s began, Kozmetsky revisited these issues in business education in testimony to a committee of Congress, using the occasion to contrast his views on education with those of the previous generation. He presented a series of new principles as his own generation's evolving challenges to the assumptions of the past—an evolution toward "new and enriched standards for education."[16] These principles underlay what he wanted to achieve at the business school: education is a universal necessity, not a privilege for the few; schools need to accept and nurture each student "to find his proper level," rather than grouping students according to one standard; education cannot be separated from the real world and is both a service to society and a shaper of society; schools are not the only educative force in society; education is not exclusively a process by which the older generation transfers knowledge to the younger generation; education is not exclusively a formal process that takes place in a classroom; and technological devices such as computers are natural extensions for the individuality of teaching and for creativity.

These principles reflect the society-wide changes that were elements of the social and political upheavals of the 1960s and 1970s. Apart from the theoretical or philosophical basis for these principles, Kozmetsky was concerned about the strictly practical question of how the capitalist system could be sure to produce an appropriately educated workforce capable of dealing with rapidly emerging technologies. He often cited reports that by the year 2000 more than 60 percent of the US workforce would be engaged in "nonroutine" industries—a number equal to the entire workforce of 1969.[17] Kozmetsky's interest in education for nonroutine industry merited a mention in futurist Alvin Toffler's best-selling book *Future Shock*, in a chapter on emerging types of nonhierarchical, ad hoc organizations.[18] ("Routine" jobs, such as working on an assembly line or doing traditional office work, mostly involve repetitive actions; in the twenty-first century routine jobs have continued to give way to work that is nonroutine, such as in the service, entertainment, and information sectors, or other activities that cannot be easily automated. A study in 2015 found that the entire job growth in the United States since 2001 had been in nonroutine work.)[19]

Despite the growing acceptance of the new principles and the pressure for change among the college-age generation, Kozmetsky noted that the main problem facing higher education was continued resistance to new ways of thinking, or "widespread, habitual, institutionalized resistance to needed change," and he was aware that he wanted to push for the new principles "faster than some of us may want to go, for some of us feel that we are not capable of meeting the demanding accelerated rate of change."[20]

The change that Kozmetsky saw as essential was what he called "integrative education," by which he meant education that employed the new techniques of systems analysis and broke down the barriers separating the traditional academic disciplines, leading, ultimately, to new professions and new types of higher education institutions.[21]

Kozmetsky advocated greater concentration in business schools on research into strategic areas related to the new type of workplace and business organization based on technological change. The research areas (also to be reflected in the curriculum) included management of productivity, efficiency, and competitiveness; management of innovation, research, and development; management of strategic relationships and social responsibilities; entrepreneurship, business development, and capital venturing; management of information; management of the environment in the interests of quality of life; development of new growth industries; and assessment of the influence of technology on organization, education, and training.

Business schools needed to accept three broad responsibilities for carrying out such research goals if they were to teach people how "to manage our human resources in a technologically based society in such a way that we anticipate change and not just accept or react to it," Kozmetsky wrote. Those responsibilities were to emphasize "situational and strategic management controls" based on links between basic science and management practice, educating a new type of entrepreneurial manager able to understand both scientific development and social needs; to place new emphasis on comprehensive audits that produce a greater level of accountability; and to expand the state of scientific knowledge by developing new methods and techniques for dealing with complex problems such as pollution, scarcity of resources, social welfare, energy, and public risk.[22] Kozmetsky identified such problems as requiring new management skills appropriate to "large-scale projects" in engineering.

Kozmetsky's Vision for Capitalism

In 1970, four years after he became dean and seven years before he established the Institute for Constructive Capitalism, Kozmetsky set forth in a brief paper his vision for a democratic, socially responsible, and technologically innovative brand of capitalism, which would require a new kind of business manager, who would, in turn, require a new kind of business education. Kozmetsky's vision for how to reform business education, and how to place the University of Texas business school at the forefront of such reform, cannot be understood apart from his vision for a new kind of capitalism. Kozmetsky spoke and wrote on many occasions about various aspects of these ideas, but this nine-page paper may be the clearest and most succinct account of his thinking regarding the intersection of business, education, and society.[23]

Most of the concepts and terminology that preoccupied him for the rest of his life are prominent in this paper, including constructive or creative capitalism, innovative management, new intellectual resources, nonroutine tasks (also later referred to as unstructured problems), technological entrepreneurship, and collaboration among business, government, and education. He didn't mention the techniques that he was to develop in the 1980s and 1990s—technology incubators, technology venturing, regional venture capital funds, and so forth—but he pointed in their direction by emphasizing the need for new "complexes" of private and public institutions comparable to the "military-industrial complex" that had arisen in the 1950s and 1960s.[24]

Kozmetsky asserted that the new generation of entrepreneurs and business managers who rose to prominence after World War II had already begun the work of creating a new kind of capitalism based on new technologies, a new sense of social responsibility, and new democratic business practices. He located most of these innovators in California, and while he didn't mention any names, he could only be referring to his contemporaries at Hughes, Litton, Teledyne, and numerous other innovative companies, such as TRW. One of the hoped-for byproducts of the changes that he wanted to see in business education would be to make the trends in such companies better known and better understood in the larger society.

Kozmetsky identified these "vanguards of the evolutionary American businessmen" as college graduates of the previous two decades who "had been educated to think for themselves," and "consequently they established goals and high ideals beyond the stereotyped materialism of the entertainment media. They are innovative managers rather than the 'professionals' of the new industrial state." These new managers dispelled "the image of rigid and insensitive bureaucracy and the classic organization man," developing new ways of sharing their companies' equity growth with both outside investors and employees, and mentoring employees who later left to establish their own companies.[25]

The Statistics of Change

A variety of statistical measurements bring many of the changes at the University of Texas business school into sharp relief.[26] Some changes reflect the results of policies introduced or refined by Kozmetsky; others reveal the broad social, economic, and political forces that were affecting the nation's business schools and higher education generally from the mid-1960s to the early 1980s.

One of the most fundamental changes at the school between 1966 and 1982 was the growth in enrollment, including dramatic increases in the number of women students. During that period, the total enrollment at the University of Texas at Austin grew by 20,694—from 27,345 in the fall of 1966 to 48,039 in the fall of 1982 (a 75.9 percent gain). Enrollment at the business school grew by 7,129—from 3,733 in 1966 to 10,862 in 1982. This was an increase of 191 percent and accounted for almost 35 percent of the overall campus growth. The peak in business enrollment during the Kozmetsky years came in 1980, with 11,596 students, just before major enrollment-control measures went into effect.

There was a corresponding increase in the number of degrees conferred during these years. In 1969–1970, for example, the business school awarded a total of 980 undergraduate and graduate degrees. The number grew to 2,385 by 1980–1981, after which there was a gradual decrease as enrollment controls took effect.

The increases in enrollment reflected several factors, including the growing academic reputation of the school, growth in the Texas population (by 16.2 percent from 1970 to 1980, surpassing the 10.2 percent growth in the US population), and a nationwide trend of greater interest among students in professional, career-oriented education. Across the nation from 1970 to 1980, the number of students earning an undergraduate business degree grew by 51.7 percent, while the number graduating from master's programs in business grew by 126.6 percent.[27]

When Kozmetsky became dean there were only 198 women in the undergraduate business program and only six women in the MBA and doctoral programs. Campus-wide, about one-third of the enrollment was female, but the number of women in many other University of Texas colleges and schools was almost as low as in business. In engineering there were only 22 women (among a total of 2,330 students), and in law there were only 62 women (among a total of 1,558). Most female students were concentrated in the traditional fields of education, communication, and fine arts—all of which had majorities of female students. (The University of Texas at Austin School of Nursing did not open until 1968, although nursing courses were taught on the campus beginning in 1960 through an arrangement with the University of Texas Medical Branch at Galveston.)

These statistics on the enrollment of women mirrored national trends, as did the statistics by 1982—after the first wave of a national and international revolution in women's higher education. In the University of Texas graduate business programs in 1982, there were 418 women and 880 men, and among undergraduate business students, there had been an even greater movement toward parity, with 4,292 women and 5,272 men.

Although the university began a series of affirmative action programs in the 1970s with the goal of increasing the number of African American and Hispanic students, the results never measured up to the hopes of administrators who advocated the programs. This was nowhere more true than at the business school, which under Kozmetsky never made significant progress in enrolling minority students. In the fall of 1982, just after Kozmetsky stepped down from the deanship, there were only 270 African American students and only 773 Hispanic students among the business school's total enrollment of 10,862. That was 2.5 percent and 7.1 percent, respectively. Over the next three decades African American enrollment in the business school never climbed much above 3 percent of the total, although Hispanic enrollment showed slightly larger gains (standing, for example, at 12.2 percent in 2014). These percentages were fairly close to the overall percentages for the university.

As the business school's overall enrollment increased, so did, of course, the number of semester credit hours it produced. From 1966 to 1974, for example, the number of semester credit hours increased by 97 percent, from 72,950 to 143,980. The student-faculty ratio increased dramatically during these years, as the business school failed to add enough faculty to keep pace with enrollment growth. The problem was only partly eased by increasing the dependence on nonfaculty instructors (assistant instructors and teaching assistants).[28] In 1968 the student-faculty ratio at the business school (faculty members only) was 23.9. The ratio reached a high of 37.0 in 1979 before dropping to 30.8 in fall 1982 (just after Kozmetsky stepped down from the deanship). Including assistant instructors and teaching assistants, the ratio was 25.6 in 1982—still higher than the student-faculty ratios of the 1960s. These high student-faculty ratios were a major reason that the business school faced accreditation problems in the 1970s and early 1980s.

The school saw major increases in its budget during the Kozmetsky years, in both actual and inflated dollars, although there usually seemed to be a shortage of money for recruiting and retaining faculty members. The instructional budget, made up mostly of salaries, rose from $1.4 million in 1966 to almost $8.5 million in 1982. The increase was more than twice the rate of inflation during those years. Expenditures for research also surged when Kozmetsky was dean, with the greatest percentage increases coming in the early years—a result of the shift in faculty hiring decisions to place more emphasis on faculty members who were interested in conducting advanced research programs. From 1969–1970 to 1974–1975, for example, research expenditures at the business school more than tripled, from $282,443 to $882,935. Campus-wide research expenditures grew by about 44 percent during these years, from $25.8 million to $36.8 million.

How Good Was the Business School under Kozmetsky?

Well before the end of Kozmetsky's sixteen years as dean, the impact of his initiatives began to be reflected in the business school's rising national reputation. There were numerous ways of attempting to measure that reputation, all of them inexact, but a consensus emerged among other business school leaders nationwide, and among business executives and the news media, that dramatic improvements were under way at the University of Texas.

When Ransom and the regents made it clear to Kozmetsky in 1966 that they expected him to elevate the business school to the ranks of the five best business schools in the nation, they might not have realized how difficult that would be, given the enrollment pressures on the University of Texas at Austin, the erratic nature of state financial support, and the increasing competition from other institutions around the country. They also could not have foreseen the new ways that all academic institutions would be ranked in the next two decades, as publications began to offer their own evaluations aimed at the needs of parents and students, the newly defined "consumers" of higher education.

After Kozmetsky left the deanship, he recalled for his students his early goals for the business school and the uncertainty of measuring the attainment of those goals:

> When I came here as dean the Texans laughed at me. I said that in
> the next decade we were going to be one of the top ten outstanding
> graduate schools of business in the United States. At that time we were
> unranked. I remember the faculty being very traditional and saying,
> "How do you measure it?" I said, "You don't. People will tell you. You
> don't even have to waste your time to measure." They asked, "Well, how
> do you get the people to say you are amongst that?" I said, "Each of us
> has to do the best of what we think we can do. If each of us does our
> best, we each make our contribution in research and teaching and in
> community relations, we will make it." One day somebody announced
> that we were number seven. . . . I know the *Wall Street Journal* some-
> time during the holidays had us amongst the top twenty. All I can say
> to you is I don't know how they measured it, but they couldn't leave us
> out, could they? They can't talk about world class business schools today
> without putting us in. . . . Greatness to me is measured very simply.
> Who asks for your services? Does the president of the United States ask
> for our services? Are our faculties and students out on commissions?
> Who wants us? Does the state use us or does it go outside and bring in
> outside consultants?[29]

Kozmetsky acknowledged the difficulties inherent in assessing the business school's progress, but he remained optimistic. Just three years after becoming dean, he gave a glowing report to the school's advisory council regarding the achievements up to that time: "The academic years 1966–1969 were truly years of building on the foundations of Deans Fitzgerald, Spriegel, and White to continue an ever-increasing search for the quest of recognized excellence for our college, its graduate school, and graduate programs. Our sometimes over-simplified objective of becoming one of the five outstanding schools of business in the nation is no longer considered by many of us as unreachable or even overly optimistic. The three specific steps outlined to reach this objective in our first meeting of 1966 bears repeating. They were, namely: (1) to initiate an outstanding research program; (2) to supplement our then sound teaching/research faculty with other equally outstanding faculty members; and (3) to develop a curriculum to adequately train our students in current and innovative business skills and social leadership for today's and tomorrow's industrial world."[30]

Kozmetsky noted that more than fifty people had been added to the faculty and research staff in those three years; major revisions had been made to the PhD and MBA curricula; new undergraduate courses had been created; and students had been given much greater choice in selecting their courses, both within and outside the business school.

Several formal studies were made during the years that Kozmetsky served as dean to compare the quality of the nation's business schools. One survey in the early 1970s sent a questionnaire to 1,180 deans of professional schools asking them to list the top five schools in their field. The sixty-one business deans in the survey mentioned Harvard most often, followed by Stanford, University of Chicago, University of Pennsylvania, and Carnegie-Mellon. The published results did not indicate how often other schools were mentioned.[31]

An evaluation of US business schools compared publication of scholarly articles in professional journals in 1961–1965 (the five years just before Kozmetsky became dean) and in 1966–1971 (the first six years of Kozmetsky's deanship). The rankings were based on each school's percentage share of the available pages in journals in various specializations. The University of Texas made significant gains in the rankings in most of the journals in the surveys. In two accounting journals, the university rose from twentieth place to twelfth. In three marketing journals, it rose from fifteenth place to fifth. In the journals *Management Science* and *Operations Research*, the university rose from no ranking at all to fifteenth. In the *Journal of Risk and Insurance*, it rose from fourteenth to ninth. The University of Texas did not show up in the top fifteen schools in 1966–1971 in journals in the fields of finance, personnel management and administrative science, and industrial and labor relations, nor in the multidisciplinary *Journal of Business*. Overall, the University of Texas had an average ranking of 20.1. The University of California, Berkeley, was in first place overall.[32]

A study of graduate education first conducted in 1966 by Allan Cartter of the University of California, Berkeley, and continued in 1976 by Lyman Porter of the University of California, Irvine, showed a dramatic rise for the University of Texas at Austin. The Graduate School of Business was ranked ninth in the nation among public universities that were included in the 1976 survey, which asked several hundred deans and professors for their assessments of the academic quality of graduate programs at fifty-one PhD-granting institutions. The assessments regarded faculty quality (faculty research competence) and "educational attractiveness." That category encompassed the reputation and accessibility of the faculty, the quality of curricula and students, the presence of innovative programs and library resources, the prominence of alumni, and other factors.[33]

Cartter's methodology was the basis of a survey, published in 1974, of more than 1,100 accounting faculty members, who were asked for their assessment of the nation's doctoral programs in accounting. The University of Texas accounting department was ranked fourth in the quality of its faculty (behind Stanford, Chicago, and Berkeley) and third in the effectiveness of its graduate programs (behind Stanford and Chicago). The University of Texas had risen from sixth place in a similar survey published in 1968.[34]

More national evaluations came as Kozmetsky's deanship began to draw to a close. A nationwide survey in 1979 of four thousand faculty members ranked the University of Texas business school faculty as the seventh best in the country.[35] Also ranked seventh was the University of Texas MBA program, according to a survey of the chief executive officers of the nation's largest companies.[36]

A survey of the deans of ninety-two of the nation's accredited business schools in 1980 concluded that the University of Texas undergraduate business program was the fifth best in the nation[37]—an assessment that seemed to belie accounting professor C. Aubrey Smith's early forecast that Kozmetsky would neglect the undergraduate program. The University of Texas was tied for fifth with the University of Illinois. Ranked ahead of Texas and Illinois were the University of Pennsylvania; University of Michigan; University of California, Berkeley; and Indiana University. In another part of that study, conducted by faculty members at the University of Virginia, personnel executives at forty-two large corporations ranked the University of Texas undergraduate program as the ninth best in the country.[38]

Other studies from the late 1970s placed the university's business school among the top twelve schools nationwide from which major companies recruited students, and in the top ten business schools among US public universities.[39]

Although Kozmetsky had often relied on opinion surveys in touting the academic progress of the business school, his next-to-last annual report as dean contained a note of caution about the validity of such studies: "These types of surveys have many limitations and are subject to unwarranted interpretations. Such surveys, however, tend to attract attention as well as students to the College and Graduate School of Business."[40]

As noted in chapter 8, rankings of business schools and other academic programs by the mass media did not begin until 1988, when *Businessweek* published its first annual rankings of MBA programs. Other publications—*U.S. News and World Report*, *Forbes*, the *Financial Times*, and the *Economist*—soon followed with their own rankings. It was clear from the rankings in these publications that Kozmetsky's deanship set the business school on a course of competitiveness with the best schools in the nation and laid a foundation on which subsequent deans continued, and continue, to build.

CHAPTER 10

TRANSFORMING THE BUSINESS SCHOOL II

Faculty Recruitment and Research

Realizing Kozmetsky's vision for business education required major advances on many fronts, not the least of which was strengthening the quality of the faculty. Together with broadening the business school's research presence and increasing its endowment, enhancing the faculty was fundamental to the broad transformation of the school that Kozmetsky was seeking. He played a central role in developing the faculty, and one of his main tasks was to serve as the chief recruiter of established scholars from other universities—people who were in midcareer or even toward the end of their careers, often at the nation's most prestigious institutions, but who could be enticed to take part in a new academic venture in Texas. The process was akin to the front office of a baseball club enticing seasoned "free agents" from other clubs, through financial incentives or other opportunities, to make a career move.

Kozmetsky recorded several stunning successes in attracting such faculty members to the University of Texas, particularly in the early years, drawing from among his wide network of friends and colleagues at other higher education institutions or within business and government. When possible, he lured these faculty members to the university with an endowed chair or professorship, special research funding, limited teaching requirements, and other attractions.

Each academic department, through its budget council or executive committee, was largely in charge of the effort to recruit highly promising new PhDs to serve as assistant professors, but Kozmetsky was the main recruiter of senior faculty members who had already established themselves in fields in which he had the most expertise, and he often played an important part in recruiting faculty members whose work cut across the traditional academic disciplines.

Early Plans for Strengthening the Faculty

After Kozmetsky had been dean for a year he provided Harry Ransom and Norman Hackerman with a detailed list of what might be called his faculty "dream team"—the people whom he hoped to recruit from the academic areas in which he wanted to establish endowed positions during the next five to ten years. Ransom had asked for such a list from all the deans to aid in planning and fundraising. Already in his first few months as dean, Kozmetsky had recruited three highly regarded faculty members, but the outline that he sent to Ransom and Hackerman makes it clear he was dreaming on a scale of much larger proportions.[1]

Kozmetsky's list included several national and international stars whom he succeeded in bringing to the University of Texas. Among those were Abraham Charnes and William W. Cooper, Kozmetsky's old friends in the field of management science; William C. Leone and James R. Bright in the field of management of technology; and Andrew C. Stedry, a precocious scholar whose work crossed several disciplinary lines.

There were also significant names whom Kozmetsky failed to lure away from other institutions, but they help reveal his high aspirations. They included two of the country's most eminent scholars in behavioral science and organizational theory—Herbert A. Simon (a future Nobel laureate in economics) and James G. March. In the field of financial management, Kozmetsky dreamed of attracting scholars such as Jacques Dréze, Myron J. Gordon, and Franco Modigliani, all economists of international stature. Modigliani won the Nobel Prize in economics in 1985.

For these and other hoped-for faculty, Kozmetsky advocated establishing endowed chairs or professorships that would have required at least $1.9 million in new funding. The ambitious plans that he conveyed to Ransom and Hackerman are all the more striking when considered in light of the university's overall number of endowed positions in 1967. The entire campus had only three endowed chairs that had been established with private donations (in geology, law, and chemistry); only thirteen privately endowed professorships (two in business, six in law, and one each in chemical engineering, sociology, psychology, American studies, and comparative literature); and only three endowed lectureships (in business, law, and arts and sciences). The entire University of Texas System had less than forty endowed faculty positions.[2]

The number of endowed positions at the business school and across the university would soar in the late 1970s and early 1980s, when the regents established a program to match endowment gifts with money from the Permanent University Fund as part of the University of Texas at Austin's extended celebration of its centennial.

Faculty Recruiting Successes

The first senior faculty member that Kozmetsky recruited was Eugene B. Konecci, whom he had met while consulting with NASA on a study of automation and the interaction of people and machines. Konecci arrived at the university in December 1966 and was named to a professorship funded by the Kleberg family foundation of Kingsville.[3] Konecci, who was controversial among some University of Texas faculty (see chapter 11), held a doctorate in medical physiology from the University of Bern and also had done graduate work at the University of Chicago and in the air force. He had a varied background in government, business, and academia, and his interdisciplinary interests made him one of Kozmetsky's most trusted colleagues.

Konecci had been the senior staff member at the National Aeronautics and Space Council in Washington, serving as chief adviser to President Johnson on the space program. Earlier, he had been director of NASA's Biotechnology and Human Research Office. Before joining NASA he headed Douglas Aircraft Co.'s life sciences and human factors engineering section, where he led a marketing study that was reminiscent of the one Kozmetsky had done at Hughes Aircraft.

In addition to his appointment as a professor of management at the University of Texas at Austin, Konecci was named a professor in the university's aerospace engineering department and a clinical professor of bioengineering at the university system's new medical school in San Antonio. Through the years, Konecci took on numerous special assignments for Kozmetsky, becoming one of a small group of people whom Kozmetsky relied on again and again for a new initiative or to troubleshoot an existing one. In Konecci's early days at the university he also served as a special assistant to Chancellor Ransom.[4]

Another early recruiting success was Albert Shapero, who moved to the university in the fall of 1966 to become a professor of management and business statistics and was also named chairman of the Department of Management.[5] He had directed technology management programs at the Stanford Research Institute, where he gained recognition for his work in the management of science and technology projects. He brought research projects with him to the University of Texas, including a study of the needs for retraining engineers whose skills had previously been employed in defense projects. His other research included the role of science and technology in the development of economic and social institutions and the process of technology transfer, particularly diffusion of defense technology in the civilian economy.[6]

Eugene Konecci, the first senior faculty member that Kozmetsky recruited when he became dean. 1971. Austin *magazine*.

Shapero, who held degrees in engineering from the University of California, Berkeley, specialized in teaching and research on entrepreneurship and published widely on that subject as well as on economic and industrial development. He was active since the early 1950s in professional organizations for operations research and management science. While at the University of Texas he chaired the first International Meeting on Entrepreneurship and Economic Development in 1975. He stayed at the university until 1978, when he moved to Ohio State University for the rest of his career.[7]

A third important recruit during Kozmetsky's first year at the University of Texas was Thomas E. Burke, who was appointed as the Eugene McDermott Special Research Associate in Cognitive Processing. McDermott, the former head of Texas Instruments, had established the research position "to advance the management aspects of computer concepts and their impact on industry and commerce." At first Burke came to the University of Texas on a leave of absence from the NASA Electronics Research Center in Massachusetts, but in 1968 he accepted a permanent position at the university. He worked with Konecci on research into advanced computer concepts,

William C. Leone, whom Kozmetsky recruited to teach at the business school soon after he became dean. *Texas Student Publications (Daily Texan).*

multiprocessing methods, and computer interactions with people, but he would also take on many special assignments for Kozmetsky, including serving as an adviser on computer purchases for the business school. In 1970–1971, he worked with Kozmetsky on a research project called Cognitive Processing in Management Education, which aimed at developing computer techniques for teaching problem-solving skills.[8]

Kozmetsky resorted to an unconventional approach in attracting William Leone to the business school to teach a weekly three-hour graduate seminar in production management. Leone was on Kozmetsky's September 1967 wish list for an endowed position, but that fall he was persuaded by Kozmetsky to fly to Texas every week to share with University of Texas students his insights into managing complex industrial production tasks. Such a commute was not easy in those days, when there were no direct flights between Los Angeles and Austin.[9]

Leone had the kind of varied background to which Kozmetsky was attracted. The two had met as faculty members at the Carnegie Institute of Technology, and they had later worked together at Hughes Aircraft, where Leone managed the industrial systems division. Leone had three engineering degrees from Carnegie Tech and had been a vice president at Rheem Califone Corp., a maker of tape recorders and teaching machines, including language-lab equipment. At the time of his University of Texas appointment he was vice president and general manager of Remex/Rheem Electronics. His book *Production Automation and Numerical Control* was published in late 1967.[10]

Kozmetsky reached into the management science talent at the Carnegie Institute of Technology to hire Andrew Stedry, a widely published young researcher who came to the University of Texas in September 1967 with the rank of professor in the Department of General Business (at that time the academic home of most of the business school's experts in management science) as well as professor of computer science. Stedry had been one of William Cooper's first students at Carnegie Tech, and he had published research with both Abraham Charnes and Cooper. He was the author of a landmark book in behavioral-quantitative budgeting and accounting research. In addition to teaching at Carnegie Tech, he had been on the faculties at George Washington University and the Massachusetts Institute of Technology, and he had been a consultant for three federal agencies. Stedry stayed at the University of Texas only through 1972–1973, after which he moved to Oakland University in Rochester, Michigan. He died in a traffic accident in New York in 1978.

Kozmetsky's focus on interdisciplinary learning was reflected in the hiring of several senior faculty, including David L. Huff, a geographer who came to Texas from the University of Kansas in 1968 to become a full professor with appointments in the Department of Marketing and the Department of Geography (now the Department of Geography and the Environment, a unit of the university's College of Liberal Arts). The University of Texas position was attractive to Huff because of the opportunities it afforded him to pursue his research. At Kansas he had been a professor of business administration and the director of a regional studies center. Huff specialized in geographical and ecological aspects of consumer behavior, trading areas, and channels of distribution.[11] He was known for creating the Huff Model, a widely used analytical tool that employs multiple variables about consumers to help companies make business decisions, such as determining the best location for retail and service facilities. Huff introduced the model in 1963, and it is still widely used for analyzing geographic data.[12]

One of Kozmetsky's biggest early successes was persuading Abraham Charnes to move to the university. Charnes accepted the job offer in June 1968. Since his early days at Carnegie Tech, Charnes had moved first to Purdue and then to Northwestern, where he had strengthened his reputation as a pioneer in developing advanced mathematical methods for solving management problems in manufacturing, government, engineering, medicine, and other fields.[13] He moved his research projects from Northwestern to the University of Texas, and he also brought along students and associates, perhaps most notably Darwin Klingman. The research projects transferred from Northwestern included work on "Extremization Theories and Number Analysis," "Mathematical Methods in Manpower Management," "Temporal Planning and Management Decision under Risk and Uncertainty," and "Nonlinear Problems in Operations Research."

It would be twelve more years before Kozmetsky could persuade William Cooper to come to the business school, but Charnes by himself was enough to put the University of Texas instantly on the map in management science. The recruitment of Charnes helped give the business school a dramatic boost in credibility.[14]

Charnes had been a professor of applied mathematics at Northwestern. At the University of Texas he held the Jesse H. Jones Professorship in Biomathematics and Management Science, funded with $100,000 from the Houston Endowment. He also held the title of University of Texas System professor, a position through which he worked on biomedical research and other projects with the system's health-science institutions. The business school and the University of Texas System shared paying his salary.

In an essay for Charnes's seventieth birthday, Kozmetsky cited three reasons for recruiting and keeping faculty members like him: to build a business school known for developing new methods and concepts and moving in new academic directions; to educate doctoral students who will be employed by other first-tier institutions; and to establish a research program that attracts funding from federal agencies, foundations, corporations, and other private-sector institutions.[15]

Kozmetsky summarized the challenges of having scholars such as Charnes on the faculty: "A dean has a responsibility to faculty members who are creative and innovative, especially those whose work encompasses unstructured problems. These unique faculty members generally do not want to teach within regular class-load regulations so that they have more time for research and for work with their doctoral students. They, more often than not, have the ability to generate their own funds for research, as well as funds for graduate students and other faculty members. They also do not want to be constrained by bureaucratic red tape in allocating and administering these research funds. It is surprising what good managers of research and development they become. These issues require deans to walk fine lines and still live within the policies of the university administration and the policies adopted by their college faculties."[16]

Kozmetsky could not hope to score many successes comparable to recruiting Charnes, and there were many years in which no senior faculty members were attracted to the business school, with new hires being limited to entry-level assistant professors who were recent recipients of a doctoral degree. Many of these, as their careers developed, would make major contributions to the academic stature of the business school. The academic year 1976–1977 was notable, however, for Kozmetsky's success in attracting two additional scholars who had been leaders in the fields of operations research and management science.

One was Charles C. Holt, a friend of Kozmetsky's from the Carnegie Institute of Technology who had since established a reputation as a leading economist and statistician, with faculty positions at the Massachusetts Institute of Technology, the London School of Economics, the University of Wisconsin, and the Urban Institute, a Washington think tank that researches economic and social policy. At the University of Texas, Holt became a professor of management as well as the director of the Bureau of Business Research, and his appointments greatly strengthened the business school's quantitative research capabilities. Holt was an expert on computer simulation, macroeconomics, and operations research. In 1957, in a highly influential publication with the humdrum title of "Office of Naval Research Memorandum Number 52," Holt had developed the basis for one of the most important forecasting methodologies for operations research. The methodology used weighted moving averages to forecast economic trends, a sophisticated mathematical technique that was used for planning production lines, inventory, and workforce needs. The methodology was the centerpiece of a landmark 1960 book titled *Planning, Production, Inventory, and Workforce*, which Holt cowrote with Herbert Simon and other Carnegie Tech colleagues.[17]

Another recruiting victory in 1976–1977 was drawing Leon Lasdon away from the prestigious operations research program at Case Western Reserve University to serve as a professor of statistics and operations research at the University of Texas. Lasdon's first appointment was in the Department of General Business, which after several reorganizations became the current Department of Information, Risk, and Operations Management in 2005. Holder of the David Bruton Jr. Centennial Chair in Business Decision Support Systems, Lasdon specializes in decision support systems, decision theory, management science, operations research, optimization, and supply chain management. His many achievements include being the codeveloper of the Microsoft Excel Solver, embedded in Microsoft Excel since 1991.

Lasdon said that although Darwin Klingman had taken the lead in recruiting him from Case Western, Kozmetsky was "the leader who created the forward momentum for the school" that had made the University of Texas position attractive to him.[18] Klingman and Kozmetsky also recruited another distinguished Case Western faculty member in operations research, Peter Mevert, who came to the University of Texas at the same time as Lasdon but soon joined the faculty at the Free University of Berlin.

Kozmetsky persuaded James R. Bright to come to the University of Texas from Harvard, first as a distinguished visiting professor in 1968–1969, and then the following year as a permanent faculty member with the rank of professor. Bright, who specialized in the study of technological innovation, technology planning and forecasting, automation, and related subjects, was also appointed associate dean for long-range planning and coordination of the graduate curriculum.[19] Bright's research included ways of anticipating technological progress. He organized conferences on technology forecasting and published several books on the subject, including *A Guide to Practical Technological Forecasting* (Prentice Hall, 1973). Bright stayed at the University of Texas through 1975–1976, after which he continued to do research at a consulting firm in Austin.

Kozmetsky took several steps to strengthen the research capability of the Department of Finance, considered by some in the 1970s to have the weakest research program of any department in the business school. One of those steps was to hire Stephen Magee from the University of Chicago in the fall of 1976 as a visiting full professor. Magee—whose research interests have included tariffs and trade, the economics of intellectual property, the economic effects of legal systems, and the economics of mergers—gained tenure at the University of Texas a year after serving as a visiting professor and went on to chair the Department of Finance from 1980 to 1984, continuing to serve in both the finance and economics departments and to hold an endowed chair.

Magee recalled the important role Kozmetsky played in bringing him to the university. Lawrence L. Crum, then chairman of the finance department, called him in Chicago after he had visited the campus, and Magee soon discovered that Kozmetsky was also on the line. "Larry said, 'We are making you an offer to be a visiting associate professor of finance.' Kozmetsky interjected, 'No you will be a visiting full professor of finance.' Larry then said my salary would be a certain amount, and Kozmetsky

A CIVIC ENTREPRENEUR

interjected, 'No, your salary will be $4,000 more than that.' So George Kozmetsky overrode the finance department decisions to make sure I would come here." Magee said he had been also considering an offer to be the personal economist to David Rockefeller, then president of Chase Manhattan Bank in New York, but he was persuaded by Kozmetsky to come to Austin instead.[20]

Kozmetsky continued to help recruit outstanding mathematicians to the finance department after Magee became chairman. These included Patrick L. Brockett, now director of the business school's Risk Management and Insurance Program, and Leslie Young, who had earned his doctorate in mathematics from Oxford University at age twenty. Young left the University of Texas in the early 1990s to accept an endowed chair at the University of Hong Kong, and he is now a professor at the Cheung Kong Graduate School of Business in Beijing.

The effort to recruit Young demonstrated Kozmetsky's willingness to ignore standard procedures in order to achieve his purposes. Magee said the finance department's budget council had opposed Magee's desire to hire Young. Magee explained to Kozmetsky about Young's credentials and the opposition of the budget council, and Kozmetsky responded, "Well let's just you and I hire him anyway and not tell your Budget Council and the rest of the department about it until the President's Office has approved it." They proceeded with that plan, and months later when Magee informed the budget council, the members were very upset. "I let them yell at me for what seemed a very long time," Magee recalled. "I knew they were a bit afraid to confront George so letting them blow off steam at me helped them get over it."[21]

Toward the end of Kozmetsky's deanship, Kozmetsky helped the finance department and Magee recruit Vijay Singh Bawa, one of the world's leading finance theorists. In addition to enhancing the reputation of the business school through his research, Bawa was a highly regarded teacher whose graduate seminars were often attended by faculty colleagues eager to hear his ideas. He held an endowed professorship sponsored by the College of Business Administration Foundation. The promise of a distinguished career at the university was cut short when Bawa died in 1983 after a long battle with diabetes.

Bawa, who was born in India, earned a doctorate from Cornell University in operations research in 1970 and then joined the technical staff of Bell Laboratories, where he stayed until moving to the University of Texas. At Bell Labs his jobs included leading the economics and financial research department. From 1978 to 1981 he was also a professor at New York University.[22]

The presence of researchers and teachers such as Brockett, Young, and Bawa rapidly elevated the reputation of the Department of Finance, Magee said: "When top finance faculty from the top schools such as Yale, Harvard, and Chicago would come to present papers, these guys would correct their math and improve their work. This quickly changed the impression of senior national finance scholars . . . that a lot was going on here at Texas."[23]

As important as any of these recruitment successes was Kozmetsky's ability to hire William Cooper from the Harvard Business School in 1980—the culmination of efforts that Kozmetsky had been making ever since he became dean. Cooper was sixty-six when he came to the University of Texas, but his career was far from over, as he continued to teach, conduct research, and produce publications in the ever-broadening field of management science until his death in 2012 at age ninety-seven, even though he officially retired in 1993. During his University of Texas years, Cooper published more than 325 articles, including one just a few weeks before he died. Kozmetsky acknowledged the breadth of Cooper's research by appointing him in 1980 to three departments—management, finance, and accounting. Although Cooper's colleague Charnes was equally distinguished as an innovator in the interdisciplinary field of management science, Cooper had also made a name for himself as an administrator at both the Carnegie Institute of Technology and Harvard.[24]

Cooper, Charnes, and Kozmetsky had been working together on various projects since their days at Carnegie Tech and continuing through Kozmetsky's years in business in Southern California. Cooper and Charnes had been collaborating on research since the early 1950s even though they were for many years at different institutions, and they continued working together at the University of Texas without missing a beat, although their professional collaboration was also tinged with personal rivalry. Charnes was notoriously difficult to work with, and Cooper said he thought Charnes was too insistent on always having his name appear first in the credits on their joint publications, regardless of which person had made the greatest contribution.[25] The two continued to collaborate for the next ten years despite the personal tension, but eventually they stopped speaking to one another.[26]

"I never knew what happened or when," wrote Sten Thore, an economist at the IC[2] Institute who worked closely with both of them. "First, people around them assumed that it was just a matter of some passing hot temper. Eventually the awful truth sank in. Everybody was baffled: of course they had strong personalities and they were both uncompromising in their scientific rectitude and honesty. But they had been friends for so many

William W. Cooper, a leader in the field of management science, whom Kozmetsky recruited for the business school faculty. *Photograph by Dan Kallick, University Photography Services.*

years and they were both charming and open-minded persons. The two families knew each other intimately, and their wives Kay Charnes and Ruth Cooper were longstanding, good friends. My wife Margrethe has reminded me of the following episode: When she, together with Ronya and George Kozmetsky, and a few close friends, arranged a festive dinner for Ruth on her 75th birthday in 1990, the Charnes couple was not present."[27]

Despite the problems in his working relationship with Charnes, in 1980 Cooper found the opportunity to collaborate with him more closely, and to reunite with Kozmetsky, highly appealing. Kozmetsky said that both the University of California, Los Angeles, and Duke University had offered Cooper a higher salary than what the University of Texas was able to pay, but he decided to come to Texas anyway.[28]

In May 1982, just days before he announced that he would be stepping down from the deanship, Kozmetsky was working on efforts to lure econometrician Henri Theil away from his endowed position at the University of Florida to lead a proposed University of Texas Center for Econometrics and Business Research. Kozmetsky had proposed to the university's central administration that Theil hold an endowed chair for which funds were still being raised (the Harkins & Company Chair) and that Theil's annual salary be $110,000 (almost $286,000 in 2017). A university official called that compensation "high but not unreasonable in relation to his current salary at Florida."[29]

There was no doubt among University of Texas officials that Theil was worth such a high salary, as well as an endowed chair and his own research center, although it was recommended that a formal offer be delayed until funding for the chair had been completed. Theil, a native of the Netherlands, had taught at the University of Chicago, and in 1981 he was appointed to an endowed chair at the University of Florida in Gainesville. Theil made numerous contributions to econometrics, a field that applies mathematics, computer analysis, and statistical methods to economic data. He invented several mathematical techniques that bear his name.

Magee was among those advocating that the university try to recruit Theil. "He had been a very distinguished colleague of mine at the University of Chicago," Magee recalled. "In general, George got very excited about hiring superstars. He was all for building an Ivy League–quality faculty here at Texas."[30] The effort to recruit Theil was renewed in the months after Kozmetsky left the deanship, but Theil elected to remain at the University of Florida.

Also indicative of the distinguished scholars that Kozmetsky hoped to attract to the faculty was George C. Eads, an economist who had been a member of the President's Council of Economic Advisers during the Carter administration and had also served with Kozmetsky on the National Commission on Supplies and Shortages in the mid-1970s. Theil, Eads, and any number of others declined whatever Kozmetsky had been able to offer them.[31]

Apart from recruiting distinguished senior faculty, the business school made progress during the Kozmetsky years in attracting outstanding entry-level faculty members who would go on to build their careers at the University of Texas. Departmental committees might have been more important than the dean in finding and recruiting these younger faculty members, but Kozmetsky often played a major role in the sometimes-delicate process of retaining them.

Among the many faculty members who were hired as assistant professors when Kozmetsky was dean and who stayed at the business school for at least a significant portion of their careers were the following:

Timothy W. Ruefli came to the university's Department of Management in 1967–1968, about a year before earning his PhD from the Carnegie Institute of Technology. Ruefli became one of Kozmetsky's most trusted associates, helping him start the IC² Institute and serving as its first associate director. His research was in high-technology strategic management, information systems, management science, and microeconomics. He also created the business school's Classroom 2000, which included a computer at each student's workstation, and he helped Kozmetsky create the master's program in technology commercialization.[32]

Robert E. Witt joined the Department of Marketing in 1968 and would go on to serve as dean of the business school for nine years, as well as president of the University of Texas at Arlington, president of the University of Alabama, and chancellor of the University of Alabama System.

Darwin Klingman was hired by the Department of General Business in 1969–1970 and would eventually hold an endowed chair and become an internationally recognized authority on the application of mathematical models and computer technology in policy and decision-making. In addition to being a professor of management science and information systems, he served as director of the university's Center for Business Decision Analysis and the master's program for information systems management.

William H. Cunningham was hired in 1970–1971 in the Department of Marketing. He became associate dean for graduate programs under Kozmetsky and then was his immediate successor as dean, before serving as president of the University of Texas at Austin and chancellor of the University of Texas System.

Robert A. Peterson came to the university as an assistant professor of marketing in 1971. He worked with Kozmetsky on several research projects and has held a variety of university administrative positions, including serving as associate vice president for research. He was associated with the IC² Institute from its beginning in 1977 and served as the institute's director from 2013 to 2016.

Robert S. Sullivan was recruited to the university management department in 1976 and held a succession of faculty and administrative posts through 1995. He was dean of the business school at Carnegie Mellon University from 1995 to 1997, when he returned to the University of Texas to succeed Kozmetsky as director of the IC² Institute. In 1998 he moved to the business deanship at the University of North Carolina, and in 2003 he became the first dean of the school of management at the University of California, San Diego.

Reuben R. McDaniel Jr. came to the University of Texas in 1972 as an assistant professor of management as well as an associate dean of students. He served as an associate dean for undergraduate programs and planning beginning in 1976. He eventually held an endowed chair in health-care management, and his areas of expertise included decision-making within complex organizations. He founded the interdisciplinary McCombs School of Business Health Care Initiative.

McDaniel, one of the few African American faculty members at the University of Texas, was recruited by Kozmetsky even though his degrees were in mechanical engineering and higher education administration, not in business. McDaniel said he believes his interdisciplinary and nontraditional background were factors in Kozmetsky's support for him as a faculty member and later as an associate dean. "George had his eyes on me from the first day," McDaniel said. "He wanted me to get my feet on the ground, and then he tapped me for a role within the college."[33]

Kozmetsky played an important role in promoting those younger faculty members whom he and various departments wanted to keep on the faculty. The first step was promotion to associate professor (which meant receiving tenure) and then to the rank of full professor, with the final decision on such matters being up to the university president. The entire process could take many years, although some faculty members were definitely on a fast track for promotion.

One of those on a fast track was Cunningham, who was promoted to associate professor only three and a half years after coming to the University of Texas in 1971 and then was recommended for promotion to professor only three years after that. Kozmetsky approved the recommendation of the Department of Marketing in 1977 that Cunningham be made a full professor and forwarded it to President Lorene Rogers, even though Cunningham himself thought the promotion was a little premature. Rogers turned it down, and the next year the same recommendation came from the department and Kozmetsky, and again Rogers said no. Cunningham speculated that his promotion might have gotten caught up in one of the frequent power struggles between Rogers and Kozmetsky, and he recalled that he was quite upset about not receiving the promotion that year, enough so that he entertained thoughts of leaving the university and pursuing his career elsewhere.

Kozmetsky, however, intervened in a dramatic way, as Cunningham has written: "Kozmetsky knew that I would be very unhappy about the decision [by Rogers]. He gave me the news at the office and then I went home. Later that day he came out to our house and sat with me and Isabella for about an hour and talked about how confident he was that I would be promoted the next year and how important I was to him and the college. The fact that Kozmetsky thought enough of me to come to our house and ask me to stay at the university sealed the deal. I loved UT, and I enjoyed working with Kozmetsky. The university had been good to me, and down deep in my heart I did not want to leave. However, I was hurt by

Rogers's decision, and without Kozmetsky's show of interest and affection, I probably would have left the university. I was promoted to full professor the next year, and all was forgiven."[34]

Kozmetsky took unusual actions on other occasions to protect the faculty that he and his colleagues had developed. One of the most extraordinary episodes concerned Darwin Klingman, who by 1980 had become one of the brightest international stars on the faculty. In November of 1980 Klingman wrote a nine-page letter to Kozmetsky criticizing his management of the business school—a letter that reads much like the outpouring of a faculty member who is so upset that he has decided to burn all his bridges. Klingman's exchange with Kozmetsky is revealing not only for the details about faculty dissent on a variety of issues and the way it offers a behind-the-scenes view of the business school, but also for the way Kozmetsky's immediate and long-term responses illustrate key aspects of his management style, including his determination to do whatever he could to pacify an important faculty member like Klingman.

Klingman's complaints, which at the time remained largely within the confines of the business school and the university's central administration, had particular force because of his stature as a scholar—and also because he worked in an area that was dear to Kozmetsky's heart. Klingman specialized in applying mathematical models and computer programs to policy and decision-making. His work was adopted by more than one hundred companies and government agencies, and he established the university's highly ranked information science program and was largely responsible for putting into practice Kozmetsky's desire to incorporate information science into the standard education of business managers. Klingman's complaints also surprised some people within the business school because Klingman had been perceived as one of Kozmetsky's close allies.[35]

Sending copies of his letter to his colleagues Lanier Cox, Gaylord Jentz, and Ray Sommerfield, Klingman detailed the "major weaknesses" that he perceived in Kozmetsky's leadership. He began by writing that some colleagues had advised him not to send the letter because Kozmetsky "only hears what he wants to hear" or "George's ego won't let him acknowledge managerial weakness." Then he presented a catalogue of examples of the school's pervasive "mediocrity," which he said resulted from an "impersonal atmosphere" for which Kozmetsky was responsible, and instances of the school's "slow but steady" deterioration since the early 1970s.

The long list of complaints included an inconsistent reward structure that benefited Kozmetsky's "favorites," Kozmetsky's use of "inconsistent" statistics in the school's annual report, a perception among the faculty that Kozmetsky worked hard but "spreads himself too thin" between his

Kozmetsky with students at the business school, 1970s. *Texas Student Publications (Cactus).*

duties as dean and outside interests, a lack of precision and coherence in Kozmetsky's recent speeches, questionable decisions by Kozmetsky on faculty hiring, and unresponsiveness to student needs by the dean's office.[36]

The letter, along with similar complaints from other faculty members, appears to have shaken Kozmetsky. A few days after Klingman wrote the letter, Sommerfield sent a copy to Robert Mettlen, assistant to President Peter Flawn, with this handwritten note attached: "You might find the attached of some interest. Klingman told Sommerfield he did not object to having the letter shared with me. I'd feel uncomfortable, though, in distributing this copy any more widely. While obviously self-serving, the letter is particularly noteworthy because of its source. Klingman has always been recognized as a 'F.O.G.'—friend of George. It helps explain why Koz has been somewhat more unsettled than usually so in the last week. Ray [Sommerfield] tells me the 'noise level' in the [business school] is as high as he's ever seen it—with some faculty even explicitly inquiring about the procedures for a 'no confidence' vote or a mid-year change in the deanship. There's obviously much ado about something—how critical the something is remains to be revealed."[37]

A Civic Entrepreneur

Kozmetsky's immediate response was to write a six-page letter to Klingman (beginning "Dear Dar"), taking issue point by point with his complaints and defending himself as "doing the best I can." He sharply disagreed with Klingman's assertion that the business school was on the decline, especially with regard to faculty recruitment and promotions. "Maintaining a balanced and diversified excellent faculty between teaching and research has been a hallmark of my administration," Kozmetsky wrote. "There is no way of satisfying individual faculty members as to the selection, promotion, and appointment to professorships."

He also rejected the idea that he was engaged in so many activities that he was failing to pay enough attention to the business school. "I put in more than the traditional 40 hours in a normal five-day week," he said. "There are a number of reasons for this," one being to achieve excellence in the business school's programs. He defended as beneficial to the school his many other roles, including serving on corporate boards and national commissions and doing work for the board of regents. Kozmetsky closed his letter with a dig at Klingman for lacking information about the business school because he often failed to attend various committee meetings, and he took a good-natured swipe at the business school's self-appointed "critics in residence."[38]

However much Kozmetsky disliked the criticism, he did not hold the comments against Klingman. In fact, he took steps to enlarge and strengthen Klingman's role as a key member of the faculty. Kozmetsky continued to place a very high value on Klingman's contribution to the faculty as a teacher and researcher. He was concerned in 1982 about efforts by Texas A&M University to hire Klingman, and he asked Flawn for help in countering an A&M offer.[39]

Far from retaliating against Klingman, Kozmetsky rewarded him with various academic plums. He appointed Klingman to a professorship in the application of computers to business and management, and he made Klingman chairman of a committee on computers and communication, which in 1982 developed a plan for expanding the use of computers in classes as well as in research and administration. Kozmetsky also was a strong advocate, near the end of his deanship, of a Decision Support Systems Center, a research unit that Klingman would lead.

Research

Greater emphasis on research by faculty and students was one of Kozmetsky's highest priorities as dean, as is clear from the kind of people he was most interested in recruiting for the faculty. Research resulting in peer-reviewed publication, far more than good teaching and other faculty activities, would prove to be the central factor by which the growing reputation of the business school was judged. Early in his tenure at the university, Kozmetsky established a "working paper" series through which faculty members circulated drafts of their research findings.

After his first year as dean, Kozmetsky could claim that he had laid a sound foundation for an expanded research program through the hiring of Konecci and Shapero, but he also acknowledged that "considerable work remains to be done in developing an appropriate research environment which is so essential for the advancement of management research."[40] He cited research projects that were in various stages of development and for which he was seeking further funding, all of which had been initiated during his first year as dean and a few of which he was participating in directly as one of the investigators. The projects included those by Shapero on the mobility of scientists and the retraining of defense engineers, as well as projects on an international business model, a health maintenance center model, integer programming, chance constraint programming, management of technological and intellectual resources, and information systems. In addition, he summarized three other major projects that were under way: a project with the School of Architecture to produce a "generalized university model" related to the planning of new university campuses, a "cognitive processor" project (early work by Thomas Burke on artificial intelligence), and a symposium on the industrial potential of marine sciences, part of Kozmetsky's work with the Board of Regents.[41]

Kozmetsky's recruitment of Charnes had a far-reaching effect on expansion of research conducted at the school. About a year after his arrival, Charnes sought approval from President Hackerman for the establishment of an International Center for Cybernetic Studies, the kind of interdisciplinary center of advanced research that Kozmetsky advocated. The center would become (without the "international" in the title) the first of what were called "organized research centers" to be created at the business school during Kozmetsky's deanship. Such centers were administrative units that facilitated interdisciplinary projects and the winning of research grants and contracts. Perhaps because Charnes was not asking the University of Texas for any money to get the center started, Hackerman approved it only eight days after Charnes's letter.[42] Charnes named Eugene Nelson, a longtime University of Texas professor of business law, as his first associate director, perhaps to take advantage of his knowledge of the university's administrative procedures.

As Charnes described the center, it would provide a vehicle for continuing his research "on the theory and practice in regard to complex systems of many kinds" with the aim of establishing the University of Texas at Austin "as an acknowledged world leader in this activity." He said the center was designed to cut across fields—from urban and environmental affairs to life and biomedical sciences and engineering.

Kozmetsky secured a gift of $100,000 for the center from Farah Manufacturing Co. of El Paso. The work of the center was also supported through Charnes's ongoing research funding, including grants from the Office of Naval Research, the Office of Civilian Manpower Management, and other federal agencies.

One of Konecci's first assignments was to serve as "director of project research," which involved responsibility for several multidisciplinary research projects and centers involving advanced systems planning and management. One of those was development of an "international business model" that the University of Texas at Austin was undertaking with other US universities (UCLA, Carnegie Tech, Northwestern, and Stanford) and the National University of Mexico. Another was the Research Center for Intellectual and Technological Resources, which Konecci directed.

Kozmetsky's interest in regional economic development was reflected in research that began in 1967–1968 on behalf of the Ozarks Regional Commission, a federal/state agency that worked during the 1960s and 1970s on long-range economic development plans for parts of Arkansas, Kansas, Missouri, and Oklahoma. The research included developing a planning system for the commission, an information management system, and services for the commission to implement in areas such as transportation.[43] This project was a forerunner of many of the economic development activities of the IC² Institute.

Researchers at the business school also contracted with a Texas regional medical planning group to help develop a computerized data-management system and other services.[44] And Kozmetsky was involved with two faculty members, Andrew Stedry and J. Barry Gertz, in a project to develop a computer program to assess the performance of mutual-fund portfolio managers.[45] Kozmetsky and Gertz worked together on research that led to the development of a computer simulation to aid decision-making in mergers and acquisitions.[46]

Another early research endeavor was the Oral Business History Project, which focused on Texas-based business and industry. An extension of an oral history project on the Texas oil industry from the 1950s, the project that began under Kozmetsky's deanship in 1969 was led by Floyd S. Brandt, a professor of management, and included participation by students. Among the early subjects for oral history interviews were such Texas business leaders as Walter F. Woodul Sr., former lieutenant governor and University of Texas regent who was credited with legislation that helped build a "well-funded University System"; Max Levine, retired chairman of Foley's Department Stores; Houston Harte, leader of the newspaper company Harte-Hanks Inc.; William Thomas Eldridge, developer of Sugarland Industries, which became Imperial Sugar Co.; W. Duke Walser, executive vice president of Tenneco; and Ben Love, a Houston banker who would become chairman of Texas Commerce Bank.

Other companies that were the subject of oral histories included Steck Co. printers, Sakowitz department stores of Houston, Lone Star Brewing Co. of San Antonio, M. L. Leddy & Sons Bootmakers of San Angelo, American General Life Insurance Co. of Houston, Adams Extract Co. of Austin, and Farah Manufacturing Co. The project also produced an oral history by Morris B. Zale, a founder of the Dallas-based Zales Jewelers, as well as a history of the company's first fifty years. Interviews were conducted with more than sixty business leaders during the six years of the project, and some interviews were used as source material by the *Handbook of Texas*, a publication of the Texas State Historical Association.[47]

Kozmetsky participated in—or at least lent his name to—many research projects that were largely conducted by others. One of these projects that drew the widest attention was a series of surveys of public opinion on capitalism led by marketing professor Robert A. Peterson, beginning when Kozmetsky was dean and continuing through the 1980s. The research began with a survey of public perceptions of whether the news media were biased, either for or against business, in covering business stories. One of the findings was that a perception of bias against business increased with a person's education and income level.[48] Another survey found disparity in the percentage of business editors and the general public who perceived a bias toward business in news coverage. More than two-thirds of the editors perceived the news media to be unbiased, but fewer than four in ten general public respondents thought so.[49]

That study was followed by a survey that found that only about one-third of Americans could define capitalism correctly, but that people were more likely to give correct definitions of terms such as "free enterprise," leading to the authors' conclusion that capitalism was undergoing an "identity crisis."[50] "This boils down to the fact that people really don't have much understanding of business and economics," Peterson and his coauthors said. "However, it doesn't mean that people aren't capitalists. Rather, their general attitude seems to be, 'I can't tell you what I like, but I know it when I see it.'"[51] After further studies of public opinion, the ten years of research were summarized in a book that tracked a decline in positive views of capitalism among Americans during the 1980s, a finding that was surprising in light of the embrace of capitalism by former communist countries after the demise of the Soviet Union.[52]

Kozmetsky also collaborated with Isabella Cunningham on several research projects beginning in the mid-1970s, including a book of readings on asset management related to an informal class that Kozmetsky taught.[53] "George was a very capable scholar, and he was always interested in understanding and helping scholars, but there was also always a very practical side to him," Cunningham said. "He was always especially interested in research that could help solve society's problems and that would make life better for people."[54]

When Kozmetsky stepped down from the deanship in 1982, he could look back on the past sixteen years as a period of extraordinary transformation of the quality of the business school's faculty and the contributions that faculty members were making to research. In these respects, the school bore little resemblance to the institution that Kozmetsky had inherited, a contrast that also applied to the university as a whole. In neither case—the business school nor the university as a whole—had this transformation been achieved without being threatened by serious issues, from budget problems to enrollment crises to administrative turmoil. The way Kozmetsky dealt with these challenges constitutes another aspect of his legacy.

CHAPTER 11

TRANSFORMING THE BUSINESS SCHOOL III

Endowments, Enrollment, and Curriculum Issues

Closely related to Kozmetsky's plans for strengthening the faculty and broadening research were his efforts to increase the business school's endowment through donations from the private sector. Other issues that had a direct impact on the quality of teaching and research were efforts to control the mushrooming growth in the number of students and to overhaul the undergraduate and graduate curricula to reflect the trends in business and society that had concerned Kozmetsky since his own days as a business school student.

FUNDRAISING AND ENDOWMENTS

Faculty recruiting and retention were advanced through the creation of endowed chairs, professorships, and other positions during Kozmetsky's deanship. Compared with the work that his predecessors had done, fundraising from among alumni, foundations, and other private-sector sources was significantly expanded during these years, although compared with the progress made under subsequent deans, beginning with William H. Cunningham in 1982, Kozmetsky barely scratched the surface. Cunningham has suggested that Kozmetsky's great personal wealth might have made him reluctant to ask others for donations.[1]

The entire university was slow to emphasize private-sector fundraising until the university's centennial period, which began in 1981. Higher education philanthropy had been mostly a matter that concerned private institutions until well into the postwar era. At the University of Texas business school, the first endowment to support an academic position was not established until the fall of 1966. This was a professorship in accounting named for Kozmetsky's predecessor as dean, John Arch White. It was followed in 1968 with a gift from the Houston Endowment for the

Kozmetsky and William H. Cunningham, who served as associate dean of the business school when Kozmetsky was dean. *AP Photo*/Austin American-Statesman, *David Kennedy.*

Jesse H. Jones Professorship in Mathematics and Management Science, named for the Houston publisher.[2] Abraham Charnes became, in 1968, the first appointee to that professorship, which aided in his recruitment by Kozmetsky.[3] In 1967, the business school acquired two other private-sector endowments—the Alice G. K. Kleberg Annual Professorship and the Richard J. Gonzalez Lectureship.

From those modest beginnings, the business school gradually began to accumulate an endowment from private-sector donations consisting of professorships, lectureships, and scholarships, as well as, much later, faculty chairs. White had created the College of Business Administration Foundation in 1964 in order to better raise money from the private sector,[4] and Kozmetsky quickly reorganized and expanded the foundation's advisory council. Kozmetsky was soon praised by the university's central development office for his broadening of the activities of the council, especially compared with most other University of Texas colleges and schools. Many of the other internal foundations were described as "inactive," "inadequate," or "short on know-how." Only the foundations supporting business, law, geology, and engineering drew unqualified praise.[5]

Kozmetsky attracted highly qualified business leaders (many of them University of Texas alumni) to serve on the advisory council. Among those on the first council that he put together were Foster Parker (who served as chairman), senior vice president of the Brown & Root construction firm of Houston; James Bayless, an executive of Rauscher Pierce Securities Group, Houston; Tom Clausen, vice president of Bank of America, San Francisco; Hardin Lawrence, president of Braniff International Airways, Dallas; Barry M. Rowles, president of M&M Candy Co., Hackettstown, New Jersey; Clyde Skeen, president of Ling-Temco-Vought Inc., Dallas; Jack G. Taylor, an investor, Austin; and Kozmetsky's old friend Arthur Rock, the venture capital pioneer.

In 1974, Kozmetsky upgraded the school's fundraising efforts with the hiring of Thomas A. Loomis, a retired navy captain, to direct the office of development and external affairs. The new position would enable the business school to better organize its fundraising efforts, as Kozmetsky wrote to university president Stephen Spurr. "For some time I have felt that we were not taking full advantage of our opportunities to publicize our programs, progress, research results, and academic achievements," Kozmetsky said. "Also, we have not followed up vigorously on opportunities to secure gift funds for student and faculty programs."[6]

Loomis, who had held public relations jobs in the navy, began his work at the University of Texas by preparing a slide show that Kozmetsky could speak from at meetings across the state. Kozmetsky, Loomis, and advisory

A CIVIC ENTREPRENEUR

council members made follow-up visits to prospective donors who had attended the luncheons.[7]

Kozmetsky had maintained an extensive statewide speaking schedule since becoming dean, but the pace of these engagements picked up after the mid-1970s. Press coverage of his appearances before potential donors and business leaders was uniformly positive. In 1977, for example, the Kilgore newspaper, reporting on a speech that Kozmetsky had given in Tyler, had these words of praise for Kozmetsky: "The dean's own dynamism is a major reason why the business school enrolls one of every five students registered at UT. Now in his 11th year at UT, he is known as a problem-solving activist who makes an adventure of solving business problems. Overcoming those challenges, he tells all who will listen, is the only way the U.S. can avoid becoming an overripe apple on the tree of international commerce. He has originated the concept of 'constructive capitalism' as a theme for the business school, this being designed to reestablish the basics of free enterprise in the light of modern national and world conditions."[8]

In 1977, the business school acquired its first endowed chair, with a gift of $500,000 from the J. M. West Texas Corp. The gift included proceeds from the eventual sale of 130 acres in Fort Bend County, adjacent to Houston, that the company gave to the university.[9] The gift was used to create the J. Marion West Chair for Constructive Capitalism, and it was held by Kozmetsky as director of the IC[2] Institute. Kozmetsky was said to donate back to the business school $25,000 from the yearly stipend that he received from the endowed chair.

When the regents established a fundraising campaign as part of the University of Texas at Austin's celebration of its centennial (1981–1983), Loomis, by then an assistant dean, helped the business school ramp up its fundraising activities to take advantage of special matching funds that President Peter Flawn had persuaded the regents to authorize. The initiative, known as the Centennial Endowed Teachers and Scholars Program, provided matching funds from the Permanent University Fund to double the value of private-sector contributions. Kozmetsky stepped down from the deanship in the middle of the campaign, but Loomis continued working on it with Kozmetsky's successor, William H. Cunningham. Kozmetsky had set a goal of raising $6 million for the business school as part of the campaign, but Cunningham doubled that goal, and then he, Loomis, Sam Barshop, and other advisory council members succeeded in raising an average of $1 million a month for the two years that Cunningham served as dean.[10]

Under the centennial campaign, the university had set goals of raising enough money to create one hundred endowed professorships or chairs, one hundred endowed scholarships, and one hundred other endowed positions.[11] As the business school's part of the campaign, the business school foundation, with an endowment committee led by Barshop, adopted Kozmetsky's goals of meeting 15 percent of the university-wide campaign—creating fifteen professorships or chairs, fifteen scholarships or fellowships, and fifteen other endowments.[12] The hope was to raise a total of $3 million by August 31, 1984, which would amount to $6 million after matching funds were added.

In a brochure outlining the school's role in the campaign, Kozmetsky observed that by 1980 the school had a total of twenty-three endowed professorships and chairs, twenty-three endowed scholarships, and $1.8 million in other endowments, such as lectureships, but that these endowments "while substantial, do not meet the college's increasing needs." The school was preparing "to move from excellence to greatness," Kozmetsky wrote. "Such a plan will require a new commitment from our alumni and friends, faculty and students, far beyond that of the past."[13]

Progress toward reaching Kozmetsky's goals was rapid, and they were substantially met by the end of 1981, when gifts and pledges totaled $3.05 million and matching funds stood at $2.89 million, for a total of $5.94 million. The endowed positions to be funded with these gifts included two chairs—one named for Kozmetsky (with the matching funds designated to be used to establish eighteen faculty fellowships) and the Harkins & Company Chair, funded by oilman and University of Texas alumnus H. B. "Hank" Harkins and his company—as well as seventeen professorships, three fellowships and lectureships, and three scholarship funds.[14]

The professorships included one in international management funded with a gift from the Kozmetsky family and named for Fred H. Moore, an oil company executive and a longtime supporter of the University of Texas at Austin and other higher education institutions. Moore retired in Austin in 1967 after a long career at Mobil Oil Co. He served two terms on the Coordinating Board of the Texas College and University System and was on the business school's advisory council. His wide interests often coincided with Kozmetsky's, as when in 1978 he arranged the donation of a Mobil seismographic research ship, the research vessel *Fred H. Moore*, to the university's Marine Science Institute geophysics research program in Galveston.[15]

The fundraising effort for the chair named in honor of Kozmetsky took unusual twists and turns. The goal was to raise $1 million to support the chair, and a committee of some of Kozmetsky's friends was organized in early 1980, without Kozmetsky's knowledge, to lead the effort. The com-

A CIVIC ENTREPRENEUR

mittee had four cochairmen—Sam Barshop, former Texas governor Dolph Briscoe, Dallas attorney and former Republican gubernatorial candidate Paul Eggers, and Houston businessman Charles Hurwitz, a longtime business associate of Kozmetsky. Others on the committee were Perry Bass, the Fort Worth oilman; Ben Love, the Houston banker; Fayez Sarofim, the Houston investor; Charls E. Walker, the former Treasury Department official who had been Harry Ransom's first choice to become dean in the mid-1960s; Glenn Welsch, a professor of accounting at the university; Bonita Wrather, the former film actress who was married to university alumnus and businessman Jack D. Wrather Jr.; and Ronya Kozmetsky and her son Greg.[16]

The cochairmen sent letters to prospects whom they knew, suggesting a donation of $25,000 by individuals and as much as $100,000 each by a few corporations and foundations, and many responded immediately with checks or pledges of at least the suggested amount. Two early pledges of $100,000 each came from Charles Hurwitz's MCO Resources and Datapoint, the San Antonio–based computer pioneer. Kozmetsky served on the boards of both companies, but the pledges were kept secret from him until that summer. The Wrather Corp., led by Kozmetsky's friends Jack and Bonita Wrather, was among several companies that quickly donated $25,000.

Bonita Wrather volunteered to write to Henry Singleton to solicit a contribution from Kozmetsky's old business partner, but she was surprised to be turned down. Kozmetsky was still on the Teledyne board, through which he and Singleton continued to see each other regularly, so Bonita had been confident that Singleton would want to contribute. "I know your pride in George," she wrote to Singleton, "and the fact that he was instrumental in helping you to found one of the great corporations of our country, Teledyne, will certainly make you desire to participate in the chair. The endowment will be for a total of $1 million, and we are sincerely hoping that you will take for Teledyne $100,000 of this commitment."[17]

Singleton responded two weeks later: "We are indeed proud of George and the work that he has done at the university. I wish we could participate in the project. But we have been following a policy here at Teledyne of directing our college and university support to special research and development programs, in areas which are of particular interest to the company. We have turned down many worthwhile opportunities (including some similar to the project for George) in order to maximize our contributions toward specific research and development. I know you will understand that we would find it very difficult to maintain our program if we made an exception in this case."[18]

Jack Wrather then took over the correspondence and tried to shame Singleton into donating:

> I know Bunny has written you about the George Kozmetsky Centennial Chair. . . . You answered her with a turn-down. I know, however, that you must consider your co-founder of Teledyne as a very special person who perhaps would not fit strictly into a precedent situation. Even though your policy of supporting research and development programs is undoubtedly a very valid one . . . I also realize how difficult it is for you to turn down a participation in . . . this chair in honor of George. It would seem to indicate that perhaps the best way out of your dilemma would be to make a personal contribution to the Business School Foundation, as many of the donors are doing. This is, of course, tax deductible. I am enclosing a list of the contributors so far and hope that you will reconsider this, Henry. It is hard to imagine a George Kozmetsky Centennial Chair contributed to in its entirety by people, none of whom have had the close and mutually profitable association with George that you have.[19]

Even this letter produced no results for almost two weeks, and Bonita Wrather was becoming increasingly frustrated. "I am disappointed to say that I haven't heard one single word from Henry Singleton in re Jack's letter to him," she wrote to Barshop. "I have tried to reach him by telephone a couple of times and the answer was, 'Not available.' I feel that Jack's letter was a pretty strong one. However, I, personally, am not very good at a hard sell. I do think pressure being put on him by people such as yourself or Dolph Briscoe just might do the trick, but, quite frankly, he is a pretty tough customer."[20] Such pressure was not necessary, because the next day Jack Wrather received a short note from Singleton saying he would make a personal donation of $10,000 for the chair.[21] (Singleton's net worth was estimated at $100 million by *Forbes* magazine in 1982.[22] That would be $252 million in 2017.)

As some university officials had anticipated when they recruited Kozmetsky to the deanship, George and Ronya became two of the business school's largest and most consistent donors. In 1972–1973, for example, they established a scholarship fund in memory of their youngest son, George M. Kozmetsky, who died in 1972. They made numerous other donations to the business school, including the Ronya and George Kozmetsky Excellence Endowment Fund, which they established in 1975 and later designated to benefit both the Graduate School of Business and the IC^2 Institute. Numerous other endowed positions were funded by the Kozmetskys personally or through their RGK Foundation.

Although they were among the most generous financial supporters of the business school, George and Ronya also were reluctant to give up complete control over their donations. The Kozmetsky endowment fund was created with the stipulation that it not be made part of the University of Texas System's Common Trust Fund (a pool of money from numerous donations) but be separately invested.[23] This would allow the Kozmetskys to track the investment returns of "their" money apart from the overall returns of university system investments. In later years, apparently thinking he could make better decisions than university officials, Kozmetsky sought to gain direct control over the investments related to his donations, but of course the university refused to cede control.[24]

For many years George and Ronya routinely made annual gifts to the business school (in addition to many other special donations to the university), and these gifts were matched by Teledyne and Gulf Oil when George served on their boards. The amounts of these annual gifts varied. In 1977 the gift was $12,000, but in 1978 it was $97,500 (consisting of one thousand shares of Teledyne stock).[25]

In October 1982 Kozmetsky and his family made one of their largest donations to the university—more than $2 million in Teledyne stock to establish twelve fellowships and a lectureship associated with the IC^2 Institute. The gift was doubled with matching funds from the centennial program.

REVISING THE CURRICULUM

As soon as he became dean, Kozmetsky set in motion a series of revisions to the undergraduate and graduate curricula that would dramatically change the classroom experience of students. Continual revisions by curriculum committees are routine, but the extent of the changes grew under Kozmetsky, especially in the early years of his deanship. The influence of Kozmetsky's ideas is evident in the new course of study that emerged from committees. The goals of the revisions included meeting the needs of business management in a time of rapid technological change as well as increasing complexity of "socio-economic systems." A related effort involved exploring new teaching methods using new technologies.

These and other changes in the curriculum took more time than other initiatives over which Kozmetsky had more direct control. Revisions in the curriculum were subject to an often long and cumbersome committee process and required the buy-in of numerous faculty leaders and other

George Kozmetsky, 1972. *Texas Student Publications (Cactus).*

administrators. Kozmetsky was eventually successful in steering this process in the direction he sought, although subsequent deans would abandon many of his innovations (see chapter 9 for details of the underlying principles that guided him in revising the curriculum).

Some of the work of revising the curriculum involved a relatively routine process of adjusting the course requirements to fit the changing times. Thus in 1966–1967 a faculty committee altered the bachelor of business administration program by reducing the sophomore English requirement and adding a course from the humanities or social sciences; dropping a course in "platform speaking" and replacing it with a choice among foreign languages, linguistics, speech, or writing; changing the prerequisites for various courses; and creating a course in business policy.[26]

A CIVIC ENTREPRENEUR

The committee later undertook a study of longer-range issues related to the undergraduates, including whether all students should be required to take courses in the behavioral sciences, business law, and managerial economics.[27] That resulted in an increase in 1968–1969 in behavioral science requirements, as well as a new emphasis on a broad foundation in the liberal arts. New courses in organizational behavior and operations management were instituted, and the overall plan of the business degree was revised with the aim of making it broader, more flexible, and more attractive to students.[28]

In 1971–1972 another committee undertook a review of the bachelor of business administration degree at the university. After an exhaustive study that included surveys of former students and other institutions, the committee recommended changes, adopted in 1973–1974, that strengthened the basic education requirements (English, history, science, etc.) and introduced a required core of upper-division courses in business law, finance, marketing, and management.[29]

Revising the master of business administration (MBA) program began in 1967 when a committee adopted goals that included a broad foundation in behavioral and quantitative concepts; an "effective level of skill" with analytic methods; an understanding of the social, legal, and economic environment within which business operates; and ability in the basic business functions of production, finance, and marketing, with an emphasis on technology and information systems. Courses in the social and managerial problems of technology and information-processing systems were planned.[30] The new program began in 1972 despite resistance from some older faculty. "Kozmetsky fought with the older guys constantly, but he got his way, said Steve Ballantyne, one of the first students in the new program. "They didn't want to change the way they had been teaching for years."[31]

The first year of the MBA program was expanded from thirty hours to thirty-six, and the old core courses were replaced with "core modules" organized in various tracks for each semester. One first-semester track, for example, included courses in computer use, management science, and microeconomics. In the second semester a student might follow a track that included planning and control, communications, and administrative organization. Other modules included data analysis, institutions and management, information flows, individual behavior, group behavior, macro-environmental analysis, social behavior, research design, and capital management. The second year remained at thirty hours, but courses in the old functional areas were supplemented with courses in "emerging areas of management," and students had fewer required courses and more electives, giving them more opportunities to specialize in a particular area.[32]

Another feature of the new MBA curriculum was a required "professional report" (similar to a thesis). This requirement placed an added strain on the school's resources, since two faculty members had to read each report and either approve it or send it back to the student for revision. Year in and year out, Eugene Konecci supervised far more of these reports than any other faculty member, and some of his faculty colleagues became skeptical about how closely he was reading them. In the five academic years from 1971–1972 to 1975–1976, for example, Konecci supervised a total of 145 professional reports, while the next most productive faculty member by this measure was management professor Kenneth W. Olm, who supervised 51 during those years.[33] Many faculty members supervised a half dozen or fewer reports each year. Konecci would have had to have been a speed reader to maintain his level of productivity, but as long as the university was continuing to admit so many MBA students, somebody had to deal with all those reports.

Another major curriculum change was the introduction of an "executive MBA" program, through which people employed full-time in business could obtain an MBA degree by taking classes on weekends. The University of Texas at Austin was slow to introduce this program, lagging behind a nationwide trend that saw a surge in executive education in the early 1970s. The business school faculty approved development of a program in 1978, by which time many other institutions already operated well-established programs. The most prominent of these included programs at Chicago, Pittsburgh, Columbia, Pennsylvania, Stanford, Illinois, Wisconsin, and Southern Methodist University.[34] The lack of a program at the University of Texas was consistent with the university's traditional focus on its statewide educational role and a general aversion to special programs designed to serve mainly Austin. For decades, for example, the university had resisted scheduling classes at night, despite repeated requests from business leaders. Kozmetsky endorsed the effort in the late 1970s to establish an executive education program, but it was not his initiative, with the leadership belonging to Cunningham, one of his associate deans.

The program was delayed by opposition from competing Texas universities as well as state regulators. The opposition was circumvented when Gerhard G. Fonken, vice president for academic affairs under Peter Flawn, devised a plan to characterize the program as merely a "scheduling option" and not a new program requiring higher approval. The "Option II" MBA program began operation in Kozmetsky's last year as dean.[35] Getting a degree under the new plan, which involved classes only on Fridays

A CIVIC ENTREPRENEUR

and Saturdays, was made feasible by a decision of the faculty to allow the dean to waive up to thirty hours of courses for students who had at least five years of full-time managerial experience.[36]

While all these developments were under way, the business school also began phasing out under Kozmetsky a series of secretarial courses that it had taught for decades. As late as 1968, the business school still offered a two-semester "secretarial improvement" course that included secretarial procedures, human relations, and letter writing. The course, taught at one time by Kozmetsky's administrative assistant, Jean Fuquay, was advertised as useful for those seeking to take the Certified Professional Secretary exam, which the university had begun administering in 1955.[37]

INNOVATIONS IN TEACHING

For several years much of the effort to reshape the educational experience of business students was organized around what Kozmetsky called "Project 75," a long-range program for integrating advanced teaching materials and techniques for a revised program of management education for "the new managers in 1975 and beyond."[38]

Project 75 funded faculty initiatives for new curricula and teaching methods. One year these activities included lectures and seminars on Latin American business, a study of cultural influences in management decision-making, a study comparing teaching machines and conventional teaching in the introductory tax course, a simulation game and course text for international business, an international conference on natural resource planning, a study of rate-making models for liability insurance, and an educational technology workshop.

Project 75 also sponsored faculty visits to other institutions to review their advances in curricula and teaching methods, use of new media, and design of new facilities. Another activity was a demonstration for the faculty of Sony's new videocassette technology adapted to classroom use (Sony had begun marketing the world's first commercial videocassette player in 1971). Faculty members were reported to have positive reactions to the technology but were concerned about whether enough content existed to make the equipment worth the cost.

Kozmetsky supported faculty members willing to try innovative teaching methods, and he found that providing even a very small grant could produce big results. Cunningham received one of these grants when he was an assistant professor. "I gave him $120 so that he could buy some tools to make his own slides so he could teach classes of 400," Kozmetsky recalled. "Then he got teaching awards and eventually became president of the university."[39]

A marketing class in an experimental classroom at the business school, 1971. *Texas Student Publications (Cactus).*

STRUGGLING TO CONTROL ENROLLMENT

One of the most troubling issues during Kozmetsky's years as dean was partly a result of the business school's academic successes. As the quality and reputation of the business school were enhanced, enrollment outstripped the school's ability to provide educational services. Beginning at least by the early 1970s, there simply were not enough faculty members, advisers, staff members, and classrooms to meet the demands of all the students who wanted to take business classes.

During most of Kozmetsky's deanship the school was one of the largest, if not the largest, of all business programs in the United States. Despite significant efforts to control enrollment growth, by the fall of 1980, the university's undergraduate business enrollment stood at 10,326, while second-place Baruch College (City University of New York) had 7,362. Arizona State was third with a reported 7,000 undergraduates, and Michigan State was fourth with 6,528. Only three other universities had as many as 5,000 undergraduates—Western Michigan (5,350), Texas A&M (5,283), and San Diego State (5,000). The University of Texas was in third place nationally in master's degree students with 1,125, behind only Harvard (1,535) and the University of Pennsylvania (1,237). The University of Texas was second in doctoral students with 222, behind the University of South Carolina (250).[40]

Enrollment more than doubled during the 1970s, beginning with a total of 5,104 in 1970 (4,577 undergraduates and 527 master's and doctoral students) and rising to a total of 11,673 in 1980 (10,326 undergraduates and 1,347 master's and doctoral students). Undergraduate semester credit hours had grown from 38,798 to 63,189, while graduate school semester credit hours had risen from 5,245 to 12,868. The student-teacher ratio rose from 27.89 to 35.11 during the decade, reflecting a lack of funds for hiring additional faculty to keep pace with growth.[41]

The growth of the business school in the 1970s far outpaced the overall enrollment increase across the university. Kozmetsky observed in the fall of 1979 that the enrollment of University of Texas students majoring in business had grown by 95 percent since 1970, while the total university enrollment had increased by almost 21 percent. The business school had accounted for 63 percent of the total growth in enrollment in those years.[42]

The increases paralleled a broad rise in the number of students at business schools nationwide. The number of MBA degrees awarded annually, for example, had been increasing ever since the end of World War II, but the 1960s and 1970s saw dramatic jumps in MBA production. About 120,000 MBA degrees were awarded nationwide in the 1960s, up from less than 50,000 in the 1950s, but in the 1970s the number soared to almost 400,000. The spectacular nationwide growth in the seventies has been attributed to several factors—a turning away from the antiwar and antiestablishment trends of the 1960s, overcrowding in other professions as more and more members of the baby boom generation pursued higher education, big increases in the number of women going to business school, increases in minority and international students in business programs, and a growing belief (perhaps related to slowdowns in the economy) that a business degree would lead to a successful career and economic security.[43]

For a while, Kozmetsky attempted to deal with enrollment increases with the temporary solution of increasing the size of classes, but he worried about the effect that would have on the quality of instruction, and he understood that large classes could be effective only if they were taught in very different ways from small classes. He also wrote about whether the business school could adapt quickly enough to the pressures created by increased enrollment: "If the traditional methods of teaching are not adjusted to these conditions, the quality of business education can imperceptibly erode. Our faculty has been among the forerunners of newer teaching methods especially for large-sized classes. These advanced developments in the past could be accomplished within our budgetary resources on a course-by-course basis. The continuing increase in overall enrollment makes it imperative that there be an increasing effort to adapt to a larger number of courses and whole programs the newer teaching methods within a very restricted time frame. It is possible that there is already a need to evaluate the possibilities of the beginnings of erosion of the quality of our educational standards."[44]

The question of quantity versus quality preceded Kozmetsky's tenure as dean and would continue to trouble the university for years after he left the deanship. A special committee that helped provide a strategic plan for the university on the occasion of its seventy-fifth anniversary in 1958 had observed: "Bigness and excellence can go hand in hand. However, size has a negative effect on quality when faculty and facilities do not keep pace with the student enrollment and other demands. Future size and scope of the university should be controlled when necessary to achieve the desired levels of quality."[45] Twenty-five years later, the special committee that helped commemorate the University of Texas at Austin centennial offered a similar observation: "The efforts of UT Austin to provide public higher education to all qualified students who want it have caused enrollment to soar. . . . Disturbing signs . . . indicate that unrestricted growth of the student body has stretched existing resources, personnel, and facilities beyond appropriate limits."[46]

Kozmetsky's efforts to deal with the enrollment problem included trying to secure budget increases that would allow him to increase the size of the faculty, building a new home for the Graduate School of Business that more than doubled the amount of space available for business programs, and increasing other services to students. But by the mid-1970s it was clear that a sustained effort was needed to better control the number of students admitted to business programs, as well as the number admitted to the university as a whole. This did not necessarily mean reducing enrollment; rather, the focus was on heading off increases of a dimension that, according to all demographic projections, threatened to overwhelm the business school. Kozmetsky, his assistants, and the business faculty were agreed that without stringent policies of "enrollment management," the school would quickly sink under the weight of its own successes.

Many faculty members and administrators across the campus in the 1970s and 1980s realized that a campus-wide enrollment-management plan was needed to address the problems in the various colleges and schools, but it took several years before a consensus was reached on such a plan—and before statewide political forces accommodated themselves to the new reality of limits on how much the University of Texas at Austin could continue to grow.

The regents had begun trying to control enrollment at least as early as 1970, when measures were taken to limit the number of freshmen and transfer students by adjusting the admissions criteria of test scores and high school rank. These efforts were only partly successful, and some populist regents continued to advocate admission by a lottery system that would disregard tests and high school grades. This policy question had still not been fully resolved by the time Kozmetsky left the deanship.[47]

As the business dean, Kozmetsky had the responsibility of officially presenting the school's enrollment-control proposals for review by campus-wide faculty advisory bodies and approval by the central administration. However, he did not devote a great deal of his own time to formulating these proposals, preferring instead to delegate that responsibility to a standing faculty committee, which was led beginning in 1975 by Cunningham, who at the time was an associate professor of marketing and would in 1976 begin six years of service as Kozmetsky's associate dean for graduate programs. While most of the correspondence with the central administration about enrollment bears Kozmetsky's name, most of the work behind that correspondence was done by Cunningham and his committee. Kozmetsky's strongest qualities included his ability to recognize talented colleagues who merited his trust, to delegate major responsibility to them, to provide them with guidance on policy and objectives, and then largely to stay out of their way. He evidently recognized in Cunningham a talent for building consensus on complex issues such as enrollment management and for representing the business school in various campus forums where business proposals would be debated and evaluated.

The appointment as chairman of the Enrollment Controls Committee was Cunningham's first major administrative assignment, and it quickly led to an increasing reliance by Kozmetsky on Cunningham as one of his key assistants. The enrollment issue was the occasion for Kozmetsky's first major step as a mentor to Cunningham, who went on to succeed him as dean and then to serve as president of the University of Texas at Austin and chancellor of the University of Texas System. The relationship between Kozmetsky and Cunningham was among numerous examples of Kozmetsky's lifelong generosity in cultivating the talents of younger people. He sometimes had trouble finding faculty members willing to work for him in administrative roles, but the people he mentored obviously benefited from the relationship, and Kozmetsky benefited as well, since he was freed from much of the day-to-day task of managing the business school and could thus concentrate on issues that were of more interest to him. Cunningham has joked that when Kozmetsky was dean, he was less interested in the details of running the business school than in focusing on national and global issues, "such as how to reorganize the World Bank."[48]

From the fall of 1966 to the fall of 1975 (when Cunningham became chairman of the enrollment committee), the number of students in the business school had grown by 102 percent (from 3,529 to 7,158), far surpassing the otherwise spectacular 56 percent growth in campus-wide enrollment during those years (from 27,345 to 42,598).[49] By almost all measures—the amount of state appropriations, the number of faculty members, the square footage of classroom space, etc.—the business school and the university had not kept pace with this growth. Cunningham's committee estimated in 1976 that enrollment in the business school would exceed 10,500 by 1980 if nothing were done by the administration to slow the rate of growth.[50]

The first plan developed by the committee, in early 1976, was aimed at cutting enrollment by setting stricter standards on test scores and class rank in high school for admission as a business major. The plan would have ended the university's practice of admitting undergraduate students according to campus-wide standards and then allowing them to select any major that they wanted. The plan died when administrators objected that it was too vague and did not justify the impact it would have on undergraduates beyond the business school.[51]

In the spring of 1977, the committee presented a new proposal, this one for gradually cutting the college's enrollment by some two thousand students by simply requiring a 2.25 overall grade point average (GPA) to take upper-division courses and to graduate, replacing the 2.0 GPA requirement that prevailed for most of the university's programs. Administrators seem to have been attracted by the simplicity of the plan and the fact that it placed no restrictions on freshman admissions, as well as by a precedent for a 2.25 GPA requirement in the College of Education, and this time President Lorene Rogers gave her approval. The plan went into effect for students entering in the fall of 1979.[52]

By the fall of 1979, however, it had become clear that the limit of a 2.25 GPA would not be enough to control business school enrollment. Cunningham's committee then proposed increasing the minimum GPA for students to take business courses to 2.50 and creating a classification of "pre-business" students who would be fully admitted to the undergraduate program (taking courses in what was called a "professional sequence") only if they successfully completed twenty-seven hours of certain introductory courses.[53] Earlier that year, Rogers had asked administrators to

Lorene Rogers, president of UT Austin from 1974 to 1979. *Texas Student Publications (Cactus).*

make recommendations for a comprehensive, campus-wide plan—a process that continued when Flawn succeeded Rogers in September 1979.[54]

Numerous plans continued to be debated for the next year and a half, and by 1980 Kozmetsky was describing the enrollment problem as creating "a state of emergency" for the business school. He was hoping to expedite changes in admissions policies and to forestall threats by the American Assembly of Collegiate Schools of Business, which was considering placing the school on probation because of its high student-faculty ratio and other factors.[55]

President Flawn accepted the claim of an emergency, and in early 1981 he approved a series of "temporary" enrollment-control measures for the business school. The plan included scheduling preferences for graduating seniors, restrictions on the number of students transferring from other institutions, and elimination of all foreign and out-of-state undergraduate admissions to the business school for 1981–1982.[56] Later that spring the university approved a requirement for a GPA of at least 2.50 for enrollment in upper division business courses. Cunningham and others were convinced that without these measures the school would have lost its accreditation by 1982.[57]

The business school's efforts to manage its enrollment were often opposed by the College of Liberal Arts because of a fear that students who would otherwise enroll in the business school would begin flooding liberal arts classes, on the theory that most students would prefer to have a bachelor's degree in any field from the University of Texas at Austin rather than transfer to another Texas university where they could get a degree in business. Some people opposed any reforms for the business school unless they were part of a campus-wide plan, but Kozmetsky and Cunningham argued that faster action was needed because of the business school's looming accreditation problem.

Kozmetsky was adept at winning sympathy for the business school from Robert D. King, who became dean of the College of Liberal Arts in 1979 and had been dean of the university's short-lived College of Social and Behavioral Sciences for three years before that,[58] thus overlapping as dean with the last six years of Kozmetsky's deanship. King said Kozmetsky had made a special effort to see how the interests of the liberal arts college and the business school could be aligned. Kozmetsky's outreach was unusual among the deans, King said, because the actions of John Silber, the controversial dean of the old College of Arts and Sciences, had "poisoned the well" for liberal arts among other deans.[59]

"I liked the way George dealt with the enrollment problem," King said. "After Silber, the other deans disliked liberal arts and were suspicious of it. All the other deans mistrusted me at first. But unlike some of the other deans, George cared about the liberal arts. He came to me [in 1979] about the enrollment problem, and after a while George and I became buddies. He called me up and invited me over to his office, and I listened to what he had to say, and for the first time I became aware of his enrollment problems. He said the president and provost would not let him deal with the problems directly, so he proposed that we figure out a way to work together."[60]

Kozmetsky's idea was to "farm out" some of his students to the College of Liberal Arts, where they could take courses in statistics and business ethics and other courses required of the business school by the accrediting agency—courses that could be taught by liberal arts departments such as economics, psychology, sociology, political science, and philosophy.

"He said, 'You've got the teachers but not enough majors in some of those subjects, while I have an enrollment problem and not enough teachers,'" King recalled. "George, in a nice way, was saying to me that

Robert D. King, dean of the College of Liberal Arts, in 1980. *Texas Student Publications (Cactus).*

he thought we could cut a deal here. Let students take statistics in the psychology or sociology department and take ethics in the philosophy department, and phase out those subjects in the business school. I said, 'George, the deal is done.' He and I ganged up on the administrators, who always seemed to say no to a solution to our problems."[61]

After Kozmetsky stepped down, additional changes to the enrollment system were adopted under Cunningham and then the next dean, Robert E. Witt—changes which together provided a longer-term solution.[62] Eventually the school became much more selective in its admissions, and enrollment was reduced significantly. In recent years the total has been about 5,500, with only about 1,100 MBA students.[63]

CHAPTER 12

TRANSFORMING THE BUSINESS SCHOOL IV

Budget Crises and Other Challenges

In September 1967, the day after Kozmetsky sent Harry Ransom and Norman Hackerman a list of endowed faculty positions he wanted to establish and the people he hoped to recruit to fill those positions (see chapter 10), Kozmetsky presented to Hackerman, who had just become president of the university, a formidable list of budget requirements of the business school for the next five years. The funds were necessary, he said, "in order to continue the transition . . . towards becoming one of the five best schools of business." His plan included a major expansion of administrative positions within the dean's office, which had been operating with only a part-time associate dean. Kozmetsky wanted to turn that into a full-time position to handle administrative details, while adding associate deans to deal with undergraduate and graduate affairs. Concerned about the business school's high student-faculty ratio as well as the need to expand the curriculum, he also proposed budget increases that would allow adding thirteen faculty positions from 1968 to 1970, including two positions for "distinguished senior faculty," five visiting professors (with the possibility of recruiting them to permanent jobs), and six new positions for assistant professors.

Kozmetsky also proposed establishing a Research Center for Management of Intellectual and Technological Resources, which he envisioned as a vehicle for recruiting senior faculty members and helping develop the younger faculty. In his first year as dean, Kozmetsky had provided $40,000 (almost $300,000 in 2017) of his own money for this kind of research, the expansion of which, he told Hackerman, "will make our college preeminent in the 1970s and will make it possible to 'leap ahead' rather than follow a practice of 'catch up.'"[1]

The new funds that Kozmetsky was requesting totaled $392,000 a year.

He also briefly discussed two capital projects (without cost estimates)—renovation of current administrative space in the Business-Economics Building and the need for a new building "by 1970." Apparently this was Kozmetsky's first mention to Hackerman of the building that would become the home of the Graduate School of Business. The building faced numerous delays and obstacles; it was not authorized by the regents until 1972 and did not open until 1975.[2]

This list of budget needs appears to be the first of a continuing series of such memos that Kozmetsky sent to administrators. A recurring theme of these memos and the responses that he received from a succession of vice presidents and presidents is that there was not enough money to achieve all his plans. Hackerman's immediate response to Kozmetsky's plans in 1967 was thoroughly noncommittal. He merely told Kozmetsky he would discuss the new budget items "when we have more information about the budget" and advised him to discuss the capital projects with the Faculty Building Advisory Committee "as soon as possible."[3]

Correspondence between Kozmetsky and his administrative superiors throughout his years as dean generally follows the pattern of this early exchange with Hackerman. Kozmetsky's expansive and dramatic proposals are sometimes met with demurral, but the prevailing response is one of caution, as administrators deflect Kozmetsky's vision and enthusiasm into the institution's more routine bureaucratic processes. This was not unusual for the relationship between deans and higher-ups, although Kozmetsky had an unusual mandate for broad and rapid improvement in the business school's academic quality. Almost all of Kozmetsky's conflict with administrators over the budget and other issues was carried on behind the scenes.

Budget Problems of the 1970s

The business school faced a series of budget problems that arose either from enrollment increases or inadequate state appropriations, or both. From the fall of 1970 through 1973, the budgets were fairly stable, but increases in enrollment had resulted in a decline in state allocations per student from $76 to $68. The biggest drop was in the Department of Accounting, where state allocations per student fell from $69 to $58.[4] Through the rest of the 1970s and into the early 1980s, the school struggled to provide enough faculty members to teach all the classes needed to meet the demands of the burgeoning enrollment. A related problem was finding the money to counteract offers of employment that other universities were making to some of the school's most prominent faculty members. Pressure on the school in the late 1970s from its national accrediting organization was a strong incentive to improve the student-faculty ratio and other measurements. The University of Texas had been, in 1916, one of the founding members of the accrediting agency, the American Assembly of Collegiate Schools of Business, and the loss of its stamp of approval would have been a serious blow to the school's academic reputation.

These financial problems arose despite steady growth—in some years quite large increases—in the school's budget. Most state appropriations were based on formulas that allocated funds according to the number of semester credit hours taught and a variety of other measures, so state appropriations would increase, at least in theory, as enrollment and other factors increased. The legislature typically reduced the portion of the formula-driven amounts that were actually funded, and in any case there were complaints that the formulas as devised were inadequate to meet the needs of University of Texas academic programs. The business school's budget was also composed of money from tuition and fees, research grants and contracts, and other sources, but much of this revenue was designated for purposes other than faculty salaries. This helps explain why the school experienced a shortage of faculty and difficulty in retaining some of its best faculty members even though the overall budget kept rising.

In the late 1960s, before the biggest increases in enrollment, Kozmetsky persuaded Hackerman of the advantages of increasing class sizes in the business school because that would allow taking money that had been allocated to faculty salaries and using some of it to pay faculty in the summer to develop new courses, and it would allow the school to spend money to upgrade its computer facilities. "Thank goodness we had Norman Hackerman as president. . . . That is how we got the [new] computer in the business school and how we began building up some of the new things," Kozmetsky said later. "It takes time to do that. We have used our savings and invested in new projects."[5] Increasingly in the 1970s, however, different budget strategies were needed because class sizes were about as high as they could be, given the available classroom space, and because of growing national competition for faculty.

The records of the president's office are replete with long letters from Kozmetsky with details of budget problems and, more often than not, replies from the provost or the president that no more money would be available until after the next legislative session, if then. Kozmetsky tended to persist in the face of these negative responses, as if he believed that by complaining loud enough and long enough he could pry loose more money for the benefit of the business school. Sometimes this complaining succeeded with Hackerman, but after he left the presidency in 1970, his immediate successors (Bryce Jordan, 1970–1971; Stephen Spurr,

Stanley R. Ross, provost under President Stephen Spurr, 1971. *Texas Student Publications (Cactus).*

1971–1974; and Lorene Rogers, 1974–1979) were generally less amenable to Kozmetsky's budget requests.

One of the most serious waves of budget problems arose in 1973 as the business school began to experience the ill effects of steep enrollment increases. Undergraduate enrollment rose by 13 percent from 1970 to 1973, while enrollment in master's programs grew by 17 percent. Some departments saw much steeper increases than the average. In accounting, for example, undergraduate enrollment surged by 58 percent. Faced with budget shortages across the campus, President Spurr advised deans that they should find money for merit raises by eliminating unfilled faculty positions, but Kozmetsky found this approach inadequate. Increasing the size of the faculty was, for Kozmetsky, the only good answer to the problem. The alternatives were limits on enrollment, closing academic programs, or continuing to increase class sizes (although he said that would be difficult because of a shortage of large classrooms).[6]

These arguments seemed to have little effect on Spurr and his provost, Stanley R. Ross, perhaps because the financial resources available to them were inadequate, but it also appears from their correspondence that they doubted the problems were as severe as Kozmetsky said. The best Ross could recommend was for Kozmetsky to use more teaching assistants in small-group discussion sections as a way of dealing with the negative effects of increased class sizes. "When I suggested this to George, he gave me a typically flamboyant statement rejecting my idea, and stating that he had come up with the best teaching program anywhere," Ross wrote.[7]

Kozmetsky and other deans were generally not on good terms with Ross, who also served under Lorene Rogers. The deans felt that Ross had an outsized ego, and Kozmetsky thought actions by Ross, whose field was Latin American history, demonstrated that he had little regard for business education.[8]

Later that year, Spurr did transfer money from a reserve account to provide special merit raises for four of six faculty members that Kozmetsky had said were most deserving, but no overall solution to the budget problems was forthcoming.[9]

Spurr was dismissed by the regents in 1974 and was succeeded by Lorene Rogers, who served for the next five years. Rogers was a controversial president, partly because faculty members objected to the regents' procedures in hiring her. She tangled over many issues with faculty and deans, including Kozmetsky, and on one occasion the faculty gave her a vote of no-confidence. Rogers's successor, Peter T. Flawn, said Kozmetsky was "the leader among the deans" who had helped organize a deans' group that met separately from the routine meetings of the official deans' council with the president. "Rogers didn't like it," Flawn said.[10]

The budget and enrollment problems continued during most of the Rogers years, and Kozmetsky was usually disappointed in the responses of Rogers and her new vice president for academic affairs, William L. Hays.[11] In early 1979, the administration approved six new business faculty positions at an average starting salary of $19,000, but Kozmetsky noted that schools against which the University of Texas was competing were paying salaries as high as $22,000 to recruit new PhDs. The salary problem was exacerbated because even more money was needed to hire and keep tenured faculty for the growing graduate programs. Kozmetsky also complained that the administration had not addressed other pressing needs of the business school, such as renovation projects to provide more faculty office space. "Bill, when one has greatly exceeded the capacity of his faculty, facilities, and staff resources, incremental and piecemeal solutions are not adequate," Kozmetsky wrote in one typically exasperated letter to Hays.[12]

Embedded in all these interactions was Kozmetsky's general lack of confidence in the judgment of Rogers and her first two vice presidents

Kozmetsky with Gerhard Fonken, an administrator during the terms of seven presidents at the University of Texas at Austin. He was the chief academic officer during Kozmetsky's last years as dean of the business school. *Photo by Dan Kallick, University Photography Services.*

for academic affairs, Ross and Hays—feelings that were widely shared by other deans.[13] Kozmetsky had much better relations with Hays's successor, Gerhard Fonken, and the difficult relations with the central administration that had characterized much of Kozmetsky's early years as dean were greatly improved under Flawn, who kept Fonken in his administration as vice president for academic affairs and research.

When Flawn became president in September 1979, Kozmetsky continued to argue forcefully for increased funds for hiring new faculty, providing more competitive salaries, and meeting other needs. Under Flawn and Fonken, Kozmetsky had somewhat better success than under the previous administrations. His main arguments continued to be that the student-faculty ratio had risen so high (from 20 in 1965 to 38 in 1979) that the school did not have "the resources that are required to provide a first-class education"; that the school was unable to compete for faculty; and that the school's accreditation was in jeopardy. By 1979, an accreditation review said the school was seventeen faculty members short of the number needed to meet national standards.[14]

Some relief came in December 1979 when Flawn approved an allocation of $196,800 for merit raises, but Kozmetsky quickly replied that he needed $81,000 more to keep from falling further behind other universities. He told Flawn that average starting salaries nationally for assistant professors with new doctorates were in most cases higher than what the University of Texas was paying assistant professors who had been on the faculty for four years.[15] The money that Flawn was able to provide helped some, but not enough to keep up with the competition, Kozmetsky said. As he wrote to Flawn: "By the time we extended our first offers to candidates, it became obvious that our offers—although $1–2,000 higher than last year—were too low to attract the five to ten better Ph.D. candidates from the 15 first-tier universities from which we recruit our faculty."[16] Flawn approved additional increases the next year, allowing the school to offer as much as $26,000 for new PhDs in accounting and finance and slightly less for new faculty in other fields. Fonken advised Kozmetsky that further relief was anticipated after the 1981 legislative session, when it was hoped that a special allocation of $200,000 for raises would be possible.[17]

Faculty Retention Problems

Given these long-running budget problems, it was not surprising that the business school sometimes had trouble keeping faculty members who were targets for recruiting by other universities. Kozmetsky said that in his first ten years as dean, the school had not lost, "in any significant numbers," any faculty members whom it wanted to keep, but that record began to change by 1977. Many other distinguished universities—or institutions that aspired to enhancing their academic standing—were paying new and experienced faculty members much more than the University of Texas, and they were often offering higher academic ranks, more research money, lower teaching loads, and other benefits. Kozmetsky sent Hays long letters in the spring of 1977 with details of offers that other institutions had made to some of his most accomplished faculty members.

Sometimes the problem was a refusal by the central administration to approve a promotion. One such case, involving marketing faculty member William H. Cunningham, was discussed in chapter 10, but there were many others. Some within Rogers's administration were concerned that Kozmetsky was recommending promotions at a pace that was out of line with the practice in other University of Texas colleges and schools. That was the opinion of Irwin C. Lieb, vice president and dean of graduate studies, who urged Rogers "to bring promotions in the College of Business Administration into consonance with the promotion schedule in the other colleges."[18]

A Civic Entrepreneur

Irwin C. Lieb, vice president and dean of graduate studies in the 1970s. *Texas Student Publications (Cactus).*

That was the reason given for denying a promotion to Barry Cushing, an associate professor of accounting, who was described by his chairman, Ed Summers, as "our most outstanding associate professor." Cushing left the university in 1977 for the University of Utah, which offered him a professorship, research money, and a smaller teaching load than at the University of Texas. Kozmetsky wrote to Hays in early 1977 about Cushing's case, as well as examples of at least fifteen other faculty members (in accounting, marketing, finance, and other fields) who were being courted by other universities. At least five of those decided to leave the university, accepting offers from such varied employers as the University of Oklahoma, Emory University, Southern Methodist University, Oak Ridge National Laboratory, and International Paper Company.

"I do not think we have seen the end of the raiding of our faculty for this year and perhaps the next two to three years," Kozmetsky wrote. "We will have difficulty staffing our classrooms under any workload if we cannot make the appropriate adjustment in salaries and starting rates. We respectfully request your timely reply. Time is of the essence. To date, I have asked individual faculty members to withhold their decision making or resignations over the next few weeks in the hope that we can make the appropriate counter-offers."[19]

William L. Hays, vice president for academic affairs under President Lorene Rogers. *Texas Student Publications (Cactus).*

In the midst of these offers and counteroffers, Hays wrote a plaintive letter to Rogers about his inability to provide Kozmetsky with a solution to the problem: "I know that experience has taught you, as it has me, to be somewhat skeptical of cries of alarm that come from the academic units from time to time about the dangers of losing their faculty. . . . [However,] my considered opinion is that the College of Business Administration is extremely vulnerable at this time to raiding at various levels. I am constantly being pressed by George Kozmetsky and his faculty for some sort of response to these communications, but I fear I have very little in the way of encouragement to offer. I wish I had a definite recommendation to make, but I do not."[20]

On the same day, Hays responded to a request from Kozmetsky for at least $230,000 in new funds for 1977–1978 for salary increases to meet the competition: "You are probably correct in your assessment of the salary increase moneys that would be required to restore a measure of stability to this situation. Frankly, however, in this appropriations year so far I

A CIVIC ENTREPRENEUR

have seen no signs that this sort of money is going to become available. In fact, the best word we have received is to look for little or no increase money at all. Being a natural optimist, I still hope that things will turn out better than that, but hope is a pretty weak basis for making firm commitments. President Rogers is aware of these problems and of your deep concerns. I am sure she is going to do everything in her power to try to resist these losses."[21]

There were some cases in which everyone concerned realized that the loss of a particular faculty member would do lasting harm to the university. One of those instances concerned Darwin Klingman, the temperamental computer expert and professor of management science whom Kozmetsky had sought to pacify in 1980. In 1982 Texas A&M offered Klingman an endowed chair and reduced teaching duties, as well as ample time on the university's mainframe computer, with a terminal in Klingman's office (an unusual arrangement at that time).[22]

Kozmetsky, Flawn, Fonken, and others were united in the effort to make a counteroffer that would lead Klingman to resist Texas A&M. A raise of almost 25 percent was part of the counteroffer. The University of Texas also provided $4,000 in computer time, and Kozmetsky promised that "should you need additional computer time, I will gladly entertain any additional request." Kozmetsky also named Klingman to chair the business school's faculty computer committee, and Klingman immediately began an ambitious plan to expand the school's computing equipment for student and faculty use. Klingman also was named to the committee that would plan the renovation of the business school's buildings, and he received Kozmetsky's endorsement for a research institute in the emerging field of decision support systems. This package satisfied Klingman.[23]

STRUGGLES WITH THE BUREAUCRACY

Kozmetsky's relationships with key members of the university's central administration were often strained, partly because of an inclination by administrators to micromanage some of the decisions that one might expect to be handled at a lower level, and partly because Kozmetsky had little interest in bureaucratic procedures, however necessary they might be in managing public funds and satisfying legislators. He also seemed to have little understanding of or interest in the intricacies of academic politics. "He didn't want to play the game," said Isabella Cunningham. "He was bigger than that."[24]

Kozmetsky's disputes with President Rogers were more frequent than any problems he faced with her predecessors or successors. Rogers, who served as interim president in the 1974–1975 academic year and then president until 1979, was unpopular with many faculty members and students and was perceived by some as overbearing and sometimes arbitrary in her decisions.

Much decision-making at the university was decentralized, but sometimes minute matters required complex bureaucratic procedures and approvals from above—whether because of state law, rules made by the regents, or the predilection of administrators in the Main Building. When he first arrived at the university, Kozmetsky would have been struck at once by the fact that the university was organized in a very different way from the decentralized, "free-form" structure of Teledyne. The contrast with entrepreneurial decision-making was often dramatic.

Examples of micromanagement were wide-ranging. In one case a dean needed approval from the university president to spend fifty dollars on an educational film.[25] In another, Chancellor Harry Ransom himself supervised payments to a feedstore for the upkeep of Bevo, the longhorn steer that was the university's mascot.[26] In the business school Kozmetsky's assistant, Seymour Schwartz, needed the president's permission, under a rule promulgated by the regents, to charge students five cents a copy to use the Xerox machine in the dean's office and put the money in a special account.[27]

Kozmetsky could run afoul of the university's procedures at almost any turn, and some of his greatest difficulties involved working with Rogers, often on detailed matters far removed from the level of strategic planning on which he preferred to focus. In 1976 he asked Rogers for approval to produce and sell to students a programmed instruction manual for a course involving computer use. The plan worried Rogers. "We are very much of the opinion that if we set up such revolving funds and start selling materials to students, we will soon find ourselves in real difficulty with the legislature," she wrote, suggesting that Kozmetsky have the manual produced and sold by the campus bookstore, as other departments were supposed to be doing.[28]

On other occasions, there seemed to be no particular rule against what Kozmetsky wanted to do, but Rogers opposed him anyway, as when he wanted to employ a temporary worker to organize the elaborate dedication ceremony for the Graduate School of Business, including the handling of such details as thank-you notes to the participants. Rogers rejected this plan and informed Kozmetsky that one of the people in her office would handle the event.[29]

Sometimes a dispute with Rogers involved a much more serious matter, as with irregularities that she found in a 1977 contract between the business school and Sonatrach, the large, Algerian state-owned oil and gas company. Rogers complained that the contract, for consulting services provided by faculty members, was not drawn up until well after the work had begun. She was also upset about the amount of "overhead" costs that the university could recover under the contract, and she believed the job descriptions in the contract had been manipulated to reduce the recoverable costs. (The overhead payments in a research or consulting contract are designed to allow a university to recover indirect expenses associated with a project, such as the cost of utilities and office space.) University of Texas System officials approved the contract on the condition that the indirect costs be computed differently in future contracts. Rogers testily informed Kozmetsky that she had signed the contract but did so reluctantly. "Would you . . . make sure that in the future such contracts are submitted for approval well before the beginning date," she wrote.[30] The sentence is phrased as a question, but Rogers's omission of a question mark is revealing.

A major conflict arose over Kozmetsky's plan in 1977 to create an external foundation for handling some donations to the business school. At the time, the only other external foundation at the University of Texas was associated with the School of Law. Rogers strenuously objected to Kozmetsky's proposal. She was uncomfortable with the idea of external foundations, which were independent nonprofit entities, because the university lacked control over their operations, and she wanted to prevent other colleges and schools at the university, such as business and engineering, from copying the law school. As legally separate entities, external foundations were not subject to state and regental regulations governing public agencies and institutions. This gave them certain advantages over state-controlled entities, such as freedom to invest their funds and disburse the proceeds without regard to state or university limitations. This very freedom was one of the reasons that Rogers was concerned, but it was also one of the main appeals of an external foundation for Kozmetsky, who tended to think the state was a poor manager of its investment assets and wanted to make his own decisions about how to use donated funds. Proponents of an external foundation said it would have more success in appealing to some major donors.

Rogers and others in her administration worried that Kozmetsky, working with the directors of the external foundation, would be able to provide salary supplements and other support for faculty members outside the usual procedures and standards established for the campus—and outside the supervision of the president. "When there is internal control of salary levels," Rogers wrote to Allan Shivers, chairman of the regents, "the amount of each individual salary is arrived at through a set of checks and balances involving departmental budget councils, department chairmen, deans, vice presidents, and the president, with subsequent review and concurrence of the [chancellor] of the UT System and the Board of Regents. In cases where an external foundation exists . . . the whole process of trying to arrive at fair and equitable levels of compensation can be misdirected. Not only is this unfair to other individuals in the university, but the practice is subject to . . . abuse and generates major internal management problems."[31]

Rogers was also concerned about losing centralized control over fundraising and feared that an external business school foundation would approach donors without coordinating its activities with the university's overall fundraising program and without regard for the fundraising priorities of the president.[32]

Kozmetsky's plan had strong support from members of the advisory council of the business school's internal foundation, particularly James Bayless, then president of Rauscher Pierce Securities Corp. in Dallas, who took the lead in working with attorneys and others in setting up the new entity and helping Kozmetsky allay the concerns of University of Texas System officials.[33]

The proposal was considered by the regents at their meeting in Tyler on November 11, 1977. Although it was clear that Shivers, always one of Kozmetsky's strongest allies, and other regents were prepared to approve Kozmetsky's plan, Rogers spoke against it at the meeting. This may be the only known example of a University of Texas at Austin president and dean openly taking opposite sides of a proposal before the regents. Rogers was described as angrily expressing her opposition to Kozmetsky's proposal as the regents sat in silence. "I don't see how you can give a president responsibility for the whole institution and then make it possible for one unit in that institution to operate outside all of the university policies and procedures," Rogers told the board. In the end, the regents voted unanimously for the external foundation, known simply as the Business School Foundation.[34]

"George greased the skids on that proposal with the chairman of the board of regents," said Kozmetsky's friend Robert D. King. "Rogers knew her term was coming to an end. She had the guts to get up and speak against it at the regents meeting, knowing she was going to lose."[35]

Rogers received support from the *Daily Texan*, which said in an editorial that Kozmetsky's "charismatic personality and proven abilities" probably persuaded the regents to vote for his plan, but that "the structures of a great university cannot be built around or reformed for outstanding personalities. The foundation will continue long after Dean Kozmetsky leaves office."[36]

Kozmetsky might have faced opposition on one occasion from Frank Erwin, the powerful chairman of the regents from 1966 to 1971 (he was on the board from 1963 to 1975). Kozmetsky's name was mentioned in connection with the turmoil that surrounded Erwin's firing of the dean of the College of Arts and Sciences, John Silber, in 1970. In the aftermath of the firing, the university campus was swirling with rumors, including talk about who might be named to replace President Hackerman, who was leaving to become president of Rice University. Kozmetsky was among other university deans who were rumored to be in danger of losing their jobs. The Austin newspaper reported on a wire service story that suggested Kozmetsky could be fired soon, along with Alan Taniguchi, dean of the School of Architecture, and Page Keeton, dean of the School of Law. In Kozmetsky's case, the report had quoted an unnamed source as saying that Erwin objected to Kozmetsky's fundraising trips around the state (a report that seems suspect, given Kozmetsky's overall strong support from the board). Chancellor-elect Charles A. LeMaistre and University of Texas at Austin president ad interim Bryce Jordan responded to the wire service story by saying, "There is no truth to the rumor that other deans at UT Austin will be removed." The rumors then fell out of the news.[37]

Opportunities for Women and Minorities

Kozmetsky served as dean during a period of dramatic new demands for educational opportunities for women and members of ethnic minorities. The enrollment of women surged in the business school during the Kozmetsky years, as it did across most of the campus, as a result of society-wide social and economic forces. Some professional programs, such as the nation's engineering schools, found it necessary to institute special recruitment programs in an effort to attract women to fields that had previously been unwelcoming, but business schools had no such difficulty in attracting female students. The situation was quite different at the University of Texas at Austin, including at the business school, with regard to attracting African American and Hispanic students, for whom a series of affirmative-action recruitment and retention programs were begun in the 1970s.

The dramatic growth in enrollment of women at the business school reflected large-scale changes in the status of women that happened to coincide with Kozmetsky's deanship. In the summer of 1966, just as Kozmetsky was moving to Austin to begin work as dean, the National Organization for Women was created in a Washington, DC, hotel room rented by Betty

Friedan. Many of the women who met with Friedan were attending a White House conference on the status of women, organized partly out of frustration with the way the federal bureaucracy was failing to enforce provisions of the 1964 Civil Rights Act pertaining to women. The National Organization for Women was one response to increasing demands by women for greater social and economic opportunity—a movement that quickly overwhelmed almost all aspects of society, including higher education.

Kozmetsky often proclaimed himself a feminist who welcomed the new opportunities for women,[38] and, indeed, he had shown himself to be an advocate for women's education since at least his years as a teacher at Radcliffe College. During his earliest years as dean, however, he followed a much more traditional or paternalistic approach, even organizing, with the help of his wife, Ronya, a graduate student wives club.[39] By the mid-1970s, many of these wives had become students themselves at the business school. In those days the school also had a faculty wives club, which held teas and other social events.

As opportunities for women increased across the country, women not only began enrolling in business schools in larger numbers but also began to take leadership roles at those schools. In 1972, Kozmetsky appointed the business school's first female department chair, Elizabeth Lanham, who led the management department through 1977. Lanham earned MBA and doctoral degrees from the University of Texas at Austin and began teaching personnel management and organizational behavior in 1947, becoming the school's first female professor.[40] Also early in the 1970s, Kozmetsky supported the membership of the first two women on the advisory council of the business school's foundation—Nancy B. Negley (whose family controlled Brown & Root) and Margaret Scarbrough Wilson (president of Scarbrough's Department Store of Austin).[41]

In 1969, the year the student wives club was organized, George and Ronya also began teaching a noncredit Executive Futures Seminar for graduate business students and their spouses, focusing on practical issues of raising a family when one of the adults is pursuing a high-stress and time-consuming career in business management. Much of the course in the early years was oriented around the idea that the wife would be staying at home while the husband pursued a business career,[42] but it later incorporated the possibility that the wife could be the business executive. In imparting advice to the students, the Kozmetskys drew heavily on their own experiences from the years when George worked at Hughes, Litton, and Teledyne. After twelve years of teaching the seminar, they gathered much of their advice into a book, *Making It Together: A Survival Manual for the Executive Family* (Free Press, 1981), which was mostly written by Ronya.[43]

A CIVIC ENTREPRENEUR

Elizabeth Lanham, the first woman to chair a department at the business school, 1973. *Texas Student Publications (Cactus).*

Ronya Kozmetsky also was responsible for several other activities at the business school in support of opportunities for women, including serving as an adviser to the graduate student wives club and meeting regularly with the spouses of faculty members. Friends and colleagues established the Ronya Kozmetsky Centennial Lectureship for Women in Business in her honor in 1983 to bring business leaders to the campus to present lectures that would be "meaningful in terms of advancing the knowledge [and] providing encouragement and role models of future women managers." Bonita Granville Wrather, the Kozmetskys' friend from Los Angeles who served on the school's advisory council, chaired the fundraising campaign for the lectureship.[44]

Members of minority groups had been lobbying for some form of affirmative action in University of Texas admissions since the mid-1960s, but little was done until the next decade. As early as 1967, President Hackerman received a request from Mexican American members of the legislature to relax admission standards for minority students to take into account deficiencies in the state's public school system. "We recommend that members of minority groups be admitted without qualification, other than graduation from high school, for their first two semesters; and that, if on the basis of early examination they are found to have academic deficiencies, appropriate remedial programs be instituted for the University," the legislators wrote. Hackerman referred the proposal to the university's Educational Policy Committee, and nothing more was heard of it. In the late 1970s, the university adopted a "provisional admissions program" that incorporated some features of the earlier proposal.[45] The business school, of course, participated in this program, but Kozmetsky appears not to have taken a position on it.

In 1969, Kozmetsky helped establish one of the business school's first minority-oriented programs—the Community Business Advisory Program, through which student volunteers advised minority-owned small businesses on bookkeeping, marketing strategies, loan applications, and other tasks. Founded by graduate students Steven Estrin and John Burnham, the program began as a way to help black and Hispanic entrepreneurs in East Austin manage their businesses more effectively. [46] The Mobil Oil Foundation gave a grant to the program in 1970, and the Small Business Administration became a partner with the program in 1972.[47]

The university placed much more emphasis on trying to increase minority enrollment under the administration of President Flawn and his successors than it had in previous years, but Kozmetsky rarely addressed the issue publicly. In his detailed annual reports of activities at the business school, as well as in his many speeches, Kozmetsky was mostly silent on the subject of minority opportunity in business education, although he did encourage, in the mid-1970s, the creation of a Black Business Student Association and a Chicano Business Student Association to provide greater cohesion among minority students.[48] He also helped persuade donors to support minority opportunity at the business school. One of those was Sam Barshop, founder of La Quinta Motor Inns and a member of the school's advisory council, who in 1978 endowed two scholarships for Hispanic or black students. Barshop wrote to Kozmetsky about the donation: "Our entire state will benefit by encouraging bright young people of ethnic minority backgrounds to become business-oriented, and we trust this program of grants will be of some assistance in such a long-range goal."[49]

The next year Kozmetsky and the Business School Foundation provided matching grants for an endowed scholarship fund for Mexican American business students. Students at the business school and in the student senate contributed money to the endowment and helped raise contributions from minority-owned businesses and others.[50] Another initiative at the school was participation in LEAD (Leadership Education and

Development), a national summer program to encourage minority high school students to pursue higher education in business. The University of Texas business school joined the program in November 1980 after LEAD began at the Wharton School of Finance. Other major business schools, such as those at Northwestern University and the University of Michigan, soon joined the effort.[51]

Such initiatives to expand minority opportunity were part of the university's response to the long-running federal desegregation lawsuit *Adams v. Richardson*,[52] which was filed by the NAACP to try to make the federal government enforce the provision of the 1964 Civil Rights Act that required an end to segregation at higher education institutions. The case, which applied to Texas and other states with a history of segregated colleges and universities, led in the late 1970s to the first in a series of plans, supervised by a federal court and developed with the US Office of Civil Rights, to increase the representation of African American and Hispanic students in Texas universities. During the last years of Kozmetsky's deanship, he and other university administrators were involved in carrying out the first of those desegregation plans by developing programs to promote recruitment and retention of minority students.

While Kozmetsky was dean, one of the official goals under a resolution from the Board of Regents, adopted in connection with the desegregation plan, was to strive to reduce by 50 percent the disparity between the proportions of African American and Hispanic high school graduates and the proportion of white high school graduates entering undergraduate study at Texas universities. Despite many affirmative-action programs at the business school and across the university, that goal was never reached. Other goals set by the regents were less specific—to achieve an annual increase in undergraduate, graduate, and professional programs for minorities and to reduce the disparity in graduation rates between minority and nonminority students. There, too, progress was hard to achieve (see enrollment data in chapter 9).[53]

New Facilities for the Business School

For the first nine and a half years that Kozmetsky was dean, the business school's only classroom and office space was in the Business-Economics Building (now named the College of Business Administration, or CBA) on the northwest corner of Twenty-First Street and Speedway, a building that the school shared with the large Department of Economics, which was a unit of the College of Liberal Arts. As enrollment and the size of the faculty grew, along with increasing demands for space for computers, research assistants, and student services, the need for additional facilities became a critical problem. Kozmetsky had predicted to Norman Hackerman as early as 1967 that a second building would be needed as the business school expanded its operations, and he had originally hoped the new building could open by 1970, but planning for a new facility was slow to begin—delayed by funding problems and the university's other priorities. Planning finally got started in 1970, and regents approved the new building in 1972, to be built on a site adjacent to the Business-Economics Building.[54]

The new home of the Graduate School of Business and related offices opened in the fall of 1975 and was dedicated, with much fanfare, on March 26, 1976. The building, with a main entrance on Twenty-First Street between Wichita and Speedway, adjoined the existing Business-Economics Building.[55] The location had once been the site of Pearce Hall, which had opened in 1908 and was being used for classrooms before it was demolished in 1974 to make way for the business building. The older building, before it was renamed Pearce Hall, had been the home of the School of Law until 1953, when the law school moved to the newly constructed Townes Hall, on the north side of the campus.[56] The regents had planned at first to place the new business building across the street from the Business-Economics Building, where the university's main library now stands, but were persuaded that having it connected with the other business school facility would be preferable.[57]

The elaborate dedication program, organized by Barbara Vackar of Lorene Rogers's office, included comments by Lady Bird Johnson, who was then a member of the board of regents; former Texas governor Allan Shivers, then chairman of the regents; and Joseph W. Barr, US treasury secretary in the administrations of Presidents Kennedy and Johnson. The ceremony ended a week of events that included guest lecturers and classroom visits by business executives.

The $6 million, 146,000-square-foot building, an angular modernistic structure of limestone and bronze-tinted glass, incorporated the latest teaching technologies, including multimedia and audiovisual equipment and computer facilities. Each classroom was equipped with a closed-circuit TV system, and the building had a computer laboratory. Kozmetsky was particularly proud of the building's "free-form" interior plan that "while projecting a somewhat corporate-like image, conveys a sense of 'openness' that encourages an unregimented interaction between faculty and students, and between students and students."[58]

Among the building's innovations were several features to assist "handicapped" people (the term then in use), fifteen years before the federal Americans with Disabilities Act made a more comprehensive list of such design elements mandatory. All of the restrooms accommodated people in wheelchairs, and the elevators included floor numbers in Braille. The aisle seats in a lecture hall were designed for the note-taking needs of left-handed students.[59]

The building also housed the business school's computers, which in 1976 included a Control Data 3100 computer system and two PDP 11/40 computers, as well as an interface with the university's central CSC 6600/6400 dual computer system. The school was also in the process of acquiring a Datapoint 5500 system that included an interface with three Datapoint 2200s to form a network for research in database management. In those days before the Internet, the school maintained a large library of taped databases, including the Compustat financial information service, inaugurated in 1962. The tapes provided annual and quarterly financial information on 1,800 US industrial companies, 150 utilities, and 100 banks.[60] Today the online Compustat database covers tens of thousands of global securities.

The building provided much-needed classrooms for the overcrowded business school, but enrollment growth was such a problem that even after the building opened, students sometimes had to sit on the floor or at the back of classrooms in folding chairs.[61] To help alleviate such problems, Kozmetsky began planning for another classroom building to be used largely by the business school, this one located across Twenty-First Street adjacent to the Perry-Castañeda Library. This building, known today as the University Teaching Center, which opened in 1984, was the subject of a fundraising proposal, discussed by Kozmetsky and Flawn, that would have involved a major gift from South Texas oilman and University of Texas alumnus H. B. "Hank" Harkins in exchange for naming the building after him or possibly naming the entire complex of business school buildings for him. Negotiations with Harkins never came to fruition.[62]

When Kozmetsky stepped down from the deanship in 1982, the regents recognized his role in transforming the business school by naming its complex of buildings the George Kozmetsky Center for Business Education. This included the Business-Economics Building, the Graduate School of Business, and the University Teaching Center, which was then under construction.[63] Many people who were close to Kozmetsky have said privately that he would have preferred that the business school itself (as an academic entity, not just a collection of buildings) be named for him. In 2000, in a step that testified to the added value that Kozmetsky and his successors imparted to the business school, the regents named the school for San Antonio businessman Billy Joe "Red" McCombs in recognition of his gift of $50 million.

CHALLENGES FROM ACCOUNTING

Although Kozmetsky had a strong background in accounting and had been recognized for years as an authority on the controller's function in corporations, he had continuing problems throughout his deanship in relations with the business school's large and independent-minded Department of Accounting and some of its most powerful professors. The problems dated even to before Kozmetsky entered the dean's office, when his appointment was opposed by longtime accounting faculty member C. Aubrey Smith, who feared that Kozmetsky would neglect the undergraduate program. Smith remained critical of the way Kozmetsky handled the dean's job, but he was only one of the most vocal of the opponents within the department, which was the largest department within the business school, had been for many years the school's most prestigious academic unit, and fiercely guarded its independence.

After Kozmetsky arrived in September 1966, Smith watched and waited to see how the new dean would approach his job, but that honeymoon period lasted no more than six months. By February 19, 1967, Smith could no longer remain silent, and he wrote to Hackerman (typing the letter himself so no one else would see it) with a list of complaints and a recommendation that Hackerman lecture Kozmetsky on how a dean ought to act.

Smith advised Hackerman, who was still serving as Ransom's vice chancellor with broad responsibilities for the Austin campus, that he was not alone in being displeased with Kozmetsky, and that there was "considerable unhappiness" with his performance so far, both within the faculty and among the state's business community. He said faculty members were upset because of Kozmetsky's "ineptness in dealing with staff," and he cited complaints about Kozmetsky's decisions on promotions, a feeling "among many young teachers that one cannot get the ear of the dean [and] even when an audience is had it is claimed that the words of the visitor go unheard," and a sense that Kozmetsky and his associate dean, Glenn Welsch, were only giving "lip service" to the cause of good teaching.

The reaction to Kozmetsky off the campus was no better, according to Smith, who wrote that businessmen "around the state" were objecting to Kozmetsky's approach to undergraduate business education. "I refer to contacts I have had with ex-students and alumni who are bankers, local real estate and insurance people, merchants, local C.P.A.'s, those in local service organizations, and the like," Smith wrote. "These people fear that emphasis will be placed strictly on training the top leaders and managers for big business and that the needs of the 65% to 75% out of bachelor degree people (including pre-law) who normally move into small business will be overlooked or materially reduced in importance."[64]

This was also Smith's own fear and had been since Kozmetsky's name had first surfaced during the search for a dean a year and a half earlier. He was right in that Kozmetsky's personal interests lay more in educating the leaders of large corporations than in training those who would become small-town merchants, but the much-feared "neglect" of the undergraduate program never materialized. The undergraduate business program continued to be one of the largest in the nation, and considerable effort was spent throughout the Kozmetsky years in revising its curriculum and upgrading services to students, and its national academic reputation rose steadily while Kozmetsky was dean. Nevertheless, the idea persisted among some critics that Kozmetsky had slighted undergraduates in favor of the graduate program and faculty research.

Smith offered Hackerman several suggestions for fixing the problems as he perceived them. He returned to the idea that he had proposed in late 1965, that separate academic structures be created for the undergraduate and graduate programs, with two deans. Short of that, he recommended that a "strong" associate dean be appointed with the power to run the undergraduate program "without too much direct control by the dean." These ideas quickly disappeared from the correspondence files of the university administration, although Kozmetsky did appoint a series of associate deans who oversaw the undergraduate program.

One of those associate deans, Reuben R. McDaniel Jr., who assumed responsibility for the undergraduate program in 1976, said some of the criticism from Smith and others was justified. "I don't think George had a very deep understanding of undergraduate education," McDaniel said. "His background did not give him a good grip on it. But one reason he put me in the position of associate dean was that I did understand it and I knew how to solve management problems that had frustrated others. He cared deeply about the students and wanted them to have a good experience. Some of the problems we faced seemed almost insurmountable, such as the large numbers of students and problems with registration and academic advising, and George told me to bring order to the system and get it under control. He approved of all the steps I wanted to take, and he supported me when some faculty complained. Sometimes he would come to me and say that I had really pissed off so-and-so, but he legitimized my effort and he always backed me up one way or another."[65]

Others in the department besides Smith also longed for change, and they found an opportunity in the mid-1970s through a proposal to separate the accounting department from the business school and make it a separate academic unit with its own dean. For a while during that decade there were efforts among many in the accounting profession nationwide to establish separate schools of accounting, on the theory that secession from business schools could result in greater prestige for accounting education and more focused attention on the field's particular needs, which, it was argued, were poorly served by the more diverse interests of business schools as they had developed after World War II. It was also argued that accountants and their firms might be more likely to make financial contributions to a university accounting program if it had its own identity separate from a business school.[66]

Major accounting associations and some large accounting firms backed the idea, but it drew opposition from academic leaders who raised concerns about overly narrowing the education that accounting students would receive, as well as about the prospect of extra administrative expense.[67]

As happened at other institutions, an alternative plan emerged at the University of Texas to rename the accounting departments as a school but keep it within the purview of the dean of the business school, an organizational structure that might achieve some of the goals of the secession movement without its drawbacks. This compromise was backed at the University of Texas in the late 1970s by the chairman of the accounting department, Robert G. May, and by associate dean William H. Cunningham, who knew that Kozmetsky would be averse to any plan that separated accounting completely from the business school.[68] (Both Cunningham and May would later serve as deans of the business school.)

The reorganization plan was approved by all levels of the university administration and the regents, but eventually it was turned down by state regulators. Numerous other Texas universities were also seeking to reorganize their accounting departments and establish new independent schools, and the more modest University of Texas compromise plan was caught up in the opposition to the other institutions' proposals.[69] The University of Texas accounting department continued with its old administrative structure, although several innovative approaches to the master of professional accountancy degree were implemented. In time, the national trend toward independent accounting schools faded away.[70]

Kozmetsky's long-running difficulties with the Department of Accounting sometimes spurred him to make contemptuous remarks about the department to his fellow deans. "George told me," said Robert D. King, dean of the College of Liberal Arts and one of its predecessor colleges,

A CIVIC ENTREPRENEUR

"that if I wanted some lessons about how to deal with difficult departments, I should talk to him about accounting."[71]

An Official Evaluation

Some of the most intense criticism of Kozmetsky came from a committee that began meeting in early 1977 to conduct an official evaluation of his work as dean. Deans of the University of Texas colleges and schools were appointed for one year at a time, but at least by the end of a six-year period, each dean, if he or she wanted to continue in office, was supposed to be evaluated by a committee that would make a recommendation to the president on the reappointment. Kozmetsky underwent two of these reviews, in 1971 and 1977. The first committee, chaired by Stanley A. Arbingast, a professor of marketing who was director of the Bureau of Business Research from 1969 to 1975, recommended that Kozmetsky be reappointed as dean, but the committee's report is not in the papers of the president's office as preserved in the university archives. The committee reported that it had destroyed all its working papers, including all correspondence and testimony from faculty members, alumni, and business leaders.[72]

The complete report of the second evaluation committee, whether by design or oversight, is in the archives, and it provides a highly unusual inside account of what the individual faculty of one of the university's schools thought about its dean—or what a faculty member might say when confident his or her identity would be protected.

The candid and sometimes highly critical comments about Kozmetsky that the 1977 committee sent to President Rogers were not made public at the time, with only the president's final decision—agreeing with the overall recommendation to reappoint Kozmetsky—announced to the world. The committee noted that its recommendation was not unanimous, but it did not provide details of how the members voted. It did, however, include results of a campus-mail straw poll of the business faculty—forty-seven faculty members (52.8 percent) voted for Kozmetsky to be reappointed for another term, thirty-seven (41.6 percent) said no, and five (5.6 percent) were undecided.[73] The eighty-nine faculty members who returned ballots were about half of the total business school faculty.

Rogers appointed seven faculty members and three students to the committee. Six faculty members were from the business school—Arbingast, chairman of the first evaluation committee; Lawrence L. Crum, professor of finance who had also served on the 1971 committee; Gaylord A Jentz, professor of business law; Elizabeth Lanham, chair of the management department; Kermit D. Larson, professor of accounting; and Robert

E. Witt, professor of marketing. Others on the committee were G. Karl Galinsky, professor of classics; and students Fred Raschke, David Lear, and Vicki Wimberley. The committee met for the first time in January 1977 and chose Jentz as its chairman. At first Rogers asked for a written report by March 28—only two months away—but the committee asked for and received an extension until May 2.

Kozmetsky disliked the faculty review process and, like some other deans, might not have even read the 1977 committee's report.[74] The report briefly called attention to the environment in which Kozmetsky had served, suggesting that the previous eleven years were a time of unusual difficulty. Kozmetsky had served under four presidents or acting presidents, dealt with "phenomenal growth" in business school enrollment, faced a "skyrocketing" student-faculty ratio of 36-to-1, "and all of this has taken place during a period when funding to the entire university has been limited, total enrollment . . . has leveled off or even decreased, and research funds have been more difficult to acquire."[75]

The committee then provided a long list of criticisms of Kozmetsky, based on interviews with faculty, administrators, and other constituencies, but sometimes qualified with comments to Kozmetsky's credit. The criticisms included the following:

Faculty members faulted Kozmetsky for failure to provide direction for committees. "After appointment, it appears that each committee is left to chart its own course," leading to a lack of coordination or inaction. It was also said that Kozmetsky often failed to listen to recommendations of committees, "even to the point of the discourtesy of ignoring committee action completely and/or rendering decisions contrary, without even an explanation." On the other hand, Kozmetsky made it a practice to ask faculty members each year which committees ought to be eliminated, usually with little faculty response, and had strongly supported committees dealing with revision of the curriculum.

The chairmen of academic departments were generally favorable but did fault Kozmetsky for being inconsistent in communicating his decisions to them. Faculty members said Kozmetsky's decisions about promotions were handed down without explanation, particularly when he rejected recommendations for promotion. He was also criticized for failing to communicate his reasons for making budget decisions and for not consulting with the chairmen when he moved money from one department to another, as well as for allocating money for merit raises in a way that circumvented the work of departmental budget councils.

Kozmetsky was praised for helping recruit outstanding faculty members, although some faculty thought he devoted his energy exclusively to a few areas in which he was particularly interested and neglected others. Kozmetsky's busy schedule was blamed for some problems related to retaining these outstanding faculty members, with some departing faculty members complaining that they'd had so little contact with the dean that they were uncertain whether he supported them.

Some faculty had the impression that Kozmetsky was intent on exercising "corporate executive authority," as opposed to the collegial management approach they expected, and his speaking style was also criticized. "Many faculty, some students, and some in the business community indicated that they found it difficult to interpret what the dean says," the committee wrote. "Although he impressed persons with words, quantity of paper distributed, diagrams, etc., they simply did not understand the message he was attempting to get across."

A lack of dialogue with small businesses was another criticism, as it was felt that Kozmetsky concentrated his attention on large corporations. There was a suggestion that this had hurt the business school's relationship with minority-owned businesses and caused image problems among prospective minority students. At the same time, Kozmetsky was praised for his good relations with business and government leaders across the country, which had led to increased sources of funds for the business school. Faculty members complimented Kozmetsky on his fundraising efforts but some said they were "left in the dark" about the use of these funds.

Minority students said Kozmetsky was inaccessible and had not met with minority student organizations or business owners. They also faulted Kozmetsky for giving little attention to financial assistance for minority students, neglecting recruitment of minority faculty, and failing to encourage minority-business recruiting on campus. Other groups of students and faculty also complained that Kozmetsky was inaccessible. He was available, when he was in town, between 7:00 and 8:30 a.m. without an appointment, but the committee noted that "these hours seem to be inconvenient for most faculty and students." Getting an appointment with him at other times could take two weeks or more.

A limited survey of business leaders found strong support for Kozmetsky's leadership of the business school, except within the accounting profession, where he had the same kind of difficult relationship that he had with the Department of Accounting. Overall, the committee praised Kozmetsky's leadership in enhancing the national reputation of the business school: "It is generally felt that the dean's success in business, his numerous relationships with business and government agencies, and the dynamic way in which he does things has given the college visibility and contributed substantially to the national reputation of the college as a whole."[76]

Although the committee recommended that Kozmetsky be reappointed, it also advised Rogers that several changes in Kozmetsky's management of the business school were needed. Chief among these was a recommendation that Kozmetsky appoint an "executive dean" with authority for day-to-day management of the school. This new person would "be available at all times, particularly when the dean is absent, and must have the confidence . . . that his decisions will be backed by Dean Kozmetsky."[77]

Rogers reappointed Kozmetsky, but no action was taken on this proposal for an "executive dean." However, Kozmetsky did rely more and more during the next five years on his associate dean for graduate programs, William H. Cunningham, who had been appointed in the summer of 1976 and would gradually become responsible for more of the day-to-day operations of the business school before he succeeded Kozmetsky as dean.

The committee offered a long list of other recommendations for changing the way Kozmetsky ran the business school, from keeping faculty and students better informed about his schedule to exercising closer consultation with budget councils and communicating with faculty about major fundraising efforts. There is little evidence that Kozmetsky made any major changes in the operation of the school as a result of these recommendations.

Reuben R. McDaniel Jr., one of Kozmetsky's associate deans in the latter part of his deanship, offered an assessment of Kozmetsky that agrees in part with the evaluation of the 1977 committee. He said Kozmetsky's "stock with the faculty was very high in the early years and then it gradually went down. There was without doubt an erosion of support from the faculty in the later years."

McDaniel said that Kozmetsky "was a visionary with great ability, and he was a very compassionate person and had genuine love for the business school and its people. He could inspire people by his vision and his understanding of quality performance, and he was a man who could make things happen. But he did not understand the kind of power he could have marshalled by working with the faculty to better utilize what he had built. One example was with the PhD program. He wanted a broader range of students, a much more diverse curriculum, and more internships in industry and government, and he wanted graduates to become leaders at top universities, in business, and in the public sector. But he couldn't bring the faculty together to achieve that. The faculty's vision, by

A Civic Entrepreneur

A display honoring Kozmetsky's legacy at the business school. *Photograph by Monty Jones.*

The Graduate School of Business was built during George Kozmetsky's deanship adjacent to the business school's older building (right). *University of Texas at Austin photograph.*

and large, stayed on the same narrow path, and he was not able to get them to share his vision, which was unique."[78]

Peter Flawn had a somewhat different assessment. "I think it is fair to say that George had an entrepreneurial approach to being dean, rather than an academic one," Flawn said, "and he certainly had an inner circle of trusted colleagues, a 'Friends of George' group. He used the deanship as a bully pulpit, and he had national stature. George was very independent, and he had strong support from the Board of Regents. I think he did what he had been hired to do. When you hire a businessman for a position such as dean, you take a risk that he can't function in an academic community, but he was able to do that. He certainly was able to recruit some outstanding people for the faculty, as well as some who were not so outstanding."

Flawn said, "I recognized what we had in George, and I never wanted to just say no to him. I usually tried to give him something when he came to me with requests. The university gave him a great opportunity to build something, and I think he took advantage of that opportunity."[79]

A CIVIC ENTREPRENEUR

CHAPTER 13

ADVISING THE BOARD OF REGENTS

As executive assistant for economic affairs for the University of Texas System Board of Regents, George Kozmetsky filled a position that was created to take advantage of his unique mix of talents. The job gave him responsibility for formulating long-range plans for the development and management of the university system's economic resources, meaning primarily the investments of the Permanent University Fund. He also served, in effect, as the regents' one-person strategic planning committee. During the thirty years that he worked with the regents, Kozmetsky took on numerous special assignments—from economic development initiatives at university system campuses, to advising on the expansion of high-performance computing facilities, to producing reports on long-term planning for dealing with economic and social changes. He said that about 10 percent of his time was devoted to this advisory role with the regents, but it is clear that the time he spent on the regents' business varied greatly over the years. His work with the board also was consistent with a well-established pattern in Kozmetsky's career—as he provided expert advice on public policy issues across a diverse range of subjects through his service on many government commissions, task forces, and special projects. Many of the projects Kozmetsky worked on for the regents overlapped with advising he did for other state and federal agencies.

Kozmetsky developed close relationships with several regents, beginning with W. W. Heath, who was the chairman of the board when Kozmetsky was hired as the dean of the business school. Others with whom Kozmetsky was close through the years, and who had deep trust in his judgment, included Allan Shivers, a former governor of Texas who was a regent from 1973 to 1979; Bernard Rapoport, a regent from 1991 to 1997;

Louis Beecherl, who was on the board from 1987 to 1993; and Janey Briscoe, a regent from 1981 to 1987, whose husband, Dolph, had been governor of Texas from 1973 to 1979.

Kozmetsky's role with the regents gave him extraordinary clout on the University of Texas at Austin campus—power that was so widely recognized that he rarely had to exert it overtly. "I frequently sat next to George at meetings of the deans' council," said Robert D. King. "I would just think to myself that if I said something the president would say, 'Screw you, Bob,' but no one said that to George. They'd have to lay off George because he would be talking to the regents. When a contentious issue came up, Flawn wouldn't take it out on George, but he would on me." Still, according to King, Kozmetsky never used his power arrogantly and never "played his regents' card" in meetings.[1]

University deans must often divert their time and energy away from personal academic pursuits—teaching, research, and service—to concentrate more fully on their administrative responsibilities. Kozmetsky generally found time to continue doing everything, although as was seen in chapter 12, he was sometimes criticized for spreading himself too thin and for being remote or unavailable when the administrative work of the dean's office needed attention. Fortunately, he hired capable associate and assistant deans and other staff members who could deal with that work when he was occupied elsewhere.

Particularly in the early years of his association with the University of Texas System, Kozmetsky participated in the system's fundraising activities. In December 1969 he and Harry Ransom spoke in Southern California at a lunch for friends and alumni of the University of Texas. The lunch was hosted by the former actress Bonita Granville Wrather and her husband, Jack D. Wrather, a Los Angeles oilman and entertainment entrepreneur and a graduate of the University of Texas at Austin. Jack had earned a degree in fine arts from the university in 1939. He and his wife were close friends of George and Ronya, and he joined the University of Texas System Development Board in 1967, later serving as its vice chairman.[2] Among guests at the 1969 event were business, foundation, and financial leaders, many of whom knew Kozmetsky from his years with Teledyne. Such events might not have included a direct passing of the hat, but they did serve to build and reinforce the network of contacts essential for a long-term fundraising effort. Kozmetsky also helped the Development Board expand its contacts in San Francisco and New York, where he had numerous former business associates.[3]

A CIVIC ENTREPRENEUR

Charles A. LeMaistre, vice chancellor for health affairs, in 1970, the year before he was named chancellor. *Texas Student Publications (Cactus).*

MARINE SCIENCE

Kozmetsky participated in numerous special committees that the regents formed to study new academic and research initiatives. One of the most ambitious of these was a five-person committee led by then vice chancellor Charles A. LeMaistre formed in 1969 to explore ways that the university system could expand its involvement in marine studies.[4] The committee benefitted from a study of marine science that Kozmetsky organized at the business school.[5] The committee's recommendations included two proposals that were undertaken by the regents and bore significant fruit over the years—a major expansion of the work of the University of Texas at Austin's Marine Science Institute at Port Aransas and the creation of a "Gulf Marine Medicine Institute" in Galveston, which became in 1969 the Marine Biomedical Institute, a unit of the University of Texas Medical Branch at Galveston. The institute has become a major research organization specializing in study of marine invertebrates whose nervous systems are useful for understanding comparable systems in humans, and which are a source of biomedically important substances.

"George had a deep interest in marine studies, particularly the potential for research that was relevant to medicine," said LeMaistre, who served as chancellor of the university system and president of the system's M. D. Anderson Cancer Center in Houston. "He understood that potential as few people did, and he made a very valuable contribution to that committee. The results continue to benefit medical research more than forty years later."[6]

The marine studies committee grew out of a symposium that Kozmetsky held in Houston in June 1967 to explore the industrial potential of the marine sciences, with particular focus on the Gulf of Mexico. The symposium brought marine scientists and technologists together with business and investment leaders "to discuss the commercial and industrial aspects of new products, new businesses, [and] rejuvenation of existing marine enterprises." The symposium deserves recognition as the first of a long series of such University of Texas gatherings, extending over the next three and a half decades, in which Kozmetsky convened diverse leaders from academia, government, and the private sector to exchange information and ideas and, Kozmetsky always hoped, to stimulate new relationships that would lead to viable business enterprises.[7] Kozmetsky and Eugene Konecci organized a second marine science symposium in September 1968, this time in Corpus Christi, with Governor John Connally as the main speaker. Kozmetsky moderated a panel on business opportunities and drew on his network of longtime business associates as participants.[8]

Another of Kozmetsky's contributions to public policy in marine science came soon after he arrived at the university, as both he and Konecci advised a panel on marine engineering and technology of the national Commission on Marine Science, Engineering, and Resources. The commission, created in 1966, led to major federal legislation, such as the National Sea Grant College Program, the Marine Mammal Protection Act, and legislation on clean water, endangered species, and marine research.[9]

Kozmetsky's interest in marine science made him a natural choice as one of six lay members of a Texas House of Representatives Interim Committee on Oceanography, which convened in 1970 to begin a yearlong study of coastal and marine issues. The committee also consisted of five house members, including Ray Lemmon of Houston, the committee's chairman. Lemmon also chaired a Council on Marine-Related Affairs, a twelve-person body created by the legislature in 1971 to provide state government with expert advice on marine-related problems. Kozmetsky was appointed to the council as its representation for education. The committee's work included studying the possibility of creating a new state institution for oceanography, but state initiatives in that area were confined to existing institutions.

A CIVIC ENTREPRENEUR

Planning for the 1980s

Typical of the larger-scale strategic planning that Kozmetsky performed for the regents was a report he produced in August 1979 titled "The Eighties: A Decade of Challenge and Achievement." He began by identifying four major state trends—continuing rapid population growth, increased enrollment at universities, continued strong demand by community college students to transfer to University of Texas System institutions, and rapid changes in technology and societal values.

Kozmetsky emphasized the potential growth in nontraditional students, especially those who had begun their careers but needed retraining, maintenance of their professional credentials, and other advanced education. Drawing on a 1972 study that he had conducted for the Conference Board (see chapter 14), Kozmetsky advised the regents that instead of people experiencing three distinct phases of education, career, and retirement, the rapidly growing trend was toward serial careers and education—perhaps as many as three or four periods of education and career alternating through a lifetime. "Studies I have made in the past have shown the potential market for this category is four times as large as the currently accepted market for the traditional university student," he wrote.[10]

Kozmetsky listed seven broad areas of new technology that the regents should consider as areas for academic preeminence. Within each area he cited specific topics that presented promising opportunities: microelectronics (advanced chips, advanced software applications, and personal computers); medicine (biotechnology, psychotherapy, transplantation, and birth control); materials (special application designs, photosynthesis, super-cold technology, industrial and scientific instruments and robots, and automated batch production); energy (solar, fusion, coal-mining technology, and power stations); defense technologies (electronic warfare); agricultural technologies (genetic selection, electrostatic spraying, waste management, and nuclear radiation); and other technologies, including airwaves, communication, and construction.

Kozmetsky saw several differences between these emerging technologies and those of the recent past. "The technologies of the 1960s and 1970s were not dominated by innovations and discoveries at the universities," he wrote. "Few of the nation's leading research institutions were concerned with scientific advances. . . . Much of the past technologies of mass production and electronics were developed 'in house' or through invention and exploitation of advances made in other countries or companies. The Board of Regents will need to determine the role and support that the UT

System will provide for the education required by the technologies of the 1980s and 1990s."[11]

Another difference, according to Kozmetsky's report, was that in the earlier decades "economic support was generated by the public sector as well as by large companies. Today support is not as abundant as in the past. There are many reasons government support is being focused into other areas than science and technology. Many of our major companies are facing unique economic conditions under intense international competition, double digit inflation, and increased government regulations. Providing laboratories with sophisticated equipment and facilities for these newer technologies requires large amounts of capital investments as well as significant annual operating funds. The coupling of higher education research with the needs of the private sector is one of the major issues for the 1980s. Such sectors need to have respect for each other's abilities as well as their mutual dependence on each institution's contributions if the U.S. is to regain its technological leadership in the free world."

In other parts of his report, Kozmetsky outlined his projections for needed expenditures through the 1980s in instruction, research, community service, and modernization and cost-effectiveness. He advised that priority should be given to graduate student housing, library materials and knowledge databases, computer and communications equipment, satellite and microwave communications, endowed faculty positions, and support for faculty housing. Some of his projections for the decade must have seemed daunting to the regents, such as $846 million in capital expenditures for facilities to replace aging buildings and meet new space demands, $266 million for library materials, up to $90 million for new graduate student housing, more than $50 million in matching funds for endowment donations, and $60 million for capital expenditures on computers, plus up to $90 million for computer operations.

His projections of needed expenditures to advance the cause of research at University of Texas System institutions were no less ambitious. He recommended $50 million to $100 million in new expenditures to support research in the newer areas of technology; up to $15 million for purchase of land for at least two or three university/industry research parks; and $20 million to $50 million for a high-technology business development fund. He recommended that the pattern for such a fund could be similar efforts undertaken by Stanford University, the Massachusetts Institute of Technology, and other institutions. "This could serve as a major future funding source in the 21st century when our oil and gas run out," he wrote. "Most investor-specialists do not recognize that $20 million in less than a quarter of a century would grow to $1.4 billion in current dollars. This is equal to the value of the [Permanent University Fund] in 1979." The University of Texas System did not establish such a fund, although in subsequent years the state took several steps to help fund high-tech business development, including creation of the Texas Growth Fund in 1988. Many other research recommendations in Kozmetsky's report eventually came to pass in one form or another.

Kozmetsky also recommended that the system promote community service at each of its institutions, with an expenditure of up to $30 million through the 1980s for staff and programs. He saw these expenditures as largely offset by a projected increase in revenue from expanded educational services for older students returning to universities for retraining and continuing education. He saw that the need for such programs was growing because of an increased rate of "knowledge obsolescence as well as the need for an expanded knowledge data base for the key leadership of all professions."

A final need for increased expenditures in the 1980s was aimed at saving money through increased cost-effectiveness and productivity. In this regard, Kozmetsky foresaw the emphasis on cost savings that would preoccupy the University of Texas System and its institutions from the late 1980s to the early twenty-first century, largely in response to demands from the state legislature during times of shortages in state revenue.

Kozmetsky did not add up all his forecasts and estimates for the new decade, but any regent with a pencil could have quickly found that he was calling for new capital and operating expenditures of almost $1.7 billion through the end of the 1980s. If Kozmetsky had anticipated several other key areas that would demand major expenditures in the 1980s and 1990s—such as supercomputer purchases, expansion of "distance education" through computerized instruction, and expansion of South Texas educational and medical programs—his cost estimate would have been even greater. Kozmetsky presented the needed expenditures as part of a strategic vision that sought to take advantage of retrenchment in education in other states. "While other state university systems in the nation are consolidating academic programs, merging facilities and locations, the UT System can 'programmatically' plan for quality growth," he wrote.

Kozmetsky concluded the report with a piece of advice that eventually resulted in a diminished need for a one-man strategic planning office such as he was providing, as he called for an expansion of the system's planning and analysis function. Regents and chancellors in the 1990s and early in the twenty-first century might not have been aware of Kozmetsky's 1979 report, but they saw the same need for a more formal planning process. Many functions undertaken by a greatly expanded business affairs office served to institutionalize the kind of studies that Kozmetsky had undertaken on an ad hoc basis.

ASSET MANAGEMENT

A similar transition occurred with regard to the management of the financial assets for which the regents were responsible. In the early part of his tenure as executive associate to the regents, Kozmetsky played a much larger role in providing advice about investments and investment policy than he did toward the end of his tenure, when the asset-management function of the university system had been expanded and transformed—first into a highly professional in-house investment office and then into a separately administered "company." As these developments played themselves out over the years, there was less and less need for someone like Kozmetsky to provide a separate channel of advice about asset management.

Kozmetsky was called on from time to time to study management issues for the university system staff or the regents and to present recommendations for new policies or organizations. Thus, as sort of an in-house consultant, he performed the kind of independent studies that an outside consultant might be engaged to conduct today. One of those studies, undertaken in 1979, concerned the management of the 2.1 million acres of land in West Texas, known as the University Lands, which with its mineral wealth provided the underlying strength of the Permanent University Fund (PUF). During the 1980s, the growth of the PUF became more a function of its investments in securities and other instruments than a result of direct income from the lands, but maximizing that income through improved management techniques was always a goal. Kozmetsky offered his views on how that could be done in a four-page memo to Chancellor E. Don Walker and Board of Regents chairman Dan C. Williams in October 1979.[12]

The memo focused on changes in the organizational structure and the division of responsibilities among various offices that helped manage the lands. The approach outlined by Kozmetsky was partly reflected in organizational changes in 1980, although additional reorganization came later in the decade. Kozmetsky's first recommendation was for the creation of the position of vice chancellor for land management, who would direct a staff with particular expertise in three areas: oil, gas, and minerals; surface development, including agricultural and nonagricultural uses of the land; and lands held in trust by the University of Texas System apart from the acreage in West Texas. Other staff members would be responsible for economic analysis, short- and long-range business planning, and alternative policy recommendations.

Kozmetsky then recommended a clear division of responsibilities between the new vice chancellor for lands and other university system offices, particularly the vice chancellor for business affairs and the general counsel. These three positions at the vice chancellor level would share the oversight of the lands and investments, with an executive director for investments and trusts reporting to the vice chancellor for business affairs. In addition, Kozmetsky recommended that the chancellor establish two new functions within the chancellor's office—an annual internal audit of finances and operations of the lands, and a regular legal review and analysis (apart from the work of the general counsel) to ensure compliance with all relevant laws.

The organizational chart did not materialize exactly as Kozmetsky envisioned it in 1979, with the main difference being that the manager of University Lands was a vice chancellor reporting instead through the executive vice chancellor of business affairs. Another difference came in the mid-1980s, when the investment function was assigned to a new vice chancellor for asset management. It is clear that Chairman Williams and Chancellor Walker, and their successors, considered Kozmetsky's recommendations for how to draw a new organizational chart to be just one of many possible arrangements, but they did move in the direction of clearer lines of authority and greater professionalism, two principles inherent in Kozmetsky's recommendations in 1979. However, the thrust of those recommendations was finally realized (without a direct reference to Kozmetsky's old proposals) in the twenty-first century, when, in 2014, the regents created the position of chief executive officer of University Lands.[13]

Kozmetsky and others advocated for many years a broadening of the types of investments that could be made by the Permanent University Fund, before changes were finally allowed through a constitutional amendment. In 1982, Kozmetsky had served on a special task force of bankers and investors appointed by the regents' Land and Investment Committee to make recommendations for changing the limitations that the state constitution placed on PUF investments. The limitations that the task force examined dated to 1956, when PUF investments in corporate securities were first allowed, and they included these provisions: no more than 1 percent of PUF assets could be invested in the securities of one company, a stock was not eligible for purchase unless it had paid a cash dividend for five consecutive years, most eligible stocks had to be listed on an exchange registered with the US Securities and Exchange Commission, no more than 5 percent of the voting stock of a company could be held, and only stocks in US corporations were eligible.

The task force concluded that those restrictions had had "a serious detrimental effect on the operation and investment potential of the Permanent University Fund . . . [and] the continuation of such restrictions could have an even greater negative impact on the Fund's potential growth in the future." The task force advocated that investments be governed only by the "prudent person rule," which had been in effect in theory since 1968 but was still impinged upon by the 1956 limitations. The task force advised that by having the limitations lifted, the PUF would be free to invest in real estate, securities that had not paid a dividend, the sale of stock options, and the lending of owned securities. "Under the 'prudent person rule,' the Board of Regents would have full authority to adjust the investment objectives and activities of the Fund in order to take advantage of the ever-changing investment environment," the task force said.[14]

Despite a similar recommendation from a task force on state trusts and asset management appointed by Governor Bill Clements, no immediate legislative action was taken on the issue after Clements lost the governorship to Mark White in November 1982. A constitutional amendment lifting the restrictions on PUF investments was not passed by the legislature and approved by voters until 1988, after Clements had returned to the governor's office for his second term. PUF investment policy was not necessarily a partisan issue, but the issue did lose momentum after the change in governors in January 1983 and regained momentum after the 1986 gubernatorial election.

When the regents took up the issue again in 1988, it was part of a proposed constitutional amendment that included the Texas Growth Fund, designed to provide state grants to companies for plant and facility expansion and to support new companies with venture capital—the kind of fund that Kozmetsky had been advocating since at least the late 1970s. The amendment allowed the PUF and other state funds to invest up to 1 percent of their assets in the Texas Growth Fund. By providing that investment decisions would be governed by the standards of "prudent investors," the amendment also tracked closely with the recommendations of the task force on which Kozmetsky had served in 1982.

By 1988, the investment functions were under the authority of an executive vice chancellor for asset management. Michael E. Patrick, the first person to hold that position, advocated that the regents endorse the proposed amendment, using arguments reminiscent of the earlier task force report but casting the issue in a sharper light. The limitations on PUF investments had been "specifically tailored to the markets of 35 years ago," Patrick told the regents. "There was no NASDAQ, no commercial paper, and large foreign corporations did not trade on major U.S. exchanges and comply with the rules of the Securities and Exchange Commission. Today the 1956 amendment limits the Permanent Funds to 1,200 corporate names from over 7,000 available. Fully 20 percent of 101 names from the Standard & Poor's 500 list of the largest and most diversified companies are prohibited investments. . . . In effect the Permanent Funds are denied access to the growth industries of today and the future."[15] Texas voters approved the amendment in November 1988, with 63.3 percent voting yes.[16]

Kozmetsky provided advice to the regents on another issue related to the PUF in 1990, when the board was evaluating its relatively new "private placement" investment program, which provided an alternative to the traditional investments in publicly traded securities. The system had begun investing a portion of its assets in private placement and venture capital deals in 1988 in hopes of outperforming the growth rates expected from more traditional investments and taking advantage of a changing market environment. By 1990, some regents had begun to feel that too great a share of the system's assets was being invested in private placements, and they wanted to slow down the program. Others saw a need to review the progress of the program and consider new guidelines. Patrick and Kozmetsky made presentations to the board on these issues in June 1990—both advocating that the private placement program continue, but with a new policy in place to guide the investing. They also advised that the regents and the staff, as well as the Investment Advisory Committee (a group of outside advisers with expertise in investing and finance), evaluate other nontraditional investments, such as international securities and equity real estate.

Kozmetsky presented a slide show at that meeting of the regents, providing an overview of how the PUF operated, a review of investment policies before and after passage of the 1988 constitutional amendment, reasons for reviewing the investment policy in 1990, and a review of short-term policies. He recommended that the board and the Investment Advisory Committee "begin an active and cooperative study to develop a five- to ten-year investment policy and the goals to be assigned to such a policy." He added that "the national and international economic communities were undergoing considerable change and that with the board's increased ability to use nontraditional investments, there was a need for a close review of how these techniques should be integrated within an overall investment policy for the PUF."[17]

The board's Land and Investment Committee worked with Patrick and Kozmetsky, as well as the outside advisory committee, the rest of that year. In December, Shannon Ratliff, chairman of the Land and Investment Committee, presented a detailed policy governing private placement investments. The policy stated the goals of the program as to generate long-term capital appreciation in excess of the return expected from pub-licly traded stocks and to provide a means of prudent diversification. Lim-its were placed on the percentage of funds that could be part of the private placement portfolio, on the amount of new investments in the portfolio each year, and on how much of the portfolio could be invested in any single entity. The policy also listed types of investments to be avoided, such as highly leveraged transactions closely tied either to the economy or to a specific industry cycle. Other prohibited investments included hostile takeovers and high-tech start-up companies that had no venture capital backing.

Although the new policy was highly specific, the regents wanted more oversight. Chairman Louis A. Beecherl Jr. and Vice Chairman William F. Roden told Patrick that Kozmetsky "should be fully informed and involved in these private placement evaluations as one way to insure that the board is comfortable with this process." Kozmetsky assured them that he had a close working relationship with Patrick and would be pleased to continue his involvement in the private placement portfolio.[18]

Patrick recalled the consistent support that Kozmetsky gave to the new private placement program and said his advice had been valuable in per-suading the regents to undertake the new initiative and to strengthen it through the years. "He understood the importance of the program, and he understood how to communicate with the regents, and it is clear that they trusted his advice implicitly," Patrick said.[19]

For several years after the private placement program was inaugu-rated in 1988, University of Texas System staff members who coordinated the program visited with Kozmetsky in his office at the IC^2 Institute to review investment proposals that they wanted to present to the regents. The proposals were usually highly complex investment deals, but Kozmetsky grasped the scope of each proposal at once and always asked incisive questions that helped clarify the details and sharpen the staff's presentations, said Austin M. Long III, the first director of the private placement program. "There were many instances in which Kozmetsky's sophisticated understanding of what we were proposing was important in gaining the buy-in of the regents. We were fortunate to have someone of his experience and expertise to review our work, and the high level of confidence that members of the board had in him was a decisive factor," Long said.[20]

SUPERCOMPUTERS AND ENERGY POLICY
Access to the high-speed computers known as supercomputers was one of the most costly demands on University of Texas System resources in the

1980s and 1990s. Supercomputers, meaning simply the fastest scientific computers at any given time, had been used primarily by the military and the oil industry until the 1980s, when there was a rapid expansion of use of the machines by other industries and by university researchers. Those years also witnessed an extremely rapid evolution of supercomputer speeds. Kozmetsky was one of the people the regents relied on for advice when, in the mid-1980s, they began considering whether to buy a super-computer and, if so, what kind of equipment to purchase. Others who provided advice to the regents on the first purchases of a supercomputer and later upgrades were Charles Warlick, who was the university's top administrator for computing facilities from 1970 to 1996; Gerhard Fonken, executive vice president and provost at the university; and University of Texas System chancellor Hans Mark. In 1990 Kozmetsky also helped bring in as consultants two experts from the San Diego Supercomputer Center, a national supercomputing resources center supported by the National Science Foundation.[21]

Less than a dozen US universities had their own supercomputers when the University of Texas System bought its first one in 1985, and the technology was developing so rapidly that the regents were called on every few years to make major additional purchases. These were difficult decisions for some regents, as they pondered whether to authorize a multimillion-dollar purchase now or to wait until a newer and much faster model hit the market in a couple of years, or even in only a few months. Kozmetsky mostly remained in the background as the board considered these pur-chases, while officials such as Warlick and Fonken bore most of the responsibility for explaining details of the staff proposals to the regents, but Kozmetsky was a comforting presence for some regents, giving them reassurance that they were acting in the best interests of the university, its faculty, and its advanced research programs. By that time Kozmetsky was among the national experts who were called on regularly by the US Con-gress to testify on national policies on the development of supercomput-ers and related technologies, and his advice to the regents on these issues tracked what he had said during congressional hearings.[22]

When the regents paid a total of $20 million for the university sys-tem's first supercomputer in 1985 and an upgrade in 1988, Kozmetsky was one of the few witnesses to the regents' decisions who had been follow-ing the spectacular advances in scientific computing since the early 1950s. Kozmetsky had had a front-row seat for much of that history as it related to the use of advanced computers in industry, beginning as early as his work on computers at Litton Industries. Kozmetsky was in an almost unique position for fully appreciating the excitement of bringing advanced computing capabilities to the university and placing the University of Texas on the frontier of research that required supercomputers.

Kozmetsky joined other University of Texas officials and Governor Mark White in celebrating the unveiling of the first University of Texas supercomputer at Balcones Research Center in April 1986. White hailed the machine as "a magnet for new research and business coming to Texas," and he nicknamed it "Santa Rita No. 2," after the oil well known as Santa Rita No. 1 that first started the flow of oil money into the university's endowment.[23]

University researchers on energy issues were among those who had need of advanced computing facilities. Kozmetsky had been active in this field since 1972, when he began chairing the advisory committee for the university's Energy Research Group, which brought together faculty members from engineering, business, and other fields to concentrate on the frontiers of energy research, issues of energy and economic growth, and public policy related to energy. The regents, probably in response to the OPEC oil embargo of 1973 and related aspects of the "energy crisis" facing the United States, had a strong interest in the work of the Energy Research Group, and they encouraged Kozmetsky to pursue the project vigorously. At one time the regents had even suggested that Kozmetsky give up his limited teaching duties so he could devote more time to the subject of energy.[24]

The Energy Research Group focused on energy production, an energy database, energy models, and energy education. Participants included the university's Bureau of Business Research, Bureau of Economic Geology, Bureau of Engineering Research, Center for Plasma Physics and Thermonuclear Research, Energy Systems Engineering Program, Environmental Health Engineering Laboratories, and LBJ School of Public Affairs. The interdisciplinary focus of the group had obvious appeal for Kozmetsky.

Kozmetsky helped organize a conference at the university in 1973 titled "The Implications of Nuclear Power in Texas," which included speakers from federal agencies and energy companies and featured discussions of all the major issues of nuclear power, from power plant design to safety issues to management of high-level nuclear waste. At the time of the conference, the use of nuclear power to generate electricity was expanding in the United States, and one estimate was that Texas would need fifteen nuclear plants by 1985 to keep up with demands for electricity.[25] Only two nuclear plants were being planned in Texas at the time of the conference, and they remain the only nuclear plants in the state. Construction began in 1974 on the Comanche Peak plant near Fort Worth and in 1975 on the South Texas Nuclear Project near Bay City.

A CIVIC ENTREPRENEUR

Economic Development Initiatives

After Kozmetsky left the deanship in 1982, much of his work with the regents focused on a range of economic development projects. Most of his economic development initiatives were undertaken through the IC² Institute, but they also included special efforts requested by the regents. Especially after the success of the university's role in attracting the MCC consortium to Austin (see chapter 16), the regents wanted to extend that campus's success as an economic development engine to other University of Texas institutions. Business and political leaders in the cities with University of Texas campuses were eager to get in on the high-tech trend exemplified by the relationships between the University of Texas at Austin and the computer industry. The institutions themselves were also eager to be involved, and Kozmetsky was a willing advocate for these community and campus aspirations.

Jon Newton, chairman of the regents, paid tribute to Kozmetsky's leadership in working with cities outside Austin when he announced in October 1984 that agreements had been reached with groups in San Antonio and Tarrant County (part of the Dallas–Fort Worth area) to establish economic development projects. Building on the academic and economic history of these communities, the projects were the Institute of Biotechnology (established in association with the University of Texas Health Science Center at San Antonio) and the Advanced Robotics Research Institute in Fort Worth (established as a research and teaching unit of nearby University of Texas at Arlington).

The regents had met in June 1984 with San Antonio mayor Henry Cisneros and officials of the Texas Research and Technology Foundation and the San Antonio Medical Foundation regarding plans for an Institute of Biotechnology in association with the Health Science Center. In August, the regents met with a delegation of business and civic leaders from Fort Worth regarding plans for the robotics center. Each of these plans involved a donation of land and other local financial support. "In each case," Newton said at the October board meeting, "these community groups recognized the importance of high technology programs to their future economic/business development and recognized also the importance of strong university related academic and research participation."[26]

Many years of planning and fundraising were still required before the initiatives began operation. A key development in San Antonio was the donation in 1986 of more than 1,200 acres for the Texas Research Park, which would be the home of the fledgling Institute of Biotechnology. The institute began operations in its new building at the research park in 1991, with a focus on the genetic causes of cancer and other diseases. Through the 1990s and beyond, the institute and the research park sought to attract the kind of synergistic economic development that Kozmetsky had envisioned, including a company that conducted clinical trials of anticancer drugs, a biomaterials manufacturing plant, an anticancer-drug manufacturing plant, and additional research facilities operated by the Health Science Center.

Jay Stein, who was chairman of the Department of Medicine at the Health Science Center, was selected by the institution's president, Frank Harrison, to work with Kozmetsky on the early plans for the research park. "One day Harrison called me into his office and introduced me to George, and we had a discussion about the I-35 corridor and about what MCC [which had recently selected Austin for its headquarters] would mean for the region," Stein recalled.

> George was wise enough to say we needed a medical school complex involved in these efforts, and that helped start the idea of the biotechnology research park. I don't know why Harrison picked me to work with George, and at first I had a hard time understanding him, but I got used to the way he thought and talked and we worked together very well. He would be all over the place in his conversation, with a new idea about every tenth of a nanosecond. Over the years I brought many people from San Antonio to talk with George at his office at IC², and they would often come away saying they didn't understand him. He was always at the blackboard as he talked, and I think that helped his ideas become clearer. After George, I was at the blackboard all the time myself. His vision, understanding, and enthusiasm made him an important catalyst for the projects related to economic development that the Health Science Center was engaged in.[27]

Stein became a fellow at the IC² Institute, and he made Kozmetsky a faculty member at the Health Science Center, where, among other projects, Kozmetsky helped organize a conference on artificial intelligence and biotechnology.

The vision for the Texas Research Park as a nationally prominent center of biotechnology was never fulfilled, perhaps partly because the park was located twenty-three miles from the campus of the Health Science Center. After twenty-five years of effort, the research park had attracted only one permanent resident, the Health Science Center's Barshop Institute for Longevity and Aging Studies, which had been established with a gift from the former regent Sam Barshop and his wife. In 2016, the regents authorized the sale of the institute's six buildings and the remaining vacant land at the research park, with plans by the Health Science Center to relocate the institute to a new building on the main campus.[28]

True to Kozmetsky's accustomed role as a behind-the-scenes generator of ideas that others acted on (or as a "first-level influencer," in David Gibson's terminology), various leaders of the University of Texas at Arlington credit Kozmetsky with introducing them in the early 1980s to the idea of a robotics institute that would be a collaborative effort of the university, private industry, and civic and business leaders from Fort Worth. "Dr. Kozmetsky deserves a lot of credit for conceiving the idea, and then the rest of us for running with it," John Rouse Jr., dean of engineering at the Arlington campus from 1981 to 1987, told a newspaper on the tenth anniversary of the robotics center.[29]

When ground was broken on the center, Kozmetsky related to his students at the University of Texas at Austin the behind-the-scenes involvement of the IC² Institute. Discussing the fundraising campaign and the research strategy of the center, Kozmetsky asked, "Where was that problem structured? At IC². What did IC² do? It held two workshops bringing that community together, and they had a lot of informal meetings. Who got the credit? The University of Texas at Arlington. We didn't take any of it."[30]

Another similarity with the San Antonio project was that the robotics initiative built on the academic history of the local campus, where engineering had long been a strength and a robotics program had been established in the early 1980s, and the initiative dovetailed with the economic history of the region, which since World War II and the 1950s had included a strong manufacturing base focused mainly on aircraft and automobiles.

As with the biotechnology initiative in San Antonio, the success of the robotics idea depended heavily on the ability of local leaders to contribute financially. A campaign led by the Fort Worth Chamber of Commerce bore fruit with a donation of 18.5 acres for the robotics center on the east side of Fort Worth by brothers David and Kenneth Newell, and other contributions came from established Fort Worth businesspeople, such as Edward Bass and W. A. "Tex" Moncrief, and area foundations, such as the Amon G. Carter Foundation and the O'Donnell Foundation. Computers and other equipment were donated by companies including IBM. It took two years after the regents' 1984 announcement before ground was broken on the robotics center and another two years before the center opened. In the first decade after it opened, the center had conducted research for more than 1,500 companies and government agencies and was estimated to have contributed more than $400 million to the Dallas–Fort Worth economy.[31]

Kozmetksy also pursued his interest in robotics in other ways. While the University of Texas at Arlington center concentrated on applied projects dealing with specific industry needs, Kozmetsky developed a close working relationship with Delbert Tesar, a faculty member at the University of Texas at Austin who was an international leader in fundamental robotics research. Tesar became a fellow of the IC^2 Institute, and Kozmetsky regularly visited his classes to discuss issues of technology and the economy.[32]

Kozmetsky provided not only some of the initial ideas but also assisted with some of the hands-on management for another University of Texas System economic development initiative, the Center for Energy and Economic Development (CEED) at the University of Texas of the Permian Basin. This center, located between Midland and Odessa, was a response to the boom-and-bust cycle of the oil industry. It was an effort to support the oil industry by serving as a conduit for research, such as at the Bureau of Economic Geology at the University of Texas at Austin, and to promote a more diverse economy for the Permian Basin region. Kozmetsky worked with local leaders, such as Bill Roden, a member of the Board of Regents from Odessa, to establish CEED, which in addition to its research functions included a center for small-business development and an initiative to support economic development efforts with other public entities. CEED began in 1986 with donated land and a $500,000 grant from the Odessa Industrial Development Corp., but several years were required before its building was completed and all its programs were inaugurated.

Assigned by the regents to have a hands-on role in management of the center, Kozmetsky worked closely with Warren Gardner, University of Texas of the Permian Basin's vice president for academic affairs, and traveled to CEED frequently to consult with staff, entrepreneurs, and local officials. "George would fly in and spend a day or two once or twice a month, letting people bounce all their ideas off him," Gardner recalled. "He was a hard task-master. He would call up and say, 'Do you have my schedule lined up? I don't want any delays. I don't want these people to have to wait.'"[33]

The final economic development center that Kozmetsky worked on in his capacity as an adviser to the regents, even after he no longer held an official position with the board, was the Cross Border Institute for Regional Development (CBIRD), located at the University of Texas at Brownsville but also with offices in Monterrey, Mexico (only two hundred miles south of Brownsville). CBIRD began in April 1999 with an expansive vision of building "a knowledge-based, technology-linked region through new institutional alliances and public-private partnerships."[34]

The institute was a collaboration among the IC^2 Institute, the University of Texas at Brownsville, the Houston Advanced Research Center, and the Monterrey Institute of Technology and Higher Education. Kozmetsky and Robert Ronstadt, his successor as director of the IC² Institute, traveled to Monterrey with other Texas officials in April 1999 for a ceremony announcing the collaborative effort.

Kozmetsky said the new institute was designed to foster strategic partnerships among business, government, academic, and philanthropic sectors in order to focus on critical problems facing the US-Mexico border region, such as education and training, infrastructure, telecommunications, affordable housing, quality-of-life issues, human resources, and financial capital. "We will cooperate wherever possible in areas of economic development, technology commercialization, high-tech industrial park creation, research, education, training, venture capital, and other sustainable development activities," Kozmetsky said in a joint press release announcing the initiative. "It's the most exciting program that I can think of. We want to get things done. We want people to see that it works."[35]

In an arrangement that Kozmetsky worked out with Baylor University president Robert B. Sloan, Baylor faculty member Corey Carbonara (a former student of Kozmetsky's and a fellow at the IC² Institute) was loaned to CBIRD as its director of new technology and community networks. Carbonara traveled with Kozmetsky to the Lower Rio Grande Valley on many occasions to work on the project, which he said Kozmetsky envisioned as a way to support the unique culture of the Valley and foster new economic opportunity in a region that had been left out of much of the progress Texas had made since the early 1980s. Carbonara worked with the Texas State Technical College on an infrastructure assessment of the border region focused on using digital technology to increase the quality of education and entrepreneurship in the region.

"CBIRD was part of George's hope for shared prosperity," Carbonara said. "He was very serious about trying to do something constructive for the region. He told me that earlier in his career he had worked on many weapons systems that were used to destroy things, but now he was determined to build something. He wanted to build community."[36]

Juliet Garcia, president of the University of Texas at Brownsville, used some of Kozmetsky's terminology to describe the importance of the project: "The ideas that come out of this institute . . . will make a difference. CBIRD will function as a cross-border catalyst center that is both a 'think' and 'do' tank where creative ideas are studied analyzed, disseminated, and implemented."[37]

As with some of Kozmetsky's other brainchildren, CBIRD lost its momentum after his initial push to get it started, and it might have fallen victim to continuing rivalries among the cities of the Lower Rio Grande Valley. The institute produced a few reports but did not achieve the broad influence that Kozmetsky had envisioned.

Kozmetsky's involvement in so many and such diverse projects on behalf of the Board of Regents over thirty years sometimes resulted in his getting credit for achievements that were not his and that he never claimed. Occasionally the *Daily Texan*, the student newspaper at the University of Texas at Austin, would list Kozmetsky as a tenth member of the Board of Regents, and some people believed that he had been responsible for just about every economic development project that came along, including the idea of establishing a winery on the University Lands in West Texas. In reality, Kozmetsky was a supporter of that endeavor when it was being considered by the regents, but it had not been his idea.[38]

The Board of Regents was only one of many entities that benefitted from Kozmetsky's advice. Throughout the years that he advised the regents on a host of policy and planning questions, Kozmetsky also continued his work as a consultant to numerous other government and private-sector organizations across the country—work that enhanced his stature as a strategic thinker and a resourceful advocate for new approaches to old problems.

CHAPTER 14

CONSULTING ON PUBLIC ISSUES

Well before he served as dean of the business school and an adviser to the university regents, Kozmetsky had been recognized as an expert adviser to business and government on a variety of strategic planning and public policy issues, many having to do with computers or other technical subjects. While Kozmetsky was sometimes criticized for being involved in more projects than he could effectively manage—taking him away from Austin many days each year—his ongoing participation in national commissions and advisory groups and other special consulting projects obviously brought him personal satisfaction and was widely perceived as enhancing the reputation of the business school and the university. These activities were also consistent with Kozmetsky's vision of the business school as a force for change in society.

Among the host of appointments that Kozmetsky undertook were service on the management advisory panel of NASA, membership on the board of directors of the Adlai Stevenson Institute (a Chicago-based public policy organization), leadership of a panel on technology at the White House conference "The Industrial World Ahead," and membership on an American Council on Education task force on international business.[1] Kozmetsky participated in many other ad hoc projects organized by business organizations or government agencies, as summarized in this chapter.

COMPUTERS AND PRIVACY

Toward the end of his management career at Teledyne, Kozmetsky was appointed to a task force organized by the US Bureau of the Budget to study whether the government should have a centralized data center that would bring together statistical information from all federal agencies in one computerized database. His appointment to the database task force is evidence that—perhaps through his work on digital computing at Hughes and Litton, his 1956 book on computers and business management, and his other activities—he had become recognized as one of a still-small group of experts on the use of computers in the management of large organizations. Many of the issues studied by the data-center task force continue to be debated more than fifty years later, and the twenty-first-century debate follows much the same pattern as in the 1960s.

Advocates of the proposed "national data center" argued that it would take advantage of the available technology for computer storage and analysis of information, thus supporting advanced research into economic and social issues, increasing government efficiency, and improving decision-making related to government policy and budgeting. Opponents concentrated on the risks to privacy that a centralized data center could pose. In the end, Congress killed the idea in 1967 after a series of hearings by subcommittees of the House Government Operations Committee, the Senate Judiciary Committee, and others.[2]

Although the proposals of the task force were ultimately rejected, its recommendations and the debate surrounding them remain of interest because of the continuing public discussion about government information and privacy during the ensuing half century. The task force worked in the now-antique era of IBM punch cards and magnetic data tapes, but the issues it confronted remain relevant and unresolved today.[3]

The chairman of the task force was Carl Kaysen, an economist who had worked at the Office of Strategic Services during the war and was at the time of the task force's report the director of Princeton's Institute of Advanced Study. Other members were Richard Holton, an economist who had been assistant secretary of commerce and was dean of the business school at the University of California, Berkeley, from 1967 to 1975; H. Russell Morrison, a statistician at Standard Statistics Co., a computer subsidiary of Standard & Poor's; Richard Ruggles, an economist who had also worked at the Office of Strategic Services; and Charles C. Holt, an economist at the Urban Institute at the University of Wisconsin and a former colleague of Kozmetsky at the Carnegie Institute of Technology, as well as a future colleague at the University of Texas.

The Kaysen task force was formed by the Bureau of the Budget (an agency in the Executive Office of the President) after a private organization, the Social Sciences Research Council, proposed in 1965 that the government set up a centralized data bank. As envisioned by that group and endorsed by the task force, the data bank would allow agencies such as the Census Bureau, the Internal Revenue Service, and the Social Security Administration to store and integrate statistics in one computer, thus helping social scientists and government workers analyze economic and social issues. As usually described, the data center would store information that was only statistical in nature, such as Census Bureau population data, without the names of individuals attached, but critics worried that it could grow into a collection of highly detailed electronic dossiers on every person in the country.

The task force presented its report to the Bureau of the Budget in early fall 1966, just after Kozmetsky had moved to Austin, but the proposed data center had already drawn the attention of several members of the US Congress. The House Government Operations Committee's Special Subcommittee on Invasion of Privacy held hearings on the proposal in July 1966. The hearings featured prominent opponents of the idea of a data center. One was Vance Packard, a writer popular for a series of books that critiqued the consumer economy and other features of postwar society. Packard's book *The Naked Society*, which raised alarms about computer technology and privacy, had been published in 1964. In his testimony to the subcommittee Packard warned that the data center would encourage the depersonalization of life in America, lead to greater distrust of the government by citizens, create "a suffocating sense of surveillance" by the government, make it likely that negative and perhaps incorrect information about individuals would follow them forever, and allow too much power "to rest in the hands of the people in a position to push computer buttons."

"My own hunch," Packard said, "is that Big Brother, if he ever comes to these United States, may turn out to be not a greedy power seeker, but rather a relentless bureaucrat obsessed with efficiency. And he, more than the simple power seeker, could lead us to that ultimate of horrors, a humanity in chains of plastic [computer] tape."[4]

The task force addressed these worries in its report, which strongly advocated the creation of a new centralized agency (to be known as the National Data Center) for the computerized collection, storage, and analysis of information, but with safeguards built in to protect individual privacy. The task force found the current decentralized "federal statistical system" to have three principal inadequacies—the time lag between gathering information and making it public, the loss of details in the process of aggregation and tabulation, and the lack of a uniform policy on individual privacy across all agencies. Major inefficiencies in the system, according to the task force, were duplication in the collection of information, failure to collect data in a form that could be used by all agencies, and failure to take advantage of the efficiencies of greater centralization. The task force also concluded that much of the government relied on obsolete technology for handling and storing information, with the result that agencies were unable to meet the growing demand for timely and useful information.[5]

The task force proposed that Congress deal with the issues of privacy and confidentiality through legislation replacing the current diversity of policies across agencies and defining "a general statutory standard governing the uses of information that is collected on individuals." The director of the new National Data Center would be given responsibility for monitoring compliance with the uniform standard by both the data center itself and all other federal agencies.[6]

After Congress declined to institute a uniform, government-wide approach to the collection and use of data, agencies continued their piecemeal efforts to deal with the problems that the task force had described. Much of this work was centered in the Census Bureau and the Bureau of the Budget's Office of Statistical Standards.[7] A comprehensive approach to the issues dealt with by the task force would have to wait for another day.

NATIONAL SYNTHETIC FUEL PROJECT

Kozmetsky's role as an adviser to the regents on issues that included the management of the university's oil lands in West Texas, as well as his position as chairman of the advisory committee for the University of Texas at Austin's Center for Energy Studies, might have contributed to his selection as one of the leaders of a project in 1973–1974 to study ways that the federal government could stimulate the production of synthetic fuels. The fact that Kozmetsky was eager to use the resources of the business school, including its large number of management and policy experts, to work on the project was also a plus. The Incentives Preference Project was organized by US government organizations in response to a national energy plan announced by President Richard Nixon in November 1973, just after the Arab countries that belonged to OPEC imposed an oil embargo. Nixon's plan was called Project Independence, and its goal was to make the country self-sufficient in energy.

The National Science Foundation and the Federal Energy Administration set out to determine what incentives the federal government could best use to accelerate the commercial production of synthetic fuels, or "synfuels," from four sources—oil from oil shale and three kinds of fuel from coal. Phase one of their study involved a survey of leaders of energy companies, utilities companies, and banks to get their views on the issues. Phase two, in which Kozmetsky and the University of Texas business school played a major part, included a simulated negotiation between a "government team" and an "industry team," with the goal of analyzing six proposed government incentives for the synfuels industry. The busi-

278   A CIVIC ENTREPRENEUR

ness school and a private consulting firm in Arlington, Virginia, were in charge of the second phase of activities. Kozmetsky led the industry team, and he and others from the university took part in a week of role-playing exercises in the fall of 1974 that produced a set of recommendations for government action. Kozmetsky also served as the chief negotiator for the industry team during the simulated negotiations.[8]

The six possible incentives studied by the teams dealt with ways of helping finance a synthetic-fuel plant through different types of grants, loan guarantees, or other mechanisms. After debating each incentive, the simulated negotiations resulted in a list of "five crucial roadblocks" that could prevent the effective use of any of the incentives. The roadblocks included the need for enabling legislation, the availability of capital, the complex "scope of work" needed to bring some synfuel operations into being, the environmental impacts of the projects, and legal issues such as patent rights. In each case, detailed recommendations were made for eliminating these roadblocks. The project could not, of course, anticipate the technological and market changes of the twenty-first century that resulted in a revolution in the production of oil from shale, changing much of the debate over this resource; the project did, however, discuss in detail the environmental issues that are still familiar with oil shale today.[9]

President Carter's National Energy Plan

In the spring of 1977, just as he was busy getting the IC^2 Institute off the ground, Kozmetsky was among a small group of faculty and administrators who were asked by University of Texas president Lorene Rogers to respond to an urgent request by Governor Dolph Briscoe for advice on a newly proposed National Energy Plan from the administration of President Jimmy Carter. The plan, developed in the midst of the long-running "energy crisis" that had begun with the OPEC oil embargo, called for a series of conservation measures to reduce consumption of oil and gas, greatly increased production of conventional and alternative energy sources, and various tax incentives and disincentives designed to make the country less dependent on foreign energy resources (imports accounted for about half of the country's consumption of oil in 1977). The Carter plan had major implications for Texas and other southwestern and Gulf of Mexico states because of its call for sharply increased oil and gas production in those regions.

The university's response to Briscoe's request was to put together, within three weeks, a four-hundred-page report that critiqued the Carter plan by drawing mostly on existing research, much of which had been conducted at the business school or at University of Texas research centers in geology and energy.[10] Kozmetsky was one of the organizers of the project, along with economics professor Walt W. Rostow; William L. Fisher, director of the Bureau of Economic Geology; and Herbert W. Woodson, director of the Center for Energy Studies and a future dean of engineering at the university. Briscoe relied heavily on the report in congressional testimony on the National Energy Plan.[11] Kozmetsky and Rostow helped write Briscoe's prepared remarks for the congressional hearings, and Kozmetsky traveled to Washington with the governor to serve as an on-the-scene adviser,[12] although it is clear from Briscoe's give-and-take with members of Congress after his prepared statement that he had a full grasp of the issues.

An overview of Carter's plan—written by Rostow, Kozmetsky, and Fisher—criticized it as calling for "a rather desperate two-front war with both conservation and production fronts." The overview criticized proposals for a ceiling on the price of natural gas and an "all-out" increase in oil and gas production in Texas and other southwestern states while leaving largely untapped the petroleum resources on federal lands in the West. The overview also questioned whether projections of increases in energy production over the next ten years were realistic, and it challenged assumptions about investments needed for meeting production targets in oil, gas, coal, nuclear, and other energy sources. Other criticisms included the omission of any proposal for increased use of mass transit and the plan's call for seventy-five new nuclear power plants by 1985 (more than doubling the number of plants operating in the United States).[13]

Kozmetsky cowrote three other sections of the report—an analysis of the economic implications of the call for weight limitations on automobiles, written with graduate student Chris Wrather and associate professor of general business Po-Lung Yu (a paper that would be published in 1978 in the journal *Policy Sciences*); an analysis of the investments required in order to meet the ambitious energy production goals, written with Eugene B. Konecci; and a discussion of capital needs for economic growth in the Southwest in the next decade, written with associate professor of international business Hossein Ashari. Other sections were written by faculty members in the business school and researchers at the Center for Energy Studies. Kozmetsky's associate dean, William H. Cunningham, contributed a summary of his research that was relevant to the plan's proposal for a tax increase on gasoline of five cents a gallon every year that national consumption did not decline. Cunningham concluded that a five-cent tax would not be enough to spur drivers to reduce consumption.[14]

In 1978, Congress incorporated portions of Carter's plan in five pieces of legislation collectively known as the National Energy Act of 1978. Many

A CIVIC ENTREPRENEUR

provisions, such as price controls on natural gas, were short-lived, but others, such as conservation measures, had a more lasting impact. These measures included fuel-efficiency standards for cars, tax credits to encourage business to invest in conservation, an assistance program to weatherize residences, and energy-efficiency standards for new construction.

INFORMATION TECHNOLOGY

Kozmetsky often advocated research and academic programs across the traditional academic disciplines, and he pursued a variety of interests that went well beyond the usual academic bailiwick of the business school. These multidisciplinary interests were frequently focused on information technology.

Kozmetsky's interest in information technology found expression in many projects during his years at the university. One of these came in the late 1960s, when Kozmetsky collaborated with his friend Roland Gommel Roessner, a University of Texas architecture professor who would work on several design projects for Kozmetsky, in a large student design project aimed at developing ideas for "an educational campus for the next decade." The project was called the Generalized University Model, or GUM, and involved an interdisciplinary study of how technology could support student learning.[15] Innovations resulting from the project were reported to have been implemented on university campuses nationally, and ideas from the multimedia section were used in the "model teaching laboratory" that was incorporated into the design for the Graduate School of Business that opened in 1976.[16]

Applying emerging communications technologies to classrooms and other learning environments was a subject that intrigued Kozmetsky throughout his years as dean, and it was one topic that drew his early attention to Cunningham, then a young faculty member in marketing, who was one of the relatively few faculty members making intensive use of slide presentations in his classes. Cunningham remembers how flattered he felt as an assistant professor when Kozmetsky would stroll into his office from time to time to talk about their mutual interest in adding visual elements to lectures as a way of capturing and holding the students' interest. Visits to faculty members' offices by the dean were rare, and Cunningham recognized that these sessions had special meaning.[17] Kozmetsky's emphasis on the importance of technology in business education was reflected in the facilities that were built during his tenure as dean, notably the "Classroom 2000" that was incorporated in the new building for the Graduate School of Business and the multimedia features of classrooms in the University Teaching Center.

Kozmetsky's interest in information technology played out on a national scale beginning in 1970, when he and faculty member Timothy W. Ruefli took part in a large study sponsored by the Conference Board (a business and economics research organization) aimed at developing an overview of the rapidly emerging field and making policy recommendations for communities in business, government, education, and science. The study involved dozens of business and university leaders and resulted in a 235-page report focused on challenges for all sectors of society in the 1970s and 1980s.[18] Kozmetsky and Ruefli were given a follow-up assignment—to digest the report, looking for short-term action items, with emphasis on initiatives that needed immediate attention from decision makers in the public and private sectors. They produced a twenty-six-page report whose goal was to set the information technology agenda for business, government, and academia in the last part of the twentieth century.[19] They also wrote a closely related report that provided a context for analyzing the problems presented by information technology and presented a long-range program for managing its effects.[20]

The University of Texas would not have been in a position to participate in this project in 1970 and subsequent years if Kozmetsky had not, during his first four years as dean, established a strong presence for management science and cybernetics studies within the faculty and the research program of the business school.

By the late 1960s governments and business organizations around the world were grappling with the organizational and policy implications of the computer era, which was barely twenty years old but had begun to affect larger and larger segments of society. There was a widespread perception that for the industrial world, a revolution in communications and information was imminent, and that this revolution would transform economies, create new centers of wealth and power, require new types of education, and form the basis of new levels of competition among nations and regions—all themes that preoccupied Kozmetsky for years. The Conference Board study was one of the earliest efforts to come to grips with the issues presented by such a revolution. There was a certain urgency to the study, partly as a result of the nature of the problem itself, but also because other parts of the world were also focusing on the changes being wrought by information technology. A group in Japan had produced a report in 1970 that helped set that country on the path of membership in the worldwide "information society," with a set of national policies and actions related to computers comparable in scale to the US Apollo space program. A 1971 study by the European Organisation for Economic Co-operation and Development had set forth a comparable urgent agenda for

A Civic Entrepreneur

the countries belonging to that organization. Even in the Soviet Union, a "crash program" had been ordered in 1972 for greatly expanding training programs for computer scientists and computerizing the country's economy by the 1980s. These developments—and the clear message that the United States was entering a new era of global competition—informed the focus by Kozmetsky and Ruefli on "decisions that cannot wait" in the United States. Thanks to Kozmetsky, the University of Texas business school was squarely at the center of these global developments.

Kozmetsky and Ruefli presented a ten-item "can't wait" agenda for dealing with the challenges of information technology. The first of these was for greater understanding among decision makers about what information technology is—as an industry, as "emergent national resources," and as a source of economic and political power. As he did so often, Kozmetsky saw a need to approach this problem in comprehensive, strategic terms rather than piecemeal. This led to the second proposal, an independent center that would make continuing study of information technology issues and formulate a national policy.[21]

Other proposals dealt with broad information technology issues that remain concerns in the twenty-first century, including a need for a better understanding of privacy issues, particularly as concern for individual privacy may conflict with actions seen in other respects to be in the national interest; a need for "constantly updated comprehension" of the way developments in information technology are changing group and institutional values, including changes in ideas about corporate profits and social responsibility, work and leisure cycles, scientific developments, and individual aspirations; and a need for more attention to standardized and coordinated technologies to make technologies compatible with one another and more efficient.

The remaining agenda items were relevant to the nation's system of education at all levels, including educational issues that Kozmetsky was dealing with at the business school. These included a call by Kozmetsky and Ruefli for an interdisciplinary study of how information technology would affect management styles, skills, and performance. A related initiative called for expanded use of information technology to implement a "systems approach" to solving large, complex, "unstructured" problems, including the tasks of clarifying a problem, setting priorities, and allocating time and resources. This would mean tackling social and economic problems with a systems approach similar to the one used by NASA. Closely tied to that initiative was a call for expanded support for research and development in information technology.

Another agenda item was a need for all types of educational institutions to develop new programs and instructional methods necessary "to meet the manpower requirements of an information-dependent society and prepare the talent to manage this emerging national resource." Consistent with this was a call to "close the literacy gap" between users and nonusers of communications technology, particularly the gap between the skills and understanding of the top management of companies and the "technologists" who work under them. Kozmetsky and Ruefli also identified an information technology literacy gap between older managers who rely on empirical judgments to solve problems and a younger generation "who increasingly will substitute 'decision models' for experience." They found another gap between the producers and users of information: "The misunderstanding or limited understanding of information technology that clouds the public mind must be dispelled if the myths and threats, real or imagined, are not to create unwarranted antagonism against 'elite experts' and against information technology in general."[22]

To combat these problems and smooth the way for a more unified public vision of the uses and benefits of information technology, Kozmetsky and Ruefli recommended university courses to teach future managers about the new techniques of "information collection, storage, transfer, and use as a resource, as an industry, and as a tool for policy formulation and resource allocation." They noted that the University of Texas business school, "as a result of its participation in this study," was planning to introduce such courses in its graduate curriculum in 1973. This was a reference to revisions in the MBA curriculum that included new interdisciplinary electives, including several related to information technology.

The report was widely distributed among influential leaders in business, government, and higher education, and Kozmetsky made presentations about the report on numerous occasions. He incorporated the main ideas from the study into a presentation in February 1972 at a White House conference on the future of US business and industry,[23] and in June 1972 he spoke on these "decisions that cannot wait" at a conference titled "The Information Society of the 70s and 80s—A Transatlantic Assessment." The US Information Agency arranged for Kozmetsky to speak in 1972 to embassy staffs in various European countries on information technology and the management of world resources.

There were indications that the world was far from ready for the work that Kozmetsky and Ruefli did on developing policies for the new field of information technology. Many years later, Kozmetsky recalled the difficulty he'd had in getting corporate executives—even the leaders of major technology companies—to grasp the revolution in information technology and its implications for society.

"The thing was that in 1972 we couldn't get the senior executives of the major corporations in this country to even understand it," Kozmetsky said in 1985. "I remember IBM got so mad at me when I said that we no longer have a 'real world' out there, we have an 'informational world.' If you are going to be a part of it, regardless of its value and worth, you have got to 'plug in' or you are going to be left out. So they ran ads selling their products: 'We are selling reality . . .' Remember, they had this couple walking on the beach. That was reality. So I think I can't blame anyone, because we were not good enough to get people to understand it."[24]

Corporate Social Responsibility

Another area highlighted in the Conference Board study was the broad impact of information technology on the way the private sector viewed profits to include not only a company's direct costs and benefits but also the effect on society of the company's actions. Kozmetsky and Ruefli included these ideas in the first report of the study and elaborated on them in a later working paper.[25] They argued that the rise of information technology as a management tool and as a national resource would be likely to affect both the measurement and the concept of corporate profits.

Their theory was that the availability of information technology as a management tool would lead managers to start extending their assessment of profits in terms of direct costs and benefits to also include secondary and tertiary effects. The result would be a redefinition of costs and benefits to include, for example, factors such as environmental pollution, government regulations, and public opinion as influenced by environmental organizations.[26] By profitability, as distinct from profits, Kozmetsky and Ruefli were referring to the larger social consequences of a company's actions, consequences that, as they rippled through society, amounted to a new national resource.

Kozmetsky and Ruefli's definition of profitability included benefits that "can be measured outside the company's accounting measure of profits":

> For example, a company that had developed an effective internal education system to train its own personnel; e.g., computer programmers or managers skilled in information technology who, through attrition, go to other firms or government agencies and utilize such skills as represent a contribution to profitability. There are also secondary and tertiary effects to profitability. In the above example, a secondary effect is to reduce the need for educational institutions because of such corporate actions. A tertiary effect is that such corporate programs can provide materials, examples, as well as instructors for educational institutions.

A key point is that there exists the ability to transfer technology (information process) developed for one purpose to meet other needs. In other words, the notions of corporate profits must be extended to profitability which includes societal demands. The notion of profitability allows formulating decisions on where it is best to produce goods and services for society under changing internal and external environments, ranging from war to prolonged peace.[27]

This concept of "profitability" (an assessment of a company's society-wide benefits and detriments) apart from a company's "profits" (as shown on a balance sheet) underlay Kozmetsky's continued insistence that "making a buck" was not, by itself, the final word on a company's value. The broader idea of profitability explains his statement that "if all business does is make a buck . . . they won't be in business, and if they don't make a profit, they won't be in business. Therefore, making a buck is not the objective of business."[28] Today it is routine for corporations to proclaim their dedication to social responsibility through philanthropic and service activities aimed at establishing a company as not only a profitable enterprise but also as a "good corporate citizen." Such practices were much less common in the 1960s and 1970s, when Kozmetsky was promoting a new concept of profits and profitability.

SUPPLIES AND SHORTAGES

Kozmetsky dealt with some public issues that had only short-lived importance. One of these was the widespread and severe (but, as it turned out, temporary) shortage of commodities—everything from strategically important metals to food crops—that the world's industrialized nations mysteriously experienced in 1973–1974. Kozmetsky was among five non-government appointees named by President Gerald Ford to serve on the National Commission on Supplies and Shortages, established by Congress to study the causes of shortages. The commission also included four members of Congress and four senior officials from the executive branch, including Treasury Secretary William Simon and Alan Greenspan, who was then chairman of the president's Council of Economic Advisers.

The commission held a public hearing and contracted with economics research firms to produce case studies of various commodities that had been in short supply—titanium, aluminum, steel scrap, pulp and paper, livestock and feed grains, fertilizer, low-sulfur coal, and petroleum products. The commission concluded in its 1976 report that the causes of the shortages were not fully understood but included three complex factors: a worldwide surge in demand that had begun in 1972; a decline in investment, beginning in the mid-1960s, in the industries that processed natural resources; and a "shortage mentality" that acted as a self-fulfilling prophecy and led to hoarding and profiteering (although the commission's report avoided such politically charged language). The report concluded that a variety of government policies—including price controls, expanded farm acreage, and environmental regulations—had contributed to the shortages by inhibiting investment while also stimulating demand.[29]

The commission recommended improvements in collection and analysis of data about commodities markets; a broader and more informed approach to government policy making related to commodities; creation of an "economic stockpile" of various commodities, similar to the strategic petroleum reserve that was created in 1975 in response to the OPEC oil embargo; an expanded national emphasis on recycling; and expanded research and development related to new materials. Kozmetsky agreed with the majority of the commissioners on these recommendations, but Greenspan, Simon, and James Lynn, who was the director of the Office of Management and Budget, dissented over the issue of economic stockpiles.

Journalist Robert J. Samuelson critiqued the work of the commission and its "modest" recommendations, and he took comfort from the fact that the commissioners did not advocate any radical measures but concentrated on "administrative and technical" recommendations. "Mostly the report seems valuable as a text: a guide to the lessons of the 1973–74 shortages," he wrote. "This is more important than it seems, for nothing would be easier than drawing the wrong lessons from that experience."[30]

The shortages had eased by the time the report was made public in January 1977, and soon there were even worldwide surpluses in many of the commodities that had been so scarce in 1973–1974. The reasons for the surpluses might have been as poorly understood as the earlier shortages, but once the sense of a crisis had passed, the government failed to adopt the most fundamental implication of the commission's work—that there should be a coordinated national policy for natural resource management. Whether dealing with technology R&D, information technology, natural resources planning, or other policy issues, Kozmetsky consistently advocated a coordinated, strategic, national approach. The typical government response, however, was to try piecemeal solutions or to postpone action altogether.

COMPETITIVENESS

From 1987 to 1989, Kozmetsky served on a task force organized by the American Electronics Association (AEA) to develop strategies for improving the international competitiveness of the US electronics industry, which for a decade had been facing increasing challenges from companies in Japan and other countries. The association, the main trade group for US electronics manufacturers, representing some 3,500 electronics and information-processing companies,[31] set up the task force just as the industry was planning for the creation of Sematech, a research consortium to work on semiconductor manufacturing technology, much the way the Microelectronics and Computer Technology Corporation (MCC) had been set up to conduct research on computer software (see chapter 16).

Competitiveness in electronics had been the study of a major report from the Office of Technology Assessment, a research arm of the US Congress, in 1983. That report concluded that although the United States remained a world leader in electronics, the US industry was not likely to return to the preeminent international position it held in the early 1970s. Nevertheless, the Office of Technology Assessment said the country could continue to be competitive, and Congress could take the initiative—through a wide range of policy decisions outlined in the report—to ensure the health of the industry.[32]

The AEA task force was created partly in response to a decline in the US share of exports among eleven major electronics-exporting countries. The United States was in second place with 22.4 percent of electronics exports in 1986, down from 25.5 percent in 1984, while Japan had increased its lead from 30.6 percent to 31.1 percent. The trends "show clearly the shrinking of our country's share of international electronics trade," said J. Richard Iverson, the association's president. "It is an accurate indicator of the diminishing competitiveness of U.S. high technology companies in the global marketplace."[33]

Kozmetsky was the only member of the task force from an academic institution, although his status as a high-technology business leader and venture capitalist gave him the credentials needed to contribute to the group's work, quite apart from his years of work as an educator and a scholar of technology issues and industrial policy. The task force was led by Ed Zschau, a former member of the US Congress from California and a venture capitalist. The panel included Kozmetsky's old friend Roy Ash, as well as Robert N. Noyce of Intel Corp. (later the first leader of Sematech) and other business executives.

The agenda set for the task force by the AEA read like the topics for discussion at one of Kozmetsky's conferences—to define what competitiveness means and to develop a way of measuring it; to develop a framework for thinking about the issues that would shape public discussion; to develop a public policy agenda that would stimulate enhanced competitiveness within the US electronics industry; and to develop private-sector initiatives that would enable US companies to compete in the global marketplace.

A few months after the task force went to work in spring 1987, a consortium of semiconductor companies announced the creation of Sematech, a move endorsed by the AEA as a way to benefit suppliers and their customers. The association said Sematech met criteria identified by the competitive task force, including collaborative research programs supported in part by temporary government funding.

In late 1988 the task force reported to the AEA, identifying a "competitiveness crisis" facing the industry as a result of the nation's uncertain response to a changing international business environment, the high cost of capital, and the declining quality of US education. The report recommended government action, including taking a strategic approach to trade, reducing financial risk in innovation, reducing the cost of capital, setting new initiatives in education, taking a multinational approach to dealing with depletion of the earth's ozone layer, and strengthening the nation's industrial capabilities related to defense. The AEA used the recommendations in its extensive lobbying efforts in Washington, but with only mixed success.[34]

The competitiveness of US companies involved in high-technology research, development, and manufacturing continued to be a prominent political issue into the 1990s. In a study issued in 1990, the US Commerce Department acknowledged the problem of a declining US electronics industry, relative to Japan, South Korea, and other countries. One measure of the decline was the fact that three Japanese companies led the list of companies receiving US-issued electronics patents in 1987, while only four US companies ranked among the top ten. The AEA said the report accurately described the problem but didn't go far enough in proposing ways government and industry could work together on solutions.[35]

In 1997 Kozmetsky and Piyu Yue, a colleague at the IC² Institute, published a book-length study of international competition in electronics, with detailed quantitative analysis of companies in six sectors of the industry.[36] They were more concerned with describing the current comparative strengths of companies around the world than with making recommendations, but they did endorse an earlier formulation by Kozmetsky that the economic strength of the United States "has always been grounded in the nation's ability to be scientifically creative, technologically adept, managerially innovative, and entrepreneurially daring."[37]

The Defense Technology Base

Kozmetsky served in the late 1980s on an advisory panel that worked with the Office of Technology Assessment (OTA) to study US technology capabilities and resources necessary to provide for the nation's defense. This "defense technology base" had been under study periodically since 1967, when Defense Secretary Robert S. McNamara asked Kozmetsky's old friend Simon Ramo to lead a special panel that sought to predict the future technology needs of the military. McNamara believed that the United States should have foreseen technological problems related to fighting the war in Vietnam, and he wanted the Department of Defense to do a better job of anticipating such problems.[38] The OTA project had a similar mission. It began in 1987 after the US Senate Armed Services Committee expressed concern about whether the United States was staying competitive in the development of technology.[39]

The twenty-three-member advisory panel was led by Walter B. LaBerge, vice president of corporate development at Lockheed Corp., and it included Kozmetsky's friend Bobby R. Inman, who at the time of the defense study was chairman and CEO of the Austin-based Westmark Systems Inc. William J. Perry, who also served with Kozmetsky on the concurrent American Electronics Association project, was a member of the OTA panel. Other academics and defense company officials rounded out the panel.

The project resulted in two reports, in 1988 and 1989, that were written by the OTA staff with input from the advisory panel, as well as three workshops in which other defense industry managers and scientists from universities participated. The final report discussed national and international trends that called into question the ability of the United States to maintain its worldwide lead in military technology. These included an expansion of foreign companies in high-tech markets; a growing dependence of the United States on foreign sources for defense equipment; the increasing importance of the civilian sector of the US economy, as opposed to government labs, as a source for defense technology; progress that the Soviet Union had been making in catching up in its defense technology; and the increasing complexity of defense systems that were high priced, took a long time to develop, and often did not work properly.[40]

The report identified seven issues that needed congressional attention and provided a range of policy options that lawmakers could consider. The issues were reforming the defense acquisition system; compensating civilian contractors for their R&D; reforming the Department of Defense labo-

A Civic Entrepreneur

ratory system; reforming strategic planning of R&D programs; reforming government personnel practices that affect defense technology; fostering greater coordination between defense and civilian R&D programs; and addressing international trends in high-tech industries.[41]

The report said Congress had been responsible for weaknesses in defense technology by passing laws giving priority to competing interests, such as environmental protection, accountability, minority business interests, protection against conflicts of interest, and protection of constituent interests. More efficient procurement of defense systems could require Congress to give up some of its oversight authority or to curtail some of the powers of the executive branch, the report said.[42] Congressional opposition to aspects of the OTA report came swiftly. Representative Patricia Schroeder said Congress should demand "more accountability, not less," and she cited problems with development of the B-2 bomber as an indication that Congress ought to be even more involved in the management of defense technologies.[43]

The National Technology Initiative

The administration of President George H. W. Bush sponsored in 1992 a series of seminars across the country (in communities with a concentration of high-tech industries) called the National Technology Initiative. This was an effort to strengthen US economic competitiveness through faster commercialization of technologies developed at federal labs and other research centers. The initiative was organized by the US departments of energy, defense, commerce, and transportation and included presentations by federal officials on opportunities for licensing innovations resulting from the some $70 billion in research that the federal government sponsored each year. The seminars also included presentations by local and regional experts on technology transfer and related topics, and when the initiative made a stop in Austin, Kozmetsky was invited to address the meeting on the subject of raising capital for technology-based start-up companies.[44]

Kozmetsky spoke from a series of slides on "technology venturing," his term for the relatively new institutional arrangements for promoting small and "take-off" companies seeking to market technological innovations. Technology venturing included the work of industrial R&D consortia, collaborations between business and universities, state venture capital funds, risk capital networks, business incubators, and other activities (discussed in more detail in chapter 16). Compared with those engaged in technology venturing, the traditional venture capital community was composed of "amateurs" whose emphasis on short-term profitability failed to meet the challenge of supporting a new class of entrepreneurs who understood new technologies, Kozmetsky said.[45]

Kozmetsky's ideas on technology venturing were fully developed through work by him and his colleagues at the IC^2 Institute, the economic development think tank that he founded at the University of Texas at Austin. The next three chapters trace the history of the institute under Kozmetsky's leadership.

THE IC² INSTITUTE I

The Theory and Practice of Economic Development

George Kozmetsky had been interested in establishing an economic development think tank at the University of Texas at Austin for years before the creation of the Institute for Constructive Capitalism in 1977. Many of the ideas that lay behind the institute, eventually to be known simply as the IC² Institute (IC² being Kozmetsky's shorthand for Innovation, Creativity, and Capital), can be seen in his earliest plans for the business school's research programs. As early as 1966, Kozmetsky dreamed of establishing a Research Center for Management of Technological and Intellectual Resources, and he provided his own money to support research in this area by Eugene Konecci, the first senior faculty member whom he recruited to the business school.

Long before the IC² Institute became what Kozmetsky called a "think and do tank,"[1] with an emphasis on practical, hands-on economic development activities as well as academic research—and long before any research was actually conducted into the conditions of high-technology economic development—Kozmetsky had identified most of the pieces of the puzzle. And well before many others in Austin began promoting the city's high-tech future, Kozmetsky was busy trying to educate business leaders, bankers, politicians, and academics about Austin's potential. He carried on this campaign for years, with a few like-minded Austinites, before it began to bear fruit in the early 1980s. Some within the Austin Chamber of Commerce and other groups were longtime allies of Kozmetsky in this effort, and the chamber, under the leadership of Vic Mathias, had been promoting Austin as a home for science-based companies since the early 1960s, but no one had a more comprehensive vision of Austin's potential than Kozmetsky.

Celebrating the IC² Institute's twenty-fifth anniversary. *IC² Institute photograph.*

Despite the groundwork laid by the chamber and Kozmetsky in their own ways, it took a long time for the idea of Austin as a potential high-tech center to be understood and accepted by the larger community, said Neal Spelce, who has published a newsletter about the Austin economy since 1979. "Many people didn't understand the potential that we had in Austin, particularly with regard to the strength of the University of Texas and the way it could contribute in practical ways to diversifying the economy," Spelce said. "It took some time for these ideas to sink in."[2]

A CIVIC ENTREPRENEUR

The vision behind the IC^2 Institute, as well as most of the essential elements in the emergence of the Austin technology-oriented economy, were clear to Kozmetsky as early as 1971, just five years after he first visited Austin. In a speech to the chamber's Economic Development Council on September 27 of that year—at a dinner at the Gondolier restaurant in the downtown Ramada Inn—Kozmetsky shared that vision.

Austin could become a regional technological manufacturing center, he said, if the city could figure out how to attract and nurture entrepreneurs. He then laid out nine steps toward that goal: connect entrepreneurs with people at the University of Texas who have technical knowledge and skills, thus reining in the export of that university talent to other parts of the country; educate banks about new technologies so they will understand investment opportunities; exert political pressure to get the university to offer night classes in technological subjects; think and act regionally, particularly in collaboration with San Antonio; develop research parks in advanced electronics and management sciences; educate the Austin print- ing and publishing industry about new opportunities related to packaging knowledge for new ways of teaching; improve transportation, including highways and air travel; enhance the quality of life in ways that will appeal to the employees of high-tech businesses; and concentrate on developing new products in locally owned businesses.

Kozmetsky told the chamber audience that opportunities for Austin to become an important high-tech manufacturing center were so great that he was surprised it had not already happened. "It is strange," he said, "that so little manufacturing has started here in light of Austin's resources [and] quality of life, and since so many Texans want to live in Austin."[3]

Some effort is required to recapture the newness of Kozmetsky's ideas for his audience in 1971. His description of what Austin needed to do includes all the major elements of the economic development around Stanford University and San Jose, California—an area that was just begin- ning to be known as Silicon Valley. The forces at play in that region were not widely understood elsewhere. In fact, the first use of the term "Silicon Valley" has been attributed to the trade journal *Electronic News* just nine months before Kozmetsky's speech in Austin.[4]

Kozmetsky would spend the following years repeating the messages that he delivered at that dinner, and eventually enough other people began to understand what he was talking about—enough to begin turning the ideas into action in Austin and many other locations. The IC^2 Institute became an important focal point for Kozmetsky's message, the elements of which remained remarkably consistent through the years. The institute would conduct research into those elements and would participate in new institutional arrangements stemming from Kozmetsky's vision for Austin, although the institute also maintained a global orientation.

Apart from Kozmetsky's early technology-related research center at the business school, there were at least two other attempts at the University of Texas at Austin, before the IC² Institute, to establish research centers dealing with issues of economic development. The university's economics department operated a Center for Economic Development as a research unit for a while in the 1960s and early 1970s, until the center fell victim to state budget cuts.[5] Another initiative was a Labor and Management Education Center, which Ray Marshall, an economics professor and later a US secretary of labor and a faculty member at the LBJ School of Public Affairs, wanted to establish in the early 1970s to bring together businesses and unions to work on research and education projects. The proposal had strong support from the Texas AFL-CIO but was caught up in legislative politics, and by 1972 it had been dropped from state appropriations.[6] Marshall later became a fellow of the IC² Institute. The fate of those projects may have been a reason Kozmetsky wanted to use only private donations to support his institute.

A VISION FOR KOZMETSKY'S INSTITUTE

Kozmetsky's early descriptions of the Institute for Constructive Capitalism included the goals that it would underwrite advanced research on issues such as determining the role of capitalism in society, encouraging business enterprises to contribute more toward solving societal problems and improving quality of life, nurturing entrepreneurship and gaining a better understanding of the role of small business in a capitalist society, and promoting better public understanding of business, including improving business education in public schools.

The scope of the center would be redirected and broadened several times, with the early emphasis on research, conferences, and publications evolving in the 1980s into a more proactive role of spurring economic development. As the institute began to become a "think and do tank," its advocates hailed it as the first organization of its kind "to combine technology, entrepreneurship, and innovative education to understand wealth creation and the evolution of capitalism."[7]

Kozmetsky kept the institute's focus on the future. In 1994, he wrote of three possible approaches to commercializing science and technology. The first was the laissez-faire approach that let markets dictate decisions and gave government a minor role, confining federally sponsored R&D to basic research and leaving commercialization to private industry. At the other extreme of economic theory was the approach that advocated

A CIVIC ENTREPRENEUR

a "national industrial policy," with the government intervening in strategic decisions about technology and serving as a manager of trade. The final approach was the one that Kozmetsky advocated, involving a national commitment to advancing the realms of science and technology through extensive collaboration among government, business, education, and labor.

Collaborations of this type were at the heart of the research and practical projects undertaken by the IC² Institute, and this approach lay at the core of Kozmetsky's vision of a peaceful world based on "shared prosperity." As Kozmetsky wrote, "To prepare for the twenty-first century, countries and communities will have to implement new strategies that will take into account globally competitive market systems. The next millennium must be a round of collaboration and competition between different forms of market-driven economies. Shared prosperity at home and abroad must be the goal."[8]

In 1975 Kozmetsky and Konecci produced a paper that incorporated ideas for the institute as Kozmetsky had originally conceived it. The main issues that they concentrated on had preoccupied both of them for many years—the extraordinary pace of change in society, driven by the advances in technology, and the effect of rapid change on efforts to manage business enterprises and to prepare the next generation of business leaders. They also focused on a perceived lack of support for business within American society, and explored ways of strengthening society's understanding of the role of private enterprise.[9]

Founding the Institute

Kozmetsky had been talking to faculty members about a research center to concentrate on such issues, and he had been lining up potential financial backers from among his business contacts on the advisory council of the school's fundraising foundation and elsewhere for some months before his earliest written communication to President Lorene Rogers, in the fall of 1975, about his plans.[10] He wrote that his ideas "had generated interest and enthusiasm" and that he had already secured a matching grant from the "George Brown Foundation" for $100,000 to start an endowment that would support the institute without a need for university funds.[11] He had also been discussing his plans in speeches for several months.[12]

Another issue that he took care to mention to Rogers was the possibility of criticism of such a research center on the grounds that it would not produce objective research or that the center's funding sources might "result in inherent bias or [support for] preconceived positions and principles." He referred to such concerns as typical of attitudes of the 1960s and 1970s, but he expressed hope that such criticisms could be countered if the institute could raise a permanent endowment providing all its support, "rather than being subject to annual grants, budgets, or special contracts from specific government, private agencies, or foundations."[13]

In her response, Rogers thanked Kozmetsky for informing her about the progress "on your efforts toward an Institute for Constructive Capitalism. I appreciate your sensitivity to possible criticism for such an institute. I shall be interested in future developments."[14]

By early 1977 Kozmetsky had developed his idea well beyond its embryonic stage and was ready for the institute to be established formally as what the university called an "organized research unit." This meant it needed a formal charter setting out its mission and structure, and it needed to be approved by a faculty committee known as the Research Council; by the vice president for research, Eldon Sutton; and, ultimately, by Rogers. When Rogers wrote to Kozmetsky that all these steps were complete, she included the disconcerting information that she had also approved a recommendation by Sutton and the Research Council to change the name to the Institute for the Study of Capitalism.[15] They had taken Kozmetsky's more dramatic name, with its suggestions of action and advocacy (and a bit of salesmanship), and had reduced it to the nondescript, neutral, and noncommittal language of dispassionate academic scholarship. Rogers almost certainly knew Kozmetsky well enough to realize that the name change would be galling to him.

The ploddingly academic name that university officials proposed suggests they were worried about the idea of an institute that would be "for" something besides mere study and were troubled by the possible meanings of "constructive." They might have had legitimate concerns about departing from a university's traditional role of objective pursuit of truth and venturing into a role of advocacy. In calling his think tank the Institute for Constructive Capitalism, Kozmetsky had given his brainchild a brand name, and the university bureaucracy had proposed stripping it down to its generic fundamentals. He must have felt they had not only neutralized it, but had also neutered it.

Kozmetsky promptly wrote back to Rogers that he and the business school's advisory council had been promoting and raising money for the institute for more than two years and that the term "constructive capitalism" had been an effective selling point in gaining the interest and support of private business leaders. "President Rogers," he wrote, "we are not dealing with only a name; but more importantly, with a concept that many business and other supporters of the University of Texas at Austin, members of our faculty, and other scholars here and at other universities have interpreted as an innovative area of research involving business and society."[16]

Rogers didn't like it, but she acceded to Kozmetsky's wishes. Apparently forgetting their correspondence from two years earlier, in which she had approved of his early fundraising activities, she also used this occasion to take him to task for overreaching his authority, as she saw it. "I am authorizing the change in name of the Institute for the Study of Capitalism to the Institute for Constructive Capitalism. In reaching this decision I have taken into account your statements that you have been raising money for more than two years for an institute with the latter title even though you did not have institutional approval for either the institute or the title. Surely, you have been a part of this institution long enough to know the proper procedures in such instances, and we would very much appreciate your adhering to them in the future."[17]

The records of the university president's office give no indication of a response from Kozmetsky to this irritable reprimand. Presumably, he thanked Rogers the next time he saw her and went ahead with plans for inaugurating the institute on his own terms. He could have argued that Rogers had known since September 1975 that he was raising money "for constructive capitalism," that she had never objected until the last minute, and that he might have taken her friendly encouragement in 1975 as enough of a "proper procedure" to authorize his continued work on the project. But there is no evidence that he argued with her about the issue any further, having already gotten his way.[18]

The use of "constructive" to describe a kind of capitalism was open to interpretation, but for Kozmetsky it invited thoughts of a new, broadly envisioned purpose for capitalism as an economic system that would not merely earn a profit for shareholders but also help to solve society's problems. He also sometimes wrote about what he called "creative capitalism," by which he meant an enlightened economic system that met people's needs in a nonexploitative manner. As he explained in a presentation to a committee of the US Congress: "Creative capitalism must advance our society beyond the need for imperialism or exploitation of people. Creative capitalism's success depends on its creation of wealth in a manner that truly establishes the community of humanity as the goal of our society. Wealth produced under creative capitalism must be distributed in a manner which makes it possible to increase the standard of living of all the people. . . . The new institutions or complexes upon which creative capitalism is based will make it possible to solve in a timely basis our social problems simultaneously while creating wealth and providing for meaningful leisure for all people in the world."[19]

Kozmetsky was not the only person talking about "constructive capitalism" in the 1970s, although he might have been the first to use the term widely. Arie Y. Lewin, a business professor at Duke University, also liked the term, but he seems to have given it a more politically conservative twist than Kozmetsky did. Lewin, who later contributed to several publications of the IC^2 Institute, advocated an aggressive campaign by business leaders to influence public policy with procapitalist positions and not simply to react negatively on issues such as environmental regulations, minority job opportunities, and consumer product safety. He argued that the defensiveness of corporations on such issues had helped fuel a widespread antibusiness bias and left the door open for government initiatives that were bad for business.[20]

The University of Texas announced creation of the institute in April 1977. A university press release, which abbreviated the institute's name as "ICC" (not a form adopted by Kozmetsky), emphasized the role of the research center in providing the private sector with ideas for how it could help solve society's problems "in a time of rapid socio-economic and cultural change." Examples of such problems cited in the press release included the energy crises that were of such concern in the 1970s and economic or ethical issues resulting from new technologies. The press release identified four broad areas of research that the institute expected to focus on—policy issues and analysis, with emphasis on areas where the public and private sectors overlap; a "dynamic small business" and entrepreneurship program, including advisory services to small businesses; educational materials for high schools to help students better understand capitalism; and research into cultural, ethical, and institutional issues related to the private sector and "the leadership role of capitalist institutions in American society."

Kozmetsky, who was, of course, the institute's first director, and Timothy Ruefli, its first associate director, expressed the hope that the institute would quickly become nationally recognized, on the order of the Brookings Institution in Washington, DC, which focuses mostly on governmental policy issues.[21] Kozmetsky remained director of the institute until 1995, when he was seventy-seven, but after stepping down he continued to serve on its advisory board, kept an office in its building on San Gabriel Street, and was influential in selecting its leaders for the rest of his life.

The institute's own publicity materials would provide a somewhat different summary of its purposes. Looking back after the institute had been in operation for ten years, the organization traced its origins to three basic needs—to assess the impact of technology and ideology on society, to bring new analytical methods to bear on problems affecting

A CIVIC ENTREPRENEUR

The IC² Institute in Austin, designed by Kozmetsky's friend Roland Gommel Roessner and donated by George and Ronya Kozmetsky to the University of Texas in 1995. *Photograph by Coral Franke, IC² Institute.*

the nation and society, and to evaluate emerging industries, the viability of business enterprises, and the role and purpose of private- and public-sector institutions.[22]

In addition, the institute said there were six characteristics that made it a unique research organization, characteristics that Kozmetsky emphasized throughout much of his career: dealing with "unstructured problems," which were complex issues for which there was no clear and accepted framework for resolution; developing multidisciplinary "think teams" for the solution of complex problems; going beyond the traditional subjects of business education (finance, marketing, accounting, etc.); linking theory and practice through multidisciplinary conferences, initiatives for public and private collaboration, and the involvement of "experienced practitioners"; providing new opportunities for solving problems while remaining within a university environment; and transferring research results to other institutions, such as new professional organizations, rising academic disciplines, and other research centers.[23]

The institute's first home was a room full of cubicles on an upper floor of the Graduate School of Business. Most of those cubicles were occupied by graduate students who served as research assistants, but there was also an ever-changing group of visiting scholars, institute fellows, and even corporate officials who did research at the business school relevant to their companies.

Kozmetsky's fundraising efforts for the institute had yielded almost $1.5 million in donations by the spring of 1977. The total included $500,000 from the J. M. West Texas Corp. for an endowed chair in constructive capitalism, reserved for the institute's director, and $500,000 from the Sid Richardson Foundation. Other large gifts included $100,000 from the Brown Foundation, $100,000 from H. B. "Hank" Harkins for a professorship to be held by the associate director, $50,000 from the Abel-Hanger Foundation, and $50,000 from Mrs. Paul Turnbull. Smaller amounts were contributed by other Texas foundations and companies, including Harte-Hanks Newspapers, Tenneco, Central Texas Iron Works, Hayden Head Sr., and the Mobil Foundation.[24] Kozmetsky had dreamed of raising $20 million, but his fundraising never reached that level. A portion of the proceeds from the George and Ronya Kozmetsky Excellence Endowment Fund, which had been established to support various University of Texas projects, was also dedicated to the institute.[25] Kozmetsky's own financial contributions, as well as grants from the RGK Foundation to underwrite the cost of conferences and other activities, continued to be important sources of support for the institute.

EARLY VIEWS OF THE INSTITUTE FROM OUTSIDE

The first extensive media attention attracted by the IC[2] Institute came from The *Texas Observer*, a politically liberal biweekly published by Ronnie Dugger, whose 1973 book *Our Invaded Universities* offered a leftist/populist critique of the University of Texas at Austin and other universities that Dugger saw as having compromised their academic integrity through intimate connections with corporate America. An *Observer* article on the IC[2] Institute in the summer of 1977 reflected that view of the university and its business school, making for a decidedly hostile introduction of the institute to the magazine's readers.[26] The article, which was based on the mistaken assumption that the institute was intended as a center of propaganda for big corporations and a defender of traditional capitalism against all criticism, would become important as one of the founding documents of a small but loud anti-Kozmetsky campaign on the university campus in the 1980s and 1990s. The article was frequently quoted during those years by critics from the political left as if it contained the truth about Kozmetsky's institute (see chapter 19).

Kozmetsky declined to be interviewed for the *Observer* article, but the authors were able to talk with Ruefli. Both Kozmetsky and Ruefli were suspect for the *Observer* because of their common background working with companies with defense contracts. The suspicions were returned. Ruefli joked with the authors that he would try to "say something really reactionary" to give them something to write about, and he commented, "I hope you won't say anything too good about us. That would kill us at the box office," meaning it could hurt fundraising efforts. As it turned out, the authors found nothing good to say about the institute. They found fault with its fundraising campaign among corporate leaders (with the hoped-for goal of raising $20 million), criticized its publicity materials as being vague about the institute's goals, and questioned the scholarly validity of any studies that would be underwritten with corporate funding.

"A troubling question: when does scholarship become toadyism?" the authors wondered. "All this bigtime money may not buy academics, but it certainly buys an entrée. And ICC's corporate-funded 'studies' boosting big business will have an aura of scholarship and legitimacy that ought not to be for sale at any price."[27] It appears that the *Observer* never returned to the subject of the institute's scholarship to see if its many publications over the years were actually the kind of pro-big-business propaganda that the 1977 article warned about.

The *Observer* was not alone in assuming that research centers such as the IC[2] Institute would promote a simplistic view of the virtues of free-market capitalism. Indeed, the former US treasury secretary William E. Simon, in a widely noted speech in 1976, urged universities to do just that, and he criticized what he perceived as a prevailing leftward bias against capitalism among faculty members. Partly in response to complaints such as Simon's, major corporations by 1979 had provided financial support for more than thirty academic centers or endowed chairs of free enterprise.[28] Although Kozmetsky had been planning the IC[2] Institute long before this movement emerged, the national media perceived the institute as part of the trend. Other research centers or chairs related to the study (or promotion) of capitalism—all established a year or two before or after the IC[2] Institute—included those at the University of Southern California, Cornell University, Kent State University, and Texas A&M University.[29]

Some of the other academic initiatives related to capitalism might have been designed to defend laissez-faire capitalism as it then existed, but that was never Kozmetsky's goal, even though media coverage tended to obscure his real interests, which included developing a new brand of capitalism. Among Kozmetsky's persistent criticisms of capitalism as it was reflected in large corporations were those organizations' insufficient attention to "social responsibility," reluctance to adopt new techniques of management, and resistance to technological change.

Eventually the IC^2 Institute began to attract a more objective brand of media attention than that seen in the early *Observer* article, and most of the institute's subsequent publicity, focusing on the work of faculty, graduate students, and corporate researchers, was extremely positive. The *Christian Science Monitor* noted in 1982 that when the institute was established, "some critics quickly put it in the corporate propaganda camp. After all, its name didn't do much to dispel that notion. Nor did locating it in laissez-faire Texas." But the *Monitor* also said the institute had overcome that image and was "slowly emerging as a no-nonsense evaluator of the nation's economic health."

"In a cubicled fourth-floor room of the university's graduate school of business, researchers explore the roots of capitalism, its current status, and ways it can be improved," the newspaper wrote. "At any given time some 40 people, blue-jeaned graduate students and pinstriped professors, are working on projects. Even by its own yardstick the institute is far from achieving one of its original goals: to be a respected advocate of private enterprise. Yet the reports from this self-styled economic think tank are being more widely circulated in Washington and some corporate boardrooms."[30]

The newspaper observed that the institute had sponsored workshops on topics such as the Texas economy and entrepreneurship and had published some three hundred papers and studies in five years, and "only a few have been called shallow." Kozmetsky was described as "a small but energetic man who likes to jot notes on a legal pad. Dr. Kozmetsky sees the institute as one of the few academic centers involved in purely 'objective' research of the capitalist system."

Projects of the institute highlighted by the newspaper included bringing business executives in for several weeks to focus on a research topic, such as a plan for reorganizing data processing at San Antonio's Datapoint Corporation (where Kozmetsky was a board member) and a marketing strategy for an oil company. Companies paid a $6,000 fee to send their "corporate scholars" to the institute to work on such projects. Other projects involved studying free enterprise in developing countries and gathering data on the "corporate trees" of the one hundred largest US corporations—information on acquisitions, mergers, reorganizations, and financial status—with a goal of creating a computer database that could help analyze corporate behavior.[31]

Research for Innovation and Creativity

Despite the adamancy with which Kozmetsky had fought for the original name of his think tank, he decided by 1985 that the name "has become unwieldy, somewhat confusing and at times misleading." He came up with a new name that would preserve the original initials but change what they stood for, employing two of his favorite words: "innovation" and "creativity." The name "IC² Institute" was conceived to "more correctly reflect our research mission and program objectives," Kozmetsky said. "In this context, 'I' stands for Innovation, 'C' stands for Creativity and 'C' stands for Capital. Constructive change requires creativity and innovation through the utilization of capital."[32]

Sten Thore, who was a researcher at the institute from 1978 to 1996, has offered a fuller explanation for the name change. His view is that "capitalism" was such a dirty word for many academics from other countries that Kozmetsky decided to drop the word from the name of the institute. Thore himself had been attracted to the institute because of its original name, since one of his continuing research goals had been to reveal the economic realities behind the propaganda of the anticapitalist Soviet Union and its allied governments in Eastern Europe. "I grieved when the name of our institute . . . was changed," Thore wrote. "It was done to placate Europeans. . . . In retrospect, perhaps it was necessary. My own teacher from England, Frank Hahn, did no longer want to shake my hand. I had badly betrayed the great don of leftist Cambridge, by working for an 'institute of capitalism'!"[33]

Also in 1985, the institute began leasing the first and third floors of the RGK Foundation building at 2815 San Gabriel Street, about twelve blocks northwest of the business school. Kozmetsky continued to manage the institute from his office on the second floor. Later the foundation would move to offices on Twenty-Fifth Street near Lamar Boulevard, and the Kozmetskys donated the building on San Gabriel to the university for use by the institute.

From the beginning, Kozmetsky named an executive committee of faculty members to assist him in achieving the institute's goals, as well as an advisory board of private-sector representatives. The first members of the executive committee were Nelda Garcia, associate professor of business education; Kermit Larson, professor of accounting; Stephen Magee, professor of finance; Reuben R. McDaniel Jr., associate dean and associate professor of management; and Robert A. Peterson, associate professor of marketing.[34] Peterson would join Kozmetsky in several research projects and in 2013 would become the institute's fifth director.

When the institute began, it focused its research on four areas—small business and entrepreneurship (directed at first by Ernest Walker, professor of finance); cultural, ethical, and institutional studies (directed by Eugene Konecci); policy issues and economic analysis (directed by Timothy Ruefli); and studies in private enterprise education (directed by Diane E. Downing). In the first five years, the institute produced hundreds of publications on these topics, as well as conducted many conferences, seminars, and academic courses. During the second five years, from 1982 to 1987, the institute shifted its focus to additional areas: addressing the broad topic of "creative and innovative management," which included the management of technology and which Kozmetsky hoped to see recognized as a distinct academic discipline; measuring the state of society, including studies of small-business problems and global markets; exploring economic analysis and management science; and conducting "exploratory research and advanced academic development," which included new applications of computers in business, the development of business databases, and studies of venture capital and business incubators.[35]

The institute's fellows, a network of scholars and practitioners, formed the "intellectual center" of the institute's interdisciplinary work on high-tech entrepreneurship. In the early years, the fellows included several prominent faculty members from the business school, but professors in other fields such as medical chemistry, economics, botany, and physics also participated. Kozmetsky had a flare for attracting some of the university's best-known faculty members from outside the business school to serve as fellows, including botanist Tom J. Mabry, chemist and Nobel laureate Ilya Prigogine,[36] and economist Walt W. Rostow. Kozmetsky also recruited many fellows from among his contacts across the United States and other countries—a way of institutionalizing his global network of personal relationships.

The fellows that Kozmetsky recruited made an impressive group. Sten Thore has written of his first meeting with them: "We had all assembled on the second floor of the newly completed IC^2 building, seated around the enormous glass table in the boardroom. 'We' were all the freshly baked centennial fellows, each one of us holding a fellowship honoring Kozmetsky's business associates, friends, or family. I had been part of the research staff at the institute since its inception. My new colleagues were world-class researchers, handpicked by Kozmetsky from across the entire university, representing departments as diverse as medical chemistry, economics, management science, marketing, government, biotechnology, and robotics. And there was Ilya Prigogine, director of the Center for Studies in Statistical Mechanics. Watching them all, I felt extremely proud—and humble. This was indeed a Learned Academy."[37]

The institute provided support for an ongoing series of visiting scholars, drawn from other higher education institutions, government agencies, and private businesses. They were in residence at the institute for varying lengths of time, some for several years. Some came to the institute primarily to study its methods of promoting economic development, while others conducted research closely aligned with the research of the institute's permanent staff. Many of the visiting scholars were from abroad and had been recruited by Kozmetsky during his frequent attendance at international conferences. One of the most prominent of these foreign scholars was Nikolay Rogalev, who first worked at the institute in 1992–1993 while on leave from the faculty of the Moscow Power Engineering Institute (where he is now the president). He studied the methods of the IC^2 Institute related to science and technology commercialization, technology transfer, management, and entrepreneurship, and he worked with the institute and the Austin Technology Incubator on collaborative projects involving the institute and his home institution.[38]

Among the conferences held during Kozmetsky's years as director of the institute were several that claimed to be the first academic meetings in the world on their topics. These included conferences on creative and innovative management (1982); data envelopment analysis (1985), a technique in management science for evaluating the efficiency of complex production activities; the "technopolis" trend in regional economic development (1987); computational economics (1991), another new field that brings together computer science, economics, and management science; e-commerce (1994); and electronic marketing (1996).

The institute also sponsored, among other gatherings, the first conference in Texas on biotechnology (1982) that brought together university researchers, private businesses, and state agencies; the first US-China "venture fair" and conference on science and technology commercialization, in Beijing (1997); the first international conference on technology policy and innovation, in Macau (1997); and the first international conference on technology commercialization, in Saint Petersburg, Russia (1997).[39] The RGK Foundation was a financial partner in these conferences, as well as in many others that the institute sponsored either at its Austin offices or at other institutions.

Because of his and Ronya's family backgrounds, Kozmetsky had a particular interest in the Russian economy, a topic that was reflected in several activities of the IC^2 Institute. One of the earliest of these was the management of a three-day seminar, sponsored by the National Science Foundation, that brought a delegation of economists and planners from the Soviet Union to Austin in December 1978 to discuss regional planning issues, including problems of applying computers to such planning. The conference was one of a series of exchanges under a science and technology agreement that followed President Richard Nixon's 1972 trip to the Soviet Union. A follow-up conference was scheduled to take place in Moscow in January 1982, but it was canceled along with other US-Soviet academic exchanges in the wake of the Soviet crackdown on the Solidarity labor movement and the imposition of martial law in Poland in December 1981.[40] The IC² Institute published both sides' papers from the 1978 conference and the US papers from the canceled 1982 meeting, including a paper by Kozmetsky on the management of technological change.[41]

The institute's early interest in supporting private enterprise education for elementary and secondary schools as well as the general public was phased out after several years of activities, perhaps because other groups were already active in such efforts. While the institute was still involved in this public education initiative, it cosponsored events such as a 1977 debate on the UT campus between liberal economist John Kenneth Galbraith and conservative business professor Michael C. Jensen, both faculty members at Harvard; a conference at the LBJ School of Public Affairs on partnerships between government and business; and a series of workshops for senior executives of large companies. Other projects included programs on "economic literacy" with the Texas Federation of Women's Clubs; a "Free Enterprise Teaching Calendar," which included children's illustrations of basic economics concepts; and a bilingual tape-slide program on free enterprise, designed for nationwide use in high schools. [42]

A Theory of Economic Growth through Technology

By the mid-1980s, Kozmetsky and his colleagues had developed an elaborate theoretical framework for how new technologies spur economic development, either by a series of largely unplanned forces and relationships or through deliberate management of those elements. This "framework for technology commercialization," as Kozmetsky called it, was one of the earliest achievements of research at the IC² Institute, and it was the foundation that underlay a large part of the institute's further research, as well as its eventual efforts to actually stimulate economic development in addition to studying and elucidating the process. By the mid-1990s this framework had evolved into what Kozmetsky and his colleagues called the "Austin Model," a detailed strategy for economic development that was based on studies of Austin's experience and aimed at extending and sustaining the region's technology-based economy.

Working closely with other researchers—including Raymond Smilor, David Gibson, Michael D. Gill Jr., and Eugene Konecci—Kozmetsky devised in the 1980s a series of complex tables that illustrated the process of fostering economic growth through technology diversification. This process dealt with the relationships among technology, expansion of existing companies, creation of start-up companies, community infrastructure, and private-sector goals—all leading to centers of innovation and manufacturing. Kozmetsky's elaborate tables, which satisfied his predilection for visual presentation of ideas, showed how these factors were involved in "four dimensions of relationships" that interacted simultaneously.

The four dimensions were the linking of research and development with public and private institutions; the fostering of institutions that serve as the public and private "infrastructure" for economic development; the linking of support activities and aspects of entrepreneurship with centers of innovation and manufacturing; and the monitoring of the "outputs" of resource development, economic wealth, expanded markets, and job creation.[43]

For each of these dimensions, Kozmetsky provided a detailed picture of relationships in action. For the first dimension, for example, the private and public institutions included an educational base of elementary and secondary schools, vocational schools, higher education, and continuing education; public entities such as utilities, transportation, and government labs; private entities such as service clubs, trade associations, venture capital, and consulting services; traditional financial institutions such as commercial banks, investment banking, and the like; and business networks, including professional associations, ad hoc groups, mentors, and business angels. Kozmetsky emphasized the necessity of complex linkages among all these elements, linkages that "can only be accomplished by conscious design and cooperative efforts."[44]

The second dimension of relationships—that of the public and private infrastructure—included the institutional development of private capital, including private partnerships, corporate financial or industrial firms, small business investors, international venture capital firms, business development firms, R&D limited partnerships, leveraged buyouts, and mergers and acquisitions. Another category of this infrastructure involved what Kozmetsky called "technology venturing" and included at least nine new types of institutional developments: industrial R&D consortia, academic and business collaboration, university/industry centers of excellence, university commercialization of intellectual property, business incubators, small-business innovation programs, state venture capital funds, risk capital networks, and formal collaboration among academia, government, and business.

Kozmetsky defined technology venturing as "a collaborative strategy for economic growth" and argued that the nine new kinds of institutions that he had identified were providing a new set of coherent relationships among the key organizations concerned with economic growth and technological diversification. He saw the emergence of these new institutions as being stimulated by a variety of factors, including an increase in foreign competition, a shortage of highly trained scientists and engineers, the difficulty of staying up-to-date with technological developments, gaps in the transfer of new technologies to the marketplace (especially when research from more than one traditional academic discipline was involved), a need to diffuse new technologies by developing commercial products, a desire to expand basic research at universities, and a determination to spread R&D activities across wider geographic areas.[45] These were the "drivers" of the development of new institutions related to technology venturing.

The third dimension of relationships involved "facilitators" or "bridge builders" who linked support activities and entrepreneurship with centers of innovation and manufacturing. Support activities included the work of public entities such as industrial development organizations, research parks, municipal commissions and task forces, and state offices for international trade, while important elements of entrepreneurship included management talent, technology, capital, and "know-how," a highly prized skill that Kozmetsky thought was usually in short supply.

The fourth dimension of relationships involved close interactions among the key "outputs" of economic activity—resource development, wealth generation, market growth, and job creation. Kozmetsky said technological resources were often viewed as the "stepchild of economic thought" and argued that their value in attaining wealth ought to be more appreciated: "The technologies for the 1980s and 1990s must be viewed as a national and a world resource, as a generator of economic wealth, as the means to increase productivity and international trade, as an area for assessment of public and private risk taking and risk sharing, and as an influential factor for change in the organization, education, and training of the workforce."[46]

Kozmetsky and others at the IC² Institute spent years elaborating on and refining this framework, as well as working to apply it, in one permutation or another, to actual problems of economic development. The Austin economy was an important initial focus of these activities, but

A CIVIC ENTREPRENEUR

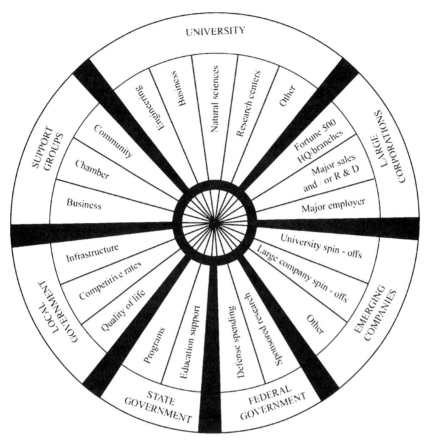

The Technopolis Wheel, the IC² Institute's visualization of the process of high-tech economic development. *IC² Institute.*

the institute also quickly expanded its work of economic development consulting to the state of Texas as a whole, to other US states, and around the world.

Smilor and Gibson devised an influential visual depiction of high-technology economic development that they called the "Technopolis Wheel." This was a rotational diagram, employing the centuries-old tradition of the wheel as a metaphor for relationships of all kinds.[47] The Technopolis Wheel illustrated the relationships among higher education, the three levels of government, community and business support groups, large corporations, and emerging companies in fostering the area of regional economic development known as a technopolis.[48] Gibson and Smilor, sitting in the office next to Kozmetsky's on the second floor of the institute, made the first attempts to sketch these relationships in a diagram that became the Technopolis Wheel. They had been motivated by Kozmetsky's habit of "drawing a picture" to explain ideas.[49]

Based on an analysis of the emergence of Austin as a center of high-technology economic activity, including success in winning the research consortia MCC and Sematech (in 1983 and 1988, respectively), Smilor, Gibson, and Kozmetsky emphasized that the seven main segments of the wheel and the smaller divisions within each segment were linked through key individuals, or "influencers," who in effect set the wheel in motion. It was within this framework that Gibson and Everett Rogers described Kozmetsky himself as one of the main "first-level influencers" responsible for long-term changes in Austin's economy.[50]

The institute's research into the processes by which a technopolis develops, as depicted by the Technopolis Wheel, has been influential around the world. Scholars from China, Japan, Korea, Israel, Russia, and many other countries have acknowledged this influence.[51]

COLLEAGUES AND COLLABORATORS ON RESEARCH

Kozmetsky built a team of close associates who shared his vision for the IC² Institute and had special interests in its fields of research. Many of these associates were also faculty members at the business school, but Kozmetsky also brought in researchers and administrators with backgrounds in other disciplines.

Konecci and Ruefli were two of the most important early colleagues at the institute. In the early days of the institute, Ruefli's research included a study of national policy on natural gas, an analysis of international competition in the microelectronics industry, and an exploration of new ideas about profits that took into account a company's social responsibilities. In later years, Ruefli joined with Kozmetsky in creating the institute's Master of Science in Technology Commercialization program, for which he taught a course on technology commercialization.

In the institute's second year, Kozmetsky hired Harvey J. McMains, who had been a director of corporate planning for AT&T for twenty-nine years, to work with him on gathering economic data for a project on the state of American capitalism. McMains did other research at the institute and, when he became the associate director for administration, helped manage the institute and served as a public spokesperson. He also held an adjunct teaching position at the business school.

McMains's impressive résumé included serving as vice president and executive director for the National Bureau of Economic Research in Cambridge, Massachusetts. Materials published by the IC² Institute and oth-

Kozmetsky and other board members of the IC² Institute in 2000, with the institute's third director, Robert Ronstadt, on the left and Laura Kilcrease on the right. Standing, left to right, are Glenn West, Mark Calhoun, Mike Todd, Dale Klein, Jeff Swope, and Charles Teeple. *IC² Institute photograph.*

ers said McMains held degrees in physics, math, and law,[52] but after he left the institute in 1983 to become interim director of the Houston Area Research Center (known as HARC, a project of oilman George Mitchell in the Woodlands), it was discovered that the only degree he held was a bachelor's in physics from the University of Texas at Austin. When the facts about McMains's background were printed by the *Houston Post*, McMains resigned from HARC as well as from his job as a lecturer in management in the University of Texas business school.[53]

"I hired him for administration, which had nothing to do with degrees, but with his experience," said Kozmetsky, who had recommended McMains to Mitchell, "I don't understand why Harvey would have embellished the details of his academic background."[54]

Raymond Smilor joined the institute in 1979 as a research associate and quickly became one of Kozmetsky's most trusted colleagues. He stayed until 1992, serving for much of that time as the executive director. After McMains left in 1983, Smilor had responsibility for administrative services and publications, program analysis, liaison with other organizations, and conferences and workshops, while Kozmetsky concentrated on planning and development.[55] Smilor also transferred many of the institute's research interests to the classrooms of the business school, and he was one of the early developers of the business school's Moot Corp., a business-plan competition that has become international in scope. In addition to conducting research on entrepreneurship, technology transfer, and the management of technology, Smilor was a faculty member in the business school, where he developed a graduate school concentration in technology management and entrepreneurship.[56] Smilor also helped ensure that the institute complied with university rules—a task that Kozmetsky didn't like tending to personally.

Smilor, like Konecci, Ruefli, and a few others before and after him, became one of Kozmetsky's protégés and confidants and a person upon whom Kozmetsky relied for help with a wide range of initiatives. "Our relationship evolved through the years and it became a deep and loving relationship," Smilor said. "We worked together on one project after another, and we traveled extensively all over the world. With George there was always an intense working environment. . . . Every few years Ronya would come to me and ask, 'How do you do it?' She knew how demanding and exhausting working with George was. He and I worked shoulder to shoulder. He was relentlessly driven, and I was, too. He was good at coming up with ideas, and I was able to follow up and implement them. For some reason we just clicked."[57]

Kozmetsky's focus was "always on the next ideas and the next challenges, and he drove and drove and drove, and many people couldn't keep up," Smilor said. "He had inexhaustible stamina, and he sometimes wore out other people, but for some reason he didn't wear me out. It was clear that he personally cared about making a difference in the world. He wanted to make things better, and that had a way of making other people care, too. He and Ronya both felt a deep obligation to give back and make a difference."[58]

As demanding and driven as he was, Kozmetsky was also a patient teacher for whom any question could become a learning experience. "When I first came to IC² George asked me to do some background research on economic issues for a speech that he was going to deliver in Europe," said Smilor, who had earned a doctorate at the University of Texas at Austin in history. "He told me to do a matrix for him on economic issues, and I said, 'What's a matrix?' His response was, 'Let me show

A CIVIC ENTREPRENEUR

you,' and he drew a picture for me and explained it perfectly. I never hesitated to ask him a question when I didn't understand something, and he never hesitated to explain. He was a true teacher and mentor and encouraged me to grow."[59]

In 1992 Smilor was recruited to lead the Kauffman Center for Entrepreneurial Leadership at the Ewing Marion Kauffman Foundation in Kansas City. Kozmetsky sought to keep Smilor at the University of Texas and wrote to administrators praising his contributions to the institute and seeking a $10,000 salary supplement for him,[60] but Smilor decided to move to the Kauffman Center, where he could be in charge of an entrepreneurship program. From the Kauffman Center he became executive director of the Beyster Institute, which promotes employee ownership as a business model, at the business school of the University of California, San Diego. In 2009 he joined the management department at the Neeley School of Business at Texas Christian University.

Fred Y. Phillips was another longtime associate of Kozmetsky who rose to a leadership role at the IC² Institute and then moved to faculty and administrative positions at other leading institutions. He first met Kozmetsky when he was a seventeen-year-old high school student visiting Austin from Evanston, Illinois, where he was a classmate of Abraham Charnes's daughter and worked for Charnes in the summers at Northwestern University doing computer programming and other jobs. After Charnes moved to the University of Texas at Austin in 1968 he persuaded Phillips to enroll at the university.

"I came down to Austin during spring break in 1969, and Abe introduced me to George," Phillips said, "and I got the first of many of my chalk talks from George." Kozmetsky ended up paying for Phillips's university education through a scholarship from the dean's discretionary fund.[61] After graduate school at the University of Texas (with a PhD in mathematics and management science) and a fellowship in Japan, Phillips returned to Austin and became the first postgraduate research assistant at the IC² Institute. After a period away from the institute, including a stint at Dell Computer Corp., Phillips returned and served as the institute's research director from 1988 to 1995. He was involved in organizing the Austin Software Council and the Austin Technology Council, helped develop the curriculum for the institute's master's degree program in the commercialization of technology, and worked on many other initiatives. He also served as a "translator" for some of Kozmetsky's more obscure statements, putting them into language anyone could understand—a role performed by several of Kozmetsky's colleagues through the years.

While working for Kozmetsky had many rewards, it was also trying,

Phillips said. "Working next to George was like getting a second PhD," he said. "But George was very possessive about the people he had mentored, and he could be very manipulative. One thing I did right was that I never kissed his ass, but the thing I did wrong was that I let him intimidate me. Abe warned me, 'Just wait, George will walk all over you,' and I saw that happen."[62] Kozmetsky's manipulation ranged from tactics such as promising a person a secretary as a recruitment tool and then taking the secretary away a few months later, to more career-changing activities, such as controlling the direction of a person's research interests to satisfy Kozmetsky's needs.

In 1995 Phillips became dean of management at the Oregon Graduate Institute of Science and Technology, then a private institution, which has since been incorporated into the Oregon Health and Science University. He is a distinguished professor in the College of Management at Taiwan's Yuan Ze University, where he manages the college's international affairs.

David V. Gibson, who earned a doctorate in sociology from Stanford in 1983, was recruited to the University of Texas at Austin as one of Kozmetsky's last faculty hires during his final year as dean. Kozmetsky had read Gibson's dissertation, "Determinants of Organizational Structure and Process: Technological Versus Cultural Explanations Concerning Innovation Management." During Gibson's recruitment visit, Kozmetsky talked about his vision for the IC² Institute.

"I was immediately captured by his vision and energy and the idea of multidisciplinary research and theory application focused on regional development," Gibson said. "He knew members of my dissertation committee—Dick Scott, my chair; and Jim March, who had been at Carnegie Mellon; and Bill Ouchi, who had recently been hired by UCLA's business school and was living near the Kozmetsky home in Santa Monica. My other committee member, Everett M. Rogers, had recently published *Silicon Valley Fever: Growth of High-Technology Culture*, and during my first year in Austin I introduced Rogers to Kozmetsky, after which Ev was invited to be an IC² fellow. Ev encouraged me to research Austin's emergence as a high-tech center, and we decided to publish a book on Austin's winning the national competition for MCC, the nation's first for-profit R&D consortium, and the resulting challenges of technology transfer."[63]

After becoming a fellow of the institute in 1986, Gibson participated in numerous "think and do" projects to better understand and to promote technology-based economic development in Austin, nationally, and internationally. During the 1990s he traveled extensively with Kozmetsky to Russia, China, Taiwan, Korea, and South America. Gibson held a series of positions at the institute, including director of the multidisciplinary

Kozmetsky with Everett M. Rogers, an authority on technological innovation and a senior research fellow at the IC² Institute. *IC² Institute photograph.*

technology transfer research program, director of publications, director of global programs, and director of research. He is currently an associate director and senior research scientist and serves as chair of the International Conference on Technology Policy and Innovation, which he founded with IC² fellow Manuel Heitor (currently minister of science, technology, and higher education for Portugal). Gibson was a Fulbright Scholar to Portugal's Technical University in 1999–2000.

Gibson collaborated with Kozmetsky and others on some of the institute's most important publications focusing on regional development and technology commercialization. These include *Creating the Technopolis: Linking Technology Commercialization and Economic Development*, with Smilor and Kozmetsky (1988); *Technology Transfer: A Communication Perspective*, with Fred Williams (1990); *Systems and Policies for the Global Learning Economy*, with Chandler Stolp, Pedro Conceição, and Manuel Heitor (2003); and *Global Perspectives on Technology Transfer and Commercialization: Building Innovative Ecosystems*, with John S. Butler (2011).

Kozmetsky wrote three well-received books on macroeconomics with another collaborator, Piyu Yue, who came to the University of Texas from China in the 1980s to pursue a doctorate in economics. She worked as a research assistant for Kozmetsky for three years while in graduate school, and in 1991, after two years as a researcher at the Federal Reserve Bank of St. Louis, she joined the IC^2 Institute as a full-time researcher and writer. Kozmetsky had chaired her dissertation committee, which also included others associated with the institute and the economics department at the university. The dissertation, which dealt with monetary analysis and management issues in international business, was completed with financial assistance and research databases provided by the institute.[64]

Her later work with Kozmetsky included the books *Global Economic Competition: Today's Warfare in Global Electronics Industries and Companies* (1997); *Embracing the Global Demographic Transformation 1950–2050: Sharing Peace and Prosperity in the Global Marketplace* (2000); and, completed after Kozmetsky's death, *The Economic Transformation of the United States, 1950–2000: Focusing on the Technological Revolution, the Service Sector Expansion, and the Cultural, Demographic, and Ideological Changes* (2005). Yue returned to China with her family after that last book was published.

Sten Thore, an economist who was a native of Norway and had been a colleague of Abraham Charnes and William Cooper at Carnegie Mellon University, learned about the IC^2 Institute from Charnes during a symposium in Austin in 1977 honoring Charnes on his sixtieth birthday. He joined the institute in 1978 as a research fellow and in 1983 was named to one of the institute's centennial fellowships. He held the fellowship named for Gregory A. Kozmetsky until 1996.

Much of Thore's research involved applying the mathematical and computer techniques developed by Charnes and Cooper to practical problems in economics and business.[65] He published papers with Kozmetsky on data envelopment analysis, including "DEA and the Management of the Product Cycle: The U.S. Computer Industry" (*Computers and Operations Research* 23, no. 4 [1995]) and "The Effects of Defense Spending on the Texas Economy: An Example of Concave Programming" (*Journal of Policy Modeling* 6, no. 4 [1984]). The institute also sponsored the publication of Thore's book *Economic Logistics* (Quorum Books, 1991).

Isabella Cunningham, wife of William H. Cunningham, worked on research with Kozmetsky beginning in the mid-1970s and continued her association with him as a fellow of the IC^2 Institute. The Cunninghams came to Austin in 1971, both with new doctorates in marketing from Michigan State University, and Bill joined the faculty of the University of Texas marketing department while Isabella became an assistant professor and then an acting dean at St. Edward's University. Isabella became a visiting assistant professor in the University of Texas marketing department in 1974 and began working with Kozmetsky on several projects, including helping him with a Saturday morning noncredit class in investing techniques—a class that drew wide interest for Kozmetsky's personal approach to investing. She and Kozmetsky also worked on his early plans for the IC² Institute, and she collaborated with him and others from the university faculty on research. One of those research projects, led by marketing professor Robert A. Peterson, was on public and news-media perceptions of capitalism and led to several journal and book publications. Isabella Cunningham and Kozmetsky also coedited a book, *Funds Management and Managerial Research: A Book of Readings* (Institute for Constructive Capitalism, 1979).

Kozmetsky offered Cunningham a job as assistant dean in 1974,[66] but she was interested in a permanent teaching and research position and was soon hired as a faculty member in the University of Texas advertising department (a unit of the College of Communication).

"George was a very capable scholar, and he was anxious to understand and help scholars with their research and their careers, but as much as he supported people doing traditional scholarship he always had a very practical side and was always interested in what would benefit society. His greatest interest was in how to make life better for people," Isabella Cunningham said.[67]

Beginning in 1989, Laura Kilcrease was one of Kozmetsky's most trusted colleagues at the institute, first as a leader of the Austin Technology Incubator and then in other roles. Her work at the institute is discussed in more detail in chapters 16 and 17.

Two administrative assistants that Kozmetsky relied on to keep up with his correspondence, scheduling, and a host of other details in making the institute run smoothly were Ophelia Mallory and Patti Roe. They began working for Kozmetsky when he was dean of the business school and stayed with him throughout his years at the institute. Roe has recalled her first encounter with Kozmetsky. It was one of her first days of work in the dean's office, but she had never met him, having been hired by Mallory as her assistant. Kozmetsky was supposed to be out of town, and Mallory was away from the office, so Roe was uncertain about what to do when a strange man approached the dean's door with a key.

"Not having seen any picture of Dr. Kozmetsky (as yet) and based on the name alone, I envisioned a very tall, broad-shouldered Russian with dark, bushy eyebrows," she wrote. "Here entering the office is a very

Robert A. Peterson, an early collaborator with Kozmetsky on research at the IC² Institute and the institute's fifth director. *IC² Institute photograph.*

quiet, unassuming silver-haired gentleman standing 5'6". Needless to say, I was caught off guard by this turn of events but—as Dr. Kozmetsky requested—I managed to get the FedEx envelope to the nearest post office without wrecking my car."[68]

Kozmetsky was succeeded in 1995 as director of the institute by Robert S. Sullivan, who had been a faculty member at the University of Texas business school and then served as dean of the business school at Carnegie Mellon. He directed the institute until 1997 and later served as dean of the business schools at the University of North Carolina and the University of California, San Diego. He was succeeded at the institute by Robert Ronstadt, an academic leader and entrepreneur who had taught entrepreneurship at Babson College and Pepperdine University. Ronstadt left the institute in 2003 to be director of a new Technology Commercialization Institute at Boston University.

One of Kozmetsky's last acts at the IC² Institute was to persuade John S. Butler, a professor of management and sociology at the University of Texas, to become the institute's next director. "George came to me and said he needed me to run the institute," Butler said. "He wanted the institute to return to research that would have an impact on society. He said

A CIVIC ENTREPRENEUR

we had a lot in common and he trusted me. We had both been medics in the army, and I had studied immigrant entrepreneurship, which was of great interest to him. He told me he saw himself as an immigrant entrepreneur. He identified himself as an immigrant (being born so soon after his parents immigrated), and he said, 'I am so wealthy because I am an immigrant.' He had been interested in my work for many years and had asked me to be a fellow at IC² in the early eighties, and later he suggested we do a conference and a book on entrepreneurship."[69]

The institute's fifth director, Robert A. Peterson, had been associated with the institute since its earliest days, having been a member of its first executive committee and having collaborated with Kozmetsky on research into public perceptions of capitalism and other topics. He had also served as associate vice president for research at the University of Texas, as well as associate dean for research in the business school and chairman of the marketing department. Peterson returned to his faculty position full-time in 2016 and was succeeded by interim executive director Gregory Pogue.

Kozmetsky refocused the institute in the late 1980s with greater involvement in generating economic development, apart from merely conducting research into its processes. Development of the high-tech industry in Austin and encouragement for local entrepreneurs were the immediate objectives, soon followed by similar activities well beyond Austin.

CHAPTER 16

THE IC² INSTITUTE II

The Austin Technopolis

During the 1980s the IC² Institute began to move beyond research on economic development and its related conferences and publications, adding a series of initiatives to actually carry out the process of economic development—the "do" part of the institute's long-term "think and do" mission. These initiatives were a natural outgrowth of the institute's early research interests. In the early 1980s, for example, the institute's research subjects included ideas for commercializing technologies from the Strategic Defense Initiative (the "Stars Wars" missile defense program) and other defense research and development programs; arguments in favor of a national technology commercialization act; and methods of accelerating the process of diffusing new technologies.[1] For Kozmetsky, it was a small step from those studies of the process of economic development to getting involved in the process itself.

Kozmetsky and his colleagues said their research into the process of economic development, especially as an outgrowth of technological innovation, had identified at least eight "emerging institutional developments" that fostered the relationships necessary for economic growth to occur. These were industrial R&D joint ventures and consortia, academic-business collaboration, government-university-corporate relationships, business incubators, industry-university research and engineering centers of excellence, small-business innovation research programs, state venture capital funds, and commercializing of university-college intellectual property.[2] This list offered a rich menu from which the institute would eventually select a series of projects for its own work.

The economic development initiatives originated in Kozmetsky's personality, eventually to be institutionalized and implemented by dozens of entrepreneurially spirited people whom he recruited or encouraged.

Laura Kilcrease, the first director of the Austin Technology Incubator. *IC² Institute photograph.*

Kozmetsky's own entrepreneurial abilities, as well as his openness to new ideas and people, his enthusiasm and optimism, his tirelessness, and his ability to cultivate wide networks of talented people—all these traits were the beginning point for the institute's economic activities, and they helped sustain the initiatives during their critical early years. There are several examples of initiatives that began to wither when Kozmetsky withdrew his energy to focus on new projects, or after he became ill in his last years— testimony to the importance of his presence as a sustaining force.

One of Kozmetsky's talents was finding capable people to implement a new project, but every idea did not come to fruition. "George's approach was to throw out a lot of seeds and see what grew, and then tend those that grew and ignore the others," said Laura Kilcrease, whom Kozmetsky chose as the first director of the Austin Technology Incubator.[3]

The "think" and the "do" activities under Kozmetsky's leadership gave the IC² Institute a deep sense of community, Kilcrease said. "People felt they were working for a greater good. There was a collective sense of purpose, and people went about their work with a sense of happiness and inclusiveness. What would happen was not always predictable, but people were open to the unpredictable, to encourage diverse ideas and seize opportunities as they arose."[4]

THE BEGINNING OF THE AUSTIN TECHNOPOLIS

The Austin Technopolis, as Kozmetsky and his colleagues began calling the region in the 1980s, had a long formative period. Some have traced its origin to soon after World War II, when the federal government transferred to the University of Texas at Austin the land in north Austin that has been developed into the J. J. Pickle Research Campus. Another convenient starting point is the founding in 1955 of the defense electronics company that would become known as Tracor Inc. The company, established by University of Texas faculty members, became the city's first homegrown company traded on the New York Stock Exchange and included on the Fortune 500 list of the nation's largest companies. Tracor spun off more than twenty other Austin technology companies.[5]

One of the most important early milestones came in 1958 with decisions by the University of Texas at Austin and the university system Board of Regents to begin a long-term enhancement of the campus's academic stature, including its commitment to graduate education and advanced research. These decisions, an outgrowth of the university's commemoration of its seventy-fifth anniversary, laid the foundation for the University of Texas at Austin's ability to become a partner with the private sector and other government agencies in economic development initiatives many decades later. The regents, with the leadership of Chancellor Harry Ransom, began implementing this plan in 1960 with a decision to pour millions of dollars into a construction program for academic buildings in all fields. The university took another leap forward during the commemoration of its centennial in 1981–1983, a period that included a fundraising campaign fueled by a decision by the regents to shift a portion of the university's oil-based endowment fund into grants to match private donations for the support of hundreds of new endowed faculty positions. The fundraising campaign was capped in 1984 with the announcement of the creation of thirty-two endowed chairs in science and engineering, using funds donated by the O'Donnell Foundation of Dallas and five other Texas foundations, as well as matching money from the regents.[6] Much of the Austin region's economic transformation from the 1980s onward was directly related to this previous twenty-five-year period of sustained expansion and enhancement of the University of Texas at Austin's academic programs. The transformation of the university business school during Kozmetsky's deanship was an important aspect of this larger movement at the university.

Many other events from the 1960s through the mid-1980s helped set the stage for the region's transformation, and Kozmetsky was often involved in these early steps. The founding of the university's computer science department happened to coincide with Kozmetsky's arrival at the university in 1966, and he served as a professor in the department in addition to his position at the business school. In 1971 Kozmetsky provided strategic advice to computer science professor James C. Browne as he established Information Research Associates, a company that marketed a technology for the evaluation of computer systems.[7] Kozmetsky also was an early adviser to James Truchard, who in 1976 with other researchers from the university's Applied Research Laboratory founded National Instruments Corp., which produced automated test equipment and related software. Other technology firms that were founded in Austin during these early years included MRI Systems, a database software developer that is considered the first significant software spin-off company from the University of Texas at Austin; BPI Systems, a personal computer software company; the Rubicon Group, Austin's first technology incubator; and Austin Ventures, which would become the largest institutional investor in local high-tech start-ups.[8]

Another early trend was the growing number of established technology companies that decided to locate branch offices or factories in Austin, often drawn by the proximity of the university's engineering, computer science, and business programs. These companies included Texas Instruments in 1966 and IBM in 1968, followed by a host of other companies, such as Motorola, Data General, Advanced Micro Devices, Schlumberger, Lockheed, and 3M.

The publication in 1985 of an economic development study sponsored by the Austin Chamber of Commerce has often been described as of pivotal importance in giving direction to the organizations and people, such as Kozmetsky, that were most involved in Austin's transformation. The study, which dealt with Austin's potential as an "idea city" with realistic opportunities for expansion of high-tech industries, laid out a path for attracting Japanese companies and pointed the city toward a broadened network of organizations involved in promoting technology-based industry.[9] The study, prepared by SRI International, a research organization in Silicon Valley, was titled "Creating an Opportunity Economy," and it presented a long-range plan that "anticipated rapid technological change and the emergence of new industries, then unknown."[10]

Despite such developments, Austin as late as 1982 was still sometimes referred to merely as one of a group of US cities that had begun developing clusters of high-tech industries but lagged far behind the two powerhouse centers of high technology—Silicon Valley and the Route 128 area of Boston.[11] It was not until the 1983 decision by the research consortium known as the Microelectronics and Computer Technology Corporation (MCC) to locate in Austin that the city's long-nascent trend toward high technology began to come to fruition. The trend then accelerated rapidly, leading to a cascade of events that transformed the region. Kozmetsky and the IC² Institute provided much of the inspiration and guidance for this transformation, serving as a center of ideas, programs, and networks that helped shape and direct the changes.

The IC² Institute and the Austin Technopolis

By winning the national competition for MCC in 1983, followed by the decision in 1988 by another consortium, Sematech, to set up its headquarters in the city, Austin found itself with a vastly enhanced reputation that began to rival the older high-tech centers in California and Massachusetts. That reputation had begun forming a little before the arrivals of the MCC and Sematech consortia, as Austin had started to attract national attention as one of the nation's "new cities," where factors such as an entrepreneurial spirit, community leadership, attractive natural resources, and the presence of a major research university were seen as contributing to broad economic change. In 1982, the *Christian Science Monitor* included a profile of Austin in a series of articles about "cities on the rise," midsized urban centers that had the potential for changing the nation's urban landscape. Austin was identified as the center of a "silicon prairie," and Kozmetsky, who was in his final months as dean of the business school, was prominently quoted on the city's potential and its mix of "idea people and widget builders." "Here we've got the research and development, entrepreneurs, as well as the production facilities and marketers," Kozmetsky said.[12]

Twenty years later, with the Austin area firmly transformed into a technopolis, some of the other cities discussed in that newspaper series were questioning why Austin had fulfilled its promise of the early 1980s and they had lagged behind. And once again, Kozmetsky, by then officially retired and entering the final year of his life, was called on to help explain to a newspaper reporter what had happened. He advised the leaders of other cities that they must take risks and set bold and specific goals, and then hold themselves accountable. "Everyone hates to be measured, but you'd better do it, or else you don't know what the hell you're doing" he said. "If your leaders aren't ready to do that, don't waste your time. Wait for them to retire."[13]

Despite the importance of MCC, Sematech, and other recruiting victories, Kozmetsky emphasized in that 2002 interview the importance of cultivating homegrown companies, with a high-technology incubator and courses in entrepreneurship at the University of Texas at Austin as part of the foundation of that effort. "What the hell got this country going?" Kozmetsky asked. "Small businesses."[14] (Or, as he could have added, companies such as Teledyne that had necessarily started small but aspired to, and achieved, bigness.) He also paid tribute to a culture of determination to make something new in Austin, with effort from leaders in the fields of venture capital, politics, and education. "It takes people with fire in their belly," Kozmetsky said. "If you don't have people with that fire, it ain't gonna happen."[15]

The newspaper identified Kozmetsky as a visionary leader who'd had a central role in the transformation, particularly in response to the economic troubles of the 1980s following a collapse in oil prices—a downturn that had affected banking, real estate, and most other sectors of the Austin and Texas economies: "At the brink of collapse, one of the most well-known and respected minds in town saw a chance for his lifelong vision to finally become reality. The visionary was George Kozmetsky. . . . Long before Austin's economy was in turmoil, Kozmetsky had envisioned his city as something more than it was: a technopolis. And he knew it was time to act. Now 84 years old and using a cane to get to meetings, brainstorming sessions, and mentoring opportunities six days a week, Kozmetsky remembers growing up in the Depression. 'I didn't want to die in one,' he said."

Kozmetsky also alluded to Austin's large supply of university graduates who were unemployed or underemployed and were available for opportunities in new industries. But those opportunities often failed to materialize, he said, because the state's economy was still focused on the traditional strengths of oil and cattle. He had been talking for years about the need to change that focus, and by the mid-1980s a critical mass of people had finally gotten the message. Kozmetsky had many allies in that campaign, including people whom he recruited to the effort. One of those was Laura Kilcrease, who thought of a novel way to get the message across to the Texas Legislature. She and colleagues went to the capitol and left microchips with tiny cows on them at each legislator's desk. An attached card said, "This is your new chip for Texas."[16]

Seeing the new economy in terms of comparing the old to the advantages of the new was a common technique for explaining the changes that awaited Austin and other parts of the state. Among many others who had gotten the message about a new kind of economy for Texas were Governor Mark White (who served from 1983 to 1987) and his aide Pike Powers, both of whom had been deeply involved in recruiting MCC to Austin. After Kozmetsky had helped persuade the University of Texas regents to spend an initial $14 million on a supercomputer in 1985 and 1986, White celebrated the installation of the equipment at the Balcones Research Center, asserting that the research center and its computing facilities were "going to be the new oil field of Texas, and the knowledge produced here will be a renewable resource."[17] The supercomputer was an apt symbol of the complex changes in Austin and Texas throughout the 1980s and 1990s, moving toward a new era in which information and technology were at the forefront. It reflected the way that Kozmetsky's diverse activities can be seen as part of a coherent whole.

At the beginning, relatively few people beyond Kozmetsky and his colleagues at the IC[2] Institute understood the potential changes to be the development of what was being called a "technopolis." The word had been used as early as 1946 to refer to a technology-oriented economic and cultural center,[18] and several incipient technopolises emerged in the early postwar period (such as the area that would become known as Silicon Valley and the "science city" known as Sophia Antipolis in France), but the first organized effort to create such centers using the term "technopolis" appears to have begun in Japan in 1980, when the Ministry of International Trade and Industry initiated a nationwide technopolis program. The program evolved to include plans for integrated development of industry, research universities, and housing at twenty sites, each of which was to concentrate on regionally specific technologies and would receive national tax incentives and other government underwriting.[19] Kozmetsky followed these developments in Japan closely, partly through his association with Hirofumi Matsuo, an assistant professor in the University of Texas business school and a research fellow at the IC[2] Institute. Among other activities, Matsuo organized an extended seminar cosponsored by the IC[2] Institute on Japanese business, with an emphasis on high-technology industries.[20]

Other contacts that Kozmetsky made among scholars also kept him apprised of the Japanese development of the technopolis idea. These contacts included the Japanese-American business consultant Sheridan Tatsuno and the physicist and historian Kunio Goto, both of whom participated in conferences at the IC[2] Institute in the 1980s and 1990s. Since 1993, Goto has been a fellow of the institute, which that year published a book by him on Japanese science and technology. The book also included a case study of the Japanese Kansai Science City project, which was planned to include a complex of three new academic institutions and a group of eight

A CIVIC ENTREPRENEUR

research institutes on topics ranging from energy to urbanization to food production. Goto wrote that Kozmetsky quickly accepted his request in 1991 to do research at the IC² Institute, and that Kozmetsky, David Gibson, Raymond Smilor, and others at the institute supported and encouraged his work on Japanese industrial policy. Kozmetsky and colleagues from the institute would make several trips to Japan to observe the progress of Kansai Science City.[21]

MCC and Sematech

The transition of the IC² Institute from an academic research center to a center of both research and practical action can be seen in Kozmetsky's contributions to the campaign to persuade MCC to make its home in Austin. The selection of Austin in May 1983 as the home of MCC—a research and development consortium of microelectronics companies, brought together to enable the United States to better compete with Japan—was a major milestone that propelled the city into the top ranks of centers of high-technology and set it on a course toward becoming a full-fledged technopolis. A detailed account of how MCC selected Austin for its home has been told by David Gibson and Everett Rogers, who described the involvement of a large number of Austinites and other Texans who played a direct role in putting together the proposal and interacting throughout the spring of 1983 with the consortium's selection committee.[22] In addition to this nucleus of "influencers" who worked together effectively to promote technology-based economic development, Gibson and Rogers identified two other key factors in Austin's surprise victory in attracting MCC. These were the development of the University of Texas at Austin as one of the nation's leading research universities (allowing MCC to be connected with a center of science and technology talent) and Austin's high quality of life (supporting MCC's need to recruit and keep researchers from the older technology centers on the East and West Coasts).[23]

Among those who participated daily or almost daily in the effort to attract MCC were Governor White and Pike Powers, and a host of others are credited with playing critically important direct roles at many junctures, including Dallas businessman H. Ross Perot; University of Texas president Peter Flawn; university faculty members Ben Streetman, Herbert Woodson, and Cliff Drummond; university vice president for research and academic affairs Gerhard J. Fonken; university system chancellor Don Walker; university system Board of Regents chairman Jon Newton; and San Antonio mayor Henry Cisneros. These and a host of others organized a thorough campaign that far surpassed the efforts of other cities competing for MCC and impressed the consortium's leaders with the depth,

Kozmetsky with Fred Phillips (left) and David Gibson (right), his colleagues at the IC²
Institute, early 1990s. *IC² Institute photograph.*

breadth, and ingenuity of Austin's commitment, said Neal Spelce, who
turned over the conference room of his advertising agency as a war room
for the effort.[24]

Kozmetsky also played an essential role, even if he was not among the
small group for whom the five-month national competition was an almost
all-consuming endeavor. Instead, he served as what Gibson and Rogers
refer to as a "first-level influencer." This was a person who could "set the
vision, inspire, and get things started" and then largely leave the details of
acting on that vision and inspiration to others, the "second-level influencers."[25] This visionary and largely strategic, rather than tactical, role that
Kozmetsky played is credited by those who were closely involved as being
of decisive importance.

Bobby R. Inman, a retired navy admiral and senior intelligence and
national security official who was named the first chief executive officer of
MCC in January 1983, agrees with the description of Kozmetsky as a highly

A CIVIC ENTREPRENEUR

important "first-level influencer." During the months that MCC was considering where to locate its operations, Inman had his first encounter with Kozmetsky. That occurred in Tallahassee, Florida, where the IC² Institute was one of the sponsors of a conference in March 1983 on the potential for commercializing the results of research and development undertaken by the Department of Defense. The conference brought together corporate leaders, defense department officials, politicians, and university scholars to discuss a range of issues, and Kozmetsky invited Inman to speak at the meeting on the subject of competition with Japan. The two had never met, but Inman said he was deeply impressed with both George and Ronya during his brief time at the conference.

"Ronya met me at the airport with a limousine to take me to the meeting, and then I met George at the hotel and then we went to the conference the next day," Inman said. "In introducing me, George described my new research venture in precise terms and said any community worth its salt

Admiral Bobby R. Inman, USN (Ret.) speaks at a reception in 1994 honoring Kozmetsky on receiving the National Medal of Technology. Inman met Kozmetsky in 1982 during the search process for a home for the Microelectronics and Computer Technology Corporation. *Photo by Dan Kellick, University Photography Services.*

would be competing for it. I left the conference with the clear impression that this was not just one professor in Austin who understood what we wanted to do with MCC, but that the entire community definitely had some very high-powered support."[26]

After the meeting in Tallahassee, Inman did not see Kozmetsky again until after the site selection had been announced later that spring, but he was aware that Kozmetsky was involved in one way or another as the process moved forward. "George was one of the people that our advance team met with as we prepared to visit the four cities that were finalists, and he was hovering in the background throughout this whole process," Inman said.

Kozmetsky's role in bringing people together and serving as a catalyst for others to take action is discussed in detail by Gibson and Rogers. One of the early turning points was a meeting at the IC^2 Institute in mid-March 1983 between Kozmetsky and San Antonio mayor Henry Cisneros, who was seeking advice on how San Antonio might win MCC. Kozmetsky ended up persuading Cisneros to join a state-led initiative under the leadership of the office of Governor White. Kozmetsky also met with University of Texas chancellor Don Walker later that week to help prepare him for a meeting with the governor. One of Kozmetsky's selling points for getting the state involved was that the consortium would help Texas keep its university graduates contributing to the Texas economy rather than see them migrate to other states. The strategy that Kozmetsky discussed with Walker included raising money to endow faculty positions in computer and electrical engineering at the University of Texas at Austin to strengthen programs involving microelectronics research. "This strategy amounted to Texas throwing a forward pass and then running out to catch it," Gibson and Rogers wrote.[27]

George and Ronya also had dinner that week with Austin lawyer Sam Winters, University of Texas at Austin president Peter Flawn, Lieutenant Governor Bill Hobby, and other academic and business leaders to discuss MCC. That meeting helped to win over a few skeptics, such as Flawn, and to consolidate the plan that Austin would be the focus of a highly coordinated statewide campaign.[28]

Kozmetsky stayed in the background of the campaign as Governor White and his aide Powers led the effort, which involved a host of leaders from higher education, government agencies, and the business community. Fifty-six other cities in twenty-seven states also entered the competition. Eventually, Austin was named one of four finalists for the consortium (along with San Diego, Atlanta, and Raleigh-Durham), and then, on May 17, was named the winner.

A CIVIC ENTREPRENEUR

Powers, who managed the involvement of the governor's office in the campaign to win MCC, credits Kozmetsky with being much more than a behind-the-scenes visionary as the competition unfolded that spring. "We were talking a lot throughout that time," Powers said. "George had several roles in planning and carrying out the effort. One of the things he did was enable the MCC team to evaluate Austin in a different light. George added a visionary element, and his presence validated our work and gave it credibility. His involvement was understood and appreciated by MCC, and his presence was icing on the cake for us. It made Austin's bid for MCC believable and doable."[29]

Powers said he believes Kozmetsky's reputation as a businessman and an academic leader "gave him a cachet that others lacked," but his intellect was even more important. "He was the smartest person in the room, and it could be intimidating for everyone else," Powers said. "George could command a room on intellect alone. He was a force of nature."[30]

Although Powers and Kozmetsky worked together on many projects with great success, there was one idea by Powers that never attracted Kozmetsky's support. That was Powers's hope that an area of north Austin that has since been developed as the retail, office, and residential complex known as the Domain could become a concentration of venture capital firms like the fabled Sand Hill Road area in Menlo Park, California. Powers thinks Kozmetsky failed to understand the real estate issues or recognize the potential for that piece of land, which is near MCC and the University of Texas at Austin's Pickle Research Campus and was formerly owned by IBM.[31]

Kozmetsky and the IC² Institute were also closely involved in the successful competition for Sematech in 1987, a national semiconductor research consortium, although many others who had worked on bringing MCC to Austin appear to have been more involved than Kozmetsky in attracting Sematech. Kozmetsky might have had a smaller role in this new effort, but he continued to serve as a fatherlike figure and a source of inspiration. One of the most active participants in the Sematech proposal was William H. Cunningham, Kozmetsky's protégé at the business school. By this time, Cunningham had become president of the University of Texas at Austin, and unlike his predecessor, Flawn, he did not hesitate to have the university involved in alliances with the private sector. Under Cunningham, the university became fully engaged in the kind of university-government-business collaborations that Kozmetsky always championed, using its resources to strengthen the financial incentives and technical capabilities that laid the foundation for Austin's bid for Sematech. Those activities even included using the university's bond and credit standing to facilitate purchase of land and a building, including paying for renovations, for use by the consortium.[32]

AUSTIN'S CIVIC ENTREPRENEURS

Those who participated directly in the competition for MCC, Sematech, and other Austin economic development efforts have often observed that the city benefitted during the 1980s and 1990s from an unusual confluence of talented individuals who worked together as a team for common purposes. Chance played a part in the fact that this assemblage came together when it did, just when it was most needed to achieve, first, the MCC victory, and then a string of other successes. Many have speculated that if the electronics industry had organized MCC only five years earlier, Austin probably would have been poorly prepared to compete for the consortium, because all the people who helped make the city's eventual bid a success were not yet in place in the positions they would hold by 1983. Kozmetsky would certainly have been ready to work on such an effort five years earlier, but many other key players were not yet on the scene. Other cities, as well as the leaders of MCC and Sematech, took note of the highly collaborative spirit that motivated Austin leaders as they each contributed in their own ways to the united campaigns, and Kozmetsky was usually mentioned as one of the most important of these leaders.[33]

Glenn E. West, who came to Austin from Macon, Georgia, in 1987 to lead the Greater Austin Chamber of Commerce after running chambers in Missouri, Kansas, and Georgia, described Kozmetsky as a key member of "a cadre of people in leadership positions who liked one another, spent a lot of time together on economic development issues, and collaborated on one project after another."[34]

"George was an extraordinary resource for the chamber and for everyone else in this group of people," West said. "He was connected with everyone, and all these people together formed a real community. Everyone was intimately involved, and we got together regularly and communicated easily and informally. The focus was on everyone contributing toward solving problems. One of the reasons Austin was so successful during this period was the presence of this extraordinary community of leaders, and one reason other cities were not so successful was that they lacked a community of this kind."[35]

Pike Powers agreed with the importance of this community of leadership. "The chemistry of this group was extraordinary," Powers said. "We liked each other and worked together to accomplish things for purposes that were bigger than any one of us. It was a unique moment in many ways. There was a collaborative environment that encouraged people to give their time and energy and money for the greater good of the community, and George was at the center of that with a force of will and enthusiasm that was all-important."[36]

This community of civic leaders, as it emerged in the 1980s, can be traced in part to a long-standing attitude of openness and inclusiveness that characterized Austin and set it apart from many other Texas cities, said Neal Spelce, who has been active in economic development efforts since the 1970s. "Austin has always been a welcoming city," he said. "It has a history of being an open city, not at all a closed community. Collaboration was inherent in the way we always operated, with encouragement for new people and new ideas."[37]

Austin did not win every economic development competition in the 1980s and 1990s. A third US industry research consortium, focusing on the computer display industry, chose San Jose, California, over Austin and Ann Arbor, Michigan, for its headquarters. With Powers, West, and others, Kozmetsky had been active in the recruitment effort for the US Display Consortium, which had backing from the Department of Defense, and he had helped secure space at the Austin Technology Incubator and other support from the university as part of the incentive package for attracting the consortium. It was reported that the consortium chose San Jose in October 1993 because of the large number of equipment suppliers and display users in that area.[38]

The leadership community that West and Powers talked about has been singled out as an example of a national trend of "civic entrepreneurs" banding together to transform a local economy, adapting to new technologies or changing economic conditions in an era of increasing globalization. The main scholarly study of this trend does not mention Kozmetsky or the IC[2] Institute, but West, Powers, Neal Kocurek (a Radian founder and longtime civic volunteer), and others who worked closely with Kozmetsky do figure prominently in the study.[39]

Kozmetsky, Powers, and Kocurek are a focus of another study, from the perspective of political science, that analyzes a new form of local governance based on the presence of a highly active group of civic entrepreneurs who respond to the challenges of developing competitive, knowledge-intensive industries. These new governance networks involve "a mix of mostly local actors who take a strategic interest and role in shaping the long-term economic prospects of a locality. Through mobilizing and developing knowledge assets in support of targeted industries, drawing down resources from upper levels of government, and helping resolve multi-jurisdictional regional governance problems related to sector development, these networks help regional firms adapt to ever-changing global high-tech markets."[40]

Kozmetsky has been identified as one of the best known of these civic entrepreneurs, both in Austin and beyond. He is credited with "building up the institutional capacity for developing new firms out of the knowledge base within the region, contributing a considerable amount of his own money. To Kozmetsky, creating firms was preferable to 'stealing' them, as he claimed the chamber has done through its recruitment practice. Kozmetsky also took on the role of mentor to many new technology firms in the region."[41]

THE CENTER FOR TECHNOLOGY VENTURING

One of the earliest formal initiatives of the IC² Institute to foster economic development through new institutions came in the spring of 1988 with establishment of the Center for Technology Venturing, a joint project of the institute and the business school's Bureau of Business Research.[42] The center was created "to address the challenge of a hypercompetitive environment, spurred on by the globalization of markets, which directly affects the economic well-being of Texas and the rest of the nation."[43] The term "technology venturing," apparently coined at the IC² Institute in the early 1980s,[44] was defined by Kozmetsky and his colleagues as "a collaborative entrepreneurial process for commercializing science and technology through innovative institutional arrangements."[45]

Technology venturing, wrote Kozmetsky and his colleagues, "is the process by which major institutions take and share risk in integrating and commercializing scientific research and various technologies. It is a primary means of generating innovative products and services of economic value, particularly through a vibrant venture capital industry. To compete effectively in the global economic arena, we need to find creative and innovative ways to link public-sector initiatives and private-sector investments. What entrepreneurship does for small business, technology can do for corporations, universities, consortiums, and governments. Thus technology venturing is a catalyst for a broad-based emergent entrepreneurial spirit in America."[46]

The IC² Institute had sponsored a conference in Dallas on technology venturing in 1984, with speakers that included officials of the US Department of Commerce, Department of Defense, Army Corps of Engineers, National Science Foundation, and NASA, as well as executives of Bechtel Corp. and other companies.[47] The institute also sponsored several publications on the subject in the mid-1980s, including *Initiatives for Trans-*

Kozmetsky at a conference at the IC² Institute, late 1990s. *IC² Institute photograph.*

forming the American Economy (IC² Institute, 1984), based on the Dallas conference.

Kozmetsky had presented at that conference a broad vision of the concept of technology venturing and how it could transform the economy. He linked the concept to the promotion of large-scale or macroengineering projects (see chapter 18), development of a "national technology agenda" (an idea that he and Eugene Konecci had advocated for years), transfer of technology from government programs to commercially viable products in the private sector, expansion of high-technology research at universities, new types of private-public collaborations, and transformation of education to meet the workforce needs of the new economy.[48]

The Center for Technology Venturing became the administrative vehicle through which these activities were carried on. The center began under the joint direction of Kozmetsky and Robert S. Sullivan, who was associate dean for graduate programs at the business school (and would be director of the IC² Institute from 1995 to 1997). The center started with teaching programs in entrepreneurship, applied research (such as a marketing study for Tracor Inc. and a technology transfer study for MCC), an executive development program, and a risk capital network that set up a database to link entrepreneurs and private investors. Within a year of its founding, the center spawned the Austin Technology Incubator.[49]

The term "technology venturing" was widely copied. Other centers and academic programs arose with "technology venturing" in their titles, including at the University of North Carolina at Chapel Hill, the University of Southern California, and London's Imperial College Business School. The government of Wales opened a "technology venturing" office, as did the Chinese province of Zhejiang, and companies began including "technology venturing" among investment strategies in managers' portfolios.

The Capital Network

One of the first activities of the Center for Technology Venturing, in 1989, was to establish a database that linked entrepreneurs with private investors, with the aim of expanding the pool of seed capital available to emerging companies. Consistent with Kozmetsky's practice of creating alliances among diverse institutions and community organizations, this "risk capital network" was a collaboration with Leadership Texas (a women's business-training nonprofit), the Texas Women's Alliance, and the Texas Lyceum (a public-issues discussion forum).[50] George and Ronya Kozmetsky were active in these organizations. Meg Wilson, who worked with the Austin Technology Incubator and later managed business development for MCC, was recruited by Kozmetsky to steer the network until it was large enough to hire its own director. At the time, she was president of the Texas Lyceum and was active in Leadership Texas.[51]

Kozmetsky had conceived of the network in the early 1980s, but it took three years to get it started and several more years before it was functioning smoothly. The network was first called the Texas Capital Network, but by 1994 it had expanded nationwide and changed its name to the Capital Network. The network made its first match between an investor and an entrepreneur in 1991. Within six years of its founding, the network had helped companies raise more than $25 million. By 1994 the database had attracted six hundred companies seeking money and two hundred investors looking for companies.[52] It was recognized that year as the nation's largest nonprofit venture capital network.[53]

One of the advantages of the network, in comparison with most for-profit venture capital funds, was that its services were available to companies seeking relatively small investments, sometimes as little as $10,000. One of the network's perceived disadvantages was that it acted simply as a neutral matchmaker and was prevented by federal securities regulations from participating in negotiations between an investor and a company.[54]

The potential for a conflict between the network, as a public-university entity, and private business interests had raised eyebrows among University of Texas administrators, but Kozmetsky overcame objections by

assuring officials that the network would not be involved in giving investment advice, negotiating contracts, or handling investment money, but
would serve only to connect entrepreneurs and investors.[55]

THE AUSTIN TECHNOLOGY INCUBATOR

One of the most successful activities of the IC[2] Institute has been the Austin Technology Incubator (ATI), founded by Kozmetsky in 1989 to assist
new and potentially fast-growth companies. The incubator provided
companies with strategic advice, mentoring, financing, marketing, public relations assistance, employee benefit programs, and office and manufacturing space for as long as three years, after which it was hoped the
companies would be strong enough to "graduate" as independent companies with marketable products or services. As an incubator, ATI aimed at
reducing the failure rate of new businesses by making it easier for them to
weather the early stages of development.

ATI proved to be one of the most successful incubators, but it did not
pioneer the concept. Some of the earliest efforts to support new businesses
through private-sector incubators began in Great Britain in 1975 as a
response to widespread layoffs in the British steel industry. Beginning with
space for new entrepreneurs in vacant steel plants, the incubator movement spread to other countries in Europe, and in 1984 the firm that had
organized the first British incubators opened one in Flint, Michigan.[56] The
movement expanded quickly in the United States, and by the time the IC[2]
Institute got involved, beyond its studies of the movement,[57] there were
incubators of one kind or another in at least twenty-eight US states and
many foreign countries. In 1986, Pennsylvania led the states with twenty-
five incubators, while California had fourteen, and Michigan and Minne-
sota had nine each. The US Small Business Administration had conducted
national conferences on the incubator idea, and by 1985 the movement
had developed enough to support the establishment of the National Business Incubation Association.[58] The next year, the Small Business Administration published a detailed guide on how to organize an incubator.[59]

Austin had been represented in this movement as the home of a for-
profit incubator known as the Rubicon Group, founded in 1983 by Stephen Szygenda, a former chairman of the University of Texas at Austin
Department of Electrical and Computer Engineering, and J. Jette Campbell, an Austin business consultant. Rubicon, which provided management services, business education, and other assistance to entrepreneurs
with technology backgrounds but with little or no business experience,
raised funds from a variety of investors and began by supporting ten new
companies, six of them in the software business.[60] The incubator closed in

1986 without showing a profit or graduating a successful company. Lessons from Rubicon's failure were not lost on Kozmetsky.

Kozmetsky got involved in starting an incubator through his first meeting, in 1987, with Glenn West, who had just moved to Austin. West had compiled a list of one hundred people that he should meet in Austin as soon as possible, and Kozmetsky was high on the list. On his first day in Austin, West happened to run into Kozmetsky in a hallway at the old chamber building next to Palmer Auditorium (now the Long Center), where Kozmetsky was attending the first meeting of the Sematech recruiting committee. West told Kozmetsky, "We need to talk," and Kozmetsky, always open to expanding his network of associates, agreed at once.

When that chance encounter led to their first conference, West brought up the subject of business incubators. "I had watched the creation of a technology incubator at Georgia Tech, and I asked George why there was no incubator in Austin," West said. "He told me about how people had tried and failed, and then he said to me, 'You know about incubators, and I have a building. Let's start one.' That led to a fundraising campaign so the chamber could be a partner in supporting the new incubator."[61] It was typical of Kozmetsky to immediately and enthusiastically endorse an idea such as West's and then figure out a way to engage other people in the project. He rarely said no as a first response to a new idea.[62]

Kozmetsky worked out part of the early funding for the incubator in a hurried conversation in the parking lot of the IC^2 Institute. He called Austin mayor Lee Cooke and said he needed to speak with him at once. Cooke was on his way to speak to a neighborhood group, but he stopped by at the institute, and Kozmetsky came down and told him through the car window that he needed money from the city, the chamber, and the university to start the incubator, although he said he was prepared to put in his own money if he couldn't get the University of Texas to participate. "I didn't have the authority to approve it on my own, but I assured George that the city and the chamber would do their part," Cooke said.[63]

In another example of George and Ronya Kozmetsky's highly productive network of colleagues and friends, and their equally productive relationship as partners, George was assisted by Ronya in recruiting Laura Kilcrease to lead the incubator. Kilcrease had moved to Austin in 1984 to become an executive at Nova Graphics International Corp., a software company, after nine years at Control Data Corp. in her native London. She met Ronya through a series of monthly professional development seminars that Ronya helped organize for women in management. The seminars were recorded, and one day while driving Ronya listened to a tape of Kilcrease giving a presentation at one of the sessions.

A CIVIC ENTREPRENEUR

Kozmetsky lecturing at the IC² Institute. *IC² Institute photograph.*

"When she got home she woke up George and said he needed to listen to this woman because she makes a lot of sense," Kilcrease recalled.[64]

Other people, such as Cathy Bonner [a marketing executive and political activist] also told George about me, and one day he called me out of the blue. I had never met him. He called me at 11:00 a.m. and said he had an idea he wanted to talk to me about. My response was give me a clue about what it is about, and he said no, he'd rather talk to me about it in person. I said OK, and then he said how about one thirty today, in a couple of hours. I told him I was not available that day but how about 2:00 p.m. the next day. We met then at his office at IC² and it turned out he wanted me to work with him on the Austin Technology Incubator as a volunteer, to help get it started and line up support within the Austin business community. I agreed to do that volunteer work, and we worked on that from the end of 1988 to the early part of 1989. George didn't have time to do the work that I did, and he also realized that he wasn't the right person. I had to go to the Chamber of Commerce and the county and others to get the money for it. When a project, like this one, needed the integral contributions of other groups, George thought they should come to the table with money to support the project. He ran a very lean operation and believed strongly that the entire community should contribute.[65]

Kilcrease said Kozmetsky was cautious about starting the incubator, particularly in light of the failure of the Rubicon project three years earlier. That caution led him to insist on commitment to the incubator by a broad range of public and private participants who could help develop not merely a successful company here and there but also an entrepreneurial start-up culture. Kilcrease said, "He wanted us to learn from the problems that other incubators had had, and he was determined that if we started the incubator it would be a success. Failure was not something he was interested in. After several months of working on the idea, I told George it would work, but that he would have to find the right person to be the director. Then he asked me to be the director, and I was reluctant because it would be a nonprofit and that was not in my experience. My mind didn't work that way. But he said, 'Why run one business when you can run twelve?' And he told me this project would make a difference in the landscape of Austin. So he persuaded me."[66]

The incubator, which was organized through the Center for Technology Venturing and the Bureau of Business Research, opened officially in February 1989 with initial funding from a variety of sources—$50,000 from the City of Austin, $50,000 from the Kozmetsky family, $25,000 from the Chamber of Commerce, and $163,000 in in-kind services from the university and about thirty local companies, including banks and accounting firms. The next year, Travis County commissioners contributed $70,000.[67] Close association with the business school's technology entrepreneurship program, as well as the "know-how" network of business professionals who volunteered to consult with the new companies, were fundamental to the plans for the incubator.

The incubator was an immediate success and soon gained a reputation as one of the nation's leading organizations of its kind. Kozmetsky mostly left Kilcrease alone to run the incubator in its early days, but his interest in the project rose as she demonstrated it could be successful. "As soon as George saw how successful it was becoming, he became even more enamored with it," she said. "For the first few months I would be calling him to let him know what was going on, but after the early record of success he was calling me every day."[68]

Early tenants who benefitted from the incubator's services credited Kilcrease's leadership as well as the credibility with investors and established businesses that resulted from Kozmetsky's involvement.[69] The success came despite an uneven record among the numerous incubators that had been started in the United States since the mid-1980s and a rising level of criticism over the way many of them were being managed.[70]

One major difference between ATI and Rubicon was that Kilcrease and Kozmetsky required applicants to have a written business plan in addition to a promising new technology or service, while Rubicon had concentrated heavily on the technological expertise of would-be entrepreneurs. Raymond W. Smilor, then serving as Kozmetsky's executive director at the IC² Institute, had been a consultant to Rubicon and had analyzed the record of it and many other incubators, and he lent his expertise on the strengths and weaknesses of various types of incubators to the new project run by Kilcrease.[71]

Within seven months of the start of ATI, at least eighteen other incubators of various types had opened in Texas, and others were being planned. The Southeast Business Incubator, designed to help minority- and women-owned businesses, opened in Austin soon after ATI, and Huston-Tillotson University, a historically black university in East Austin, was planning an incubator (the Enterprise and Development Center) to assist small businesses owned by students and alumni. By September 1989, four incubators had opened in Houston, with others in Dallas, San Antonio, and smaller cities. Only a few of these were dedicated, like ATI, exclusively to high-tech ventures.[72]

Some of the earliest tenants of ATI needed relatively little assistance to become independent, a fact that helped give the incubator a quick record of success. The first tenant was a subsidiary of Pencom Systems of San Jose, California, whose mission was to design software for the UNIX operating system. Pencom joined the incubator May 15, 1989, and graduated only a year later, moving into its own facilities in northwest Austin. The company became known as PSW Technologies and completed an initial public offering in 1997, raising $25 million. The company, which changed its name to Concero in 2000, went out of business in 2003.[73] Another early success, also graduating in May 1990, was Desk Top Manufacturing Corp. (DTM), a maker of three-dimensional laser printers.[74] DTM was founded by University of Texas at Austin graduate Carl R. Deckerd, a developer of the 3-D printing technique known as selective laser sintering.

Among other early successes at ATI was Evolutionary Technologies International (ETI), a software company cofounded by Katherine Hammer, who served as CEO and president from the company's inception in 1991 until 2005. ETI began as a three-year research project at MCC and then became the consortium's first commercial spin-off, moving into ATI in January 1991 and graduating in December 1992. The company specialized in middleware—software that facilitated data exchange among otherwise incompatible systems—and sold its products to companies in banking, insurance, telecommunications, retail, and health care.

Hammer said Kozmetsky's mentoring was important in the company's success. "George provided us with unbelievably helpful counsel and guidance," she told *Entrepreneur* magazine. He also connected ETI with his network of associates, including Inman, who became one of the company's early investors. In addition to providing the usual financial support and management assistance, the incubator gave Hammer and her cofounder, Robin Curie, a nurturing environment that allowed them to resist early financing proposals that would have meant losing control of the company. They kept control through third-stage financing. "We were lucky," Hammer said. "We were able to build the foundation of the business according to our vision."[75] ETI was eventually acquired by Versata Enterprises Inc., a unit of Trilogy Inc.

ETI and its founders were the subject of national press coverage that has become legendary in the history of Austin's rise as a technology center. Hammer was on the cover of *Forbes* magazine in 1996 for a story that began about working women but turned into a feature about Austin and its new high-tech economy.

Other ATI successes during Kozmetsky's lifetime included Applied Science Fiction (ASF), which marketed an image auto-correction technology developed at the IBM Research Center in Austin and was acquired by Eastman Kodak in 2003; Haystack Laboratories, which specialized in security technology for Internet sites and was acquired in 1997 by a company that eventually evolved into McAfee Inc.; Isochron Data Corp., which was founded by two University of Texas at Austin business students and integrated wireless communication technology into vending machines; and Evity Inc., which developed a product that enabled e-commerce companies to monitor the performance of a website the same way a customer would perceive it, and which was sold to BMC Software for $100 million in 2000.[76]

ATI found it necessary to relocate to larger office space three times within its first three years. Two of those locations, on North Mopac Expressway and on Business Park Drive, were owned by the Kozmetsky family and were provided to the incubator at such a discount below market rates that the incubator was able to charge its tenants only fifty cents per month per square foot.[77] (There was, however, a significant surplus of office space in Austin during much of the early development of ATI.) Eventually the incubator settled into offices in the building that the University of Texas at Austin had constructed for MCC near the Pickle Research Campus and remained there until a move closer to the university's main campus in 2016.

In 1991, ATI carried Kozmetsky's message of shared prosperity to Mexico, where ATI helped establish a high-tech incubator at the Monterrey Institute of Technology and Higher Education. At the time, the number of US business incubators had grown to more than four hundred, but Mexico had only two, both run by the government.[78] Many other countries also were assisted by ATI in starting business incubators. In 1993, for example, a delegation from Indonesia visited ATI and other US incubators in a program sponsored by the United Nations.

Drawn by the success of ATI, the National Business Incubator Association held its annual conference in Austin in 1992. More than four hundred people from around the country came to the conference to learn more about the example of ATI, which the association's director called "a premier program in the United States."[79] In 1994, the incubator's fifth year, it was named the nation's best incubator in a competition sponsored by the Coopers & Lybrand accounting firm, as rated on its economic impact, graduating tenants, business successes, service programs, and contributions to the industry. By that time, ATI had assisted forty-four new businesses and graduated fifteen, generating more than 640 jobs and $44 million in annual sales by the companies.[80]

When Kilcrease stepped down as director in 1997, the number of graduating companies had risen to forty-two, with five having had public stock offerings. The total number of jobs credited to the companies had risen to 1,300, and annual revenues of the companies had reached $130 million.[81] In Kozmetsky's lifetime the incubator graduated more than eighty companies that generated over 2,500 jobs in the Austin area. The companies had attracted more than $600 million in venture capital (sometimes from Kozmetsky himself) and generated revenues of more than $1 billion. The success of the incubator made it a model for similar efforts around the world, and its track record was important in a decision by NASA in 1993 to select Kozmetsky and Kilcrease to help the space agency start technology commercialization programs (see chapter 17).

AUSTIN TECH NETWORKS

Kozmetsky led a group of entrepreneurs in establishing the Austin Entrepreneurs' Council, which began meeting in the fall of 1991 as a forum for executives of start-up companies to discuss challenges and issues of their emerging businesses. The first impetus for the organization came when Kozmetsky learned that the Massachusetts Institute of Technology was planning to bring to Austin its MIT Enterprise Forum, a series of workshops and other continuing education programs offered to entrepreneurs in cities across the country. "Kozmetsky responded by telling civic leaders in Austin that we could do this ourselves," said David Gibson. The local organization was first called the Austin Enterprise Forum, but the name was soon changed to the Austin Entrepreneurs' Council out of concern about infringing on MIT's trademark.[82]

The group began with forty charter members who paid $100 a year in membership fees and gathered for quarterly meetings at the IC^2 Institute or the Austin Technology Incubator. In addition to the council serving as a catalyst to help new companies succeed, Kozmetsky said he hoped the group would serve as a source of information on new technologies and government regulation, as well as a vehicle for networking with people in government, academia, established companies, and professional firms. The council continued to meet during the 1990s, but as the Austin entrepreneurship scene expanded, a series of more specialized networking organizations emerged.

An outgrowth of the Austin Entrepreneurs' Council was the establishment of the Austin Software Council. Most of Austin's early strength in the new technology-based economy had been in electronic devices, computer hardware, manufacturing, and research, but by the early 1990s a significant presence in the software industry had also developed. Kozmetsky and the IC^2 Institute contributed to this industry, and to stimulating the further growth of Austin as an international center of software development, through creation of the Austin Software Council. At the request of computer science faculty members at the University of Texas at Austin and leaders in the software industry, the institute sponsored meetings in 1991 on the future of software engineering and the prospects for Austin's growth as a software center, and this conference spurred formation of the software council. Fred Y. Phillips, research director at the IC^2 Institute, organized a conference that brought together regional leaders in software development and researchers from the University of Texas, MCC, and Sematech. That led to monthly dinner meetings at MCC that included entrepreneurs in discussions of software research, marketing, finance, and start-ups, and those meetings soon led to formation of the software council.[83]

The council began as a unit within the IC^2 Institute and was intended to serve as a unifying force for the four hundred companies that were then engaged in software development in Austin, as well as for lawyers, investors, academic groups, and others interested in collaborating with software developers. Through its networking opportunities and monthly meetings and workshops with guest speakers, the council hoped to nurture a supportive environment that would assist the current software companies and help attract new ventures in the field. Kozmetsky summed up the aim of the council: "We want a friendly environment in Austin for people who want to devote their futures to make things happen through software."[84]

A strategic plan for the organization (developed in late 1993 through discussions among some seventy-five representatives of the university, the IC[2] Institute, MCC, Sematech, state government agencies, and private companies) embodied Kozmetsky's vision for the software industry and its place in the Austin regional economy. The strategic plan also adopted the institute's Technopolis Wheel as a model for how to realize the goals of its initiatives in developing a world-class technology and human-resource base, marshaling capital investment, and promoting the image of Austin as an internationally important software center.[85]

Unlike most of the projects that the IC[2] Institute undertook, the Austin Software Council had difficulty achieving the purposes that Kozmetsky envisioned. Software developers were eager to participate at first but found by the late 1990s that the group was less helpful than they had anticipated. Within a few years the organization's meetings had become dominated by other professions, and the software industry's issues seemed to be of less importance than making business connections. A joke among the software community was that "the best place to find a lawyer, accountant, or consultant was at an Austin Software Council meeting." In 1997 the council sought to refocus its energies to better fulfill its original purpose and concentrate more on serving the needs of software companies and promoting Austin as a center of the industry.[86]

Less than a year later, at the beginning of a major boom in technology industries, the council shifted direction again by separating from the IC[2] Institute and the university and becoming an independent nonprofit organization. One motive for the change in structure was to give the group more leeway in lobbying and other political activities in support of the software industry, making it more of a standard trade association. This political emphasis was said to align the council more with similar groups in other major centers of the industry, such as Boston, Seattle, and Silicon Valley.[87] The University of Texas did maintain a representative on the council's board.[88] Another metamorphosis of the council came in the spring of 2002, when it changed its name to the Austin Technology Council, reflecting a broadening of its activities beyond software companies. By then, only about half of the participants were software companies.[89]

Kozmetsky as a Business Mentor: Dell Computer

During the years that Kozmetsky was most active at the IC[2] Institute in "doing" economic development in and beyond Austin, he was deeply involved in strategic planning within Dell Computer Corp., by far the most successful of all the technology companies started in Austin. The company got its start in 1983 when Michael Dell, then an eighteen-year-old freshman at the University of Texas, began selling upgraded IBM personal desktop computers and add-on components from his dorm room, marketing his products direct to customers through newspaper classified ads and word-of-mouth contacts. At the time, personal computers were sold primarily through retail computer stores at a high markup but with little or no customer support. Dell left the university in May 1984 without graduating and concentrated on expanding his business, which first relocated to a condominium and then to a small office space in north Austin. Within a few months Dell switched from upgrading existing IBM machines to assembling custom-built clones from stock parts.

The business was an immediate success and kept expanding rapidly, supported by a private placement of stock in 1986 and an initial public offering in 1988. Dell had known of Kozmetsky since the earliest days of his career as an entrepreneur, but the two began an extended period of intense collaboration in 1986 when the company expanded its board, which until then had consisted simply of Dell. Until then the company had been financed largely through a line of credit that Dell's president, Lee Walker, had arranged through Texas Commerce Bank, but greater resources were soon needed to keep up with customer demand.[90]

"The company was going from maybe $60 million or $70 million in revenue to $150 million, and we needed to raise some capital, so we decided to do a private placement of shares with Goldman Sachs," Dell recalled.

> At the time the board of directors of the company was just me—a board of one—and Goldman said we needed to have more than one director. I asked them how many, and they said four and maybe the investors will bring another one. So the president of the company at the time, Lee Walker, and I were sitting around and we said how are we going to get four directors, and we said I'll be one and you'll be another, so that's two, so we needed two more. We asked ourselves who would be great for this, and I knew of George Kozmetsky and Admiral Bobby Inman, and they were the people we picked as our first choices.
>
> I had heard George speak once or twice, and Lee knew Inman well, so I said I'll go after Kozmetsky and you go after Inman and we'll see how we do. So I went to see George at his office and explained what we were doing and told him that with his experience he would be very helpful to the company. He came out to our office and we spent some

time talking about the business, and shortly thereafter he agreed to join the board, and so did Inman.[91]

In remarks at a memorial service for Kozmetsky in 2003, Dell recalled that arranging a meeting with Kozmetsky in 1987 had taken several attempts, but that when Kozmetsky visited the company's facilities he had many detailed questions for Dell and insisted on a tour of the computer lab. "He wanted to see where the action was. He kind of reminded me of Curious George," Dell said.[92]

Inman and Kozmetsky also talked with one another about Dell and his company before agreeing to join the board. Inman had been reluctant to join the board when first approached because of his other commitments and the small size of the new company, but Kozmetsky sparked his interest in Dell. "At least meet the founder," Inman recalled Kozmetsky telling him. "George said he'd join the board if I would."[93]

"I would often meet with George in his office at IC² to talk about MCC, and at one of those meetings he said he had a company he was fascinated by, and he asked me to look at it and [said he] would like to have me involved," Inman said. "George told me that [Michael] Dell 'is the most intriguing youngster I have met in years, and if you are as intrigued as I, we'll both put some money in it, and we can be on the board.'"

Inman said he met with the company's founder and "was immediately impressed by his entrepreneurial spirit. He was young and needed help, and I told George that I would be pleased to serve with him on the board. I told George, 'I'll take the compensation committee, and you can take the audit committee.'"[94] After the private placement in 1987, venture capitalist Paul Hirschbiel, then a vice president of Prudential Equity Investors, also joined the board. The private placement was a prelude to the company's initial public offering the next year, a transaction that raised $30 million in capital.

As with most companies, Dell and members of his board almost always declined to discuss publicly the inner workings of the board, but Dell often paid tribute to the contribution that Kozmetsky made to the guidance of the company and as one of his most important mentors, adding that Kozmetsky and Inman brought immediate benefits for the company. "Their presence gave us a huge boost in credibility; young companies like Dell typically don't have such a strong board starting out. As the original board members, George and Bob set a precedent of sage advice and valuable counsel that has helped carry us to where we are today."[95]

Especially in the early period of Kozmetsky's service on the board,

Kozmetsky at a meeting of the IC² board of directors. *IC² Institute photograph.*

Dell often visited Kozmetsky at his home on Seventeenth Street or at his office at the IC² Institute to discuss company strategy. The importance of the Kozmetsky house as a site for such meetings was one reason that the City of Austin approved a historic landmark designation for it in 2010. Dell recalled how these discussions helped to guide him through the early development of his company:

> George was definitely a person with a big global vision, and he had a lot of insights and ideas—not all of which I understood, by the way—but I could talk to him about what we were doing and bounce things off him, and he would provide ideas. I would often go see him, either at IC² or at his home and sort of explain things I was thinking about doing, such as expand here or going in this area, and he'd provide his ideas and thoughts. Having been a part of some great big businesses, he had made plenty of successes as well as failures and he had a lot of experiences to offer, and he was a great sounding board for new ideas.
>
> He also talked with me a lot about Teledyne and Litton and about Henry Singleton and all the early adventures in his life. And he talked about philanthropy, and of course his kids and his grandkids. He was

A CIVIC ENTREPRENEUR

obviously a person who deeply believed in the entrepreneurial spirit and innovation and the value of new ideas. He just loved the whole process of creating new companies.[96]

Dell said Kozmetsky was an ideal board member. "George knew that the role of the board was not to run the company. He wasn't trying to do that. He was trying to be helpful and to make sure that he provided sound advice and good ideas and gave his feedback if he thought we were doing something well or weren't doing something well. He would always speak up. One of the things it's hard to get in a board member is someone who has been there and done that, in large companies, and has already seen a number of the challenges that we would face."[97]

Another contribution that Kozmetsky made was in using his far-flung contacts to assist the company with its international expansion, which began with operations in the United Kingdom in 1987. "He had many contacts that were helpful to us as we were expanding around the world," Dell said. "We would have our board travel to overseas locations periodically, and whether we were in Japan [which Dell entered in 1992] or somewhere else, George would be able to invite important customers to meet with us. He was very helpful in establishing the company's reputation in foreign markets, using his own influence and reputation."[98]

The company from time to time encountered crises and downturns involving issues that paralleled problems Kozmetsky had experienced at Teledyne, Litton, and Hughes Aircraft. These included issues of inventory control and cash flow, struggles to keep up with rapidly advancing technology, quality-control issues with vendors, design glitches in new products, special problems that required solutions from outside management talent, and efforts to find the right pace for growth.[99] Kozmetsky was also on the board when Dell began sales through the Internet, in 1994, the same year that Amazon.com Inc. was founded. There had been no Internet, of course, when Kozmetsky had been in business in California, but he and the IC² Institute had been early advocates for e-commerce. At a 1996 conference on e-commerce at the IC² Institute, Kozmetsky said, "The new challenge for the 21st century is to recognize electronic commerce as the driving force that will change the basic tenets of business management."[100]

Kozmetsky remained on the Dell board for ten years, until July 1997, when he became the company's first director emeritus. By the time he left the board, the company had nine thousand employees in the Austin area and was adding more than one hundred a week. It was the second-largest private-sector employer in the area, behind Motorola, which had 10,500 employees. The company had revenues of $7.7 billion in its 1997 fiscal year and was in the midst of a major expansion of its online business, with sales of $2 million a day on the Internet in July 1997, twice as much as six months earlier.[101] That month, the shareholders approved increasing the number of shares of common stock from three hundred million to one billion, resulting in Dell's fourth stock split in the past five years.[102] Dell had become a Fortune 500 company by 1992. The year before, Michael Dell had joined *Texas Monthly* magazine's annual list of the one hundred wealthiest Texans, with an estimated net worth of $265 million. Two other Austinites were on the list, CompuAdd founder Bill Hayden ($460 million) and Kozmetsky ($210 million).[103] Over the years, the Kozmetsky and Dell families developed close ties. One aspect of their relationship involved philanthropy, as George and Ronya set an example for the younger couple (as they did for others in Austin) and sometimes provided advice based on their experience.

EnterTech

The IC² Institute joined in the late 1990s with an Austin company called Human Code (a "digital content studio" that produced software for e-commerce, learning systems, and other activities) to develop EnterTech, a training program to help workers develop high-tech skills and make them more employable in the new economy—thus helping to bridge the "digital divide" that kept otherwise capable workers out of high-tech industries. The three-week training program combined Internet instruction with classroom sessions that included simulations of on-the-job experiences inside a typical technology company. Since the mid-1960s Kozmetsky had often spoken about the need to extend the benefits of high-tech economic development to people of all socioeconomic levels, and the EnterTech experiment fit well with his long-standing commitment to "shared prosperity," but EnterTech was one of the few initiatives that he was involved in that was actually designed to address the problems identified by those theories.

Human Code and the IC² Institute developed the program based on surveys of high-tech employers to gather information about the criteria for successful entry-level workers, as well as interviews and focus groups with workers and job hunters. EnterTech was funded in 1998 with a three-year grant of $2.1 million from the Texas governor's office and the Texas Workforce Commission.[104]

Kozmetsky and Dewey Winburne, an Austin educator, philanthropist, and multimedia innovator, had come up with the idea for EnterTech in 1996 as they discussed the need for low-skilled workers in the Austin area to be trained for jobs in the region's rapidly expanding technology sector.

A CIVIC ENTREPRENEUR

Their idea was to seek government funding for development of a training program, but to develop it in close cooperation with major Austin employers, who were facing critical shortages of qualified workers.[105] Kozmetsky arranged for Winburne to work on the project from an office at the Austin Technology Incubator. The relationship between Kozmetsky and Winburne was another example of Kozmetsky's practice of developing contacts with younger people with innovative ideas and a lot of energy and encouraging them to put their ideas into practice. Perhaps partly because they were more likely to share his impatience for change, he often seemed more attuned to younger people than to members of his own generation. After Winburne died, Kozmetsky found a new partner for the digital-divide project in Human Code. "Human Code brought the required knowledge and experience to the EnterTech program team," Kozmetsky said. "Their expertise in multi-media instructional design and web delivery combined with exceptional creativity, commitment and compassion for tomorrow's training is invaluable."[106]

Kozmetsky and Deaton Bednar, who directed the project for the IC[2] Institute, won support from Dell, Samsung, 3M, Raytheon, and even fast-food companies like Taco Bell and Pizza Hut—all of which reviewed the curriculum and allowed the project to videotape their workplaces and interview entry-level workers. In all, some eighty employers, community organizations, educators, and policy makers signed up to help with the program.

Kozmetsky also enlisted friends to study ways to incorporate interactive digital technology into the EnterTech project, making it unique for training programs at the time. Baylor University faculty members Corey Carbonara and Michael Korpi, as well as David Smith in Austin (all of them senior research fellows at the IC[2] Institute), recommended using CD-ROM and DVD technology that enhanced the quality of the video segments incorporated into the project.[107]

The curriculum included basic math, reading, and writing, as well as more advanced technical training and other workplace and interpersonal skills. The content, which in some cases included the most fundamental job skills, such as dressing appropriately and conveying a positive attitude, was presented with high-quality computer graphics that could compete with video games and other popular media. After months of development, including tests at a variety of Austin schools, the IC[2] Institute pilot tested the program in 2000 at sites throughout Texas, including high schools, community colleges, and adult learning centers.

Over the three years of the program, 178 of the 193 people who enrolled completed the forty-five-hour program.[108] Of those, 67 percent gained employment or enrolled in continuing education, and 15 percent received raises or changed jobs and received higher salaries. One-third of welfare recipients who participated were taken off welfare, resulting in an annual savings to the federal government of $3,848 per person. Some employers reported that EnterTech graduates were easier to train, more productive, and more likely to stay on the job than other employees.[109]

Despite increasing illness, Kozmetsky kept working on various e-learning projects in the last two years of his life. In the spring of 2002, he worked with Alex Cavalli, a research scientist at the IC² Institute, to establish E-Learning and Training Labs (ELT Labs) as a "collaboratory" bringing together transdisciplinary teams from academia, business, and various levels of government to research and develop workforce development, training, and learning programs. Building on the success of EnterTech, ELT Labs focused on "identifying leading-edge economic issues, quickly finding solutions and creating self-sustaining business models that other research and development institutes can utilize," said Robert Ronstadt, director of the institute. Kozmetsky observed: "Breakthroughs in technology are what generate the prosperity and higher-paying jobs of the future. . . . ELT Labs' main goal will be to empower local communities to shape their own futures through dynamic civic entrepreneurships that form 21st century partnerships for economic development."[110]

Kozmetsky was active in other efforts to promote use of the Internet and expand online access by people with low incomes and other disadvantages. He was a strong supporter, for example, of a City of Austin proposal in 1994 to build a citywide fiber-optic network open to anyone for commercial use and providing access for people of all economic levels. "A feasible information highway is in my opinion necessary if we're to achieve sustainable economic growth and become a world-class software center and more," Kozmetsky said. Faced with opposition from some network providers and telephone companies, the city's idea did not go forward.[111]

The "Austin Miracle"

By the last years of Kozmetsky's life, Austin had achieved an economic transformation that in many ways met or even exceeded the vision that he had long held for the region. By almost any measure, Austin and its surrounding area had joined the ranks of the nation's most important high-tech regions. By the mid-1990s, the region had more than 275 technology manufacturers, 60 percent of which were in the computer and electronics industry. By 1998 about 20 percent of the city's employment was in high-tech industries, up from a negligible level thirty years earlier. The leading employers were Dell (14,000 workers) and Motorola (12,000).[112] More than 150,000 jobs had been created from 1990 to 1998, with significant growth in both the manufacturing and service sectors. The software industry accounted for much of the growth in service jobs, employing more than 154,000 people in the region.[113] The number of patents registered in the Austin region grew from about 350 in 1990 to almost 1,600 in 2000, more than those registered in much larger regions, such as Seattle, and about twice as many as in Raleigh-Durham. The R&D and product development units of four companies—IBM, Advanced Micro Devices, Motorola, and Dell—accounted for 65 percent of the region's patents in 1999.[114]

The dramatic changes in the Austin economy in the last quarter of the twentieth century drew worldwide attention. Politicians, economists, academic researchers, journalists, and delegations from chambers of commerce and similar organizations began to visit Austin in a steady stream to learn firsthand about how the city had been transformed into a high-technology powerhouse. Delegations arrived from Dallas, Houston, and other cities across Texas, from cities and regions throughout the nation, and from highly developed countries, as well as those in the Third World—all hoping to identify the causes of what was often called the "Austin Miracle." The IC² Institute and its Austin Technology Incubator were always prominent stops on these tours, and Kozmetsky was highly sought after for his insights into the city's transformation and his advice on whether other cities could achieve a similar record of change.

One of the most notable of these visits came in 1997, when a delegation from Seattle led by Bill Gates Sr. arrived for a series of meetings with Austin entrepreneurs and university faculty members and administrators, including Kozmetsky. An official of the Technology Alliance of Washington said of the visit: "We were particularly interested in learning about IC² and the Austin Technology Incubator and talking to entrepreneurs and venture capitalists who were building a technology-based economy in a similar-sized city."[115]

Visitors who sought a precise template on which to craft their own economic miracles would be disappointed, just as were those who had made earlier efforts to duplicate exactly the experience of Silicon Valley and the Route 128 corridor, but Kozmetsky and his colleagues at the IC² Institute did offer a detailed analysis of the Austin transformation— a framework of theory and practice that they said constituted a "road map" for similar transitions of local and regional economies based on the advance of technology. In the 1990s they called this road map the Austin Model, and in addition to explaining it to visiting delegations they carried it around the world as they consulted with local and national government agencies, government-industry collaborators, entrepreneurs, and others (see chapter 17).

Numerous scholars have studied the events on which this model was based and have presented summaries of Austin's transition. These studies tend to agree on the main elements of that transition: well-organized community planning, with early leadership from the Chamber of Commerce; a close-knit community of leaders with shared goals (with Kozmetsky being one of the most prominent of these "civic entrepreneurs"); a self-conscious effort by these leaders to develop in Austin an "information-based economy" (something Kozmetsky had been promoting on a broader scale since the 1960s); consistent leadership over an extended time, reinforcing the city's institutional memory; close interaction among the private sector, government, and higher education, with the University of Texas at Austin playing a central role at almost every turn; and a willingness to adapt the city's economic development planning to changing conditions, along with an ability to anticipate future needs (another of Kozmetsky's long-standing priorities).

Kozmetsky is consistently credited with being at the center of the events on which the Austin Miracle was based, mainly through his activities at the IC² Institute and three of the main institutions that he created as "experiments" in economic development—the Texas Capital Network, the Austin Technology Incubator, and the Austin Software Council. The combined work of these entities has been seen as fulfilling a main recommendation of the 1985 report from SRI International by "creating a climate for innovation as well as improving links between sectors of the technopolis. The IC² Institute, for example, has become one of the central governance forums in the region, holding workshops and meetings and maintaining close contacts with government, the community, the mayor's offices, as well as the chamber."[116]

One study of the region's transformation has identified three stages of growth—first, from 1968 to 1984, the development of the area as a center of branch plants of established technology companies based in other parts of the country; then, from 1984 to 1995, transformation of the region into an advanced manufacturing center, often with significant local R&D operations; and third, beginning in 1995, a shift in the local economy toward greater agglomeration and local innovation that heralded an increasingly internal process of development.[117] With this third stage of development, the region began to more fully achieve Kozmetsky's long-held emphasis on the importance of local innovation and homegrown companies, rather than a reliance on attracting companies from outside.

Many studies emphasize the role of the University of Texas at Austin in the region's high-tech transformation. This important contribution has been attributed mainly to the university's endowed chairs in science and engineering, its expenditures on research and development, and its technology licensing and spin-off activity. Among many other factors that help explain the growth of the Austin technopolis, the presence of key "influencers" has been found to be essential: "The 'momentum' for success within the Technopolis Framework comes from key influencers—visionaries and champions—in each sector or sub-sector working together to connect and leverage otherwise unconnected and perhaps competing sectors for a common purpose. First-level influencers [such as Kozmetsky] are usually successful leaders in their sector, who also maintain extensive personal and professional network links to other sectors and who effectively cross sectors with credibility and influence. First-level influencers also tend to mentor and 'protect' second-level influencers as they network across different public-private sectors to structure and implement action-oriented activities that often challenge institutionalized rules, procedures, and established expectations of conduct. Second-level influencers act as communication bridges to first-level influencers while initiating boundary-spanning activities with their colleagues and trusted friends in other sectors."[118]

In Kozmetsky's view, research at the IC² Institute led to the conclusion that new institutional alliances (such as a technology incubator and a venture capital network) could serve as surrogates for a national industrial policy "to encourage scientific research, enhance diffusion through technology transfer, and generally create an ecosystem that fostered the success of private enterprise. Indeed, the major purpose of the Austin regional alliances was to be a catalyst to unite academic and business institutions for diffusion of innovations that flowed from a process founded on cooperation and collaboration. . . . With the Austin region as its laboratory, the IC² Institute devised a strategy to pull government, business, and academic institutions together to build technology-based firms."[119]

Even as they focused on Austin as their first laboratory for economic development, Kozmetsky and the IC² Institute were also carrying the same messages and techniques to other parts of the country and around the world.

CHAPTER 17

THE IC² INSTITUTE III

Beyond Austin

The emphasis that Kozmetsky placed on economic development in the Austin region, for which he may be best known beyond the academic world, should not obscure his equally ardent interest in promoting economic prosperity elsewhere. A commitment to "shared prosperity," which Kozmetsky dreamed of encompassing the entire world, was one of the fundamental elements of his way of thinking and his diverse projects for practical action. "Austin was George's laboratory, but it was never his focus," said Raymond Smilor, his colleague at the IC² Institute. "He wanted to change the world."[1]

From its earliest days the IC² Institute was involved in the study of economic development well beyond Austin. In 1980, for example, researchers at the institute helped plan the White House Conference on Small Business, the first of four such conferences in the 1980s and 1990s.[2] When the institute expanded its mission beyond research, conferences, and publications, the new practical initiatives reached throughout Texas, the nation, and the world. In the process, the institute became an international institution, drawing overseas visitors and establishing a vibrant presence as a consultant and partner in many countries.

PLANNING FOR THE NEW TEXAS ECONOMY

Until the 1980s, the Texas state government was involved in promoting economic development in only a very limited way. One early initiative was an annual Governor's Conference on Industrial Expansion, begun by Governor John Connally and continued by his successor, Preston Smith. These events attracted up to 1,500 Texas industrial leaders. Kozmetsky took part in a panel discussion at one of the conferences.[3]

Such early efforts were broadened in the early 1980s, when governors and the legislature began sponsoring strategic planning projects that focused on economic development issues such as expanding the state investment in science and technology, strengthening the quality of higher education, and increasing collaboration between government and the private sector. A consistent leader in the legislature on all of these issues was William P. Hobby Jr., who was lieutenant governor from 1973 to 1991. Kozmetsky and the staff at the IC^2 Institute participated in all of the planning projects, and many of the recommendations of special committees and commissions that were at the center of the projects reflected programs that Kozmetsky had been advocating since the 1960s.

The first of these strategic planning projects was the Texas 2000 Commission, organized during the first term of Governor William P. Clements Jr. with the purpose of reestablishing the planning function of the governor's office that Clements's predecessor, Dolph Briscoe, had discontinued. Clements was said to be aghast that the state's principal effort at planning was limited to the two-year budget cycle, and he wanted to extend the planning horizon at least to the end of the century.[4] The commission's charge was "to address certain critical issues relating to the continued economic growth and development" of the state and to propose "a long-range state development investment strategy."[5]

Harvey McMains, then associate director of the IC^2 Institute, served on the thirty-member commission and chaired its committee on research and development. The commission oversaw two reference volumes that provided statistical portraits of the state and to which the IC^2 Institute contributed, *Texas Trends 1980* and *Texas Past and Future: A Survey*.

Meg Wilson, an LBJ School of Public Affairs graduate who had been working in the Texas General Land Office but was loaned to the governor's office for the Texas 2000 project, said Kozmetsky and the institute "were absolutely integral in putting together the reports of Texas 2000."

"We reached out to many people to help with research, and our first UT foray did not get a very friendly response," Wilson said. "Then Vic Arnold [executive director of the Texas 2000 Commission] suggested that we talk to George, and George immediately said he could help us with research on several topics. He volunteered for IC^2 to do a statewide survey for us on research and development. Until then no one had looked at R&D in the state as a whole, and George thought that would provide IC^2 with an interesting baseline of data."[6]

The research and development survey—written by Wilson, McMains, and Smilor—advocated an increase in research and development projects by expanding the relationships among governments, business, and universities, particularly in "the three most critical industries in Texas—

energy, high technology, and agriculture." The survey provided details of R&D in Texas by agencies, universities, industry, and foundations, and it included a list by Kozmetsky of "Technology for the 1980s"—areas that he identified as having increasing scientific and economic importance. They included microelectronics, medicine, materials, energy, defense technologies, and agricultural technologies.

The R&D survey also set guidelines for a comprehensive state strategy to support scientific and technological research and development, and it made ten recommendations for action by the state government, all consistent with the blueprint for economic development and diversification that Kozmetsky and the IC^2 Institute had been working on. Indeed, the proposals could have been borrowed from publications of the institute. They included allowing companies to take R&D tax deductions; allowing sole-source contracts for companies with innovative solutions to major problems; expediting government contract negotiations when new technology is involved; establishing a state business development corporation to help develop innovations; supporting establishment of university research parks; and similar measures through which state government could provide leverage to stimulate the new economy.[7]

The final recommendations of the commission were less explicit, but they did include proposals for increased R&D funding at universities, changes in faculty compensation policies to provide incentives for research, state assistance to small business and entrepreneurs, and state and federal tax credits for R&D by private industry. Recommendations related to water, energy, agriculture, and transportation also called for increased R&D expenditures by the state.[8]

Issues raised by the Texas 2000 Commission, such as the state's investment in research and development, received considerable public attention, at least in the state's largest newspaper,[9] but when Clements was defeated for reelection in 1982 by Mark White, less attention was paid to the work of the commission, since the new administration had its own priorities. And when Clements returned to the governor's office after the 1986 election, many of the remaining proposals of the Texas 2000 Commission were largely sidetracked in the legislature by the fiscal crisis resulting from a steep decline in oil prices and by other issues.[10]

Before that crisis struck, however, the Texas 2000 project did provide a boost for Kozmetsky's ideas about a new, diversified Texas economy based on high technology, driven in part by vigorous government action. Another important forum for Kozmetsky to explain his ideas to increasingly receptive audiences came with the establishment in 1980 of the Texas

Lyceum Foundation, a leadership organization on public policy issues. According to Wilson, the confluence of Texas 2000 and the Texas Lyceum stimulated a proliferation of economic diversification projects. Kozmetsky spoke at the Lyceum's early meetings about his vision for a new state economy, speaking engagements that Wilson identifies as of fundamental importance in educating Texas community leaders about the state's changing economic landscape.

"Everyone had heard about economic diversification from George's presentations and from Texas 2000," Wilson said, "and when Austin's bid for MCC was successful [in May 1983] people across the state said, 'Aha!' The state was ready for it. People understood what George had been saying, and all of a sudden the whole agenda of IC² was front and center in Texas."[11]

White might not have adopted Clements's Texas 2000 agenda, but he did promote other technology-related economic diversification projects, including establishing in 1984 a Texas Science and Technology Council, a thirty-member panel charged with making recommendations for enhancing the state's competitive position in science, new technologies, research and development, technology transfer, venture capital, and related areas.[12]

Wilson continued to work in the governor's office after the change in administration and helped organize the council. She said Kozmetsky would have been an obvious candidate to serve on the council, but she thought his talents would be more useful as an outside adviser rather than a member of the group. "I didn't recommend him for it because I wanted to see what the other members would come up with without being influenced by George's preconceived notions. I knew that George had such standing and was so passionate about his ideas that other members of the council naturally would have deferred to him. He would have taken over the deliberations."[13]

Many of the council's members were well acquainted with Kozmetsky. They included chancellors of the state's university systems (including Hans Mark of the University of Texas System), other university administrators, corporate leaders, Bobby Inman of MCC, San Antonio mayor Henry Cisneros, and Pike Powers of the governor's office. Kozmetsky made presentations to the council, and the staff went to him and the IC² Institute for information, and in the end the council's recommendations reflected his ideas.

The legislature in 1985 enacted a package of technology proposals that the council had endorsed and that were consistent with the policies advocated by Kozmetsky—as well as reflecting a new statewide consensus on high-tech economic development issues for which Kozmetsky had been laying the groundwork. Among the measures were a Texas National Research Laboratory Commission, which led the state's successful effort to attract the federal Superconducting Super Collider; the Texas Advanced Technology Research Program, a $35 million grant program for universities; a Center for Technology Development and Transfer at the University of Texas at Austin; and a Select Committee on Higher Education, which reviewed the state's colleges and universities, including their role in economic development, and led to further legislative reforms.

Several other proposals from the Science and Technology Council related to technology and research issues—including a venture capital bill, a bill related to funding of research grants, and a bill to revise university faculty workload regulations—failed to pass that year.[14]

Two years later, the Science and Technology Council continued this movement of state involvement in economic development with a report that made comprehensive recommendations for encouraging the emergence of a high-tech economy for Texas by the end of the 1990s. The report emphasized one of Kozmetsky's longtime goals—to have Texas develop a new technology-based economy from within, by growing its own start-up companies rather than relying on the old strategy of attracting branch manufacturing plants from established companies based in other states or abroad. The key to prosperity, the report said, required technology plus entrepreneurship—a clear connection to the formula that Kozmetsky had been promoting since he arrived in Texas.[15] Another link to his approach was a proposal for a state agency that would foster statewide partnerships between private business and government. Other proposals included increased funding for research and development at universities, new approaches to technology transfer involving results of university research, and expansion of technical training programs.

During the first term of Governor George W. Bush, Kozmetsky again was called on to help organize the state's initiatives related to economic development based on science and technology. He was the cochair (with W. Arthur Porter, CEO of the Houston Advanced Research Center) of a conference in Austin called the Texas Technology Summit, which was promoted by Bush to highlight the problems and opportunities related to technology industries and make the state more competitive in developing and attracting high-tech businesses. The IC^2 Institute and the RGK Foundation were among twenty sponsors of the conference, an outgrowth of a Technology Initiative Working Group. The working group included many people with whom Kozmetsky had been collaborating for years on economic development issues, including Meg Wilson (who by that time

A CIVIC ENTREPRENEUR

had become vice president for business development at MCC) and Richard Seline (then managing partner of the Jacob-Louis Group, a business consulting firm).

The Texas Technology Summit, which met in September 1996, brought together 170 government, academic, and industry officials. One purpose of the meeting was to lay the groundwork for new initiatives in nine industry sectors—aerospace, agribusiness, biomedicine, electronics and information technology, energy and environment, finance and professional services, manufacturing, multimedia, and telecommunications.[16]

Kozmetsky addressed the conference on its first day, speaking on "growing the twenty-first-century technopolis." He traced seven items of good economic news for Texas since the recession of the 1980s. Most of these were related to technology: (1) technology is dramatically changing the way Texans work, plan, and live; (2) Texans are headed toward technologically "smart" products for learning and leisure, distance learning, health delivery, and Internet commerce; (3) the state's "can-do" culture is evolving into "technology entrepreneurism"; (4) Texas has become a leader in modern manufacturing and services for computers, telecommunications equipment, and other technology; (5) Texas companies and research centers are at the forefront of emerging technologies; (6) more than four out of five Texans live in metropolitan areas; and (7) all levels of Texas government are "rethinking, reshaping, and restructuring" how they partner with business and education in a "cold peace era."[17]

At the end of the Texas Technology Summit, Bush reconstituted the Texas Science and Technology Council and named Kozmetsky to the new panel. More than half of the council's thirty members were corporate executives, which may help explain the fact that the group's analysis of the state's economic needs and its recommendations, issued in 1998, were heavily weighted toward strengthening the ability of the state's workforce to meet industry's needs.

Working with Texas Cities

Kozmetsky was often involved in economic development initiatives in cities and regions throughout Texas. Sometimes these initiatives were concentrated at university campuses within the University of Texas System, as with the projects discussed in chapter 13 involving Arlington, San Antonio, Midland-Odessa, and the Lower Rio Grande Valley. Kozmetsky was also frequently invited to speak to business and civic groups around Texas, and audiences were often most interested in hearing about how they could promote their local economies.

Kozmetsky tended not to just tell these audiences what they wanted to hear, but to give them a realistic assessment of their situation as he saw it. Such was the case in 1975 when he spoke to a "State of the City" conference in Galveston. He said most people around the country had an image of Galveston that was more suitable to the 1930s than the 1970s, and he urged civic leaders to discard their insular attitude and make the city more attractive to tourists and business investors. Major improvements in the urban infrastructure were needed, from transportation between the island and the mainland to basics such as better street lighting and drainage. And he suggested a need for new hotels and retail shops to attract visitors.[18]

Kozmetsky also had some involvement in the early plans of Houston oilman and real estate magnate George P. Mitchell to establish the Houston Area Research Center (now the Houston Advanced Research Center, known as HARC) in the Woodlands, Mitchell's master-planned city north of Houston that was established in 1974. HARC opened in 1982 as part of Mitchell's visionary "Research Forest." Although it was modeled mostly on the research enterprises in Silicon Valley, along Route 128 in Massachusetts, and in the Research Triangle in North Carolina, Mitchell did consult with Kozmetsky on his plans for the center, which would bring together universities in a technology-focused research consortium that, it was hoped, would lead to commercially viable collaborations with private industry.[19]

Kozmetsky played a major role in an effort by higher education institutions and the local chamber of commerce in Waco to try to expand the city's technology-based economy. Much of that effort began in the 1990s and culminated in an economic development study sponsored by the chamber and a "technology planning group" that included Baylor University, McLennan Community College, and the Texas State Technical College (TSTC). The IC^2 Institute and Angelou Economics, an Austin-based economics planning firm, conducted the study.[20]

Although Kozmetsky was no longer a central player in the daily management of the IC^2 Institute, his presence was deeply felt within the Waco community, as a source of encouragement and inspiration regarding the potential of the city's economy and, in particular, the role its higher education institutions could serve. His reputation in Waco was as high as it was anywhere in the world, with long-term, well-established relationships with officials at Baylor University (including Chancellor Herbert Reynolds and President Robert Sloan) and strong ties with the leaders of the community college and the TSTC, as well as local business leaders.[21]

Kozmetsky's influence was particularly strong at the TSTC System, which has a campus as well as its headquarters in Waco. Kozmetsky was instrumental in giving the college a new direction through the hiring in

1998 of Bill Segura as its chancellor. Kozmetsky and Segura had worked together when Segura was president of Austin Community College (ACC) from 1993 to 1996, before he left to become chancellor of the nine-campus Los Angeles Community College.

It was actually Ronya who brought the two of them together after she met Segura at a program on women in technology at ACC. "The RGK Foundation was the main founder of the program, and at one of its events I made remarks about how women were in high demand in technology jobs," Segura recalled. "Ronya took me aside, and we had a long talk, and later she introduced me to George. There had been a perception that ACC was sort of stand-offish regarding the technology industry in Austin, at least before the collaboration between Sematech and ACC, and George was extremely interested in new programs at ACC to make better connections between industry and technology training."[22]

The relationship between the Segura and Kozmetsky families continued after Bill Segura took the job in Los Angeles, and one evening in 1998 George invited the Seguras to dinner at the Kozmetskys' Santa Monica house. During the meal George asked Bill how his career was going, and Bill talked about his dissatisfactions with his Los Angeles job, which he'd had for less than two years. He said he found the college and the local political system mired in bureaucracy and corruption and not fully committed to making the changes he thought were necessary, and then he said he was looking around for a new opportunity and had heard the chancellor's job at TSTC was open.

"George's face lit up when I said that, and he said he thought I would be great for that job," Segura said. "At the same time I saw Ronya's face fall. The contrast between the two of them was funny. Ronya argued against George, and she told me I couldn't leave LA and that this was the perfect stage for me to try to make a difference in reaching across racial lines and dealing with the problems of the city." The community college had just recently been selected to run the remaining programs of what had been known as Rebuild LA (an economic development initiative that was a response to the rioting that followed the Rodney King incident in 1992), and Ronya saw this as an opportunity that Segura shouldn't pass up. There was no doubt that George and Ronya had not conspired in talking about Segura's future.[23]

Segura decided to apply for the Texas job, and several months after he had accepted an offer from the TSTC regents, he learned from a member of the board that George's support for his candidacy had been decisive. George had called the regent and learned that the board had not been able to make a decision about the chancellor's job because it was split between

Segura and another candidate. "The regent told me that George had said, 'You'd be a bunch of damn fools if you don't hire Bill Segura,' and after the regent relayed that to his colleagues they offered the job to me. I had no idea George had done this, but the board had so much respect for his opinion that he tipped the balance of the scales in my direction."[24]

Ronya "forgave" Segura for leaving Los Angeles and became an active supporter of Segura's efforts to strengthen TSTC. Her main interest was in broadening opportunities in technical education for single mothers and other women, and she helped finance a women's resource center to provide assistance to female students, including a child care program and scholarships.[25] Her legacy at TSTC in Waco includes a continuing set of women's programs in the Department of Student Life, including mentoring and networking activities, education in women's issues, career services, and the Women in Technology student organization.

There was no immediate surge of economic activity in Waco resulting from the reports by the IC[2] Institute and Angelou Economics, but ten years later (and after a further study by economist Ray Perryman) local organizations began to create a research and industrial park that bore most of the characteristics of Kozmetsky's vision for homegrown economic development. The park arose from an old General Tire plant that Baylor University acquired and, with its partners, turned into the Baylor Research and Innovation Collaboration, known as BRIC. TSTC was a major partner, along with support from the Waco Chamber of Commerce, the community college, and others. Baylor University moved its mechanical and electrical engineering research labs to the site, as well as related academic programs and the university's recently established Innovative Business Accelerator, a business incubator built largely on Kozmetsky's Austin Technology Incubator model. Combining access to TSTC's workforce development programs and Baylor's research and graduate school personnel, the plan included efforts to attract industrial partners to the site or to adjacent land.[26]

National Center for Manufacturing Sciences

In 1986, when the US government, auto industry leaders, and others were planning a national R&D consortium to improve the country's competitiveness in manufacturing, Kozmetsky and others hoped to attract the project to Texas. Instead, the consortium's headquarters was located in Ann Arbor, Michigan, close to the traditional center of the auto industry, but Kozmetsky continued to have an interest in the project, which overlapped with many of the activities of the IC[2] Institute. He became friends with the consortium's first president, Edward A. Miller, and the two began a long relationship that included numerous collaborative efforts between the consortium and the institute.

Kozmetsky began working with the board of the consortium, the National Center for Manufacturing Sciences (NCMS), and Miller became a fellow of the IC^2 Institute.[27] Kozmetsky often spoke at annual meetings of the NCMS, and the institute conducted an advanced manufacturing program that was relevant to the work of the center in Michigan. Activities that the institute counted as part of its advanced manufacturing program in the 1980s and 1990s included Delbert Tesar's robotics research, a variety of academic studies of project management, and consulting work with a manufacturing technology center at the TSTC.[28]

The NCMS organized a fleet of vans, called Manufacturing Technology Laboratories, that were designed to travel to schools to promote the development of job skills among students who might not be headed to college. Kozmetsky connected this project with one that Walt and Elspeth Rostow had begun for improving education and social services in Austin's low-income neighborhoods, and one of the NCMS vans operated in East Austin, as well as in Brownsville. Kozmetsky praised this "school-to-work" project as a way of helping students plan their futures, but he warned that schools needed to do more to change their approach to education.[29] "I cannot use the old methods and the old body of knowledge and be living in this new world that I'm already in," he said.[30]

East Tennessee and the Energy Department

In 1994 and 1995 Kozmetsky and others from the IC^2 Institute made trips to East Tennessee (the designation for the eastern third of the state) to confer with officials about the potential for high-tech economic development in the region. The officials were concerned about a possible decline in federal funds at national institutions in the region, including Oak Ridge National Laboratory in Tennessee and the Redstone Arsenal in Alabama, as a result of the end of the Cold War. Like leaders in other parts of the country, they were eager to replace lost spending on national defense by emulating the successes of the established centers of high-tech business— and the rapidly developing center in Austin. Part of their strategy was to engage the IC^2 Institute as a consultant to provide research and planning that would aid in setting realistic goals and taking specific steps to turn their goals into reality. A regional organization known as Tennessee Resource Valley also hired the economic analysis firm DRI/McGraw-Hill to work with the institute.

Kozmetsky jumped into this drive to create an East Tennessee technopolis with a presentation in October 1994 in Knoxville to an international trade meeting known as the East-West '94 Conference. Kozmetsky spoke on the subject of technology transfer and what was needed to strengthen East Tennessee's role as a participant in the "triad world" of the North American free trade zone, the Asia-Pacific region, and the European Community. The meeting was the largest of three trade conferences that the US Chamber of Commerce and the University of Tennessee sponsored in the early and mid-1990s. These conferences represented a major thrust to put the area's economy on the world map, and Kozmetsky's participation in 1994 signaled an increasingly close involvement by him and the institute. The meeting had been in the works since early 1994, while the institute was also considering possible avenues of collaboration with the Oak Ridge National Laboratory, the Energy Department's largest science and energy laboratory.

Much of what Kozmetsky said would have been familiar to anyone who had heard him speak about high technology and economic development in the previous twenty years, but his comments seemed informed by a new urgency resulting from his extensive trips abroad in 1993 and 1994. "We are entering an era of a new hypercompetitive regionalized world rather than a period of globalization," he told the conference attendees. "World financial capital is flowing to enhance a period of regionalism. ... The long and short of globalization versus regionalization is that leaders of Tennessee ... need to break the mold of how they go about doing business as well as how they commercialize science and technology in the globally competitive market. ... Leaders can no longer afford to be passive about or take for granted the commercialization of technology nor can they ignore regionalization of science and technology resources."[31]

Kozmetsky listed ways the East Tennessee region could accelerate the process of turning new technologies into commercially viable products or services. Most of these techniques had been important in Austin's development, such as technology incubators, "angel networks" that link entrepreneurs with investors, industrial R&D consortia, university technology transfer programs, technology literacy programs, and links between companies and other R&D entities, such as federal labs and universities.[32]

Many people in the Knoxville area were introduced to the concept of a technopolis—and the possibility of turning East Tennessee into one—through contacts with Kozmetsky in 1994. A couple of weeks after Kozmetsky's talk at the trade conference, more than seventy business, government, and university leaders from East Tennessee made a three-day visit to Austin designed to inform them about how the city had acquired its status as a burgeoning center of technology-oriented industry. University of Texas at Austin officials, including representatives from the IC^2 Institute and the Austin Technology Incubator, were prominent among those who discussed the city during the tour. The visitors came away with the idea that East Tennessee had many of the same basic ingredients as Austin but needed to emulate the qualities of community leadership and collaboration that had been so important in Austin.[33] A group organized by the Chattanooga Chamber of Commerce visited Austin a year later to get their own briefing on the city's success. Kozmetsky made presentations to that group on his ideas about forging partnerships to stimulate economic growth and on the work of the IC^2 Institute as a vehicle for economic change.

During 1995 Kozmetsky made at least six trips to Knoxville or Chattanooga, all but one using his private airplane. David Gibson, Laura Kilcrease, and others from the IC^2 Institute often accompanied him, and they also made numerous other visits to the region without him. These staff members spent many hours working with groups in the region to prepare for the meetings that Kozmetsky would attend and to develop the projects that made up the overall initiative. They were assisted by Richard Seline, a business and economic consultant with whom Kozmetsky contracted to provide planning and logistics for the initiative. Projects that they worked on throughout 1995 included a genealogy report tracking the history of high-tech industries in the region; an inventory of technologies "on the shelf" or in development at Oak Ridge National Laboratory, Martin Marietta Corp., the Tennessee Valley Authority, and other entities; a survey of businesses regarding their technology needs and their assets for advancing technologies; creation of a venture capital program with links to Austin's Capital Network; and planning for a technology conference. Another project was an effort to promote "wealth-building" and entrepreneurship, including an entrepreneur's council similar to the one in Austin. Seline reported in March 1995 that business faculty at the University of Tennessee were skeptical about getting the region involved in an entrepreneurship initiative because previous efforts had failed, but they were enthusiastic about trying again if Kozmetsky was involved. One faculty member told Seline that "George is the kind of person we need to get the community behind this."[34]

In June 1995 Kozmetsky spoke again to East Tennessee leaders as the keynote speaker for the Oak Ridge Summit "Charting America's Competitive Future," which focused on how the federal government's billions of dollars in weapons research in the region could spur private-sector business development, as well as how the region could make the transition to an era in which defense expenditures were expected to decline significantly. Kozmetsky advised the attendees that East Tennessee could become the nation's next technology center, but that if the region did not take advantage of the fifty-year federal investment in technology in the region, the resources of the area would move to other regions. A major step toward the collaboration that Kozmetsky advocated was announced at the conference when the City of Chattanooga and the Department of Energy agreed to coordinate research and development efforts.[35]

Kozmetsky spoke to the summit just seven months after Republicans had swept the midterm elections and taken control of the US House of Representatives for the first time since 1955—including victories in East Tennessee and surrounding congressional districts. The nationwide conservative trend was not lost on Kozmetsky, and his speech recast his long-held approach to private-public collaboration in terms that would be palatable to a conservative audience.

Kozmetsky participated in November 1995 in another discussion in Tennessee on innovation and partnerships at federal laboratories. The meeting focused on the future of the Oak Ridge lab, and Kozmetsky discussed with the group a report earlier that year that had criticized Department of Energy labs as inefficient and as having accounting and morale problems. He suggested that new forms of management for the labs might be necessary. A follow-up discussion was organized in Washington with many of the same speakers. Kozmetsky moderated a panel that addressed how to implement a plan for private-sector partnerships involving the labs.

The June conference in Knoxville had been organized by Zach Wamp, who had been elected the previous November to the US House of Representatives from Tennessee's Third Congressional District and would be one of the region's main advocates of high-tech industry for the next two decades. Kozmetsky had challenged members of the region's business and political communities to exert leadership toward developing an East Tennessee technopolis, and Wamp answered the call. A conservative Republican who served sixteen years in Congress, Wamp was a strongly bipartisan advocate for the Department of Energy and its operations at Oak Ridge and for efforts to capitalize on the lab as an engine of private-sector economic growth. He found an ally for these efforts in his fellow Tennessean Vice President Al Gore, and he frequently credited Kozmetsky with the underlying vision that guided his activities related to economic development. One of Wamp's initiatives that bore Kozmetsky's stamp was the creation in 1995 of the Tennessee Valley Corridor, a regional economic development organization that promotes commercialization of technology stemming from federal research labs, military programs, and universities. The organization has expanded over the years to include parts of Middle Tennessee and adjacent portions of Kentucky, Virginia, North Carolina, and Alabama.

Wamp summarized Kozmetsky's contributions to the region this way: "Without question, Dr. Kozmetsky's vision led directly to the creation of the Tennessee Valley Corridor, which has existed since 1995, won many awards including the U.S. Department of Commerce award in 2004 for enhancing regional competitiveness, and spawned extraordinary advanced technology investments in our region. As a young business guy and civic activist, I followed trends from our nation's greatest futurists, so I attended meetings when Dr. Kozmetsky came to our area in 1994 to listen, learn, and lead. He spoke of a 'technopolis' . . . between the hubs of Oak Ridge and Huntsville following years of federal R&D investments in energy, defense, and space. He even compared this infrastructure to the Research Triangle and Silicon Valley."

Wamp recalled what happened the day after he was elected to the US Congress in November 1994:

> I held a press conference in Oak Ridge and a reporter named Paul Sloca asked me what I intended to do about the threat of losing important missions in the region due to budget cuts and a new wave of conservative political leaders elected across the nation the day before. I quickly laid out a plan to hold a series of "summits" across the region to pull together the best minds and talent with a goal of forging a technology corridor between Oak Ridge and Huntsville.
>
> By the spring of 1995, the first of now more than 30 summit meetings was held in Oak Ridge. We assembled some 600 of the region's leaders and invited Dr. Kozmetsky to address this conference to remind us all what was at stake and the advantages we had in parlaying our glorious past into an even more competitive future. Needless to say, "the rest is history" as we have enjoyed one of the most resilient economies not just in the South but in the entire nation over the last 20 years.[36]

It was on one of their many trips to Knoxville and the hilly campus of the University of Tennessee that Laura Kilcrease noticed Kozmetsky, who was then in his late seventies, beginning to slow down. "We were going up and down those hills, and I turned around and he was far behind. That may have been the first time that I saw him tired," Kilcrease said.[37]

The IC² Institute and DRI produced extensive research reports on the region's economic development. The first, in February 1995, was about a survey, led by David Gibson, that summarized evaluations of industry partners of cooperative R&D programs run by Martin Marietta Energy Systems, the manager of the Oak Ridge lab.[38] Other reports—also under the leadership of Gibson and with assistance from the University of Tennessee and others—dealt with details of a "twenty-first-century jobs initiative" for the region and a detailed plan for job creation, which offered a guide to how the broad principles enunciated by Kozmetsky could be translated into strategies and programs for building on the education and research base of the region.[39]

The principles of economic development that Kozmetsky helped instill in the region continued to guide the political and business leaders of East Tennessee long after Kozmetsky and the IC² Institute completed their work there. Wamp chose to compete for the Republican nomination for governor in 2010 instead of running for a ninth term in Congress. His successor in the Third District was Chuck Fleischmann, another strongly conservative Republican whose general opposition to the growth of federal spending did not include Oak Ridge and other federal installations in the region. The Department of Energy's programs continued to draw bipartisan support in East Tennessee, where there was little doubt about the impact of the agency on public- and private-sector job growth and private-sector industrial development. The links among government R&D, university education and research programs, and private-sector entrepreneurship appear to have become an article of faith among leaders in the region, transcending traditional partisan approaches to government spending.

Kozmetsky was involved in other projects related to the Department of Energy. One of those that overlapped with his work in Tennessee was the effort by the Bechtel Corp. of San Francisco to win the management contract for the Nevada Test Site, a large nuclear experimentation center sixty-five miles northwest of Las Vegas. Kozmetsky had known Bechtel managers since the 1950s, and his activities related to technology transfer, energy policy, and federal contracting made him a valuable consultant to Bechtel as it put together its bid to run the 1,350-square-mile test site. During numerous westward trips in 1995—whether to California, Washington, or Alaska—Kozmetsky often included stops in San Francisco or Nevada to consult with Bechtel officials.

Bechtel won the five-year, $1.5 billion contract in October 1995 and continued to manage the site, now known as the Nevada National Security Site, until 2006. In late 2000, Bechtel also won the contract to manage the Yucca Mountain nuclear waste storage project in Nevada.

A CIVIC ENTREPRENEUR

Kozmetsky with four colleagues at the IC² Institute at a conference in 1993. The colleagues, from left, are Sten Thore, an economist who has been a fellow of the institute since 1978; Tom J. Mabry, a botanist at the University of Texas; David Gibson, senior research scientist at the institute; and Michael Wakelin of the Bechtel Corp. *IC² Institute photograph.*

Alaska

In 1989, just as the IC² Institute was beginning its early practical efforts to stimulate economic development in Austin, Kozmetsky began serving as one of two non-Alaskan members of the board of the Alaska Science and Technology Foundation, established by the state in 1988 to promote economic development through peer-reviewed research and other initiatives. Similar in some ways to the advanced research and technology programs that Texas established in the mid-1980s, the Alaska foundation awarded research and development grants to companies and public agencies from a $100 million endowment created with proceeds from the state's oil revenues. Kozmetsky served on the board into the twenty-first century, often speaking to civic groups and consulting with entrepreneurs in Alaska as well as attending foundation board meetings.

State initiatives to promote economic development had caught on across the country in the 1980s, and Kozmetsky was recognized as one of the founding fathers of the movement, mainly as a result of the research and conferences sponsored by the IC^2 Institute and publications such as *Creating the Technopolis*, which Kozmetsky edited with Raymond Smilor and David Gibson. When Alaska governor Steve Cowper, a Democrat, asked Kozmetsky to serve on the foundation, there were signs that Alaskans had begun to "think big" about the future of the state—on a scale and with a boldness that appealed to Kozmetsky. At about the time of his appointment, an Alaska nonprofit public affairs forum known as Commonwealth North sponsored the development of futurist goals for the state. The group came up with a twelve-point agenda that was seen as a way to look beyond the catastrophe of the *Exxon Valdez* oil spill in March of that year and to envision a time when Alaska would be a forceful player in the world economy. The agenda included establishing an Arctic research center on global climate change, developing the state's role in world trade, promoting the state as a "new Geneva" for international conferences, attracting the Winter Olympics, developing deepwater ports as hubs for a North Pacific marine transportation system, and collaborating among state government, universities, and the private sector on economic development, environmental protection, and other initiatives.[40]

Kozmetsky did not participate in the forum that developed this agenda, but the breadth of its thinking was consistent with his own approach to the future. (The fact that, almost three decades later, little of the agenda has been realized is in some ways beside the point.) The agenda also meshed well with Kozmetsky's long-standing interest in the Pacific Rim and greater economic and cultural links between the eastern and western parts of the Pacific. Given this context of bold thinking by Alaskans about their place in the world, Kozmetsky was a natural choice to serve on a major new effort by the state to support research oriented toward economic development. Kozmetsky's involvement in Alaska also connected with his early life in Seattle, which along with the rest of Washington had always had close links to the frontier to the north, so much so that many people had long thought of Alaska as sort of a colony of Washington.[41] Alaskans also habitually looked to their west, toward Siberia and Russia, for cultural, economic, and natural-resource ties—another connection with Kozmetsky's own family heritage.

Kozmetsky saw similarities between Alaska and Texas, as he discussed

A CIVIC ENTREPRENEUR

at a meeting of Commonwealth North when it announced its agenda. The connections included both states' traditional economic dependence on natural resources, as well as a pressing need to develop new strategies for economic development in light of increased global competition, and a need to create economic opportunities that would keep each state's talented young people at home. Among the strategies he recommended for Alaska was an increased emphasis on Pacific Rim trade and exports.[42]

Kozmetsky participated in six board meetings of the Alaska Science and Technology Foundation each year (usually four in Anchorage or Juneau and the others in smaller cities or sometimes by conference call). Although the foundation had an executive director and a professional staff, board members were heavily involved in the grant decisions, and, judging from the group's agendas and minutes, board membership required a significant commitment of time. Kozmetsky led the board's peer-review committee, in charge of finding and organizing experts from around the country to evaluate grant proposals, and he took his turn at every meeting discussing a selection of proposals before the board voted on whether to award a grant. At one meeting he was responsible for presenting a detailed review of twelve grant proposals that included projects to enhance sockeye salmon production, to find uses for recycled glass, to generate power from "low-rank coal-water fuels," and to improve feeding techniques on elk and reindeer farms.[43]

Although most grants concerned the application of new technologies to traditional Alaskan industries, such as mining, fishing, and lumbering, the foundation also ranged far afield from such activities and took part in projects that fit better with Kozmetsky's own high-tech interests. The foundation provided early funding for the Alaska Aerospace Development Corp.'s Kodiak Launch Complex, a rocket launch facility on Kodiak Island that had a successful record of satellite launches for the US government and private industry until the state halted the project in 2014 due to budget shortages. Another project of the foundation was Alaska Growth Capital, a development bank established in 1998 with the Arctic Slope Regional Corp. The capital provider was credited with creating more than one thousand jobs in rural or other high-risk areas in its first five years.

The foundation also helped establish InvestNet, a venture capital program inspired by Kozmetsky's Austin-based Capital Network. InvestNet was started with a grant to the Juneau Economic Development Council in 1998, and Kozmetsky worked closely with the organization as a mentor and a member of its advisory board. He met on more than one occasion with potential investors to explain the program, which, like the Capital Network, sought to match "angel" investors with commercial ventures that were beyond the stage of research and development but not far enough along for traditional financing.

Throughout the 1990s and early 2000s, Kozmetsky was a familiar figure at Alaska economic development events and was well-known to readers of Alaska newspapers and magazines. He was regularly described as having adopted Alaska as a third home state behind Texas and California, and he was reliably optimistic about the future of Alaska in interviews with the news media. As the *Juneau Empire* reported: "Kozmetsky said the next three years could mark the dawn of a new era in which Alaska's wealth is more heavily invested in local high-tech start-ups. Wealthy Alaskans, who have made timely profits in real estate, retail or natural resources enterprises, must learn the economic and social value of long-term investment within a community, he said. 'I think we're at a critical turning point,' said Kozmetsky, a Texas and California resident who nonetheless uses 'we,' 'us' and 'our' in speaking of Alaska. 'People have to be ready. We're getting there. People are beginning to buy in. . . . And yes, I'm very confident and optimistic.'"[44]

Kozmetsky's trip to Juneau at that time was mainly for a meeting of the foundation's board, but he also spoke with half a dozen potential investors at a private home, and he met privately with state legislators and Governor Tony Knowles. Reporters were not at those closed meetings, but Kozmetsky's message (which would have been quite familiar to Texans who knew him) was evident in the rest of his interview with the Juneau newspaper: "Although reticent about what advice he might have given . . . Kozmetsky emphasized encouraging trends in Alaska. The use of computers in schools is among the highest in the nation, the state is well-wired into the Internet, Alaskans who have left the state are returning, and the 'middle-aged leadership' in the business community is committed to the state, he said. 'Now the question is, how do we take knowledge and create value? . . . We've got most everything going, except we need more knowhow.' The challenge is not to develop technology, but to make use of cutting-edge technologies as they occur, Kozmetsky said. And while he wouldn't call it philanthropy, Kozmetsky said, 'a sharing and caring society' would be the result of the investment attitude he's encouraging. 'Those are women qualities men have to learn.'"[45]

Kozmetsky had a similar message when he spoke in June 1999 to Commonwealth North, urging Alaskans to think globally, to tap into world markets, and to look to people under thirty-five for the best ideas about potential new directions in business. In keeping with his overall views about the proper function of capitalism, he also emphasized the importance of being "civic entrepreneurs." "For those of you who have made it, it's the satisfaction of giving back to society," he said. "Your satisfaction is not money, your satisfaction is to see others make it."[46]

In some ways the high-tech advance of Alaska was slow going, with the state's great distances, small population, and challenging terrain often cited as drawbacks, but Kozmetsky and other promoters never gave up on the state's potential. In 2000, after eleven years on the board of the foundation, Kozmetsky was urging government officials to reaffirm their support of the foundation for the sake of Alaska's future. "Alaska has the talent, though perhaps not yet the mindset, to create a vibrant high-technology sector through 'angel' investments in homegrown business startups," he said. He predicted that the next three years could be the beginning of a new economic era in which investors would place more of the state's wealth in high-tech ventures.[47]

Kozmetsky's influence in Alaska continued to be felt in the twenty-first century. John Wanamaker, a leader of Venture Ad Astra, a venture capital firm in Anchorage, traced part of the firm's inspiration to Kozmetsky. He recalled Kozmetsky telling him not to be discouraged by the lack of capital for investment in Alaska, because investors would show up if the state could boast just one successful technology venture. "He said, 'You just need to do it. You just need one. You just need a Dell,'" and then the money would follow, Wanamaker told the *Alaska Journal of Commerce* in 2005.[48]

Kozmetsky also linked his work in Alaska with the resources of the IC^2 Institute. In the fall of 2002, for example, he sponsored a research fellowship at the institute for Jeanne Huang, a participant in InvestNet's entrepreneur-in-residence program. At the institute, her work included a study of lessons learned from the economic transformation of Austin, with an eye toward how Austin's experience could be useful to Alaska.[49]

The foundation was brought to a close in June 2003, just a month after Kozmetsky died, when Governor Frank Murkowski, a Republican, decided to transfer the $87 million remaining in the foundation's endowment to the state's general operating budget. Murkowski said the foundation had funded some good projects but that its performance had not been up to expectations in the number of jobs created and successful businesses started. Others disputed his statistics about the foundation's record. Shutting down the endowment followed efforts through the years to raid the fund to benefit the state's yearly budget. In addition to the Kodiak Launch Complex and the venture capital network, the foundation's successes included funding innovations in fisheries research and processing technology, a process to make a liquid fuel from coal, a project to help mining companies deal with environmental problems, and grants to wire schools for Internet service.[50]

SOUTHERN CALIFORNIA

The Kozmetskys maintained their deep connections with Southern California through all the years that they were in Texas. In addition to keeping their home in Santa Monica and having family ties in the Los Angeles area, they remained involved in the region's business community (not least through George's continued membership on the Teledyne board) and its higher education institutions. Economic development was also a focus of their interest in the region.

Kozmetsky joined other investors and high-tech enthusiasts in late 1999 to create the $400 million Tech Coast Superfund to help finance technology start-up companies in Southern California. News reports described the fund as an effort to borrow some of the entrepreneurial magic of Silicon Valley and the San Francisco Bay Area. The fund planned to invest in early-stage and growth-stage companies, projects to commercialize university research, and a technology incubator.[51]

Kozmetsky was described by the media as one of the "heavy-hitters" among the backers of the superfund, which was organized as a "fund of funds." He was among six fund directors, who also included leaders and former leaders of large institutional investment groups, such as the California public employee retirement system.

The president and CEO of the superfund was an old friend of Kozmetsky's from the Alaska Science and Technology Foundation, John Sibert. After leaving the Alaska project, he had been chief operating officer of the California State University Institute and chairman of the National Association of State Venture Funds.[52] Despite its flashy start in the news media and its array of investment-savvy participants, the fund appears to have had little luck in finding growing companies to back, and it soon disappeared from Southern California news coverage.

More productive was the relationship that Kozmetsky and the IC² Institute developed with the University of California, San Diego, particularly with its Connect program, an initiative that shared many traits with the IC² Institute, such as encouraging entrepreneurship and encouraging the availability of venture capital for start-up companies. In the early 1990s, Kozmetsky and Laura Kilcrease met frequently with Mary Walshok, a University of California, San Diego, administrator involved in the early days of Connect, and with others in San Diego to share ideas.

"A personal trust relationship was built between the innovative programs at Connect and IC², and we happily collaborated," Kilcrease said.

"We were part of a relatively small group of pioneers, doing leading-edge things, and George was quite happy to find these leaders in San Diego with ideas that fit so well with his own ideas. The two organizations became very close, hosting each other's conferences, and working together on many projects."[53] In 2005 Connect became an independent trade association, giving it the ability to engage in political lobbying.

Another of Kozmetsky's activities in Southern California was his service as a "mentor and navigator" for the advisory board of Global Business Incubation, a nonprofit corporation that sought in the late 1990s to create an incubator for start-up businesses in entertainment, media, and technology—part of an effort to bring a new era of entrepreneurship to downtown Los Angeles.[54]

South Florida

The openness to new people and ideas that characterized so much of Kozmetsky's life was reflected in his involvement in efforts by the University of South Florida to enhance its position as a center of discussion of economic and social issues facing Florida. The IC[2] Institute largely paid for a symposium in October 1988 that was the central event in the inauguration of the university's new president, Francis Borkowski. Kozmetsky and Borkowski met by chance in Washington, DC, in 1987, soon after Borkowski was appointed to the presidency, and Kozmetsky became interested in his plans for the university, particularly for its role in working on issues affecting the growing metropolitan area of Tampa and Fort Myers. "The president not only has a vision for the university, but he also has a vision for how it fits into the community," Kozmetsky said. "This is not a common thing in our country."[55]

The symposium was an attention-grabbing departure for the university, which had not had much of a public face. The meeting featured discussions of ensuring the quality of life amid economic growth, promoting equal opportunities for women, and increasing the ability of Florida to compete in a global market. Kozmetsky drew on his contacts to put together the speaking program.

Among the speakers were Kozmetsky's friends Everett M. Rogers, a faculty member at the University of New Mexico and a frequent collaborator on IC[2] Institute projects; Stephen L. Gomes, a manager of technopolis development for the Bechtel Corp.; Meg Wilson, at that time the coordinator of the Center for Technology Development and Transfer at the University of Texas at Austin; and Martha P. Farmer of Leadership America. Kozmetsky spoke on the prospects for the Tampa–Fort Myers region to become a technopolis. The institute also helped publish the proceedings.[56]

Kozmetsky's influence was again in evidence in 1989 when Borkowski proposed the establishment of a campus think tank modeled on the IC^2 Institute. Borkowski's plan, which did not come to fruition, was to call the think tank IC^3 ("IC cubed"), with the Cs standing for Creativity, Capitalism, and Commercialism. The goal was to establish a center for multidisciplinary research on "Suncoast" issues, such as the aging population, the water supply, and growth.[57] In later years, the university did establish an economic development center, known as USF Connect, that includes an incubator and other services to entrepreneurs.

"George was a great believer in what we were trying to do at the university, and he was extraordinarily generous with his time," Borkowski said. "He was an inspiring figure for me and, I believe, the entire campus and region."[58]

NASA

Kozmetsky's long relationship with NASA, which began while he was a business executive in California, reached new milestones through contracts awarded by the space agency to the IC^2 Institute.[59] One of the most important of these was a \$5.4 million grant in 1993 for the development of technology commercialization centers at the Johnson Space Center in Houston and the Ames Research Center at Moffett Field in Northern California.

The three-year contract was a response to increasing pressure on federal agencies to transfer technologies to the private sector. The contract included a marketing study of NASA technologies and incubators to support new businesses based on space-related technologies. NASA said it selected the IC^2 Institute for the contract because of its track record with spin-off and start-up companies in Austin.[60] "The pioneering work being done in Texas at the Austin Technology Incubator was a key factor in receiving this award," Kozmetsky said. "NASA considered the lab-to-market model we developed and currently operate as a pivotal selling point."[61]

In addition to accelerating the technology commercialization process, the project aimed at bolstering "entrepreneurial spirit" throughout the NASA organization. In Houston, much of the relevant technology was related to medical science and aerospace research, while at Ames the focus was on computing skills and hardware, as well as materials. The centers were planned with the hope that they could take advantage of related industries in each region. The sites represented strong contrasts in NASA culture but were both in regions with strong technology infrastructure.[62]

Kozmetsky got the centers started with the help of Laura Kilcrease, who applied the skills she had used as director of the Austin Technology Incubator. At the beginning, they made frequent trips together to Houston and San Jose on Kozmetsky's private plane, often with Greg Kozmetsky serving as the pilot, since there was not yet a nonstop commercial flight from Austin to San Jose. To get to the NASA site in California, they would typically be at the Austin airport by 3:00 a.m., take off by 4:00, and be in California by 7:00 or 7:30. Then they would work all day at the office in San Jose and head back to Austin at about 6:30 p.m., arriving home at midnight.[63]

The California project turned out to be more successful than the one in Houston, where the space agency had more trouble finding practical, marketable applications for technology developed at the Johnson Space Center.[64] At the Ames incubator, thirty-two companies were started during the three-year contract, and nineteen technologies were licensed for private-sector development. The incubator helped raise $55 million in seed capital for the new companies.[65]

The Ames incubator included a network of established executives and professionals to mentor new entrepreneurs, as well as a computerized networking service that matched entrepreneurs and investors. Among the companies that got their start through the incubator were a developer of scheduling software and a maker of innovative de-icing systems for aircraft.[66]

The work that the IC² Institute did for NASA laid the groundwork for the establishment of the agency's extensive nationwide network of technology transfer programs by the end of the century, often in collaboration with higher education institutions. NASA established six regional technology transfer centers, as well as nine business incubators, each associated with a major NASA research center or other facility. Complementing those operations were establishment of a small-business innovation research program and a small-business technology transfer program; participation in a national robotics engineering consortium and a federal lab consortium; and creation of the NASA Scientific and Technical Information Program, for dissemination of NASA research results to the public.[67]

Near the end of the contract with NASA, Kozmetsky organized a meeting in Washington, DC, for officials from the space agency, agents of the federal departments of energy and commerce, and representatives from Congress, as well as employees of companies that managed federal labs and others, to discuss ways of promoting technology-based partnerships. The meeting included discussions of proposals that could attract broad support in government and industry related to technology transfer, outsourcing, and joint ventures between agencies and companies.[68] Congress later approved funds for several technology transfer initiatives at federal agencies, including at the National Oceanic and Atmospheric Administration.

MASTER'S DEGREE IN SCIENCE AND TECHNOLOGY COMMERCIALIZATION

Partly as a result of the IC² Institute's experience in working with NASA and other entities on the commercialization of technologies, Kozmetsky concluded that there was a pressing need for a formal educational program on methods for transferring technology from government and academic research programs to the marketplace. The result was a program administered by the institute offering a master of science degree from the University of Texas at Austin in science and technology commercialization. The program, which began in 1996, was among the earliest degree programs of its kind. It was designed mainly to meet the needs of working professionals, allowing them to obtain a master's degree in twelve months while continuing their jobs. The program was offered in Austin as well as at the Defense Systems Management College at Fort Belvoir, Virginia.

In a bureaucratic tangle reminiscent of some of the conflicts Kozmetsky encountered as dean of the business school, the IC² Institute arranged for the program to be taught at Fort Belvoir without getting prior approval of state higher education officials in Texas or Virginia. That omission raised questions about whether the program would be properly accredited, but those questions were eventually resolved to state officials' satisfaction.[69] The program remained under the auspices of the IC² Institute until 2014, when it was moved to the University of Texas business school.

The program had two precursors from Kozmetsky's early days at the business school. One was an interdisciplinary doctoral program in the management of technology, which began in the early 1970s and included a contingent of students from France. The other was a Community Business Advisory Service that was funded by the US Small Business Administration. Lessons from these early "experiments" in technology education and community service later influenced the scope of the master's program.[70]

SOUTH CAROLINA

In the mid-1990s the IC² Institute began working with officials in Charleston, South Carolina, to develop a greater high-technology presence in the region's economy. The effort was largely prompted by the community's need to overcome the economic losses resulting from the decision in 1993 to close the Charleston naval base and its related shipyard and to downsize other navy installations in the city. The closures, which were completed in April 1996, had been estimated to mean the loss of up to thirty-six thousand jobs and more than $1.1 billion in the local economy.[71]

A CIVIC ENTREPRENEUR

Because of initiatives of Charleston leaders and other actions, the effects of the base closures were not that dire, but the city's work with the IC^2 Institute was seen as an important part of the region's response. A group organized by the Charleston Metro Chamber of Commerce visited Austin in 1995, including a stop at the institute, to study local economic development activities.[72]

The centerpiece of the institute's work was a proposal to collaborate with the National Oceanic and Atmospheric Administration (NOAA), a significant presence in the region through its Center for Coastal Ecosystem Health, on efforts to encourage the commercialization of technology developed by the agency. Building on the institute's success with its NASA contract, Kozmetsky, Kilcrease, Gibson, and others produced a proposal for NOAA to fund a technology commercialization center at the Center for Coastal Ecosystem Health. The proposed center was mainly a technology incubator modeled on the one at the IC^2 Institute.[73]

The grant proposal also included plans for a benchmarking study of the high-tech industry in the region, a study of NOAA's technology transfer policy, a marketing study of coastal environmental technology, development of networks for venture capital and business expertise, and an initiative to leverage the IC^2 Institute's relationship with NASA's Ames Technology Commercialization Center.[74]

The institute's work with NOAA was first financed through Congress in 1997, with the incubator known as the Center for Technological Innovation. In its third year the NOAA grant was transferred to the Charleston Metro Chamber of Commerce, which eventually began funding the incubator on its own. The incubator underwent several changes in structure and was eventually renamed as ThinkTEC.[75]

Another part of the institute's work in Charleston was a "technology portfolio analysis," using a methodology developed by the institute to identify technologies within local research organizations with the greatest commercial potential. One report focused on technologies associated with research at the Medical University of South Carolina in Charleston.[76]

The technology benchmarking study included a survey of business leaders to assess the entrepreneurial climate of the region, including accessibility of knowledge and expertise, availability of capital, quality of education, and presence of physical infrastructure. The study assessed existing technology-intensive business clusters, higher education resources, and technology indicators, such as the level of federal R&D funding. The study also offered an account of how the NOAA incubator could be the catalyst for new companies and economic development alliances.[77]

International Reach of the IC² Institute

The IC² Institute expanded its international initiatives beginning in the mid-1980s, and throughout the next decade Kozmetsky helped promote collaborations with countries around the globe. The most intensive relationships were with universities, businesses, and government agencies in Japan, China, and Russia, but the institute also maintained significant programs with organizations in Hong Kong, India, South Korea, Taiwan, Israel, Ukraine, Great Britain, France, Germany, Italy, Portugal, Chile, Brazil, Mexico, and Australia.[78]

In Brazil, for example, the institute established cooperative arrangements with Brazilian higher education institutions in 1993 that led to an executive development program for Brazilian bankers and plans for programs related to technology transfer and commercialization, as well as a student exchange program, joint research projects, and short-term academic programs.[79]

The institute's relationships with organizations in Japan and China formed a cornerstone of a conference on economic development in the Pacific Basin that the institute and the RGK Foundation cosponsored in Apia, Samoa, in 1988. Another sponsor was the University of the South Pacific, which has campuses in Samoa, Fiji, the Marshall Islands, and on other islands.[80]

That meeting and similar conferences that Kozmetsky organized throughout the Pacific Basin were influential in the development of the Asia Pacific Economic Conference, an annual meeting of the leaders of nations throughout the region. The conference began in 1990 at the suggestion of Australian prime minister Bob Hawke, but in 1993 President Bill Clinton was influential in reorganizing the conference to include the heads of state of the participating countries. The reorganization of the conference was along lines recommended to Clinton by Kozmetsky, said Edward A. Miller, who traveled with Kozmetsky on one of his trips to China.[81]

Beginning in 1985 the institute and the RGK Foundation cosponsored a series of International Technical Innovation and Entrepreneurship Symposiums, which were held in a different country each year. Another program with roots at the institute is the International Moot Corp. competition, started in the early 1980s by two MBA students at the University of Texas at Austin and now connected with entrepreneurship programs at universities around the globe. Students in the competition develop a business plan for an enterprise and make presentations to a panel of judges consisting of entrepreneurs, venture capitalists, and management consultants. Kozmetsky and the RGK Foundation supported the program financially in its early years, and Raymond Smilor led the program through its national expansion in 1989 and international expansion the next year.[82]

JAPAN

By the late 1980s the economic transformation of Austin and Texas had become a topic of international conversation, and this was nowhere more the case than among Japanese scholars, business leaders, and government officials. Japanese business executives were said to be primarily interested in two stops when they visited Texas—a tour of the superconductivity research labs of Professor Paul Chu at the University of Houston and a visit to Austin to see Kozmetsky. "Japan is now discovering Texas," Kozmetsky told a Japanese journalist in 1988. "In the past, Texas reminded everyone of oil, but today it is a high-tech state. The number of Japanese visitors to our institute has been increasing significantly. The relations between Japan and the U.S. are now moving in many highly creative directions."[83]

Kozmetsky had been reciprocating the Japanese interest in Texas. He established a high-tech joint venture with the Mitsubishi Research Institute, Mitsui & Co., and other companies. He had visited Japan frequently and was planning another trip when the Japanese reporter talked to him in 1988, and "Prof. Kozmetsky's appointment book is already overflowing."[84]

Kozmetsky and Robert E. Witt, dean of the University of Texas business school, visited three Japanese cities on that 1988 trip, which resulted in collaborative ties including programs with the Japanese Association for the Promotion of International Cooperation, the National Institute for Research Advancement, the Japan External Trade Organization, and the Long-Term Credit Bank of Japan.[85]

During another visit to Japan, in 1992, Kozmetsky spoke at a conference on technology incubation that included representatives of seventy-five major Japanese companies. Kozmetsky discussed the Austin Technology Incubator as a community collaborative effort, and Fred Phillips talked about interactions between the incubator and the University of Texas at Austin.[86]

The IC² Institute's Japan Industry and Management of Technology Project, which was established in 1993, was funded through a grant from the US Air Force. The project sponsored conferences on cross-cultural education and research, new strategies for Japanese industry, the growth of Japan as a "techno-economic superpower," and the human side of technology. The project also conducted research and held workshops on the Japanese technology industry.[87]

Relationships such as these led to several Japanese scholars establishing long collaborations with the IC² Institute through its fellowship program.

China

The IC² Institute was involved in research and consulting on economic changes in China in the last two decades of the twentieth century. Kozmetsky and others from the institute made several trips to China to participate in conferences on economic policy and to consult with Chinese academic and government leaders on techniques for building a new economic system. Kozmetsky was warmly received in China, where he developed friendships with many scholars and government officials, most notably with Song Jian, director from 1985 to 1998 of the State Science and Technology Commission (now the Ministry of Science and Technology).

Kozmetsky and Smilor visited China in the summer of 1987 as guests of science and technology agencies—a trip that came just as China was preparing to adopt policies related to economic development, including a greater commitment to private enterprise. Kozmetsky said the agencies were dealing mainly with issues of government policy, new technologies, and collaboration between developing and developed countries. Before audiences of thirty to sixty people, Kozmetsky and Smilor lectured on economic development, small-business development, business incubation, high-tech marketing, technopolis development, and the role of women in corporate management and entrepreneurship.[88]

After a week of discussions and site visits, Kozmetsky observed that China was "clearly in an expansive experimental mode" and was "willing to try many things within reason." He added, "There is an emerging private enterprise thrust in the country, but its future is uncertain." He also noted that the Chinese had their own nascent "Silicon Valley" in Beijing. "This is a section of the city . . . where many small, private, computer-related companies are springing up."[89]

Kozmetsky and Smilor also met with entrepreneurs and leaders of the Ministry of Aeronautics, the center of the country's space program. Much like NASA, the Chinese agency was being expected to do more to commercialize its technology.

Kozmetsky summed up his impressions of China: "China seems at a crossroads. There is an emphasis on decentralization, expansion of academic and business ties to the U.S., and experimentation in the development of small and medium-sized technology companies. But many issues are still being evaluated, and there is no consensus about . . . policies."[90]

One of the agencies agreed to partner with Kozmetsky on cooperative activities with the IC² Institute, including support for a graduate student working at the institute, faculty and student exchanges, and an exchange of publications. Another result of that trip was a conference sponsored by the IC² Institute in Beijing in March 1989 on US and Chinese perspectives on the commercialization of science and technology. Kozmetsky and Smilor attended the conference, which included two days of presentation of papers; two days of workshops on high technology, emerging industries, and policy issues for regional economic development; and visits to universities and businesses. The conference, which was related to the free-market reforms promoted by Zhao Ziyang, secretary general of the Chinese Communist Party, came just weeks before the large-scale protests by students, intellectuals, and others that culminated in Zhao's downfall and the Tiananmen Square crackdown in early June.

China's State Science and Technology Commission led the Chinese delegation, which included representatives of three dozen universities, companies, and government agencies. The US delegation included organizations with which Kozmetsky had long-standing relationships, such as the University of Texas at Austin, Teledyne Industries Inc., Bechtel Civil Inc., Paine Webber Development Corp., and the Kozmetsky family's KDT Industries.[91]

The conference led to tentative agreements between the University of Texas at Austin and Chinese institutions for educational exchanges and other cooperative activities. An agreement with the University of Science and Technology of China called for exchanges in the fields of natural science, technology, engineering, and social science. A joint program between that university's school of management and the University of Texas at Austin Graduate School of Business was discussed, as were joint projects involving the IC² Institute, the Chinese Institute for Industrial Economics, and the Chinese Academy of Social Sciences. Among other results of the conference, the institute established a China Industry and Management of Technology Program, which offered internships and courses similar to those of the institute's Japan program.

At the close of the conference, the US delegation met with Zhao at his official residence, and Kozmetsky spoke frankly on lessons learned at the conference, including the following: Chinese enterprises were ready to participate in joint ventures, with "huge opportunities" for such ventures existing in computers, software, and biotechnology; China needed to resolve intellectual property issues; China must make sure its first-time exports of high-tech products and services were of high quality; and China needed to improve its ability to compete within an international market, bringing its skills in marketing, sales, manufacturing, and finance up to a higher level.[92]

Kozmetsky also told Zhao that members of the US delegation were interested in assisting China in expanding its management "know-how," including a possible IC² Institute management-training program in collaboration with the State Science and Technology Commission. Kozmetsky said improved management skills would be essential for the success of China's Torch Program, an economic development program inaugurated in 1988.[93]

Kozmetsky has been credited with inspiring the early activities of the Torch Program, one of China's most successful efforts for transforming its economy. The program, which continues into the twenty-first century, includes high-tech industrial development zones, research and development in high-tech fields, development of technology industry "clusters," science and technology incubators, industrial parks, and other measures. The program, first directed by Dinghuan Shi, a member of the State Council of China, was started by China's Ministry of Science and Technology (formerly the State Science and Technology Commission) to promote market-based commercialization and industrialization of high-tech research results, concentrating on microelectronics, biotechnology, new materials, energy, and information and communication.[94] Omega International Group, a San Antonio consulting firm with ties to China, was hired to study business models, incubators, and other economic development programs in the United States, and the work of the IC² Institute became an important focus of the consultants' advice to the Ministry of Science and Technology. Kozmetsky and the Austin Technology Incubator provided the ministry with case studies of the commercialization of technology, and the incubator became a model for the Torch Program's initial activities, according to Dinghuan Shi.[95]

By 2006, the Torch Program had established 53 national science and technology industrial parks and 465 business incubators, generating more than 3.5 million jobs and $200 billion in revenues (for 2003)—18 percent of China's gross domestic product that year.[96]

Contacts between the IC² Institute and Chinese agencies expanded greatly after the 1989 conference. China regularly sent visiting scholars to the institute to conduct research or do graduate work, and larger delegations visited Austin with some frequency. Fifteen members of the Chinese Young Entrepreneurs' Association visited the institute in September 1995, and Kozmetsky moderated a program at which four Chinese professors and business leaders discussed high-tech business opportunities in China. The association signed an agreement through which the institute would host a visiting scholars program, provide executive training in management and technology transfer, consult with Chinese companies on tech-

Kozmetsky with a delegation from the Chinese Young Entrepreneurs' Association, visiting the IC² Institute in 1995. *IC² Institute photograph.*

nology and marketing projects, and collaborate with the entrepreneurs' association on other projects.[97]

Kozmetsky returned to Beijing in May 1997 for another symposium on science and technology commercialization and to sign a new agreement with the Ministry of Science and Technology designed to advance the goals of the Torch Program. Kozmetsky reaffirmed the IC² Institute's long-term commitment to help China commercialize its high-tech achievements through exchange programs, research, and training.[98]

Russia

Kozmetsky was a frequent visitor to the Soviet Union and, after its dissolution in 1991, to Russia, to discuss economic development with government officials, academic researchers, and the country's emerging entrepreneurs. In the 1990s Kozmetsky told his friend Edward A. Miller that he had decided to work on economic development in the country of his and Ronya's ancestors while they were taking a river cruise in Russia. He was thinking of the contrasts between the economies of Russia and America, and it struck him that Russia could advance economically and that he could influence it. "From that, he began bringing Russian academics to the United States to train them in his model of economic development and to take what they learned back to Russia," Miller said.[99]

One of the earliest of Kozmetsky's Russian projects involved collaboration with Soviet officials on the use of computers in economics and management of large systems, a program that resulted from a 1972 science and technology agreement between the United States and the USSR. The IC² Institute hosted Soviet delegations in 1978 and 1980 for seminars on using computers in regional economic planning, and in 1982 Kozmetsky, Smilor, and McMains traveled to Moscow for a week of meetings on this topic.[100]

In 1990 Kozmetsky met with the USSR State Committee for Public Education in Moscow to plan a 1991 seminar for evaluation of business plans for start-up companies, to arrange a workshop on commercializing technology in global markets, and to develop a graduate program for managing in market-driven systems.[101] The institute also participated in the first workshop in the USSR on science parks and incubators, held in Tomsk, Siberia, in June 1990. Tomsk was the site of the country's first science park, established in February 1990, and others were being planned for Moscow, Leningrad, and Minsk. Kozmetsky later expressed reservations about whether the scientists and bureaucrats with whom he had met understood the concepts of economic development promoted by the IC² Institute: "At times I felt they did not comprehend what it means for individuals to build technology-based companies. There was no discussion on using science parks and incubators to develop products and services for domestic needs. There was mention of building jobs in Siberia and having people leave the farms or big cities in the western part of the USSR to provide the required labor. They seem to think only about research and innovation. How the innovation was to be implemented was not discussed other than through . . . patents and joint ventures."[102]

Kozmetsky also noted that he saw no products that could be transferred directly to the US market, and that Soviet design abilities were old-fashioned. "Their laboratories and medical facilities have equipment that reminds me of the 1950s and 1960s," he wrote. "There were no obvious gold mines. There were, in my opinion, no giant markets waiting to be exploited."[103]

In June 1991, amid the turmoil of the last months of the USSR, Kozmetsky and Smilor attended a second conference on science parks and incubators, this time in St. Petersburg.[104]

A CIVIC ENTREPRENEUR

The contacts with Russia led to the appointment of Nikolay Rogalev, a faculty member from the Moscow Power Engineering Institute, as a visiting scholar at the IC² Institute in 1994 and 1997. Rogalev studied the institute's approaches to science and technology commercialization, technology transfer, management, and entrepreneurship, and he worked with the Austin Technology Incubator on collaborative projects with the Moscow Power Engineering Institute.[105] Rogalev, now president of the power institute, has been a fellow of the IC² Institute since 1996.

The Kozmetskys' fluency in Russian served them well on their visits to Russia and in playing host to Russian visitors to the United States. In 1990 they opened their Santa Monica home to Gennady Filshin, an economist who was the deputy premier of the Russian Federation. Filshin was in California to attend the IC² Institute's fourth International Conference on Creative and Innovative Management. Ronya Kozmetsky helped show Filshin around the Los Angeles area, and the visit earned a mention in the society pages of the Austin newspaper: "What does a Soviet honcho want to do when he comes to America? The first two choices of Gennady Filshin . . . were visiting Disneyland and swimming in the ocean. So report Dr. George and Ronya Kozmetsky. Ronya took him to Mickey Mouse Land where he thoroughly enjoyed six rides. And the Kozmetsky grandchildren taught him to ride a 'boogie board' in the Pacific."[106]

Filshin was a reformer under Boris Yeltsin, president of the Russian Federation (while Mikhail Gorbachev was still leading the USSR), and when Filshin returned to Moscow he was among those advocating a dramatic five-hundred-day push toward a market economy. He resigned in early 1991, charging that the KGB was trying to discredit Yeltsin and the reform program.[107]

Kozmetsky was elected in 1992 to the International Academy of Sciences of Higher Education of the Russian Commonwealth.

PORTUGAL

The IC² Institute's long relationship with Portugal began in 1994 with faculty and student exchanges with the Superior Technical Institute (IST), a graduate science and engineering institute at the Technical University of Lisbon. Manuel Heitor, a faculty member at IST concentrating on technological innovation and public policy, initiated the relationship with the IC² Institute and became a fellow of the institute in 1996. In 2015 Heitor was named to head the Portuguese Ministry of Science, Technology, and Higher Education. David Gibson was also an early participant in the exchanges, lecturing at IST and conducting research with Portuguese faculty and students. The two institutions were cosponsors of the first International Conference on Technology Policy and Innovation, held in Macau in 1997. The second conference in the series was in Lisbon in 1998, and the third was in Austin the following year.[108]

Sten Thore, who had been a researcher at the IC² Institute for eighteen years, moved to IST in 1997 to hold a faculty chair and participate in a master's program on engineering policy and technological innovation. The institute's activities in Portugal deepened in the twenty-first century through creation of the University Technology Enterprise Network, a collaboration with the Portuguese government to commercialize science and technology for international markets.

CHAPTER 18

NEW ACADEMIC FRONTIERS

From his earliest days in Southern California, Kozmetsky was active in the development of new academic disciplines—fields that involved new ways of posing and solving problems. The first of these was the field of management science, in which Kozmetsky was involved as a founder of the Institute of Management Sciences in 1953. This was an organization of academics, business executives, and government officials that sought to institutionalize an emerging quantitative approach to management through scholarly meetings and a journal.

Beginning when he was dean of the business school at the University of Texas at Austin, Kozmetsky was also an advocate of what he called "creative and innovative management," an approach to business management tailored to the conditions of the information age and global competition. Closely related was "transdisciplinary studies," which carried interdisciplinary or multidisciplinary studies a step beyond merely uniting aspects of established disciplines in collaborative projects and sought to develop a truly hybrid, new approach to organizing knowledge.

Another new field that Kozmetsky helped promote was "design and process science," which focused on the concept of process across many traditional disciplines in the sciences and engineering, with the aim of developing new ways of addressing complex problems.

Finally, Kozmetsky was a proponent of the development of special management techniques for "large-scale projects," which were simply the largest and most complex of all scientific and engineering endeavors (NASA's Apollo project being a prime example) and which, so Kozmetsky and others argued, required new techniques for successful management.

The close relationships among these fields were clear. All involved an interdisciplinary outlook, and all were based on the assumption that the new information and new technologies of the post–World War II era had produced new classes of problems that demanded new approaches to problem-solving. Whether these new approaches really deserved to become new academic disciplines within university bureaucracies was a subject of debate, but they did develop their own traditions, publications, research centers, university courses, and professional organizations.

Another common thread was that Kozmetsky was present in their formative years, serving as an organizer, practitioner, researcher, and teacher, and sometimes as a financial backer.

MANAGEMENT SCIENCE

Kozmetsky's association with William W. Cooper and Abraham Charnes led to his participation in founding the Institute of Management Sciences (known to its members as TIMS). Kozmetsky's role in organizing TIMS began with discussions among his colleagues while he was still on the faculty at the Carnegie Institute of Technology, but the efforts to establish the association really began only after he had moved to California to work at Hughes Aircraft. The organization is an example of how Kozmetsky maintained close contacts with the academic world during the fourteen years that he worked at private-sector corporations. Whether through volunteer work with TIMS or research and writing, Kozmetsky was never completely separated from academic endeavors.

The role that Kozmetsky played in TIMS while in the private sector was not unusual, as many forward-thinking companies in the 1950s and 1960s participated in the new theories and techniques TIMS promoted. Three technology companies—IBM, Burroughs, and Remington Rand—as well as General Foods Corp., were early institutional members, and executives of many other companies held membership in the early days. These included officials from aerospace and computer companies of the West Coast, as well as stalwarts of the older industrial Northeast and Midwest, such as General Electric, Westinghouse Electric, and Ford Motor Co.[1]

The links that TIMS fostered between academia and private business were mirrored by many of the research projects undertaken by Cooper, Charnes, Herbert Simon, and other advocates of the new discipline. It was typical of their research to collaborate with private companies and, indeed, to design academic research projects around the need to solve problems faced by industry. One of the first motives for computer programming innovations by Charnes and Cooper had been to assist Gulf Oil Co. in solving the complex scheduling problems of producing aviation fuel at the company's refinery in Philadelphia.[2] In this and in many other ways, management science broke through the old barriers between the ivory tower and the factory floor, and the Institute of Management Sciences provided an organizational structure for bringing the two worlds together, as well as for engaging them in collaborations with the federal government.

Melvin E. Salveson, then a faculty member in the business school at the University of California, Los Angeles, is credited with the original idea of establishing a professional association to bring together people involved in the new field of management science, regardless of which traditional academic discipline they participated in or whether they were working in academia, government, or the private sector. Another somewhat similar group, the Operations Research Society of America, had been established in 1952 by professors at the Massachusetts Institute of Technology who had participated in research on antisubmarine warfare during World War II and wanted to transfer to academic settings the management techniques they had applied in that wartime program. (A related organization began meeting in Britain in 1948 as an outgrowth of war research there.)

Salveson, along with Cooper, Kozmetsky, and Andrew Vázsonyi, a mathematician who was to become a colleague of Kozmetsky's at Hughes Aircraft, thought the Operations Research Society of America was too narrow in its focus and membership requirements, emphasized military problems at the expense of civilian business management, and was dominated by people with little knowledge of the private sector and little interest in using computers in the management of businesses. They advocated a new organization that would include people from the behavioral sciences and any other discipline that could contribute to a scientific understanding of management. The new group was to be named the Institute of Management Sciences.[3] (Through the years the differences between the two organizations were often blurred. Many people belonged to both groups, and many referred to operations research and management science as if they were interchangeable terms. In the early days they represented two approaches to management issues, but in time the distinction dimmed, as illustrated by the merger of the Operations Research Society and the Institute of Management Sciences in 1995 to create the Institute for Operations Research and the Management Sciences, or INFORMS.)

Salveson, who had managed a submarine construction program in San Francisco during the war, had been pursuing the new management approach after the war without having a definite name for it. At the core of the new approach was an effort to move beyond the "intuitive, nonrigorous practice" that Salveson and others had pursued in their war-production work and develop a more scientific and efficient approach to managing supply lines, allocating manpower, coordinating the stages of a manufacturing process, and other demands. Others had the same idea, and by the early 1950s a network of scholars had developed with seven main centers of activity. These were the Carnegie Institute of Technology, the Case Institute of Technology, RAND Corp., Columbia University, IBM Corp., and the University of California at Berkeley and Los Angeles.[4]

Salveson taught management at the University of California, Los Angeles, from 1949 to 1954 and established the university's pioneering center for management science research. He organized a meeting of a small group of people in the summer of 1953 to discuss the need for a new professional organization, partly in order to sponsor an academic journal that would be receptive to research in the new field. Charnes and Cooper happened to be in the Los Angeles area on a consulting project for Kozmetsky at Hughes Aircraft, which Kozmetsky had recently joined, and the three were among those with whom Salveson met.[5] The meeting led to a decision to move forward with the planning of a new organization, and Kozmetsky was assigned to study its financial feasibility and to report at a larger meeting at Columbia University later that year. Also at that meeting in Los Angeles was Paul Kircher, with whom Kozmetsky would collaborate to write an important early work on computers (see chapter 6).

Kozmetsky's financial report was favorable and helped persuade the people at the New York meeting to establish what would be called the Institute of Management Sciences. Cooper became the first president, and Kozmetsky the first secretary and treasurer. Kozmetsky managed the correspondence and financial affairs of the organization from his office at Hughes Aircraft, and he got the company's commercial artists, working on company time, to design the cover of the new journal, *Management Science*. He also arranged for the company to produce the first issue of the journal while TIMS negotiated with publishers. Kozmetsky organized a process for safeguarding the institute's funds and drew up the first plans for a nationwide membership drive.[6] He continued to have an active role in the organization for many years and was elected its fifth president in 1958, while he was at Litton Industries.[7]

Early membership lists for TIMS make it clear that the field of management science was predominantly an East Coast and West Coast activity in the early 1950s. Of the fifty-three members in February 1954, just two months after the organization was established, thirty were from the Northeast and ten were from California.[8]

An Application of Management Science: Weapons System Management

Before leaving his management role at Teledyne, Kozmetsky compiled a series of "notes" that he and three of his colleagues had written from 1963 to 1966 on the subject of weapons system management, with the goal of capturing the company's approach to "the control of large-scale weapons systems [and] space systems" as a precursor of "industrial management control systems of large-scale multi-divisional and multi-product organizations" (in other words, companies that shared these organizational features with Teledyne, whether or not they were military contractors). It is unclear whether the 190-page report was shared with anyone outside the company, but the report provides a detailed and in places highly technical summary of how to manage the research and development phases of complex weapons systems and, by implication, the R&D operations of any large-scale industrial concern. In many ways, the report reads like a blueprint for how to run the core business of a company such as Teledyne in the 1960s, and it would have been invaluable for new employees seeking to learn Teledyne's corporate culture. It also offers a case study of applying principles from management science to an actual business operation.[9]

The authors begin by noting that the use of a large-scale digital computer was essential for managing the complex projects that Teledyne undertook—a statement that might seem like a forgone conclusion, if the report had not included the observation that many industrial concerns had not yet bought in to the use of computers (at least by 1963, when parts of the report were written): "To date there has been a hesitancy in Weapon System Management Systems to use the mechanization and automation of information handling now available to the fullest extent. Those techniques would include computer systems, data communication, information storage and retrieval, and presentation devices and machines."[10]

In addition to using the computer to do calculations related to decision-making in engineering and management, the computer would be "the central means of providing an information system for the engineering, financial, logistic, testing, reliability and maintainability operations as well as provide that information required for mission analysis, war-gaming, and tactical evaluation of new systems, subsystems, and equipment through computer simulation."[11]

The authors include sections on strategic planning as part of the R&D process for weapons systems but state that their techniques are applicable to broader industries. Kozmetsky's old friends Abraham Charnes, then at Northwestern University, and William Cooper, then at the Carnegie Institute of Technology, provided continuing assistance to Kozmetsky's management team by helping apply the techniques of chance-constrained programming to the strategic-planning issues that Teledyne faced.[12] This analytic tool was aimed at giving Teledyne the assurance that its reports on a weapon system had "the characteristic of prediction in the sense of providing a measure of confidence that certain goals could be obtained if certain selected strategies were followed."[13]

During the early 1960s Teledyne drew heavily on an advanced computer technique that Charnes, Cooper, and others had developed for making financial decisions about the marketing of new products. The technique was named DEMON, for Decision Mapping via Optimum Networks, and Charnes and Cooper had developed it in collaboration with David Learner of the advertising firm BBDO.[14]

One of the technique's analytical strengths was its incorporation of all accumulated information about a product at each stage that a decision was required—thus taking into account a quantity of information (engineering tests, financial data, scheduling issues, etc.) that would have been impossible to integrate without a computer. The application of computer-based decision-making techniques to the management of Teledyne's weapons contracts is only one example of the career-long interest by Kozmetsky, Charnes, and Cooper in using the disciplines of operations research and management science to solve real-world problems.

Creative and Innovative Management

"Creativity" and "innovation" were watchwords for Kozmetsky and his associates throughout his University of Texas years. One of the earliest uses of the terms came in one of the business school's three-day seminars for business executives in 1971, when Robert E. Anderson (director of the management development program), faculty member Albert Shapero, and others made presentations about "creativity and innovation" and how to remove blocks to creativity within business organizations.[15] These and related themes were continued in the 1980s and 1990s in the graduate management course that Kozmetsky taught one semester each year.

For Kozmetsky, "creative" and "innovative" had distinct meanings, the first involving the invention of ideas or methods, and the second involving the application of those inventions to problem-solving—particularly the interdisciplinary "unstructured problems" arising from technological change. Kozmetsky, who attributed this terminology to Charnes and Cooper, eventually came to blend the two concepts into the term "transformational management." He believed this way of analyzing the problemsolving process held a key to management in an era of rapid technological change and in what he called the "hypercompetitive environment" of the global technology-based economy.

"Building new companies on the one hand and expanding existing companies on the other have become the cornerstone of competitive strategy for economic development," Kozmetsky wrote. "Creative and innovative managers must establish a new framework for economic growth through technology. There are four dimensions of this framework: (1) R&D linkages with public and private institutions, (2) institutional infrastructure for economic development, (3) support activities for entrepreneurial elements and innovation and manufacturing centers, and (4) economic wealth generation, resource development, markets and job creation."[16]

Kozmetsky maintained that these and other aspects of creative and innovative management were not merely the product of theorizing but were based on the conclusions of research conducted at the IC^2 Institute. The institute promoted the diffusion of this research, and sought to encourage further studies in the field, through a series of conferences. The first of these, in 1982, began an effort to make creative and innovative management into a distinct discipline.[17]

That conference, which commemorated Kozmetsky's sixty-fifth birthday and the end of his tenure as dean, led to the conclusion that three preconditions were needed for turning creative and innovative management into a new discipline. One of these involved eliminating outworn distinctions—between entrepreneur, manager, and academic administrator; between academia and the world of use and practice; between teaching small- and large-scale creativity; and between management practices and scientific R&D, from conception through commercialization.

Also necessary was the development of new management approaches, such as improving methods for reaching consensus on issues, broadening the use of strategic planning, and adopting new planning models that emphasize flexibility and adaptability rather than only efficiency and effectiveness. The final requirement was the redesign of business and social institutions to deal with modern international competition, as well as the design of new kinds of collaboration among government, industry, and academia.[18]

Other conferences were to follow, sponsored by the IC^2 Institute and the RGK Foundation and held at the University of Texas at Austin or other institutions, such as Carnegie Mellon University, that had faculty members with an interest in the subject. Kozmetsky and others edited a series of books that consisted mostly of the papers presented at these conferences, volumes that constituted a basic library on the field.

The graduate management class that Kozmetsky taught often focused on creative and innovative management. The class met at the IC^2 Institute's building and was usually limited to about fifteen students. One of those students in the spring of 1987 was Corey Carbonara, who worked at Baylor University in Waco and was pursuing a doctoral degree in the radio-television-film program at the University of Texas College of Com-

Corey Carbonara, a Baylor University professor who worked closely with Kozmetsky. *Photograph by Steven Poster.*

munication. Carbonara developed a close relationship with Kozmetsky, eventually taking over the teaching duties for the course that Kozmetsky had developed, and today teaches a course at Baylor University based on the same principles.

"The title of George's class caught my eye, and I went to see him to ask if I could be in the class," said Carbonara, who had worked on high-definition television at the Sony Corp. before joining the staff at Baylor University. "He asked me why I should be in the class, and I said I had made a lot of mistakes at Sony and liked the positive sound of taking a 'creative and innovative' approach to management. He liked my answer and said I was in."[19]

Carbonara said the class was even more useful than he had expected: "[It] exceeded all my expectations. George was fascinated by my background in engineering and television production, and he took me under his wing and I became one of the group of people that he called his 'special children.' He became one of the cochairs for my dissertation, and I worked on several research projects at IC² that became part of the dissertation."[20] The dissertation, "A Historical Perspective of Management, Tech-

A CIVIC ENTREPRENEUR

nology, and Innovation in the American Television Industry," was the first to incorporate Kozmetsky's ideas on creative and innovative management.

By the end of 1990, Kozmetsky was ready to stop teaching his management class, and he persuaded Carbonara to continue it. "I told him I couldn't fill his shoes, but he said his footprints will still be there," said Carbonara, who also taught in the IC² Institute's master of science program in science and technology commercialization. When Carbonara returned to Baylor University full-time, he designed his own course in creative and innovative management. One of Kozmetsky's disappointments was that the new discipline did not spread more widely as a formal part of management education, Carbonara said.[21]

Transdisciplinary Studies

Kozmetsky's long-held interest in interdisciplinary education merged in the 1990s with a new trend known as transdisciplinary studies, which goes a step beyond interdisciplinary approaches to knowledge and seeks to develop truly hybrid syntheses of diverse disciplines, as opposed to merely juxtaposing them. The theory has been that a transdisciplinary approach will counteract the drawbacks of overspecialized scholarship and better reflect the complex relationships among bodies of knowledge in the world outside educational institutions. The goal is a true integration of knowledge yielding transformative solutions to problems.[22]

Kozmetsky had many possible inspirations for this approach to knowledge, including the seminal treatise *Cybernetics* by computer pioneer Norbert Wiener. Kozmetsky had an early edition of this book in his library, a gift from his friend Albert Shapero and heavily underlined by one or both of them. Early in that book Wiener observed that advances in the study of computers required people to be conversant in multiple disciplines, including, at the least, mathematics, statistics, electrical engineering, and neurophysiology, and that progress would be most likely through the development of a common language among such fields.[23] It seems a short step from that insight to development of transdisciplinary studies toward the end of the century.

The term "transdisciplinary" has been associated with opposition to the fragmentation of knowledge and is "characterized by its hybrid nature, non-linearity, and reflexivity, transcending any academic disciplinary structure."[24] Transdisciplinary work also enables "the cross-fertilization of ideas and knowledge from different contributors that promotes an enlarged vision of a subject, as well as new explanatory theories. . . . Transdisciplinarity is a way of achieving innovative goals, enriched understanding, and a synergy of new methods."[25]

George and Ronya Kozmetsky pursued their interest in this approach to learning in several ways, including by underwriting an endowed faculty position (the George and Ronya Kozmetsky Transdisciplinary Chair) at Claremont Graduate University (CGU), in Claremont, California, adjacent to the east side of Los Angeles. Kozmetsky served on the university's board of trustees on two occasions, from 1976 to 1982 and again from 2000 until his death—continuing the Kozmetskys' long interest in supporting the educational programs of relatively small higher education institutions. The home of the Claremont Transdisciplinary Studies Program is in a modest building (formerly a private residence) known as Kozmetsky House. The university credits Kozmetsky with introducing the concept of transdisciplinary studies to the campus, leading to establishment of the academic program.[26]

According to Claremont, in 2000 Kozmetsky "observed that the term 'interdisciplinary' was outmoded. And, he argued, the growing interconnection among academic disciplines and the explosion of knowledge emanating from the use of technology had transcended specific academic fields. Kozmetsky suggested CGU use the term 'transdisciplinary' to organize and pursue scholarly interests within the university."[27]

The Kozmetskys' donations in 2002 also supported a program of annual fellowships for faculty members to pursue research and other activities in transdisciplinary studies. One of the tasks of the Kozmetsky Fellows in the first year of the program was to organize a conference on poverty, capital, and ethics.[28] The program in transdisciplinary studies annually selects an overarching theme to help organize the students' work, and in the 2015–2016 academic year the theme happened to be "innovation and creativity"—although this topic was chosen without an awareness of the particular importance of those words for Kozmetsky.[29]

A related initiative that Kozmetsky undertook at about the same time as his involvement at CGU was the founding of the Academy of Transdisciplinary Learning and Advanced Studies (ATLAS), established in 2000 with financial support from Kozmetsky, who was also one of the first board members of the organization. Kozmetsky's longtime colleagues Herbert Simon, Raymond Yeh, and C. V. Ramamoorthy also participated in starting the academy, which publishes the *Transdisciplinary Journal of Engineering and Science.*

Since 2011, the academy has sponsored the George and Ronya Kozmetsky Memorial Lectures and also awards an annual George and Ronya Kozmetsky Memorial Medal to commemorate the couple's "shared passion for innovation, service, and global prosperity." In 2012, the academy established the annual George Kozmetsky Innovation and Entrepreneurship Award.[30]

Closely related was Kozmetsky's involvement with the Santa Fe Institute, a private research institution founded in 1984 in New Mexico. Although the institute did not use the term "transdisciplinary" in its early literature, its approach was consistent with that trend. The institute sought to "bring the tools of physics, computation, and biology to bear on the social sciences, reject departmental and disciplinary stovepipes, attract top intellects from many fields, and seek insights that were useful for both science and society"—all goals in accord with Kozmetsky's broad interests.[31] Kozmetsky joined the institute's board of trustees in 1987 and contributed to its work financially.

DESIGN AND PROCESS SCIENCE

Kozmetsky also played a pivotal role in the establishment in 1995 of the Society for Design and Process Science, a professional association dedicated to interactions among engineers, scientists, business managers, and public policy decision makers. When various scholars were contemplating the creation of the organization, Kozmetsky quickly grasped the relevance of this new interdisciplinary field to the broad issues that he had focused on for most of his life—issues such as how to frame the relationship between innovative technology and economic development; how best to approach complex, unstructured problems; and how to instill in new generations of managers an ability to embrace his ideas about "creative and innovative management."

Kozmetsky's involvement in the early days of the society happened by chance. It began at a conference of the Institute of Electrical and Electronics Engineers in São Paolo, Brazil, in 1994, when Murat Tanik, who would become one of the founders of the society, happened to meet David Gibson from the IC[2] Institute. Tanik, who was on the engineering faculty at the University of Texas at Austin, talked to Gibson about his ideas for a new professional organization that would concentrate on the concept of process across multiple disciplines. Gibson was intrigued and suggested that Tanik talk with Kozmetsky when they returned to Austin.

Tanik's first meeting with Kozmetsky in his office was a little intimidating. He recalled that he tried to impress Kozmetsky by dropping the names of important figures whose work related to process science, including that of C. V. Ramamoorthy, the legendary computer science pioneer at the University of California, Berkeley. At Ramamoorthy's name, Kozmetsky leaned back and said, "Well, tell Ram to give me a call and we'll talk."[32]

It turned out that Kozmetsky and Ramamoorthy had known each other since the late 1960s when Kozmetsky was the new dean of the University of Texas business school and Ramamoorthy was a young faculty member in electrical engineering and computer science.

The two old friends' subsequent conversation about process science convinced Kozmetsky to support the new organization, including donating $40,000 to the society to support its first annual meeting, held at Kozmetsky's invitation at the IC^2 Institute. Kozmetsky attended every annual meeting of the society until his death, and spoke at several meetings. He also enlisted Herbert Simon as an early supporter of the society, and several members became fellows of the IC^2 Institute or maintained other relationships with Kozmetsky.

The organization publishes the quarterly *Journal of Integrated Design and Process Science* and in other ways promotes the idea that process science ought to be recognized as an academic discipline in its own right, or at least ought to become the guide for adapting the field of engineering to the complex problems of the twenty-first century. The society argues that engineering is still largely based on the science of the nineteenth and twentieth centuries, and that newer "integrative" approaches are needed to expand the design possibilities of the engineering profession.[33]

LARGE-SCALE PROJECTS

Beginning in the early 1980s Kozmetsky and his colleagues at the IC^2 Institute began to participate in a new discipline in engineering and management concerned with the planning and development of "large-scale" projects. By "large-scale" they simply meant the very largest technological and scientific challenges—extremely complex projects that required an inordinate degree of planning, were very expensive, and demanded the expertise of people from numerous traditional disciplines. Kozmetsky believed that by their very nature such projects called for sophisticated new management techniques, well beyond simply "scaling up" the techniques for more modest endeavors. Many people and institutions around the globe were involved in the development of large-scale projects as a field of study and a subject for theorizing (a field also known as macroengineering), and the IC^2 Institute was one of the main centers of such activity.

The participation of Kozmetsky came mainly through the founding of the Large-Scale Projects Institute (LSPI)—a nonprofit professional organization incorporated in Texas in early 1985 for the purpose of encouraging research and education in the field, sponsoring conferences, and obtaining R&D grants from organizations (such as NASA) engaged in large-scale projects. Kozmetsky was the founding president of the organization (which had its headquarters at the IC² Institute) and he recruited University of Texas System chancellor Hans Mark to chair the board of directors. Stewart Nozette, an assistant professor of aerospace engineering at the University of Texas and a former NASA official, was vice president.[34] The institute also began with affiliations with the University of California, San Diego, and seven other institutions—the University of Texas at Austin, the University of Texas at Arlington, the University of Arizona, Georgetown University, Auburn University, the University of Florida, and the Massachusetts Institute of Technology. Other institutions, including Alaska Pacific University, later joined.

Kozmetsky said the LSPI was founded in response to a lack of programs in the United States for the training of people to manage large-scale projects.[35] The official goal of the organization was "to foster cross-disciplinary coordination, political mediation, and public understanding for the successful identification and implementation of public and private large scale programs." The institute planned to analyze the strengths and weaknesses of historic and current large-scale projects and to develop programs for educating managers of future projects.[36]

The LSPI operated out of the IC² Institute building, although it began with no formal ties to the University of Texas at Austin. Kozmetsky wrote to President William H. Cunningham in 1986 requesting a formal relationship between the institute and the university, and Cunningham was encouraging, asking Kozmetsky for a copy of the institute's charter or an equivalent document. It appears that Kozmetsky did not respond to this request until the next year.[37] Whatever the organization's official status at the university, it continued to operate as a special project under Kozmetsky's supervision. A collaborative research and education agreement was finally signed by Kozmetsky and sent to Cunningham in August 1987.[38] The agreement was mainly useful to the LSPI because its grant proposals could now identify the institute as a University of Texas at Austin affiliate.

The LSPI was one of two major organizations in the United States for the study and promotion of large-scale engineering projects. The other group, the Society for Macro-Engineering, was established in 1982 by Frank P. Davidson, a professor at the Massachusetts Institute of Technology and generally acknowledged as the most prominent leader in the field of large-scale projects. Among his many activities related to large-scale projects, Davidson began advocating for construction of the Channel Tunnel in the late 1950s and celebrated its opening in 1994 with other macroproject enthusiasts. For many years he led a research program that specialized in analyzing the reasons for failure or success of large projects.[39]

Kozmetsky, who was a founding member of the board of directors of the Society for Macro-Engineering, had at least four books edited by or about Davidson in his personal library. The oldest of these was a 1978 compilation, edited by Davidson and others, of papers presented at a symposium sponsored by the American Association for the Advancement of Science.[40] Another of the books, a compilation of lectures on macroengineering delivered at the Massachusetts Institute of Technology in the 1980s and 1990s, includes a chapter by Kozmetsky that presented his assessment of the field in the United States and its future directions. Kozmetsky summarized research at the IC^2 Institute that focused on the potential for commercializing technologies involved in macroengineering projects. He also emphasized the need to learn how to better manage the commercialization process, which he liked to call "technology venturing." Another of his topics was the interactions between public and private institutions required for most large-scale engineering projects.

Kozmetsky also listed steps that were needed for moving macroengineering beyond its fledgling status, including establishment of a research consortium of universities engaged in the field, development of a "national technology agenda" that would focus US resources on future needs, expansion of technology transfer programs related to government-sponsored projects, and expansion of university research on public infrastructure projects.[41]

Although the LSPI was a new organization in 1985–1986, there was nothing new about humans' desire to plan and build large-scale projects. Engineering projects on a vast scale (in proportion to the technical capabilities of their times) were as old as the ancient pyramids, and plans for projects that would even more dramatically alter the landscape of the earth proliferated in the nineteenth and twentieth centuries. Particularly for Kozmetsky's and some of his colleagues' generations, which came to maturity before the mid-twentieth-century environmental movement, dreams of radically transforming the earth through massive engineering projects were often alluring.

"All of us who grew up remembering World War II were used to large projects," Hans Mark said, "such as the Manhattan Project and the development of radar. I wanted nothing more than to run a project of that size and importance, and I think George had always been fascinated by the management of big projects. I had written a book about the management of research institutions such as government laboratories[42] and had worked on some very large projects at NASA, and I think that led George to ask me to get involved in this new organization."[43]

Soon after it was published in 1954, Mark had acquired a first edition of a book by Willy Ley that described some of the most dramatic of the

Hans Mark, chancellor of the University of Texas System from 1984 to 1992, worked with Kozmetsky on the Large-Scale Projects Institute. *Photo by Dan Kallick, University Photography Services.*

then-unbuilt proposals for large-scale feats of engineering. These included some projects that have since become a reality—a tunnel under the English Channel, large arrays of solar panels for tapping into the sun's energy, and the International Space Station—but Ley also wrote about several projects that remain fantasies. One of those was a proposal to lower the level of the Mediterranean Sea with a series of dams, including one across the Strait of Gibraltar, to create vast new coastal lands and to generate electricity.[44]

Mark still keeps Ley's book within reach. The book also influenced Masaki Nakajima, president of the Mitsubishi Research Institute (Japan's leading think tank and business consulting organization, which collaborated with Kozmetsky), as he promoted his ideas for a "global infrastructure fund" that would involve large-scale engineering projects designed to revolutionize economies around the world. Nakajima also called his plan a "Global New Deal."[45]

Although Kozmetsky had cultivated a boyish interest in big engineering projects such as hydroelectric dams since the 1930s, his academic involvement in problems of managing large-scale projects can be traced to

1969, when he recruited Abraham Charnes to join the business school faculty and administer the Center for Cybernetic Studies. Charnes's research included the development of theories and practices for managing large-scale design and production facilities, including computer-based solutions to large production scheduling problems.[46] The big production and logistics problems that Charnes worked on were related to traditional industrial organizations, but the relevance of his work to managing macroengineering was clear.

Kozmetsky also interacted with Japanese scholars and business leaders concerning their interest in large-scale engineering projects. Beginning in the late 1970s, Japan was a major center of planning and study of potential macroengineering projects, mainly through the work of the Mitsubishi Research Institute. In December 1984, Kozmetsky had an opportunity to learn about the growing interest in Japan about macroengineering when he attended a joint Japan-US Conference on Macro Projects at the Imperial Hotel in Tokyo. He met with three Japanese scholars who were leaders in the establishment of the Japan Institute for Macro-Engineering, as well as with the former president of the Science Council of Japan and executives of Mitsubishi Corp., Nippon Steel Corp., and the Long-Term Credit Bank of Japan—all of whom were interested in the possibility of large, privately financed engineering projects. Kozmetsky also met with the mayor of Osaka, which had joined an international macroengineering association. Among the proposed projects of interest to the Japanese scholars and business leaders were factories in space for producing semiconductors and pharmaceuticals and a solar power generator in space.[47]

In most of Kozmetsky's writings about large-scale projects, it is clear that he is focusing on discrete engineering challenges that happen to require massive amounts of planning, time, materials, and manpower. On a few occasions he also included less specific challenges under the heading of large-scale projects—immense social problems that, unlike building a dam or making a trip to the moon, had no definable beginning or end and pervaded economic and political debate. "An example of such a problem is the allocation of world resources to meet the needs and secure the rights of all humans," Kozmetsky wrote. "Other macroengineering problems include concerns about pollution, scarcity, social welfare, energy, and public risk."[48]

Kozmetsky thought large-scale projects called for an approach to management that was different from methods appropriate to managing simpler projects. "The management of such large systems requires that the leaders of our institutions exhibit the abilities to conceptualize multiple objectives, to interact with other economic, social, and cultural institutions, and to operate within a highly dynamic environment," he wrote. "Research in education should, therefore, be directed toward establishing a way in which man and society will reconstruct the world based on the technological change that is taking place."[49]

The visit to Osaka in 1984 made a lasting impression on Kozmetsky, who met on that trip with the head of the city's planning department. Kozmetsky asked him what the city's "planning horizon" was, and the official said five hundred years. "I have a reputation for being a way-out thinker," Kozmetsky recalled, "but I don't think anybody in the U.S. has ever made it more than 30 years." A member of Osaka's planning staff soon spent a year at the IC^2 Institute studying the management of large-scale projects.[50]

Further interest by Japan in participating in large-scale engineering projects was expressed at a conference on global infrastructure projects that Kozmetsky and others from the IC^2 Institute attended at Alaska Pacific University in Anchorage in July 1986. Sponsors of the conference included the Mitsubishi Research Institute and the International Federation of Institutes for Advanced Study, based in Solna, Sweden, as well as the LSPI. Kozmetsky spoke at the conference on how to define the boundaries of a large-scale project. James Michener, who was in the state researching and writing his novel *Alaska*, also participated in the conference.

The conference featured discussions of actual megaprojects (such as a huge flood-control project in the Netherlands and the Aswan High Dam in Egypt), as well as visionary ideas that were being promoted by Japan's Global Infrastructure Fund. The proposals included a second Panama Canal and a transcontinental "ice highway" across the North Pole.[51]

In 1989 Kozmetsky represented the IC^2 Institute at a meeting in San Francisco to discuss organizing a North American Global Infrastructure Fund that would work with the Japanese project.[52] By 1991, the institute was working with the Japanese to establish a similar fund based in Europe. Kozmetsky attended another conference on the Global Infrastructure Fund in Tokyo in 1991, this time at the Palace Hotel, where he spoke on "academic approaches for realizing the GIF [Global Infrastructure Fund]." Japanese officials promoted the megaprojects envisioned by the Global Infrastructure Fund as peaceful and humanitarian uses of the country's economic power, but the projects proposed by the Japanese consistently met opposition around the world on political, economic, environmental, and technological grounds, and financial partnerships with other wealthy nations, including the United States, were not forthcoming.[53]

The IC^2 Institute and the RGK Foundation helped sponsor conferences and workshops in Austin exploring research priorities for large-scale programs, including strategies for commercializing defense technologies, particularly those associated with the Strategic Defense Initiative (the "Star Wars" program).[54]

In 1986, Kozmetsky tried to raise money among Austin businesses to help support the activities of the LSPI. In a fundraising letter he mentioned the institute's "pilot program" with the Defense Department and the Commerce Department "to address key technology and technology transfer issues in the SDI [Strategic Defense Initiative] Program." He said that if the potential of that effort "is fully realized, it could result in the eventual development of major cutting-edge research activities in Austin similar to a national laboratory." Recipients of the letter were advised that a contribution of $2,500 would entitle them to "early notification of and invitation to" all LSPI conferences as well as access to the institute's publications.[55] Little came of the fundraising effort.

The LSPI did attract funding through research grants and contracts, including an initial grant from NASA in 1985 to develop a computer model for integrating all the major systems involved in a manned base on the moon. The grant was one of many that NASA awarded for work related to a lunar base, which at the time was widely discussed as the next big national space goal and a potential stepping-stone for manned trips to Mars.[56] NASA said many US companies were interested in development of a lunar base as a way to stimulate industrial technologies. Interest was expressed, for example, by MCC in benefits that a lunar base could bring to the microelectronics industry.[57]

LSPI used its NASA grant to engage engineers and computer programmers in the task of designing software simulating the challenges of building a lunar base, including detailed lists of questions that would have to be answered about work to be done on the lunar surface, the number and types of workers needed, production schedules, and technical requirements.[58]

The software allowed engineers, scientists, and astronauts to be sure they were using common assumptions as they planned techniques of building and operating a lunar base. The software used Lotus 1-2-3 spreadsheets, which IBM supported from 1983 to 2014, and it represented NASA's first use of PC technology to link data. At one time NASA was hoping to be operating a manned base on the moon by 2010.[59]

The NASA research grant produced at least one commercial spin-off—a computer game called Moonbase marketed in 1990 by an Austin company, Wesson International Inc., which also sold air-traffic-control simulators. The game was used for a while by Kozmetsky in his graduate course in management "as a relatively painless way to initiate managers to the complexities of planning large-scale projects."[60] According to the *New York Times*, the game, which sold for $49.95, "works best on a 386SX or faster computer with a color monitor, a mouse, a hard disk, and at least 640 kilobytes of system memory."[61]

A player, designated as Moonbase Commander, was given seed money and then had to invest it wisely in providing shelter, power, thermal control, and supplies for a largely self-sustaining lunar base. The player had to choose a source of power and build a power station, hire a crew and negotiate labor contracts, look for sites for commercial mining operations, avoid disasters such as nuclear meltdowns, and carry out other management duties. A player was advised that he could "get on NASA's good side" by placing scientific research facilities on the moon even though they might not generate income.[62]

The Large-Scale Projects Institute, which remained active through the 1990s, received a variety of other grants for work for NASA, the army, the National Science Foundation, and private industry. The work included several projects in conjunction with KDT Industries, a Kozmetsky family company.[63]

CHAPTER 19

PHILANTHROPY AND BUSINESS INTERESTS

George and Ronya Kozmetsky had been inclined toward helping others from the earliest days of their marriage, but the wealth that George, with Henry Singleton, accumulated as a cofounder and major stockholder of Teledyne suddenly by the mid-1960s put the Kozmetskys in a position to make major financial contributions to the charitable causes that interested them. Their new wealth also gave them the opportunity to invest in other business ventures, just as it provided George with the independence and security he required to return to the academic world. Among all the business ventures that Kozmetsky participated in after 1966, only Dell Computer achieved success on a scale that equaled or exceeded Teledyne, or rivaled the impact on society that was achieved by Kozmetsky's academic pursuits or the couple's philanthropic endeavors.

Philanthropy

Ronya told friends that they had been planning to use their wealth to finance a business school that George had dreamed of establishing since his days at Harvard, independently from any existing institution, but that after the opportunity to lead the University of Texas at Austin school developed in 1965 they realized they could use their money for other charitable purposes.[1] For the rest of their lives they spread their wealth among medical and educational institutions, community projects, and other causes, using their RGK Foundation as the vehicle for many of their gifts but also making many donations, often in the form of Teledyne stock, as individuals. The foundation, overseen by succeeding generations of the Kozmetsky family, continued the traditions that George and Ronya began.[2]

The Kozmetskys established the RGK Foundation in the fall of 1966, after George had left the management of Teledyne and had begun serving as dean of the business school. The initial motive for creating the foundation was to support research into scleroderma, or systemic sclerosis, a chronic autoimmune connective-tissue disease that can be life-threatening and that George and Ronya's daughter, Nadya, had been diagnosed with when she was in high school. Doctors warned that the disease could damage vital organs and lead to death, but Ronya said she was determined to keep that from happening. "I told her not to believe anybody. I was not going to allow that to happen," Ronya told a reporter years later, recalling the origins of her commitment to supporting research into the disease.[3] It turned out that the diagnosis was mistaken and Nadya was facing instead the much less serious problem of juvenile arthritis, but the foundation continued to underwrite research into scleroderma and related diseases, as well as many other medical research initiatives.[4] The foundation also broadened its focus to include all levels of education as well as a broad range of community programs, such as social services for women and children and cultural arts programs. The IC^2 Institute and its extensive program of academic conferences and publications were also regular beneficiaries of the foundation during George's lifetime.

Ronya took the lead in running the foundation (and managing the family's investment portfolio) while George focused on the business school and other endeavors, and she continued to serve as the foundation's president until 1996, when she turned the leadership role over to her son, Greg. George and Ronya served as trustees of the foundation until their deaths. In 1999, the national Association of Fundraising Professionals gave the foundation its annual Award for Outstanding Foundation.

Research into ALS (amyotrophic lateral sclerosis, or Lou Gehrig's disease) was a major emphasis of the foundation, especially after George's death as a result of the disease (his sister, Luba, had also died of ALS). The ALS Therapy Development Institute, a research organization in Cambridge, Massachusetts, received several RGK Foundation grants, including $1 million in 2008 to support the institute's efforts to use the latest gene therapy technology in fighting the disease. In 2003, just after George's death, the foundation gave the institute $1 million for its drug discovery and testing program as well as for a knowledge-sharing initiative.[5] ALS research at the Burnham Institute for Medical Research in La Jolla, California, was supported with a $1 million grant from the foundation in 2006.[6] In 2013, the foundation gave $1 million to the Methodist Hospital Foundation of Houston to support ALS research.[7]

The foundation's other support for medical research and medical care has included grants for the study of Alzheimer's disease at the Center for

BrainHealth at the University of Texas at Dallas and genetics at the University of Texas Health Science Center at Houston (home of the Kozmetsky Family Chair in Human Genetics). Ronya and her children gave $5 million in 2005 to help build the Dell Children's Medical Center in Austin, which replaced a children's hospital that had also been supported by the Kozmetsky family.

Either individually or through the foundation, the Kozmetsky family had donated $30.4 million to the University of Texas at Austin through the fall of 2016, placing them among the university's most generous donors. More than $21.2 million of that total was donated during George's lifetime.[8] The total does not include more than $3 million in in-kind donations, mainly the land and building of the IC^2 Institute, given to the university in 1995. Throughout his years at the university, George also made numerous informal contributions, such as often paying his own travel expenses.

The business school and the IC^2 Institute were major beneficiaries of the Kozmetskys' university-related gifts, with more than $15.3 million being donated to the institute and more than $1.3 million given to other programs in the business school through the fall of 2016. In 1982 the Kozmetskys donated $2 million to the IC^2 Institute to establish twenty four endowed fellowships that became a major source of support for the institute's research programs. The endowments were supplemented with matching funds from the regents' centennial endowment program. Twenty-two of the fellowships were named for people who had been important to the Kozmetskys in their careers and personal lives, including University of Texas System chancellors Harry H. Ransom, E. D. Walker, and Charles A. LeMaistre; Board of Regents chairmen W. W. Heath, Frank C. Erwin Jr., Jon Newton, and Jack Blanton; regents Sam Barshop and Janey S. Briscoe; university administrator Gerhard J. Fonken; business school faculty member Judson Neff; Teledyne executives Henry Singleton and George A. Roberts; Texas businessmen Charles E. Hurwitz and William B. Blakemore II; Los Angeles oil executive Richard Seaver; Los Angeles friends Jack and Bonita Granville Wrather; and family members Gregory A. Kozmetsky, Nadya Kozmetsky Scott, Cynthia Hendrick Kozmetsky, and Michael Scott. Two other fellowships were named for George and Ronya and for the RGK Foundation.[9]

The Kozmetskys donated to many other departments and programs at the university, in fields that included architecture, art, astronomy, athletics, education, engineering, fine arts, geology, law, liberal arts, literacy, natural sciences, nursing, social work, and women's studies.

After the IC^2 Institute, the largest beneficiary of Kozmetsky family donations at the university was the LBJ School of Public Affairs, which in 2000 received the first installment of a $5 million gift from the RGK Foundation for the establishment of the RGK Center for Philanthropy and Community Service. The center operates a graduate program in nonprofit studies to educate new generations of leaders of nonprofit and philanthropic organizations. The center also offers an executive education program, and it conducts research on issues in philanthropy, nonprofit management, social entrepreneurship, and civic activity. Before the RGK Foundation was split into two new organizations in late 2016, it made its final grant, for $750,000, to the center.

Consistent with the Kozmetskys' broad commitment to education and their egalitarian spirit, the foundation also provided grants through the years to smaller, private higher education institutions, including, in Austin, St. Edward's University, Huston-Tillotson University, and Concordia University Texas, and, in the Los Angeles area, Pepperdine University, Loyola Marymount University, and Claremont Graduate University. In Waco, they supported projects at Baylor University, McLennan Community College, and the Texas State Technical College.

At St. Edward's, the Kozmetskys made a $3 million donation in 2002 to establish the Kozmetsky Center of Excellence in Global Finance, which focuses on issues of social justice through economic policy. Goals of the interdisciplinary center include supporting "sustainable financial stability" around the world and expanding the international perspective of students at St. Edward's. The center's recent lectures and conferences have dealt with political and economic issues in Ukraine, climate change, religion and international security issues, the role of social media in political campaigns, and environmental issues on Native American land.

Pat Hayes, president of St. Edward's from 1984 to 1998, has said that the Kozmetskys were the university's first major donors and encouraged others to support the school. "Their role was probably the single biggest factor in putting St. Edward's in another league in philanthropy," she said. "Ronya always said, 'Pat, you've got to get people to move the decimal point.'"[10]

Huston-Tillotson, a historically black university, received several grants from the Kozmetskys and the RGK Foundation beginning in the 1970s. Ronya Kozmetsky became a trustee of the university in 1976. Among the foundation's early gifts was a grant for the purchase of IBM Selectric typewriters and other office machines for use in office management classes.[11]

Gifts to Concordia University Texas over the years have totaled more than $495,000. They include $350,000 in 2009 to help fund faculty recruitment and other start-up costs of a bachelor's degree program in nursing.[12] Five years later, the foundation provided $60,000 to help start a master's program in nursing. Another gift was $85,600 for a program that matches student teachers with students in English-as-a-second-language classes.[13]

The foundation provided most of the financing for a "mobile technology laboratory" that the Austin school district operated as part of the Austin Project, a public education and social issues initiative led by the Kozmetskys' friends Walt and Elspeth Rostow. The laboratory, developed by the National Center for Manufacturing Sciences, was housed in a thirty-six-foot trailer and moved from campus to campus in the school district to provide students with hands-on experience in robotics, laser optics, computer-aided design, and other technologies.[14] The foundation helped sponsor other programs connected with the Austin Project, such as the Center for Development Education and Nutrition, an Austin nonprofit that sought to improve prenatal care, child development education, and parenting skills.

The endowment fund of the Austin Children's Museum received $1 million from George and Ronya in 2002. The fund was used to support the downtown museum's programs, such as art and science education for young children, as well as the programs of the Thinkery, its successor museum in the Mueller Development.[15] Another Austin cultural institution supported by the Kozmetskys was the Joe R. and Teresa Lozano Long Center for the Performing Arts. The Kozmetskys gave $1.5 million to help renovate and expand an older city auditorium to become the Long Center, home to the Austin Symphony and other arts organizations.

The foundation gave $500,000 to the Austin Center for Battered Women (later Safe Place, and now the Safe Alliance) in 1996, when the center was raising money to expand its emergency shelter capacity and build an apartment complex where victims of domestic violence and their children could stay temporarily.[16] Greg Kozmetsky and the RGK Foundation also were credited with helping attract $1.5 million from other foundations for the fundraising drive.[17] Many other women's causes received financial support from the Kozmetskys. Ronya supported the civic networking and training organizations known as Leadership Austin, Leadership Texas, Leadership California, and Leadership America. She also gave $3 million to the Women's Museum in Dallas (see chapter 20).

The Kozmetsky family name can be found throughout Austin, reflecting the various causes supported by the foundation, such as the Seton Kozmetsky Community Health Center, the Kozmetsky Center for Child Protection (named for Ronya, who donated $2 million to the center in 2006 and was a founding member of the center's board), and the George M. Kozmetsky Campus of the K–12 charter school operated by the University of Texas at Austin. The campus, named for George and Ronya's youngest child, is located in an emergency shelter for families who are survivors of domestic or sexual violence.

A special interest for the Kozmetskys was the Claremont Graduate University, which received a gift in 2002 to support "transdisciplinary" studies—a new approach to education that goes a step beyond interdisciplinary studies and seeks to synthesize the content and methods of various academic disciplines. George had been elected in 1976 to the board of fellows of the Claremont University Center, the central coordinating institution for the five undergraduate Claremont Colleges, the Keck Graduate Institute, and the Claremont Graduate University, all in Claremont, California, on the east side of Los Angeles. He was a member of Claremont Graduate University's board of trustees at the time of the 2002 gift.

The gift left university administrators free to organize an initiative in transdisciplinary studies as they thought best. The Kozmetskys "had a hands-off approach," said Patricia Easton, a philosophy professor who is codirector of the program. "They had the vision for transdisciplinary work and saw it as a remedy for overspecialization, but they gave us the freedom to figure out how to do it. Their gift and the vision that inspired it have had a major impact on this institution."[18]

Pepperdine University in Southern California was also a beneficiary of the Kozmetskys' philanthropy. In 1995 their support helped the university's business school begin the Kozmetsky Prize competition for business plans, an award that generally increased a new company's ability to attract venture capital.[19]

The Kozmetskys were also donors to their alma mater, the University of Washington, most notably with a gift of $100,000 in 1968 to establish the university's first endowed professorship, honoring George's mentor, Grant I. Butterbaugh.

One of the Kozmetskys' least known philanthropic activities was their support for the Oxford Center for Hebrew and Jewish Studies, established at the University of Oxford in 1972 for the study of Jewish history, literature, and languages. The RGK Foundation began supporting the center in 1983 with a gift of $25,000 to the center's endowment fund, and George later helped organize additional fundraising activities in the United States. Charles Hurwitz, George's friend and business associate in Houston, introduced George to the center's founder, David Patterson, in 1982, and George and Ronya visited the center the next year. Ronya was enthusiastic about supporting the center and persuaded George to participate.[20] George later joined Hurwitz as a member of the center's board of governors.

During their 1983 trip to Oxford University, the Kozmetskys were courted by Patterson with intimate visits with some of the nine-hundred-year-old university's most distinguished scholars, including philosopher Isaiah Berlin, historian Robert Blake, and Oriel College provost Zelman Cowen. When he sent the $25,000 donation a few weeks later, Kozmetsky wrote: "Ronya and I feel strongly that it is imperative that a positive understanding and appreciation of the Judeo-Christian tradition should be developed and nurtured, particularly to replace the vacuum caused by the Holocaust and its destruction of so much of Jewish cultural and scholarly intellectual heritage."[21] The Kozmetskys returned to Oxford for two days in 1984 along with their granddaughter Bethany Scott, who was ten at the time. Ronya and Bethany went sightseeing while George talked academic and fundraising business with Patterson.[22]

Stanford University was another recipient of the Kozmetskys' largesse, including a gift of $1 million in 1999 for Stanford's Institute for International Studies. The money supported an interdisciplinary program to help scholars, government officials, and business leaders understand the knowledge-based economy and its potential benefits to developing countries. The program was started by the Bechtel Foundation with the goal of better understanding the interactions of political, economic, social, and technological changes. Kozmetsky joined the advisory council for the program. When the gift was announced, Kozmetsky said: "Technological innovation has been the main driver of our economy. The best way we may be able to foster global growth, change, and prosperity is to make learning, knowledge, and the ability to innovate indigenous to institutions and organizations in developing regions of the world."[23]

The last major gift to higher education during George Kozmetsky's lifetime was announced just a few days before he died. This was a $6 million donation to establish the Kozmetsky Global Collaboratory at Stanford University to focus on technology innovation and commercialization.[24] The gift was announced with much fanfare (at a news conference at the IC[2] Institute attended by Kozmetsky and university officials) as involving a partnership between Stanford University and the University of Texas at Austin, but Stanford always had the leading role, and little, if any, of the money was spent at the University of Texas.[25] Some people associated with the University of Texas, who might not have been familiar with the breadth of the Kozmetskys' support for higher education through the years, speculated that the Stanford gift implied a criticism of the University of Texas, but such speculation may reflect only their own expectations.

BUSINESS INTERESTS

Whether as an entrepreneur, investor, manager, or board member, Kozmetsky was active in private business for more than fifty years. Beyond

John Butler, the IC² Institute's fourth director, joins Kozmetsky at the announcement of a major gift to Stanford University and the University of Texas at Austin in April 2003. *IC² Institute photograph.*

the two extraordinary successes of Teledyne and Dell, Kozmetsky also participated in a host of other business ventures. These varied greatly in their level of success, with some ultimately falling far short of their great initial prospects. Most of these ventures were attempts to market innovative technologies.

Kozmetsky was often a member of corporate boards. His longest-running board memberships were at Teledyne and Dell, but he served on other boards as diverse as La Quinta Motor Inns (run by University of Texas alumnus Sam Barshop), computer pioneer Datapoint, Gulf Oil, Heizer Corp. (a large venture capital company active in the 1980s), and companies controlled by Houston financier Charles E. Hurwitz. Kozmetsky sometimes served on eight or more boards at one time, a pattern of board service that is even rarer today than in the past. A survey in 1983 of eight thousand publically held companies found only seventeen people (Kozmetsky among them) with eight or more directorships.[26]

Michael Dell and George Kozmetsky at the Austin Technology Incubator, 1997. *IC²
Institute photograph.*

In addition to promoting new forms of venture capital to encourage
high-tech economic development, Kozmetsky was a notable venture capitalist in his own right. He was a partner in the highly successful Davis and
Rock investment firm of San Francisco—a firm that had been an early
investor in Teledyne—and late in his life he participated in another California venture capital effort, the Tech Coast Superfund.

In the late 1980s and early 1990s, Kozmetsky and Bobby Inman served
on the board of directors of PaineWebber Development Corp., a subsidiary of PaineWebber Group Inc. that specialized in high-technology
investments. Other board members included Richard Hodgson, a founder
of Intel Corp., and Joshua Lederberg, a president of Rockefeller University
and a Nobel laureate in chemistry. The company managed some $550 mil-
lion in investment funds in 1989.

Kozmetsky was active in Texas-based businesses from the early days
of his deanship. These included Texas State Bank, where he was named a

A CIVIC ENTREPRENEUR

director in 1967,[27] and Hyperformix, an information technology consulting firm in which Kozmetsky invested in the 1970s. Over the years Hyperformix shifted to the development of information technology software, specializing in "capacity management," or the process of analyzing and using efficiently the full range of a company's information technology resources. The company retained its connections to the Kozmetsky family, with Greg Kozmetsky serving on its board. Hyperformix was among eight companies acquired in 2010 by CA Technologies of Islandia, New York, as part of CA's initiative to strengthen its cloud technology.

Another Austin high-tech company in which Kozmetsky invested was Scientific and Engineering Software Inc., a supplier of software for systems analysis, design, and performance modeling. James C. Browne, a faculty member in the University of Texas Department of Computer Science, was the founder and chairman of the company, and Kozmetsky served on its board in the 1990s. Kozmetsky invested in the company through KozFund Limited, a subsidiary of the family's KMS Ventures. [28]

In the early 1970s Kozmetsky joined the board of Farah Manufacturing Co., which for a while in the 1970s was said to be the world's largest manufacturer of men's and boy's slacks. The company, with headquarters in El Paso, was established in 1920 by a family of immigrants from Lebanon and after the 1960s operated factories in El Paso and San Antonio as well as in other countries. At one time, the company employed more than nine thousand workers in El Paso. Labor unrest and subsequent battles for control of the company by the Farah family and its creditors characterized much of the period in which Kozmetsky was a director.[29] Kozmetsky's friend William C. Leone, who like Kozmetsky had been a director of the company since 1973, replaced William F. Farah as CEO in July 1976, but turmoil over control continued. Kozmetsky, Leone, and two other directors resigned from the board in March 1977 while Farah was fighting to be reinstated as CEO. Leone remained as CEO briefly, but was succeeded by two more people in the next few months, until Farah finally returned as CEO in April 1978.[30]

The Farah family and the company had other connections with the University of Texas at Austin during Kozmetsky's deanship. Kozmetsky persuaded the company to donate $100,000 to help support Abraham Charnes's Center for Cybernetic Studies, and the company was the subject of one of the oral histories produced by the business school's Oral Business History Project.

Kozmetsky and Inman were among the early investors who put a total of $2 million into Dryken Technologies, which sought to market software to e-commerce companies for managing customer relationships.

Kozmetsky also advised the company's founders, Ingrid Vanderveldt and Lyn Graft, on their business plan.[31] Vanderveldt had earned an MBA at the University of Texas at Austin in 1996. The company, which changed its name in 2001 to Studios 212, was founded in Tennessee in 1997 and in 1998 moved its headquarters to Austin, where venture capital was more available. The company's Storekeepers software helped online marketers keep track of customers' buying habits and use that information to update their websites. Although Studios 212 eventually attracted an additional $5.7 million in venture capital, the company came to an end after two of its major investors withdrew in late 2001.[32] Vanderveldt, who also counted Ronya Kozmetsky among her mentors, later served as "entrepreneur in residence" at Dell Inc., where she started a $100 million venture capital fund.[33]

Some of Kozmetsky's major investments could be traced to his position as a leading shareholder of Teledyne. In 2001, for example, Kozmetsky filed paperwork with the US Securities and Exchange Commission (SEC) reporting a 5.98 percent stake (four million shares) in Unitrin Inc., a Chicago-based insurance and consumer-finance company that was formed in 1990 from insurance companies that been acquired by Teledyne.[34] (In 2011 Unitrin changed its name to Kemper, an old insurance company that had sold much of its business to Unitrin in 2002.)

THE WRATHER CORPORATION

In March 1977, Kozmetsky was elected to the board of directors of the Wrather Corp., a Los Angeles company led by University of Texas alumnus Jack D. Wrather Jr. The company had diverse interests in oil, television and movie production, real estate, resort hotels, and other fields, and at one time it owned the *Queen Mary* ocean liner and held a lease on Howard Hughes's *Spruce Goose* airplane, both of which were operated as tourist attractions in Long Beach, California. For a few years in the 1960s, Wrather owned the A. C. Gilbert Co., a Connecticut toy maker famous in the postwar era for its popular Erector and chemistry sets. Other Wrather interests included ownership of the *Lassie* and *Lone Ranger* TV shows.

Wrather, a native of Amarillo who graduated from the University of Texas at Austin in 1939, reconnected with his alma mater in the 1960s, partly through his friendship with Kozmetsky. Wrather and his wife, Bonita Granville, a Hollywood actress in the 1930s and 1940s, became loyal donors to the business school and helped raise money for many university causes. Jack Wrather became a member of the University of Texas Chancellor's Council, a fundraising group, and sometimes offered the Disneyland Hotel, which his company owned, as a site for the council's meetings.[35]

Another connection between Kozmetsky and the Wrathers involved their son, Chris, who became a student at the University of Texas through Kozmetsky's persuasion. Chris attended the University of California, Berkeley, in his freshman and sophomore years, studying math and computer science, but when Kozmetsky visited San Francisco in 1972 to make a speech to a group of University of Texas alumni, he urged Chris to transfer to Texas. "George said I could come to UT and be his research assistant, and I thought that sounded great," said Wrather, who earned a doctorate at the university in statistics and operations research. The job as a research assistant was less glamorous than he had envisioned, with his duties including serving as an aide to Kozmetsky for a Saturday seminar that he taught on investment techniques. Kozmetsky continued as one of his mentors and supervised his dissertation, which dealt with buyer-seller bargaining.[36]

All these relationships between Kozmetsky and the Wrather family had numerous benefits for the University of Texas at Austin, but they also tested Kozmetsky's business principles when he and Jack Wrather had what Chris called "sort of a falling out." Jack Wrather had strong ideas about how to run the company he had founded, and even after it became a publically traded company he often continued to act as if it was still a proprietorship, Chris said. Sometime after 1980 a disagreement developed between Wrather and members of the board over one of his plans for the company, and in the confrontation it became clear that Wrather was thinking of the board as mostly a ceremonial body, while Kozmetsky insisted on the need for the board to uphold its fiduciary duty and protect what he saw as the interests of the shareholders. In the end, Kozmetsky resigned from the board on principle rather than acquiesce to Wrather's plan.[37] The dispute did not lead to a complete rupture in the Kozmetsky-Wrather relationship, as, for example, Kozmetsky later honored Jack and Bonita by naming fellowships at the IC[2] Institute after them.

DATAPOINT

Kozmetsky was among the early investors in Datapoint Corp. of San Antonio, a pioneer in the technology underlying personal computers. The company, founded in 1968 as Computer Terminal Corp. by two former General Dynamics engineers, Austin "Gus" Roche and University of Texas at Austin graduate Phil Ray, was for more than fifteen years a leading designer and manufacturer of computer hardware, including desktop computers and office automation systems. Kozmetsky joined Datapoint's board in November 1973 and remained on the board for twelve years. William C. Leone was also a board member for most of those years.

Datapoint's innovations included the first successful general-purpose video terminal (1969); the first general-purpose desktop computer (1971); and the first local area network (LAN) system (1977), which allowed a company's entire workforce to communicate electronically and share disk drives and printers. The company's goal was to produce machines and services that would result in an "integrated electronic office."[38] Some writers have said that all personal computers in use today trace their origins to the Datapoint 2200 terminal, patented in 1972.[39]

Kozmetsky joined the board as part of efforts to strengthen the company's financial posture and accountability. Those efforts included a new management team that led a decade of spectacular increases in revenues and strong growth in the stock price. The successes were tarnished in 1982 when irregularities in sales and accounting practices were discovered, problems that were said to be the result of intense pressure on the sales staff to continue to produce record gains.[40] Discovery of the problems led to the dismissal of several executives and, in 1984, an agreement by the company and one sales executive to commit no more violations of SEC regulations. No one was indicted in the scandal, but Datapoint's reputation on Wall Street never fully recovered. The scandal caused so much turmoil within the company that "there were board meetings where every board member brought their own lawyer," as the board and management wrestled with the question of who was to blame, according to one executive.[41]

Datapoint's stock price declined dramatically as a result of the scandal, creating an opportunity in 1984 and 1985 for Asher Edelman, a New York investor, to seek to gain control of the company. Edelman began buying Datapoint stock aggressively, stating that his goal was to liquidate the company. Datapoint's board tried to prevent the takeover, but by March 1985 Edelman was powerful enough to force concessions from the board, which, after three days of negotiations in New York, named him chairman and agreed to give him control over half the seats on the board.[42] Kozmetsky and Leone left the board in April to make way for Edelman's new members.[43] Soon Edelman changed his strategy and decided to keep the company together and operate it under new management, but a long period of decline ensued.

By the time Edelman took control, the company had begun losing its position as a technology innovator, and it never regained that status. The company went bankrupt in 2000, after which a holding company that owned Datapoint's patents survived until 2005.[44]

Gulf Oil Corporation

One of the most trying experiences that Kozmetsky faced as a corporate board member came in 1975 and 1976 when Gulf Oil Corp. was dealing with a scandal involving a secret slush fund that had been used for years by top executives to make illegal political campaign contributions and bribes to foreign government officials.[45] Kozmetsky joined the board in October 1975, two years after the slush fund had come to light during the US Senate's Watergate investigation and just a few weeks before an internal review ordered by the SEC exposed the full extent of the illegalities, so there was never any allegation that he had been involved. He was, however, a close ally of Robert R. Dorsey, the Gulf Oil chairman and CEO, who was ousted by the board in January 1976 as a result of the scandal. Kozmetsky was reported to be among at least three directors who fought against the ouster during a dramatic two-day board meeting.[46]

The existence of the slush fund was revealed when Gulf Oil's illegal contributions to the reelection campaign of President Richard Nixon were discussed in hearings held by the special Senate committee investigating the burglary of Democratic Party Headquarters at the Watergate building in Washington, DC. The subsequent investigation ordered by the SEC faulted Dorsey and other executives and concluded that the board had failed in its fiduciary duty to shareholders by ignoring warning signs about the payments. The bribes to foreign officials had been made to win decisions favorable to Gulf Oil's worldwide operations and included money paid to influential figures in South Korea, Italy, Sweden, Turkey, Canada, and other countries.[47]

In January 1976 the board forced Dorsey and three other executives to resign because of their roles in the scandal. The board's action came at 1:15 a.m. on January 14 after sixteen hours of deliberations in the boardroom on the thirty-first floor of Gulf Oil's headquarters in Pittsburgh. According to a newspaper report the next day, Kozmetsky and two other board members had supported Dorsey, but five directors associated with the Mellon family, which owned 15 percent of Gulf Oil stock, led a majority to vote against Dorsey and the other executives. The newspaper account said the atmosphere at the meeting was "sort of like a jury room" and that Kozmetsky and other allies of Dorsey had tried "to the last minute" to save his job. They proposed several alternatives to his dismissal, including making him part of a three-person team that would run the company or leaving him as a mostly honorary chairman while a vice chairman would be placed in charge. In the end, the Mellon faction prevailed and the board named Jerry McAfee, president of Gulf Oil's Canadian affiliate, to be the new chairman.[48]

Kozmetsky's loyalty to Dorsey stemmed from a close friendship that had developed through their connections to the University of Texas at Austin. Dorsey graduated from the university in 1940 with a degree in chemical engineering. As he rose through the ranks during his more than thirty-five years at Gulf Oil, Dorsey maintained close ties with the university, and he was named a distinguished alumnus in 1968. Dorsey credited Kozmetsky with persuading one of his sons to enroll in the university's Graduate School of Business instead of at Harvard, which had been his first choice.[49] Dorsey moved to Austin after leaving Gulf Oil and spent his retirement years on philanthropy and volunteer work

The SEC sued more than two dozen companies, including Gulf, to force changes in their behavior with regard to illegal campaign contributions. The commission concluded that more than four hundred US companies had made questionable or illegal payments to foreign officials. One result, in 1977, was the Foreign Corrupt Practices Act, which made it a crime to bribe foreign government officials and revised accounting procedures and internal controls of publicly traded companies.[50]

KDT INDUSTRIES

In the 1980s the Kozmetsky family started KDT Industries, which provided systems and software services for commercial, aerospace, and military customers. KDT was a family-run holding company that had operations in Texas, California, and Vermont as diverse as rebuilding turbochargers for locomotives, manufacturing electrical wiring harnesses and other "low-end" electronics components, making digital signal processors, and adapting global positioning system (GPS) technology to the task of managing a company's vehicle fleet. In 1993 KDT joined the computer research consortium MCC as part of an initiative to offer membership to small businesses and universities at sharply reduced dues.[51]

A 1992 strategic plan for KDT envisioned expanding the company's locomotive refurbishing operations in California and its electrical cable and switch business in Vermont, but the greatest hopes were placed in the company's GPS technology, which it had developed into a fleet-management system known as Fleetcon, as well as in two related software innovations—a method of integrating computers and databases and a method of data handling designed to improve the flow of information within architecture and construction projects.[52]

These software products were managed through KDT's Austin-based Arrowsmith Technologies subsidiary, which employed more than 120 people in its efforts to market GPS-related hardware and software to cable companies and other utilities companies for managing their fleets. Arrowsmith, which was established in 1991, sought to help cable companies overcome their reputation for slow customer service by tracking their fleets by satellite and dispatching trucks with the aid of a computer. Arrowsmith worked with researchers at the University of Texas at Austin to apply GPS and other technologies to the problems of fleet management. The company was one of the pioneers in marketing GPS technology, which had been developed by the US military and was made available for civilian use beginning in the mid-1980s.

By 1995 Arrowsmith had made deals with seven of the eight largest cable companies and was considered the leader in this market. Arrowsmith "linked several technologies—global positioning systems, radio communications, and advanced computer systems—by using its proprietary object-oriented software as well as off-the-shelf database and geographic information systems software." The goal of these efforts was "to build a computer information hub that initially handles customer service but can be expanded to other functions."[53]

Arrowsmith had dreams of quickly growing to more than $100 million in annual sales, but estimates were that sales of the privately held company were never more than about $10 million a year. Developing the technology appeared to be less of a hurdle than financial problems in the cable TV industry, slowing the industry's ability to invest in new technology. It was said that heavy debt and cash flow problems among cable companies had undermined Arrowsmith's sales and left it unable to collect on several million dollars owed by some customers. In early 1997 the company began reevaluating its prospects and in June dismissed 90 of its 122 employees. It was said that Kozmetsky and other investors "had lost confidence in the company's ability to become profitable in the near term without a substantial downsizing."[54]

The terminated workers were given sixty days of salary and benefits and help in finding new jobs. "We've always tried to create jobs in Austin and protect the people and get more high-tech jobs in Austin. I guess you don't win them all," said Laura Kilcrease, the former director of the Austin Technology Incubator who had been named chief operating officer of Arrowsmith in February 1997 in an effort to see if the company could be saved.[55] By the end of the summer a decision was made to shut down the company.

The Kozmetsky family business was engaged in many other ventures. Kozmetsky proved that he could be a hard-nosed negotiator. Charles Teeple, an Austin real estate developer who met Kozmetsky as a student at the business school and later worked for the Kozmetsky businesses, recalls a meeting with the owners of a California company to discuss a possible sale of the enterprise. "Greg and I were in the meeting with him, and we thought we had an agreement, and then the other side asked for something more that was a deal-breaker," Teeple said. "At that point George

Charles Hurwtiz, CEO of Maxxam Corporaion and a longtime business partner with Kozmetsky, in 1986. *AP Photo/ The Houston Chronicle.*

stands up, slams his folder on the desk, and storms out of the room. We followed him out and got in the car, and he turned to us and said, 'How did I do?'"[56]

Charles E. Hurwitz

Kozmetsky and Charles E. Hurwitz, a Houston financier, philanthropist, and longtime friend of the Kozmetsky family, had numerous business relationships, a few of them considered controversial by environmental groups or federal regulators.

The first of their business relationships was the Hedge Fund of America, a public hedge fund that Hurwitz managed and that included Kozmetsky among its investors. The hedge fund was formed in 1968 when it raised $54 million in a public offering.[57] Along with many other hedge funds, the Hedge Fund of America suffered in the 1969–1970 recession, and it later merged with a fund run by the Oppenheimer investment company.

Hurwitz took the initiative to meet Kozmetsky and discuss his plans for the hedge fund soon after Kozmetsky became dean of the business school.

I had followed his career, and I read in the paper that the University of Texas was hiring him to be dean of the business school, and I was impressed that the university was able to attract someone of his caliber and national stature. I wanted to do the first public hedge fund and wanted to talk to George about my plans, so I called his office to see if I could come and see him, and his longtime secretary, Ophelia [Mallory], said he was very busy and maybe he could see me in about a year. I knew one of the regents . . . so I called him, and we got an appointment to see George on a Saturday.

We walked into his office, where he had a big chalkboard set up, the way he always did. He said, "OK, describe this to me and tell me why you want to do it." We had an hour blocked off, and five or six hours later he agreed to sit on my board.[58]

That meeting began a business relationship and friendship that continued until Kozmetsky's death. Hurwitz was only twenty-six and Kozmetsky was forty-nine when they met, and their relationship is reminiscent of Kozmetsky's association with Michael Dell and with other young entrepreneurs. From the 1970s through the 1990s, Hurwitz and Kozmetsky were involved in a series of corporate takeovers and other deals, and Kozmetsky often served on the boards of companies controlled by Hurwitz, considered one of the leading "corporate raiders" of that era.[59]

Hurwitz said that as a board member Kozmetsky "was very inquisitive and always asked excellent questions. He didn't talk just to be heard like a lot of people, but if he had something to say he would speak up. He always made a contribution, always made a difference."[60]

One of the earliest deals that Hurwitz undertook was the 1973 takeover of Federated Development Co., a New York holding company whose new board members included Kozmetsky. Hurwitz used Federated Development and other companies that he controlled in the hostile takeovers of many other companies, including Los Angeles–based McCulloch Oil Corp., in 1978; Simplicity Pattern, a maker of home-sewing patterns, in 1982; United Savings Association of Texas, in 1982; Pacific Lumber Co., owner of old-growth redwood forests in Northern California, in 1985; and Kaiser Tech, the parent company of Kaiser Aluminum, in 1988. After the acquisition of McCulloch Oil, Hurwitz's business interests were organized as units of a new company called MCO Holdings and, after 1988, as part of Maxxam Inc. McCulloch's founder had wide-ranging business interests, including ownership of London Bridge, which had been dismantled and moved, stone by stone, to Arizona in 1967.

William C. Leone was sometimes named to the boards or the management teams of companies taken over by Hurwitz. Harvey J. McMains, at the time an associate director of the IC² Institute, served on the board of the company that succeeded McCulloch Oil.[61]

The collapse in 1988 of United Savings Association of Texas (one of the many savings-and-loan casualties of the Texas oil and real estate bust of the 1980s) resulted eventually in a long-running lawsuit by federal regulators against Hurwitz—a lawsuit that would entangle Pacific Lumber and its controversial plans for cutting old-growth redwood for lumber. The Federal Deposit Insurance Corp. (FDIC) sued Hurwitz in 1995, charging that he was to blame for the United Savings failure and seeking at least $250 million. Also in 1995, the Office of Thrift Supervision charged in a lawsuit that Hurwitz and other board members of United Savings and United Financial Group had contributed to the demise of United Savings by making high-risk investments. The Office of Thrift Supervision, which said the failure of United Savings had cost taxpayers $1.6 billion, sought to recover $821 million.

Hurwitz was chairman and CEO of United Financial Group, the parent company of United Savings, and Kozmetsky served on the boards of both companies for different periods in the 1980s. Kozmetsky testified in the FDIC lawsuit that Hurwitz had not interfered in the management of United Savings. "I would never say that Charles forced the board to do anything," Kozmetsky told an administrative law judge in federal court in Houston in 1997. "Never once did he ask me to rubber stamp anything." Kozmetsky also answered, "Absolutely not," when asked if Hurwitz had benefited personally from the actions of United Savings.[62]

Kozmetsky gave a deposition in the Office of Thrift Supervision lawsuit in September 1995. Although the agency had sought $821 million, it settled in 1995 with United Financial Group for restitution of $9.45 million, and in 1999 several former directors settled with the agency for another $1.03 million. Hurwitz and Maxxam Inc. settled in 2002 for $206,000. They did not admit wrongdoing but agreed to restrictions on their involvement in bank management.[63]

The FDIC dropped its lawsuit in late 2002, but Hurwitz then sued the agency, claiming that its suit had been undertaken in bad faith as part of a plan to pressure him into giving Pacific Lumber's redwood acreage to the government in return for forgiveness of his debts. A federal district judge in 2005 agreed with Hurwitz that he had been the victim of a government scheme to force him to give up control of the redwood acreage, and the FDIC was ordered to pay Hurwitz $72 million for his legal costs. An appeals court reduced that award to no more than $15 million, and the case was settled in 2008 for $10 million.[64]

A CIVIC ENTREPRENEUR

When Hurwitz won control of Pacific Lumber in 1982, he incurred the wrath of environmental groups that protested his plans for dramatically increasing the harvesting of old-growth redwoods, said to be part of his plan to reduce the debt from the takeover. Led by the radical group Earth First!, the protesters used a variety of extreme tactics—including occupying the forest, blockading logging trucks, and staging sit-ins at company offices—that continued for twenty years. In 2001, a congressional committee that investigated the FDIC and Office of Thrift Supervision litigation agreed with Hurwitz that the claims against him and his companies were partly fueled by environmentalists seeking to limit the cutting of redwoods by Pacific Lumber. Some of the impetus for the protests was removed in 1999 when the California and federal governments paid Pacific Lumber for a 9,500-acre area known as the Headwaters Forest. The protests continued at Pacific Lumber's other redwood forests, finally ending only when the company went into bankruptcy and was bought, in 2008, by a group that adopted new forest-management policies.[65]

The sale of the Headwaters Forest in 1999 came after years of negotiations with the federal government, which made what it called a "debt for nature" proposal, under which the government would agree to drop its case related to the demise of United Savings in exchange for a portion of Pacific Lumber's old-growth redwood acreage. Hurwitz, insisting he had done nothing wrong, resisted the deal. He later told a reporter that Kozmetsky, then a board member of Maxxam, had urged him to accept the government's offer. "George used to tell me every day to get rid of it at any cost," Hurwitz told Christopher Helman of *Forbes* magazine. "He said, 'It's not worth fighting the government. Our energies should be spent in other ways. Whatever it cost, we can make that money back; just move on.'" When Hurwitz finally agreed to sell some of the acreage in 1999, the sale was not accompanied by a deal for the FDIC to drop its lawsuit. As part of the sale, Hurwitz accepted restrictions on how he could harvest his remaining forests.[66]

CRITICS FROM THE LEFT

Kozmetsky's business dealings with Hurwitz, particularly the issue of the redwood forests, and some of his other business and university activities aroused the fury of a group of student political and environmental activists at the University of Texas at Austin in the 1980s and 1990s and brought Kozmetsky a level of criticism that had been absent from his early years in business and academia. Kozmetsky's critics from the left of the political spectrum were never numerous and never attracted much attention beyond their own circle and alternative newspapers, but for a few years they made a lot of noise and were very energetic, and they have left for posterity a detailed—if greatly distorted—online critique of parts of Kozmetsky's career.[67]

At the height of the protests in 1990, members of Earth First! held a demonstration outside the IC^2 Institute, spraying red paint on the front of the building. The demonstration was a slight echo of the large sit-ins and rallies that Earth First! organized against Pacific Lumber in Northern California. As someone who prided himself on defending freedom of speech and other rights, Kozmetsky took the protest in stride, according to Greg Kozmetsky.[68] Earth First! also staged a small protest at a talk that Hurwitz presented at the business school at about the same time. Earth First! was probably best known in Austin for occupying three environmentally sensitive caves in northwestern Travis County in 1988 as part of an effort to protect them from development of a nearby shopping center.[69]

Criticism of Kozmetsky in the 1980s and 1990s surfaced mostly in a series of small alternative publications. Even this amount of public criticism was rare in Kozmetsky's career. Given his background in defense contracting, having worked for two major military contractors and having cofounded a third, it is ironic that during his leadership of the business school from 1966 to 1982 he almost entirely escaped the notice of the antiwar movement, student radicals, and the counterculture. He presented a large potential target for the Vietnam generation's antiwar campaigns because of his career-long participation in and even advocacy for the "military-industrial complex" and his continuing support for military-related research and development.

Kozmetsky was simply off the radar of early activist organizations, as leaders of the antiwar movement at the University of Texas were unaware of his background in business.[70] Two important scholarly studies of the student radical movement at the university—*The Politics of Authenticity: Politics, Christianity, and the New Left in America* by Doug Rossinow (Columbia University Press, 1998) and "History of Student Activism at the University of Texas, 1960–1988," a master's thesis by Beverly Burr (University of Texas, 1988)—make no mention of Kozmetsky or the business school. Both portray the University of Texas at Austin as one of the nation's most important centers of student activism, comparable in size and influence to movements at Berkeley and Columbia. Another irony is that the main antiwar organization on the campus, Students for a Democratic Society, routinely reserved a large classroom in the Business-Economics Building, just down the hall from the dean's office, for its meetings.[71]

The activist students generally wrote off the business school as a lost cause in their efforts to find allies and organize students and therefore never noticed who occupied the dean's office, just a few blocks from the scene of some of the largest antiwar demonstrations on any campus.[72] Some business school students and a few of the faculty might have affected at least a toned-down version of the counterculture style, but the portion of the movement that was composed of the radical left and the antiwar groups did not gain much traction at the school.

Not until the 1980s and the rise of a new generation of student protesters did the political left pay much attention to Kozmetsky. There were earlier exceptions, but they were not widely noticed at the time. Early criticism of Kozmetsky and the IC^2 Institute in the *Texas Observer* has been discussed in chapter 15. Other occasional criticism surfaced in the pages of the *Rag*, an alternative newspaper that was one of the country's most important underground papers of the era.[73] Kozmetsky was also criticized in a book by James Ridgeway, an associate editor of the *New Republic*, who placed many of Kozmetsky's aspirations as dean in the context of a supposed conspiracy between big business and higher education, evidenced by numerous entrepreneurial activities by campuses, from Stanford University's industrial park to business start-ups organized by professors at the Harvard Business School. Drawing mostly on published accounts, Ridgeway found sinister implications in Kozmetsky's interest in research that was relevant to the real world of business, his ideas about how the regents could better exploit the university's West Texas land, and his vision of expanded industries based on marine science.[74]

When a new wave of leftist student activism swept over parts of the University of Texas at Austin campus in the 1980s and 1990s, most of the new activists' energies were concentrated on research and writing, rather than street demonstrations. There were a few large campus demonstrations in the era, particularly against University of Texas investments related to South Africa, but the student activism of the period was more often expressed in the pages of alternative publications and on Internet sites. The main vehicles were *Polemicist*, a pamphlet-like off-campus magazine, and, by the 1990s, the website maintained by a group known as UT Watch. Kozmetsky and the IC^2 Institute were targets of both of these underground media outlets.

The critique of the university offered in these publications was heavily influenced by Ronnie Dugger's book *Our Invaded Universities* (Norton, 1974). Pursuing themes that Dugger had explored, the new activists hammered tirelessly on the dangers of "corporate control" of higher education, university policies that were environmentally suspect, links between university research and the military, an alleged lack of moral and ethical principles in university investments, and the "dehumanizing" effects of computers and other advanced technology.

Kozmetsky and the business school apparently were not mentioned in Dugger's critique of the University of Texas at Austin (the 457-page book has no index), but the work contains numerous starting points for finding fault with Kozmetsky's contributions as a dean and, indeed, his life's work.[75] On several key issues, the book set the stage and served as a guide for the later critics of the university and Kozmetsky, such as Dugger's argument that research and teaching were antithetical activities and that great public universities ought to function as populist institutions that concentrate their energies on introducing the masses to the core "arts and sciences" curriculum, with professional schools not to be taken seriously as much more than job-training programs.

The *Texas Observer* article and Dugger's book were fundamental texts for the leftist critique of Kozmetsky that arose in the 1980s, particularly in the pages of *Polemicist,* which was founded and run by University of Texas students Scott Henson and Tom Philpott. *Polemicist,* published irregularly from 1989 to 1992, ran several long articles devoted to "exposing" Kozmetsky's relationships with the defense industry, his promotion of the high-tech economy, his personal business dealings, and other aspects of his career in business and academia.[76] Two other off-campus publications that briefly succeeded *Polemicist*—the *Other Texan,* published in 1992–1993, and *(sub)TEX,* published beginning in 1993—continued the assault on Kozmetsky.

Kozmetsky's business relationships with Hurwitz were also a favorite target of *Polemicist* articles, which tended to recount various complicated stock deals, buyout attempts, shareholder lawsuits, and SEC inquiries with little citation of sources, although there were occasional nods to articles in the *Wall Street Journal,* the *New York Times,* and other mainstream media outlets. One article concluded that those dealings added up to a "long and sordid history," and it indicted capitalism as "a place where a few men gamble with the production of all the others." The article noted with dismay that while corporate raiders of the 1980s such as Michael Milken and Ivan Boesky had been sent to prison, "Kozmetsky and Hurwitz roam the streets of the corporate world freely."[77]

Another article rose to the level of caricature in depicting Kozmetsky's career: "Along with Hurwitz, Kozmetsky exemplifies everything vile about American capitalism: greed, avarice, obsession with short-term gain, and paper entrepreneurship. They deserve to be lashed, but instead they get rich. Constructive capitalism indeed."[78]

The most extreme criticism of Kozmetsky and Hurwitz in Austin's alternative press surfaced in a 1990 interview with Earth First! organizer Darryl Cherney, who made the bizarre implication that Kozmetsky and Hurwitz might have been responsible for a pipe bomb that exploded in Oakland, California, in a car occupied by Cherney and fellow activist Judi Bari. Cherney was quoted as saying that Kozmetsky and Hurwitz "are very wrapped up in the military-industrial complex [and] they're actually people who make bombs, and who actually use bombs all the time during their normal everyday operations. . . . So, in a sense they are bombers, they're bombers of the Earth. The question is are they bombers of people, and certainly [the] track records of their friends would indicate that we can't rule that out."[79] The bombing case, which was never solved, took many twists and turns, and in 2002 the FBI and Oakland police lost a civil rights lawsuit over their actions in the investigation.[80]

The most comprehensive attack on Kozmetsky is found in the pages of a doctoral dissertation by Robert Ovetz, a graduate student in sociology at the University of Texas at Austin in the 1980s and 1990s.[81] Ovetz's thesis was that the university was being transformed into a new sort of profit-making multinational corporation and as such was a model for what he saw happening at universities across the country. One of his chief interests in studying this "entrepreneurialization" of universities was the way it threw light on "the international accumulation of capital and the importance of students in the class struggle." Thus Ovetz presents his analysis of the University of Texas at Austin (and Kozmetsky's role as founder and director of the IC^2 Institute) as fodder for a campaign against capitalism, particularly multinational corporations and global markets.

For Ovetz, Kozmetsky's interest in the commercialization of technology is linked, at every turn, with an increasing militarization of research and technology transfer as well as increased uses of higher education institutions to serve military purposes. The IC^2 Institute thus was "a test case for technology transfer and the development of a 'technopolis,' the further subordination of all aspects of life, work, leisure, government, and education to the high tech industry."[82] Ovetz maintained that these developments at the University of Texas at Austin and other universities should be seen from the larger perspective of the "remilitarization" of higher education by the Department of Defense (primarily through research funding), a trend that "has served to reverse many of the advances culled by the [student] movements of the 1960–70s."[83]

The Texas Legislature, in Ovetz's view, was complicit in this counter-revolution through passage of a series of bills in the 1980s that promoted advanced scientific and technological research, the commercialization of technology from university labs, and the creation of commercial ventures in which universities were partners—all measures that were advocated by Kozmetsky and that helped advance the economic development projects of the IC^2 Institute.[84]

Kozmetsky weathered these attacks without difficulty and was probably not even aware of all of them. Perhaps because their views were confined by the limits of an unyielding anticapitalist ideology, these critics failed to understand Kozmetsky and his life's work, including his insistence on fostering a new, "constructive" form of capitalism based on the principles of shared prosperity, social responsibility, creative and innovative management, entrepreneurship, alliances among formerly contending groups, and the promise of technology.

CHAPTER 20

THE FINAL YEARS

The last decade of George Kozmetsky's life was as busy and productive as any earlier period as he continued to pursue his central interests—global economic development based on advanced technology along with a commitment to social responsibility that sought universal prosperity. These were not utopian dreams for George and Ronya, but practical projects. As US Representative J. J. "Jake" Pickle noted in the late 1990s, "George was a practical visionary."[1]

George and Ronya were both generally optimistic about the prospects for success in these undertakings, and their shared enthusiasm and positive attitudes were often infectious. Nevertheless, toward the end of his life George appeared to some people to grow more and more doubtful about global trends and fearful about the world his grandchildren would inherit.[2] He sometimes surprised his students by saying that he felt a sense of urgency about his message of economic development and shared prosperity because the alternative was World War III—a global confrontation between the haves and the have-nots.[3] These darker visions of what the future held might have stemmed from a realization that his life was drawing to a close, together with an impatience to get as much more accomplished as he could while there was still time.

Many of his colleagues sensed that the cheerfulness that prevailed for most of his life reflected an inner joy, but according to his own testimony it was also a result of a deliberate effort to present himself to the world in a positive light. As he once explained to his students at the University of Texas at Austin: "As you probably know, I do a lot of thinking. I have some bad habits when I think. One of my bad habits is that my eyebrows furrow and I get a stern look. I would walk out of my office [at Teledyne] and people would think the company was going bankrupt. In actuality, I

Darius Mahdjoubi, Kozmetsky's last doctoral student. *Photograph by Coral Franke, IC² Institute.*

was having the most wonderful thoughts! I had to teach myself to put on my 'Mickey Mouse' smile. I have had to train myself to walk out as if there isn't a care in the world."[4]

As he grew increasingly ill in the last two years of his life, so that the loss of control over his muscles left him in a wheelchair, he slowed down but he never retired. Just a few months before he died he was still advising his last doctoral student, Darius Mahdjoubi, about his dissertation, an interdisciplinary study of the intersection of knowledge, innovation, and entrepreneurship.[5] Mahdjoubi would meet with Kozmetsky in his office at the IC² Institute to discuss refinements in his treatment of the evolution of new business ventures in Austin since 1990. Kozmetsky's mental powers were not diminished, but he needed an assistant to turn the pages of the dissertation that was propped up before him.[6]

This picture of Kozmetsky, at age eighty-five, still pursuing his work as a professor, epitomizes the way Kozmetsky thought of himself—simply as a teacher, despite his outsized reputation and the multiplicity of his roles through his career. One of his granddaughters recalled that she had been told all her life that he was "a great man, a visionary, an entrepreneur," and that she asked him one day what he did for a living. "I'm a teacher,"

A CIVIC ENTREPRENEUR

he answered. She wasn't impressed and asked him again, "What do you do for a living?" "I'm a teacher," he insisted.[7]

Explaining Himself

For someone whose lifelong preoccupations involved conveying ideas to others and mobilizing collaborations, Kozmetsky had a style of communicating that many people found difficult. It was common for people to leave a meeting with him impressed with the breadth of his knowledge but not quite certain about what he had been getting at. There are numerous accounts of people looking at each other after hearing him speak and asking something like, "What was that about?" People at all levels—staff members, professors, university presidents, regents, politicians, business leaders—were regularly impressed, if not awestruck, by the quickness of his mind and the range of topics on which he was well informed. Still, there was a frequent reaction of not quite grasping his point, failing to understand how all the things he said fit together, and sometimes suspecting that they might not fit together at all.

Some accounts of this phenomenon have become legendary. At one meeting of President Peter T. Flawn's executive council, Kozmetsky spoke at length, and after he finished Flawn said, "George, I didn't understand a god-damned word you said." At a meeting in Japan between a delegation from the University of Texas and a group of Japanese university and government officials, Kozmetsky made a lengthy presentation, after which all the Japanese attendees applauded with enthusiasm but Kozmetsky's own colleagues simply looked at one another in puzzlement.[8]

One theory to account for Kozmetsky's seemingly oracular style of speaking is that he would throw out parts of an argument or pieces of an idea to see what the other person would say, hoping to find someone who could understand the whole topic without having to be led along step by step. A variation on that theory is that he often liked to try out an idea on another person, even if he hadn't yet worked it out in detail in his own mind. Some people believe Kozmetsky's mind worked so quickly that he would begin speaking faster and faster as his words raced to keep up with the runaway pace of his thoughts. Another view is that he would often be thinking of three or four things at once and that he skipped among them as he tried to put them into words, often not slowing down enough to fill in the gaps.

Another observer who knew Kozmetsky well, Robert A. Peterson, recounted a backstage conversation in which Kozmetsky, just before a faculty meeting, was discussing the ideas he wanted to present to the faculty, and everything made perfect sense. Then when Kozmetsky stood before the faculty and made his presentation, Peterson said he was left wondering what relation the talk had to the preview that Kozmetsky had given him.[9]

Kozmetsky took very seriously the need to communicate, however some might have thought he had a cavalier attitude toward it. Greg Kozmetsky relates the story of Kozmetsky at a blackboard in his home in California during the Teledyne days, with his own children as well as children from the neighborhood assembled on the floor in front him as he drew diagrams and sketched ideas, trying to explain to his small audience a relationship or a trend or the dimensions of a problem. Kozmetsky would say that if he could explain it to the nine- and ten-year-olds, he would have a chance of explaining it to the adults at work the next day.[10]

Kozmetsky was aware of his reputation for obscurity. "I have certain weaknesses," he told one of his University of Texas classes. "I have had a tendency all my life to try to crystallize and capsulize what I think, and I don't add enough noise into my communication so that it communicates."[11]

The difficulty that Kozmetsky often had in tailoring his words to the needs of his audience might have resulted in his sometimes being given less credit than he deserved for the influence of his ideas, and despite his sometimes weak communication skills he had a commanding presence in a room, said Neal Spelce. "Despite everything, Koz had a charisma about him," Spelce recalled. "His reputation was phenomenal when he first came to Austin, and his reputation helped overshadow any other shortcomings."[12]

Despite the frequent observations that people weren't quite sure what Kozmetsky was talking about, there are others who report that they never had any significant problem in understanding him. "I always understood what he was saying," said Robert D. King, dean of liberal arts for part of the time that Kozmetsky was dean of business, and a good friend of Kozmetsky's, "but I do remember that other people would be confused, as if he was talking beyond them. I would hear people say, 'We're only mortals,' as if George needed to come down to the ordinary level of human beings. But if you listened to him carefully he was always connecting the dots. He carried on a linear discussion, from point to point to point."[13] Other colleagues who found Kozmetsky's conversations easy to follow often served as informal translators for those who needed help. Fred Y. Phillips and Laura Kilcrease sometimes filled this role at the IC² Institute.

Between these extremes was the experience of Isabella Cunningham. "I could understand him, but I had to listen intensely," she said. "Sometimes he would talk for a week before he would come back to where he started. I did stop him at times and ask him to clarify something. His mind seemed almost like a net, with him at the center, reaching in all directions."[14]

A CIVIC ENTREPRENEUR

Another positive account of Kozmetsky's speaking style is provided by historian Joe B. Frantz:

Once he and I rode together on a plane to Dallas (on Braniff Airways). . . . I sat in one seat while George sat opposite. He started on an idea about multiplication of capital at his mile-a-minute pace. . . . [M]y view of George was regularly blocked (by flight attendants and passengers who were moving around) and sometimes the confusion interfered with my hearing, but he lectured on. I wished I had brought a tape recorder so that I could take it home, listen to it for fourteen hours, and absorb all the ideas he threw my way in an hour's ride.

Business administration is not considered one of the verbal disciplines, but no one ever informed Kozmetsky. He never seems to lose patience or geniality, nor does he engage in trivia. He just gushes on like the fountain in Beulah Land that never runs dry. I find him the most continually fascinating talker the campus has ever had, with the possible exception of Harry Ransom and Roy Bedichek. His talk is inventive, interesting, and often challenging. He opens the doors of the mind.[15]

Sometimes Kozmetsky's talk simply overwhelmed. As Floyd Brandt, who taught in the University of Texas management department, recalled, "I would go to George's office to talk to him about a leaky canoe, and he would send me back to my office with plans for a battleship."[16] Brandt told that joke to Frantz, who used it in a book about the university, but without attribution to Brandt. "I don't think George liked that quote very much. It got under his skin," Brandt said.[17]

DRAWING A PICTURE

The story about Kozmetsky teaching children at a blackboard is revealing of one of his ways of thinking through a question for himself and then trying to explain it to others. His thought process was highly visual, and working at a blackboard, where he could draw diagrams and symbols as he talked, was a favorite technique. Every office that he had—at the business school, at the IC² Institute, or at home—was equipped with blackboards (or whiteboards in later years), and they were usually filled with lists of key words, drawings, arcane symbols, and a maze of lines and arrows showing how everything was connected. Several photographs show Kozmetsky standing at a blackboard juggling a piece of chalk. Kozmetsky's assistants and colleagues at the IC² Institute often photographed a blackboard after Kozmetsky had covered it with ideas—and before it was erased for the next conversation. David Gibson's office at the institute still contains a blackboard filled with Kozmetsky's diagrams and writings. Another of his blackboards—from his house in Santa Monica—has been preserved by a granddaughter.

When no blackboard was available, a yellow legal pad would do. His personal papers are filled with arcane schematic drawings, often difficult to decipher, that represent his ideas, and he sometimes engaged artists to produce a more polished depiction of historical processes or complex relationships from among his thoughts. He also worked at drafting tables at the business school and the IC^2 Institute (as well as when he was at Teledyne) to construct illustrations that combined an engineer's precision, an artistic flair, and a futuristic visual vocabulary. One of his early illustrations depicts the extraordinary growth of information in the twentieth century represented by the number and size of filing cabinets required to store everything, as well as a complex graph of interactions among broad areas of learning such as the natural sciences, technology, and the arts. A viewer who has doubts about how to interpret the fine details of one of

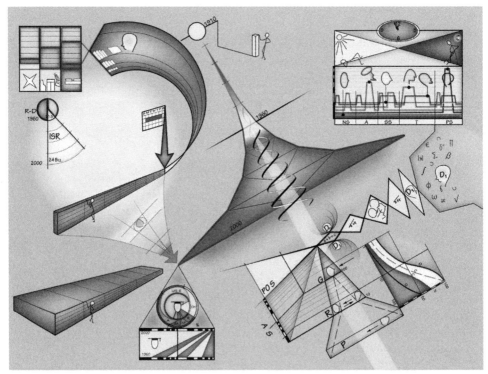

A depiction by Kozmetsky of technological innovation and the explosion of knowledge in the twentieth century. *IC^2 Institute.*

A CIVIC ENTREPRENEUR

these drawings may be relieved to learn that Kozmetsky himself sometimes explained them in different ways.[18]

Sometimes Kozmetsky resorted to larger formats, such as rolls of butcher paper, to contain his ever-expanding ideas and plans. He used those large sheets to lay out his "road maps" involving the future of technology or to sketch his networks of actual and hoped-for colleagues.

Kozmetsky often urged others to think visually as he did, to sharpen their ideas. "Draw me a picture," he would tell his grandson Jordan Scott and his partners as they sought advice on their business plans. "If you can't draw it, you don't know what you are saying."[19]

An Early Start

Kozmetsky's daily work habits also set him apart from many colleagues. Since his days in Southern California Kozmetsky had been in the habit of getting to the office well before dawn, sometimes as early as 3:00 or 4:00 a.m. This might have been so he could work for a while without interruptions, but it also could have been necessary in Los Angeles when he needed to talk with bankers in New York or bureaucrats in Washington.

When he was Kozmetsky's associate dean, William H. Cunningham found it advisable to meet with Kozmetsky before usual work hours if he wanted to get his full attention. Many others who called Kozmetsky's office to set up an appointment found themselves scheduled for a 5:00 a.m. meeting, even if that meant getting up in the middle of the night to drive from San Antonio or Houston. Corey Carbonara relates a story of arriving at the locked IC[2] building for an early morning appointment (after driving in from Waco) and trying to get Kozmetsky's attention on the second floor by tossing pebbles against the lighted window. When that didn't work he tried larger stones. Finally, Kozmetsky came down and let him in and said, "I was wondering how big those rocks were going to get before you stopped."[20]

Susie Brown, now an associate dean of the University of Texas business school, said getting to the office before Kozmetsky was unlikely when she worked with him at the IC[2] Institute in the 1990s. "He might start his day at 3:00 a.m. I would usually come at seven, and he would greet me by saying, 'Good afternoon, Susie,' with a twinkle in his eye. I think I beat him to the office two or three times."[21]

Edward A. Miller, who lived with the Kozmetskys on weekdays for a year in 1995 after he left the National Center for Manufacturing Sciences and was working with George at the institute, recalls that they left home every day at 3:00 a.m. so they could get to the institute when the *Wall Street Journal* was delivered at 3:15. George would put the coffee on, and they would have wide-ranging discussions until others started coming in.[22]

Visitors to Kozmetsky's office sometimes walked in while he was on the phone to a prominent person on another continent—Margaret Thatcher, for example. He would motion for them to sit down while he finished the conversation. While they waited they might sneak a look at the elaborate diagrams on his blackboard or admire his assortment of antique seafaring instruments—chronometers and sextants—that stood as literal examples of his efforts to navigate the world of technology and economic development.[23]

GEORGE AND RONYA

The life story of George Kozmetsky cannot be understood without an appreciation for the role that his wife, Ronya, played in shaping his outlook, sharing his values, and working side by side with him on numerous endeavors. Previous chapters have discussed many of Ronya's contributions, such as her role in advancing George's social conscience, supporting his wish to move to Southern California and enter the world of private business, helping to coordinate academic conferences, managing their philanthropic endeavors, and serving with him as a mentor to students and entrepreneurs.

The couple's friends viewed Ronya as a force every bit as powerful as George, a "person in her own right" who displayed an unstoppable determination, especially when it came to helping others. "Ronya wants to be not the person who solves other people's problems in a way that doesn't help them to grow as leaders, but that gives people an edge, gives people a little help so they can take the next step," said Pat Hayes, president of St. Edward's University from 1990 to 1999. Cathy Bonner, whom Ronya assisted in starting leadership training organizations, observed, "If she decides that she is going to put hope in you and that she believes in you, she is not going to let you fail."[24]

The Kozmetskys' marriage was a partnership that weathered early financial uncertainty, the stresses of George's rise in the business world and his frenetic activity, the loss of their youngest child, and the fact that both of them were strong-willed, ambitious, and highly energetic personalities. Other family members could not imagine one without the other. In 1988, on their forty-fifth wedding anniversary, forty-five roses arrived from Nadya in California, and then Greg called and invited them to dinner at Tarry House, a private dining club. When they arrived, they found both children and seven grandchildren waiting to help them celebrate.[25] Many old friends, some of whom they had not seen for decades, sent congratulatory letters on their fiftieth anniversary.

A CIVIC ENTREPRENEUR

A picture of their partnership is presented in their book *Making It Together: A Survival Manual for the Executive Family* (Free Press, 1981), which resulted from a noncredit "Executive Futures" course that they began teaching in 1970 for graduate business students and their spouses. They sought in the book and the course (which met on Saturdays several times during a semester) to draw on their own experiences as an "executive couple" when George was working in the electronics industry in Los Angeles and Ronya was a homemaker and a schoolteacher.

Their advice for how to manage a marriage was based largely on the traditional pattern of the husband having a demanding and time-consuming career outside the home and the wife being mostly responsible for taking care of the family, but they also put their own twist on that tradition—based on their commitment to their marriage as a true partnership, relying heavily on the force of Ronya's personality and her strength of will. Even though Ronya also worked outside the home, it was clear that George's work was the highest priority, and, indeed, he was often away from home during the years in Southern California. On many occasions, it was Ronya's determination that made everything work. "The way you handle yourself is going to make a great deal of difference in your husband's career," Ronya said. "The key to your husband's success is the degree of tolerance with which you cope with trying situations."[26]

Although the book draws its lessons from a time before the prevalence of two-career marriages and single-parent households, it does offer a realistic look at the risks of affluence—when a career can take precedence over family plans, when being forced to move from city to city can threaten family stability, and when overwhelming work schedules isolate family members from one another. Ronya joked that the book could be subtitled "A Guide to a Disaster."[27]

Her sense of humor was indispensable. She often joked that George was merely "on probation," and that she would decide each year whether to continue the partnership. When George and Henry Singleton decided to go into business together in 1960, she said to George, "I can't change you as much as I think you should be changed, but I've decided to live with you for the rest of my life. And in order to do that I've got to have a career of my own."[28] With all three of her children in school, she went to the University of California, Los Angeles, and got a teaching certificate and began teaching social studies in Los Angeles public schools, a career that she pursued until George moved to the University of Texas at Austin. The teaching job had a very practical purpose because in the early years of Teledyne George wasn't bringing home much, if any, income. The children depended on her paycheck in those days for their small allowances.[29]

After the move to Austin, Ronya continued to work outside the home, but as the leader of the RGK Foundation.

Greg Kozmetsky acknowledges that his father was often absent from family life during his years as a business executive but expressed admiration for what George was accomplishing outside the home in the 1950s and 1960s. "His was a time that was very important in our history. He and his peers were building things that people today don't know much about," Greg said. "But if you needed him he would be there. When I was injured in Vietnam he went to UCLA to talk to specialists there, and then he flew to Japan to talk to my doctors. He was always busy building companies, and he had many concerns, but he made time for you when you needed him."[30]

Few details remain about Kozmetsky's daily routine while in the private sector, but in later life he kept to a frenetic schedule that reflects a lifelong pattern of crowded projects and exhausting interests. Well into his seventies, Kozmetsky maintained a travel schedule that would have been daunting for many younger people. In the second week of October 1988, for example, just after he celebrated his seventy-first birthday, Kozmetsky crisscrossed the North American continent at a breakneck pace. He left Austin at 8:00 a.m. on Monday of that week to fly to San Angelo to speak to a group of local business leaders, after which he flew to Anchorage (via Dallas–Fort Worth and Salt Lake City), arriving in Alaska after 10:00 p.m. On Tuesday he attended an all-day meeting of the board of the Alaska Science and Technology Foundation, and on Wednesday he left Anchorage at 7:05 a.m. headed for Tampa (via Seattle), arriving in Florida at 11:50 p.m. local time. He began Thursday with a midmorning presentation at a symposium that he had helped organize at the University of South Florida, and then he left in the early afternoon on a flight to Dallas, where he was inducted that night into the Texas Business Hall of Fame. On Friday morning he flew home to Austin, having covered more than 8,700 miles during the week.[31]

His travel schedule when he lived in Southern California might not have been that hectic every week, but he spent long hours at his office and did make regular trips to Washington to talk with defense officials or to New York to visit bankers and investors. On some of those trips he liked to take one of his children along, but they were sometimes left to explore the city for themselves while their father was in meetings. Nadya remembers going with him to New York when she was sixteen and visiting the New York World's Fair by herself while he was working. On other trips she toured historic sites such as Williamsburg, Virginia, or entertained herself in hotels, ordering from room service, while he was in meetings.[32]

Even at home he encouraged independence in his children. Nadya said that during the summer when she was eleven and was taking classes in a special program at the University of California, Los Angeles, she had lunch with him at the Beverly Hilton Hotel, and then he dropped her at a bus stop at the university, assuming she could find her way home from there.[33]

Kozmetsky made time when he could for family meals when the children were growing up, enjoying Ronya's hearty but mostly simple cooking (a homey salmon loaf was one of her specialties) and making a game of quizzing the children about current events as they ate. On weekends he liked to take the family to hamburger joints, and to celebrate the children's good grades he would take the family to a steakhouse in Culver City. The family made regular trips to Seattle to visit George's sister and other relatives, and they developed a tradition of spending Easter at Palm Springs.

The couple often joked about Ronya being the more talented of the two, and George was always quick to give her credit as an equal partner in all their activities. Many of their friends considered Ronya as the fundamental social conscience of the partnership, exerting a powerful influence on George's commitment to corporate social responsibility, broad educational opportunity, women's rights, and other social causes. This influence surfaced quite early in their relationship, when Ronya persuaded George to provide accounting services to immigrant entrepreneurs in the Seattle area. She also influenced his progressive views on opportunities for women in education and business—views that emerged as early as his days as a faculty member at Harvard and an instructor at Radcliffe College. Ronya told friends she was not happy at Harvard, where she felt the sting of discrimination (perhaps because she was a woman, or perhaps because of her Jewish heritage), and was happy when George joined the faculty at the Carnegie Institute of Technology.[34]

The Kozmetskys shared many interests, including a taste for luxurious cars—one of the few extravagances in their mostly quiet and inconspicuous lifestyle. Ronya preferred sporty models and was known to scare more than one of her grandchildren by speeding up and down the Pacific Coast Highway.[35] George drove a Jaguar V12, a notoriously temperamental model, in his early days at the University of Texas and at some point switched to a Lexus. He bought a new Jaguar in 1971 and traded it in for another new one in 1976. That car, only two weeks old, was stolen after burglars broke a window and entered the house on Seventeenth Street and took the car keys from a kitchen drawer. No one was home (George was out of town), and the house was ransacked. The car, said to be worth $20,000 (over $85,000 in 2017), was found late the next day in a parking lot. A witness said she saw two teenage boys driving the car, but no one was arrested.[36]

Kozmetsky told friends the theft had been foiled because the car had broken down. On another occasion, demonstrating George and Ronya's ability to deal with just about any circumstance, they were on a drive through the Hill Country west of Austin when the Jaguar stopped running. They got out and flagged down a pickup, and they sat in the bed of the truck as the driver carried them back to Austin.[37]

Kozmetsky was a passionate sports fan and loved watching University of Texas games on television (and shouting at the screen), but his devotion did not often encompass some of the university's quaint traditions. One of those involved the practice of making the "Hook 'em Horns" sign at various public events, such as football games and graduation ceremonies, while singing "The Eyes of Texas." The sign consists of extending the index and pinky fingers of the right hand into the air while keeping the three other fingers bent, thus imitating a longhorn steer's horns. Kozmetsky was rarely observed making this sign—an omission of school loyalty and unity that might have actually damaged a career if committed by a younger and less powerful faculty member.

Robert King related a discussion they had about the "Hook 'em Horns" sign. "Ronya and George used to enjoy going to the women's basketball games," King said, "and Karen [King] and I and our kids would often go and would sit next to the Kozmetskys. Everyone would be making the Hook 'em Horns sign, but not George. One time I took his hand and showed him how to make the sign. I said, 'Look, George, you stick your little finger out this way, and you stick your [index finger] out on this side, and you bend your other fingers down this way, and you wave your hand in the air, and it's called the Hook 'em Horns sign. Now why can't you do that?' He said, 'Because it looks stupid and ridiculous.' He said he might do it at an athletics event but never at an academic event, such as commencement. That gave me the courage to stop doing it myself at academic ceremonies, although I still do it at athletic events."[38] In his later years, Kozmetsky softened his aversion to the sign, as a photograph of him taken in front of the IC² Institute attests.

For someone with so many preoccupations that stretched around the world, George could also display a decidedly domestic side. He and Ronya were often seen having breakfast or a hamburger at a Holiday House in west Austin, and he liked to drive with Ronya to small towns outside Austin to have dinner. He would also make time to go with Ronya on shopping trips to upscale places like Grace Jones's dress shop in Salado or a shop at the Beverly Hills Hotel.[39]

POLITICS

The Kozmetskys' interests coincided with regard to politics. Although some colleagues assumed from George's business background that he was a conservative who naturally favored Republican candidates, the available record of George and Ronya's political contributions indicates otherwise. Throughout their Texas years, the Kozmetskys were consistent contributors to progressive politicians, women's issues, and the Democratic Party, with only an occasional donation to a Texas Republican, such as Senator John Tower, Senator Kay Bailey Hutchison, and Governor Rick Perry. Most of their documented political contributions were in Ronya's name, but family members observe that it was probably a result of the simple fact that Ronya handled the family checkbook, and not an indication that George was in disagreement with Ronya's preferences among political causes. An additional explanation is that as an official of a public university, it was in George's interest to keep a low profile in partisan politics. He worked with politicians of both parties in support of issues related to higher education and economic development.

The Kozmetskys were regular donors to Emily's List, a political action committee that supports pro-choice Democratic women candidates. From 1989 until 2008, the Kozmetskys gave at least $54,000 to Emily's List. In addition, the Women's Campaign Fund, a nonpartisan political action committee supporting women candidates, received over $9,000 from the Kozmetskys in the 1990s.[40]

The Kozmetskys also were notable donors to Democratic Party organizations. They gave more than $16,000 to the Democratic National Committee from the late 1980s to the early 2000s, as well as more than $16,000 to the Democratic Congressional Campaign Committee, $3,000 to the Democratic Senatorial Campaign Committee, and $2,400 to the Texas Democratic Party. Individual candidates who received their financial support included US Representative Lloyd Doggett of Austin, his predecessor in Congress, J. J. "Jake" Pickle, and many other local Democratic politicians. They also supported many Democrats from other states, including Hillary Clinton, Patty Murray, Barbara Boxer, Dianne Feinstein, Debbie Stabenow, Barbara Mikulski, Barbara Ann Radnofsky, Geraldine Ferraro, Al Gore, Richard Gephardt, Chuck Robb, and John Kerry.[41]

WOMEN'S ISSUES

The Kozmetskys' partnership included efforts to advance the cause of women's rights and expanded educational and economic opportunities for women. These projects included support for a host of community,

The IC² Institute sponsored a series of forums on women's issues in the early 21st century. Speaking at a conference on "Breaking the Glass Ceiling" in May 2001 were, left to right, UT advertising faculty member Isabella Cunningham, Austin entrepreneur Karen Thompson, IC² Institute staff member Melissa Brown, UT sociology faculty member Mournia Charrad, Ronya Kozmetsky, and attorney Sarah Weddington. *IC² Institute photograph.*

service-oriented, and political organizations, such as the Texas Lyceum, Emily's List, and training and networking organizations such as Leadership Texas, Leadership California, and Leadership America.

Ronya often took the lead in these efforts. One of her most ambitious activities was helping organize the Women's Museum, an affiliate of the Smithsonian Institution that opened in Dallas in September 2000. The RGK Foundation contributed $3 million toward the project when it was being planned, with the money helping finance a technology project at the museum to help young girls excel in math and computing. The museum was the inspiration of Cathy Bonner, an entrepreneur and community activist who was president of the Austin-based Foundation for Women's Resources and had been a member of the first class of Leadership Austin.

The museum was officially known as the Women's Museum: An Institute for the Future, and its programming and educational arm was named in honor of Ronya. "Our history books don't explore what women have

A CIVIC ENTREPRENEUR

accomplished," Ronya said. "The museum is going to show what wonderful things women have done and can do."[42]

Despite the ambitious hopes with which the museum began—and a successful $30 million fundraising campaign for renovation of its historic building in Fair Park—the museum began running deficits by 2005 and was closed in 2011.[43]

The Kozmetskys' work on behalf of women evolved with the times. In the mid-1960s it was considered a step forward to organize clubs for the wives of students in the business school. Both George and Ronya were active in promoting and advising these clubs, which were eventually phased out after women began enrolling in large numbers as students and began preparing for their own careers in fields such as finance or marketing instead of merely serving as part of their husbands' support system.

Those social activities may seem quaint today, but they did serve as a form of networking that could be important in advancing women's careers. Ronya's early commitment to those careers was recognized in 1982 when a group of her friends, led by Bonita Granville Wrather, organized a secret fundraising campaign to endow the Ronya Kozmetsky Centennial Lectureship for Women in Management at the business school. When the endowment was announced, Ronya wrote to Sue McBee, another committee member: "What makes me especially proud is that the U.T. has taken the lead in recognizing women managers as professionals and has made the profession legitimate. I have always felt that it is so important for women managers to have *women* as role models. This lectureship should attract some fantastic women in management that the U.T. women students can definitely relate to."[44]

Several years later, Ronya distilled her thoughts on women in management in a book, *Women in Business: Succeeding as a Manager, Professional or Entrepreneur* (Texas Monthly Press, 1989). The book was based in part on discussions that Ronya and attorney Sarah Weddington organized among women in Austin to help women compete with men in leadership roles—one of many projects that the two collaborated on through the years in support of opportunities for women.

Ronya might have written only one letter to a newspaper editor. It was a passionate defense of Hillary Clinton, who as First Lady had been criticized for her health-care proposal and other initiatives. "I am outraged that First Lady Hillary Clinton has been so severely criticized and denigrated by the American people," Ronya wrote.

She should be applauded and praised for caring so much that she has placed herself in the position of "deliberate victim" for supporting social service programs that would benefit those in our society who need it most.

The women of America should thank Mrs. Clinton who had the courage and conviction to be a person in her own right. Because of her independence she has made it easier for presidents' wives of the future to be separate and individual thinking people who will make important contributions to society. Our country, which is going through a period of upheaval and confusion, needs these kinds of people as role models. Women, historically, have been the healers and nurturers of the world. Our men leaders need their wisdom and humanism. Women of sensitivity and compassion like Mrs. Clinton do not deserve to be demonized.

Contemporary women owe a great debt to women who historically have been victimized for their beliefs. Because of other courageous women, young women today can be anything they want to be. I say hooray for women of courage and conviction.[45]

Such public outspokenness from Ronya might have been rare, but it did not surprise those who knew her. One of her friends, Cynthia Smith, observed, "Upon meeting Ronya for the first time, one sees a quiet unassuming person who is slightly uncomfortable when attention is directed toward her. But just bring up an issue that deals with the welfare of others. All of a sudden you see this dynamo who becomes a catalyst for a myriad of projects."[46]

George's support for women's issues and expanded opportunity in business was strongly influenced by Ronya, but he also told friends that he traced his views to his experiences after his father died when George was five. "George's mother had to go to work, and he had to help with the housework and cooking," said Kay Hammer. "He told me, 'I know how hard a woman's life is and how talented they are. That's why I am supportive of women.'"[47] Both George and Ronya often mentioned their belief that women had a deeper and more nuanced understanding of the world than men, and that all aspects of society needed the benefit of their talents.

RECOGNITION

Both Kozmetskys received numerous awards and honors recognizing their contributions to their community and the larger world. They were recognized as Austinites of the Year by the local Chamber of Commerce in 1993, and many other civic and community organizations paid similar tribute. One of the largest local tributes came in 1998 when they were guests of honor at a dinner organized by the Chamber of Commerce and others at the Frank Erwin Center.

A CIVIC ENTREPRENEUR

President Bill Clinton and Vice President Al Gore present Kozmetsky with the National Medal of Technology, 1993. *White House photograph.*

George Kozmetsky's contribution to promoting the transfer of technology from laboratories to the marketplace was recognized in 1988 with the Thomas Jefferson Award of the Technology Transfer Society. The award recognized Kozmetsky's role in developing computers at Litton Industries, his service on state and national advisory boards, and his publications on the subject of technology transfer.[48]

In September 1993 Kozmetsky was among nine people honored by President Bill Clinton with the National Medal of Technology, the nation's highest honor for technological achievement. The medal is awarded annually for outstanding contributions to the country's economic, environmental, and social well-being and recognizes those who "have made lasting contributions to America's competitiveness, standard of living, and quality of life through technological innovation, and to recognize those who have made substantial contributions to strengthening the nation's technological workforce." First awarded in 1985, the medal also is intended to inspire people to prepare for and pursue technical careers to enhance the country's global technology and economic leadership.[49]

At the same time that Kozmetsky received the technology medal, former University of Texas at Austin president Norman Hackerman, a chemist who had also served as president of Rice University, was awarded the National Medal of Science.

In a Rose Garden ceremony at which Clinton presented the medal to Kozmetsky and other honorees, most of them from the corporate world, the president noted that Kozmetsky was being honored "for his commercialization of various technologies through the establishment and development of over one hundred technology-based companies that employ tens of thousands of people and export over one billion dollars worldwide."

Larraine Segil, an entrepreneur and business consultant who has been a fellow of the IC² Institute since 1991, organized the nomination materials for the medal. The nomination process, managed by the US Department of Commerce, required detailed information about a candidate's background, and the first year Segil nominated Kozmetsky he was not selected.

"I was determined to bring Dr. Kozmetsky's achievements to the attention of the review committee," Segil said. "I wanted them to understand, as I did, the way he had dedicated his life to creative and innovative thought and to mentoring and motivating others in developing new technologies and transferring them to the marketplace. I wanted them to have a clear picture of the wide influence he had had on so many individuals, including myself, and his important role in fostering entrepreneurship."[50]

Kozmetsky commented on receiving the medal: "As a first-generation American, I find it very humbling—indeed beyond my imagination—to be given this award. Whatever I have accomplished is the result of being an American plus great good fortune. I had wonderful parents. I have had a wife and children who were always with me, an excellent education, wise mentors, friends who inspired and supported me, exciting entrepreneurial ventures, and the opportunity to participate in cutting-edge progress and projects that link the academic, business, and government sectors for the general welfare. Mrs. Kozmetsky and I feel very strongly that individuals who have been so privileged ought to contribute to society. To be honored for simply being a responsible citizen is overwhelming, and I am deeply grateful."[51]

The Institute as a Family

As they had done with faculty and staff members at the business school, George and Ronya treated many colleagues at the IC² Institute as mem-

Lady Bird Johnson and Luci Baines Johnson congratulate Kozmetsky at a reception after he was awarded the National Medal of Technology. *Photo by Dan Kallick, University Photography Services.*

bers of an extended family. There were always a few staff members who were particularly close to the Kozmetskys, making frequent trips with them on the institute's business, serving as sounding boards, staying at their home in Santa Monica, and going on excursions to the beach or other local areas of interest. George sometimes called these colleagues his "special children."

The Kozmetskys could become closely involved in the lives of their colleagues and their families. For example, they personally provided the financing for a bridge loan to help Raymond Smilor complete the purchase of a house, and Ronya provided David Gibson with a loan to help him pay his mortgage.[52]

Ronya also often stepped in to solve a problem or look after the needs of George's employees or faculty colleagues. On one occasion she called the Cunninghams' home and learned that Bill was out of town and Isabella was at home with a bad cold. "Within the hour Ronya was at my door with a bowl of soup," Isabella said. "We lived in northwest Austin, and the Kozmetskys lived on Seventeenth Street, so it was quite a drive up to our house. Ronya was that kind of person, always wanting to do whatever she could to help."[53]

The Kozmetskys sought to bring together the staff, fellows, and others associated with the institute through regular social events that they hoped would foster a sense of collegiality in an atmosphere that was more relaxed than the high-pressure world of work. When George was dean of the business school, these social activities included an annual black-tie dinner and dance at the Driskill Hotel in downtown Austin. Later, when he was director of the IC² Institute, George hosted an annual picnic for the institute and the RGK Foundation at his family ranch west of Austin.

Sten Thore has written about attending those events. "Even by Texas standards it was a respectable 'spread' that included an entire river," Thore said. "To go there you had better bring your pickup truck because the river was fairly deep and you had to splash right through it! The excursion was for the people working at the RGK Foundation and the IC² Institute. [Greg Kozmetsky] would organize the annual softball game pitting the RGK and IC². Every able-bodied person had to participate. The barbecue itself was served up by the nearby Cow Town, on a steam-driven rebuilt agricultural tractor from the 1930s. As night fell, we would all sit on the low wall of the circular pit, lazily looking at the flames of the huge log fire."[54]

Even at that late hour, amid the night breezes and the woodsmoke, the fertile minds of some of Kozmetskys' scholar friends kept churning. Thore remembers Ilya Prigogine entertaining (or mystifying) the crowd around the campfire with talk of his "dissipative structures," concepts that he was using to revise some of the principles of Newton's physics.[55] The picture Thore presents convinces that Kozmetsky had recreated in the Texas Hill Country the kind of broadly diverse community of thinkers that had been so important to him on the East Coast and in Southern California.

When he was dean of the business school, Kozmetsky often sat in on informal discussion groups among faculty members that must have reminded him of those earlier interchanges. One such group was organized by physicist John Wheeler and linguistics professor Winfred Lehmann. The group met once a month with a guest speaker, and Kozmetsky sometimes sat in, although he tended not to speak.[56]

Kozmetsky's embrace of other disciplines and his family-like friendships with people outside the field of business included the wide range of scholars whom he recruited to serve as fellows of the IC² Institute. One of those was Delbert Tesar, a leading researcher in robotics, whose classes were frequently visited by Kozmetsky for discussions about the future of manufacturing. Tesar said Kozmetsky called him soon after Tesar was recruited to an endowed chair at the University of Texas in 1985. "George wanted me to be involved in the campus and at the IC² Institute," Tesar said. "He didn't want me to feel left out, and I appreciated his friendship and his willingness to come and talk with my graduate students. George was always very enthusiastic, and he wanted to help everyone succeed. He was not like academic bureaucrats, who seem to want you to fail, but a genuinely caring person who wanted to help."[57]

Another IC² Institute fellow who developed a close friendship with Kozmetsky was Walt W. Rostow, an economist who had worked in the Johnson administration and later taught at the University of Texas. Rostow and Kozmetsky were born almost exactly a year apart, and they often celebrated their birthdays together by going out to dinner together with their wives. (Walt's wife, Elspeth, was dean of the LBJ School of Public Affairs from 1977 to 1983.) Their last birthday together was in 2002. Rostow died February 13, 2003, two months before Kozmetsky.

ILLNESS

Soon after the turn of the century, Kozmetsky began to feel the early effects of the disease that would take his life—amyotrophic lateral sclerosis (ALS), a progressive neurodegenerative disease that also, in a different form, took the life of his sister. Also known as Lou Gehrig's disease, ALS attacks cells in the brain and spinal cord that carry messages to the muscles, resulting in progressive muscle weakness. As the disease advances, a person can lose the ability to control arm and leg muscles and even to breathe unassisted. In Kozmetsky's case, the first sign of the disease was a gradual weakening of his right arm, a problem that at first he thought might be only a pinched nerve. In time, he lost the use of that arm, and then the disease affected other parts of his body. In his last months, Kozmetsky used a wheelchair, and one of his grandchildren, Jordan Scott, moved to Austin from Dallas to assist him with everyday tasks.

In the early stages of the disease, before it was diagnosed, Kozmetsky began having trouble with ordinary tasks requiring the use of his hands. Sometimes he would ask a friend to help tie his tie before he made a speech. On one trip to Southern California, Corey Carbonara, Kozmetsky's former student and an IC² Institute colleague, went with him to a medical center to get an MRI to try to find out what was happening to his body.

Kozmetsky remained intellectually alert to the end. In addition to conferring with his last graduate student, Darius Mahdjoubi, he continued to go to meetings and keep up with his reading interests. One of the last books that caught his attention—and that he recommended to friends— was *A Mind at a Time* by pediatrician Mel Levine.[58] The book, published in January 2003, was subtitled *America's Top Learning Expert Shows How Every Child Can Succeed*—a theme that was close to Kozmetsky's heart, having been himself a late bloomer in schooling and having devoted much of his life to promoting opportunity for people of all backgrounds.

In his last years Kozmetsky also continued to work on book projects. One of those was *Immigrant and Minority Entrepreneurship: The Continuous Rebirth of American Communities* (Praeger, 2004), coedited with John S. Butler, which examines how immigrants and American minorities develop businesses and advance economically. Another collaboration was *Zero Time* (Wiley, 2000), coauthored with Raymond Yeh and Keri Pearlson, a study of how businesses can guarantee that they consistently meet the needs of customers. The book draws heavily on Kozmetsky's experience with Dell Computer Inc. One of the last books with which Kozmetsky was associated was *New Wealth: Commercialization of Science and Technology for Business and Economic Development* (Praeger, 2004), a collaboration with Frederick Williams and Victoria Williams.

In 2002, Kozmetsky was part of a team that put together Austin's successful bid to host the 2006 World Technology Congress on Information Technology, a biennial gathering of technology and government leaders.[59] Three years after Kozmetsky died, the conference brought to Austin 2,100 high-tech leaders from eighty-one countries.[60]

As the ALS progressed into the first months of 2003, many friends called on Kozmetsky at his and Ronya's tenth-floor condominium at Ninth Street and Lamar Boulevard. (They had moved the previous fall to the condo overlooking a city park, envisioning that it would simplify their lives and be a short walk from shopping, such as at a Whole Foods grocery and a large local bookstore.) These visits were a way of saying goodbye, a last opportunity to exchange private thoughts and express again to Kozmetsky how important he had been as a mentor and friend.

One of the most striking reports of these visits comes from Corey Carbonara. Just a few weeks before Kozmetsky died, Carbonara visited him with two other friends—Jeff Cook, president of the Texas Association of Broadcasters,[61] and Ramiro Pena Jr., pastor of Christ the King Baptist Church in Waco. Kozmetsky, who was never demonstrative about religion, knew that Carbonara was Catholic, and since 2000 he had been a friend of Pena, whom he called "Padre," so he might not have been surprised when his visitors asked if they could pray at his side. He said OK, and afterward he expressed some wonder over the fact that "people are praying for me."[62]

Kozmetsky's last public event came five days before he died, when he made a presentation to a group of officials from Mexico who visited the IC² Institute.[63]

He was still working hard three days before he died, even though breathing was becoming increasingly difficult. Carbonara visited again, this time with another friend from Waco, Bill Segura, chancellor of the Texas State Technical College. They stood on either side of Kozmetsky's bed, "both of us with pads in our hands to write down his ideas for a digital platform for certifying technicians' skillsets and his ideas for training using digital multimedia elements. We did all we could to keep up with his ideas!"[64]

Two days later, Edward A. Miller spent an hour and a half on the phone with Kozmetsky talking about the problem of how developed and developing countries can interact without either being taken advantage of. "We talked about that many times but never reached a conclusion," Miller said. "That day he told me to never stop working on that problem until it is solved."[65]

On Wednesday, April 30, 2003, Ronya asked Jordan Scott to stay with George until noon, when another grandson, Daniel Kozmetsky, was scheduled to drive George to a regular doctor's appointment—to get the latest test results and see if George would need to get a tracheotomy and start using a ventilator. George and Jordan spent the morning talking about a business venture of Jordan's called Flightlock, and George was offering advice about how to make the business successful. When Daniel arrived, the three of them and Ronya headed for the doctor's office, with George in the front seat. They drove north on Lamar, past the turnoff for the house at Seventeenth Street and then past the RGK Foundation at Lamar and Twenty-Fifth Street. As they neared the IC² Institute at Lamar and San Gabriel, Daniel heard George take a deep breath. When they arrived at the doctor's office he didn't respond to efforts to wake him, and they called 911 as Jordan tried giving CPR until George's doctor and then the EMS arrived. "In all the commotion and chaos, I sat and held my grandfather's hand, and told him in my mind that things were OK, that we were here with him and with my grandmother, and that we would take care of everything. Eventually the commotion slowed and the EMS technician looked to our family doctor and shook his head."[66]

Remembrances

Kozmetsky's adopted-hometown newspaper published a 1,700-word obituary that paid tribute to him as "a tireless entrepreneur, scholar, investor, and philanthropist who laid the groundwork for Austin's emergence as a technology center."[67] Newspapers in other cities where Kozmetsky had lived also took note of his death, as did the *New York Times* and a host of more specialized publications. On Sunday, May 4, five hundred mourners gathered at the university's Erwin Center for a memorial service. The remembrances ranged from Michael Dell recalling Kozmetsky's first visit to his then-small company, to recollections from his grandchildren that he was notorious for cheating at rock-paper-scissors.[68]

The most unusual tribute came on November 10, 2005, when the University of Texas Wind Ensemble performed a twenty-minute symphony, titled *American Visionary*, that commemorated Kozmetsky's love of technology, family, and community. The performance was a collaborative effort on a truly Kozmetsky scale. Robert Freeman, dean of the university's College of Fine Arts, first conceived of a musical work that would include narration performed by San Antonio businessman Red McCombs, who agreed to participate if the theme could be the life of Kozmetsky, his friend and business adviser. Freeman then commissioned the music from Dan Welcher, a professor of composition at the university, and they recruited Robert L. Kuhn, a longtime colleague of Kozmetsky and a fellow at the IC² Institute, to write the narration. Kuhn searched through Kozmetsky's writings for appropriate quotes.

The work began with McCombs reading Kozmetsky's words about the future of Texas: "Texas—think beyond cattle, cowboys, and oil. To see the future, Texas, link intellect, technology, and enterprise." At its conclusion, the performance received a standing ovation from the audience in the packed, seven-hundred-seat Bates Recital Hall.[69]

Ronya outlived George by eight years. She died at home on October 25, 2011, four months after her ninetieth birthday. Pike Powers remembered her as "a completely gracious lady who was every bit a match for George's personality."

"They made a great team," Powers said. "She had a mind of her own and thought quite independently. I thought they were a wonderful couple, but she was a special spirit in making that couple work."[70]

Laura Kilcrease recalled the "phenomenal balance between George and Ronya," and observed that they had been "equally strong with different strengths. She was generous, giving, and a proponent of those who were less fortunate," Kilcrease said. "There was a strong sense of 'We are immigrants and we did well, and we should give back.'"[71]

THE KOZMETSKY LEGACY

In 2017 the IC² Institute observed the one hundredth anniversary of George Kozmetsky's birth, as well as the fortieth anniversary of the institute. Fellows of the institute gathered in Austin to pay tribute to Kozmetsky for his central role as a civic entrepreneur who helped to shape the Austin technopolis and as a passionate advocate for creative and innovative applications of technology in the furtherance of global prosperity. They remembered him as an inspiring figure whose expansive personality was able to draw together disparate forces, stimulate creative and critical thinking, and infect his associates with his own optimism and energy.

Scholars and entrepreneurs from across the United States as well as from Australia, Canada, China, India, Iran, Mexico, Taiwan, and the United Kingdom mused on Kozmetsky's achievements and on what might come next. A common theme of those discussions was Kozmetsky's ability "to see beyond the horizon," whether forecasting developments in technology, planning for changes in education to address the needs of new generations, or thinking of new kinds of organizations and vehicles to further his goal of expanding economic opportunity in his adopted hometown and around the world. Some in attendance had not known Kozmetsky, but all sensed the continuing influence of his long life and varied activities as they worked in their own ways to carry forward one aspect or another of his vision, as if Kozmetsky's life were a prism that now revealed an overwhelmingly diverse spectrum of endeavor.

As the beneficiaries of that vision, they celebrated together a complex man—a millionaire businessman who was most comfortable among young, creative entrepreneurs trying to build something from scratch; an early advocate of the military-industrial complex who was intent on making capitalism a constructive force in society; a child of immigrant parents of modest means who rose to leadership roles in business, education, and civic life; a broadly knowledgeable scholar absorbed with the unstructured problems of the real world; a lifelong teacher whose overriding message was the need to break down barriers between contending academic disciplines; an enthusiastic and optimistic believer in technology with broad faith in an eventual technological solution to human problems, even as in his later years he feared for the world in which his grandchildren would live; a partner for sixty years with his wife, Ronya, in creating a legacy of service to society and support for broad economic advancement.

Today the multifaceted influence of George Kozmetsky continues to be felt around the globe, from the Austin technopolis to the science cities of Japan, from Beijing to Lisbon, from New Delhi to Monterrey. Despite his influence, many people in many nations continue to resist his vision of the world as a community and a family in which educational and economic opportunity are within the reach of all. For him, that resistance would probably be just one more reason to get up early and go to work.

NOTES

CHAPTER 1

1. Transcript of Management 385, "The State of American Capitalism," Spring 1983, February 9, 1983, p. 2, Kozmetsky Papers, IC² Institute. Kozmetsky was actually forty-seven in August 1965.

2. "Deep in the Heart of Texas," *Economist*, May 27, 1997.

3. The idea of civic entrepreneurship in this sense has been explored by Douglas Henton, John Melville, and Kimberly Walesh, *Grassroots Leaders for a New Economy: How Civic Entrepreneurs Are Building Prosperous Communities* (San Francisco: Jossey-Bass, 1997); Stephen Goldsmith, *The Power of Social Innovation: How Civic Entrepreneurs Ignite Community Networks for Good* (San Francisco: Jossey-Bass, 2010); and Tijs Creutzberg, "Governing a Knowledge Economy: Scalar, Civic, and Strategic Dimensions of Contemporary Economic Governance in North America" (PhD thesis, University of Toronto, 2006).

4. Interview with Laura Kilcrease, April 4, 2012.

5. Ibid.

6. Interview with Robert D. King, September 27, 2011.

CHAPTER 2

1. Letter from Art and Barbara Jenkins for George and Ronya's fiftieth wedding anniversary, 1993, Kozmetsky Papers, IC² Institute. The reminiscences provided by family friends on the occasion of George and Ronya's anniversary were compiled by Nadya Scott in an anniversary book, now in the library at the IC² Institute.

2. Letter from Gladys Fogel for George and Ronya's fiftieth wedding anniversary, 1993, Kozmetsky Papers, IC² Institute.

3. Greta N. Slobin, *Russians Abroad: Literary and Cultural Politics of Diaspora (1919–1939)* (Boston: Academic Studies Press, 2013), 14.

4. Ibid., 53.

5. "Russians Will Hold Festival," *Seattle Times*, February 17, 1925.

6. *Seattle Municipal News* 7, no. 45, October 5, 1918.

7. John Douglas Marshall, *Place of Learning, Place of Dreams: A History of the Seattle Public Library* (Seattle: University of Washington Press, 2004), 65–71. Also see Paula Becker, "Seattle Public Library Fires Foreign-Books Librarian Natalie Notkin," April 6, 2012, www.historylink.org/File/3971.

8. Margaret Kay Anderson, "Analysis of the Attempts of Workers in the Seattle Needle Trades to Organize and Bargain Collectively under Section 7 (A) of the National Relief Administration" (Seattle: Digest of Theses, University of Washington, 1938).

9. Interview with Kenneth D. Walters, October 30, 2015.

10. William H Mullins, *The Depression and the Urban West Coast, 1929–1933* (Bloomington: Indiana University Press, 1991), 8.

11. Ibid., 9.

12. Ibid., 77.

13. "Hoovervilles and Homelessness," in *The Great Depression in Washington State*, a multimedia web project based at the University of Washington, http://depts.washington.edu/depress/hooverville.shtml.

14. US Census, 1920. The census report gives Nadya's entry date as 1915, but it is given as September 27, 1916, in immigration papers for her second husband, Stanley Liszewski, and in other documents, including an affidavit that she signed in 1942.

15. Spelled "Grodna" in "George Kozmetsky: A Brief Biography," an unpublished manuscript in three parts prepared in 1995 by IC² Institute staff member Nancy Ritchey and based on interviews with Kozmetsky. The manuscript is in the archives of the IC² Institute. This important source will be cited as "Brief Biography" in subsequent references. The names of locations and other proper nouns related to Belarus are spelled in various ways, depending on whether they are being referred to in Belarusian, Russian, Polish, Lithuanian, Yiddish, or another language.

16. Communication from Stephen Gomes, April 28, 2017.

17. Also spelled Szeresowo in some historical documents and spelled Sarasova on some present-day maps.

18. Written reminiscences of Nena Running, provided by her niece Elaine Wiley.

19. Ibid.

20. Ritchey, "Brief Biography," 1:2–3.

21. US Census, 1920. The author is indebted to Karla Walters of Bellevue, Washington, for locating this census record despite the family name being listed incorrectly.

22. Application for delayed certificate of birth (for Nena Nehoda), May 18, 1942, State Archives, Bellevue, Washington.

23. The borders of the nations in Eastern Europe have changed frequently. Grodno has been at various times in Poland, Lithuania, Russia, and Belarus.

24. Application for delayed certificate of birth (for Nena Nehoda), May 18, 1942, State Archives, Bellevue, Washington.

25. *Kroll's Atlas of Seattle*, 1920 and 1930.

26. *Polk's Seattle City Directory*, 1919, 1920, 1921, and 1923.

27. Letter from Nena Running for George and Ronya's fiftieth wedding anniversary, 1993, Kozmetsky Papers, IC² Institute.

28. Ritchey, "Brief Biography," 1:3.

29. Ibid.

30. Ibid.

31. Interview with Elaine Wiley, October 30, 2015.

32. Interview with Greg Kozmetsky, April 19, 2010.

33. Interview with Elaine Wiley, October 30, 2015.

34. Interview with Laura Kilcrease, April 4, 2012.

35. Immigration and naturalization records, National Archives and Records Administration, Seattle.

36. Film of the SS *Kaiserin Auguste Victoria* is on YouTube at https://www.youtube.com/watch?v=V9qdUAQKvmI.

37. Interview with Elaine Wiley, October 30, 2015.

38. Immigration and naturalization records, National Archives and Records Administration, Seattle.

39. The draft registration card (serial no. U6349) confirms Stanley's birthdate as April 12, 1896, and states that he was living at 1402 Ninth Avenue South. The card is in the collection of the National Archives and Records Administration.

40. "18 State Firms Aid Ship Output," *Seattle Times*, October 30, 1942.

41. *Kroll's Atlas of Seattle*, 1920 and 1930.

42. Interview with Elaine Wiley, October 30, 2015.

43. *Polk's Seattle City Directory*, 1921–1936; *Pacific Telephone and Telegraph Directory*, 1955.

44. Interview with Laura Kilcrease, April 12, 2012.

45. "Nettie Liszewski," *Seattle Times*, March 28, 1978.

46. Interviews with Nadya Scott, April 28, 2015, and Elaine Wiley, October 30, 2015.

47. The spelling "Keosiff" will be used here, even though records cited may give a different spelling.

48. Immigration and naturalization records, National Archives and Records Administration, Seattle; and ship records of the Museum of History and Industry, Seattle, accessed through Archive Engine West.

49. This may be the Ukrainian city of Berdyansk, a port city on the Sea of Azov. Fedor registered for the draft in 1942 (serial no. U1872). His employment is listed as "The Ship" in Olympia.

50. Immigration and naturalization records, National Archives and Records Administration, Seattle.

51. David Wolff, *To the Harbin Station: The Liberal Alternative in Russian Manchuria, 1989–1914* (Stanford, CA: Stanford University Press, 1999), 1–4.

52. Immigration and naturalization records, National Archives and Records Administration, Seattle.

53. University High School yearbook, 1966, accessed through ancestry.com.

CHAPTER 3

1. In the early 1930s, it was routine for a group of "February Freshmen" to transfer to high school in midyear. *Tolo Weekly* (Franklin High School newspaper), February 8, 1933, Seattle School District Archives.

2. Records of George Kozmetsky, Seattle School District Archives.

3. Ritchey, "Brief Biography," 1:4.

4. Letter from Nena Running for George and Ronya's fiftieth wedding anniversary, 1993, Kozmetsky Papers, IC[2] Institute.

5. Nile Thompson and Carolyn J. Marr, *Building for Learning: Seattle Public School Histories, 1862–2000* (Seattle, WA: Seattle Public Schools, 2002), 97–101; Seattle Public Schools, *Successful Living* (Seattle, WA: Seattle Public Schools, 1935), 39.

6. *Tolo Weekly*, February 8, 1933.

7. Seattle Public School Archives.

8. Seattle Public Schools, *Successful Living*, 11.

9. Seattle Public School Archives.

10. Ritchey, "Brief Biography," 1:5–6; and Seattle Public School Archives.

11. "1998 Induction," Franklin Alumni Association and Foundation, http://www.franklinalumni.net/1998-induction/.

12. Ritchey, "Brief Biography," 1:6.

13. "Fund Donor Warns of College Need," *Seattle Times*, May 11, 1968.

14. "Faculty Endowment Donor Information," fundraising document, Foster School of Business, University of Washington.

15. Interview with Kenneth D. Walters, October 29, 2015.

16. Ritchey, "Brief Biography," 1:7; "$100,000 Grant Honors Former U.W. Professor," *Seattle Times*, April 28, 1968.

17. George Kozmetsky, "The Grant I. Butterbaugh Professorship," *University of Washington Business Review*, Summer 1968, pp. 9–11.

18. University of Washington Catalogue, 1934–1935 and 1936–1937.

19. Interview with Kenneth D. Walters, October 29, 2015.

20. See, for example, Woody Guthrie, *Columbia River Collection* (Rounder Records C1036, 1987; first published 1941); and *Grand Coulee Dam* (DVD, *The American Experience*, PBS and WGBH, 2012).

21. Letter from Nena Running for George and Ronya's fiftieth wedding anniversary, 1993, Kozmetsky Papers, IC² Institute.

22. Ibid.

23. Not to be confused with the better-known Vancouver in Canada, Washington's Vancouver is across the Columbia River from Portland, Oregon, 165 miles south of Seattle.

24. "Russians End Polar Flight; Land at Vancouver, Wash.," *New York Times*, June 21, 1937.

25. Ibid.

26. "George Kozmetsky Interprets Airmen's Words to World," *Seattle Post-Intelligencer*, June 21, 1937.

27. Ibid.

28. Georgy Baidukov, *Russian Lindbergh: The Life of Valery Chkalov*, trans. Peter Belov (Washington, DC: Smithsonian Institution Press, 1991).

29. Ritchey, "Brief Biography," 1:7–8.

30. "Russians End Polar Flight; Land at Vancouver, Wash.," *New York Times*, June 21, 1937.

31. John McCannon, *Red Arctic: Polar Exploration and the Myth of the North in the Soviet Union, 1932–1939* (New York: Oxford University Press, 1998), 68–73.

32. Ritchey, "Brief Biography," 1:9.

33. Ibid., 1:10–11.

34. "Destroyer History—Seattle Tacoma Shipbuilding, Todd Pacific Shipyards, Seattle, WA," Destroyer History Foundation, http://destroyerhistory.org/destroyers/seatac/.

35. Interview with Greg Kozmetsky, April 19, 2010.

36. "Business School Leadership Banquet Honors Three Alumni," *UW Business*, Fall 2001.

37. Ritchey, "Brief Biography," 1:11–12.

38. Letter from Herman Feinberg for George and Ronya's fiftieth wedding anniversary, 1993, Kozmetsky Papers, IC² Institute.

39. Letter from Gladys "Cappy" Fogel for George and Ronya's fiftieth wedding anniversary, 1993, Kozmetsky Papers, IC² Institute.

40. Ritchey, "Brief Biography," 1:12–13.

41. "PSS History," Phi Sigma Sigma, www.phisigmasigma.org/aboutus/heritage/psshistory.

42. Craig L. Torbenson and Gregory S. Parks, *Brothers and Sisters: Diversity in College Fraternities and Sororities* (Madison, NJ: Fairleigh Dickinson University Press, 2009), 217.

43. Ronya Kozmetsky obituary, *Austin American-Statesman*, October 27, 2011.

44. Ritchey, "Brief Biography," 1:13.

45. Ibid., 1:14.

46. Ibid., 1:14–15.

47. Interview with Elaine Wiley, October 30, 2015.

48. Washington Marriage Records, 1865–2004, www.ancestry.com.

49. "Evangeline Starr; Retired Judge," *Seattle Times*, January 31, 1990.

50. Late in his life, George recounted the shopping trip to Corey Carbonara, one of his graduate students and later a colleague at the IC^2 Institute.

51. Bernard Rapoport, *Being Rapoport: Capitalist with a Conscience* (Austin: University of Texas Press, 2002), 58, 71.

52. Washington Marriage Records, 1865–2004, www.ancestry.com; "Croatian Union to Dance," *Seattle Times*, April 20, 1938; "Croatians to Meet," *Seattle Times*, May 13, 1948; "Anton Susanji and His Tamburitza," *Seattle Times*, April 15, 1962.

53. Interview with Elaine Wiley, October 30, 2015.

54. Ibid.

55. Ibid.

56. Ibid.; and homepage of www.grunion.org.

CHAPTER 4

1. Interview with Greg Kozmetsky, April 19, 2010.

2. Transcript of graduate management class, January 22, 1986, p. 8., Kozmetsky Papers, IC^2 Institute. Kozmetsky was inexact about the term MASH (mobile army surgical hospital). The army introduced mobile hospitals close to the front lines during World War II, but they were not designated as MASH units until the Korean War. See Booker King and Ismail Jatoi, "The Mobile Army Surgical Hospital (MASH): A Military and Surgical Legacy," *Journal of the National Medical Association* 97, no. 5 (May 2005): 648–656.

3. Transcript of graduate management class, January 22, 1986, Kozmetsky Papers, IC^2 Institute.

4. "The 1973 Fire, National Personnel Records Center," National Archives and Records Administration, http://www.archives.gov/st-louis/military-personnel/fire-1973.html; and correspondence to the author from the National Personnel Records Center, August 17, 2012.

5. Correspondence to the author from the National Personnel Records Center, August 17, 2012; and "Combat Interviews, Battle of Hurtgen Forest, 16 November–3 December 1944," US Army Medical Department, Office of Medical History, http://history.amedd.army.mil/books-docs/wwii/HuertgenForest/4thIDCIHF.htm. The original typescripts of the interviews are in the National Archives, Records of the US Army Adjutant General's Office.

6. Ritchey, "Brief Biography," 1:16.

7. US World War II Army Enlistment Records, 1938–1946, National Archives, College Park, Maryland, accessed through ancestry.com.

8. "Historic California Posts, Camps, Stations and Airfields: Lemoore Army Air Field," California State Military Museums, http://www.militarymuseum.org/LemooreAAF.html.

9. Richard V. N. Ginn, *The History of the U.S. Army Medical Service Corps* (Washington, DC: US Government Printing Office, 1997), 122.

10. Ibid., 125.

11. Ibid.

12. Ibid., 132.

13. Ibid., 132–133.

14. Ibid., 132.

15. The site, seven miles southeast of downtown San Antonio, closed in 2011 as a military base and is now a mixed-use community known simply as Brooks. The base was a different facility from the Brooke Army Medical Center at Fort Sam Houston, also in San Antonio.

16. Ritchey, "Brief Biography," 1:16–17.

17. Ginn, *History of Medical Service Corps*, 141.

18. John S. Mailer Jr. and Barbara Mason, "Penicillin: Medicine's Wartime Wonder Drug and Its Production at Peoria, Illinois," Illinois Periodicals Online, www.lib.niu.edu/2001/

iht810139.html; Patricia W. Sewell, ed., *Healers in World War II: Oral Histories of Medical Corps Personnel* (Jefferson, NC: McFarland, 2001), 50.

19. Douglas B. Kendrick, *Blood Program in World War II* (Washington, DC: US Government Printing Office, 1964), 265.

20. "Order of Battle of the United States Army, World War II, European Theater of Operations," US Army Center of Military History, http://www.history.army.mil/documents/ETO-OB/ETOOB-TOC.htm.

21. Michael Reynolds, *Hemingway: The Final Years* (New York: Norton, 1999), 101–125.

22. Interview with Jordan Scott, July 29, 2015.

23. Robert Sterling Rush, *Hell in Hürtgen Forest: The Ordeal and Triumph of an American Infantry Regiment* (Lawrence: University of Kansas Press, 2001), 92.

24. "22nd Infantry Regiment History World War II," excerpt from *22nd Infantry Regiment Yearbook* (1947), 1st Battalion 22nd Infantry Regiment Society, http://1-22infantry.org/history2/regthistory.htm.

25. David Rothbart, *A Soldier's Journal: With the 22nd Infantry Regiment in World War II* (New York: ibooks, 2003).

26. William S. Boice, ed., *History of the Twenty-Second United States Infantry in World War II* (n.p., 1959); "22nd Infantry Regiment History," http://1-22infantry.org/history2/regthistory.htm.

27. Rush, *Hell in Hürtgen Forest*, 3.

28. Edward G. Miller, *A Dark and Bloody Ground: The Hürtgen Forest and the Roer River Dams, 1944–1945* (College Station: Texas A&M University Press, 1995), 206–210.

29. Rush, *Hell in Hürtgen Forest*, 3.

30. Ibid., 270, 359.

31. "22nd Infantry Regiment History," http://1-22infantry.org/history2/regthistory.htm.

32. Charles B. MacDonald, *The Siegfried Line Campaign* (Washington, DC: Office of the Chief of Military History, US Army, 1963), 444–445.

33. "Combat Interviews, Battle of Hurtgen Forest, 16 November–3 December 1944," http://history.amedd.army.mil/booksdocs/wwii/HuertgenForest/4thIDCIHF.htm.

34. Ibid.

35. Ibid.

36. Ibid.

37. Hugh M. Cole, *The Ardennes: Battle of the Bulge* (Washington, DC: US Government Printing Office, 1965), 238.

38. Ibid., 251.

39. James Marion Kirtley, *Kirtley Kronicles* (Crawfordsville, IN: Montgomery County Historical Society, 1997), 127.

40. Ibid.

41. Stanley A. Kornblum, "Nearsighted and Flatfooted," in *Healers in World War II: Oral Histories of Medical Corps Personnel*, ed. Patricia W. Sewell (Jefferson, NC: McFarland, 2001), 51.

42. Boice, *History of the Twenty-Second Infantry*, quoted in Gerald Astor, *The Bloody Forest: Battle for the Huertgen, September 1944–January 1945* (Novato, CA: Presidio Press, 2000), 206–208.

43. Robin Neillands, *The Battle for the Rhine: The Battle of the Bulge and the Ardennes Campaign, 1944* (Woodstock, NY: Overlook Press, 2005), 247–248.

44. "U.W. 'Prof' Fixes Wounds in Front Lines," *Seattle Times*, February 7, 1945.

45. Charles B. MacDonald, *The Last Offensive* (Washington, DC: Office of the Chief of Military History, US Army, 1973), 86–88.

46. Ibid., 89.

47. Kozmetsky family papers in possession of Greg Kozmetsky.

48. Correspondence from the National Personnel Records Center, August 17, 2012.

49. Interview with Greg Kozmetsky, August 16, 2016.

50. Ritchey, "Brief Biography," 1: 20.

51. Ritchey, "Brief Biography," 1:18–19.

52. Rothbart, *A Soldier's Journal*.

53. The author is grateful to Gary Hoover of Austin, Texas, for his research into air, train, and bus schedules from 1945.

CHAPTER 5

1. The business school did offer financial help to some students through its own loans, scholarships (ranging from $300 to $1,000), and campus part-time jobs, "which enable a student to earn in the neighborhood of $10 a week." Harvard University, Official Register of the Graduate School of Business Administration 42, no. 29 (December 15, 1945), 65.

2. Ritchey, "Brief Biography."

3. Transcript of graduate management class, April 12, 1989, p. 1, Kozmetsky Papers, IC² Institute.

4. Harvard University, Official Register (1945), 65.

5. U-Haul, the nation's first one-way rental company for do-it-yourself movers, was started in Portland, Oregon, in the summer of 1945 by a war veteran and his wife who faced a moving problem similar to the one that the Kozmetskys faced, but there were no U-Haul trailers in the Seattle area until the end of 1945. "Our History: An Idea to Meet a Need," U-Haul, http://www.uhaul.com/About/History.aspx.

6. Ritchey, "Brief Biography," 1: 23–24.

7. Communication from David Smith, April 29, 2017.

8. "Harvard Business School Will Cover Management," *New York Times*, August 25, 1945.

9. "Business Methods Applied to Air War," *New York Times*, October 21, 1945.

10. "Annual Report of the Dean of the Graduate School of Business Administration for 1946–47," Official Register of Harvard University 46, no. 30 (December 1, 1949). Each annual report was published in the Official Register several years after it was first sent to the president.

11. Ibid., 468.

12. "Annual Report of the Dean for 1947–48," Official Register of Harvard University 47, no. 12 (May 16, 1950), 445.

13. Geoffrey Jones, "Debating the Responsibility of Capitalism in Historical and Global Perspective" (Harvard Business School Working Paper 14-004, July 8, 2013), 16.

14. Donald K. David, "Business Responsibilities in an Uncertain World," *Harvard Business Review* 27, no. 3 (May 1949): 1–2.

15. Transcript of graduate management class, February 23, 1983, p. 13, Kozmetsky Papers, IC² Institute.

16. Official Register (1945), 29–43; "Harvard Opening Business School," *New York Times*, January 31, 1946.

17. "Electronic Computer Flashes Answers," *New York Times*, February 15, 1946.

18. "World's Fastest Calculator Cuts Years' Task to Hours," *Boston Globe*, February 15, 1946.

19. "Harvard Opening Business School," *New York Times*, January 31, 1946.

20. "History and Timeline," US Department of Veterans Affairs, www.benefits.va.gov/gibill/history.asp.

21. Ritchey, "Brief Biography," 1:24.

22. Ibid.

23. Biographical note included in the nomination materials for the National Medal of Technology, notebook on the 1993 National Medal of Technology, Kozmetsky Papers, IC² Institute.

24. Transcript of Management 385, Spring 1983, Kozmetsky Papers, IC² Institute.

25. Interview with Fred Phillips, April 23, 2015.

26. Transcript of Management 385, Spring 1983, pp. 25–26, Kozmetsky Papers, IC² Institute.

27. Transcript of graduate management class, February 15, 1986, p. 10, Kozmetsky Papers, IC² Institute.

28. UT press release, April 29, 1970.

29. "MBA Program at Harvard Business School, 1963–1970: The Co-ed Experience," Harvard Business School, http://www.library.hbs.edu/hc/wbe/exhibit_mba-program.html.

30. "Harvard Goes Co-ed, but Incognito," New York Times, May 1, 1949.

31. Interview with Edward A. Miller, May 5, 2017.

32. Ritchey, "Brief Biography," 1:25.

33. Transcript of graduate management class, September 19, 1990, pp. 18–19, Kozmetsky Papers, IC² Institute.

34. Interview with Janey Lack, November 6, 2013.

35. Ritchey, "Brief Biography," 1:25–27.

36. Ibid., 1:28.

37. Subrata Dasgupta, It Began with Babbage: The Genesis of Computer Science (New York: Oxford University Press, 2014), 225–230.

38. George Kozmetsky, "Unions' Financial Reporting," Harvard Business Review 22, no. 1 (January 1949): 14.

39. George Kozmetsky, "What Operating Data for Collective Bargaining?," NACA Bulletin 30, no. 22 (1949): 1317–1324.

40. Gerald Mayer, "Union Membership Trends in the United States" (Congressional Research Service, August 31, 2004); data for 2015 from the Bureau of Labor Statistics, Current Population Survey.

41. George Kozmetsky, Financial Reports of Labor Unions (Boston: Harvard University, 1950), vii; abstract prepared by the Division of Research of the Harvard Business School.

42. Ibid., 10–14.

43. Solomon Barkin, book review, Industrial and Labor Relations Review 5, no. 3 (April 1952): 462–463.

44. Herbert G. Heneman Jr., book review, Accounting Review 26, no. 1 (January 1951): 129–130.

45. Unsigned book review, Labor Law Journal 2, no. 5 (May 1951): 385.

46. Ritchey, "Brief Biography," 1:27.

47. Mandatory retirement ended for most federal employees in 1978 and for most other employees in 1986. Universities were given until 1994 to comply. Kozmetsky never did fully retire.

48. The Carnegie Institute of Technology merged in 1967 with the Mellon Institute of Industrial Research to form Carnegie Mellon University. In 2004, in recognition of a $55 million gift from hedge fund manager David A. Tepper, the GSIA was renamed the Tepper School of Business.

49. "$6,000,000 Grant for Carnegie Tech," New York Times, January 18, 1949.

50. Mie Augier and James G. March, The Roots, Rituals, and Rhetorics of Change: North American Business Schools after the Second World War (Stanford, CA: Stanford Business Books, 2011), 123.

51. Ibid., 61–63.

52. Ibid., 131.

53. George Kozmetsky, remarks on the occasion of William W. Cooper's seventy-fifth birth-

day, in *Bill and Ruth Cooper and Their Friends*, ed. Yuji Ijiri and Rona A. Watts (Pittsburgh: Carnegie Mellon University Press, 1990), 42.

54. Ritchey, "Brief Biography," 1:30–31.

55. UT Austin press release on the occasion of the gift of the IC² Institute building to the university, November 14, 1995.

56. Herbert A. Simon, George Kozmetsky, Harold Guetzkow, and Gordon Tindall, *Centralization vs. Decentralization in Organizing the Controller's Department* (1954; repr., Houston: Scholars Book Co., 1978).

57. Kozmetsky, in Ijiri and Watts, *Bill and Ruth Cooper*, 46.

58. "Controllers Plan Accounting Study," *New York Times*, October 1, 1950.

59. Autobiography of Herbert A. Simon, Nobel Foundation, http://www.nobelprize.org/nobel_prizes/economics/laureates/1978/simon-autobio.html.

60. Mie Augier and James G. March, eds., *Models of a Man: Essays in Memory of Herbert A. Simon* (Cambridge, MA: MIT Press, 2004), 16–17.

61. Herbert A. Simon, *Models of My Life* (New York: Basic Books, 1991), 162.

62. Augier and March, *Models of a Man*, 72.

63. Ibid., 200.

64. George Kozmetsky, remembrances of Herbert A. Simon, Carnegie Mellon University, March 19, 2001, http://www.cs.cmu.edu/simon/all.html.

65. Interview with Greg Kozmetsky, April 19, 2010.

66. Interview with William W. Cooper, January 11, 2010.

CHAPTER 6

1. Allen John Scott, *Technopolis: High-Technology Industry and Regional Development in Southern California* (Berkeley: University of California Press, 1993), 3.

2. Ibid., 55–64.

3. "Electronics Mergers: Firms Find Two Can Live More Cheaply than One," *Los Angeles Times*, August 23, 1964.

4. "Austin Architect Brings High-Tech Tips to OC," *Orange County Business Journal*, August 25, 1997.

5. Transcript of graduate management class, April 2, 1986, p. 27, Kozmetsky Papers, IC² Institute.

6. "The Blowup at Hughes Aircraft," *Fortune*, February 1954, p. 116.

7. Simon Ramo, *The Business of Science: Winning and Losing in the High-Tech Age* (New York: Hill and Wang, 1988), 36.

8. "Blowup at Hughes Aircraft," 118.

9. This patriotic and national-security motive suffuses Simon Ramo's memoir of his years at Hughes Aircraft; see chapter 2 of Ramo, *The Business of Science*.

10. Transcript of graduate management class, January 22, 1986, pp. 8–9, Kozmetsky Papers, IC² Institute.

11. Transcript of graduate management class, February 8, 1989, p. 5, Kozmetsky Papers, IC² Institute.

12. Transcript of graduate management class, March 5, 1986, pp. 4–5, Kozmetsky Papers, IC² Institute.

13. Interview with William W. Cooper, January 11, 2010.

14. "Blowup at Hughes Aircraft," 192.

15. Ibid.

16. Interview with William W. Cooper, January 11, 2010; George Kozmetsky, "A Dean's Perspective on Abraham Charnes: The Nature of Creative and Innovative Research and Teach-

ing," in *Systems and Management Science by Extremal Methods: Research Honoring Abraham Charnes at Age 70*, ed. Fred Young Phillips and John James Rousseau (Boston: Kluwer Academic, 1992), 6.

17. Transcript of graduate management class, April 9, 1986, pp. 8–9, Kozmetsky Papers, IC² Institute.

18. Ibid.

19. Transcript of graduate management class, February 19, 1986, p. 28, Kozmetsky Papers, IC² Institute.

20. Transcript of graduate management class, February 15, 1986, p. 7, Kozmetsky Papers, IC² Institute.

21. Bethany Scott Herwegh, letter to the editor, *Los Angeles Times*, November 27, 2005.

22. Ritchey, "Brief Biography," 2:4–5.

23. "Blowup at Hughes Aircraft," 193.

24. Ibid., 193, 198.

25. Ibid., 200.

26. "Update," *Businessweek*, July 17, 1954, p. 48.

27. In late 1953, Howard Hughes created the nonprofit Howard Hughes Medical Institute and transferred ownership of Hughes Aircraft to that entity. After three decades of further success in defense contracting, the company was sold to General Motors in 1985. GM sold most of the aerospace and defense operations to Raytheon in 1997, and later various other companies, including Boeing, acquired pieces of what had been known as Hughes Aircraft.

28. Shelton W. Boyce III, "A Case Study of the Organizational Growth of Litton Industries Through Mergers and Acquisitions" (MPA degree professional report, Graduate School of Business, University of Texas, June 1967), 11.

29. "Man on the Move," *Forbes*, July 15, 1961, p. 15.

30. Fred W. O'Green, *Putting Technology to Work: The Story of Litton Industries* (New York: Newcomen Society, 1988).

31. Beirne Lay Jr., *Someone Has to Make It Happen: The Inside Story of Tex Thornton, the Man Who Built Litton Industries* (Englewood Cliffs, NJ: Prentice-Hall, 1969), 122–125.

32. Boyce, "Case Study of the Organizational Growth of Litton Industries," 1–2.

33. Ibid., 3.

34. Ibid., 11; and "Litton Names 3 Executives," *Los Angeles Times*, August 6, 1959.

35. Robert Sobel, *The Rise and Fall of the Conglomerate Kings* (New York: Stein and Day, 1984), 58.

36. Transcript of graduate management class, February 15, 1986, p. 8, Kozmetsky Papers, IC² Institute.

37. Transcript of graduate management class, May 7, 1986, p. 25, Kozmetsky Papers, IC² Institute.

38. Ibid.

39. Transcript of graduate management class, February 15, 1986, p. 16, Kozmetsky Papers, IC² Institute.

40. O'Green, *Putting Technology to Work*, 12.

41. US Patent 2,933,925, filed 1956.

42. US Patent 3,057,211, held jointly with Donal B. Duncan, filed 1958.

43. US Patent 3,062,059, filed 1957.

44. Harold Erdley, "An Autobiography of the Professional Career of Harold (Hal) Erdley," 2012, www.scribd.com/doc/111377943/My-Professional-Career-Word-2003-Formatted#scribd.

45. Ibid.

46. "A Third Survey of Domestic Electronic Digital Computing Systems" (Ballistic Research Laboratories Report No. 1115, US Department of Commerce, March 1961).

47. Kozmetsky, "A Dean's Perspective on Abraham Charnes," 6.

48. Boyce, "Case Study of the Organizational Growth of Litton Industries," 58–59, data for fiscal years 1955 and 1960.

49. Christophe Lécuyer, *Making Silicon Valley: Innovation and the Growth of High Tech, 1930–1970* (Cambridge, MA: MIT Press, 2006), 87.

50. "Turning on Tap of New Capital to Southland," *Los Angeles Times*, September 10, 1997; transcript of graduate management class, February 15, 1986, Kozmetsky Papers, IC² Institute.

51. "Turning on Tap of New Capital," *Los Angeles Times*.

52. Kircher taught at UCLA from 1952 to 1986. He was responsible for the UCLA business school acquiring its first computer, and he was one of the first professors at the university to have a personal computer, which he bolted to a desk in the student lounge so students could try using it. He was a consultant on computers to the US General Accounting Office, and in 1959 he cowrote the first report on the use of electronic computers in the federal government. John McDonough, "In Memoriam: Paul Kircher," n.d., http://senate.universityofcalifornia.edu/_files/inmemorium/html/paulkircher.htm.

53. Richard G. Canning, *Electronic Data Processing for Business and Industry* (New York: John Wiley, 1956).

54. Howard S. Levin, *Office Work and Automation* (New York: John Wiley, 1956).

55. See the bibliography in Canning, *Electronic Data Processing*.

56. Their book remains widely available in university libraries and on the used-book market.

57. "Deep in the Heart of Texas," *New York Times*, April 25, 1971.

58. Kozmetsky and Kircher, *Electronic Computers and Management Control*, iii.

59. Ibid., 2.

60. Ibid., 12. As in other publications of that era, Kozmetsky and Kircher used exclusively male terms to describe business managers and executives, while clerical workers are routinely referred to as "girls."

61. Ibid., 14–15.

62. Ibid., 59.

63. Photographs of the room-sized UNIVAC I can be viewed at http://www.computer-history.info/Page4.dir/pages/Univac.dir/index.html.

64. "Early Popular Computers, 1950–1970," Engineering and Technology History Wiki, ethw.org/Early_Popular_Computers,_1950_-_1970.

65. Kozmetsky and Kircher, *Electronic Computers and Management Control*, 91.

66. Interview with Nadya Scott, April 28, 2015.

67. Transcript of graduate management class, February 19, 1986, p. 10, Kozmetsky Papers, IC² Institute.

CHAPTER 7

1. Sobel, *Rise and Fall of the Conglomerate Kings*, 64.

2. George A. Roberts, *Distant Force: A Memoir of the Teledyne Corporation and the Man Who Created It* (n.p.: George A. Roberts, 2007), 9.

3. "Teledyne's Singleton: He Plays It Close to the Vest," *Los Angeles Times*, August 1, 1976.

4. Sobel, *Rise and Fall of the Conglomerate Kings*, 64.

5. "How Litton Keeps It Up," *Fortune*, September 1966, repr. in *The Conglomerate Commotion*, by the editors of *Fortune* (New York: Viking Press, 1970).

6. Roberts, *Distant Force*, 9.

7. "The Case for Conglomerates," *Fortune*, June 1967, repr. in *Conglomerate Commotion*.

8. Irvin M. Grossack, "An Overview of the Current Merger Movement," in *Conglomerates*

Unlimited: The Failure of Regulation, by John F. Winslow (Bloomington: Indiana University Press, 1973), viii–ix.

9. Ibid., xvi.

10. Winslow, *Conglomerates Unlimited*, 2.

11. "Teledyne: Threat to the Establishment," *Forbes*, September 15, 1967.

12. Transcript of graduate management class, January 22, 1986, p. 9, Kozmetsky Papers, IC² Institute.

13. Transcript of graduate management class, March 5, 1986, p. 2, Kozmetsky Papers, IC² Institute.

14. "The Teledyne Tech Titan Spark," *Investor's Business Daily*, May 8, 2013; "The Singular Henry Singleton," *Forbes*, July 9, 1979. Attempts to confirm the report of this autopilot invention have not been successful.

15. "Infant with a Giant Appetite," *Businessweek*, January 11, 1964, p. 67.

16. "S.F. Investor Team Bankrolls High-Flying Firms of Future," *Los Angeles Times*, August 28, 1967.

17. "Teledyne's Tender Offer Astounds Analysts," *Los Angeles Times*, May 11, 1984.

18. Interview with Charles Hurwitz, April 26, 2017.

19. Comments at IC² Institute fellows meeting, April 28, 2017.

20. The name was derived from Greek words to express the idea of "force" exerted across a "distance," an appropriate name for a company engaged in electronics.

21. Interview with William W. Cooper, August 17, 2009.

22. "Infant with a Giant Appetite," 68.

23. Ibid.

24. Transcript of graduate management class, February 1, 1989, p. 18, Kozmetsky Papers, IC² Institute.

25. "Infant with a Giant Appetite," 66.

26. Roberts, *Distant Force*, 15.

27. Ibid., 11–12.

28. Ibid., 13–14.

29. "Infant with a Giant Appetite," 66.

30. Transcript of graduate management class, January 22, 1986, pp. 24–25, Kozmetsky Papers, IC² Institute. Kozmetsky's comment about the $60,000 appears to indicate that even as a cofounder of the company, he argued over his budget with his partner Singleton.

31. Lécuyer, *Making Silicon Valley*, 216–222.

32. Ibid., 227–228.

33. Bo Lojek, *The History of Semiconductor Engineering* (New York: Springer, 2007), 184–186.

34. Isy Haas, interview by David C. Brock by phone, June 24–25, 2010, Chemical Heritage Foundation, Philadelphia, Oral History Transcript No. 0661.

35. "Oral History Interview: Jay T. Last," September 15, 2007, SEMI, http://www.semi.org/en/About/P042813.

36. Transcript of graduate management class, January 22, 1986, pp. 24–25, Kozmetsky Papers, IC² Institute.

37. Transcript of graduate management class, February 15, 1986, pp. 2–3, Kozmetsky Papers, IC² Institute.

38. Ibid.

39. George Kozmetsky, "Man-Machine Methodology: Final Report," report submitted to the Office of Advanced Research and Technology, NASA (Teledyne Systems Corp., April 1964).

40. "Minicamera Developed for NASA by Teledyne," *Broadcasting*, July 11, 1966.

41. "Interview: Jay T. Last," http://www.semi.org/en/About/P042813.

42. Communication from Corey Carbonara, April 29, 2017.

43. Class transcript of Management 385, "The State of American Capitalism," January 19, 1983, p. 15, Kozmetsky Papers, IC² Institute. Kozmetsky's comment obscures the fact that Abraham Charnes and William Cooper were the actual inventors of chance constraint programming, a method of ensuring that a decision will lead to a certain result, within specified degrees of probability.

44. Kozmetsky discussed the business management aspects of the helicopter project and implications for business education in a lecture at the Harvard Business School in 1967. See below as well as chapter 9 for details of this lecture, "Computers in Business and Education."

45. Roberts, *Distant Force*, 21; "IHAS Program May Establish Precedents," *Aviation Week and Space Technology*, June 21, 1965, p. 55.

46. The term "avionics," coined in 1949, is a combination of "aviation" and "electronics" and can refer to electronic equipment for navigation, communication, flight control, weapons control, or any other aircraft function.

47. James P. Murphy, Horace Welk, and Louis Cotton, "The IHAS Flight Control System" (paper presented at American Helicopter Society, 22nd Annual National Forum, May 11–13, 1966), 74.

48. Ibid., 70.

49. L. A. Kaufman, "Digital Flight Control Systems for Helicopter and VTOL Applications" (paper presented at Annual Aviation and Space Conference, Beverly Hills, CA, June 16–19, 1968), 698–699.

50. "IHAS Program May Establish Precedents," 41; "IHAS Uses Special Incremental Computer," *Aviation Week and Space Technology*, June 28, 1965, pp. 88–97.

51. "Infant with a Giant Appetite," 67.

52. Interview with William W. Cooper, August 17, 2009.

53. "Cost-effectiveness" was a new term in the 1960s. The *Oxford English Dictionary* cites a 1964 article for the earliest use of "cost-effectiveness" and a 1967 article (about McNamara) for the earliest use of "cost-effective."

54. George Kozmetsky, "Computers in Business and Education," lecture at Harvard Business School, April 13, 1967, repr. in *Computers and Management: The Leatherbee Lectures, 1967*, by Hershner Cross et al. (Boston: Harvard University Press, 1967), 6–7.

55. George Kozmetsky, "IHAS System Application of Bulk Semiconductor Devices" (paper presented at Third Conference on the Navy Microelectronics Program, US Navy Postgraduate School, Monterey, CA, April 5–7, 1965).

56. Roberts, *Distant Force*, 47.

57. Ibid., 58.

58. "New Teledyne Plant Will Be Built in Valley," *Los Angeles Times*, March 27, 1966; William R. Fails, *Marines and Helicopters 1962–1973* (Washington, DC: History and Museums Division, US Marine Corps, 1978), 77–80, 150.

59. Fails, *Marines and Helicopters*, 77–80, 150.

60. Ibid.

61. Carl F. Mittag et al., "Evaluation of the Teledyne Ryan Model 622 Terrain-Following Radar System Installed on an OH-58A Helicopter" (report, Army Aviation Systems Test Activity, Edwards Air Force Base, CA, November 1973), 18–20.

62. Roberts, *Distant Force*, 39.

63. "Making Big Waves with Small Fish," *Businessweek*, December 30, 1967, p. 38.

64. Teledyne annual report, fiscal year 1961.

65. "Infant with a Giant Appetite," 67–68; Roberts, *Distant Force*, 24–26.

66. "18 of Top 100 Defense Contractors in 1965 Are California Firms," *Los Angeles Times*, November 30, 1965.

67. "Defense Contractors Hail Reagan Win but Can They All Share in the Spoils?," *Los Angeles Times*, November 11, 1980.

68. "Teledyne Makes Offer for Research Company," *Los Angeles Times*, October 4, 1966; "Teledyne to Acquire Alabama Firm for $9.8 Million in Stock," *Los Angeles Times*, December 30, 1966.

69. "Teledyne Inc. Seeks Vasco in $45 Million Stock Deal," *Los Angeles Times*, March 7, 1966.

70. Roberts, *Distant Force*, 74–79.

71. Roberts, *Distant Force*, 57.

72. James D. Nisbet, *The Entrepreneur* (Charlotte, NC: Capital Technology, 1976), 83.

73. "Teledyne Posts Sharp Gains in Sales, Earnings for Year," *Los Angeles Times*, November 29, 1966.

74. "Teledyne Technologies Inc. History," Funding Universe, www.fundinguniverse.com/company-histories/teledyne-technologies-inc-history/.

75. Ibid.

76. Roberts, *Distant Force*, 286–287.

77. Roberts, *Distant Force*, 85.

78. "Teledyne to Slow Pace of Acquisition Activity," *Los Angeles Times*, March 2, 1970.

79. Roberts, *Distant Force*, 244.

80. "Teledyne History," www.fundinguniverse.com/company-histories/teledyne-technologies-inc-history/.

81. "Teledyne's Singleton," Los *Angeles Times*, August 1, 1976.

82. Transcript of graduate management class, February 23, 1983, p. 5, Kozmetsky Papers, IC² Institute.

83. Transcript of graduate management class, April 9, 1986, p. 11, Kozmetsky Papers, IC² Institute.

84. Lécuyer, *Making Silicon Valley*, 167.

85. Forbes 400, *Forbes*, September 13, 1982, and October 1, 1984.

86. Forbes 400, *Forbes*, October 12, 1998.

87. Forbes 400, *Forbes*, October 28, 1985, October 27, 1986, and October 24, 1988.

88. "Henry E. Singleton, a Founder of Teledyne, Is Dead at 82," *New York Times*, September 3, 1999.

89. Christina Singleton Mednick, *San Cristóbal: Voices and Visions of the Galisteo Basin* (Santa Fe: Office of Archaeological Studies, Museum of New Mexico, 1996), 212–213.

90. "Flammable Conditions Brought Bel-Air Fire," *Los Angeles Times*, March 11, 1962; "Bel Air–Brentwood and Santa Ynez Fires: Worst Fire in the History of Los Angeles," official report of the Los Angeles Fire Department, accessed through the website of the Los Angeles Fire Department Historical Society, www.lafdmuseum.org.

91. Interview with Greg Kozmetsky, April 19, 2010.

92. Ibid.

93. Ritchey, "Brief Biography," 2:18–19.

94. Interview with Greg Kozmetsky, April 19, 2010.

95. "Distinctive Homes Selected for Tour," *Los Angeles Times*, March 28, 1968.

96. "Landscape Contractors Honor Top Achievers," *Los Angeles Times*, August 4, 1985.

97. Interview with Greg Kozmetsky, April 19, 2010.

98. "Teledyne's Takeoff," *Time*, October 6, 1967.

99. Interview with Greg Kozmetsky, April 19, 2010.

100. Ibid.

101. Email message from Wlodzimierz Szwarc to Robert A. Peterson, April 9, 2014.

102. Interview with Elaine Wiley, October 30, 2015.

103. Richard Bellman, *Eye of the Hurricane: An Autobiography* (Singapore: World Scientific, 1984), 235–236. Szwarc noted years later that Bellman's account of the evening was correct, although he observed that Bellman made several factual errors, including misspelling Szwarc's name and getting Hoover's name entirely wrong.

104. Philosophical Society of Texas, *Proceedings of the Annual Meeting at San Antonio, December 1 and 2, 1989* (Austin: Philosophical Society of Texas, 1990), 58.

105. Interview with Nadya Scott, April 28, 2015.

106. "Josephine Ver Brugge Zeitlin, 90," *Los Angeles Times*, February 26, 2005.

CHAPTER 8

1. Interview with Adm. Bobby R. Inman, November 7, 2011.

2. Roberts, *Distant Force*, 57.

3. Class transcript of Management 385, February 9, 1983, p. 2, Kozmetsky Papers, IC² Institute. Kozmetsky was actually forty-seven at that time.

4. Judson Neff, "Notes for talk with Dr. Hackerman about Dr. Kozmetsky," November 11, 1965, UT President's Office Records, box VF 36/B.b, College of Business Administration, Recruitment of Dean, 1964, Dolph Briscoe Center for American History, University of Texas at Austin. Unless otherwise noted, correspondence in this chapter related to the search for a business dean is from this file, hereafter cited as Recruitment of Dean file, Briscoe Center.

5. Lawrence Secrest, David V. Gibson, and John Sibley Butler, "George Kozmetsky," in *Profiles in Operations Research: Pioneers and Innovators*, ed. Arjang A. Assad and Saul I. Gass, 343–362 (New York: Springer, 2011).

6. "Austin Architect Brings High-Tech Tips to OC," *Orange County Business Journal*, August 25, 1997.

7. Ritchey, "Brief Biography," 2:26–27.

8. Interview with Fred Phillips, April 23, 2015.

9. Ibid.

10. Joe B. Frantz, *The Forty-Acre Follies* (Austin: Texas Monthly Press, 1983), 282.

11. Federal law in the 1970s and 1980s eliminated mandatory retirement ages across the country.

12. UT System Board of Regents, minutes for meeting of October 21–22, 1960, pp. 17–21.

13. Alan Gribben, *Harry Huntt Ransom: Intellect in Motion* (Austin: University of Texas Press, 2008), 144. Although the ten-year plan was approved by the regents on September 24, 1960, details of the plan can be found in the minutes for the regents' meeting on October 21–22, 1960, pp. 17–21.

14. There were no regular news media rankings of academic programs in those days. *Businessweek* began its annual rankings of MBA programs in 1988 and was soon joined by *U.S. News and World Report*, *Forbes*, the *Financial Times*, and the *Economist*.

15. See Recruitment of Dean file, Briscoe Center.

16. Ransom and Hackerman to Stockton et al., October 8, 1964, Recruitment of Dean file, Briscoe Center.

17. A decision to that effect is suggested by handwritten notes on a letter from Stockton to Hackerman, May 27, 1965, Recruitment of Dean file, Briscoe Center.

18. Walker to Ransom, February 17, 1965, Recruitment of Dean file, Briscoe Center. Walker returned to the Treasury Department in the Nixon administration, serving as an undersecretary and a deputy secretary.

19. Register of the Charls E. Walker Papers, Hoover Institution, Stanford University, accessible through the Online Archive of California.

20. Interview with William S. Livingston, July 7, 2011.

21. Stockton to Ransom and Hackerman, January 22, 1965, Recruitment of Dean file, Briscoe Center.

22. Ibid.

23. Stockton to Hackerman, May 27, 1965, Recruitment of Dean file, Briscoe Center.

24. Hackerman to Stockton, June 2, 1965, Recruitment of Dean file, Briscoe Center.

25. Stockton to Ransom, June 15, 1965, and Hackerman to Stockton, June 21, 1965, Recruitment of Dean file, Briscoe Center.

26. Richard L. Norgaard to Hackerman et al., July 20, 1965, Recruitment of Dean file, Briscoe Center.

27. White to Hackerman, July 23, 1965, Recruitment of Dean file, Briscoe Center.

28. Stockton to Ransom and Hackerman, July 30, 1965, Recruitment of Dean file, Briscoe Center.

29. Hackerman to Stockton, August 18, 1965, Recruitment of Dean file, Briscoe Center.

30. Stockton to Hackerman, September 13, 1965, Recruitment of Dean file, Briscoe Center.

31. Hackerman to Stockton, September 24, 1965, and Nelson to Hackerman, September 29, 1965, Recruitment of Dean file, Briscoe Center.

32. Bickley to Hackerman, October 22, 1965, Recruitment of Dean file, Briscoe Center.

33. Cox held several high administrative positions during his long career at the University of Texas, including vice chancellor of the university system, vice president of the University of Texas at Austin, and assistant to the vice chancellor for academic affairs.

34. Craig to Nelson, November 9, 1965, and note from administrative assistant Betty Gibbons to Hackerman, November 10, 1965, Recruitment of Dean file, Briscoe Center.

35. Summary of Kozmetsky's qualifications by Judson Neff, November 4, 1965, Recruitment of Dean file, Briscoe Center.

36. Smith to Ransom and Hackerman, December 10, 1965, Recruitment of Dean file, Briscoe Center.

37. Note from "sawd" to "NH," November 9, 1965, Recruitment of Dean file, Briscoe Center.

38. Hackerman would take the title of president of the University of Texas at Austin when the office was reconstituted in 1967, with Ransom continuing to serve as chancellor of the university system until 1970.

39. Berkeley hired a new dean of engineering in 1963—longtime Berkeley faculty member George J. Maslach.

40. Judson Neff, "Notes for talk with Dr. Hackerman about Dr. Kozmetsky," November 11, 1965, Recruitment of Dean file, Briscoe Center.

41. Neff to Nelson, November 12, 1965, Recruitment of Dean file, Briscoe Center.

42. Interview with William S. Livingston, July 7, 2011.

43. Note regarding Ransom's schedule, Recruitment of Dean file, Briscoe Center.

44. Nelson to Ransom and Hackerman, December 8, 1965, Recruitment of Dean file, Briscoe Center.

45. Smith to Hackerman, December 10, 1965, Recruitment of Dean file, Briscoe Center.

46. Smith served on the university accounting faculty for forty-two years and earned BBA and MBA degrees at the University of Texas and a PhD at Columbia University. He was not related to the British actor C. Aubrey Smith.

47. Neff to Hackerman and Ransom, December 9, 1965, Recruitment of Dean file, Briscoe Center. As discussed in chapter 5, Donald K. David was dean of the Harvard Business School from 1942 to 1955. Before going to Harvard, he had been president of American Maize Products Co.

48. Sommerfield to Hackerman, December 13, 1965, Recruitment of Dean file, Briscoe Center.

49. Handwritten note by Hackerman, December 14, 1965, Recruitment of Dean file, Briscoe Center.

50. Craig to Nelson, November 9, 1965; "Confidential memorandum for the files of Chancellor Ransom and Dr. Hackerman," written by Hackerman, December 13, 1965; and "Memorandum for the file," written by Hackerman, December 16, 1965, Recruitment of Dean file, Briscoe Center.

51. Notes on telephone call from Hackerman to Balderston, December 17, 1965, Recruitment of Dean file, Briscoe Center.

52. Balderston to Hackerman, January 14, 1966, Recruitment of Dean file, Briscoe Center.

53. "Note for file" from Hackerman, January 12, 1966, Recruitment of Dean file, Briscoe Center. The next year, Kozmetsky would serve on a ten-member advisory committee that recommended to Ransom and the regents that Hackerman be named president of the University of Texas at Austin. See "Hackerman named for UT Prexy," *Austin Statesman*, October 24, 1967.

54. Neff to Hackerman, December 23, 1965, Recruitment of Dean file, Briscoe Center.

55. Hackerman's efforts to economize were not successful. When the Board of Regents approved Kozmetsky's first-year salary, it was for $30,000 for serving as dean and an additional $5,000 for his appointment as an adviser to the regents on "economic affairs." See the minutes for the regents' meeting on August 27, 1966.

56. Hackerman to Ransom, January 13, 1966, Recruitment of Dean file, Briscoe Center.

57. Note to "NH" from "sawd," February 4, 1966, Recruitment of Dean file, Briscoe Center.

58. Charles T. Zlatkovich, chairman of the Department of Accounting, to Hackerman, January 27, 1966, Recruitment of Dean file, Briscoe Center.

59. Betty Gibbons to Hackerman, April 13, 1966, Recruitment of Dean file, Briscoe Center.

60. Interview with Floyd Brandt, May 19, 2010.

61. UT Austin press release, June 15, 1966; "UT Names New Dean of Business," *Austin Statesman*, June 16, 1966.

62. Minutes of the meeting of the Board of Regents, August 27, 1966, p. 95. W. W. Heath was the chairman of the board when Kozmetsky was hired. The vice chairman was Frank C. Erwin Jr. (he would be named chairman late that fall), and the other members were W. H. Bauer, Walter P. Brenan, H. F. Connally Jr., Frank N. Ikard, Ruth Carter Stevenson, Jack S. Josey, and Levi A. Olan.

63. Market value provided by the University of Texas Investment Management Company.

64. "Kozmetsky Named CBA Dean," *Daily Texan*, June 17, 1966.

65. "The Business Deans," *Daily Texan*, June 17, 1966.

66. "Executives New Big Men on Campus," *New York Times*, July 24, 1966.

67. Ibid.

68. Remembrances of Kay Charnes for George and Ronya's fiftieth wedding anniversary, 1993, Kozmetsky Papers, IC² Institute.

69. Background material for the Austin City Council on historic zoning for the McClendon-Kozmetsky house—including research by Austin historian Phoebe Allen and comments on the design by Betsy Christian—is attached to the online agenda of the meeting of the city council for November 4, 2010, http://www.ci.austin.tx.us/council_meetings/public_meeting_agenda.cfm?meetingid=236.

70. A few years later, King would become dean of the university's College of Liberal Arts and would get to know Kozmetsky much better.

71. Unless otherwise noted, the following portrait of Austin in the mid-1960s is drawn from the extensive topical files and other historical documents of the Austin History Center, a unit of the Austin Public Library.

72. UT President's Office Records, box 85-215/37, General Files, 1976–1978, UT Historical Data, Briscoe Center.

73. "Rising Enrollment Causes 'Forty Acres' Expansion," *Daily Texan*, August 1966.

74. "UT Rated among Tops in PhD Fields," *Daily Texan*, June 7, 1966.

75. Gribben, *Harry Huntt Ransom*, 80–81.

76. "Autopsy Delays Ruling in Death," *Austin American-Statesman*, November 24, 1972.

77. Carolyn Bengston Mark column, *Austin Citizen*, July 23, 1981.

78. Interview with Nadya Scott, April 28, 2015.

79. Interview with Edward A. Miller, May 5, 2017.

CHAPTER 9

1. The early history of the business program is surveyed in C. Aubrey Smith, *Fifty Years of Education for Business at the University of Texas* (Austin: College of Business Administration Foundation, University of Texas, 1962).

2. Interview with William W. Cooper, August 17, 2009.

3. *Ex-citer* (newsletter of the College of Business Administration) 6, no. 1 (Fall 1964), UT President's Office Records, box VF 36/B.b, Budget and Departmental Files, College of Business Administration, Briscoe Center.

4. Annual report to the president from the dean of the College of Business Administration for 1965–1966, UT President's Office Records, box VF 36/B.b, Briscoe Center.

5. John Arch White, "Where Are We and Where Are We Going in Education—with Special Reference to the Use of Quantitative Methods in Training for Business," UT President's Office Records, box VF 36/A.a, College of Business Administration, Dean's Office, 1960–1966, Briscoe Center.

6. Ibid.

7. Frantz, *Forty-Acre Follies*, 282.

8. Ibid, 282–283.

9. Memo from W. W. Cooper to Floyd Brandt and Gay Jentz, February 4, 1989, personal papers of William W. Cooper (provided to the author by Cooper).

10. Transcript of graduate management class, February 9, 1983, p. 1, Kozmetsky Papers, IC² Institute.

11. See, for example, "Emergence of the Corporate Conscience," *New York Times*, January 6, 1974. The *Times* first used the term "corporate social responsibility" in 1968.

12. George Kozmetsky, "Systems Analysis for Integrative Higher Education Planning," (Walker-Ames Professor Lecture, University of Washington, May 20, 1969), 1.

13. Kozmetsky, "Computers in Business and Education," 2. The federal report cited by Kozmetsky in the lecture was "Computers in Higher Education," Presidential Scientific Advisory Committee, February 1967.

14. Ibid.

15. John Kenneth Galbraith, *The New Industrial State* (Boston: Houghton Mifflin, 1967).

16. George Kozmetsky, "Education as an Information System," testimony presented to the Committee on Science and Astronautics, US House of Representatives, January 28, 1970.

17. Kozmetsky, "Systems Analysis for Integrative Higher Education Planning," 4.

18. Alvin Toffler, *Future Shock* (New York: Random House, 1970), 121. Toffler cites a *Businessweek* article about Kozmetsky ("How a Businessman Ramrods a B-School," May 24, 1969).

19. "Is your job 'routine'?," *Wall Street Journal*, April 8, 2015.

20. Kozmetsky, "Systems Analysis for Integrative Higher Education Planning," 6.

21. Ibid., 6–7.

22. George Kozmetsky, "Perspectives on Manpower Planning and Technological Change," in *Economic Growth and Planning: Regional and National Perspectives, Proceedings of Joint U.S.-Soviet Conferences*, ed. Harvey McMains and Raymond Smilor (Austin, TX: Institute for Constructive Capitalism, 1982), 275–277.

23. George Kozmetsky, "How Much Revolution Does American Business Need?" (working paper 71-13, Graduate School of Business, University of Texas at Austin, November 1970).

24. Ibid., 6.

25. Ibid., 4. *The Organization Man*, by William H. Whyte, was one of the most popular books in the years that Kozmetsky worked in the private sector. Published in 1956, it was based on interviews with the CEOs of large traditional companies, such as General Electric. The book concluded that most Americans had a strong "collectivist" attitude and found more value in belonging to large bureaucratic organizations than in "rugged individualism." For many years, "organization man" was a familiar pejorative term in critiques of business and society.

26. Unless otherwise noted, the statistics in this section are for fall semesters and are taken from the *University of Texas at Austin Statistical Handbook*, published each year when Kozmetsky was dean by the Office of Institutional Studies (now known as the Office of Institutional Reporting, Research, and Information Systems). Each handbook tracks data across several years, so it is possible to obtain most data for 1966 through 1982 by consulting only two of the handbooks, for 1975–1976 and 1982–1983. These and other handbooks are online at the IRRIS website, reports.utexas.edu, under Resources.

27. Annual Report, 1980–1981, College of Business Administration and Graduate School of Business, UT Austin, UT President Office Records, box 88-302/34, Business Administration, 1981–1982, Briscoe Center.

28. Assistant instructors are graduate students who teach classes under the supervision of a faculty member, while teaching assistants are graduate students who do not teach classes but perform adjunct duties such as leading lab or discussion sessions.

29. Transcript of graduate management class, January 22, 1986, pp. 27–28, Kozmetsky Papers, IC[2] Institute.

30. Report to the College of Business Administration Advisory Council, October 17, 1969, UT President's Office Records, box AR 80-50/10, College of Business Administration, Office of the Dean, 1969–1970, Briscoe Center.

31. Rebecca Zames Margulies and Peter M. Blau, "The Pecking Order of the Elite: America's Leading Professional Schools," *Change* 5, no. 9 (November 1973): 21–27.

32. William R. Henry and E. Earl Bunch, "Institutional Contributions to Scholarly Journals of Business," *Journal of Business* 47, no. 1 (January 1974): 56–66.

33. Annual Report, 1976–1977, College of Business Administration and Graduate School of Business, UT Austin, p. 7.

34. Charles G. Carpenter, D. Larry Crumbley, and Robert H. Stawser, "A New Ranking of Accounting Faculties and Doctoral Programs," *Journal of Accountancy* 137, no. 6 (June 1974): 90–94.

35. "The Well-Known Universities Lead in Ratings of Faculties' Reputation," *Chronicle of Higher Education*, January 15, 1979.

36. "The Chief Executive, Background and Attitudes Profiles," Arthur Young & Company, January 1980.

37. J. David Hunger and Thomas L. Wheelen, "A Performance Appraisal of Undergraduate Business Education," *Human Resource Management* 19, no. 1 (Spring 1980): 24–31.

38. "Business College Ranks Fifth Nationwide," *Daily Texan*, June 30, 1980.

39. George Kozmetsky. "The Time for Greatness," remarks to the Century Club, November 3, 1979, Kozmetsky Papers, IC[2] Institute.

40. Annual Report, 1980–1981, College of Business Administration and Graduate School of Business, UT Austin, p. 4.

Chapter 10

1. Kozmetsky to Ransom and Hackerman, September 20, 1967, UT President's Office Records, box VF 36/B.b, College of Business Administration, Dean's Office, 1966–1968, Briscoe Center.

2. UT President's Office Records, box AR 80-50/28, Development of the University, General 1966–1968, Briscoe Center. The university also had a varying number of Ashbel Smith Professorships (ten in 1967), which were funded through the Permanent University Fund.

3. In 2015, this professorship was upgraded to the King Ranch Chair for Business Leadership through additional gifts from the Kleberg family and its King Ranch Family Trust.

4. "Aerospace Scientist Joins UT," *Austin Statesman*, December 17, 1966; development newsletter, January 1967, UT President's Office Records, box AR 80-50/28, Development of the University—General, 1966–1968; "In Memorium Eugene B. Konecci," UT Austin Office of the General Faculty, http://facultycouncil.utexas.edu/memorials.

5. The arrival of both Konecci and Shapero during Kozmetsky's first semester as dean suggests that he began recruiting them as soon as he accepted the deanship the previous June.

6. "UT Adds Stanford Researcher," *Austin Statesman*, January 9, 1967.

7. Annual Report, 1966–1967, College of Business Administration, UT President's Office Records, box VF 36/B.b, College of Business Administration, Dean's Office, 1966–1968, Briscoe Center; biographical note, *Academy of Management Review* 10, no. 3 (July 1985): 653.

8. Development newsletter, July 1967, box AR 80-50/28, Development of the University—General, 1966–1968; and box AR 80-50/72, Graduate School of Business Administration, 1970–1971, UT President's Office Records, Briscoe Center.

9. "Flying Professor Travels from LA," *Daily Texan*, October 12, 1967.

10. Ibid.

11. "Professor Emeritus David L. Huff Leaves Lasting Legacy," Department of Geography and the Environment, September 10, 2014, liberalarts.utexas.edu/geography/news/article.php?id=8323.

12. David L. Huff, "Parameter Estimation in the Huff Model," *ArcUser*, October–December 2003, www.esri.com/news/arcuser/1003/files/huff.pdf.

13. "In Memoriam Abraham Charnes," http://facultycouncil.utexas.edu/memorials.

14. "Deep in the Heart of Texas," *New York Times*, April 25, 1971.

15. Kozmetsky, "A Dean's Perspective on Abraham Charnes," 7.

16. Ibid.

17. "In Memoriam Charles C. Holt," UT Austin Office of the General Faculty and Faculty Council, http://facultycouncil.utexas.edu/memorials.

18. Email message from Leon Lasdon, September 15, 2015.

19. Annual Report, 1969–1970, College of Business Administration and Graduate School of Business, UT Austin; "UT Management Faculty Adds Six," *Austin Statesman*, October 23, 1968.

20. Email message from Stephen Magee, September 9, 2015.

21. Ibid.

22. "In Memoriam, Vijay Singh Bawa," memorial resolution of the UT Austin Faculty Council, http://facultycouncil.utexas.edu/memorials.

23. Email message from Stephen Magee, September 9, 2015.

24. "Professor William W. Cooper, Pioneer in Operations Research, Dies at 97," McCombs

Today, McCombs School of Business, UT Austin, www.today.mccombs.utexas.edu/2012/06/professor-william-w-cooper-pioneer-in-operations-research-dies-at-97.

25. Interview with William W. Cooper, January 11, 2010.

26. Interview with Isabella Cunningham, December 17, 2013.

27. Sten Thore and Ruzanna Tarverdyan, *Diagnostics for a Globalized World* (Hackensack, NJ: World Scientific, 2015), 191.

28. Kozmetsky to Peter Flawn, April 14, 1980, UT President's Office Records, box 86-209/47, College of Business Administration, 1979–1960, Briscoe Center.

29. Gerhard J. Fonken to Peter T. Flawn, May 12, 1982, UT President's Office Records, box 88-302/34, College of Business Administration, 1981–1982, Briscoe Center.

30. Email from Stephen Magee, October 2, 2015.

31. Transcript of graduate management class, March 12, 1986, p. 8, Kozmetsky Papers, IC^2 Institute.

32. Annual Report, 1967–1968, College of Business Administration and Graduate School of Business, UT Austin, p. 28; "In Memorium, Timothy W. Ruefli," Office of the General Faculty and Faculty Council, UT Austin.

33. Interview with Reuben R. McDaniel Jr., October 18, 2011.

34. William H. Cunningham, with Monty Jones, *The Texas Way: Money, Power, Politics, and Ambition at the University* (Austin: Briscoe Center for American History, University of Texas at Austin, 2013), 15.

35. "Darwin Klingman, 45, Computer Authority," *New York Times*, October 28, 1989; "In Memoriam, Darwin D. Klingman," memorial resolution of the UT Austin Faculty Council, http://facultycouncil.utexas.edu/memorials.

36. Letter from Klingman to Kozmetsky, November 3, 1980, UT President's Office Records, box 86-247/25, Robert D. Mettlen files, Business Administration, 1980–1981, Briscoe Center.

37. Mettlen to Flawn, November 7, 1980, UT President's Office Records, box 86-247/25, Robert D. Mettlen files, Business Administration, 1980–1981, Briscoe Center.

38. Letter from Kozmetsky to Klingman, November 20, 1980, UT President's Office Records, box 87-188/5, College of Business Administration, Dean, 1980–1981, Briscoe Center.

39. Letter from Kozmetsky to Flawn, January 20, 1982, UT President's Office Records, box 88-302/34, College of Business Administration, Dean, 1981–1982, Briscoe Center.

40. Annual Report, 1966–1967, College of Business Administration and Graduate School of Business, UT Austin, p. 31.

41. Ibid., 32. For the architecture project, see *Generalized University Model* (Austin: University of Texas School of Architecture, 1968–1969).

42. Charnes to Hackerman, November 5, 1969, and Gardner Lindzey to Charnes, November 13, 1969, UT President's Office Records, box AR 80-50/72, College of Business Administration, 1970–1972, Briscoe Center.

43. Annual Report, 1967–1968, College of Business Administration and Graduate School of Business, UT Austin, p. 35.

44. Annual Report, 1967–1968, College of Business Administration and Graduate School of Business, UT Austin, p. 36.

45. "Mutual Fund Eyed by UT Computer," *Austin Statesman*, February 18, 1969.

46. Bernard H. Sord, "A Merger and Acquisition Simulation," *Developments in Business Simulation and Experiential Learning* 9 (1982).

47. Annual Reports, 1968–1969 through 1974–1975, College of Business Administration and Graduate School of Business, UT Austin; and interview with Floyd S. Brandt, May 19, 2010.

48. Robert A. Peterson, George Kozmetsky, and Isabella C. M. Cunningham, "Perceptions of Media Bias toward Business," *Journalism Quarterly* 59, no. 3 (Autumn 1982): 461–464.

49. Robert A. Peterson, Gerald Albaum, George Kozmetsky, and Isabella C. M. Cunningham, "Attitudes of Newspaper Business Editors and General Public toward Capitalism," *Journalism Quarterly* 61, no. 1 (Spring 1984): 56–65.

50. Robert A. Peterson, George Kozmetsky, and Gerald Albaum, "On the Public's Perception of Capitalism," *Business Horizons* 29, no. 1 (January–February 1986): 10–14.

51. "Capitalism May Be a Dirty Word, but Free Enterprise Is Fine," *Orlando Sentinel*, May 15, 1988.

52. Robert A. Peterson, Gerald Albaum, and George Kozmetsky, *Modern American Capitalism: Understanding Public Attitudes and Perceptions* (Santa Barbara, CA: Praeger, 1990).

53. George Kozmetsky and Isabella C. M. Cunningham, eds., *Funds Management and Managerial Research: A Book of Readings* (Austin: University of Texas Graduate School of Business, 1979).

54. Interview with Isabella Cunningham, December 17, 2013.

CHAPTER 11

1. Cunningham, *The Texas Way*, 37.

2. Development newsletter, January 1967, UT President's Office Records, box AR 80-50/28, Development of the University, General, 1966–1968, Briscoe Center.

3. Development newsletter, fall 1968, UT President's Office Records, box AR 80-50/28, Development of the University, General, 1966–1968, Briscoe Center.

4. College of Business Administration Annual Report 1965–1966, UT President's Office Records, box VF 36/A.a, Office of the Dean, College of Business Administration, 1964–1966, Briscoe Center.

5. C. C. Nolen to Norman Hackerman, December 21, 1967, UT President's Office Records, box AR 80-50/28, Development of the University, General, 1966–1968, Briscoe Center.

6. Kozmetsky to Spurr, September 19, 1974, UT President's Office Records, box AR 84-171/2, Dean of Business Administration, 1974–1975, Briscoe Center.

7. "Thomas A. Loomis Endowed Presidential Scholarship," UT Austin Development Office, http://endowments.giving.utexas.edu/page/loomis-thomas-eps/2174/.

8. "Kozmetsky Shakes Dust off BBAs," *Kilgore News Herald*, October 9, 1977.

9. E. D. Walker to James A. Reichert, UT President's Office Records, box 88-308/39, Institute for Constructive Capitalism, 1981–1982, Briscoe Center.

10. Cunningham, *The Texas Way*, 36–37.

11. During the centennial campaign, the minimum in donations for establishing an endowed position was $500,000 for a chair, $100,000 for a professorship, and $50,000 for a fellowship. The matching funds could be added to these positions or used to support other ones.

12. Minutes of business school faculty meeting, November 14, 1980, UT President's Office Records, box 87-188/5, College of Business Administration, 1980–1981, Briscoe Center.

13. Fundraising brochure, UT President's Office Records, box 87-188/5, College of Business Administration, 1980–1981, Briscoe Center.

14. "Progress Report—Centennial Endowment Program," January 20, 1982, UT President's Office Records, box 88-302/34, College of Business Administration, 1981–1982, Briscoe Center.

15. "Moore, Fred Holmsley," Handbook of Texas Online, https://www.tshaonline.org/handbook/online/articles/fmo85.

16. Correspondence of the Committee to Establish the George Kozmetsky Centennial Chair, Jack and Bonita Granville Wrather Papers, series 2, subseries A, box 1, folder 6–8, CSLA-23, Department of Archives and Special Collections, William. H. Hannon Library, Loyola Marymount University (hereafter Wrather Papers, Loyola Marymount University).

17. Bonita Granville Wrather to Henry Singleton, April 25, 1980, Wrather Papers, Loyola Marymount University.

18. Singleton to Bonita Granville Wrather, May 7, 1980, Wrather Papers, Loyola Marymount University.

19. Jack Wrather to Singleton, May 13, 1980, Wrather Papers, Loyola Marymount University.

20. Bonita Wrather to Sam Barshop, May 27, 1980, Wrather Papers, Loyola Marymount University.

21. Henry Singleton to Jack Wrather, May 28, 1980, Wrather Papers, Loyola Marymount University.

22. "The Forbes Four Hundred," *Forbes*, September 13, 1982.

23. UT System Board of Regents, minutes for the meeting of February 2, 1977.

24. Interview with William H. Cunningham, September 3, 2015.

25. Kozmetsky to Charles LeMaistre, November 14, 1977, and Kozmetsky to E. Don Walker, December 23, 1978, UT President's Office Records, box AR 85-215/8, Institute for Constructive Capitalism, 1976–1977, Briscoe Center.

26. Annual Report, 1966–1967, College of Business Administration and Graduate School of Business, UT Austin, p. 36.

27. Annual Report, 1967–1968, College of Business Administration and Graduate School of Business, UT Austin, p. 41.

28. Annual Report, 1968–1969, College of Business Administration and Graduate School of Business, UT Austin, pp. 30–31.

29. Annual Report, 1973–1974, College of Business Administration and Graduate School of Business, UT Austin, pp. 111–117.

30. Annual Report, 1967–1968, College of Business Administration and Graduate School of Business, UT Austin, p. 41.

31. Annual Report, 1972–1973, College of Business Administration and Graduate School of Business, UT Austin, p. 12, and interview with Steve Ballantyne, April 10, 2014.

32. Ibid., 14.

33. These statistics are drawn from the annual reports of the business school.

34. Carter A. Daniel, *MBA: The First Century* (Lewisburg, PA: Bucknell University Press, 1998), 208–209.

35. Fonken to Kozmetsky, March 17, 1981, UT President's Office Records, box 86-247/25, Robert D., Mettlen files, Business Administration, 1980–1981, Briscoe Center.

36. Faculty meeting minutes, April 17, 1981, UT President's Office Records, box 87-188/5, College of Business Administration, 1980–1981, Briscoe Center.

37. "Secretaries to Attend UT Course," *Austin Statesman*, January 21, 1968.

38. Annual Report, 1971–1972, College of Business Administration and Graduate School of Business, UT Austin, p. 35.

39. Transcript of graduate management class, February 15, 1986, p. 14, Kozmetsky Papers, IC² Institute.

40. American Assembly of Collegiate Schools of Business fact form, UT President's Office Records, box 87-188/5, College of Business Administration, 1980–1981, Briscoe Center.

41. Semester credit hours and student-teacher ratio are from the minutes of a business school faculty meeting, April 7, 1981, UT President's Office Records, box 87-188/5, College of Business Administration, 1980–1981, Briscoe Center.

42. George Kozmetsky, "The Time for Greatness" remarks to the Century Club, November 3, 1979, Kozmetsky Papers, IC² Institute.

43. Daniel, *MBA: The First Century*, 196–198.

44. Annual Report, 1972–1973, College of Business Administration and Graduate School of Business, p. 2.

45. "Report of the Committee of 75," University of Texas, December 6, 1958, Briscoe Center.

46. "Report of the UT Austin Centennial Commission," University of Texas, September 15, 1983, Briscoe Center.

47. Minutes of meetings of the UT System Board of Regents, December 4, 1970, and December 3, 1971.

48. Cunningham, *The Texas Way*, 24–25.

49. University of Texas at Austin Statistical Handbook, 1975–1976.

50. "Enrollment Control Proposals, College of Business Administration," January 30, 1976, UT President's Office Records, box AR 84-184/22, Briscoe Center.

51. Kozmetsky to Rogers, February 20, 1976, and Rogers to Kozmetsky, May 11, 1976, UT President's Office Records, box AR 84-184/22, Briscoe Center.

52. Kozmetsky to Rogers, March 22, 1977; Gerhard Fonken to Rogers, June 14, 1977; and Rogers to William L. Hays, June 14, 1977, UT President's Office Records, box AR 85-215/3, Briscoe Center.

53. Fonken to Rogers, August 1, 1979, UT President's Office Records, box 88-302/14, Enrollment, 1980–1982, Briscoe Center.

54. Hays to Rogers, February 13, 1979; and William F. Lasher to Flawn, September 30, 1980, UT President's Office Records, box 88-302/14, Enrollment, 1980–1982, Briscoe Center.

55. Kozmetsky to Flawn, March 17, 1981, UT President's Office Records, box 88-302/14, Enrollment, 1980–1982, Briscoe Center.

56. Flawn to Kozmetsky, March 31, 1981, UT President's Office Records, box 88-302/14, Enrollment, 1980–1982, Briscoe Center.

57. Cunningham, *The Texas Way*, 17.

58. The colleges and schools at the university were reorganized several times after 1970, when the old College of Arts and Sciences was broken up.

59. Silber, who later served as president and chancellor of Boston University for thirty-two years, was famously fired in 1970 by Frank Erwin, chairman of the University of Texas System Board of Regents.

60. Interview with Robert D. King, September 27, 2011.

61. Ibid.

62. Cunningham, *The Texas Way*, 18–20.

63. University of Texas at Austin Statistical Handbook, 2015–2016.

CHAPTER 12

1. Kozmetsky to Hackerman, September 21, 1967, UT President's Office Records, box VF 36/B.b, Business Administration, 1966–1968, Office of the Dean, Briscoe Center.

2. Ibid.

3. Memo from Hackerman to Kozmetsky, October 3, 1967, UT President's Office Records, box VF 36/B.b, Business Administration, 1966–1968, Office of the Dean, Briscoe Center.

4. Annual Report, 1972–1973, College of Business Administration and Graduate School of Business, UT Austin, pp. 28–29.

5. Transcript of graduate management class, February 15, 1986, p. 17, Kozmetsky Papers, IC² Institute.

6. Kozmetsky to Spurr, November 8, 1973, UT President's Office Records, box 81-185/11, Business Administration, 1972–1973, Briscoe Center.

7. Ross to Spurr, November 12, 1973, UT President's Office Records, box 81-185/11, Business Administration, 1972–1973, Briscoe Center.

8. Interview with Robert D. King, October 11, 2011.

9. Spurr to Kozmetsky, June 4, 1973, UT President's Office Records, box 81-185/11, Business Administration, 1972–1973, Briscoe Center.

10. Interview with Peter T. Flawn, October 20, 2011.

11. The title of the chief academic officer under the UT Austin president varied through the years.

12. Hays to Kozmetsky, January 24, 1979, and Kozmetsky to Hays, January 30, 1979, UT President's Office Records, box 86-209/34, Business Administration, 1978–1979, Briscoe Center.

13. Interviews with Robert D. King, October 11, 2011, and Ernest Gloyna, October 17, 2011.

14. Kozmetsky to Fonken, September 17, 1979, UT President's Office Records, box 56-209/47, Business Administration, 1979–1980, Briscoe Center.

15. Kozmetsky to Flawn, December 19, 1979, UT President's Office Records, box 56-209/47, Business Administration, 1979–1980, Briscoe Center.

16. Kozmetsky to Flawn, April 14, 1980, UT President's Office Records, box 56-209/47, Business Administration, 1979–1980, Briscoe Center.

17. Fonken to Kozmetsky, December 17, 1980, UT President's Office Records, box 56-209/47, Business Administration, 1979–1980, Briscoe Center.

18. Lieb to Rogers, March 3, 1977, UT President's Office Records, box 85-215/13, Business Administration, 1976–1977, Briscoe Center.

19. Kozmetsky to Hays, February 22, 1977, and March 10, 1977, UT President's Office Records, box 85-215/13, Business Administration, 1976–1977, Briscoe Center.

20. Hays to Rogers, March 18, 1977, UT President's Office Records, box 85-215/13, Business Administration, 1976–1977, Briscoe Center.

21. Hays to Kozmetsky, March 18, 1977, UT President's Office Records, box 85-215/13, Business Administration, 1976–1977, Briscoe Center.

22. William V. Muse, Texas A&M vice chancellor and dean of business, to Klingman, February 9, 1982, UT President's Office Records, box 88-302/34, Business Administration, 1981–1982, Briscoe Center.

23. Kozmetsky to Klingman, February 22, 1982, and Klingman to Flawn et al., March 1, 1982, UT President's Office Records, box 88-302/34, Business Administration, 1981–1982, Briscoe Center.

24. Interview with Isabella Cunningham, December 17, 2013.

25. William R. Muehlberger to Hackerman, February 1, 1968, UT President's Office Records, box VF 37/C.a, Graduate School, 1965–1968, Briscoe Center.

26. Ransom to Maguire, August 14, 1968, UT President's Office Records, box AR 80-50/35, Student Activities, 1966–1968, Briscoe Center.

27. Schwartz to Hackerman, January 16, 1970, UT President's Office Records, box AR 80-50/10, College of Business Administration, Office of Dean, 1969–1970, Briscoe Center.

28. Rogers to Kozmetsky, June 22, 1976, UT President's Office Records, box AR 84-184/72, College of Business Administration, Office of Dean, 1975–1976, Briscoe Center.

29. Kozmetsky to Rogers, December 15, 1975, and Rogers to Kozmetsky, December 29, 1975, UT President's Office Records, box AR 85-215/16, College of Business Administration, Office of Dean, 1975–1976, Briscoe Center.

30. Rogers to Kozmetsky, November 4, 1977, UT President's Office Records, box AR 86-209/4, College of Business Administration, Office of Dean, 1977–1978, Briscoe Center.

31. Rogers to Shivers, September 8, 1977, UT President's Office Records, box AR 86-209/4, Business Administration, 1977–1978, Briscoe Center.

32. Warren Gould to Rogers, October 19, 1977, and Rogers to Shivers, September 8, 1977,

UT President's Office Records, box AR 86-209/4, Business Administration, 1977–1978, Briscoe Center.

33. John C. Holton to Rogers, October 31, 1977, and Gould to Rogers, October 14, 1977, UT President's Office Records, box AR 86-209/4, Business Administration, 1977–1978, Briscoe Center.

34. "Rogers, Regents Row over Business Fund," *Daily Texan*, November 15, 1977; minutes of the meeting of the UT System Board of Regents, November 11, 1977; UT Austin press release, November 11, 1977, UT President's Office Records, box AR 86-209/4, Business Administration, 1977–1978, Briscoe Center.

35. Interview with Robert D. King, September 27, 2011.

36. "Foundation's College or Home Rule?," *Daily Texan*, November 16, 1977.

37. "Letters Named Prof, Deans Prexy Choices," *Austin Statesman*, July 29, 1970.

38. "Graduate School Enrollment Figures Increase for Women," *Dallas Morning News*, December 19, 1974.

39. Report by Kozmetsky to the College of Business Administration Advisory Council, October 17, 1969, UT President's Office Records, box AR 80-50/10, Office of the Dean, Business Administration, 1969–1970, Briscoe Center.

40. UT Austin press release, January 13, 1972; and "In Memorium, Elizabeth Lanham," http://facultycouncil.utexas.edu/memorials.

41. UT Austin press release, December 4, 1973.

42. "10 Tips for Executive Wives," *Alcalde*, February 1971.

43. "Executive Families—Communication, Humor Strongest Glue," *Austin American-Statesman*, October 27, 1981; Carolyn Mark column, *Austin Citizen*, July 23, 1981.

44. UT Office of Public Affairs Records, box 4Ab87, Ronya Kozmetsky biography file, Briscoe Center; Lee Kelly column, *Austin American-Statesman*, November 4, 1982.

45. Minutes of the meeting of the dean's council, August 15, 1967, UT President's Office Records, box AR 80-50/26, Dean's Council, 1966–1968, Briscoe Center.

46. UT Austin press release, August 5, 1969.

47. UT Austin press releases, December 17, 1970, and November 20, 1972; "Focusing on the Real World," *Texas Business*, September 1977.

48. "Focusing on the Real World," *Texas Business*, September 1977.

49. UT Austin press release, March 1, 1978.

50. UT Austin press release, February 9, 1979.

51. UT President's Office Records, box 87-188/5, College of Business Administration, 1980–1981, Dean, Briscoe Center.

52. 480 F.2nd 1159 (D.C. Cir. 1973). Adams v. Richardson was dismissed by a federal judge in 1987 for a variety of reasons, and efforts to diversify UT Austin and other universities moved on to new phases.

53. "Resolution of the Board of Regents of the University of Texas System Regarding Equal Educational Opportunity," December 12, 1980. Minutes of Meeting No. 772, UT System Board of Regents, pp. 111–112.

54. "Regents Approve Plans, Memorials," *Austin Statesman*, September 11, 1972.

55. A miscalculation was discovered during construction, as part of the third floor of the new building was a little higher than the third floor of the old building. See "Mistake Found in New School," *Daily Texan*, February 15, 1974.

56. "Old Law Building (Pearce Hall)," UT School of Law: Buildings in Photographs, Tarlton Law Library, tarlton.law.utexas.edu/exhibits/buildings/index.html.

57. UT press release, January 29, 1971.

58. Annual Report, 1975–1976, College of Business Administration and Graduate School of Business, p. 110.

59. Dedication program, included in Annual Report, 1975–1976, College of Business Administration and Graduate School of Business, UT Austin.

60. Annual Report, 1975–1976, College of Business Administration and Graduate School of Business, UT Austin, pp. 20–23.

61. "Committee Suggests Cuts in Business Enrollment," *Daily Texan*, November 2, 1976.

62. Kozmetsky to Flawn, September 12, 1981, and Flawn to Kozmetsky, October 21, 1981, UT President's Office Records, box 88-302/34, College of Business Administration, 1981–1982, Dean, Briscoe Center.

63. UT System press release, August 13, 1982.

64. Smith to Hackerman, February 19, 1967, UT President's Office Records, box VF 36/B.b, College of Business Administration, 1966–1968, Office of Dean, Briscoe Center.

65. Interview with Reuben R. McDaniel Jr., October 18, 2011.

66. Daniel, *MBA: The First Century*, 209–211.

67. Rogers to John S. Bickley, a professor at the University of Alabama, February 7, 1977, UT President's Office Records, box 85-215/3, College of Business Administration, 1976–1977, Office of the Dean, Briscoe Center.

68. Interview with Robert G. May, April 18, 2011; Cunningham, *The Texas Way*, 31–32.

69. William S. Livingston to Flawn, June 29, 1982, UT President's Office Records, box 88-302/34, College of Business Administration, 1981–1982, Accounting, Briscoe Center.

70. Daniel, *MBA: The First Century*, 209.

71. Interview with Robert D. King, October 11, 2011.

72. Arbingast to Bryce Jordan, May 10, 1971, UT President's Office Records, box AR 80-50/10, College of Business Administration, 1970–1971, Evaluation of Dean, Briscoe Center.

73. Report on the Evaluation of Dean George Kozmetsky, May 16, 1977, UT President's Office Records, box AR 85-215/3, College of Business Administration, 1976–1977, Office of Dean, Briscoe Center.

74. Interview with Robert D. King, October 10, 2011.

75. Report on the Evaluation of Dean George Kozmetsky, May 16, 1977, UT President's Office Records, box AR 85-215/3, College of Business Administration, 1976–1977, Office of Dean, Briscoe Center.

76. Ibid.

77. Ibid.

78. Interview with Reuben R. McDaniel Jr., October 18, 2011.

79. Interview with Peter T. Flawn, October 20, 2011.

CHAPTER 13

1. Interview with Robert D. King, September 27, 2011.

2. The Wrathers had many other connections with Kozmetsky. Jack Wrather was named a Distinguished Alumnus of UT Austin in 1975. Bonita Granville Wrather was elected to the advisory council of the Business School Foundation in 1978. Kozmetsky served for a while on the board of the Wrather Corp., and the Wrathers' son, Chris, was recruited by Kozmetsky to come to the university as a student and served as one of his research assistants. The Kozmetsky family donated money in 1983 to establish two centennial fellowships named for Jack and Bonita Wrather to benefit the IC² Institute.

3. UT System Board of Regents minutes, September 13, 1967, and December 12, 1969.

4. UT System Board of Regents minutes, April 19, 1969.

5. UT System press release, February 19, 1970.

6. Interview with Charles A. LeMaistre, June 17, 2013.

7. Annual Report, 1966–1967, College of Business Administration and Graduate School of Business, UT Austin, p. 32.

8. *Ex-citer* newsletter, College of Business Administration, Fall 1968, UT President's Office Records, box VF 36/B.b, Business Administration, 1966–1968, Briscoe Center.

9. Commission on Marine Science, Engineering, and Resources, "Keys to Ocean Development," panel reports by the commission (Washington, DC: US Government Printing Office, 1969); William J. Merrell, Mary Hope Katsouros, and Jacqueline Bienski, "The Stratton Commission: The Model for a Sea Change in National Marine Policy," *Oceanography* 14, no. 2 (2001): 11–16.

10. George Kozmetsky, "The Eighties: A Decade of Challenge and Achievement" (UT System Board of Regents, General Reports, August 31, 1979), Office of the UT System Board of Regents.

11. Ibid.

12. Memo from George Kozmetsky to Dan C. Williams and E. D. Walker, dated October 9, 1979, but stamped "Received" by the Office of the Board of Regents on October 12, 1981, UT System Board of Regents, General Correspondence, Office of the UT System Board of Regents.

13. "Board of Regents Hires CEO for University Lands Office," UT System press release, February 10, 2015.

14. UT System Board of Regents minutes, December 2–3, 1982, pp. 85–88.

15. UT System Board of Regents minutes, September 14, 1988.

16. "Constitutional Amendment Top Vote-Getter in Texas," Associated Press, November 10, 1988.

17. UT System Board of Regents minutes, June 14, 1990, pp. 174–175.

18. UT System Board of Regents minutes, December 6, 1990, p. 79.

19. Interview with Michael E. Patrick, June 4, 2012.

20. Interview with Austin M. Long III, May 20, 2012.

21. UT System Board of Regents minutes, October 12, 1990.

22. See, for example, Kozmetsky's testimony to the US House Committee on Science and Technology on November 15, 1983, and June 10, 1985, and to the US Senate Committee on Commerce, Science, and Transportation on January 1, 1987.

23. "UT Heralds New Era with Supercomputer," *Austin American-Statesman*, April 4, 1986.

24. Letter from Stanley R. Ross to Stephen H. Spurr, January 29, 1974, UT President's Office Records, box 81-185/11, Business Administration, 1973–1974, Briscoe Center.

25. "The Implications of Nuclear Power in Texas," conference proceedings, University of Texas at Austin, March 1–2, 1973, Kozmetsky Papers, IC² Institute.

26. UT System Board of Regents, minutes for the meeting of October 11–12, 1984.

27. Interview with Jay Stein, November 29, 2011.

28. UT System Board of Regents agenda, May 12, 2016.

29. "Reaping the Rewards of Determination," *Dallas Morning News*, March 1, 1998.

30. Transcript of graduate management class, February 15, 1986, p. 5, Kozmetsky Papers, IC² Institute.

31. Ibid.

32. Interview with Delbert Tesar, September 30, 2013.

33. *Midland Reporter-Telegram*, August 25, 2003.

34. "Cross Border Institute for Regional Development Launched," UT Austin press release, April 7, 1999, https://news.utexas.edu/1999/04/07/cross-border-institute-for-regional-development-launched.

35. Ibid.

36. Comments at IC² Institute fellows meeting, April 28, 2017.

37. "Research Center Will Tackle Issues in Border Region," *Houston Chronicle*, December 14, 1999.

38. Interview with Steven Hartman, former director of University Lands, June 10, 2014.

CHAPTER 14

1. UT press release, August 16, 1968; email message from the Adlai Stevenson Institute, February 8, 2012; UT press release, December 12, 1971; UT press release, December 31, 1976.

2. The work of the 1966 task force and the issues raised in public debate over the proposed data center are discussed in detail in "Privacy and Efficient Government: Proposals for a National Data Center," an unsigned note in *Harvard Law Review* 82, no. 2 (December 1968): 410–417.

3. "IC²'s Four Program Areas of Research," *Texas Business*, April 1982, p. 117.

4. *Hearings on the Computer and Invasion of Privacy, Before the House Committee on Government Operations, Special Subcommittee on Invasion of Privacy*, 89th Congress, 2nd session, July 26, 1966, pp. 11–13; "Center for Data on Everybody Recommended," *Washington Post*, July 13, 1966.

5. "Report of the Task Force on the Storage of and Access to Government Statistics" (Executive Office of the President, Bureau of the Budget, October 1966). The report is reproduced on pp. 25–37 of *Hearings on Computer Privacy, Senate Committee on the Judiciary, Subcommittee on Administrative Practice and Procedure*, 90th Congress, 1st session, March 14–15, 1967.

6. Ibid.

7. Ibid.

8. Annual Report, 1974–1975, College of Business Administration and Graduate School of Business, UT Austin. The final report of phase two was copublished with the business school's Graduate Management Research Center. See FEA/NSF Incentives Preference Project, *Spurring Synthetic Fuel Production* (Arlington, VA; Austin, TX: Don Sowle Associates; University of Texas Graduate School of Business, 1975).

9. FEA/NSF Incentives Preference Project, *Spurring Synthetic Fuel Production*, 55–59.

10. "Preliminary Assessment of the President's National Energy Plan," University of Texas at Austin, May 11, 1977.

11. See *Hearings on National Energy Act, House Committee on Interstate and Foreign Commerce, Subcommittee on Energy and Power*, 95th Congress, 1st session, May 13, 1977; *Hearings on Natural Gas Pricing Proposals of President Carter's Energy Program, Senate Committee on Energy and Natural Resources*, 95th Congress, 1st session, June 13, 1977.

12. "IC²," *Texas Observer*, August 12, 1987.

13. "Preliminary Assessment of the President's National Energy Plan"; and "Carter Proposal Shredded by UT Experts on Energy," *Austin American-Statesman*, May 15, 1977.

14. "Preliminary Assessment of the President's National Energy Plan."

15. Garland Anderson Jr., Thomas E. Burke, and Sam P. Drago, "Architectural Design Criteria for Multi-Media Educational Space," in University of Texas School of Architecture, *Generalized University Model*, vol. 3 of 7 (Austin: University of Texas, 1968).

16. Brochure to support fundraising for the Roland G. Roessner Centennial Professorship. Architecture Archive, SOADV box 12, UT School of Architecture, Alexander Architectural Archives.

17. Interview with William H. Cunningham, August 25, 2011.

18. Conference Board, *Information Technology: Some Critical Implications for Decision Makers* (New York: Conference Board, 1972).

19. George Kozmetsky and Timothy W. Ruefli, *Information Technology: Initiatives for Today—Decisions that Cannot Wait*, Conference Board report no. 577 (New York: Conference Board, 1972).

20. George Kozmetsky and Timothy W. Ruefli, *Information Technology and Its Impacts* (Austin: Graduate School of Business, University of Texas at Austin, 1971).

21. Kozmetsky and Ruefli, *Information Technology: Initiatives for Today*, 3–4.

22. Ibid., 20–23.

23. George Kozmetsky, "Technological Transfer," in *A Look at Business in 1990: A Summary of the White House Conference on the Industrial World Ahead* (Washington, DC: US Government Printing Office, 1972), 172–176.

24. Robert Lee Chartrand, ed., *Critical Issues in the Information Age* (Metuchen, NJ: Scarecrow Press, 1991), 76–77.

25. Conference Board, *Information Technology: Some Critical Implications for Decision Makers*; and George Kozmetsky and Timothy W. Ruefli, "Newer Concepts of Management, Profits, and Profitability: Summaries and New Directions" (Working Paper 74-1, Graduate School of Business, University of Texas at Austin, October 1973).

26. Kozmetsky and Ruefli, "Newer Concepts of Management, Profits, and Profitability," 13.

27. Ibid., 14–15.

28. Transcript of graduate management class, February 9, 1983, p. 1, Kozmetsky Papers, IC² Institute.

29. US National Commission on Supplies and Shortages, *Government and the Nation's Resources* (Washington, DC: US Government Printing Office, 1976).

30. Robert J. Samuelson, "Coping with Shortage," *National Journal*, January 29, 1977.

31. The American Electronics Association merged in 2008 with the Information Technology Association of America to form a new trade group called TechAmerica.

32. *International Competitiveness in Electronics* (Washington, DC: US Congress, Office of Technology Assessment, OTA-ISC-200, November 1983), 5–11.

33. "U.S. Firms Lose Export Share in Electronics," *Journal of Commerce*, August 19, 1987.

34. "American Electronics Association Statement on Competitiveness Crisis in U.S. Electronics Industry," US Newswire, April 3, 1989; "The Setback for Advanced TV," *New York Times*, September 30, 1989.

35. "Report Warns of Decline of U.S. Electronics Industry," *New York Times*, June 9, 1990.

36. George Kozmetsky and Piyu Yue, *Global Economic Competition: Today's Warfare in Global Electronics Industries and Companies* (Boston: Kluwer Academic, 1997).

37. Ibid., 398.

38. Simon Ramo, *The Business of Science: Winning and Losing in the High-Tech Age* (New York: Hill and Wang, 1988), 220–222.

39. *The Defense Technology Base: Introduction and Overview—A Special Report* (Washington, DC: US Congress, Office of Technology Assessment, OTA-ISC-420, April 1989), iii.

40. Ibid.

41. *Holding the Edge: Maintaining the Defense Technology Base* (Washington, DC: US Congress, Office of Technology Assessment, OTA-ISC-420, April 1989), 9–14.

42. "Study Warns on Military Superiority," *New York Times*, May 17, 1989.

43. Ibid.

44. "Administration Plans Push to Commercialize Government Technology," Dow Jones Newswires, January 22, 1992.

45. "Highlights from the National Technology Initiative First Meetings," *Technology Access Report*, April 1, 1992; George Kozmetsky, "Partnerships for Long-Term Investments and Financing: A University Perspective," March 4, 1992, Kozmetsky Papers, IC² Institute.

CHAPTER 15

1. Kozmetsky apparently first heard the expression "think and do tank" from a Japanese visitor and liked it so much he adopted it as his own. Interview with Fred Y. Phillips, April 23, 2015.

2. Interview with Neal Spelce, August 11, 2017.

3. "Organizers Said Must for Austin," *Austin Statesman*, September 28, 1971.

4. Don C. Hoefler, "Silicon Valley U.S.A.," *Electronic News*, January 10, 1971. *Electronic News* eventually became an online-only publication and then merged with the online magazine *EDN*. Despite that 1971 article, the *Oxford English Dictionary* states the earliest printed use of the term "Silicon Valley" is in a 1974 article in *Fortune*.

5. UT President's Office Records, box AR 80-50/16, Economic Development, 1970–1971, Briscoe Center.

6. UT President's Office Records, box AR 80-50/16, Labor and Management Education Center, 1971–1972, Briscoe Center.

7. IC² Institute, "IC² Institute 'Firsts' and Other Major Accomplishments, 1977–1999," December 1999.

8. George Kozmetsky, foreword to *R&D Collaboration on Trial: The Microelectronics and Computer Technology Corporation*, by David V. Gibson and Everett M. Rogers (Boston: Harvard Business School Press, 1994).

9. George Kozmetsky and Eugene B. Konecci, "Society's Responsibility to Business as an Institution" (Working Paper 75-36, Graduate School of Business, University of Texas at Austin, June 1975).

10. Kozmetsky to Rogers, September 16, 1975, UT President's Office Records, box AR 84-184/22, Business Administration, 1975–1976, Dean, Briscoe Center.

11. The name of the foundation is actually the Brown Foundation, established by brothers Herman and George R. Brown and their wives, of the Houston construction giant Brown & Root Inc.

12. "Society vs. Business: Wanted: A Few Guidelines," *Dallas Morning News*, June 13, 1975.

13. Kozmetsky to Rogers, September 16, 1975.

14. Rogers to Kozmetsky, November 21, 1975, UT President's Office Records, box AR 84-184/22, Business Administration, 1975–1976, Dean, Briscoe Center.

15. Rogers to Kozmetsky, February 15, 1977, UT President's Office Records, box AR 85-215/8, Institute for Constructive Capitalism, 1976–1977, Briscoe Center.

16. Kozmetsky to Rogers, February 18, 1977, UT President's Office Records, box AR 85-215/8, Institute for Constructive Capitalism, 1976–1977, Briscoe Center.

17. Rogers to Kozmetsky, February 21, 1977, UT President's Office Records, box AR 85-215/8, Institute for Constructive Capitalism, 1976–1977, Briscoe Center.

18. Rogers might have been even more irritated if she had been aware that Kozmetsky was claiming the institute as a sponsor of an academic conference in Washington, DC, in the fall of 1976, months before the institute was officially established.

19. George Kozmetsky, "Education as an Information System," presentation to the Committee on Science and Astronautics, US House of Representatives, 91st Congress, 2nd session, January 28, 1970.

20. Arie Y. Lewin, "A Design for Constructive Capitalism," *Businessweek*, February 13, 1978.

21. UT Austin press release on "Capitalism Institute," April 12, 1977.

22. IC² Institute, "IC² Institute: The First Decade, 1977–1987," p. 1, Kozmetsky Papers, IC² Institute.

23. Ibid.

24. *Update* (newsletter of the IC² Institute) 1, no. 1 (1977).

25. Report on meeting of the UT System Board of Regents, February 2, 1977, UT President's Office Records, box AR 85-215/8, Research, 1976–1977, Institute for Constructive Capitalism, Briscoe Center.

26. Roger Baker and Laura Richardson, "IC²," *Texas Observer*, August 12, 1977.

27. Ibid.

28. "Capitalism 101," *Newsweek*, April 30, 1979, p. 62.

29. Ibid.

30. "Capitalist Think Tank Springs Up on Campus," *Christian Science Monitor*, March 31, 1982.

31. Ibid.

32. President William H. Cunningham quickly approved the change. Kozmetsky to Cunningham, October 9, 1985, UT President's Office Records, box 93-082/7, Research, 1985–1986, Innovation Creativity Capital Institute, Briscoe Center.

33. Sten Thore and Ruzanna Tarverdyan, *Diagnostics for a Globalized World* (Hackensack, NJ: World Scientific Publishing, 2015), 188.

34. Annual Report, 1976–1977, College of Business Administration and Graduate School of Business, UT Austin, p. 122.

35. IC² Institute, "IC² Institute: The First Decade," 3.

36. Prigogine, who was born in Moscow but spent most of his career in Belgium and Austin, was nine months older than Kozmetsky and died about a month after him. He received the Nobel Prize in 1977 for his work on the importation and dissipation of energy in chemical systems—work that had important implications in physics, biology, and other fields.

37. Thore and Tarverdyan, *Diagnostics for a Globalized World*, 206–207.

38. Annual Report, 1992–1993, IC² Institute Archives.

39. IC² Institute, "IC² Institute 'Firsts.'"

40. "U.S.-Soviet Relations, 1981–1991," Office of the Historian, US Department of State, https://history.state.gov/milestones/1981-1988/u.s.-soviet-relations.

41. Harvey McMains and Raymond W. Smilor, eds., *Economic Growth and Planning: Regional and National Perspectives: Proceedings of Joint U.S.-U.S.S.R. Conferences* (Austin, TX: Institute for Constructive Capitalism, 1982).

42. Annual Report, 1977–1978, College of Business Administration and Graduate School of Business, UT Austin, p. 106; Annual Report, 1978–1979, p. 89; Annual Report, 1979–1980, p. 117.

43. George Kozmetsky, "Economic Growth through Technology: A New Framework for Technology Commercialization," in *The Technopolis Phenomenon*, ed. David V. Gibson, George Kozmetsky, and Raymond W. Smilor (Austin, TX: IC² Institute, 1990). This article overlaps with several other Kozmetsky publications, including "Economic Growth through Technology: A New Framework for Creative and Innovative Managers," in *Commercializing Technology Resources for Competitive Advantage*, ed. Eugene B. Konecci, George Kozmetsky, Raymond W. Smilor, and Michael D. Gill Jr. (Austin, TX: IC² Institute, 1986).

44. Ibid.

45. Ibid.

46. Ibid.

47. This visual-information tradition is traced by Jessica Helfand in *Reinventing the Wheel* (New York: Princeton Architectural Press, 2002).

48. Raymond Smilor, David Gibson, and George Kozmetsky, "Creating the Technopolis: High-Technology Development in Austin," *Journal of Business Venturing* 4, no. 1 (1989): 49–67. The term "technopolis" is derived from Greek words for skill and city.

49. Interview with David V. Gibson, March 4, 2016.

50. David V. Gibson and Everett M. Rogers, *R&D Collaboration on Trial: The Microelec-*

tronics and Computer Technology Corporation (Boston: Harvard Business School Press, 1994), 101, 453. The authors expanded the Technopolis Wheel with many more subsegments; see p. 102.

51. See, for example, Dinghuan Shi and Ted Y. Lei, "Torch Program: Birthed in Texas, Grown Up in China," *Texas Lyceum Journal*, November 2006; Nikolay Rogalev, *Technology Commercialization in Russia: Challenges and Barriers* (Austin, TX: IC² Institute, 1998); Akio Nishizawa and Michi Fukushima, *University Startup Ventures and Clustering Strategy* (Tohoku University Press, 2005); Michi Fukushima, *The Formation of a High-Tech Cluster and Local Initiatives: How Austin Has Grown into a High-Tech City* (Tohoku University Press, 2013).

52. *Update* 2, no. 2 (1979).

53. "HARC Director Says He Will Resign," *Houston Post*, February 26, 1984; "HARC Gets New Interim Director," *Houston Post*, March 9, 1984.

54. "UT Lecturer Resigns 2 Positions after False Credentials Disclosed," *Austin American-Statesman*, March 16, 1984.

55. Memo from Kozmetsky to IC² Institute personnel, January 24, 1983, IC² Institute Archives.

56. Kozmetsky to Gerhard J. Fonken, March 12, 1992, IC² Institute Archives.

57. Interview with Raymond Smilor, November 3, 2015.

58. Comments by Raymond Smilor at twentieth annual international conference of the Society for Design and Process Science, Fort Worth, Texas, November 3, 2015.

59. Ibid.

60. Kozmetsky to Fonken, March 12, 1992, Kozmetsky Papers, IC² Institute.

61. Interview with Fred Y. Phillips, April 23, 2015.

62. Ibid.

63. Interviews with David V. Gibson, March 4 and March 23, 2016.

64. Piyu Yue, "Two Essays on Economic Analyses" (PhD diss., University of Texas at Austin, 1990), iv–v.

65. Thore and Tarverdyan, *Diagnostics for a Globalized World*, 186.

66. Interview with Isabella Cunningham, December 17, 2013.

67. Ibid.

68. "In Celebration of George Kozmetsky, 1917–2003, by Fellows and Friends of IC² Institute," August 2003, IC² Institute Archives.

69. Interview with John S. Butler, February 17, 2016. The book that Butler and Kozmetsky coedited was *Immigrant and Minority Entrepreneurship: The Continuous Rebirth of American Communities* (Westport, CT: Praeger, 2004).

CHAPTER 16

1. Annual Report, 1982–1983, Institute for Constructive Capitalism, pp. 5–9, IC² Institute Archives; Annual Report, 1985–1986, IC² Institute, p. 3, IC² Institute Archives.

2. Annual Report, 1984–1985, IC² Institute, p. 3, IC² Institute Archives.

3. Interview with Laura Kilcrease, April 12, 2012.

4. Ibid.

5. Raymond W. Smilor, George Kozmetsky, and David V. Gibson, "The Austin/San Antonio Corridor: The Dynamics of a Developing Technopolis," in *Creating the Technopolis: Linking Technology Commercialization and Economic Development*, ed. Smilor, Kozmetsky, and Gibson (Cambridge, MA: Ballinger, 1988), 162–163.

6. "Gift by Anonymous Texan Will Help Create 32 University Chairs," *New York Times*, April 16, 1984.

7. Interview with James C. Browne by David Gibson, April 15, 2016.

8. "Austin Ciber Stories," *Austin American-Statesman*, June 14, 1998; Smilor, Kozmetsky, and Gibson, "Austin/San Antonio Corridor," 157, 162–163, 167.

9. Smilor, Kozmetsky, and Gibson, "Austin/San Antonio Corridor," 157, 167.

10. Susan Engelking, "Austin's Economic Growth: A Case Study in Futuristic Planning," *Economic Development Review* 16, no. 2 (January 1, 1999).

11. "2 Areas Show Way to Success in High Technology Industry," *New York Times*, August 8, 1982.

12. "A Lone Star City Rises in Brilliance at Sensible Speed," *Christian Science Monitor*, March 31, 1982.

13. "Orlando, Fla., Area Focuses on Transforming Low-Paying Economy," *Orlando Sentinel*, April 23, 2002.

14. "Austin's Rebirth Holds Lessons for Orlando," *Orlando Sentinel*, April 23, 2002.

15. Ibid.

16. Ibid.

17. "UT Heralds New Era with Supercomputer," *Austin American-Statesman*, April 4, 1986.

18. G. V. Jones, *Democracy and Civilization* (London: Hutchinson, 1946).

19. Sheridan Tatsuno, "Building a Japanese Technostate: MITI's Technopolis Program," in *Creating the Technopolis: Linking Technology Commercialization and Economic Development*, ed. Raymond W. Smilor, George Kozmetsky, and David V. Gibson (Cambridge, MA: Ballinger, 1988).

20. Annual Report, 1988–1989, IC² Institute, p. 11, IC² Institute Archives; Hirofumi Matsuo, ed., *The Japan Business Study Program: Understanding Japanese Business* (Austin: Bureau of Business Research, University of Texas at Austin, 1989).

21. Kunio Goto, *Science, Technology, and Society: A Japanese Perspective* (Austin, TX: IC² Institute, 1993), vii, 210–211.

22. David V. Gibson and Everett M. Rogers, *R&D Collaboration on Trial: The Microelectronics and Computer Technology Corporation* (Boston, MA: Harvard Business School Press, 1994).

23. Ibid., 126–178.

24. Interview with Neal Spelce, August 11, 2017.

25. Ibid., 101. In describing these types of "influencers" in their book about MCC, Gibson and Rogers draw on *Creating the Technopolis* (Ballinger, 1988), a work edited by Raymond W. Smilor, George Kozmetsky, and David V. Gibson.

26. Interview with Adm. Bobby R. Inman, November 7, 2011.

27. Gibson and Rogers, *R&D Collaboration on Trial*, 116–117.

28. Ibid.

29. Interview with Pike Powers, July 21, 2015.

30. Ibid.

31. Ibid.

32. The university's involvement in recruiting Sematech is described in Cunningham, *The Texas Way*.

33. See, for example, "The Rise of the Texas Tekkies: Austin's Emergence As a Computer Center Offers Some Lessons in Industrial Policy," *Washington Post*, November 29, 1992; "Why Did Austin Prosper and Orlando Stumble?," *Austin American-Statesman*, May 26, 2002; "State Seeks Technology Center Status," *Aviation Week and Space Technology*, August 4, 1984.

34. Interview with Glenn E. West, July 7, 2015.

35. Ibid.

36. Interview with Pike Powers, July 21, 2015.

37. Interview with Neal Spelce, August 11, 2017.

A CIVIC ENTREPRENEUR

38. "Cities Compete for Display Consortium," *Austin American-Statesman*, September 13, 1993; "San Jose Rises in Display Bidding," *Austin American-Statesman*, September 25, 1993; "Display Consortium Picks San Jose," *Austin American-Statesman*, October 9, 1993. Austin also lost the competition for a flat-screen manufacturing plant, which went to Michigan. The US Display Consortium changed its name to the FlexTech Alliance in 2008.

39. Douglas Henton, John Melville, and Kimberly Walesh, *Grassroots Leaders for a New Economy: How Civic Entrepreneurs Are Building Prosperous Communities* (San Francisco: Josey-Bass, 1997).

40. Creutzberg, "Governing a Knowledge Economy," ii–iii.

41. Ibid., 106.

42. The Bureau of Business Research, founded in 1926, conducts applied economics research. It became a unit of the IC² Institute in 2005.

43. Annual Report, 1987–1988, IC² Institute, p. 3, IC² Institute Archives.

44. See, for example, Michael D. Gill, "Technology Venturing: The Japanese Fifth-Generation Computer Program" (MBA report, University of Texas at Austin, 1983).

45. George Kozmetsky, Michael D. Gill, and Raymond Smilor, *Financing and Managing Fast-Growth Companies* (Lexington, MA: Lexington Books, 1985), xxii.

46. Ibid., 82.

47. Conference program, "Technology Venturing: American Innovation and Risk Taking," February 5–7, 1984, UT President's Office Records, box 90-242/47, Research, 1983–1984, Institute for Constructive Capitalism, Briscoe Center.

48. George Kozmetsky, "Technology Venturing: The New American Response to the Changing Economy," in *Technology Venturing: American Innovation and Risk-Taking*, ed. Eugene B. Konecci and Robert Lawrence Kuhn (New York: Praeger, 1985).

49. Annual Report, 1988–1989, Center for Technology Venturing, Bureau of Business Research, UT Austin.

50. Annual Report, 1988–1989, IC² Institute, p. 5, IC² Institute Archives.

51. "An Answer to Their Prayers," *Austin American-Statesman*, August 19, 1990.

52. "Where Ideas Get Help with Financial Reality," *Austin American-Statesman*, June 9, 1995.

53. "Regional News Note," *Technology Transfer*, October 1, 1994.

54. Ibid.

55. Gerhard J. Fonken to William H. Cunningham, July 25, 1988, and Kozmetsky and Sullivan to Robert E. Witt, July 16, 1988, IC² Institute Archives.

56. Renee A. Berger, *The Small Business Incubator: Lessons Learned from Europe* (Washington, DC: OPSI, US Small Business Administration, 1984).

57. Raymond W. Smilor and Michael D. Gill of the IC² Institute wrote one of the earliest comprehensive studies of the incubator trend, *The New Business Incubator: Linking Talent, Technology, Capital, and Know-How* (Lexington Books, 1986). The study was conducted with grants from the US Small Business Administration and Peat, Marwick, Mitchell & Co.

58. Smilor and Gill, *The New Business Incubator*, 1–3.

59. US Small Business Administration, *Small Business Incubators: A Handbook on Startup and Management* (Washington, DC: OPSI, US Small Business Administration, 1986).

60. Smilor and Gill, *The New Business Incubator*, 115–121. The authors provide a case study of Rubicon through 1986.

61. Interview with Glenn E. West, July 7, 2015.

62. Interview with Laura Kilcrease, March 26, 2012.

63. Comments by Lee Cooke at IC² Institute fellows meeting, April 28, 2017.

64. Interview with Laura Kilcrease, March 26, 2012.

65. Ibid.

66. Ibid.

67. "Incubator Starts the Ball Rolling," *Austin American-Statesman*, February 3, 1989; "County Approves $70,000 for Technology Incubator," *Austin American-Statesman*, September 6, 1990.

68. Interview with Laura Kilcrease, April 12, 2012.

69. "Sorry, There's No Room at the Incubator," *Austin American-Statesman*, December 17, 1990.

70. "Business Incubators Suffer Growing Pains," *Wall Street Journal*, June 16, 1989; "Business Incubators Turn In Spotty Initial Track Records," *Austin American-Statesman*, September 11, 1989.

71. "Business Incubators Turn In Spotty Initial Track Records," *Austin American-Statesman*, September 11, 1989.

72. "Texas Business Incubators," *Austin American-Statesman*, September 11, 1989.

73. Bureau of Business Research, "The Economic Impact of Austin Technology Incubator Companies on Travis County, 2003–2012" (Austin: University of Texas at Austin, 2014).

74. "Nurturer of High-Tech Firms Hatches First Success Stories," *Austin American-Statesman*, May 4, 1990.

75. "Fertile Ground," *Entrepreneur*, August 1, 1997.

76. Bureau of Business Research, "Economic Impact of Austin Technology Incubator Companies."

77. "Incubator Beset by Growing Pains," *Austin American-Statesman*, June 3, 1991.

78. "Austin Technology Incubator Introduces High-Tech Incubators to Mexico," *Marketing Computers*, April 1, 1991.

79. "Incubators in Town to See How It's Done," *Austin American-Statesman*, May 16, 1992.

80. "Incubator Honored as Best in the Nation," *Austin American-Statesman*, May 14, 1994.

81. "High-Tech Incubator Sends Off Its Brood," *Austin American-Statesman*, September 23, 1997.

82. Interview with David Gibson, August 23, 2016.

83. Fred Y. Phillips, *Social Culture and High-Tech Economic Development: The Technopolis Columns* (London: Palgrave Macmillan, 2006), 18–21.

84. "Council Formed to Support Software," *Austin American-Statesman*, February 13, 1993.

85. Austin Software Council Planning Group, "Strategic Plan for Software Prominence (Summary) 1993–1998," December 1993, Kozmetsky Papers, IC² Institute.

86. "Austin Software Council Reboots to Its Roots," *Austin American-Statesman*, June 16, 1997.

87. "Independence from University of Texas Adds Politics to Software Council's Sphere of Possibility," *Austin American-Statesman*, March 2, 1998.

88. "UT Picks Representative for Software Council," *Austin American-Statesman*, June 22, 1999.

89. "Technology Council Shifts Focus to Older Companies," *Austin American-Statesman*, November 11, 2002.

90. Michael Dell, with Catherine Fredman, *Direct from Dell: Strategies that Revolutionized an Industry* (New York: Harper Business, 1999), 11–21.

91. Interview with Michael Dell, May 21, 2013.

92. "Professor Remembered for Belief in Efforts," *Austin American-Statesman*, May 5, 2003.

93. "Dell's Board Gains Respect with Growth," *Austin American-Statesman*, July 24, 2000.

94. Interview with Adm. Bobby R. Inman, November 7, 2011.

95. Dell, *Direct from Dell*, 21.

96. Interview with Michael Dell, May 21, 2013.

97. Ibid.

98. Ibid.

99. Dell, *Direct from Dell*, 36–45.

100. "Electronic Markets Workshop to Address Research and Industry Agenda for Electronic Commerce," Business Wire, October 9, 1996.

101. "Dell Aims to Keep Its Stock Climbing," *Austin American-Statesman*, July 19, 1997.

102. "Dell Computer Shareholders Authorize Share Increase," PR Newswire, July 18, 1997.

103. "Who's the Richest of 'Em, Ya'll," *Austin American-Statesman*, August 15, 1991.

104. "Human Code and IC^2 Deliver E-learning to Bridge the Digital Divide," PR Newswire, August 17, 2000.

105. "Perfecting Job Training in the Age of Video Gaming," *Austin American-Statesman*, April 3, 2000.

106. "Human Code and IC^2 Institute Bridge the Digital Divide through E-learning," PR Newswire, June 27, 2000.

107. Interview with Corey Carbonara, March 30, 2015.

108. "Perfecting Job Training in the Age of Video Gaming," *Austin American-Statesman*, April 3, 2000; EnterTech, "The EnterTech Project: Changing Learning and Lives," final report of the project (Austin, TX: IC^2 Institute, 2003).

109. "IC^2 Institute . . . Launches E-learning and Training Collaboratory," PR Newswire, April 29, 2002.

110. Ibid.

111. "Proposed City Fiber Optic Network Draws Praise, Skepticism," *Austin American-Statesman*, July 14, 1994.

112. Bruce R. Scott and Srinivas Sunder, "Austin, Texas: Building a High-Tech Economy" (Harvard Business School Case 799-038, October 1998, rev. June 2002).

113. Data from the Greater Austin Chamber of Commerce, cited in Susan Engelking, "Austin's Economic Growth: A Case Study in Futuristic Planning," *Economic Development Review*, January 1, 1999.

114. Michael Oden and Bige Yilmaz, "From Assembly to Innovation: Learning from the Birth and Development of a High-Tech Region" (Paris: UNESCO–World Technopolis Association, 2006).

115. "Delegation of Seattle Leaders Pays Visit," *Austin American-Statesman*, November 20, 1997.

116. Creutzberg, "Governing a Knowledge Economy," 100–102.

117. Oden and Yilmaz, "From Assembly to Innovation," 98–115.

118. David V. Gibson and John Sibley Butler, "Sustaining the Technopolis: High-Technology Development in Austin, Texas 1988–2012" (IC^2 Institute Working Paper WP-2013-02.01, February 2013), 5–6.

119. John Sibley Butler, "The University of Texas at Austin," in *The Development of University-Based Entrepreneurships Ecosystems*, ed. Michael L. Fetters, Patricia G. Greene, Mark P. Rice, and John Sibley Butler (Cheltenham, UK: Edward Elgar, 2010).

CHAPTER 17

1. Comments at IC^2 Institute fellows meeting, April 28, 2017.

2. Annual Report, 1979–1980, College of Business Administration and Graduate School of Business, UT Austin, p. 117; "America's Small Business Economy: Agenda for Action; Report to the President by the White House Commission on Small Business" (Washington, DC: US Government Printing Office, 1980).

3. "Industrial Talks Set," *Austin Statesman*, May 4, 1969.

4. Carolyn Barta, *Bill Clements: Texian to His Toenails* (Austin: Eakin Press, 1996), 256.

5. Tex. Gov. Exec. Order No. WPC-22 (April 10, 1981).

6. Interview with Meg Wilson, May 5, 2015.

7. Texas 2000 Commission, *Texas Past and Future: A Survey* (Austin, TX: Office of the Governor, 1982), 150–167.

8. Texas 2000 Commission, *Texas 2000 Commission Reports and Recommendations* (Austin, TX: Office of the Governor, 1982), 29–31.

9. "Texas 2000 Group Fueling Arguments for Planning," *Dallas Morning News,* January 6, 1981; "R&D: A Key to State's Future," *Dallas Morning News,* April 15, 1982; "State R&D: An Issue for the '80s," *Dallas Morning News,* April 21, 1982.

10. Barta, *Bill Clements,* 337–339.

11. Interview with Meg Wilson, May 5, 2015.

12. Tex. Gov. Exec. Order No. MW-24 (June 21, 1984).

13. Interview with Meg Wilson, May 5, 2015.

14. Annual Report, 1986, Texas Science and Technology Council, Office of the Governor.

15. Texas Science and Technology Council, "Strategies for the New Texas Economy: Advancing Economic Development and Competitive Position through Science and Technology" (January 1987), 8.

16. "Summit Aims to Keep State a High-Tech Haven," *Austin American-Statesman,* September 17, 1996.

17. George Kozmetsky, "Texas Technology Summit: Growing the 21st Century Technopolis," Kozmetsky Papers, IC[2] Institute.

18. "Prof Calls Galveston Backward," *Austin American-Statesman,* June 18, 1975.

19. Joseph W. Kutchin, *How Mitchell Energy & Development Corp. Got Its Start and How It Grew: An Oral History and Narrative Overview* (Houston, TX: Mitchell Energy & Development Corp., 2001), 46–48.

20. "Waco Lays High-Tech Road Map," *Waco Tribune-Herald,* December 16, 2000.

21. Interview with Corey Carbonara, March 30, 2015.

22. Interview with Bill Segura, June 29, 2015.

23. Ibid.

24. Ibid.

25. Ibid.

26. "BRIC Research Center Rising out of Old General Tire Facility," *Waco Herald-Tribune,* July 3, 2011.

27. Interview with Edward A. Miller, May 5, 2017.

28. Annual Report, 1989–1990, IC[2] Institute, p. 21, IC[2] Institute Archives.

29. "Rostows Lead Austin Effort to Forge Inner-City Solutions," *Austin American-Statesman,* May 7, 1992. Ronya Kozmetsky served on the board of the Rostows' Austin project.

30. "School-to-Work Lets Students Learn About Future Earning," CNN, May 4, 1994.

31. George Kozmetsky, "Opportunities in Technology Transfer: Positioning Knoxville for the Triad Markets" (presentation to the East-West '94 Conference, Knoxville, TN, October 3, 1994).

32. Ibid.

33. "Almost Austin? Knoxville Hopes to Reach High-Tech Potential," *Knoxville News-Sentinel,* October 16, 1994.

34. Memo from Richard Seline to George Kozmetsky et al., March 27, 1995, Kozmetsky Papers, IC[2] Institute.

35. "City, DOE Tie High-Tech Knot," *Chattanooga Times,* June 2, 1995.

36. Email correspondence with Zach Wamp (now the leader of a business consulting firm in Chattanooga), July 28, 2016.

37. Interview with Laura Kilcrease, March 26, 2012.

38. David V. Gibson, James E. Jarrett, and George Kozmetsky, "Customer Assessment for Martin Marietta Energy Systems, Inc., Oak Ridge National Laboratory, CRADA Program" (Austin: IC² Institute, University of Texas, February 1995).

39. David V. Gibson, James E. Jarrett, George Kozmetsky, and Richard Seline, "East Tennessee's 21st Century Jobs Initiative: Creating Wealth for a Sustainable Economy" (Austin: IC² Institute, University of Texas, March 1996).

40. "Group Accepts Challenge to Set Agenda for Alaska," *Anchorage Daily News*, April 23, 1989.

41. Alaskans remain sensitive to "colonial" encroachments from Washington State well into the twenty-first century. See, for example, "Alaska House Leaders Take Shots at Washington State over Arctic Development," *Alaska Dispatch News*, April 10, 2015.

42. "Economist Pushes Value of Diversity," *Anchorage Times*, April 25, 1989.

43. Alaska Science and Technology Foundation, agenda for October 15–16, 1992, meeting in Anchorage, Kozmetsky Papers, IC² Institute.

44. "Financier: Alaska Could Be at Turning Point in Investment," *Juneau Empire*, February 18, 2000.

45. Ibid.

46. "Alaska Needs More Civic Entrepreneurs," *Juneau Empire*, March 27, 2000.

47. "Wireless Communication in Alaska," *Alaska Business Monthly*, April 1, 2000.

48. "Tech-Savvy Entrepreneurs Say Alaska Can Play Host to Startups," *Alaska Journal of Commerce*, August 2, 2005.

49. "Brain Circulation Should Reduce Brain Drain in Alaska," *Alaska Journal of Commerce*, November 11, 2002.

50. "Foundation Dissolved," *Alaska Journal of Commerce*, July 1, 2003.

51. "New 'Tech Coast' VC Fund Forming," *Orange County Business Journal*, November 8, 1999.

52. Ibid.

53. Interview with Laura Kilcrease, April 12, 2012.

54. "New High-Tech Business Incubator," Business Wire, June 12, 2000.

55. "USF to Step Out in Style During Inauguration," *St. Petersburg Times*, October 9, 1988.

56. Francis T. Borkowski and Susan A. McManus, eds., *Visions for the Future: Creating New Institutional Relationships among Academia, Business, Government, and Community* (Tampa: University of South Florida Press, 1989).

57. "USF to Request Hillsborough Aid for Think Tank," *St. Petersburg Times*, September 6, 1989.

58. Interview with Francis Borkowski, July 17, 2014.

59. After Kozmetsky became dean of the business school at the University of Texas, he was appointed a consultant to NASA administrator James E. Webb. NASA press release no. 68-153, 1968.

60. "Institute Receives $5.4 Million NASA Grant," *Update* (IC² newsletter), Summer 1993.

61. Ibid.

62. "NASA to Open Technology Incubators," *Technology Access Report* (University R&D Opportunities Inc.), May 1, 1993.

63. Interview with Laura Kilcrease, March 26, 2012.

64. "An Incubator for Technology Innovators," *Houston Chronicle*, March 14, 1999.

65. Interview with Laura Kilcrease, April 12, 2012.

66. "Where New Businesses Learn to Fly," *San Jose Mercury News*, October 2, 1995.

67. "NASA Technology Transfer and Commercialization," *NASA Spinoff*, 1999, https://spinoff.nasa.gov/spinoff1999/ttc2.htm.

68. "Government, Industry, Consider Prototypes for Partnering, Privatizing," *Platts Inside Energy*, March 4, 1996.

69. Master's degree in science and technology commercialization files, IC² Institute Archives.

70. Email from Helen Baca Miller, May 5, 2017.

71. "Charleston, with Long Ties to the Navy, Faces Devastation," *Atlanta Journal and Constitution*, March 13, 1993.

72. "Charleston Execs Make Trek to Study Austin," *Austin American-Statesman*, November 1, 1995.

73. IC² Institute, "Development and Implementation of a Coastal Environmental Technology Commercialization Center," proposal to the National Oceanic and Atmospheric Administration (Austin, TX: IC² Institute, March 1995).

74. Ibid.

75. "Charleston, S.C., Officials Continue Recruitment of Tech Companies," *Post and Courier*, July 9, 2001.

76. IC² Institute, "Commercialization of Technologies at the Medical University of South Carolina for the NOAA Center for Technological Innovation" (Austin, TX: IC² Institute, 1996).

77. David Gibson et al., "Benchmarking Technology-Based Entrepreneurship in the Charleston Region" (Austin, TX: IC² Institute, 1997).

78. Annual Report, 1994–1995, IC² Institute, IC² Institute Archives.

79. Annual Report, 1992–1993, IC² Institute, IC² Institute Archives.

80. Annual Report, 1988–1989, IC² Institute, IC² Institute Archives.

81. Interview with Edward A. Miller, May 5, 2017.

82. "History of the Moot Corp Competition," Center for Business Planning, http://www.businessplans.org/history.html.

83. "Superconductors Lead Japan to Texas," *Japan Economic Journal*, August 6, 1988.

84. Ibid.

85. Annual Report, 1987–1988, IC² Institute, IC² Institute Archives.

86. IC² Institute, "IC² Institute: The First Fifteen Years."

87. Annual Report, 1993–1994, IC² Institute, IC² Institute Archives.

88. Trip report, Beijing, China, July 25–August 4, 1987, Kozmetsky Papers, IC² Institute.

89. Ibid.

90. Ibid.

91. Trip report, China conference, March 13–18, 1989, Kozmetsky Papers, IC² Institute.

92. Ibid.

93. Ibid.

94. "200 Projects to Launch Torch Program," Xinhua News Agency, April 4, 1989.

95. Dinghuan Shi and and Ted Y. Li, "Torch Program: Birthed in Texas, Grown Up in China, Returning to Texas/Mexico," *Texas Lyceum Journal*, November 2006.

96. Ibid.

97. Draft of memorandum of cooperation between Chinese Young Entrepreneurs' Association and IC² Institute, Kozmetsky Papers, IC² Institute.

98. "China, U.S. Collaborate to Review Torch Project," *Asian Pacific Biotech News* 1, no. 6 (1997).

99. Interview with Edward A. Miller, May 5, 2017.

100. Trip report, January 6, 1983, Kozmetsky Papers, IC² Institute.

101. Annual Report, 1989–1990, IC² Institute, IC² Institute Archives.

102. Trip report, workshop on science parks and incubators, June 17–23, 1990, Kozmetsky Papers, IC² Institute.

103. Ibid.

104. Annual Report, 1990–1991, IC² Institute, IC² Institute Archives.

105. Annual Report, 1992–1993, IC² Institute, IC² Institute Archives.

106. Lee Kelly column, *Austin American-Statesman*, October 14, 1990.

107. "Russian Republic Reformer Resigns," *Washington Post*, February 14, 1991.

108. *Update* (IC² Institute newsletter), Summer 1998.

CHAPTER 18

1. "Membership Roster of the Institute of Management Sciences as of February. 8, 1954," Herbert A. Simon Collection, Carnegie Mellon University.

2. William W. Cooper, "Abraham Charnes and W. W. Cooper (et al.): A Brief History of a Long Collaboration in Developing Industrial Uses of Linear Programming," *Operations Research* 50, no. 1 (January–February 2002): 35–41.

3. Andrew Vázsonyi, "Milestone Manifesto," *OR/MS Today*, October 2002; Lawrence Secrest, David V. Gibson, and John S. Butler, "George Kozmetsky," in *Profiles in Operations Research*, ed. Arjang A. Assad and Saul I. Gass, International Series in Operations Research and Management Science, vol. 147 (New York: Springer, 2011), 343–362.

4. Melvin Salveson, "The Institute of Management Sciences: A Prehistory and Commentary on the Occasion of TIMS' 40th Anniversary," *Interfaces* 27, no. 3 (May–June 1997): 74–85.

5. Kozmetsky maintained his friendship with Salveson and invited him to speak at the University of Texas business school during Kozmetsky's first semester as dean. Salveson, by that time president of the Electronic Currency Corp., spoke on his invention of a comprehensive electronic credit card system for use by banks. UT press release, December 16, 1966.

6. Kozmetsky to Cooper, December 18, 1953, Herbert A. Simon Collection, Carnegie Mellon University.

7. Melvin E. Salveson, "The Founding Fathers of TIMS," *OR/MS Today*, June 2003; Bulletin (Institute of Management Sciences), June 1955, Herbert A. Simon Collection, Carnegie Mellon University.

8. "Membership Roster of the Institute of Management Sciences as of Feb. 8, 1954," Herbert A. Simon Collection, Carnegie Mellon University.

9. George Kozmetsky, Emerson Stafford, Leon Steinman, and William Wellwood, "Weapons System Management" (Hawthorne, CA: Teledyne Systems Company, 1966), Kozmetsky Papers, IC² Institute.

10. Ibid., 60.

11. Ibid., 1.

12. Ibid., 2–3.

13. Ibid., 3.

14. See Abraham Charnes, William W. Cooper, J. K. DeVoe, and D. B. Learner, "Demon: Decision Mapping via Optimum Go-No Networks; A Model for Marketing New Products," *Management Science* 12, no. 11 (July 1966): 865–867.

15. UT press release, June 30, 1971.

16. George Kozmetsky, "Growth through Technology: A New Framework for Creative and Innovative Managers," in *Handbook for Creative and Innovative Managers*, ed. Robert Lawrence Kuhn (New York: McGraw-Hill, 1988), 612.

17. George Kozmetsky, "Why New Directions for Research?," in N*ew Directions in Creative and Innovative Management: Bridging Theory and Practice*, ed. Yuji Ijiri and Robert Lawrence Kuhn (Cambridge, MA: Ballinger, 1988), 16.

18. Ibid., 16–17.

19. Interview with Corey Carbonara, March 30, 2015.

20. Ibid.

21. Interview with Corey Carbonara, June 25, 2015.

22. Jean Piaget, the Swiss psychologist, has been credited with coining the term "transdisciplinary" in 1970.

23. Norbert Wiener, *Cybernetics* (New York: Technology Press, John Wiley, 1948), 8–9. Kozmetsky's copy was the eighth printing, published in 1950.

24. Roderick J. Lawrence, "Deciphering Interdisciplinary and Transdisciplinary Contributions," *Transdisciplinary Journal of Engineering and Science* 1, no. 1 (December 2010): 125–130.

25. Ibid.

26. Interview with Patricia Easton, codirector of transdisciplinary studies, Claremont Graduate University, April 28, 2015.

27. "Knowledge Beyond Disciplines," *Flame* (magazine of Claremont Graduate University), Winter 2003, pp. 15–16.

28. "Kozmetsky Fellows Look Beyond the Disciplines," *Flame*, Winter 2003, p. 6.

29. Interview with Patricia Easton, April 28, 2015.

30. Home page of the Academy of Transdisciplinary Learning and Advanced Studies, www.theatlas.org.

31. "Something from Nothing: SFI Emerges and Synthesizes," Santa Fe Institute, http://www.santafe.edu/about/the-history/emerges/.

32. Interview with Murat M. Tanik, April 24, 2015.

33. Program of the Twentieth International Conference of the Society for Design and Process Science, November 1–5, 2015.

34. In 2012, long after he left his University of Texas faculty position, Nozette pleaded guilty to attempted espionage and was assessed a thirteen-year prison sentence after being arrested trying to deliver classified information to someone whom he thought was a representative of the Israeli government but was, in fact, an FBI agent. "Scientist Gets Thirteen Years in Spying Case," *New York Times*, March 22, 2012.

35. Transcript of graduate management class, January 18, 1989, p. 1, Kozmetsky Papers, IC² Institute.

36. *Update* (IC² Institute newsletter), Spring 1985.

37. Kozmetsky to Cunningham, February 10, 1986; Cunningham to Kozmetsky, February 27, 1986; Stephen A. Monti to Cunningham, April 14, 1986, UT President's Office Records, box 93-082/7, Innovation Creativity Capital Institute, Briscoe Center.

38. Kozmetsky to Cunningham, August 27, 1987, Kozmetsky Papers, IC² Institute.

39. "Where Engineers Think Big," *New York Times*, April 18, 1985.

40. Frank P. Davidson, L. J. Giacoletto, and Robert Salkeld, eds., *Macro-Engineering and the Infrastructure of Tomorrow*, AAAS Selected Symposium, vol. 23 (Boulder, CO: Westview, 1978).

41. George Kozmetsky, "State of the Art of Macro-Engineering Collaborative Developments and Future Directions," in *Macro-Engineering: Global Infrastructure Solutions, Massachusetts Institute of Technology*, The Brunel Lectures 1983–1992, ed. Frank P. Davidson and C. Lawrence Meador (New York: Ellis Horwood, 1992).

42. Hans Mark and Arnold Levine, *The Management of Research Institutions: A Look at Government Laboratories* (Washington, DC: NASA, 1984).

43. Interview with Hans Mark, July 30, 2014.

44. Willy Ley, *Engineers' Dreams* (New York: Viking Press, 1954), 139.

45. Maskai Nakajima, "A Proposition for the 'Global Infrastructure Fund,'" Kozmetsky Papers, IC² Institute.

46. Annual Reports, 1971–1972 and 1972–1973, College of Business Administration and Graduate School of Business, UT Austin.

47. "Professors Engaged in Mission to Spread Idea of Macroengineering," *Japan Economic Journal*, March 19, 1985.

48. George Kozmetsky, "Perspectives on Manpower Planning and Technological Change," in *Economic Growth and Planning: Regional and National Perspectives, Proceedings of Joint U.S.-Soviet Conferences*, ed. Harvey McMains and Raymond Smilor (Austin, TX: Institute for Constructive Capitalism, 1982), 277.

49. Ibid.

50. Transcript of graduate management course, January 22, 1986, p. 13, Kozmetsky Papers, IC[2] Institute.

51. "Japanese Hint at Establishment of Ambitious 'Global Marshall Plan,'" *Los Angeles Times*, July 12, 1986.

52. Annual Report, 1988–1989, IC[2] Institute, IC[2] Institute Archives.

53. The term "global infrastructure fund" has survived as a designation for an investment plan that seeks to privatize existing infrastructure projects such as airports and highways.

54. Konecci to Kozmetsky, March 28, 1986, UT President's Office Records, box 93-082/7, Innovation Creativity Capital Institute, Briscoe Center.

55. Letter from Kozmetsky to James Sexton, chairman of Texas Commerce Bank, March 18, 1986, UT President's Office Records, box 93-082/7, Innovation Creativity Capital Institute, Briscoe Center.

56. "Moon Base Gaining Support as New US Space Goal," *Aviation Week and Space Technology*, May 11, 1987.

57. "Support for Lunar Base Grows among Non-aerospace Firms," *Aviation Week and Space Technology*, October 12, 1987.

58. "To Mars, but How?," *Times* (London), July 20, 1989.

59. "Software Models Help Scientists Design Lunar Base," *Government Computing News*, October 16, 1989.

60. "The Executive Computer: Fly Me to the Moon," *New York Times*, July 21, 1991.

61. Ibid.

62. Manual for Moonbase lunar colony simulator, version 1.0, 1990, Kozmetsky Papers, IC[2] Institute.

63. Large-Scale Projects Institute, "Current Research," July 3, 1989, Kozmetsky Papers, IC[2] Institute.

CHAPTER 19

1. Communication to the author from Jami Hampton, RGK Foundation, September 20, 2016.

2. In late 2016, assets of the RGK Foundation were divided evenly between two new organizations, the Kozmetsky Family Foundation and the Reissa Foundation, representing different branches of the family.

3. "A Benefactor in Her Own Right," *Austin American-Statesman*, July 11, 1999.

4. Interview with Nadya Scott, April 28, 2015.

5. "ALS Therapy Development Institute Awarded $1M Grant," *Gene Therapy Weekly*, November 13, 2008.

6. "Lab Focuses on Science, Not Style," *Austin American-Statesman*, August 7, 2006.

7. Home page of the RGK Foundation, www.rgkfoundation.org.

8. Records of the UT Austin Development Office.

9. Records of the UT Austin Development Office; IC[2] Institute, "IC[2] Institute 1977–1992," Kozmetsky Papers, IC[2] Institute.

10. "A Benefactor in Her Own Right," *Austin American-Statesman*, July 11, 1999.

11. "Once and Future Huston-Tillotson," *Austin American-Statesman*, February 27, 1977.

12. "Concordia Receives Nursing Grant," Targeted News Service, March 25, 2009.

13. Email from Concordia University Texas development office, October 17, 2016.

14. Lee Kelly column, *Austin American-Statesman*, September 19, 1993.

15. "Children's Museum Given $1 Million," *Austin American-Statesman*, November 15, 2002.

16. "Kozmetsky Foundation Pledges $500,000 for Battered Women's Care," *Austin American-Statesman*, November 20, 1996.

17. "Bigger Better Safe Place," *Austin American-Statesman*, June 25, 1999.

18. Interview with Patricia Easton, April 28, 2015.

19. "Winners Typify the Best of Business Plans," *Orange County Register*, June 30, 1997.

20. Interview with Robert D. King, October 10, 2011.

21. George Kozmetsky to David Patterson, June 15, 1983, Kozmetsky Papers, IC[2] Institute.

22. Kozmetsky to Patterson, March 14, 1984, Kozmetsky Papers, IC[2] Institute.

23. "Kozmetsky Family Gift to Support Research on Emerging Knowledge," Business Wire, December 13, 1999.

24. "New Program Is Classic Kozmetsky," *Austin American-Statesman*, April 17, 2003.

25. Communication to the author from John S. Butler, September 22, 2016.

26. "Who's Playing the Board Game?," *New York Times*, October 9, 1983.

27. "UT Dean Director of Bank," *Austin American*, December 17, 1967.

28. Scientific and Engineering Software Inc. documents, Kozmetsky Papers, IC[2] Institute.

29. "Farah Incorporated History," Funding Universe, www.fundinguniverse.com/company-histories/farah-incorporated-history/.

30. A detailed account of these battles is included in State National Bank of El Paso v. Farah Manufacturing Company Inc., 678 S.W.2d. 661 (Tex. App. 1984).

31. "New Firm Offers Web Retailers a Personal Touch," *Wall Street Journal*, March 2, 2000.

32. "Entrepreneur Typifies Tech's Turmoil," *Knoxville News-Sentinel*, January 10, 2002; "Recycling Ideas: Intellectual Property from Failed Tech Firms Is For Sale," *Austin American-Statesman*, February 11, 2002.

33. "Dell Creates $100M Fund for Startups," *Austin Business Journal*, June 7, 2012.

34. "Unitrin Investor Kozmetsky Reports 5.98% Stake," Federal Filings Newswire, February 1, 2001.

35. Interview with Chris Wrather, April 29, 2015.

36. Ibid.

37. Ibid.

38. Austin O. Roche IV, "The Almost Forgotten History of Computer Terminal Corporation and Datapoint Corporation," San Antonio Museum of Science and Technology, April 2016, www.kuonlinedirectory.org/studygroups/wp-content/uploads/2016/04.

39. "Forgotten PC History: The True Origin of the Personal Computer," *Computerworld*, August 8, 2008.

40. "Datapoint Kept Trying to Set Records until Bubble Burst," *Wall Street Journal*, May 27, 1982.

41. Lamont Wood, *Datapoint: The Lost Story of the Texans Who Invented the Personal Computer Revolution* (Englewood, CO: Hugo House, 2010), ch. 15.

42. "Edelman Wins at Datapoint," *New York Times*, March 16, 1985.

43. "Datapoint Corp.," *Wall Street Journal*, April 22, 1985.

44. Wood, *Datapoint: The Lost Story*, ch. 18.

45. John J. McCloy, Nathan W. Pearson, and Beverley Matthews, "Report of the Special Review Committee of the Board of Directors of Gulf Oil Corporation," December 31, 1975,

Securities and Exchange Commission v. Gulf Oil Corporation, US District Court for the District of Columbia, Civil Action No. 75-0324.

46. "Gulf Officers' Ouster Was Boldly Engineered by Mellon Interests," *Wall Street Journal*, January 15, 1976.

47. "Directors Wake Up Too Late at Gulf," *Fortune*, June 1976; Ronald P. Kane and Samuel Butler III, "Improper Corporate Payments: The Second Half of Watergate," *Loyola University Chicago Law Journal* 8, no. 1 (Fall 1976).

48. "Gulf Officers' Ouster Was Boldly Engineered by Mellon Interests," *Wall Street Journal*, January 15, 1976; "A Head that Rolled," *Newsweek*, January 26, 1976.

49. "Gulf's Chief and Defender," *New York Times*, November 7, 1971.

50. Thomas Gorman, "The Origins of the FCPA: Lessons for Effective Compliance and Enforcement," *Securities Regulation Journal* (Spring 2015); Upton Au, "Toward a Reconceived Legislative Intent behind the Foreign Corrupt Practices Act," *Brooklyn Law Review* 79, no. 2 (January 2014).

51. "MCC Adds 19 Members," *Austin American-Statesman*, June 9, 1993.

52. KDT Industries Inc. Strategic Business Plan, February 1992, Kozmetsky Papers, IC^2 Institute.

53. "First in flight . . . Austin-based Arrowsmith Technologies Establishes Itself As a Major Player in Nascent Technology-Supplier Market," *Austin American-Statesman*, January 30, 1995.

54. "Kozmetskys' Arrowsmith May Be Forced to Close," *Austin American-Statesman*, June 11, 1997.

55. Ibid.

56. Comments at IC^2 Institute fellows meeting, April 28, 2017.

57. "Tree Ring Circus," *Texas Monthly*, April 2006.

58. Interview with Charles Hurwitz, April 26, 2017.

59. "Where, Oh Where, Have All the Corporate Raiders Gone?," *New York Times*, June 30, 1996.

60. Interview with Charles Hurwitz, April 26, 2017.

61. "Formation of MCO Resources Inc.—A New Company," Kozmetsky Papers, IC^2 Institute.

62. "Kozmetsky Denies Hurwitz Exploited United Savings Board," Associated Press, October 9, 1997.

63. "OTS Settled Case vs. Charles Hurwitz," *Dallas Morning News*, October 19, 2002.

64. "Maxxam Gets $10M in FDIC Suit," *American Banker*, December 10, 2008.

65. "Protesters Come Down to Earth," *Deseret Morning News*, September 24, 2008.

66. "Timber! Charles Hurwitz Took on the Federal Government and Won," *Forbes*, December 12, 2005.

67. See www.utwatch.org.

68. Interview with Greg Kozmetsky, August 16, 2016.

69. "Authorities Make Arrest at Cave Occupied by Environmentalists," Associated Press, August 31, 1988.

70. Interview with Mariann Wizard, July 1, 2014. Wizard came to the University of Texas as a freshman in 1964 and, after a brief stint as a Goldwater Republican, had a prominent role in the antiwar and counterculture movements at the university.

71. Room reservations for student organizations were made routinely by the dean of students and were based on availability and the space needs of the organization.

72. Interview with Mariann Wizard, July 1, 2014.

73. See, for example, the issue for April 27, 1968. The place of the *Rag* in the underground

press is traced in John McMillan, *Smoking Typewriters: The Sixties Underground Press and the Rise of Alternative Media in America* (Oxford, UK: Oxford University Press, 2011).

74. James Ridgeway, *The Closed Corporation: American Universities in Crisis* (New York: Random House, 1968).

75. Dugger, *Our Invaded Universities.*

76. See, for example, "George Kozmetsky and the Technopolis Concept," *Polemicist,* December 1989.

77. Kathy Mitchell, "Kozmetsky's Raiders: The Early Years," *Polemicist,* November 1991.

78. Scott Henson and Tom Philpott, "The Kozmetsky-Hurwitz Connection: A Tale of Corporate Raiders in Capitalist America," *Polemicist,* May 1990.

79. "Redwood Summer and Beyond," *Polemicist,* November 1990.

80. Steve Ongerth, *Redwood Uprising: From One Big Union to Earth First! and the Bombing of Judi Bari,* www.judibari.info/book.

81. Robert Frank Ovetz, "Entrepreneurialization, Resistance and the Crisis of the Universities: A Case Study of the University of Texas at Austin" (PhD diss., University of Texas at Austin, 1996). This dissertation is available online at utwatch.org. References here are from the online version, not the printed version available in libraries.

82. Ibid., ch. 2, p. 6.

83. Ibid., ch. 2, p. 7.

84. Ibid., ch. 2, p. 8.

CHAPTER 20

1. "Dr. George Kozmetsky Biography," YouTube video, documentary on George and Ronya Kozmetsky, posted by Russell Taylor, October 14, 2013, https://www.youtube.com/watch?v=nQutKkZkNWQ.

2. Interview with Laura Kilcrease, April 12, 2012.

3. Communication from Margaret Cotrofeld, March 30, 2017.

4. Transcript of graduate management class, March 1, 1989, p. 15, Kozmetsky Papers, IC² Institute.

5. Darius Mahdjoubi, "Knowledge, Innovation and Entrepreneurship: Business Plans, Capital, Technology and Growth of New Ventures in Austin, Texas" (PhD diss., University of Texas at Austin, 2004).

6. Interview with Darius Mahdjoubi, May 15, 2013.

7. Bethany Scott Herwegh, comments at memorial service for George Kozmetsky, May 4, 2003.

8. Interview with William S. Livingston, July 7, 2011.

9. Interview with Robert A. Peterson, August 28, 2013.

10. Interview with Greg Kozmetsky, April 19, 2010.

11. Transcript of graduate management class, March 5, 1986, p. 6, Kozmetsky Papers, IC² Institute.

12. Interview with Neal Spelce, August 11, 2017.

13. Interview with Robert D. King, September 27, 2011.

14. Interview with Isabella Cunningham, December 17, 2013.

15. Frantz, *Forty-Acre Follies,* 283.

16. Interview with Floyd S. Brandt, May 19, 2010.

17. Interview with Floyd S. Brandt, August 8, 2013.

18. Presentation by David Smith, CEO of HBMG Inc. and Strategic Pathways LLC, at IC² fellows meeting, Austin, April 24, 2015.

19. Interview with Jordan Scott, July 17, 2015.

20. Interview with Corey Carbonara, June 25, 2015.

21. Interview with Susie Brown, June 7, 2012.

22. Interview with Edward A. Miller, May 5, 2017.

23. Interviews with Susie Brown, June 7, 2012, and Corey Carbonara, June 25, 2015.

24. "Dr. George Kozmetsky Biography," https://www.youtube.com/watch?v=nQutKkZk NWQ.

25. Lee Kelly column, *Austin American-Statesman*, November 17, 1988.

26. George and Ronya Kozmetsky, *Making it Together*, 101.

27. "A Benefactor in Her Own Right," *Austin American-Statesman*, July 11, 1999.

28. Ritchey, "Brief Biography," 2:16.

29. Ibid., 2:16–17.

30. Interview with Greg Kozmetsky, April 19, 2010.

31. Travel schedule for October 10–14, 1988, Kozmetsky Papers, IC^2 Institute.

32. Interview with Nadya Scott, April 28, 2015.

33. Ibid.

34. Interview with Edward A. Miller, May 5, 2017.

35. Interview with Jordan Scott, July 17, 2015.

36. "Public Records," *Austin Statesman*, January 20, 1971; "UT Dean's $20,000 Sports Car Stolen," *Austin American-Statesman*, April 20, 1976; "Jag Recovered," *Austin American-Statesman*, January 21, 1976.

37. Comments by William H. Cunningham, IC^2 Institute fellows meeting, April 29, 2017.

38. Interview with Robert D. King, September 27, 2011.

39. Interview with Nadya Scott, April 28, 2015.

40. Center for Responsive Politics, www.opensecrets.org.

41. Ibid.

42. "A Benefactor in Her Own Right," *Austin American-Statesman*, July 11, 1999.

43. "Women's Museum at Fair Park in Dallas to Close after History of Financial Struggles," Associated Press, October 5, 2011.

44. Ronya Kozmetsky to Sue McBee, November 8, 1982, Frank and Sue McBee Papers, Austin History Center, Austin Public Library.

45. "Mrs. Clinton Earns Praise," *Austin American-Statesman*, December 22, 1994.

46. "Mentoring and Leadership: Ronya Kozmetsky," *Austin American-Statesman*, June 5, 1994.

47. Comments at IC^2 Institute fellows meeting, April 28, 2017.

48. Francis W. Wolek, Technology Transfer Society, to Kozmetsky, June 15, 1988, Kozmetsky Papers, IC^2 Institute.

49. "National Medal of Technology and Innovation (NMTI)," US Patent and Trademark Office, www.uspto.gov/learning-and-resources/ip-programs-and-awards/national-medal-technology-and-innovation-nmti. The name of the medal was changed in 2007 to recognize achievements in both technology and innovation.

50. Interview with Larraine Segil, November 6, 2013.

51. Ritchey, "Brief Biography," 3:2.

52. Interview with Raymond Smilor, November 3, 2015; interview with David Gibson, March 4, 2016.

53. Interview with Isabella Cunningham, December 17, 2013.

54. Thore and Tarverdyan, *Diagnostics for a Globalized World*, 207–208.

55. Ibid.

56. Interview with Robert D. King, September 27, 2011.

57. Interview with Delbert Tesar, September 30, 2013.

58. Interview with Kenneth D. Walters, October 30, 2015.

59. "Global Gathering Is Bound for Austin," *Austin American-Statesman*, February 28, 2002.

60. "City, Tech Firms Eager to Charm Captive Crowd," *Austin American-Statesman*, April 30, 2006.

61. Kozmetsky, Carbonara, and Cook cochaired a committee on the future of broadband technology for the broadcasters' association. The committee was guided by Kozmetsky's vision that broadcasters needed to see themselves in the larger role of infrastructure providers for mobile and other wireless communication systems.

62. Interview with Corey Carbonara, March 30, 2015.

63. "George Kozmetsky 1917–2003," *Austin American-Statesman*, May 1, 2003.

64. Email from Corey Carbonara, May 1, 2017.

65. Interview with Edward A. Miller, May 5, 2017.

66. Jordan Scott, comments at memorial service for George Kozmetsky, May 4, 2003.

67. "Entrepreneur Gave Austin Its Tech Wings," *Austin American-Statesman*, May 1, 2003.

68. "Professor Remembered for Belief in Others," *Austin American-Statesman*, May 5, 2003.

69. "A Cowboy Goes to the Symphony," *Chronicle of Higher Education*, December 9, 2005.

70. "Donor Led with Grace, Passion, Fire," *Austin American-Statesman*, October 26, 2011.

71. Ibid.

ACKNOWLEDGMENTS

This biography of George Kozmetsky would not have been possible without access to the resources of libraries and historical archives in Austin and on the East and West Coasts. Of fundamental importance in my research has been the University of Texas archives that are housed at the Dolph Briscoe Center for American History. These archives have been particularly valuable in tracing Kozmetsky's activities as dean of the university's business school and as an adviser to the University of Texas System Board of Regents. I also relied heavily on the Briscoe Center's many other resources, including its collections of the papers of many university leaders and Texas politicians, its newspaper archives, and its extensive topical files. I am also grateful to Don Carleton of the Briscoe Center for his decision to publish this book and for the assistance of the center's outstanding staff, notably Margaret Schlankey, head of reference services, and Holly Taylor, editor and head of publications. They and their staffs were unfailingly helpful.

The library resources at the University of Texas at Austin—particularly the Perry-Castañeda Library, the Collections Deposit Library, and specialized libraries in architecture, engineering, and law—were extremely useful in researching the wide range of subjects that were important in Kozmetsky's life.

The collections of the Austin History Center, the local history archive of the Austin Public Library, helped provide an understanding of the enormous changes in Austin since 1966, when George and Ronya Kozmetsky moved to the city.

Other archives that I relied on were the online historical resources of the Harvard Business School and Carnegie Mellon University; the George A. Roberts Collection at Carnegie Mellon; the William H. Hannon Library of Loyola Marymount University (home of the papers of Jack and Bonita

Granville Wrather); the university archives housed at the Allen Library at the University of Washington; the historical archive maintained by the Seattle Public Schools (a model archive that school districts across the nation would do well to emulate); the Seattle Collection at the Seattle Public Library; the Museum of History and Industry in Seattle; the Pearson Air Museum in Vancouver, Washington; and the Seattle offices of the National Archives and Records Administration. The staffs of all these institutions were attentive and resourceful. I want to offer special thanks to the staff of the National Archives in Seattle, who responded with aplomb during a power outage that struck while I was using their digitized records.

Francie A. Frederick and her staff at the office of the University of Texas System Board of Regents assisted me with research related to minutes of the regents' meetings and other board records.

The extensive historical files and publications of the IC² Institute were of inestimable value in my research. Most of these resources have now been transferred to the Briscoe Center, where they will be available to future researchers. The RGK Foundation also graciously made available documents and information from its files.

The beginning point for the research for this book was "George Kozmetsky: A Brief Biography," a valuable eighty-page manuscript produced in 1995 by Nancy Ritchey, an editor at the IC² Institute, based on interviews with Kozmetsky. The only copy of this manuscript that I know of is among the Kozmetsky Papers at the institute.

This project was conceived by three friends and colleagues of Kozmetsky—Robert A. Peterson, John Sibley Butler, and William H. Cunningham. They recruited me to undertake this biography and provided advice and guidance based on their many years of close association with Kozmetsky at the University of Texas at Austin business school and at the IC² Institute. Gregory Pogue, interim director of the institute; Bruce Kellison, director of the institute's Bureau of Business Research; and David Gibson, senior research scientist, as well as others at the institute, including Margaret Cotrofeld and Coral Franke, supported and assisted with the project in numerous ways.

The IC² Institute has supported this project financially, underwriting the costs of research and writing through my employment by the institute and providing a portion of the publication costs. Everyone associated with the project at the institute gave me complete control over the research and the writing of the book. The institute's goal was to produce a comprehensive, objective, balanced, and thoroughly documented biography of George Kozmetsky. I am deeply grateful for the suggestions that I received throughout the project from those who knew Kozmetsky well, but I alone am responsible for the contents of the book, and any shortcomings are my responsibility alone.

Many people graciously consented to my interview requests, including members of the Kozmetsky family—George and Ronya's surviving children, Greg Kozmetsky and Nadya Scott; George and Ronya's grandson Jordan Scott; and George's cousin Elaine Wiley. They also generously provided me with access to family papers and photographs that remain in their possession.

Others whom I interviewed or corresponded with and who generously shared their insights include Debra Amidon, Steve Ballantyne, Francis Borkowski, Floyd Brandt, Susie Brown, Dan Burck, Corey Carbonara, William W. Cooper, Isabella Cunningham, Michael Dell, Arthur H. Dilly, Patricia Easton, Mark Eaton, Peter T. Flawn, Stan Gatchel, David Gibson, Ernest Gloyna, Steven L. Gomes, Steven Hartman, Thomas Hatfield, Jess Hay, Gary Hoover, Charles E. Hurwitz, Adm. Bobby R. Inman, USN (Ret.), Laura Kilcrease, Robert D. King, Janie Lack, Leon Lasdon, Charles A. LeMaistre, William S. Livingston, Austin M. Long III, Stephen Magee, Darius Mahdjoubi, Hans Mark, Sandra Martin, Bob May, Billy Joe "Red" McCombs, Reuben R. McDaniel Jr., Edward A. Miller, Helen Baca Miller, Michael E. Patrick, Fred Young Phillips, Pike Powers, Larraine Segil, Bill Segura, John Sibert, Raymond Smilor, David Smith, Neal Spelce, Jay H. Stein, Murat Tanik, Charles Teeple, Delbert Tesar, Karla Walters, Kenneth D. Walters, the Honorable Zach Wamp, Tom Weber, Glenn West, Meg Wilson, Mariann Wizard, and Chris Wrather.

Many who were associated with George and Ronya Kozmetsky have written about or recorded their experiences, and I have benefited greatly from their perceptive reminiscences. These include Cathy Bonner, Pat Hayes, J. J. "Jake" Pickle, Sten Thore, and Ingrid Vanderveldt.

I benefited more than I can say from comments offered by those who read all or parts of the manuscript. Their special knowledge of the Kozmetskys and their sustained interest in this project have made it a much better book than it would have been without their help, although they cannot, of course, be held responsible for my final editorial decisions. These readers are John Sibley Butler, Corey Carbonara, Margaret Cotrofeld, William H. Cunningham, Bruce Kellison, Laura Kilcrease, Gregory A. Kozmetsky, Robert A. Peterson, Gregory Pogue, Pike Powers, Nadya Scott, and Meg Wilson.

The costs of publication of this book have been partially underwritten by friends of the Kozmetskys. The IC^2 Institute and I are grateful to them for their generosity and their interest in the life story of George and Ronya. The donors to the project are James L. Bayless Jr.; Sophia,

G. W., and Michelle Brock; William H. and Isabella Cunningham; Susan Dawson; Frank Denius and the Cain Foundation; Fred Hegi and the Hegi Family Foundation; Woody L. Hunt and the Hunt Family Foundation; Adm. Bobby R. Inman, USN (Ret.); Kenneth M. Jastrow II; Herb Kelleher; Gregory A. Kozmetsky; Vijay Majahan; Hans Mark; Red McCombs; and Charles and Mary Teeple.

INDEX

anniversary, forty-fifth and fiftieth wedding, 444
ANT-25 monoplane, 34
antiques, 444
anti-Semitism, 78, 447
antitrust regulators, 113
antiwar movement, 432
Apollo project, 122, 393
Arbingast, Stanley A., 249
Arctic Slope Regional Corp., 375
Ardennes and Ardennes Offensive, 51, 53
Arlon, Belgium, 57
Army Air Forces, 47, 70. *see also* US Air Force
Army Air Forces Statistical School, 70
Arnold, Vic, 359
Arrowsmith Technologies, 426–427
Art, Ben, 41
Art's Jewelers, 41–42
Ash, Roy, 66, 90, 91, 93, 111–113, 288
Ashari, Hossein, 280
Asia Pacific Economic Conference, 384
Asia-Pacific region, 368
Association of Fundraising Professionals, 413
Atlanta, 332
ATLAS (Academy of Transdisciplinary Learning
    and Advanced Studies), 402–403
atomic bombs, 64
Austin, TX: and Austin Technology Incubator,
    342; city council, 159, 350; drug culture in,
    164; and economic boom, 325–326; fiber-optic
    network plans, 354; and high tech economy,
    161, 293–295, 312, 354–355; historic landmark
    designation for Kozmetsky home, 159, 350; and
    IC² Institute, 295–296, 310–311; as "idea city,"
    325; international attention, 355, 385; leadership
    of, 327, 334–336; and MCC competition, 329;
    mobile technology laboratory, 367, 416; as
    "new city," 326; in 1966, 161–164; openness and
    inclusiveness of, 335; population growth of,
    161; reputation of, 326; tech networks, 345–347;
    as technopolis, 322–357, 368–369; and urban
    renewal program, 162; World Technology Con-
    gress on Information Technology, 458
Austin-Bergstrom International Airport, 162
Austin Center for Battered Women, 416
Austin Chamber of Commerce, 293–295, 325, 334,
    342, 356. *see also* Austin, TX
Austin Children's Museum, 416
Austin City Council, 159, 350. *see also* Austin, TX
Austin Community College, 365
Austin Enterprise Forum, 345–346
Austin Entrepreneurs' Council, 345–346
Austinites of the Year, 452
"Austin Miracle." *see* Austin Technopolis
"Austin Model," 308–312, 355–356
Austin Project, 367, 416
Austin Software Council, 315, 346–347, 356
Austin Statistical Metropolitan Area, population
    of, 161

Austin Technology Council. *see* Austin Software
    Council
Austin Technology Incubator (ATI), 307, 339–345,
    380, 391
Austin Technopolis: "Austin Miracle," 354–357;
    and Austin Technology Incubator, 339–345;
    beginning of, 324–326; and Capital Network,
    338–339; civic entrepreneurs, 334–336; and Dell
    Computers, 347–352; early technology com-
    panies, 325; economic potential of, 328–329;
    and EnterTech, 352–354; growth stages, 356;
    international attention of, 355; and MCC, 288,
    326, 329–333; and oil price collapse, 327; reputa-
    tion of, 326; technology networks, 345–347;
    technology venturing, 337–338; and University
    of Texas, 354, 356, 357
Austin Ventures, 325
auto industry, 366–367
autopilot for jet fighters, 114–115
aviators, Russian, 12
awards and recognition, 5–6, 38, 46, 61–62,
    452–454

B

Bach, George Leland, 84, 85
bachelor of business administration program,
    214, 215
Baidukov, Georgy, 36
Baker Scholar, 75
Balcones Research Center, 268, 328. *see also* Pickle
    Research Campus
Balderston, Frederick F., 150, 153, 154–155
Ballantyne, Steve, 215
ballroom dancing, 98
Bank of America, 109
Bari, Judi, 435
Barr, Joseph W., 244
Barshop, Sam, 209, 210, 211, 242, 270, 414, 419
Barshop Institute for Longevity and Aging
    Studies, 270
Baruch College, 218
basketball games, women's, 448
Bass, Edward, 271
Bass, Perry, 211
Bates Recital Hall, 460
battalion surgeon, assistant, 50
Battey, Jim, 119
battle fatigue, 55
battlefield, miniature, 49
Battle of Hürgten Forest, 54–59
Battle of the Bulge, 53
Battle of the Hedgerows, 52
Bawa, Vijay Singh, 193–194
Bayless, James, 208, 238
Baylor Research and Innovation Collaboration
    (BRIC), 366
Baylor University, 273, 364, 366, 399–401, 415
Beacon Hill Elementary school, 26

Bechtel Corp., 336, 372, 387
Bechtel Foundation, 418
Bedichek, Roy, 162
Bednar, Deaton, 353
Beecherl, Louis A., Jr., 255–256, 266
behavioral sciences, 77, 157, 167, 215, 395
Beijing conference, 387
Bel Air–Brentwood wildfire, 45, 134–135
Belarus, 18–19
Belarusian Soviet Socialist Republic, 18
Belgium, 51, 53
Beliakov, Alexander, 36
Bell, Spurgeon, 166
Bellman, Richard E., 138
Bell Telephone Laboratories, 86, 93, 193
benchmarking study for Charleston, 383
Bergstrom Air Force Base, 162
Berlin, Isaiah, 418
Beverly Hills offices, 116
Bevo (mascot), 236
Beyster Institute, 315
bias, antibusiness, 204, 300
Bickley, John V., 146, 150
big business. *see* conglomerates; corporations
biography of Kozmetsky, 1990s, 45–46
biotechnology: conferences and seminars, 270, 307; and IC² Institute, 306; Institute of Biotechnology, 269–270; Kozmetsky's interest in, 4, 9; opportunities in, 259, 387, 388
blackboards, 136, 270, 429, 440, 441–442
Black Business Student Association, 242
Blair, Calvin P., 146
Blake, Robert, 418
Blakemore, William B., II, 414
Blanton, Jack, 414
Blomgren, Paul B., 149
blood plasma, dried, 51
Board of Regents. *see* University of Texas System Board of Regents
Boesky, Ivan, 434
Boice, William S., 59
Bolshevik Revolution, 13, 14, 24
Bonner, Cathy, 341, 444
Bonneville Dam, 33
books, rare, 138–139
Borkowski, Francis, 379, 380
Boston, MA, 65, 68–69, 326
Boston Globe, 74
bounded rationality, 80
BPI Systems, founding of, 325
Bradshaw, T. F., 87
Brandt, Floyd S., 156, 203, 441
Braniff International airline, 161
Brazil and IC² Institute, 384
Brentwood home, 45, 134–135, 134–138, 365, 391
bribes, Gulf Oil and, 425
bridge builders, 310
Bright, James R., 185, 192

Briscoe, Dolph, 211, 255–256, 279, 280, 359
Briscoe, Janey S., 255–256, 414
Brockett, Patrick L., 193
Bronze Star, 46, 62
Brookings Institution, 300
Brooks Field, 9, 45, 49–50
Brown, Susie, 443
Browne, James C., 325, 421
Brown Foundation, 302
budget challenges, 227–235
Bureau of Budget, 278
Bureau of Business Research, University of Texas, 89, 191, 249, 268, 336–338, 342
Bureau of Business Research, University of Washington, 31
Burke, Thomas E., 187–188, 202
Burnham, John, 242
Burnham Institute for Medical Research, 413
Burr, Beverly, 432
Bush, George H. W., 291
Bush, George W., 362, 363
business, private. *see* corporations; small businesses
Business Economics Building (BEB), 163, 167, 227, 243–244, 432
business incubators, 339, 343, 345, 366, 380, 381. *see also* technology incubators
business interests, 418–422, 419. *see also* Arrowsmith Technologies; Dell Computer Corp.; EnterTech; Hughes Aircraft Company; KDT Industries; Litton Industries; Teledyne
business model, international, 203
business policy course, 214
Business School Foundation (external), 237–239, 242
business school foundation (internal), 171
business schools: enrollment in, 218–219; Kozmetsky's plans for own school, 90, 140, 412; ranking of, 179–183; responsibilities of, 176. *see also* Carnegie Institute of Technology; College of Business Administration; education, higher; Harvard University
Businessweek, 128, 183
Butler, John S., 317, 320–321, 458
Butterbaugh, Grant I. , 30–32, 68; professorship honoring, 417
Butterbaugh Professorship, 31–32, 417

C

cable companies, 426–427
California, 91, 92, 134–139, 378–379, 430–431
California Institute of Technology, 98, 106
Cambridge Tower apartment, 158–159
camera, miniature television, 121–122
campaign contributions, illegal, 425–426
Campbell, J. Jette, 339
Camp Berkeley, 48–49
Camp Butner, 53, 63, 64

creative, definition of, 398
creative and innovative management, 306, 307, 391, 393, 398–401, 403
Crittendon Transformer Works, 129
Cross Border Institute for Regional Development (CBIRD), 272–274
Crum, Lawrence L., 192–193, 249
CSC 6600/6400 dual computer system, 245
Cunningham, Isabella, 205, 235, 318–319, 440, 455–456
Cunningham, William H.: and Carter's energy plan, 280; and Department of Accounting, 248; and enrollment control, 221–222, 224, 225; and executive MBA program, 216–217; and fundraising, 206, 209; on Kozmetsky's work habits, 443; and Large Scale Projects Institute, 405; Project 75 grant and slides, 217, 281; promotion of, 198–199, 232; recruitment by University of Texas, 197, 318–319; relationship with Kozmetsky, 198–199, 221–222, 232, 252; and Sematech bid, 333–334
Curie, Robin, 344
curriculum revision, 213–217, 250, 284
Curtiss-Wright, 132
Cushing, Barry, 233
Cybernetics, 401
Cyert, Richard, 89

D

Daily Texan, 238–239, 274
dams, hydroelectric, 5, 33
databases, taped, 245
Data General, 325
Datapoint 2000 terminal, 424
Datapoint 5500 system, 245
Datapoint Corporation, 245, 304, 419, 423–424
David, Donald K., 70–71, 74–75, 171–172
Davidson, Frank P., 405–406
Davis, Thomas J., Jr., 115, 133
Davis and Rock investment firm, 115, 133, 420
decentralized management, 101–102, 132–133
Decision Mapping via Optimum Networks (DEMON), 398
Decision Support Systems Center, 201
Deckerd, Carl R., 343
defense contractors and contracts: and activists, 303; awarding of, 92; Hughes Aircraft, 96; IHAS, 122–128; and Kozmetsky, 303; Litton Industries, 101; Teledyne, 122–129, 133, 141; Tracor Inc, 324. *see also* military-industrial complex
Defense Systems Management College, 382
defense technologies, commercialization of, 322, 410
defense technology base, 290–291
Dell, Michael, 159, 347–352, 460
Dell Computer Corp, 10, 315, 347–352, 353
Democratic Party, 10, 449
DEMON (Decision Mapping via Optimum Networks), 398

Denny Regrade, 17
Department of Accounting, 146, 167, 182, 227, 246, 247–248
Department of Defense, 92, 101, 125–126
Department of Energy, 368, 370–371, 372
Depression era, 5, 15–18, 33, 327
desegregation of university, 243
design and process science, 393, 403–404
development banks, 375
Dietrich, Noah, 94, 96, 98, 99–100
digital divide, 173–174, 352
dinner, annual, 456
dinner table discussions, 136–137
discrimination, 15–16, 39–40, 49, 78, 243, 447
Disneyland, 92, 391
Dobie, J. Frank, 162
doctorate, Kozmetsky's, 78–83
documents and records, 19–20, 30, 45, 47, 62, 135
Doherty, Robert, 84
Doriot, Georges F., 77
Dorsey, Robert R., 425–426
Douglas DC-3 airplane, 91
Downing, Diane E., 306
Dréze, Jacques, 185
DRI/McGraw-Hill, 367, 371–372
drive-in restaurants, 137, 447
drug culture, in Austin, 164–165
Drummond, Cliff, 329
Dryken Technologies, 421–422
Dugger, Ronnie, 302, 433–434
DuPont, 109
DVD technology, 353
dynamic programming, 138

E

Eads, George C., 196
Eaker, Ira C., 93
Earth First!, 431, 432, 435
Easter at Palm Springs, 139, 447
Easton, Patricia, 417
East-West '94 Conference, 368
Eckhardt, Carl J., 162
e-commerce, 307, 351
economic development: Austin Model, 355–356; CBIRD, 272–274; and community leadership, 326–327, 334–336, 356, 369; creative and innovative management, 398–399; and educational institutions, 309; four dimensions of relationships to foster, 309–310; hands-on development, 272–274, 293–321, 363–366; homegrown companies, 327, 336, 356, 362; institutional developments in, 322; policy for, 296–297, 357, 415; Rebuild LA initiative, 365; state initiatives for, 374; and technology, 3, 308–312, 362; theory and practice of, 293–321; Torch Program of China, 388; and University of Texas, 269–274; in Waco, 364. *see also* Austin, TX; IC² Institute
Economic Development Council, 295

economic growth, 308–312, 322. *see also* economic development
economic literacy programs, 308
Economic Logistics, 318
economic policy, 296–297, 357, 415. *see also* economic development
economic stockpile, 287
Edelman, Asher, 424
education: and bias against business, 204; "character education," 29; Depression era, 17, 29; and electronics industry, 289; IC² Institute efforts, 308, 336–337; importance of, 19, 21, 73; and information technology, 283–284; interdisciplinary, 9–10, 30, 73, 202, 214–216; Kozmetsky on, 158, 172–176; private enterprise education, 308; quality of, 162, 219, 220, 231
education, business: in elementary and secondary schools, 308; and Kozmetsky, 171–176; Kozmetsky's plans for own school, 90, 140, 412; lessons from IHAS project, 123; school rankings, 179–183. *see also* College of Business Administration; Harvard University
education, higher: academic entrepreneurship, 87; changing educational patterns of students, 259; collaboration with business, 357, 394–395, 433–434; controlled by corporations, 302–303, 433; and economic growth, 309; entrepreneurialization of universities, 435–436; Ford Foundation and, 85; and LSPI, 405; *vs.* private sector research, 259–260; and RGK Foundation, 212–213, 365, 414, 415–416; role in research and development, 259–260; surrogate for national economic policy, 357
education, integrative, 175
efficiency standards and energy crisis, 281
Eggers, Paul, 211
Eighth Infantry Regiment, 60–61
"The Eighties: A Decade of Challenge and Achievement," 259–262
Eldridge, William Thomas, 204
E-Learning and Training Labs (ELT Labs), 354
e-learning projects, 352–354
Electro Dynamics Corporation, 100, 101. *see also* Litton Industries
Electronic Computers and Management Control, 106–109
Electronic Equipment Division. *see* Litton Industries
Electronic News, 295
Electronic Numerical Integrator and Computer (ENIAC), 73–74
electronics industry, 91–92, 100, 287–289, 324. *see also* Hughes Aircraft Company; Litton Industries; Teledyne
elementary schools, 26, 308, 416–417
Elliott Bay squatters' community, 18
Elzey, Neil, 56
Emily's List, 450
employee ownership, 315

endowments: and Austin Technopolis, 324, 357; Butterbaugh Professorship, 31–32, 417; centennial campaign, 191, 210–213; chair for constructive capitalism, 209, 302; first endowed chair, 206, 209, 210; for free enterprise, 303; fundraising for, 206, 208–213; Harkins & Company Chair, 196, 210; honoring White, 206; Houston Endowment, 190, 206, 208; for IC² Institute, 298, 302; and Kozmetskys, 210–213, 402, 414; as recruiting tool, 185, 190. *see also* grants; Permanent University Fund (PUF)
energy crisis and policy, 278–281
Energy Research Group, 268
engineering and engineers, 104–105, 403–404, 406
English-as-a-second-language classes, 416
English Channel, tunnel under, 407
ENIAC (Electronic Numerical Integrator and Computer), 73–74
enrollment: and budget, 220, 229; in business college, 162, 177–178, 218–219; and classroom space, 245; control measures, 220–224; and GI Bill, 75; and GPA, 222–223, 223–224; growth in, 177, 178, 219; of masters students, 218–219; minorities and, 178–179; and student-teacher ratio, 219; at University of Texas, 162, 177–178, 218–219; of women, 239–240
Enrollment Controls Committee, 221, 222
EnterTech, 352–354
entry-level workers and digital divide, 352
environmental issues and activists, 279, 286, 287, 374, 430–436
Erdley Harold "Hal," 105
Erwin, Frank C., Jr., 239, 414
Erwin Center, 460
Estrin, Steven, 242
European Organization for Economic Cooperation and Development, 282–283
Evolutionary Technologies International (ETI), 343–344
executive associate for economic affairs, 156–157, 255–274
Executive Futures seminar, 240, 445
executive MBA program, 171, 216–217
Exxon Valdez oil spill, 374

F

F-86 Sabre fighter aircraft, 96–97
facilitators, for economic growth, 310
faculty: administrative positions at, 226; associate deans, 247; business school needs, 226; courted by other universities, 233–234; criticism of Kozmetsky, 246, 247, 249, 250–251; and dean search, 149; "dream team" list, 185; entry-level, 196–201; executive dean, 252; high profile members, 163; Kozmetsky and, 250–253; Project 75, 217; and promotions, 198–199, 232–233, 250; quality, 205; recruitment and retention, 145–146, 170, 181, 184–201, 206, 226, 231–235; and Rogers, 235–236; and salaries, 179, 192–193,

A CIVIC ENTREPRENEUR

Heitor, Manuel, 317, 391
Heizer Corporation, 419
helicopter avionics system, 122–128
helicopters, 122–128, 123
Hemingway, Ernest, 51
hemorrhagic shock, 51
Henson, Scott, 434
higher education. *see* education, higher
high-tech economic development. *see* economic development
high-technology business development fund, 260–261
Hiroshima, 64
Hirschbiel, Paul, 349
Hispanic students, 178–179, 239, 241–242, 243
historians, army, 55–56
"History of Student Activism at the University of Texas," 432
Hitchings, George, 30
H. J. Heinz Co., 132
Hobby, William P., Jr. "Bill," 332, 359
Hodgson, Richard, 420
Hoerni, Jean, 118, 119–120
Holiday House, 448
Holt, Charles C., 89, 191, 276
Holton, Richard, 276
Homans, George, 75, 77
homegrown technology companies, 327, 336, 356, 362
homes of, 20; Austin condominium, 458; break in at, 447–448; historic landmark designation, 159, 350; library at, 159, 160; in Seattle, 20; Seventeenth Street home, 159–161, 350, 447–448; Southern California, 134–138; visitors to, 350, 365, 391; washing machine and gardener, 109; Westgate Towers, 160; wildfire and rebuilding, 45, 134–136
honeymoon, 41
"Hook 'em Horns" sign, 448
Hoover, George W., 138
Hoovervilles, 18
hostile takeovers, 429
Houston Advanced Research Center (HARC), 273, 313, 364
Houston Area Research Center. *see* Houston Advanced Research Center (HARC)
Houston Endowment, 190, 206, 208
Houston Post, 313
Huang, Jeanne, 377
Huff, David L., 189
Huff Model, 189
Hughes, Howard, 8, 93, 94, 98, 99–100
Hughes Aircraft Company, 6, 90, 93–100, 105–106, 189
Hughes Tool Co., 94
Human Code, 352, 353
human relations movement, 77
Humphrey, Hubert H., 155
Hunter College, 39

Hürgten Forest, 57
Hurwitz, Charles E., 211, 414, 417, 419, 428–431
Huston-Tillotson University, 415
Hutchins, Robert Maynard, 84–85
Hutchinson, Fred, 30
Hyperformix, 421

I

IBM Corporation: in Austin, 161, 325, 355; computers of, 108–109, 167; and equipment for robotics institute, 271; and Georgie Kozmetsky, 164; information world *vs.* real world, 285; and Institute of Management Sciences, 394; and Litton, 104; and management science, 395; research and development, 344, 355
IBM Research Center, 344, 355
IC² (Kozmetsky's shorthand), 293
IC² Institute: anniversary celebrations, 406–461; annual picnic, 456; and Austin Model, 355–356; and Austin Software Council, 346–347; and Austin Technology Incubator, 339–345; and Austin technopolis, 322–357; building for, 305, 414; Carbonara and, 401; and CBIRD, 272–273; celebration of Kozmetsky, 461; and China, 386–389; collective purpose of, 323–324; and creative and innovative management, 399; criticism of, 297–298, 303, 433, 435–436; directors of, 320–321; Earth First! demonstration at, 432; and East Tennessee, 367–372, 369, 371–372; e-commerce advocacy, 351; and economic growth through technology, 308–312; economic literacy programs, 308; education efforts of, 308, 336–337; endowments for, 298, 302; evaluation of nation's economic health, 304; executive committee of faculty, 305; as extended family, 454–457; fellows of, 306–307, 312, 367, 391, 454; focus of research, 306; founding of, 297–302; fundraising for, 212–213, 298–299, 302, 414; and Gibson, 316–317; and hands-on development, 293; housing LSPI, 405; and Huang, 377; importance of research, 357; influence of, 358–392; and Institute for Constructive Capitalism, 296–304; interdisciplinary work of, 306; and Japan, 385–386; and Kozmetsky, 6, 303–304, 323, 459; Kozmetsky family donations, 212–213, 414; and Kozmetsky's legacy, 461; and MCC bid, 332; and militarization of research, 435; and Moscow Power Engineering Institute, 307, 391; name of, 298–299, 305; and Orange County, 106; Phillips at, 315; plans for, 303–304; practical application of theories, 310–311; promoting Austin's potential, 295–296; publications of, 317–318, 336–337; public perception of, 302–304; publishing papers, 308; and RGK Foundation, 212–213, 302, 305, 413; Ruefli and, 197; scholarship questioned, 303; sense of community, 323–324; and Society for Design and Process Science, 403–404; and South Florida, 379; Sullivan and, 197; Technology Commercializa-

tion master's program, 312, 315, 382; and Texas economic development, 359–366; theory and practice of economic development, 293–321; and University of California, 378–379; university officials' concerns, 298; vision for, 296–297; visiting scholars, 307, 388; and visitors to Austin, 355. *see also* conferences and seminars

ideas, visual presentation of, 309, 442–443

Immigrant and Minority Entrepreneurship: The Continuous Rebirth of American Communities, 458

immigrant experience: accounting services for, 447; citizenship, 14, 19, 29; discrimination against, 15–16; *Immigrant and Minority Entrepreneurship*, 458; Kozmetsky's self-identification as, 27, 321; Russian, 12–13; in U.S. schools, 27

"The Implications of Nuclear Power in Texas," 268

Incentives Preference Project, 278

incubators. *see* business incubators; technology incubators

Inertial Guidance Division, 102

inertial navigation system, 104

influencers, first and second level, 357

Information Research Associates, 325

information science program, 199

information technology, 172–173, 281–285, 363, 421, 458

information theory, 116

INFORMS (Institute for Operations Research and the Management Sciences), 395

infrastructure, public and private, 309

Initiatives for Transforming the American Economy, 336–337

Inman, Bobby R.: and advisory panel on defense technology, 290; and Dell Computer Corp., 348, 349; and Dryken Technologies, 421–422; and ETI, 344; on Kozmetsky and MCC, 330–332; and PaineWebber, 420; and Texas Science and Technology Council, 361

innovative, definition of, 398

Innovative Business Accelerator, 366

Institute for Constructive Capitalism, 296–304. *see also* IC² Institute

Institute for International Studies, 418

Institute for Operations Research and the Management Sciences (INFORMS), 395

Institute of Biotechnology, 269–270

Institute of Electrical and Electronics Engineers, 403

Institute of Management Sciences (TIMS), 31, 394–396

instruction manual, programmed, 236

Instrument Systems. *see* Teledyne

integrated circuits, 118

Integrated Helicopter Avionics System (IHAS), 122–128

intellectual property, China and, 387

interdisciplinary education. *see* education, interdisciplinary

interdisciplinary studies: and business education, 73; and business school, 166, 284; and business school faculty, 186, 189, 194, 197–198; and Center for Cybernetic Studies, 202; controllership study, 87–89; General University Model, 281; Hutchins and, 85; and IC² Institute, 301, 306; Kozmetsky's passion for, 10, 30. *see also* transdisciplinary studies

Internal Revenue Service (IRS), 276

International Academy of Sciences and Higher Education of the Russian Commonwealth, 391

international business model, 203

International Center of Cybernetic Studies, 202–203, 402, 421

International Conference on Technology Policy and Innovation, 317, 391–392

International Federation of Institutes for Advance Study, 409

International Harvester, 132

International Journal of Abstracts on Statistical Methods in Industry, 31

International Ladies' Garment Workers Union, 83

International Meeting on Entrepreneurship and Economic Development, 187

International Space Station, 407

International Technical Innovation and Entrepreneurship Symposiums, 384

inventory problems, at Hughes aircraft, 96

investing, Kozmetsky's approach to, 319

Investment Advisory Committee, 265

InvestNet, 375–376

IRS (Internal Revenue Service), 276

Iverson, J. Richard, 288

J

Jaguar, Kozmetsky's, 447–448

Jamieson, Hugh W., 101, 111

Japan, 14, 282, 288, 289, 328, 385–386, 407, 408–409

Japan Industry and Management of Technology Project, 385

Japan Institute for Macro-Engineering, 408

Japan-US Conference on Macro Projects, 408

Jensen, Michael C., 308

Jentz, Gaylord A., 199, 249, 250

Jesse H. Jones Professorship, 190, 208

jet fighters, autopilot for, 114–115

Jewish heritage, 14, 18–19, 24, 417–418

J. M. West Texas Corporation, 209, 302

job creation, 309, 310, 372, 399

Joe R. and Teresa Lozano Long Center for the Performing Arts, 416

Johnson, Lady Bird, 244

Johnson, Lyndon B., 162

Johnson Space Center, 380

Jordan, Bryce, 228

Journal of Business, 181

Journal of Integrated Design and Process Science, 404

A CIVIC ENTREPRENEUR

man-machine methodology study, 121
Manufacturing Technology Laboratories (vans), 367, 416
March, James G. "Jim," 89, 185, 316
Marine Biomedical Institute, 257
Marine Corps, 123, 127
Marine Mammal Protection Act, 258
marine science, 210, 257–258
Marine Science Institute, 210, 257–258
Mark, Hans, 267, 361, 405, 406
Marshall, George C., 34, 35–36
Marshall, Ray, 296
Martin Marietta Corp., 369, 372
Martin Marietta Energy Systems, 369, 372
Massachusetts Institute of Technology (MIT), 260, 345–346, 395, 405
master-planned city, 364
masters of business administration (MBA), 75, 171, 215–216, 284
Mathias, Vic, 293
Matsuo, Hirofumi, 328
Maxxam Inc., 429, 430
May, Robert. G., 248
Mayo, Elton, 75, 76–77
McAfee, Jerry, 425
McBee, Sue, 451
MCC (Microelectronics and Computer Technology Corporation), 288, 326, 329–333
McClendon, Anne Watt, 160
McClendon, James W., 160
McClendon-Kozmetsky house. see Seventeenth Street home
McCombs, Billy Joe "Red," 245, 460
McCombs School of Business. see College of Business Administration
McCombs School of Business Health Care Initiative, 198
McCulloch Oil Corp., 429
McDaniel, Reuben R., Jr., 197–198, 247, 252, 253, 305
McDermott, Eugene, 187
McDonald, Stephen L., 146
McGuire, Joseph W., 148, 149
McKenzie, Vernon, 49
McLennan Community College, 364
McMains, Harvey J., 312–313, 359–360, 390, 430
McNamara, Robert S., 66, 125, 290
MCO Holdings, 429
MCO Resources and Datapoint, 211
medals, military, 46, 61–62. see also awards and recognition
Medical Administrative Corps, 48
medical advances, World War II, 50–51
medical library, 9, 45, 49–50
Medical University of South Carolina, 383
medic training, 47–51
Mellon, William Larimer Sr., 84
Mellon family, 425
Mercury Transformer Corp., 129

Mettlen, Robert, 200
Mevert, Peter, 192
Mexican Americans, 178–179, 239, 241–242, 243
Mexico, 142, 203, 272–273, 345, 459
Michener, James, 409
Microelectronics and Computer Technology Corporation (MCC), 288, 326, 329–333
micromanagement, 105, 235, 236
Microsoft Excel Solver, 192
middleware, 343–344
midnight requisitioning, 97
militarization of research, 435
military-industrial complex: capitalism and, 176–177; Cold War and, 91–92, 101; and KDT Industries, 426; and Kozmetsky, 5, 426, 432, 435, 461; and post-war California, 91–92; and Teledyne, 119–120, 129. see also defense contractors; Hughes Aircraft Company; Litton Industries; Teledyne
military service, 41, 45–64
Milken, Michael, 434
Miller, Edward A., 367, 384, 389–390, 443–444, 459
mine fields, 55
Ministry of Aeronautics, China, 386
Ministry of Science and Technology, China, 388
minorities, 178–179, 239, 241–243, 251, 343
Mitchell, George P., 313, 364
MIT Enterprise Forum, 345–346
Mitsubishi Research Institute, 385, 407, 408, 409
Mitsui & Co., 385
Mobil Oil Company, 210
Mobil Oil Foundation, 242
mobile technology laboratory, 367, 416
model teaching laboratory, 281
Modigliani, Franco, 185
Moen, Al, 30
Moncrief, W. A. "Tex," 271
money, as means towards end, 90
Monroe, 105
Monterrey Institute of Technology and Higher Education, 142, 272–273, 345
moon, manned base on, 410
Moonbase computer program, 410–411
Moore, Fred H., 210
Moot Corp., 314, 385
Morris, James A., 149, 150, 153
Morris, Mark, 30
Morrison, H. Russell, 276
Moscow Power Engineering Institute, 307, 391
Motorola, 325, 351, 354–355
Mountain View, CA, 118
MRI, diagnostic, 457
MRI Systems, 325
Mueller Airport, 161–162
multidisciplinary think teams, 301
Murkowski, Frank, 377
Murphy, James P., 123
Murray, Thomas, 83

OPEC, 268, 278. *see also* oil industry
Operations Research, 181
Operations Research Society of America, 395
Option II executive MBA program, 171, 216–217
Oral Business History Project, 203–204
Orange County Business Council, 106
orchards, 116, 135
organized research centers, 202, 298
Osaka, Japan, 409
Osweiler, 57–58
OTA (Office of Technology Assessment) project, 288, 290–291
Other Texan, 434
Otis, Arthur Sinton, 26
Otis-Lennon School Ability Test, 26–27
Ouchi, Bill, 316
Our Invaded Universities, 302, 433–434
outputs of economic activity, 310
Ovetz, Robert, 435–436
Oxford Center for Hebrew and Jewish Studies, 417–418
Ozarks Regional Commission, 203

P

Pacific Basin conference, 384
Pacific Lumber Co., 429, 431
Pacific Palisades, 136
Pacific Rim, 374
Packard, Vance, 277
Page Sutherland Page, 159–160
PaineWebber Development Corp., 420
Palmer Instruments, 129
Palm Springs, 139, 447
panikhida, 23
Pardee & Fleming Landscape, 136
Paris, 52, 57
Parker, Foster, 142, 208
parking lot, 340
patents, 104, 289, 355
Paton, William A., 68
Patrick, Michael E., 264–265, 266
patriotism, 5, 95, 110
Patterson, David, 417–418
PDP 11/40 computers, 245
Pearce Hall, 244
Pearl Harbor, 47
Pearlson, Keri, 458
Pearson Air Museum, 36
Pearson Field, 33–37
Pena, Ramiro, Jr., 458
Pencom Systems, 343
penicillin, 5, 50–51
Pepperdine University, 106, 417
Permanent University Fund (PUF), 145, 157, 185, 209, 255, 262–266
Perot, H. Ross, 329
Perry, William J., 290
Perry-Castañeda Library, 245
Perryman, Ray, 366

Peterson, Robert A., 197, 204–205, 305, 319, 321, 439–440
philanthropy: and Claremont Graduate University, 417; and higher education institutions, 415–416, 418; of Kozmetskys, 10, 352, 412–418; and Moot Corp. competitions, 385; Oxford Center for Hebrew and Jewish Studies, 417–418; retaining control over donations, 213; and Stanford, 418; Teledyne stock, 412; and University of Texas, 8, 165, 209, 212–213, 226, 416–417. *see also* fundraising; grants; RGK Foundation
Philco, 100
Phillips, Fred Y., 143, 315–316, 346, 385, 440
Philpott, Tom, 434
Phi Sigma Sigma, 39–40
photographs, family, 22
Pickle, J. J. "Jake," 437, 449
Pickle Research Campus, 324, 333, 344
picnics, 106, 456
pipe bomb, 435
Pittsburgh, 85–86
Planning, Production, Inventory, and Workforce, 191
planning horizon, 409
Pogue, Gregory, 321
Polemicist, 433, 434
Policy Sciences, 280
political science and civic entrepreneurs, 335–336
politics: and activists, 431–436; conservative trend and Tennessee economy, 370; illegal campaign contributions, 424–426; of Kozmetskys, 10–11, 16–17, 449; and Saint Spiridon, 14; and Seattle, 13, 16; and US competitiveness, 289. *see also* Texas legislature
pollution, environmental, 286, 372
Porter, Lyman, 181–182
Portugal, 317, 391–392
potentiometers, 128–129
Powers, Pike, 327–328, 329, 333, 334–335, 361, 460
pre-business students, 222
Prigogine, Ilya, 306–307, 456
prisoners of war, 51
privacy, 275–278, 283
private placement investment program, 265–266
private sector, in research and development, 259–260
Production Automation and Numerical Control, 189
profits *vs.* profitability, 285–286
Project 75, 217
Project Independence, 278
prudent person rule, 264
PSW Technologies, 343
publication of research, 7–8, 181, 201–202, 273, 317–318, 336–337
public opinion and profit, 286
public schools, 27, 28–29, 308
PUF (Permanent University Fund). *see* Permanent University Fund (PUF)

A Civic Entrepreneur

A CIVIC ENTREPRENEUR

Segura, Bill, 364–366, 459
Selekman, Benjamin M., 75
Seline, Richard, 362–363, 369
Sellerich, Germany, 61
Sematech, 288, 289, 326, 333–334, 365
semiconductors: creativity of early manufacturing, 119; Kozmetsky's education about, 95; and Litton Industries, 111; and Sematech, 289, 333; Singleton's focus on, 111–112, 118–119; and Teledyne, 114, 124
seminars. *see* conferences and seminars
Serenaders (folk music group), 42
Servicemen's Readjustment Act of 1944 (GI Bill), 68
Seton Kozmetsky Community Health Center, 416
Seventeenth Street home, 159–160, 350, 447–448
Shannon, Claude E., 116
Shapero, Albert, 186–187, 202, 398, 401
Sharashova, 19
shared prosperity: business incubators, 345; and CBIRD, 273; and EnterTech, 352; and IC² Institute, 297, 352; Kozmetsky's commitment to, 4, 7, 297; urgency of need for, 437
Shi, Dinghuan, 388
ship, research, 210
Shivers, Allan, 237–238, 244, 255
S. H. Kress dime-store warehouse, 21
Shockley, William, 118
shortage mentality, 287
shortages and supplies, 286–287
Sibert, John, 378
Sid Richardson Foundation, 302
Siegfried Line, 53, 59–61
Silber, John, 224, 239
Silicon Valley, 79, 116, 133, 295, 326, 328
Silicon Valley Fever: Growth of High-Technology Culture, 316
Silver Star, 46, 61–62
Simon, Dorothea, 85–86, 89
Simon, Herbert A.: *Administrative Behavior,* 80; and ATLAS, 402; attempt to recruit, 185; bounded rationality, 80; and Carnegie Tech, 66, 87, 89; controllership study, 87–88; at GSIA, 84; and Kozmetsky, 85, 87–88, 136; Kozmetsky on, 89–90; on Kozmetsky's people skills, 88; and management science, 191, 394; as manager, 76; and Society for Design and Process Science, 404; World War II service, 66
Simon, William E., 286, 287, 303
Simplicity Pattern, 429
Singleton, Henry: appearance of, 114; autopilot for jet fighters, 114–115; blackboard in office, 136; chess enthusiast, 80; dislike of term conglomerate, 113; disputes with Thornton and Ash, 111; and donation for Kozmetsky's chair, 211–212; fellowship named for, 414; and inertial navigation technology, 102, 104; and Kozmetsky, 140; at Litton Industries, 102, 105, 112; Litton stock, 102; and press, 117; and Teledyne, 110, 113–114,

117, 128, 132, 134, 141–142; wealth of, 133–134; and wildfire, 135; on winning IHAS contract, 124; World War II service, 66
Skeen, Clyde, 208
slide presentations, in classroom, 217, 281
Sloan, Robert B., 273, 364
Small Business Administration, 242, 339, 382
small businesses: and business incubators, 339, 343; and business schools, 167; and CEED, 272; and Community Business Advisory Program, 242; critics of Kozmetsky, 251; and four dimensions of relationships, 309; and IC² Institute, 296, 300, 306; Kozmetsky on, 327, 336; MCC and, 426; and Texas economy, 360; White House Conference on, 358. *see also* conglomerates; corporations
small business innovation research program, 310, 322, 381
Smilor, Raymond: and Austin Technology Incubator, 343; consulting in China, 386; four dimensions of relationships, 309; at IC² Institute, 313–314; on Kozmetsky, 314–315, 358; loan from Kozmetskys, 455; publications of, 317; research and development survey, 359–360; and state initiatives for economic development, 374; support for Goto's research, 329; and Technopolis Wheel, 311–312; travel to Russia, 390
Smith, C. Aubrey, 146, 150–151, 153–154, 182, 246–247
Smith, Cynthia, 452
Smith, David, 353
Smith, Preston, 358
Smith, Walter Bedell "Beetle," 34, 35–36
Smith Cove Terminal, 24
Snake River, 33
Snoqualmie Falls honeymoon, 41
social justice and economic policy, 415
Social Science Laboratory, Carnegie Tech, 89
Social Sciences Research Council, 276–277
Social Security Administration, 276–277
social services for veterans, 63
Society for Design and Process Science, 403–404
Society for Macro-Engineering, 405–406
softball games, 456
software and software industry, 315, 347, 355, 356, 410–411, 422, 426
solar panels, large arrays, 407
Soldier Field, 69
Solidarity labor movement, 308
Sommerfield, Ray M., 154, 199, 200
Sonatrach contract, 236–237
Sony, 217
Sophia Antipolis, France, 328
South Africa, 433
South Carolina, 282–283
Southeast Business Incubator, 343
South Korea, 289
South Texas Nuclear Project, 268
Soviet Union. *see* Russia

speaking style, 251, 270, 315, 439–441
Spelce, Neal, 294, 329–330, 335, 440
Sperry Rand, 108
Sprague, Robert, 116
Sprague Engineering, 116
Spriegel, William R., 166
Spruce Goose, 422
Spurr, Stephen, 208, 228–229, 230
squatters' communities, 18
SRI International, 325
SS James B. Parker, 63
SS President Jackson, 23–24
Stalin, Joseph, 14
Stanford Research Institute, 186
Stanford University: business development fund of, 260; conspiracy with big business, 433; executive MBA program, 216; international business model, 203; and Kozmetsky Global Collaboratory, 418; as model for Austin and UT, 295; ranking of schools, 181, 182; and RGK Foundation, 418
Starr, Evangeline, 41
Stars and Stripes, 58
State Science and Technology Commission, China, 387
statistical planning, 69–70
statistics, 31
Stat School, Army Air Forces, 70
Steck Co. printers, 161
Stedry, Andrew C., 185, 189, 203
St. Edwards University, 415
Stein, Jay, 270
St. Lô breakout, 52
stock and stock options: Dell Computer Corp, 348–349, 352; Litton Industries, 102, 114; Teledyne, 115, 127, 128, 129, 131, 213, 412
Stockton, John R., 146, 147–148, 149–150
Stolp, Chandler, 317
Storekeepers software, 422
St. Petersburg, 390
Strategic Defense Initiative ("Star Wars" program), 322, 410
strategic planning: for Board of Regents, 255, 259–261; and chance constraint programming, 122, 202, 397–398; for Dell Computers, 347; need for, 399; and R&D process, 397–398; Texas 2000 Commission, 359–361
Streetman, Ben, 329
stretcher-bearers. *see* litter bearers and hauls
student activists, 431–436
student-faculty ratio, 179, 219, 223, 227–228, 231
student radicals, 432–433
students: business schools and, 174; "farming out," 224–225; and Konecci, 216; Kozmetsky and, 154, 158; LEAD program and high schools, 242–243; nontraditional, 259, 261; prebusiness, 222. *see also* enrollment
students, minority, 178–179, 239, 241–242, 243, 251.

see also students
Students for a Democratic Society, 432
Successful Living, 29
sulfa drugs, 50
Sullivan, Robert S., 197, 320, 337
Summers, Ed, 233
supercomputers, 266–268, 328. *see also* computers
Superconducting Super Collider, 362
superconductivity research labs, 385
Superior Technical Institute (IST), 391
supplies and shortages, 286–287
surname, misspelling of, 19–20
surpluses, understanding of, 287
Sutton, Eldon, 298
Swearingen, Eugene L., 148, 149
Sweatt v. Painter, 160
swimming pools, 137–138, 160–161
Sylvania, 109
synfuels, 278
systemic sclerosis, 413
Systems and Policies for the Global Learning Economy, 317
Szwarc, Wlodzimierz, 137–138
Szygenda, Stephen, 339

T

Talbott, Harold, 99
Tampa–Fort Myers region, 379
Taniguchi, Alan, 239
Tanik, Murat, 403–404
Tatsuno, Sheridan, 328
tax credits and energy crisis, 281
Taylor, Jack G., 154, 208
teaching assistants, 179, 230
teaching methods and innovations, 217, 219–220, 244, 281
Tech Coast Superfund, 378, 420
Technical University of Lisbon, 391
"technological fix," 4
technology: anticipating changes in, 192; and assumptions about business, 172; "dehumanizing" effect of, 434; and economic growth, 3, 308–312, 362; expectations for 1980s, 259–260; framework for, 308; higher education *vs.* private sector, 259–260; importance of, 310, 368; Kozmetsky's faith in, 2–3, 4, 72–73; as a resource, 310; solving social problems, 171. *see also* technology commercialization; technology incubators; technology transfer programs; technology venturing
Technology Alliance of Washington, 355
technology commercialization: centers for, 380–381, 383; in China, 386; and defense technology, 322, 410; and economic growth, 308–312; and federal labs, 291, 345, 380–381, 383; Kilcrease and, 380–381, 383; master's degree for, 197, 312, 315, 382; and NASA, 345, 380–381; and NOAA, 383; and Orange county, 92; and

Portugal, 392; from Strategic Defense Initiative, 322; and Tennessee Valley Corridor, 370–371; and University of Texas, 357

Technology Commercialization master's program, 197, 312, 315, 382

technology-driven management approach, 112–113

technology incubators: about, 339; Ames Research Center, 381; Global Business Incubation, 379; NOAA and, 383; Rubicon Group, 325; in Texas, 343; USSR conferences on, 391. *see also* business incubators

Technology Initiative Working Group, 362

technology licensing. *see* technology commercialization

technology networks, 345–347

Technology Transfer: A Communication Perspective, 317

technology transfer programs, 362, 380–381. *see also* technology commercialization

Technology Transfer Society, 453

technology venturing: academic programs around, 338; "angel" investors, 375–376, 377; Capital Network, 338–339; Center for Technology Venturing, 336–338, 342; definition of, 310, 336; and economic growth, 309–310; and macro-engineering, 406; need for, 309; Tech Coast Superfund, 378, 420; *vs.* traditional capital venturing, 291–292. *see also* technology commercialization; venture capital networks

technopolis, 322–357, 328, 368–369, 435–436

Technopolis Wheel, 311–312, 347

Teeple, Charles, 427–428

Teledyne: acquisitions and mergers, 113, 117–118, 130–131; Amelco, 117–118, 119; board of directors, 116, 128, 130, 132; circuit boards and pay for skill, 121; decentralized management of, 132–133; and defense contracts, 119–120, 122–129, 133, 141; diversification of, 131; financial struggles of, 116, 120, 135; financing and investors, 79, 102, 114–116, 115; Fortune 500 ranking, 131; founding of, 3, 110, 114–122; growth of, 117, 128–134; IHAS, 122–128; IHAS technology failure, 127–128; insurance money, 135; investment in other companies, 132, 133; and Kozmetsky, 6, 132, 211–212, 213, 422; and Litton Industries, 132; NASA and, 121–122; offices of, 116; orchard, 116; origin of, 114; partnership of Kozmetsky and Singleton, 116–117; religion of growth, 117; reorganization and consolidation of, 132; research and development program, 122, 132, 397; sales plan for, 120–121; and semiconductors, 117–118, 118–119; and Singleton's patents, 104; stock of, 115, 127, 128, 129, 131, 213, 412; success of, 10; Watts riots, 1, 141; weapons systems management, 396–398; work environment, 117

Teledyne Electronics Systems, 132

Teledyne Precision Inc., 129

Teledyne Relays, 116

Teledyne Systems Corp., 129

Teledyne Technologies Inc., 132

telephones, during World War II, 55

Tenneco, 204, 302

Tennessee, East, 367–372

Tennessee Valley Authority, 369

Tennessee Valley Corridor, 370–371

Terman, Fred, 3

terminology, personal, 285–286, 293, 299, 398, 401

Tesar, Delbert, 272, 367, 457

test scores, standardized, 26–27

(sum)TEX, 434

Texas: critical industries of, 359–360; economic diversification projects, 361; and economic planning, 358–363; economy of, 279, 327–328, 358–363, 360; and oil industry, 279, 327, 360; promise of, 142–143; similarities with Alaska, 374–375; and technology-based entrepreneurship, 143; and Texas 2000 Commission, 359–361. *see also* Texas legislature

Texas 2000 Commission, 359–361

Texas Advanced Technology Research Program, 362

Texas A&M University, 201, 218, 235, 303

Texas Business Hall of Fame, 446

Texas Capital Network, 338–339, 356

Texas Commerce Bank, 204, 348

Texas Federation of Women's Clubs, 308

Texas Growth Fund, 261, 264

Texas House of Representatives Interim Committee on Oceanography, 258

Texas Instruments, 122, 325

Texas International airline, 161–162

Texas legislature: and conspiracy of universities and big business, 435–436; and marine science, 258; microchips for, 327; and PUF, 264; strategic planning projects, 358–359; technology proposals of 1985, 361–362; Texas 2000 Commission, 359–361; and University of Texas admissions standards, 241–242; and University of Texas enrollment, 220–221; and University of Texas funding, 227, 228, 232, 261, 264. *see also* politics

Texas Lyceum Foundation, 338, 360–361, 450

Texas Monthly magazine, 352

Texas National Research Laboratory Commission, 362

Texas Observer, 302–303, 433, 434

Texas Past and Future: A Survey, 359

Texas Research Park, 269–270, 270–271

Texas Science and Technology Council, 361, 362, 363

Texas State Bank, 420–421

Texas State Technical College (TSTC), 273, 364–366, 367, 415

Texas Technology Summit, 362–363

Texas Trends 1980, 359

Texas Women's Alliance, 338

A CIVIC ENTREPRENEUR

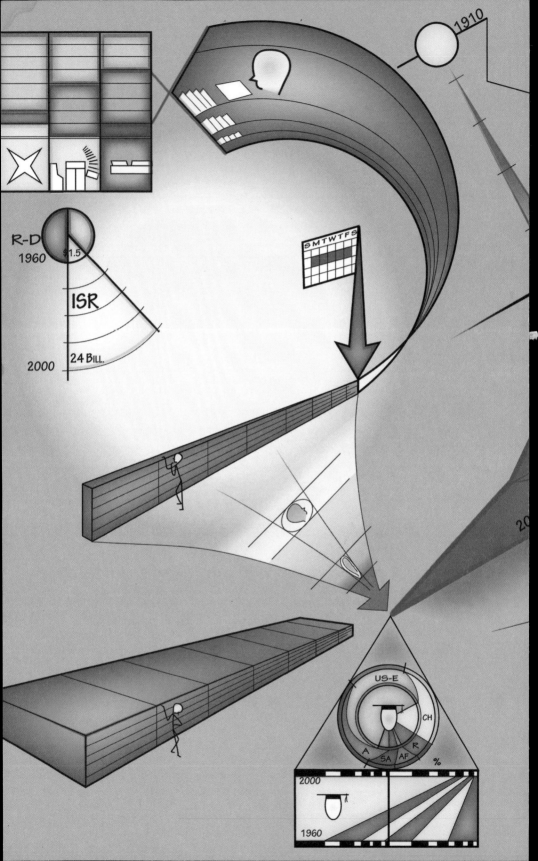